Combatting Corruption and Collusion in Public Procurement

Combatting Corruption and Collusion in Public Procurement

A Challenge for Governments Worldwide

ROBERT D. ANDERSON, ALISON JONES, AND
WILLIAM E. KOVACIC

OXFORD
UNIVERSITY PRESS

Great Clarendon Street, Oxford, OX2 6DP,
United Kingdom

Oxford University Press is a department of the University of Oxford.
It furthers the University's objective of excellence in research, scholarship,
and education by publishing worldwide. Oxford is a registered trade mark of
Oxford University Press in the UK and in certain other countries

© Robert Anderson, Alison Jones, and William Kovacic 2024

The moral rights of the authors have been asserted

All rights reserved. No part of this publication may be reproduced, stored in
a retrieval system, or transmitted, in any form or by any means, without the
prior permission in writing of Oxford University Press, or as expressly permitted
by law, by licence or under terms agreed with the appropriate reprographics
rights organization. Enquiries concerning reproduction outside the scope of the
above should be sent to the Rights Department, Oxford University Press, at the
address above

You must not circulate this work in any other form
and you must impose this same condition on any acquirer

Public sector information reproduced under Open Government Licence v3.0
(http://www.nationalarchives.gov.uk/doc/open-government-licence/open-government-licence.htm)

Published in the United States of America by Oxford University Press
198 Madison Avenue, New York, NY 10016, United States of America

British Library Cataloguing in Publication Data

Data available

Library of Congress Control Number: 2023948083

ISBN 978–0–19–285589–3

DOI: 10.1093/law/9780192855893.001.0001

Printed and bound in the UK by
Clays Ltd, Elcograf S.p.A.

Links to third party websites are provided by Oxford in good faith and
for information only. Oxford disclaims any responsibility for the materials
contained in any third party website referenced in this work.

Preface

Governments around the globe spend USD trillions on public procurement, accounting for nearly 30 per cent of all government expenditure in many countries and 10–15 per cent of gross domestic product (GDP). This expenditure relates to goods, services, works, and public infrastructure that are of immense, and everyday, importance to citizens, for example, the construction and maintenance of assets such as roads, airports, marine ports, energy and sewer systems, and military equipment; and the provision of medicines, healthcare, education, policing services, and national defence. Indeed, this spending is now taking centre-stage, and rising, as states grapple with numerous challenges, including managing the aftermath of the COVID-19 pandemic, planning for future public health crises, addressing the threat of climate change, protecting global peace and security of supply chains, and shoring up defence infrastructure.

There is serious concern, in this context, that despite the acute significance of public procurement for the well-being of nations, few jurisdictions have proved to be very successful in protecting these processes from corruption (e.g. where procurement contracts are diverted to cronies or preferred bidders in return for improper compensation) or supplier collusion (e.g. where tenderers limit price competition or share markets between them by rigging bids). Rather, and even though there have been major national and international efforts to combat these practices, corruption and collusion, whether individually or working together, continue to thwart public procurement objectives by reducing the quality and quantity of these essential public goods and services, and depleting state resources. They thus cause profound harm to society, especially its most vulnerable citizens, and, more broadly, undermine confidence in democratic governments at a time when trust in democratic institutions is already waning and authoritarianism, and populism have been on the rise.

The purpose of this book is, consequently, to consider how governments can better protect the integrity of their public procurement systems from corruption and collusion, and thereby improve their citizens' lives and instil confidence in themselves. It starts by considering why corruption and collusion are such pervasive threats to public procurement and the substantial harm they cause (Chapter 2), before examining the basic frameworks required to limit opportunities and incentives for such conduct (Chapter 3) and advocating for reforms and improvements that will help countries both generally (Chapter 4) and individually (Chapters 5–10) to shield their public procurement systems from corruption and collusion. The book highlights the need for a 'joined-up' and multifaceted approach to the problem, encompassing preventative and deterrent techniques, and national and international agencies and institutions working together to achieve a coordinated procompetitive public procurement strategy. It also recognizes, however, the need for solutions targeted at the roots of jurisdiction-specific problems.

It is true that the topics of both corruption and supplier collusion—including the context of public procurement—have already been the subject of extensive scholarly literature and debate, and numerous policy documents and reports issued by national and international organizations, such as public procurement entities, treasury departments, law enforcement agencies, the World Bank and other development banks, the Organisation for Economic Co-operation and Development (OECD), and the United Nations. Corruption, in particular, is the subject of a UN-level treaty (the United Nations Convention against Corruption) and of specific, binding provisions in the leading international trade agreement on the topic, the World Trade Organization Agreement on Government Procurement. Important anti-corruption work has also been completed by Transparency International, the Open Contracting Data Standard Organization, and other civil society groups and bodies. Yet, notwithstanding all this activity (which we draw upon and discuss throughout the book), our belief is that the problems identified merit renewed and reinvigorated attention and focus, and that a more coherent, and less siloed, approach is needed to bring them under effective control. We also consider that there are many practical lessons to be learned from the sharing of experience in this area across jurisdictions—hence, the strong international and comparative focus of the book.

We would like to extend our thanks to the Leverhulme Trust for the award to Alison Jones of a Research Fellowship which has helped to fund and support this research and to everyone who has assisted us in the research, writing, and preparation of this book. Special thanks are due to Antonella Salgueiro for her efficient and excellent research underlying several chapters of the book (especially Chapters 9 and 10) and for her painstaking work on the preparation of all of the chapters for publication, and to Maciej Bernatt and Caio Mario da Silva Pereira Neto for working with Alison on papers that provided the foundations for Chapters 7 and 8. Additionally, we thank Alberto Sanchez-Graells for helpful comments on Chapter 5 (the United Kingdom); Robert Marshall, Michael Meurer, Steven Schooner, and Christopher Yukins for their valued suggestions regarding Chapter 6 (the United States); representatives of the Anti-Monopoly Committee of Ukraine for input to Chapter 9 (Ukraine); and Don Mercer, Tom Ross, and Alan Williams for timely and helpful input to Chapter 10 (Canada). Additionally, for helpful exchanges and stimulating conversations on diverse related topics, we wish to thank Sue Arrowsmith, Michael Bowsher, Kamala Dawar, Alberto Heimler, Alina Mungiu-Pippidi, Steven Schooner, and Peter Trepte. We would also like to thank Charlotte Kershaw of OUP for her patience, encouragement, and efficiency.

Our intention was to state the law as at 6 July 2023. With the cooperation of OUP, however, we have been able to include a note of some later developments.

Lastly, we dedicate this book to our spouses, Ruth Anderson, Graeme Keen, and Kathryn Fenton, and express our sincere thanks for their support, without which the book could not have been completed.

Robert D. Anderson
Alison Jones
William E. Kovacic
6 July 2023

Acknowledgement

This work was supported by the Leverhulme Trust (RF-2021-339).

Contents

List of Tables	xiii
Table of Cases	xv
Table of Legislation	xix

1. Introduction and Overview   1

2. Corruption and Collusion in Public Procurement: Opportunities, Incentives, and Harm Caused   19

3. Basic Elements for Combatting Corruption and Collusion in Public Procurement: Well-Constructed Procurement, Competition, and Anti-Corruption Regimes   43

4. Towards a More Comprehensive Approach: Strengthening Anti-Corruption and Anti-Collusion Systems, Dealing with Systemic Corruption and the Contribution of Multi-Level Governance   83

5. Corruption and Supplier Collusion under the Waterline? Combatting Risks to Public Procurement in the United Kingdom   139

6. Persistent Corruption and Supplier Collusion in an Advanced Industrialized Country: The Case of the United States   179

7. Brazil: Lessons from Operation Car Wash   213

8. Addressing Democratic Backsliding and Increasing Corruption and Supplier Collusion Risks in Hungary and Poland: The Impact of EU Membership   239

9. Ukraine: Ukraine's Ongoing Fight Against Corruption and Supplier Collusion in Public Procurement: Relation to the Country's Broader Existential Struggle   269

10. Persistent Corruption and Supplier Collusion in Public Procurement in a (Generally) Well-Governed Country: The Case of Canada   309

11. Conclusions   343

Index   351

List of Tables

1.1	Common bid rigging practices	7
2.1	Factors rendering public procurement susceptible to supplier collusion	25
5.1	Summary of core cartel and corruption offences	149
7.1	OCW's main fronts of investigations	215
10.1	Recent bid rigging investigations by the Competition Bureau in relation to bid rigging on municipal infrastructure contracts in Quebec	338

Table of Cases

EUROPEAN UNION CASES

European Commission Decisions

Case No. IV/35.691/E-4, Pre-Insulated Pipe Cartel 21 October 1998 24
COMP/38.823, PO/Elevators and Escalators, Commission Decision of
    21 February 2007 117–18
Case COMP/39406, Marine Hoses, Commission Decision of
    28 January 2009 .... 151–52, 164–65

COURT OF JUSTICE OF THE EUROPEAN UNION

General Court (numerical)

Case T-146/09 RENV, EU:T:2016:411 151
Case T-791/19, Sped-Pro S.A. v Commission, EU:T:2022:67 ....256, 258

Court of Justice (numerical)

Case 14/68, Walt Wilhelm v Bundeskartellamt EU:C:1969:4 242
Case 145/83, Stanley George Adams v Commission EU:C:1985:323...................101
Case C-41/90, Höfner and Elser v Macrotron GmbH EU:C:1991:161...............143–44
Case C-453/99, Courage Ltd v Crehan EU:C:2001:465 ....117, 242
Case C-205/03 P, FENIN v Commission EU:C:2006:453 121
Cases C-295/04 to 298/04, Manfredi v Lloyd Adriatico Assicurazioni SpA
    EU:C:2006:461 117
Case C-70/06, Commission v Portuguese Republic, EU:C:2008:3....................261
Case C-538/07 Assitur v Camera di Commercio, Industria, Artigianato e
    Agricoltura di Milano EU:C:2009:317..91
Case C– 286/12, Commission v Hungary, EU:2012:687 259–60
Case C– 288/12, Commission v Hungary, EU:C:2014:237 259–60
C-557/12, Kone AG v ÖBB-Infrastruktur AG EU:C:2014:1317....................117–18
Case C-470/13, Generali-Providencia Biztosító Zrt v Közbeszerzési
    Hatóság Közbeszerzési Döntőbizottság, EU:C:2014:2469.....................79–80
Case C-194/14 P AC-Treuhand AG v Commission EU:C:2015:717 ....25, 121
Case C-542/14 SIA 'VM Remonts' and Others v Konkurences padome
    EU:C:2016:578 ....25, 31–32, 57
Case C-64/16, ASJP (Portuguese Judges) EU:C:2018:117..........................256
Case C-531/16 Ecoservices projektai in the 'Specializuotas transportas'
    ECLI:EU:C:2018:324 91
Case C-441/17R, Commission v Poland (Bialowieza forest), EU:C:2017:877 261
Cases C-558 and 563/18, Miasto Lowicz and Prokurator Generalny, EU:C:2020:234....256
Cases 585, 624, and 625/18, A.K. 256
Case C-619/18, Commission v Poland (Independence of Supreme Court),
    EU:C:2019:531 259–60
Case C-619/18 R, Commission v Poland EU:C:2018:1021 259–60

xvi TABLE OF CASES

Cases C-357 etc/19, Criminal Proceedings Against PM and others
  EU:C:2021:1034 . . . . 243–44, 259–60
Case C-791/19, Commission v Poland, EU:C:2021:596, see interim order
  EU:C:2020:277 and INFR(2019)2076 259–60
Case C-121/21, Czech Republic v Poland, EU:CL:2021:752 261
Case C-156/21, Hungary v Parliament and Council, EU:C:2022:97 263–64
Case C-157/21, Poland v Parliament and Council, EU:C:2022:98 263–64
Case C-204/21 R, Commission v Poland (judgment pending, interim order
  EU:C:2021:593 . . . . 259–60, 261
Case C-204/21, Commission v Poland, EU:C:2021:878 261
Case C-416/21 J. Sch. Omnibusunternehmen and K. Reisen EU:C:2022:689. 91
Case C-601/21, Commission v Poland (action brought on
  28 September 2021 judgment pending). 259–60

NATIONAL COURTS AND DECISIONS OF
RELEVANT AUTHORITIES

Brazil

CADE DECISIONS

CADE, PAC Favelas, Administrative Proceeding n° 08700.007776/2016-41 220

COURTS AND TRIBUNALS

ADCs No. 43, No. 44 and No. 54, Supremo Tribunal Federal, 7 November 2019 218–19
Brazil Supreme Court, ADI 4.650, 17 September 2015 229–30
Construction of North-South Railway (Decisions 296/2018, 2504/2019,
  930/2019, 2305/2017, and 2310/2017). 220
Criminal Appeal No. 5021365-32.2017.4.04.7000
  (Electronic Process – E-Proc V2 – TRF) (judgment 2019) 218–19
Criminal Appeal No. 5046512-94.2016.4.04.7000
  (Electronic Process – E-Proc V2 – TRF) (judgment 2018) 218–19
FAC Decisions 930/2019 220
HC No. 126,290, Supremo Tribunal Federal, 17 February 2016 218–19
STF, HC 164.493/PR. 218–19
Superior Electoral Court, Registro de Candidatura 0600903-50.2018.6.00.0000,
  1 September 2018 221

Canada

COMPETITION BUREAU CASES

Cima+ 8 December 2020 338
Dessau 19 February 2019. 338
Flour mills 7 December 1990 318–19
Génius Conseil Inc 19 June 2020. 338
Norda Stelo (formerly Roche) 5 March 2020. 338
SNC- Lavalin 19 June 2020 338
WSP Canada (formerly Genivar) 13 March 2019. 338

ROYAL COMMISSIONS, COMMISSIONS OF INQUIRY,
AND OTHER OFFICIAL PROCEEDINGS

Commission of Inquiry into the Sponsorship Program and Advertising Activities,
  'Who is Responsible? Phase 1 Report' (1 November 2005) and 'Restoring
  Accountability, Phase 2 Report' 320

TABLE OF CASES   xvii

Mario Dion, Conflict of Interest and Ethics Commissioner, 'Trudeau II report' 325
Quebec, Commission d'enquête sur l'octroi et la gestion des contrats publics
  dans l'industrie de la construction, 'Rapport final de la Commission
  d'enquête sur l'octroi et la gestion des contrats publics dans l'industrie de la
  construction', CEIC (2015) ('Charbonneau Commission Report') 311, 322–23
Royal Commission Relating to the Canadian Pacific Railway, 'Report of the
  Royal Commissioners appointed by commission, addressed to them
  under the Great Seal of Canada, bearing date the fourteenth day of
  August, A.D. 1873' 316–17

Germany

Case No. 2-06 O 464/14, Landgericht District Court 30 March 2016, Frankfurt am Main118
Case No. 16 O 193/11, Landgericht District Court 6 August 2013, Berlin. 118

Ukraine

No. 200-p, Flavoured Products 291–92
UkrGasVydobuvannya 291–92

United Kingdom

OFFICE OF FAIR TRADING AND COMPETITION AND MARKETS
AUTHORITY DECISIONS

Case 50455, Fludrocortisone acetate tablets: anti-competitive agreement 9 July 2020 . . .176
Case CA98/05/2006, Private Schools, 20 November 2006. 176
CA98/02/2009, Bid Rigging in the Construction Industry in England,
  21 September 2009 . . . . 150–52, 161
Collusive tendering for Mastic Asphalt Flat-roofing Contracts in Scotland,
  8 April 2005 151
Collusive tendering for felt and single ply flat-roofing contracts in the
  North East of England, 8 April 2005. 151
Collusive tendering for felt and single ply roofing contracts in Western
  Central Scotland, 12 July 2005 151
Flat Roof and Car Park Surfacing Contracts in England and Scotland,
  23 February 2006 151
Supply of Galvanised steel tanks: criminal investigation 151–52, 164–65, 172
Supply of precast concrete draining products: criminal investigation 151–52
Galvanised steel tanks for water storage, 19 December 2016 151–52
West Midland Roofing Contractors, 17 March 2004 151
Supply or precast concrete draining products, 23 October 2019 151–52

COURTS AND TRIBUNALS

Apex Asphalt and Paving Co Ltd v OFT (Case 1032/1/1/04) [2005] CAT 4 143–44
FP McCann v CMA (Case 1337/1/12/19) [2020] CAT 28 . . . . 151–52, 164–65
Innospec Ltd [2010] Crim LR 665 147–48
Nuclear Decommissioning Auth. v EnergySolutions EU Ltd [2017] UKSC 34 . . .57, 142–43
Prest v Petrodel [2013] UKSC 34 145
R v Bennett & Wilson [1996] 2 Cr App R(S) 879 153
R v Brian Chant, 1 February 2022 (Southwark Crown Court) 153
R v Bush [2003] EWCA Crim 480. 153
R v Ford [2011] EWCA Crim 473. 153
R v Foxley [1995] 2 Cr App R 523 153

xviii   TABLE OF CASES

R v Ozakpinar (Adam Osman) [2008] EWCA Crim 875. 153
R v Whittle, Brammar and Allison [2008] EWCA Crim 2560 151
R (Good Law Project and Every Doctor) v Secretary of State for Health and
    Social Care [2022] EWHC 2648 142–43
R (Good Law Project and others) v Secretary of State for Health and
    Social Care [2021] EWHC 346 142–43
R (Good Law Project) v Minister for the Cabinet Office [2022] EWCA 21 142–43
R (on the application of the Law Society) v Legal Services Commission
    [2007] EWHC 1848 142–43
Skansen Interior Ltd, 22 February 2018 (Southwark Crown Court) 153
Stamatis and Davies v CMA [2019] EWHC 3318 (Ch) 170–71

United States

FEDERAL TRADE COMMISSION

Boeing Co., 92 FTC 972 (1978) 192
Lockheed Corp., 92 FTC 968 (1978) 192
McDonnell Douglas Corp., 92 FTC 976 (1978) 192

FEDERAL COURTS

Colorado v Western Paving Construction Co., 833 F. 2d 867 (10th Cir. 1987) 203
McMullen v Hoffman, 174 U.S. 639 (1899) 185, 198
Northern Pacific Railroads. V United States, 356 U.S. 1 (1958) 72
Percoco v United States 598 U.S. _ , 143 S.Ct. 1130 (2023). 205–6
Petrobras Securities Litigation, In re (Case No. 14-CV-9662) (SDNY 2018) 80
United States v Addyston Pipe & Steel Co., 85 F. 271 (6th Cir. 1898), aff'd,
    175 U.S. 211 (1899). 185
United States v Aluminum Co. of America (Alcoa), 148 F.2d 416 (2d Cir. 1945) 187
United States v American Airlines, Inc., 743 F.2d 1114 (5th Cir. 1984) 199–200
United States v Aradondo Haskins et al. (April 2019) 180
United States v Champion Int'l Corp., 557 F.2d 1270 (9th Cir. 1977). 199
United States v David E. Thompson, Inc., 621 F.3d 1147 (1st Cir. 1980) 199
United States v Dynalectric Co., 859 F.2d 1559 (11th Cir. 1989). 201–2
United States v E.I. duPont de Nemours & Co., 188 F. 127 (CCD Del. 1911) 183–84
United States v Ganino Rivera Herrera et al. (6 February 2018) 181
United States v GS Caltex Corp., Hanjin Transportation Co., Ltd.,
    and SK Energy Co., Ltd. (14 November 2018) 189
United States v Koppers Co., 652 F.2d 290 (2d Cir. 1981) 199
United States v Nathan Nephi Zito, Case No. 22-cr-00113
    (D. Mt. Sept. 19, 2022) 199–200
United States v National Led Co., 63 F. Supp. 513 (SDNY 1945), aff'd,
    332 U.S. 319 (1947). 199–200
United States v Portac, Inc., 869 F.2d 1288 (9th Cir. 1989). 201–2
United States v Series Security NV, Danny Vandormael, Peter Verpoort,
    and Jean Paul Van Avermaet (29 June 2021) 189
United States v Trans-Missouri Freight Ass'n 165 U.S. 290 (1897) 185
United States v Trenton Potteries Co., 273 U.S. 392 (1927) 185
United States v United States Steel Corp., 251 U.S. 417 (1920) .183–84
United States v W.F. Brinkley & Son Construction Co., 783 F.2d 1157 (4th Cir. 1986) . . .199
US Department of Justice (case number 1:16-cr-00643) 21
Verizon Communications v Law Offices of Curtis V. Trinko, 540 US 398 (2004) 71–72

Table of Legislation

EUROPEAN AND INTERNATIONAL LEGISLATION, TREATIES, CONVENTIONS, AND CHARTERS

African Union Convention on Preventing and Combating Corruption (2003)..........67–68

Comprehensive Economic and Trade Agreement (CETA) 316

Council of Europe Civil Law Convention on Corruption (1999) 67–68

Council of Europe Convention, drawn up on the basis of Article K.3 of the TEU, on the protection of the European Communities' financial interests [1995] OJ C316/48

Art 1.........................242–43

Art 2.........................242–43

Council of Europe Council Act 97/ C 195/01 of 26 May 1997, drawn up on the basis of Article K.3(2)(c) of the TEU, the Convention on the fight against corruption involving officials of the European Communities or officials of Member States of the EU, [1997] OJ C195/1 (entered into force 28 September 2005) 242–43

Council of Europe Criminal Law Convention on Corruption (1998) 67–68

EU Charter on Fundamental Rights

Art 47........................259–60

EU Convention on Anti-Corruption (1997) 67–68

Inter-American Convention against Corruption (1996)......67–68, 335

North American Free Trade Agreement (NAFTA) 315

OECD Convention on Combating Bribery of Foreign Public Officials in International Business Transactions (Anti-Bribery Convention)........67–68, 70–71, 92–93, 97–98, 145, 242–43, 330–31, 334–35

Treaty on European Union (TEU) 266

Art 2......... 136, 243–44, 256, 260–61

Art 7................. 260–61, 266–67

Art 7(1) 260–61

Art 7(2) 260–61

Art 7(3) 260

Art 17.........................256–57

Art 19(1) 256, 259–60

Treaty on the Functioning of the European Union (TFEU) 64–65, 241–42

Art 3(1)(b).......................242

Art 26..........................64–65

Art 83(1) 242–43

Art 101......72, 79–80, 91, 143–44, 161, 164–65, 242, 244, 258

Art 101(1) 72

Art 101(3) 72

Art 102......................161, 244

Arts 258–260..................256–57

Art 258.............. 258–62, 266–67

Art 260.......................261–62

Art 260(2) 261–62

Art 278..........................261

Art 279..........................261

Art 325.......................242–43

UNCITRAL Model Law on Public Procurement (2011) 45–46, 51, 55–56, 278, 280, 310, 343

Ch VIII 59

Art 17, 1(3) 295

Art 64.........................304–5

United Nation Convention against Corruption (UNCAC) ......vi, 10, 67–68, 92–93, 120–21, 145, 242–43, 335

xx TABLE OF LEGISLATION

Arts 5–14 68–69
Art 9 . . . . .10, 68–69
Art 9(1) 68–69
Art 13 77
Arts 15–42 .68–69
Art 15 5
Arts 43–59 .68–69
United States-Mexico-Canada
    Agreement (USMCA) 341
US Free Trade Agreements 64
WTO Agreement on Government
    Procurement (GPA) . . . vi–3, 45–47,
        48–49, 51, 55–56, 140–41, 208–9,
        230, 273–75, 278, 280, 285, 296,
        305, 310, 315, 329, 343, 349
Preamble 62–63
Recitals 62–63
Art II(1) 63–64
Art II(2) 63–64
Art IV(1), (2) 62–63
Art IV(4) 62–63
Art IV(4)(a) 51
Art IX(3) 55
Art X(1) 55–56
Art X(4) 62–63
Art X(5) 62–63
Art XIII 51
Art XVIII 59, 63
Art XX(2) 63
Art XXI 63
Art XXII(7) .208–9
App I 63–64
    Annex 2, n 5 64
    Annex 7, n 1 64

EUROPEAN UNION SECONDARY LEGISLATION

Regulations

Regulation 1/2003 of 16 December
    2002 on the implementation of
    the rules on competition laid
    down in Articles 81 and 82 of
    the Treaty
Art 3 .164–65, 242
Regulation 2017/1939/EU of 12
    October 2017, implementing
    enhanced cooperation on the
    establishment of the European
    Public Prosecutor's Office
    [2017] OJ L283/1 242–43

Regulation 2018/1046 on the financial
    rules applicable to the general
    budget of the Union [2018]
    OJ L193/1 0 0 . . . . . . 64–65, 241–42
Art 61 257
Art 136(1) 265
Regulation 2020/2092 of the
    European Parliament and of
    the Council of 16 December
    2020 on a general regime
    of conditionality for the
    protection of the Union budget
Arts 3–6 263

Directives

Directive 89/665/EEC of 21 December
    1989 on the coordination
    of the laws, regulations and
    administrative provisions
    relating to the application of
    review procedures to the award
    of public supply and public
    works contracts (amended by
    Directive 2007/66/EC) . . .65, 241–42
Directive 2004/18/EC of the
    European Parliament and
    of the Council of 31 March
    2004 on the coordination of
    procedures for the award of
    public works contracts, public
    supply contracts and public
    service contracts (repealed by
    Directive 2014/24/EU)
Art 2 91
Directive 2014/23/EU of the European
    Parliament and of the Council
    of 26 February 2014 on the
    award of concession
    contracts 37, 46–47, 64–65, 91,
        104–5, 255, 266
Directive 2014/24/EU of the European
    Parliament and of the Council
    of 26 February 2014 on public
    procurement and repealing
    Directive 2004/18/EC [2014]
    OJ L 94/65 . . . . 37, 46–47, 64–65,
        91, 104–5, 140–41,
        241–42, 255, 266
Art 54 79–80
Art 57 . . . . .65, 241–42
Art 57(4) 91

Directive 2014/25/EU of the European Parliament and of the Council of 26 February 2014 on procurement by entities operating in the water, energy, transport and postal services sectors and repealing Directive 2004/17/EC 37, 43, 46–47, 91, 104–5, 241–42, 255, 266

Directive 2014/104/EU on certain rules governing actions for damages under national law for infringements of the competition law provisions of the Member States and of the EU [2014] OJ L349/1.......117–18
Art 1...........................117

Directive 2017/1371/EU of the European Parliament and of the Council of 5 July 2017 on the fight against fraud to the Union's financial interests by means of criminal law [2017] OJ L198/29 242–43

Directive 2019/1/EU of the European Parliament and of the Council of 11 December 2018 to empower the competition authorities of the Member States to be more effective enforcers and to ensure the proper functioning of the internal market [2019] OJ C11/3
Art 1(1) 242

Directive 2019/1937/EU of the European Parliament and of the Council of 23 October 2019 on the protection of persons who report breaches of Union law [2019] O.J. L 305/17................101

NATIONAL LEGISLATION AND REGULATIONS

Brazil

Bill No. 3,855/2019..............229–30
Art 63.......................230–31
CADE Resolution 21/2018
Art 12.........................236

CGU and AGU Inter-Ministerial Ordinance No. 2,278.......219–20
CGU Ordinance No. 910..........219–20
Civil Code
Art 1.134......................223
Code of Criminal Procedure (Decree-Law No. 3,689) 215
Complementary Law No. 135/2010 ('Clean Record Act') 215, 221
Art 2...........................221
Criminal Code
Art 317........................215
Art 333........................215
Art 337-B......................215
Art 337-F......................215
Decree No. 2,745/1998..............223
Decree No. 10,024/2019.............231
Federal Constitution of Brazil 1988 223
Art 33(2) 215
Art 37, XXI 213–14
Art 55.........................221
Art 70.........................215
Art 71.........................215
Art 72(1) 215
Art 74(2) 215
Art 161........................215
Art 102, I, b) 215
Art 102, I, c)....................215
Art 105, I, a) 215
Law No. 7,347/1985 215
Law No. 8,112/1990 (Public Servants Act) 224
Law No. 8,137/1990 215
Art 4.........................215
Law No. 8,429/1992 (Administrative Improbity) 215
Art 12.......................236–37
Law 8,443/1992
Art 46........................215
Art 57........................215
Art 58........................215
Law No. 8,666/1993 223
Art 28 (V) 223
Law No. 8,884/1994 215
Law No. 9,781/1999 215
Law No. 12,349/2010 223
Law No. 12,529/2011 (Competition Law)
Art 36........................215
Art 37........................215
Art 85........................215
Art 86........................215

xxii TABLE OF LEGISLATION

Art 86(7) 215
Art 87 215
Law No. 12,846/2013
    (Anti-Corruption Law) 215
Art 1 215
Art 4 215
Art 5 215
Art 6 215
Art 16 . . . . 215, 219–20
Art 17 . . . . 215, 219–20
Art 19 215
Art 22 215
Art 28 215
Art 29 233–34
Law No. 12,850/2013 (Criminal
    Organization Act)
Art 3-A 218–19
Art 3-B 218–19
Art 3-C 218–19
Art 4 . . . . 215, 218–19
Law No. 13,303/2016 229–30
Law No. 13,448/2017 225
Law No. 13,869/2019 226–27
Law No. 13,964/2019 218–19
Law No. 13,133/2021 215
Law No. 14,133/2021 (Public
    Procurement Law) 230–31
Art 9, II 223
Arti 53 230–31
Art 70 223
Art 174 230–31
Law No. 14,230/2021 226–27
Ordinance No. 33/2012 215
Presidential Decree No. 8,420
    Arts 28–40 219–20

Canada

Agreement on Internal Trade:
    Consolidated Version (2015) . . . 329
Ch 5 316
Anti-Corruption Act 331
Budget Implementation Act, 2018,
    No. 1, S.C. 2018, c 12 333
Combines Investigation Act, S.C.
    1952 supp. c. 314 . . . . 317–18, 337
Competition Act 321, 324, 334, 336
s 47(1) 337
s 47(2) 337
Constitution Act of 1867, formerly
    British North America Act 310
Constitution Act of 1982 310

Controlled Drugs and Substance Act . . . 334
Corruption of Foreign Public Officials
    Act, SC 1998, c 34 . . . . 330, 334
s 3(1)(b) 324–25
Criminal Code, RSC 1985,
    c C-46 . . . . . . 317–18, 330, 333, 334
ss 119–125 330
s 380 324–25
Defence Production Act
    (RSC, 1985, c. D-1) 313
Excise Tax Act 334
Federal Conflict of Interest Act
s 6(1) 325–26
s 7 325–26
s 9 325
s 21 325–26
Financial Administration Act 314, 334
Sch I 333
Sch I.1 333
Sch II 333
Income Tax Act 334
International Trade Tribunal Act 315
Legislation Act Respecting
    Contracting by
    Public Bodies 314
Lobbying Act 334

Hungary

Act CXCVI of 2011 247–48
Act CXLIII of 2015 on Public
    Procurement 244
Criminal Code
Art 293 244
Art 294 244

Japan

Act on Elimination and Prevention of
    Involvement in Bid Rigging,
    etc. and Punishments for
    Acts by Employees that Harm
    Fairness of Bidding, Law No.
    101 of 2002 122
Art 3, § 4 122

Poland

Penal Code
    Arts 228–230a 244
Public Procurement Law of 11
    September 2019 (in force
    since 1 January 2021) 244

TABLE OF LEGISLATION xxiii

Ukraine

Constitution 277, 290
Law No. 236/96-VR 'On the
    Protection from Unfair
    Competition' of 7 June 1996 290
Law No. 935-VIII, 'On Amendments
    to the Law of Ukraine On
    Protection of Economic
    Competition' 294
Law No. 1780-IX 'On Prevention of
    Threats to National Security
    Related to Excessive Influence
    of Persons Who Have
    Significant Economic and
    Political Weight in Public Life
    (Oligarchs)' (Anti-Oligarch
    Law) 93–94, 128–29, 229–30,
                     278–79, 286–87
Law No. 1197-VII 'on Publics' of 10
    April 2014 278
Law No. 1977-IX 'On Amendments
    to the Law of Ukraine "On
    Public Procurement" to
    Create Preconditions for
    Sustainable Development and
    Modernization of Domestic
    Industry' 293–94
Law No. 2210-III 'On the Protection of
    Economic Competition' of 11
    December 2001 290
    Art 50(1) 295
    Art 6(4) 295
Law No. 2289-VI 'On Public
    Procurement' of 1 June 2010 . . . 280
Law No. 3659-XII 'On the Antimonopoly
    Committee of Ukraine' of
    26 November 1993 290
Law No. 4851-VI 'on Peculiarities of
    Public Procurement in Certain
    Spheres of Entrepreneurial
    Activities' of 24 May 2012
    relating to the procurement of
    utilities 280

United Kingdom

STATUTES AND STATUTORY
INSTRUMENTS

Accessories and Abettors Act 1861 146
Anti-Terrorism, Crime and Security
    Act 2001 145

Bribery Act 2010 . . . . . . 92–93, 145, 152–53,
                    160–61, 162–63, 170, 174
    s 1 . . . . 145, 153
    s 2 . . . . 145, 153
    s 6 145
    s 7 . . . . 145, 153
    s 7(2) 145
    s 8 145
    s 10 146
Bribery Act 2020 . . . . 145, 160–61
Companies Act 1985 146
Companies Act 2006 146
Company Directors Disqualification
    Act 1986 143–44
Competition Act 1998 . . . . . . 151, 161, 163,
                    172, 173, 174
    Ch I 143–44
    s 2 148–49
    s 2A 148–49
    ss 25–29 148–49
    s 36 143–44
    s 40A 148–49
    s 40B 148–49
    s 47A 143–44
    s 58A 143–44
    s 59 148–49
    s 72 148–49
Crime and Courts Act 2013
    s 45 147–48
    Sch 17, paras. 7–8 147–48
Criminal Law Act 1977 . . . . 145, 146
Criminal Procedure Rules 2015,
    SI 2015/1490
    para. 5(5) 147–48
Criminal Justice Act 1987 144
Enterprise Act 2002 . . . . 143–44, 151
    Pt 4 166–67
    Pt 9 176–77
    s 188A 172
    s 188B 172
    s 190(2) 144
    ss 192–197 148–49
    s 199 148–49
    s 201 148–49
    s 204 143–44
Fraud Act 2006 146
Localism Act 2011
    s 28 142
Prevention of Corruption Act 1906 145
Prevention of Corruption Act 1916 145
Proceeds of Crime Act 2002 146
    Pt 2 146

xxiv TABLE OF LEGISLATION

Proceeds of Crime Act 2002
  (Commencement No. 4,
  Transitional Provisions
  and Savings) Order 2003,
  SI 2003/130 147–48
Procurement Act 2023 . . . .141–42, 168–69,
                      175, 177–78
  Pt 3
    Ch 1 142
    Ch 2 142
    Ch 3 142
    Ch 6 142
    Pt 4 142
    Pt 5 142
    Pt 9 142–43
    s 12 142
    s 12(1) 141
    s 12(4) 141
    s 13 141
    ss 41–43 167
    s 57 .142, 175
    ss 62–65 175
    Sch 5 167
    Sch 6 .142, 175
Public Bodies Corrupt Practices
  Act 1889 145
Public Contracts Regulations 2015,
  SI 2015/12 140–41
  reg 32 158
  reg 32(2)(c) 158
  regs 56–57 142
  reg 67 141
Public Interest Disclosure Act 1998
  s 47B 148–49
Public Services (Social Value)
  Act 2012 141
Regulation of Investigatory Powers
  Act 2000 148–49
  s 28 148–49
  s 29 148–49
Regulation of Investigatory Powers
  (Communications Data) Order 2010,
  SI 2010/480 148–49
Regulation of Investigatory Powers
  (Directed Surveillance and
  Covert Human Intelligence
  Sources) Order 2010,
  SI 2010/521 148–49
Serious Crime Act 2007
  Part II 146

Serious Organised Crime and Police
  Act 2005
  s 71 147–48
Theft Act 1968 146

United States

32 CFR
  §173.2(a) 201
  §173.2(f) 201
48 CFR
  §3.301(b) 207
  §3.303(c) 207
  §3.503-2 201
  §52.203-6 201
10 U.S.C.
  §2304(a)(1) 200
  §2305(b)(5) 207
18 U.S.C.
  §201(b) 201–2
  §201(f) 201–2
  §287 201–2
  §371 201–2
  §1001 201–2
  §1031 201–2
  §1341 201–2
  §1343 201–2
  §1346 205
  §1503 201–2
  §1505 201–2
  §1510 201–2
  §1512 201–2
  §1621 201–2
  §1623 201–2
  §1962 201–2
41 U.S.C.
  §10 a-d 208–9
  §253(a)(1) 200
  §253(b)e 207
  §8707 201–2
Anti-Corruption and Public
  Integrity Laws 201–2, 205–6
Antitrust Procedures and
  Penalties Act, Public
  Law No. 93-528, 88
  Statutes at Large
  1706 (1974) 190–91, 203–4
Buy American Act 208–9
Clayton Act
  §4 116–17
  §4A 116–17

TABLE OF LEGISLATION xxv

Competition in Contracting
Act of 1984 200

Creating Helpful Incentives to
Promote Semiconductors and
Science Act of 2022 206

Criminal Antitrust Anti-Retaliation
Act of 2019. 100

Enablers Act (H.R. 5525) 114

Federal Acquisition
Regulations 79–80, 115
§3.103-3 200
§3.301(b) 207
§3.303(a) 207
§3.11 201
§9.5 201
§52.203-2 200

Federal Civil False Claims Act . . . 101, 207–8

Federal Trade Commission Act
s 5 199–200

Federal Wire Fraud Act 205

Foreign Corrupt Practices
Act of 1977 . . . . . . 191–92, 194, 202

Foreign Corrupt Proceedings
Act, 15 U.S.C. §§ 78dd-1
(1998) 21, 69–70, 94–95

Foreign Extortion Prevention Act . . . 94–95

Inflation Reduction Act 2022 206

Infrastructure and Jobs Act 206

Office of Federal Procurement
Policy Act of 1974, 41
U.S.C. §§ 401-38 (2012) 79–80

Procurement Integrity Act. 192

Robinson-Patman Act,
15 U.S.C. §13(c) 192

Sherman Act of 1890, 15 U.S.C.
§§ 1–2 . . . . 184–85, 190, 194,
203, 310
s 1 . . . . 72, 188, 199, 200
s 2 . . . . 187, 199–200

Small Business Act 47–48

1

Introduction and Overview

A. Introduction	1	C. Corruption, Collusion, and Harm	9
B. Defining and Identifying		D. Combatting Corruption and	
Corruption and Collusion	5	Collusion: Proposals for Reform	12

A. Introduction

Across the world, many countries are struggling to ensure the continuing viability of, and citizen support for, the institutions of democratic capitalism and to counter autocracy, and the increasing trend towards it.[1] While such efforts necessarily involve renewed international engagement and collaboration, they also have an important inward-looking focus. The European Union (EU), the United States (US), and their allies can hardly succeed in their quest to promote and defend democracy abroad if their governments fail to deliver good results and a secure environment for their citizens at home. As Martin Wolf, chief economics commentator at the Financial Times, has observed:

> Trust in democratic institutions, the global market economy, and political and economic elites has faded over recent decades, not least in established high-income countries. This has shown itself in protectionism, hostility toward immigration, and, above all, a growing leaning toward authoritarian populism.[2]

Further, he considers that:

---

[1] See S. Power, 'How Democracy Can Win: The Right Way to Counter Autocracy', *Foreign Affairs* (16 February 2023), available at https://www.foreignaffairs.com/united-states/samantha-power-how-democracy-can-win-counter-autocracy (on the US government's efforts to promote democracy and deter corruption worldwide); see also B. Milanovic, 'The Clash of Capitalisms: The Real Fight for the Global Economy's Future', *Foreign Affairs* (10 December 2019), available at: https://www.foreignaffairs.com/articles/united-states/2019-12-10/clash-capitalisms, M. Wolf, *The Crisis of Democratic Capitalism* (Penguin Press, 2023); and V-Dem Institute's '2023 Democracy Report', available at https://www.v-dem.net/ (noting that, for the first time in more than two decades, the world has more closed autocracies than liberal democracies).

[2] Wolf, n. 1, 84.

2 INTRODUCTION AND OVERVIEW

the [real] enemy today is not without. Even China is not that potent. The enemy is within. Democracy will survive only if it gives opportunity, security and dignity to the great majority of its people.[3]

The steps required to rebuild belief and trust in democratic governance will involve numerous, diverse, and complex efforts. Leadership, vision, realism, and the effective countering of misinformation, disinformation, and demagoguery are all required.[4] In our view, however, one other vital means of bolstering confidence in, and strengthening the credibility of, government and ensuring the well-being of citizens is to prevent and deter misuse of public funds in the public procurement sector.[5]

Indeed, public procurement impacts on citizens' lives on a daily basis through its effect on, for example, the quality of the roads and bridges that they drive on; the airports that they use; the energy grids that they rely upon; the educational institutions that their children attend; and the public health services that they access and through ensuring that their nation is adequately defended.[6] It also entails the spending of vast sums of taxpayer—citizens'—money. Even in normal years, governments around the globe spend trillions on public procurement, accounting for nearly 30 per cent of all government expenditure in many countries (29 per cent on average in member countries of the Organisation for Economic Co-operation and Development (OECD)[7]) and 10–15 per cent of total gross domestic product (GDP).[8] This spending is now rising as governments grapple with

---

[3] Wolf, n. 1, 379.

[4] Wolf, n. 1. See also Power, n. 1.

[5] See, for related perspectives, S.E. Bosio, S. Djankov, E. Glaeser, and A. Shleifer, 'Public Procurement in Law and Practice' (2020) *PIIE Working Paper 20-14* (estimating global spending of around USD 11 trillion, accounting for 12 per cent of GDP); see also, an Open Contracting Partnership and Spend Network report estimating USD 13 trillion of spending a year, 'How governments spend: Opening up the value of global public procurement', available at https://www.open-contracting.org/what-is-open-contracting/global-procurement-spend/; A. Capobianco, 'Public Procurement and Competition Policy; Friends or Foes?', *Presentation at LEAR Conference* (10 July 2017) 6, available at http://www.learconference.com/wp-content/uploads/2017/07/CAPOBIANCO-Public-Procurement-and-Competition-Policy-Friends-or-Foes.pdf (estimating a total of USD 9.5 trillion). In 2016, EUR 1.9 trillion was estimated to have been spent on procurement in the EU, 'Rigging the Bids: Government Contracting is Growing Less Competitive, and Often More Corrupt', *The Economist* (19 November 2016), available at https://www.economist.com/europe/2016/11/19/rigging-the-bids.

[6] Consider how much damage to public confidence in government can be done by a procurement scandal on the scale of Operation Car Wash (in Portuguese, 'Operação Lava Jato'), originating in Brazil but spilling over into several adjoining economies and arguably triggering the downfall of the first government of President Luiz Inácio Lula da Silva (2003–2010), recently re-elected for a further term in office (see Chapter 7). This is not a unique situation: consider also the various corruption- and collusion-related scandals that have upended governments in Canada (see Chapter 10) and other jurisdictions discussed in this volume.

[7] See, e.g., OECD, 'Report on Implementing the OECD Recommendation on Fighting Bid Rigging' (2016), available at https://www.oecd.org/daf/competition/fightingbidrigginginpublicprocurement.htm and generally, n. 5.

[8] See OECD, *Government at a Glance* (OECD Publishing, 2019); World Trade Organization, 'WTO and Government Procurement' (5 April 2019), available at https://www.wto.org/english/tratop_e/gproc_e/gproc_e.htm; Capobianco, n. 5, 5 (OECD countries spent 28.1 per cent of government expenditures

some of the greatest challenges that they have faced in decades, such as managing the aftermath of the COVID-19 pandemic; planning for future public health crises;[9] addressing the threat of climate change; rebuilding or updating national infrastructure facilities; responding effectively to war, including that following the Russian Federation's invasion of Ukraine, and its impact on global peace, energy supply security, food security, and the cost of living;[10] and shoring up defence establishments.[11] For example, mitigating the effects of global climate change alone will necessitate enormous public investment, including in green energy technologies, production capacity and new infrastructure, the building and bolstering of sea walls, improved storm sewer systems, and measures to prevent and fight forest fires along with other international, national, and local abatement measures.[12]

When it is performed well, public procurement enables governments to maximize the value received in return for scarce public resources, while instilling confidence in themselves through the provision of the high-quality public services that citizens require. As a result, ensuring best value for taxpayer money is a core, or primary, purpose of public procurement regimes across most jurisdictions.[13]

---

on procurement in 2013); OECD, 'Roundtable on Collusion and Corruption in Public Procurement', DAF/COMP/GF(2010)6, 2. In developing countries, the proportion of GDP may be higher, up to 25 per cent; see Asian Development Bank, 'The Strategic Importance of Public Procurement' (2011), available at https://eimin.lrv.lt/uploads/eimin/documents/files/imported/lt/veikla/veiklos_sritys/viesieji-pirki mai/ADB_Brochure_Nov2011.pdf.

[9] As World Health Organization (WHO) Director-General, Dr. Tedros Adhanom Ghebreyesus, has said, 'The COVID-19 pandemic has been a seismic shock to the world, but we also know that the next pandemic is a matter of when, not if.' See WHO, 'New Fund for Pandemic Prevention, Preparedness and Response Formally Established' (2022), available at https://www.who.int/news/item/09-09-2022-new-fund-for-pandemic-prevention--preparedness-and-response-formally-established.

[10] See A. Kammer et al., 'How War in Ukraine Is Reverberating Across World's Regions', *IMF Blog* (15 March 2022), available at https://www.imf.org/en/Blogs/Articles/2022/03/15/blog-how-war-in-ukra ine-is-reverberating-across-worlds-regions-031522.

[11] See, the Stockholm International Peace Research Institute press release, 'World military expenditure reaches new record high as European spending surges' (24 April 2023), available at https://www. sipri.org/media/press-release/2023/world-military-expenditure-reaches-new-record-high-european-spending-surges#:~:text=World%20military%20expenditure%20reaches%20new%20record%20h igh%20as%20European%20spending%20surges,-24%20April%202023&text=(Stockholm%2C%20 24%20April%202023),in%20at%20least%2030%20years (noting that global military expenditure increased by 3.7 per cent in real terms in 2022, to reach a total of USD 2,240 billion) and K. Schake, 'America Must Spend More on Defense: How Biden Can Align Resources and Strategy', *Foreign Affairs* (5 April 2022), available at https://www.foreignaffairs.com/articles/united-states/2022-04-05/america-must-spend-more-defense.

[12] See, e.g., the broad panoply of actions contemplated in World Bank, 'Climate Change', available at https://www.worldbank.org/en/topic/climatechange; and in R.D. Anderson, A. Salgueiro, S.L. Schooner, and M. Steiner, 'Deploying the WTO Agreement on Government Procurement (GPA) to Enhance Sustainability and Accelerate Climate Change Mitigation' (2023) 32 *Public Procurement Law Review*, 223. See also A.E. Dessler, *Introduction to Modern Climate Change* (Cambridge University Press, 3rd edn, 2021), Chapters 11–14.

[13] It is recognized that many public procurement regimes often pursue other (sometimes referred to as 'horizontal' or 'secondary') goals, including the furthering of human rights, equity-based or sustainability considerations, and/or the provision of support for national businesses or disadvantaged groups within society. While these goals are recognized at least to a degree in many or most jurisdictions, they

4 INTRODUCTION AND OVERVIEW

Typically, this is achieved (or sought) through laws and institutions that aim to ensure compliance with fair, transparent, and reasonably open procurement processes (on the basis that sunlight is the best of disinfectants[14]), which facilitate competitive bidding by a diverse range of suppliers, deter corrupt practices, and encourage innovation. Such provisions are generally reinforced by mechanisms to debar or exclude delinquent suppliers[15] and to address (ideally in a reasonably short time frame) legitimate supplier complaints and to ensure that significant errors or abuses are remedied.[16] *Ex-post* review by auditors-general or other public accounting bodies may also be essential to detect and deter misconduct, although it generally lacks the ability to correct errors in 'real time'.

When public procurement is not done well, however, the converse is true; to the significant detriment of the nation, citizens experience poor public infrastructure and services, undergo frustration at the misuse of public money, and lose trust in government. An acute problem, therefore, is that not only are public procurement processes[17] difficult to manage efficiently (so as to ensure that public money is not wasted through mismanagement[18]), but they are also inherently vulnerable to two particular threats—corruption and supplier collusion ('bid rigging' by participating firms)—which undermine achievement of their goals. The reasons for this vulnerability are outlined in the next section and explored more fully in Chapter 2.

---

also entail potential conflicts with efficiency-based objectives. See, for discussion, C. McCrudden, *Buying Social Justice: Equality, Government Procurement and Legal Change* (Oxford University Press, 2007), see further Chapter 3.

[14] See L. Brandeis, 'What Publicity Can Do' in *Other People's Money and How the Bankers Use It* (Frederick A. Stokes Company, 1914).

[15] See S. Williams, *Fighting Corruption in Public Procurement: A Comparative Analysis of Disqualification or Debarment Measures* (Hart Publishing, 2012).

[16] See, for relevant commentary, S. Arrowsmith, *The Law of Public and Utilities Procurement, Volume 2* (Sweet & Maxwell, 2018), especially Chapter 22; and S. Arrowsmith, J. Linarelli, and D. Wallace, 'Enforcement and Remedies' in S. Arrowsmith, J. Linarelli, and D. Wallace (eds), *Regulating Public Procurement: National and International Perspectives* (Kluwer Law International, 2000).

[17] According to which governments repeatedly expend vast sums of money through government bodies and civil servants whose conduct is difficult to monitor by the intended beneficiaries of the spending or providers of the funds (citizens and taxpayers) applying rules and procedures that differ from those used for private sector purchasing; see Chapter 2.

[18] See J.A. Lynch, *Public Procurement and Contract Administration: A Brief Introduction* (Amazon Digital Services LLC, 2017); see also S. Kelman, *Unleashing Change: A Study of Organizational Renewal in Government* (Brookings Institution Press, 2005) (outlining important trade-offs between adherence to rules-based public administration, including government contracting, and the attainment of best results for citizens through institution and human capital building). On the distinction between corrupt practices and 'mere' mismanagement, see also O. Bandiera, A. Pratt, and T. Valletti, 'Active and Passive Waste in Government Spending: A Policy Experiment' (2009) 99(4) *American Economic Review* 1278. Still, it must be acknowledged that there is a continuum between outright corruption and mismanagement of public funds. Successfully addressing both challenges requires much attention to institution and human capacity building and innovation in product design and in the procurement process itself.

B. Defining and Identifying Corruption and Collusion

As described in later chapters, different cultures and national legal systems may adhere to different ethical norms and expectations and may adopt distinct approaches to the deterrence of corrupt activities (and supplier collusion). Still, there is a growing convergence and consensus around core definitions and concepts.

In a broad sense, *corruption* in public administration may be defined as the abuse by public officials, for private gain, of power that has been entrusted to them by another (the populace or an employer)[19] or as a practice involving a failure to act impartially—the putting of private interests ahead of public ones. It includes bribery,[20] the accepting and receiving of a benefit to break the rules and subvert the entrusted process, or as a condition for carrying out a process that was meant to occur,[21] and cronyism, the favouring of acquaintances, family, and friends over others. In the context of public procurement, the World Bank (WBG) has identified the core aim of corruption to be 'to steer the contract to the favoured bidder without detection',[22] so leading to restricted and unfair access to government procurement contracts. In this context, it can be achieved in a number of ways, including by: avoiding competition (e.g. through unjustified sole-sourcing or intimidating bidders); favouring a certain bidder (e.g. by tailoring specifications and sharing inside information); excluding qualified bidders (e.g. through restricted circulation of advertisements, biased evaluation purposes, or bid tampering); and avoiding detection (e.g. by negotiating the removal of audit rights).[23]

Corruption in public procurement thus typically involves procurement decisions taken not in accordance with the principles of equal treatment and non-discrimination, but in favour of particular, preferred bidders ('particularism') either in explicit exchange for improper compensation or other reciprocal benefits—often personal ones, such as bribes, lavish holidays, promises of

---

[19] See, e.g., Transparency International, 'What is Corruption', available at https://www.transparency.org/en/what-is-corruption.

[20] It may also include, e.g. fraud, illegal contribution, favouritism/particularism (such as nepotism and cronyism—preferring acquaintances, friends, and family over others), embezzlement, conflict of interest, extortion, or abuse of discretion, although legislation in a jurisdiction is likely to set out its own definition of 'corrupt action'.

[21] See S. Rose-Ackerman and B.J. Palifka, *Corruption and Government* (Cambridge University Press, 2nd edn, 2016) 9. See also the United Nations Convention against Corruption (UNCAC), Article 15, which focuses on the offering/giving to, and solicitation/receiving by, public officials of an undue advantage in order that the official act or refrain from acting in the exercise of his/her official duties. Also, see further Chapter 3. Klitgaard identifies a formula for corruption that focuses on the relationship between the monopoly of power/government and the discretion of officials and their accountability— Corruption = Monopoly + Discretion - Accountability (C = M + D-A), R. Klitgaard, *Controlling Corruption* (University of California Press, 1988).

[22] World Bank Group, *Fraud and Corruption Awareness Handbook: A Handbook for Civil Servants Involved in Public Procurement* (International Bank for Reconstruction and Development/The World Bank, 2013) 7.

[23] World Bank, n. 22, 7–8. Not all of these practices, however, will necessarily be caught by domestic anti-corruption laws; see further Chapter 3.

6 INTRODUCTION AND OVERVIEW

subsequent employment (golden parachutes), but sometimes also partisan ones, such as contribution to political funds—or as a result of cronyism. It can impact on all phases of a procurement process from the decision as to whether to purchase at all, and if so what (the pre-tender stage), to the drawing up and design of awards criteria, to the placing of suppliers on relevant lists of bidders, to the evaluation process and the award of contracts, and to the post-award contracting, implementation, or execution phase.[24] It can involve grand corruption—large sums of money and a small number of powerful players, for example, where it pervades the highest levels of government or major government contracts are awarded in return for bribes to political leaders and their allies—or petty corruption—for example, procurement contracts occurring regularly at the local level, which favour relatives or cronies.[25] Corruption in public procurement generally has both a demand-side ingredient (where a public official solicits, extorts, or receives pecuniary or other benefits from bidders, sometimes referred to as passive bribery) and a supply-side component (where businesses offer or give bribes or other advantages to public officials, sometimes referred to as active bribery).

Public procurement represents one of the highest corruption risk activities among government functions, especially as; corruption may be relatively easy to hide in this context; and such activities provide a straightforward means of transferring large (even huge) sums between the public and private sectors.[26] The susceptibility of public procurement to corruption derives, in many cases, from the fact that public purchasing differs from purchasing by private entities in that it routinely involves the taking of significant actions and decisions by persons other than those whose interests are intended to be served (a principal–agent problem).[27] As the recent COVID-19 pandemic has highlighted, the risk of corrupt practices may mount when spending is made rapidly during a crisis.[28] Further, in some countries,

---

[24] See, e.g., Ministry of Housing, Communities and Local Government, 'A Review into the Risks of Fraud and Corruption in Local Government Procurement as Committed to in the UK Anti-Corruption Strategy 2017 to 2022' (2020) 15, available at https://assets.publishing.service.gov.uk/government/uplo ads/system/uploads/attachment_data/file/890748/Fraud_and_corruption_risks_in_local_governmen t_procurement_FINAL.pdf.

[25] E. Dávid-Barrett and M. Fazekas, 'Grand Corruption and Government Change: An Analysis of Partisan Favouritism in Public Procurement' (2020) 26 *European Journal on Criminal Policy and Research* 411. Grand corruption generally involves large transactions (e.g. in construction, telecommunications, infrastructure contracts, extractive industries, and defence), including complex and sophisticated transactions.

[26] See N. Regös and M. Fazekas, 'Objective Corruption Risk Indicators Using Low and Middle Income Country Datasets', *Government Transparency Institute* (2021) 1, available at https://www.govt ransparency.eu/objective-corruption-risk-indicators-using-low-and-middle-income-country-datas ets/, and further discussion in Chapter 2.

[27] See F. Jenny, 'Competition and Anti-Corruption Considerations in Public Procurement' in *Fighting Corruption and Promoting Integrity in Public Procurement* (OECD, 2005) 29–35, Chapter 3. Related perspectives are provided in J.J. Laffont and J. Tirole, *A Theory of Incentives in Procurement and Regulation* (MIT Press, 1993). See further Chapter 2.

[28] See, for penetrating discussion, S. Arrowsmith, L. Butler, A. La Chimia, and C. Yukins (eds) *Public Procurement in (a) Crisis? Global Lessons from the COVID-19 Pandemic* (Hart Publishing, 2021) and nn. 51–53 and text.

DEFINING AND IDENTIFYING CORRUPTION AND COLLUSION   7

corruption, or particularism, may be established norms, creating a problem of 'systemic corruption', involving self-reinforcing mechanisms of rent-seeking and graft.[29]

Supplier collusion, in contrast, refers to a specific form of cartel activity,[30] in which two or more independent firms collude to rig their bids in a tendering process (bid rigging, collusive tendering, or supplier collusion). As many studies have identified, public procurement is also intrinsically vulnerable to supplier collusion,[31] partly because of the public nature of the processes, the restrictions that may apply to the right to bid and the huge and regular sums of money that are frequently involved.[32] Collusion can take a variety of different forms and involve the withholding of bids, non-competitive bidding, or joint bidding (see Table 1.1).

Table 1.1 Common bid rigging practices

Withholding of bids	Bid suppression	One or more competitors agree not to bid or to withdraw a bid to ensure that a designated firm wins
Non-competitive bidding	Cover, courtesy, or complementary bidding	One or more cartelists agree to submit bids they know will be unacceptable because they are too high or do not comply with other important tender requirements
	Market or customer allocation	Firms agree not to bid against competitors or to avoid competing for business (e.g. by submitting only complementary bids) in certain geographic areas or in relation to certain tenderers (or lots within the tender)
	Bid rotation	Cartel members all submit bids but take turns submitting a winning bid

(continued)

---

[29] A. Persson, B. Rothstein, and J. Teorell, 'Why Anticorruption Reforms Fail—Systemic Corruption as a Collective Action Problem' (2013) 26 *Governance* 449, 452.

[30] *Cartels* are frequently defined to include anti-competitive agreements or arrangements to fix prices, establish output restrictions or quotas, rig bids, or share or divide markets; see OECD, 'Recommendation of the OECD Council Concerning Effective Action Against Hard Core Cartels', C(98)35/FINAL (25 March 1998) 2.

[31] See further Chapter 2 and e.g. R.D. Anderson, A. Jones, and W.E. Kovacic, 'Preventing Corruption, Supplier Collusion and the Corrosion of Civic Trust: A Procompetitive Program to Improve the Effectiveness and Legitimacy of Public Procurement' (2019) 26(4) *George Mason Law Review* 1233; R.D. Anderson and W.E. Kovacic, 'Competition Policy and International Trade Liberalization: Essential Complements to Ensure Good Performance in Public Procurement Markets' (2009) 18 *Public Procurement Law Review* 6; R.C. Marshall and L.M. Marx, *The Economics of Collusion: Cartels and Bidding Rings* (MIT Press, 2012); and A. Heimler, 'Cartels in Public Procurement' (2012) *Journal of Competition Law & Economics* 11.

[32] See Jenny, n. 27; Anderson, Jones, and Kovacic, n. 31; Anderson and Kovacic, n. 31; Marshall and Marx, n. 31; and Heimler, n. 31.

8 INTRODUCTION AND OVERVIEW

Table 1.1 Continued

Joint bidding	Joint tendering or subcontracting	Although joint tendering and subcontracting can be legitimate (e.g. allowing firms to be able to tender at all or to tender more efficiently through joining supplementary knowledge and skills), it may constitute anti-competitive bid rigging when used in relation to projects that could be undertaken by each firm individually and as a mechanism for mitigating operational problems of collusion[33]

In most cases, the essence of bid rigging is thus to create a false impression, or illusion, of a genuine competitive bidding process,[34] whilst the bidders in fact thwart the purpose of the tendering exercise (to extract the most competitive, cost-effective bid for the products or services through tendering) by limiting price competition or sharing markets between themselves. The schemes will generally incorporate mechanisms to apportion and distribute profits among parties (a form of rent sharing), for example, through compensation, through side payments, by having the winning bidder subcontract work to losing or non-tendering firms,[35] or through the coordinated bidding structure itself.

In some jurisdictions, bid rigging impacting on public procurement is treated as a form of conduct prohibited by anti-corruption laws.[36] It is true that—in the public procurement context—supplier collusion and corruption are not infrequently found to overlap and occur together, reinforcing one another and making each other more effective and stable.[37] They are nevertheless discrete categories of conduct, which may occur independently of each other, and need to be countered

---

[33] See, generally, C. Ritter, 'Joint Tendering Under EU Competition Law' (2017) 2 *Concurrences Review* 60 (discussing how a line can be drawn under EU competition law between legitimate joint tendering or selling—e.g., where it allows two firms to produce efficiencies that outweigh the competition concerns or to be able to tender at all—and anti-competitive bid rigging); C. Thomas, 'Two Bids or not to Bid? An Exploration of the Legality of Joint Bidding and Subcontracting Under EU Competition Law' (2015) 6 *Journal of European Competition Law & Practice* 629, 630 (subcontracting is not necessarily anti-competitive, however, if it is not done in furtherance of efforts to limit competition in the award of the main contract) and the European Commission's Draft Horizontal Cooperation Guidelines, March 2022.

[34] That is, that they are competing to submit the lowest possible tender at the tightest possible margin.

[35] See, e.g., US Department of Justice, 'Price Fixing, Bid Rigging, and Market Allocation Schemes: What They Are and What to Look For' (2021), available at https://www.justice.gov/atr/file/810261/download, 2–3.

[36] Some institutions, including the World Bank Group, do sometimes refer to supplier collusion as a sub-species of corruption, and in some jurisdictions anti-corruption laws outlaw bid rigging as well as bribery; see, e.g., the position in Brazil discussed in Chapter 7.

[37] See, e.g., the experiences discussed in this book, in Chapter 6 (the US), Chapter 7 (Brazil), Chapter 8 (Hungary and Poland), Chapter 9 (Ukraine), and Chapter 10 (Canada). See also Anderson, Jones, and Kovacic, n. 31, and references cited therein.

with complementary yet often distinct remedies.[38] In general, a key premise of this book is that supplier collusion represents as great a threat to public welfare and confidence in government as corruption, while recognizing that the relative severity of each of these threats to public welfare can vary from country to country.

C. Corruption, Collusion, and Harm

Both corruption and collusion in the public procurement context may lead to wide-ranging harm—not only economic but also political, social, and environmental—so impacting negatively on human well-being.[39] Although they are distinct from poor public contracting, the latter can also have damaging effects, compound the problems of corruption and collusion, and preclude the benefits of open and transparent contracting from being reaped (unintentional waste and inefficiency is a problem that is comparable in its scope and scale[40]). There is, therefore, a spectrum and continuum of conduct from corruption and cronyism, to collusion, to mismanagement of public resources, which may undermine public procurement goals and cause significant detriment. This book focuses on corruption, cronyism, and collusion, whilst recognizing that these practices are often entangled with, exacerbated, or even facilitated, by mismanagement.[41]

It has already been seen that corrupt and collusive practices thwart the objectives of public procurement processes, increasing the cost and reducing the quality or quantity of goods, services, and works procured. They are also liable to fuel inflation, undermine the rule of law and the legitimacy of democratic political systems, and allow the proceeds of crime to enter the legitimate economy.[42] Corruption, in particular, fuels public discontent and anger, reduces trust between citizens and their public institutions, and ultimately undermines faith in, and commitment towards, democracy and the institutions of free-market capitalism.[43] Public discourse is now increasingly recognizing the importance of fighting corruption—including, in the public procurement context—and its centrality to the survival and flourishing of democracy. As observed in an United States 2021 White House policy statement:

---

[38] See Chapters 3 and 4.

[39] See further Chapter 2 and B. Rothstein, *Controlling Corruption: The Social Contract Approach* (Oxford University Press, 2021) 1.

[40] See Bandiera et al., n. 18.

[41] For example, the problem of supplier collusion in public procurement can be seen as resulting, in part, from a lack of incentives for effective managerial oversight and following up of suspicious signs. See Heimler, n. 31.

[42] See, e.g., Anderson, Jones, and Kovacic, n. 31.

[43] Wolf, n. 1. See also 'Memorandum of the Biden Administration, The Whitehouse Briefing Room' (3 June 2021), available at https://www.whitehouse.gov/briefing-room/presidential-actions/2021/06/03/memorandum-on-establishing-the-fight-against-corruption-as-a-core-united-states-national-security-interest/; and J. Pontes and M. Anselmo, *Operation Car Wash: Brazil's Institutionalized Crime and the Inside Story of the Biggest Corruption Scandal in History* (Bloomsbury, 2022) 152.

10   INTRODUCTION AND OVERVIEW

Corruption corrodes public trust; hobbles effective governance; distorts markets and equitable access to services; undercuts development efforts; contributes to national fragility, extremism, and migration; and provides authoritarian leaders a means to undermine democracies worldwide. When leaders steal from their nations' citizens or oligarchs flout the rule of law, economic growth slows, inequality widens, and trust in government plummets.[44]

Similarly, European Commission President Ursula von der Leyen has observed:

If we want to be credible when we ask candidate countries to strengthen their democracies, we must also eradicate corruption at home. That is why we will present measures to update our legislative framework for fighting corruption in the coming year.[45]

Further, Target 16.5 of the United Nations (UN) Sustainable Development Goals (SDGs)[46] commits countries to the reduction of corruption and bribery in all of its forms and accepts that the success of major elements of the SDGs is directly contingent on it. Whilst corruption contributes to impunity, injustice, and conflict, its reduction, and the building of effective, accountable, and inclusive institutions, can pave the way for sustainable development and the promotion of inclusive societies.[47] The United Nations Convention against Corruption (UNCAC)—a binding instrument of international law—recognizes the need to counteract corruption in the field of public procurement,[48] and the matters of both corruption and supplier collusion in public procurement are given prominence in relevant work of the OECD.[49]

The importance of combatting corruption has become increasingly evident in the aftermath of the COVID-19 pandemic and following the outbreak of recent

---

[44] See 'Memorandum of the Biden Administration', n. 43.

[45] See U. von der Leyen, '2022 State of the Union Address by President von der Leyen' (14 September 2022), available at https://ec.europa.eu/commission/presscorner/detail/ov/speech_22_5493 (on the EU's work to promote democracy, civil society, and the integrity of governmental institutions in its neighbouring and other countries).

[46] The SDGs were adopted by the UN in 2015 as a universal call to action to end poverty, protect the planet, and ensure that by 2030 all people enjoy peace and prosperity; see https://sdgs.un.org/goals. Goal 16 focuses on peace, justice, and solid institutions (to promote peaceful and inclusive societies for sustainable development, provide access to justice for all, and build effective, accountable, and inclusive institutions at all levels).

[47] See O. Perera, L. Casier, D. Uzsoki, and M. Ruete, 'The Role of Public Procurement in Deploying a Sustainable Infrastructure' (2016) *International Institute For Sustainable Development Discussion Paper* 5–6.

[48] See UNCAC, Article 9 and further discussion in Chapters 3 and 4.

[49] See, e.g., the multiple activities and publications cited on the OECD's website under the heading of 'Integrity in Public Procurement', available at https://www.oecd.org/gov/public-procurement/integr ity/, and those listed under the separate heading of 'Fighting Bid Rigging in Public Procurement', available at https://www.oecd.org/daf/competition/fightingbidrigginginpublicprocurement.htm.

wars across the globe, including in Ukraine.[50] Transparency International,[51] for example, has drawn attention to corruption risks in emergency government procurement of equipment needed to fight the corona virus,[52] and fraud estimates have been in the USD billions in several G20 countries.[53] The importance of a fundamental break with past corrupt practices has been highlighted repeatedly in the context of the war in Ukraine, including by President Zelensky.[54] It is also apparent that efficient public procurement will be crucial in the wake of these crises, as countries seek to rebuild their economies and to bolster their public infrastructure and legislative framework for fighting corruption in the coming year.[55]

The problems of corruption and collusion highlighted in the paragraphs above are well recognized, and jurisdictions across the world have participated in national and international efforts to combat them. Despite this, relatively few jurisdictions—whether developed, transitioning, or developing economies—are proving to be successful in protecting their public procurement processes from these problems, even (or especially) in times of crisis and emergency and even in countries that are perceived to be 'clean', or relatively clean, or that have strong democratic institutions.[56] Rather, and in spite of these efforts, many complain that the results are meagre and are not halting the practices, especially corruption when engrained within a system.[57] As Mungiu-Pippidi notes, 'the evaluations piling up after the first fifteen years of anti-corruption work showed great expectations and humble results'.[58] Further, it seems possible that the risks of such practices may actually be increasing as liberal democracies come under strain[59] and the number of

---

[50] See, regarding the latter, discussion in Chapter 9. One articulated concern is that endemic corruption may have helped to fuel Russia's authoritarian regime and military aggression; see Transparency International, US Office, 'Seven Measures Congress Can Adopt to Address Russia's Corruptly Financed Military Aggression' (3 February 2022). The commencement of conflicts may, in addition, be used as a mechanism by leaders to boost popular support and divert attention away from their own corruption, especially the misuse of domestic resources and its laundering abroad.

[51] Transparency International is a civil society organization that works, independently of governments, to promote its vision of a world without corruption, see https://www.transparency.org/en.

[52] See 'Corruption Could Cost Lives in Latin America's Response to The Coronavirus', *Transparency. org* (31 March 2020), available at https://www.transparency.org/en/news/corruption-could-cost-lives-in-latin-americas-response-to-the-coronavirus.

[53] See, e.g., 2022 OECD Global Anti-Corruption and Integrity Forum's panel on 'Protecting the integrity of public finances amid the pandemic: Taking stock of the effectiveness of external and internal audit'. See further discussion of these problems in some of the country chapters below.

[54] See discussion in Chapter 9.

[55] von der Leyen, n. 45.

[56] Rothstein, n. 39, 8 (especially so in young and fragile democracies). But consider also the experiences of the UK, the US, and Canada, as set out in subsequent chapters of this book.

[57] Rothstein, n. 39.

[58] A. Mungiu-Pippidi, *The Quest for Good Governance: How Societies Develop Control of Corruption* (Oxford University Press, 2015).

[59] See V-Dem Institution Policy Brief No. 33, 'The Case for Democracy: Does Democracy Improve Public Goods Provision?' (January 2022) ('A large body of scientific research demonstrates that democratic elections induce government to provide public goods. ... A growing body of scientific studies

12 INTRODUCTION AND OVERVIEW

autocracies (where executive restraint and the rule of law is weaker) rise[60] (see, e.g., the impact of illiberal developments in democracy and the economy in Hungary and Poland, discussed in Chapter 8).

D. Combatting Corruption and Collusion: Proposals for Reform

The purpose of this book is, consequently, to consider why corruption and collusion persist and to identify and advocate for reforms and improvements that will help countries to defend the integrity of their public procurement systems from these practices. In particular, it proposes that distinct policies, especially public procurement, anti-corruption, and competition law and policy, are more closely united around a 'joined-up' public procurement strategy and seeks to make proposals that will enable countries, with the will to do so, to achieve significant improvements in public purchasing with benefits that follow for the economic and social welfare of the nation.

One central issue addressed is the trade-offs that may be involved between the measures needed to deter 'traditional' forms of corruption in public procurement (especially bribery) and those that are needed for the prevention of supplier collusion (bid rigging). In particular, while the former rely on measures to increase transparency, economic analysis and the experience of competition agencies worldwide make abundantly clear that such measures can, in fact, facilitate bid rigging.[61] They do so by helping suppliers to overcome key challenges that, in other circumstances, work to limit the scope for cartel activity—namely the intrinsic difficulties in reaching agreement on, and enforcing, prices, output levels, and related variables.[62] This conundrum necessitates fresh approaches to public policy in this area. For example, attention is needed to the specific types of information that are made generally available for the deterrence of corruption. Carefully tailored transparency measures are less likely to facilitate bid rigging than blunderbuss approaches.

Indeed, while understanding is evolving, recent analysis suggests that the careful use of transparent electronic procurement systems (e-procurement) combined with systematic monitoring and analysis of bidding patterns may facilitate

---

now demonstrates that democratization mitigates corruption'). See also A. Mungiu-Pipiidi, *Rethinking Corruption* (Edward Elgar, 2023), Chapter 4 (rethinking corruption and democracy).

[60] See the V-Dem Institute's '2023 Democracy Report', n. 1.

[61] See Anderson, Kovacic, and Jones, n. 31; Marshall and Marx, n. 31; Heimler, n. 31; Anderson and Kovacic, n. 31; Jenny, n. 27; and discussion in Chapter 3.

[62] See, for a rigorous analysis supported by extensive, carefully researched examples, Marshall and Marx, n. 31. An early but penetrating analysis of the challenges involved in cartel formation is provided in G.J. Stigler, 'A Theory of Oligopoly' (1964) 72(1) *Journal of Political Economy* 44–61.

detection and thereby deter rather than facilitate supplier collusion.[63] 'Outside-the-box' measures can also help with the deterrence and prevention of both bid rigging and collusion. These include both: (i) structural measures to enhance the openness of public procurement markets and thereby the number and diversity of participating suppliers, for example the opening of such markets to foreign suppliers via international trade agreements, which can increase resilience to both supplier collusion and corruption; and (ii) measures to professionalize and enhance the market research and other capabilities of procuring agency staff members, which by themselves render the relevant agencies less vulnerable to collusive practices by suppliers, as they are better aware of competitive options available in the market.[64] In some jurisdictions, the risks of corrupt practices affecting public funds are of such acute proportions that tackling them may need to be prioritized—at least for a period—over the prevention of bid rigging.

To set the context for this discussion, Chapter 2 starts by exploring more fully why public procurement processes are especially prone to distortion by corruption and/or collusion. It examines the opportunities and incentives (individual and collective) that drive corruption and collusion, and how the two types of conduct may work together to create a more stable system of wrongdoing. It is only by understanding the features of public procurement that render them susceptible to these practices that (joined-up) steps and strategies to counter them can be constructed. Chapter 2 also references surveys and indicators of corruption and collusion, provides some examples of bid rigging and bribery that have been revealed in different countries across the globe, and notes indicators of the harm caused by such practices. It thus seeks to highlight the causes, size, and scale of the problem faced; how the conduct negatively impacts on citizens' life standards and their access to public services;[65] how it can be combatted; and the substantial, financial, and other benefits that can be achieved from so doing by reducing their incidences and the 'tax' they impose on public expenditure.

Chapter 3 goes on to consider the core frameworks that countries adopt to limit the scope for corruption and supplier collusion in their public procurement systems, including the basic requirements of national procurement, and anti-corruption and competition laws. These regimes tend to tackle corruption and collusion using both preventive and deterrent techniques through public procurement rules requiring the use of, where possible, open, transparent, and competitive bidding systems, which are backed up by codes of conduct, oversight mechanisms and independent enforcement mechanisms, and through the enforcement of stringent anti-corruption and competition laws by active agencies.

---

[63] J. Wachs, M. Fazekas, and J. Kertész, 'Corruption Risk in Contracting Markets: A Network Science Perspective' (2021) 12 *International Journal of Data Science and Analytics* 45. See further Chapter 4.

[64] See further Chapter 4.

[65] Regös and Fazekas, n. 26, 1.

14 INTRODUCTION AND OVERVIEW

The book recognizes, nonetheless, that robust and comprehensive systems insufficient on their own to protect public procurement from corruption and collusion. Rather, a system will not achieve its objectives if weaknesses in the implementation, coordination, oversight, or enforcement of the rules exist. For example, significant challenges arise in conducting public procurement processes. Constructing processes that deliver efficiency in contracting is complex and, as has already been seen, may require trade-offs to be made between measures designed to prevent corruption, which may have the effect of facilitating collusion on the market, and measures to prevent collusion, which may have the effect of facilitating corruption. Further, it may be difficult, without allowing corruption opportunities to arise, to enable procurement officials or to take account of evolving market developments and possibilities, or to take risks and exercise discretion, even though this may be necessary to maximize the potential benefits of public investment in infrastructure and other essential public goods and services.[66]

Alternatively, or additionally, infringements of the rules may not be prevented or deterred if the institutional framework and oversight of processes is weak or insufficient to ensure that the law is actually enforced; improvements in governance standards may be required. Further, a particular problem is that measures to combat corruption and supplier collusion in public procurement are not costless. Because significant resources are required to enable the detection, investigation, and prosecution (deterrence) of these practices,[67] a range of other mechanisms for preventing and deterring corruption and supplier collusion must be considered that do *not* entail excessive costs, including efforts to train the procurement workforce[68] and businesses, and which encourage reporting of wrongdoing and compliance.

Chapter 4 consequently reflects on the questions of how opportunities and incentives for corruption and collusion can be changed and reduced further, and how the effectiveness of public procurement, anti-corruption, and competition tools can be optimized, strengthened, and bolstered. It thus considers: how to hone the system to promote and encourage better compliance with regulatory objectives; how to prevent and deter illegal, corrupt, and anti-competitive conduct; how policy coordination, both negative (to avoid conflicts) and positive (to ensure synergies), between procurement, anti-corruption, and competition laws and agencies may contribute to a more effective system; and how to empower procurement agencies and competition and anti-corruption enforcement institutions to ensure that they

---

[66] See S. Kelman, 'Remaking the Federal Procurement' (2002) 31 *Public Contracting Law Journal* 581; S. Kelman, *Unleashing Change: A Study of Organizational Renewal in Government* (Brookings, 2005); and D. Coyle, *Markets, State and People: Economics for Public Policy* (Princeton University Press, 2020) 72.

[67] Rose-Ackerman and Palifka, n. 21.

[68] See S.L. Schooner and C.R. Yukins, 'Public Procurement: Focus on People, Value for Money and Systemic Integrity, Not Protectionism' in R. Baldwin and S. Evenett (eds), *The Collapse of Global Trade, Murky Protectionism, and the Crisis: Recommendations for the G20* (A VoxEU.org Publication, 2009), Chapter 17.

can carry out their mandates and coordinate their strategies effectively. It also discusses the problem of 'systemic corruption', in which corruption is not the result, or solely the result, of a principal–agent problem, (where corrupt procurement officials (or 'agents'), entrusted to act on behalf of a principal, act unlawfully by abusing or misusing their public office for private gain). Rather, when entrenched, corruption may derive from the deliberate actions of corrupt governmental authorities or ministers, rather than from their subordinates, and may be reinforced through 'baked-in' expectations of such conduct across a society.[69] There are some indications of such tendencies in some of the countries discussed in this book,[70] and in developing and transitioning economies more generally.

Chapter 4 thus explores the debate as to whether systemic corruption can be tackled through more law enforcement and incremental change, or whether a more all-encompassing approach is required to break a historic pattern of corruption and build new social norms, and how impetus for such reform may come about. In such circumstances, measures designed to combat corruption through changing individual incentives, for example by minimizing opportunities for wrongdoing and using law enforcement to detect, punish, and deter the conduct (so the cost of acting unlawfully, or expected punishment, exceeds the benefits of so acting taking into account the probability of apprehension), are likely to be unsuccessful and ineffective. Rather, where corruption is widespread, self-reinforcing, and based on a 'collective action' problem,[71] actors are likely to hold deeply engrained beliefs that others will act corruptly and so will generally consider it to be fruitless and pointless to act otherwise themselves—'if you expect others in your community to be corrupt, you will be incentivized to act corruptly because the individual costs of engaging in principled behaviours outweigh the individual benefits'.[72] Further, actors may be able to behave with impunity, believing that conduct engaged in, or endorsed by, senior officials or politicians will not be contested. Where this is the case, a different approach will thus be required, and it is likely to be a challenge to change beliefs that bribes must be paid and that corruption will not be investigated or sanctioned.[73]

The chapter also considers the contribution that foreign bribery and foreign extortion laws, trade liberalization, integrity pacts, and international cooperation and coordination can play in helping to combat corruption and collusion in the procurement context, particularly through changing expectations and the moral equilibrium. It thus highlights the importance of political commitment, international

---

[69] For a synthesis of relevant theoretical and empirical work, see A. Persson, B. Rothstein, and J. Teorell, 'Why Anticorruption Reforms Fail—Systemic Corruption as a Collective Action Problem' (2013) 26 *Governance* 449, 452 and see further Chapters 2–4.

[70] See the analysis in Chapters 7, 8 and 9 of this book; see also Persson et al., n. 69.

[71] See further Chapters 2, 4, and 7 and B. Rothstein, 'Anti-Corruption: The Indirect 'Big Bang' Approach' (2011) 18(2) *Review of International Political Economy* 234.

[72] See further Chapter 7 and e.g. L.D. Carson and M. Mota Prado, 'Using Institutional Multiplicity to Address Corruption as a Collective Action Problem: Lessons from the Brazilian Case' (2016) 62 *The Quarterly Review of Economics and Finance* 56, 58 and see further Chapter 7.

[73] Carson and Mota Prado, n. 72, 57.

16 INTRODUCTION AND OVERVIEW

initiatives, and collective collaboration across nations to the strengthening of procurement, competition, and anti-corruption systems.[74]

Recognizing that, even if they may embody common elements, the challenges of implementing and embedding an effective system vary across jurisdictions, subsequent chapters go on to examine the particular contexts of, and make proposals for reform in, seven discrete jurisdictions: the United Kingdom (UK), the US, Brazil, Hungary, Poland, Ukraine, and Canada (see Chapters 5–10). Given the fundamentally different nature of corruption control in non-democratic societies,[75] the jurisdictions selected for analysis constitute avowed democracies, even if concern has arisen about illiberal developments, democratic backsliding or autocratization in Brazil, Hungary, and Poland, and democracy in Ukraine is under severe stress as a result of the ongoing war.[76] Each of these chapters illustrates particular national challenges and emphasizes the importance of targeting reform measures to the specific weaknesses and problems diagnosed in each country. Nonetheless, the diagnoses and proposed reform strategies in these national case studies provide possible bases, and/or inspiration, for workable models for change in other jurisdictions facing similar or equivalent challenges. For example:

- Chapter 5 addresses the UK. It notes that, although it may constitute a relatively clean economy, there are reasons to be concerned that undetected and undeterred corruption and collusion may be distorting public procurement processes. The chapter consequently proposes reforms targeted at gaps and weaknesses identified in the system.
- Chapter 6, focusing on the US, examines recurring incidences of corruption and collusion and identifies enduring weaknesses in the public procurement system, before suggesting possible paths for reform, especially to existing statutory and regulatory tools. It notes that a significant challenge is for antitrust agencies and public procurement bodies to deepen cooperative programmes—already underway—that would strengthen the government's ability to identify, prosecute, and deter misconduct. It also proposes better data analytics, intensified study of past experiences in the prosecution of cartels, and measures to reduce barriers to entry by prospective government tenderers.

---

[74] The chapters bring together a broad variety of literature, and country experiences are used to shed light on these theoretical debates—including illustrating why existing approaches adopted in the selected jurisdictions may not be optimal, the challenges of implementing a successful system, and the challenges of introducing meaningful and successful reform in practice.

[75] See C. Carothers, *Corruption Control in Authoritarian Regimes: Lessons from East Asia* (Cambridge University Press, 2022).

[76] See, e.g., V-Dem Institute's '2023 Democracy Report', n. 1, which identifies Brazil, Hungary, and Poland as amongst the top ten autocratizing countries in the last 10 years, but noting that in both Brazil and Poland, autocratization stalled before democracy broke down (in Brazil after President Lula assumed power and in Poland because internal processes are fighting back against them).

- Chapter 7 focuses on the experience of Brazil, where Operation Car Wash (*Operação Lava Jato*) exposed one of the largest public procurement corruption and collusion scandals ever uncovered in the world. The chapter discusses the challenges of combatting corruption and collusion when it is deeply embedded in a system, and what measures can be taken to build on the steps taken to reverse this cycle or wrongdoing in Operation Car Wash.
- Chapter 8 examines the increasing corruption and collusion risks that have been emerging in Hungary and Poland as a result of illiberal developments in democracy and the economy. It traces the countries transitions from Soviet satellite states, to democracies, and Member States of the EU, and describes the political developments that have led to democratic backsliding. Recognizing that domestic political will for reform has been lacking in both countries (at least, prior to the formation of a new Government in Poland at the end of 2023), the chapter focuses on the question of what steps can be taken by the EU to protect public procurement processes in the EU, and to ensure that both countries comply with EU law and adhere to fundamental EU values.
- Chapter 9, focusing on the experience of Ukraine, underlines the nexus between that country's struggles against corruption and supplier collusion, including (very much) in the public procurement sector, and its quest for national survival, dignity, and stable democratic governance. As with the countries discussed in Chapter 8, it explores issues concerning systemic corruption and the legacy of the Soviet Union. Further, it highlights the important and positive role that e-procurement systems and the engagement of civil society have played in countering—at least to an extent—the scope for corruption in public procurement in the country.
- Chapter 10 returns to the experience of a relatively stable democracy and advanced industrial economy, namely Canada. It shows how problems of corruption and supplier collusion in public procurement can persist even in such societies, abetted by political and constitutional fault lines and gaps in policy frameworks. At the same time, it highlights progress made and insights gleaned from recent experience, particularly with respect to the suppression of bid rigging in public procurement through a more joined-up approach.

Chapter 11 draws together the book's overall conclusions and reform proposals, highlighting some core findings of the general and jurisdiction-specific discussions. Relevant themes include the real need in all jurisdictions to recognize the pervasive nature, and high risk, of corruption and collusion impacting on public procurement, and the consequent necessity for states routinely to hone and develop their systems to counter the compelling incentives for such conduct, to block opportunities for it (so highlighting the acute importance of preventative measures), and to encourage compliance with relevant laws. Most countries thus need to take further action: to bolster procurement processes to reduce opportunities

18 INTRODUCTION AND OVERVIEW

for corruption, cronyism, and collusion; to fill legislative gaps or refresh relevant legislation; to raise the stakes for those involved in wrongdoing by facilitating the identification of corrupt or collusive practices, increasing enforcement of anti-corruption and competition laws and greater use of dissuasive penalties; to ensure the recovery of misappropriated money; to encourage greater coordination and cooperation between relevant agencies and players; and to weaken links between procurers, businesses, and politicians to reduce the risk of misallocation of contracts. Consideration may also have to be given as to how to break a cycle of corruption, which becomes entrenched, without relying too heavily, or solely, on direct legal responses. As the success of any reform mechanisms proposed is dependent on the wider political and institutional context and, in particular, the existence of independent, and impartial, courts, law enforcement agencies, a free media, and respect for the rule of law, the involvement of domestic and international players may be necessary to provoke and support political and institutional reform and capacity building in some countries. Engagement of the press and civil society groups may thus be essential not only to monitor for wrongdoing but also to lobby for change and the development of new moral and legal norms.

Whilst there is abundant literature on individual aspects of these topics, relatively little work addresses these problems in a 'joined-up' fashion. By examining public procurement systems holistically, and beyond its siloed components, this book aims, at an especially sensitive moment, to make a novel contribution to the literature, advocating for an integrated and coordinated response, both generally and in identified jurisdictions, to the ubiquitous problem of corruption, collusion, or both, in distorting government procurement. The book underscores the importance not only of enhanced public investment in the effective enforcement of anti-corruption and anti-collusion measures, but also of enhancing the resilience of public procurement systems to both corruption and supplier collusion, through ensuring that procurement authorities are able, and are incentivized, to provide public goods, services, and works that represent the best value for money that is possible. As public procurement is a sphere in which even small enhancements in policy can reduce waste and the misuse of public funds, the reform proposals seek to provide mechanisms for a government to make improvements to the quality and quantity of crucial products, services, and infrastructure, which are vital to the day-to-day life of individual citizens and to the social and economic well-being of nations. This in turn may help to reverse the cycle of waning trust and belief in governments and democracy.

2

Corruption and Collusion in Public Procurement: Opportunities, Incentives, and Harm Caused

A. Introduction	19	C. Bid Rigging and Bribery in Public Procurement Markets: Surveys, Risk Indicators, and Examples	28
B. Incentives and Conditions Facilitating Corruption and Collusion in Public Procurement Markets	20	D. Harm Caused	32
i. Incentives and conditions facilitating corruption	20	i. The costs of corruption	33
		ii. The costs of bid rigging	39
ii. Incentives and conditions facilitating collusion	23	E. Conclusions	41

A. Introduction

This chapter examines the factors that render public procurement processes vulnerable to corruption and collusion. It also introduces cases, surveys, and other evidence indicating that not only are these processes intrinsically vulnerable to corrupt and anti-competitive schemes, but they are in fact frequent targets of such conduct, at huge cost to society as a whole.

By identifying the incentives and opportunities for corruption and collusion, it provides the foundations for understanding how measures to counter them should be designed. By highlighting the prevalence and generic nature of the problem, as well as its harmful consequences (economic and non-economic), the chapter also underscores the importance of combatting such conduct and the financial and other benefits that can be reaped from so doing.

20 CORRUPTION AND COLLUSION IN PUBLIC PROCUREMENT

B. Incentives and Conditions Facilitating Corruption and Collusion in Public Procurement Markets

i. Incentives and conditions facilitating corruption

For a number of reasons, public purchasing, managed not by its intended beneficiaries (individual citizens and groups of citizens) nor by those providing the funds (the taxpayer), but by public officials or civil servants acting on their behalf, is highly susceptible to disruption by corruption. These public officials, politicians, and bureaucrats, may face strong temptations to exploit their office, or to circumvent the letter of public procurement rules, in return for benefits, personal (e.g. financial rewards, holidays, or promises of subsequent employment) or partisan (e.g. for political donations)—a principal–agent problem.[1] Some argue that 'few government activities create greater temptations or offer more opportunities for corruption than public sector procurement'.[2] The large sums of money involved in government contracts, especially in certain sectors such as infrastructure, construction, and defence; the close relationships often developed with businesses; or the existence of conflicts of interest[3] make the allure of skimming powerful, particularly if '[t]he potential reward for a single contract ... can exceed the legitimate lifetime salary earnings of [a] decision-maker'[4] and the risk of the conduct being detected and penalized is low. Such incentives may be heightened where broad discretionary powers are conferred on public officials which are difficult

---

[1] The agent (a corruptible individual) purchases on behalf of its principal (the governing entity or citizens), with money that is not their own, goods, which are not for their own use, from a third party (the corrupter). Instead of advancing the principal's interest, the agent and principal may in fact be pursuing different goals, especially given their asymmetric access to information—a principal–agent problem, see, for example, S. Rose-Ackerman and B.J. Palifka, *Corruption and Government: Causes, Consequences, and Reform* (Cambridge University Press, 2nd edn, 2016) 9. See also Organisation for Economic Co-operation and Development (OECD), *Preventing Corruption in Procurement* (2016) 6, available at http://www.oecd.org/gov/ethics/Corruption-Public-Procurement-Brochure.pdf.

[2] See, for example, S. Kühn and L.B. Sherman, *Curbing Corruption in Public Procurement: A Practical Guide* (Transparency International, 2014) 4, 8.

[3] See, e.g., T. Søreide, *Corruption in Public Procurement: Causes, Consequences and Cures* (Christian Michelsen Institute, 2002) 4 and R.D. Anderson, W.E. Kovacic, and A.C. Müller, 'Promoting Competition and Deterring Corruption in Public Procurement Markets: Synergies with Trade Liberalisation' (2017) 26(2) *Public Procurement Law Review* 77.

[4] See D. Strombom, 'Corruption in Procurement', *Economic Perspectives: Corruption: An Impediment to Development* (November 1998), 20 and Søreide, n. 3. But see M. Wakui, 'Bid Rigging Initiated by Government Officials: The Conjuncture of Collusion and Corruption in Japan' in T. Cheng, S.M. Colino, and B. Ong (eds), *Cartels in Asia: Law and Practice* (Wolters Kluwer Hong Kong, 2015) 49 (procurement agents are also sometimes motivated by a desire to favour local suppliers and grow the regional economy, ensure continuity, reward suppliers with good reputation for past performance, and ensure high quality of performance; therefore, private financial interest may not be the sole or major reason for officials' involvement) and R. Klitgaard, *Controlling Corruption* (University of California Press, 1988) 75.

CONDITIONS FACILITATING CORRUPTION AND COLLUSION   21

to monitor, where monitoring and enforcement systems are weak, or where such systems are under particular stress (e.g. in times of war or national emergency).[5]

In addition to incentives for passive bribery, private firms may also face strong temptations to pay bribes or seek favours from public officials if they stand to make enhanced profits from winning lucrative, large-scale procurement contracts by cutting out competitors.[6] Although active bribery sometimes results from rogue employees acting contrary to their corporate's interests, in the public procurement context individuals may be acting according to their firm's policy and in its interests (incentivized perhaps by career, pay, and bonus systems).[7] Indeed, some of the cases discussed in this book illustrate that bribery may be a highly profitable corporate strategy. For example, in the United States (US) Foreign Corrupt Proceedings Act proceedings against the Brazilian construction firm Odebrecht (a construction giant in Latin America), the US Federal Court found that Odebrecht's USD 788 million of corrupt payments to secure procurement contracts had led it to make USD 3.3 billion in profits.[8]

In some situations, corruption may not, as just described, result from deviations from established norms of ethical universalism (providing that every citizen should be treated equally by the state and public resources distributed impartially),[9] or incentives affecting the self-interest of individual procurers and businesses on the supply side. Rather, it may sometimes occur due to a broader political and systemic problem, especially of particularism. 'Particularism exists by default, since most human societies have limited resources to share, and people tend to share them in a particular way, most notably with their closest kin and not with everyone else.'[10] In such situations, politicians may use their control over, and manipulate, the procurement system and officials (through shaping procurement laws, pressuring officials to distort their implementation, or disabling monitoring

---

[5] See, for discussion, S. Arrowsmith, L. Butler, A. La Chimia, and C. Yukins (eds) *Public Procurement in (a) Crisis? Global Lessons from the COVID-19 Pandemic* (Hart Publishing, 2021), and references cited therein.

[6] Unlike private buyers, public agents may lack the incentive to challenge these actions.

[7] OECD, *Business and Finance Outlook 2017* (OECD Publishing, 2017) 22 ('In the majority of cases, corporate management (41%) or even the CEO (12%) was aware of and endorsed the bribery, debunking the "rogue employee" myth....' (footnote omitted)).

[8] This was in relation to bribes across a number of countries, see case number 1:16-cr-00643, US Department of Justice, 'Odebrecht and Braskem Plead Guilty and Agree to Pay at Least USD 3.5 Billion in Global Penalties to Resolve Largest Foreign Bribery Case in History' (21 December 2016), available at https://www.justice.gov/opa/pr/odebrecht-and-braskem-plead-guilty-and-agree-pay-least-35-billion-global-penalties-resolve; C. Wahrman, 'Competing to be Corrupt' in P.F. Lagunes and J. Svejnar (eds), *Corruption and the Lava Jato Scandal in Latin America* (Routledge, 2020) and Chapter 7.

[9] See Report 4/2011 prepared by A. Mungiu-Pippidi et al., *Contextual Choices in Fighting Corruption: Lessons Learned* (Norwegian Agency for Development Cooperation, 2011) 7 ('Most corruption academic literature conceptualizes anti-corruption at the individual level, as do most current theories about anti-corruption. This presumes that corruption is a deviation from an otherwise established norm of ethical universalism, where every citizen is treated equally by the state and all public resources are distributed impartially'). See also A. Mungiu-Pipiidi, *Rethinking Corruption* (Edward Elgar, 2023), Chapter 1.

[10] Mungiu-Pippidi et al., n. 9.

and accountability mechanisms) in order to steer contracts towards either cronies or favoured companies in return for benefits, including bribes or other kickbacks on contracts, or donations to political parties or campaigns (for personal or partisan gain, or both).[11] Alternatively, they may turn a blind eye to corruption of subordinates and seek to derive rents from it rather than exposing and condemning it. In such circumstances, collusion between tenderers may even be encouraged as it may facilitate the operation of the scheme and reduce the risk of complaints about the conduct.

A country's political-economy context is likely to influence the operation of corruption and its impact on procurement outcomes.[12] Widespread corruption, where corruption in a country is institutionalized and not just a sum of individual corrupt acts, may be more likely to occur in countries affected by deep conflict[13] or with newer, or weaker, democratic institutions, where politicians are able to exert influence or control over bureaucrats, regulatory agencies, and the judiciary, or where past experience and weak enforcement of anti-corruption laws has led to mistrust of the government and enforcement agencies. In such countries, an expectation that corruption will occur, because it is part of anticipated and expected behaviour, may become the social norm or 'standard operating procedure' (rather than an exception to it).[14] It may therefore become a greater risk in countries where autocratization—a decline of democratic regime traits—is taking, or has taken, place and illiberal changes in politics and the economy is leading to democratic erosion or breakdown and the undermining of important checks and balances in the system.

Where a culture of corruption is perceived to exist or to be baked into a system— that is, it is widespread, persistent, subversive, or structural, and has become systemic or normalized[15]—bribes may be paid routinely even if those paying them would prefer not to do so or would be better off without so doing. Individuals or businesses engage in corrupt behaviour because others around them are also acting

---

[11] E. Dávid-Barrett and M. Fazekas, 'Grand Corruption and Government Change: An Analysis of Partisan Favouritism in Public Procurement' (2020) 26 *European Journal on Criminal Policy and Research* 411. Indeed, corruption may be a particularly acute problem where politicians need money to stay in power and the wealthy want political influence—the payment of bribes may thus serve the interests of both politicians and businesses.

[12] See M. Fazekas and J.R. Blum, 'Improving Public Procurement Outcomes: Review of Tools and the States of the Evidence Base' (2021) World Bank Group Policy Research Working Paper 9690, available at https://openknowledge.worldbank.org/handle/10986/35727 ('Public procurement is closely linked to the political economy of the country or locality as it allows for extracting a large amount of rents by a small elite (e.g. ruling family winning many large contracts), while it can also be very effectively used to distribute rents among supporters ...').

[13] See Transparency International, 'The Fifth Column Understanding the Relationship Between Corruption and Conflict' (2017), available at https://www.transparency.org.uk/publications/the-fifth-column.

[14] *See* A. Mungiu-Pippidi, 'Seven Steps to Control of Corruption: The Road Map' (2018) 147(3) *Dædalus* 20, 23.

[15] See K.E. Davis, 'Anti-Corruption Law and Systemic Corruption: The Role of Direct Responses' (2021) 17(2) *Revista Direito GV* e2129 (discussing the meaning of systemic corruption).

corruptly.[16] In the procurement context, tenderers may feel compelled in such circumstances to pay bribes, out of fear that if they do not, they will be bound to lose a contract. Firms may thus find themselves between a 'rock and a hard place'. Either their sales force use illicit means and the company risks law enforcement ... or they abstain from bribery and risk losing essential contracts'.[17] As a consequence of such unaddressed collective action problems,[18] societies may face a vicious circle of corruption that no individual alone can break, and in which even people who think corruption is wrong will take part.

The question of whether bribery in a given situation results from an individualistic, or a more systemic, problem is material, as the mechanisms for countering it will be dependent upon the incentives and factors driving it. In the latter context, a broad range of reforms may be required to enable particularism to evolve into universalism and to provoke a transition away from a corrupt equilibrium.

ii. Incentives and conditions facilitating collusion

Additionally, or alternatively, a procurement process will be threatened where private tenderers are incentivized and able to collude with competitors to rig their bids for tenders. An extensive body of scholarship identifies the conditions in which cartels, including bid rigging, are likely to flourish.[19] They establish that, to collude effectively, firms must be able to do three things:

1) cooperate in a way that allows them to align their behaviour or 'collude'—that is, reach an understanding as to how to raise price or cut their output and allocate the increased revenues from the affected market;
2) ensure the internal stability of the collusive scheme by detecting and punishing firms that cheat,[20] or deviate, from it; and

---

[16] Where a pervasive culture of corruption exists, bidders may feel compelled to offer bribes even if they would be better off without it, Søreide, n. 3, 32–3.

[17] F. Heimann and M. Pieth, *Confronting Corruption: Past Concerns, Present Challenges, and Future Strategies* (Oxford University Press, 2018), 43.

[18] Arising where a strategy that is individually rational produces an outcome that is collectively inferior; thus, although collectively society may be better off if no one is corrupt and all behave honestly, individuals may benefit personally by defecting and engaging in corruption.

[19] See, e.g. J. Tirole, *The Theory of Industrial Organisation* (MIT Press, 1988); C. Shapiro, 'Theories of Oligopoly Behavior' in M. Armstrong and R.H. Porter (eds), *Handbook of Industrial Organization, Volume 3* (North Holland, 2007); G.J. Stigler, 'A Theory of Oligopoly' (1964) 72 *Journal of Political Economy* 44; R.C. Marshall and L.M. Marx, *The Economics of Collusion: Cartels and Bidding Rings* (MIT Press, 2012); A. Heimler, 'Cartels in Public Procurement' (2012) *Journal of Competition Law & Economics* 11; and C. Harding and J. Joshua, *Regulating Cartels in Europe* (Oxford University Press, 2nd edn, 2010) 230–1.

[20] Cheating on a cartel is easier where the market is less transparent, the number of firms is greater, products are differentiated, and demand is unpredictable. The incentive to deviate from the collusive

24 CORRUPTION AND COLLUSION IN PUBLIC PROCUREMENT

3) cope with external threats that could boost supply to competitive levels, especially new entries.[21]

The art of successful collusion thus consists of both: (1) creating incentives that make cooperation, rather than unilateral action and competing, the most profitable strategy for the participants;[22] and (2) designing organizational and operational structures that cope with internal and external threats to the scheme, in particular, by monitoring the market for, and acting against, internal deviations from the collusive scheme and discouraging external competitive inroads and buyer resistance.[23] Repeated interaction and 'the shadow of the future', involving punishment and rewards, are usually essential to overcome temptations to cheat and to ensure that the expected profit from colluding outweighs the expected profit of deviating from the cooperative arrangement.[24] As most competition law systems categorically prohibit and severely punish explicit collusion (see further Chapter 3),[25] cartelists ordinarily strive to conceal their cooperation.

A number of aspects of public purchasing systems, together with their value, volume, and frequency, may combine to encourage and facilitate the creation of collusive bid rigging schemes (the alignment of behaviour) and contribute to their internal and external stability, in particular, by discouraging members from deviating from a collusive scheme, by making external competitive inroads to the arrangement more difficult through limiting the pool of bidders, and by enhancing transparency. Public procurement markets can consequently be regarded as being

---

strategy is also affected by the 'punishment' (which usually takes the form of a promise of loss of profits) that can be levied on a firm that cheats. Operating an internal enforcement mechanism is time-consuming, expensive, difficult, and indicative of the cartel being more vulnerable to detection.

[21] See Stigler, n. 19, 45–6.

[22] Harding and Joshua, n. 19 and Marshall and Marx, n. 19, 19–21.

[23] See, e.g., Commission Decision, Case No. IV/35.691/E-4, *Pre-Insulated Pipe Cartel* 21 October 1998 (noting that the cartel members had sought to win over, then threaten, boycott, and drive out a nonparticipating competitor); and J. Moore, 'Cartels Facing Competition in Public Procurement: An Empirical Analysis' (14–16 September 2012) EPPP Discussion Paper No. 2012-09, available at https://www.chaire-eppp.org/cartels-facing-competition-in-public-procurement-an-empirical-analysis-2/.

[24] See P. Dal Bó and G.R. Fréchette, 'On the Determinants of Cooperation in Infinitely Repeated Games: A Survey' (2018) 56(1) *Journal of Economic Literature* 60; but see also D. Berhnheim and E. Madsen, 'Price Cutting and Business Stealing in Imperfect Cartels' (2017) 107(2) *American Economic Review* 387 (observing two important gaps in the industrial cartel collusion scholarship: '[F]irst, apparently deliberate cheating actually occurs; second, it frequently goes unpunished even when it is detected').

[25] Collusion on a market can be *explicit*, where the mutual understanding arises through express communication among firms through verbal or other communication as to the strategies to be deployed, or *tacit*, where the mutual understanding occurs without express communication. Although most competition law systems struggle to deal satisfactorily with the latter and it is difficult to differentiate between tacit and explicit collusion, it is widely accepted that cartel activity, including bid rigging, through explicit collusion should be condemned under antitrust laws.

more vulnerable to collusive behaviour compared to other markets.[26] Further, in some cases where public officials are enlisted as corrupt agents to facilitate the operation and stability of a bid rigging cartel (e.g. by drawing up tender requirements which make it harder for outsiders to bid and alerting tenderers of new entrants), collusion and corruption may work together, reinforcing one another and creating a more stable system of wrongdoing.[27] Table 2.1 summarizes and elaborates on some of these features.

Table 2.1 Factors rendering public procurement susceptible to supplier collusion

Constant, predictable demand	Collusion is more difficult to maintain in markets where there are cyclical changes in demand[28] and/or where large orders are put in for a product occasionally rather than on a regular basis.[29] In such cases, the gains to individual firms from cheating, and consequently the temptation to cheat, are significant. By contrast, government demands in public procurement markets tend to be inelastic, and governments often resort to a regular, predictable flow of auctions and tendering events.[30] Repetitive tendering increases the opportunity for bidders to divide contracts and makes it less likely that the benefits from deviating to win a single contract will outweigh those that derive from colluding over a series of contracts. Markets with frequent contracting also make punishment and deterrence significantly easier. If, in contrast, the distance in time between tenders is long or irregular and if tender opportunities vary in size and content, successful collusion becomes more complex and harder to sustain—especially as the benefit of cheating is raised considerably.

(continued)

---

[26] B. Tóth, M. Fazekas, Á. Czibik, and I. János, 'Toolkit for Detecting Collusive Bidding in Public Procurement. With Examples from Hungary' (2014) *Corruption Research Centre, Budapest*, available at https://www.govtransparency.eu/wp-content/uploads/2015/11/GTI_WP2014_2_Toth_et_al_150 413.pdf.

[27] See A. Lambert-Mogiliansky, 'Corruption and Collusion in Procurement – Strategic complements' in S. Rose-Ackerman and T. Søreide (eds) *International Handbook on the Economics of Corruption, Volume 2* (Edward Elgar Publishing, 2013) 2 (reporting that a judge from Paris stated that there are few cases of large-scale collusion in procurement where corruption is absent, as it is frequently necessary to buy the official's silence or to achieve strategic complementarities).

[28] In these circumstances, firms may find it difficult to determine whether or not the decline in demand is due to market changes or cheating, causing deviations from the terms of the cartel.

[29] See M.C. Levenstein and V.Y. Suslow, 'What Determines Cartel Success? (2006) 44 *Journal of Economic Literature* 43, 64.

[30] Procurement markets often lack the elasticity of demand that is a primary defence of consumers: once the government has determined the need for a particular purchase, the procurement officer will generally go ahead with the procurement, provided that enough bids are made; see G.L. Albano, P. Uccirossi, G. Spagnolo, and M. Zanza, 'Preventing Collusion in Procurement: A Primer' in N. Dimitri, G. Piga, and G. Spanolo (eds), *Handbook of Procurement* (Cambridge University Press, 2006); and J. Haltiwanger and J. Harrington, 'The Impact of Cyclical Demand Movements on Collusive Behaviour' (1991) 22 *RAND Journal of Economics* 89, 92–3.

26 CORRUPTION AND COLLUSION IN PUBLIC PROCUREMENT

Table 2.1 Continued

Few competitors, barriers to entry, and (often) exclusion of foreign competitors	The more concentrated the market, the simpler it is for firms to form a consensus, detect cheating, and maintain secrecy. A smaller group of competitors are also likely to know each other well and to communicate among themselves more readily. Further, the larger the market share that each firm has, the greater the potential profits to be earned from successful collusion (the bigger the share that each will receive of the collusive 'pie'), and the more likely firms are to be willing to accept the risk of eventual detection. Procurement regulation sometimes increases concentration by artificially restricting the number of potential offerors, for example, by imposing onerous conditions or reserving contracts to domestic suppliers.[31] Requirements that exclude foreign or other suppliers may obstruct the entry of potential competitors who might undermine and destabilize collusion.[32] Procurement in emergencies may also limit competitive bidding opportunities.
Standardization and restrictive product specifications	Collusion is more likely to flourish in markets where competition mainly occurs on one dimension (e.g. price) rather than on several dimensions,[33] and when there are few or no alternatives to the product or service. In such cases, the possibility for nonprice competition through disruptive product differentiation or innovation is reduced, as are the costs of collusion. Procurement processes sometimes diminish the scope for differentiation through standardizing requirements or adopting restrictive product specifications, which can be intended to limit procurers' broad discretion and opportunities for making corrupt contract awards.[34]
Overly sweeping transparency requirements	The imposition of transparency requirements is essential to ensure the integrity of public procurement processes and to guard against corruption.[35] Nonetheless, transparency provisions, especially those mandating the disclosure of both winning and losing bids, may increase the risk of collusion by allowing suppliers to observe the terms of transactions and to monitor

---

[31] See further Chapter 3.

[32] R.D. Anderson, W.E. Kovacic, and A.C. Müller, 'Ensuring Integrity and Competition in Public Procurement Markets: A Dual Challenge for Good Governance' in S. Arrowsmith and R.D. Anderson (eds), *The WTO Regime on Government Procurement: Challenge and Reform* (Cambridge University Press, 2011) 681.

[33] R.H. Porter and J.D. Zona, 'Ohio School Milk Markets: An Analysis of Bidding' (1999) 30 *RAND Journal of Economics* 263, and R.H. Porter and J.D. Zona, 'Detection of Bid Rigging in Procurement Auctions' (1993) *Journal of Political Economy* 101.

[34] Although it can be difficult to address such measures effectively through competition law enforcement, competition law and competition advocacy have important roles to play, see generally E.M. Fox and D. Healey, 'When the State Harms Competition—The Role for Competition Law' (2014) 79 *Antitrust Law Journal* 769 and Chapters 3 and 4.

[35] See R.A. Burton, 'Improving Integrity in Public Procurement: The Role of Transparency and Accountability' in *Fighting Corruption and Promoting Integrity in Public Procurement* (OECD 2005) 23, 25.

CONDITIONS FACILITATING CORRUPTION AND COLLUSION   27

Table 2.1 Continued

	(at a lower cost) the conduct of their competitors and detect deviations from a cartel agreement.[36] Therefore, unless appropriately tailored, transparency requirements can actually facilitate bid rigging schemes.[37] In contrast, carefully designed transparency requirements can serve a variety of procompetitive purposes.[38]
Procurement models	Procurement design may also create potential risks. For example, sealed bidding tenders are easier to rig than negotiated procurements, which allow the buyer to push for better terms and thus potentially induce a cartelist to cheat. Nonetheless, negotiated procurements can also entail risks in corrupt systems where the negotiation is treated as an opportunity to broker a bribe.[39]
Incentives of procurement officials	Buyers are ordinarily well-placed to identify collusion by their suppliers. However, in many cases, procurement officers themselves may have weak or nonexistent incentives to identify cartels. 'The public official [typically] is not evaluated on how many cartels he discovers but on his ability to set up and to run bidding processes and how quickly the goods and services he purchases are actually delivered. Suspicion that there is a cartel delays the whole process of purchasing. Furthermore, the money that is being saved because of the dismantling of a cartel usually does not remain in the administration that actually discovered or helped discover the cartel, but is redistributed to the general administration's budget.'[40] If efforts to detect and deter cartels in public procurement are to succeed, this obstacle must be addressed through, for example, the provision of incentives (such as financial awards) for procurement officers who successfully detect collusive arrangements.[41]
Facilitators	Cartels sometimes enlist the assistance of trade associations and consultants to design and manage their operations. Such assistance becomes more important the greater the number of cartel members or the more complex the collusive scheme.[42] In the European Union (EU), for example, Fides/AC-Treuhand, an association-management company,

(continued)

---

[36] It is harder for bidders to collude if sensitive bid data and tenderer information are not made publicly available during the course of, or subsequent to, an auction, see Stigler, n. 19; H. Wang and H-M. Chen, 'Deterring Bidder Collusion: Auction Design Complements Antitrust Policy' (2016) 12(1) *Journal of Competition Law & Economics* 31; E. Green and R. Porter, 'Noncooperative Collusion Under Imperfect Price Information' (1984) *Econometrica* 52, 87–100; D. Abreu, 'External Equilibria of Oligopolistic Supergames' (1986) 39 *Journal of Economic Theory* 191–225.

[37] Transparency measures should not be abandoned but their ability to facilitate collusion must be recognized, see, e.g., Marshall and Marx, n. 19, 20–1 and discussion in Chapters 3 and 4.

[38] See further Chapter 3.

[39] See further Chapter 3.

[40] Heimler, n. 19, 860.

[41] See further Chapter 3.

[42] See, e.g. S. Bishop and M. Walker, *The Economics of EC Competition Law: Concepts, Application and Measurement* (Sweet & Maxwell, 3rd edn, 2010) 173–4.

28 CORRUPTION AND COLLUSION IN PUBLIC PROCUREMENT

Table 2.1 Continued

was found to have helped guide the implementation of a number of chemical-sector cartels;[43] and, in *Remonts*,[44] a sub-contractor helped to prepare bids on behalf of competitors bidding independently for a public tender. In the public procurement context, corrupt public officials may also be drawn into facilitating the operation of cartels (e.g. by manipulating tender requirements and making it harder for external tenderers to bid and for the collusive scheme to be identified) or may even encourage the operation of the cartel.[45]

In a study of bid rigging in relation to US public school milk, Robert Porter and Douglas Zona noted that the procurement market had several of the traits discussed in the preceding text that encouraged collusion.[46] For example, they found that price competition was typically the only dimension of competition; demand was inelastic and stable; bidding was a repeated game, carried out in small lots; multimarket contact was enhanced by disaggregated contracts staggered throughout the year; firms faced similar costs of production; opportunities for new entry were limited; markets were concentrated and localized given the relatively high transport costs; bids and bidders were made public after sealed-bid auctions, allowing any cheating to be observed; pricing was transparent; and parties often met through trade associations or through being customers of one another.

C. Bid Rigging and Bribery in Public Procurement Markets: Surveys, Risk Indicators, and Examples

The factors and compelling incentives described help to explain why, despite increasingly concerted efforts and initiatives by domestic and international institutions to fight cartel activity and corruption (see further Chapter 3), such practices remain alluring in the public procurement context. Although the concealed nature of collusion and corruption makes it both difficult to detect and to measure—it is not easy to know exactly how widely these practices are occurring in reality— it is common to estimate levels of these kinds of wrongdoing through indicators and indices. These tend to be derived from, for example, surveys of stakeholder

---

[43] Case C-194/14 P *AC-Treuhand AG v Commission* EU:C:2015:717, and see R.C. Marshall, 'Unobserved Collusion: Warning Signs and Concerns' (2017) 5(3) *Journal of Antitrust Enforcement* 329.

[44] Case C-542/14 *SIA 'VM Remonts' and Others v Konkurences padome* EU:C:2016:578.

[45] See, e.g., in Brazil, CADE's *PAC Favelas* case, *Administrative Proceeding nº 08700.007776/2016-41*, Reporting Commissioner Sérgio Costa Ravagnani, where the leaders of the cartel consortia are alleged to have been chosen by the state government, at the time headed by Sérgio Cabral, see further Chapter 7.

[46] Porter and Zona, n. 33.

attitudes and perceptions, reviews of institutional features controlling the conduct, or audits and investigations of individual cases. Even though it is not easy to create robust measures, and those that exist may be imperfect,[47] these indices can provide a general sense of the position. Further, as good-quality public procurement datasets are becoming more widely available,[48] some researchers are scrutinizing publicly available data to try to create more objective indications of the quality of contracting and evidence of corruption and collusion risks, rather than relying purely on surveys of perceptions and experiences.[49]

A number of jurisdiction-specific evidence is discussed in later chapters of this book. However, it can still be said that general evidence and risk indicators suggest that corruption may be occurring in many areas across the globe throughout the different stages of the procurement lifecycle—for example, by indicating that, in some jurisdictions, the overall level of competition for government contracts is falling (and that in a high proportion of cases—up to 30 per cent of large contracts—there is only a single bidder for government contracts).[50] Transparency International's (TI) Corruption Perceptions Index[51] (CPI)—a composite index based on a variety of business surveys and expert panels—also records that approximately two-thirds of countries surveyed fall below the midpoint of their scale between zero (highly corrupt) and one hundred (very clean), thereby indicating prevalent corruption across public sectors (see further discussion in

[47] 'The two most widely used perception and attitude surveys are the World Bank's Control of Corruption and Transparency International's Corruption Perceptions Index. Both have received extensive criticism.' M. Fazekas and G. Kocsis, 'Uncovering High-Level Corruption: Cross-National Objective Corruption Risk Indicators Using Public Procurement Data' (2017) 50 *British Journal of Political Science* 155, 156. See also Rose-Ackerman and Palifka, n. 1, 14–21. Transparency International's Corruption Perceptions Index is available at https://www.transparency.org/en/cpi/2022?gclid=EAIaIQ obChMIsZH3rbbSgwMVN5ZQBh1WlwcIEAAYASAAEgLr3_D_BwE&gad_source=1. See also the World Justice Rule of Law Index.

[48] See, e.g., EU's Tender Electronic Daily (TED), the publication portal for tenders covered by the EU public procurement regime, available at http://ted.europa.eu/TED/main/HomePage.do.

[49] See Fazekas and Kocsis, n. 47, 155 (developing two objective proxy measures of high-level corruption in public procurement—single bidding in competitive markets and a composite score of tendering red flags); I. Adam, A. Hernandez Sanchez, and M. Fazekas, 'Global Public Procurement Open Competition Index' (2021) Government Transparency Institute Working Paper GTI-WP/2021:02, available at https://www.govtransparency.eu/wp-content/uploads/2021/09/Adam-et-al_Evidence-paper_procurement-competition_210902_formatted_2.pdf; M. Fazekas and Á. Czibik, 'Measuring Regional Quality of Government: The Public Spending Quality Index Based on Government Contracting Data' (2021) 55(8) *Regional Studies* 1459 (assessing compliance with transparency requirements, the presence of competition at the bidding stage, administrative efficiency in contracting and control of corruption risks).

[50] See, 'Rigging the Bids: Government Contracting is Growing Less Competitive, and Often More Corrupt', *The Economist* (19 November 2016).

[51] See, Transparency International, Corruption Perceptions Index, n. 47. Transparency International also publishes a Bribe Payers Index, ranking exporting countries by reference to their likelihood to bribe in importing markets, see n. 91. Survey firms also conduct popular polls to measure perceptions and experience of corruption, see, e.g., the Global Corruption Barometer.

30 CORRUPTION AND COLLUSION IN PUBLIC PROCUREMENT

Section D).[52] Similarly, Ernst & Young's global fraud surveys[53] and PwC's Global Economic Crime Surveys (2018 and 2020)[54] report on increasing numbers of responding organizations experiencing bribery and corruption, being asked to pay a bribe, or believing that they lost a contract to a rival they think had paid one. These, combined with other evidence, suggest that significant national and international developments (discussed further in Chapter 3) which have put anti-corruption—and the enhancement of anti-corruption laws—high on the agenda may therefore be failing to deliver major positive results.[55]

Reinforcing the concerns highlighted in these surveys and reports, competition and anti-corruption agencies across the world continue, with some regularity, to expose bid rigging in public procurement contexts. This is the case even (or particularly) during moments of crisis,[56] and even in countries which are considered to be relatively clean. In a number of cases, collusion and corruption—with an insider facilitating, supporting, or orchestrating the operation of the cartel in return for bribes (e.g. by influencing the design of a tender, manipulating the selection process in favour of specific suppliers, or excluding outsiders)—have been found to operate together.

One of the most far-reaching corruption and collusion schemes that has ever been uncovered is known as 'Operation Car Wash' (*Operação Lava Jato*) (OCW). This investigation, discussed in detail in Chapter 5, revealed pervasive corruption and collusion affecting public procurement in Brazil. The case started as an investigation into the use of a car wash (hence the name) to launder money in the black market for currency exchange. However, the investigations snowballed, eventually

---

[52] See, e.g., E. Auriol, 'Corruption in Procurement and Public Purchase' (2006) 24 *International Journal of Industrial Organization* 867, 867–8 (noting that '[c]orruption is ... a major problem' and '[t]he OECD Antibribery Convention ... has apparently failed to cure it'); PwC Study, 'Public Procurement: Costs We Pay for Corruption—Identifying and Reducing Corruption in Public Procurement in the EU' (2013) 8; T. Gong and N. Zhou, 'Corruption and Marketization: Formal and Informal Rules in Chinese Public Procurement' (2015) 9 *Regulation and Governance* 63; F. Boehm and J. Olaya, 'Corruption in Public Contracting Auctions: The Role of Transparency in Bidding Processes' (2006) 77(4) *Annals of Public and Cooperative Economics* 431; and 'Rigging the Bids', n. 50.

[53] 'EY Integrity in the spotlight: the future of compliance' (15th global fraud survey) (2018) (34 per cent of UK respondents—up from 18 per cent in 2014—believe corruption to be widespread in the UK).

[54] The 2022 report focused on fraud (but reported that '[i]n the UK, 64% of businesses have experienced fraud, corruption or other economic/financial crime within the past 24 months, a substantial increase compared to 56% in 2020, and 50% in 2018').

[55] B. Rothstein, 'Fighting Systemic Corruption: The Indirect Strategy' (2018) 147(3) *Dædalus* 35, 37.

[56] Indeed, increased, rapid spending, combined with the application of more flexible procurement rules, in times of crisis may generate a spike in corruption opportunities, see Arrowsmith et al., n. 5; O. Bandiera, E. Bosio, and G. Spagnolo, *Procurement in Focus: Rules, Discretion, and Emergencies* (CEPR Press, 2021) and e.g. International Public Sector Fraud Forum, *Fraud in Emergency Management and Recovery: Principles for Effective Fraud Control* (Cabinet Office and the Commonwealth Fraud Prevention Centre, February 2020); US Department of Justice (DOJ), 'Price Fixing, Bid Rigging and Market Allocation Schemes: What They Are and What to Look For' (February 2021), available at www.usdoj.gov/atr/public/guidelines/211578.htm; and Transparency International, 'Corruption Could Cost Lives in Latin America's Response to The Coronavirus' (31 March 2020), available at https://www.transparency.org/en/news/corruption-could-cost-lives-in-latin-americas-response-to-the-coronavirus.

exposing the existence of an illegal scheme involving large construction companies, organized in cartels, paying bribes of between 1 and 5 per cent of the value of the contracts won to high-level executives of state-owned enterprises (SOEs), including Petrobras (Petróleo Brasileiro S/A), the huge SOE responsible for oil and gas exploration and production.[57] These SOE officials took a cut of the bribes, before funnelling the remainder to senior politicians responsible for their appointment and to their political parties. Following the investigation, numerous civil and criminal antitrust and anti-corruption lawsuits were brought against companies, businesspeople, procurement officials, and high-ranking politicians, including the now re-elected President Luís Inácio Lula da Silva, former Speaker of the House Eduardo Cunha, and former Governor of Rio de Janeiro, Sérgio Cabral. The huge construction company Odebrecht was found to be at the centre of the illegal activity[58] and, as well as paying corporate fines, its CEO, Marcelo Odebrecht was sentenced to nineteen years in prison for paying over USD 30 million in bribes to Petrobras.[59] Investigations also revealed that the scheme, although centred in Brazil, impacted well beyond its borders, leading Brazilian enforcers to cooperate with numerous counterparts abroad and fuelling large-scale investigations against corporations and individuals (including senior-ranking politicians in Peru and Colombia) in at least twelve other countries, including Peru, Argentina, Colombia, Mexico, Dominican Republic, Ecuador, Switzerland, the UK, Portugal, and Spain.[60]

Although headline grabbing, OCW is far from being an isolated case. Rather, serious allegations of bid rigging, bribery, or both, undermining public procurement processes, domestic or foreign, continue to be made and proven in jurisdictions across the world,[61] including in countries with some of the highest rankings

---

[57] In return for the bribes, the SOE employees helped to secure the success of the bid rigging scheme by sharing confidential information with contractors, limiting other participation on the bidding proceedings, and favouring the colluding companies.

[58] Through its internal division of Structured Operations, it used a shadow budget and a complex web of offshore companies to process the payments of bribes.

[59] See 'Brazil Petrobras Scandal: Tycoon Marcelo Odebrecht Jailed', *BBC World* (8 March 2016). See also n. 8 and text.

[60] See Chapter 8 and e.g. E. Cordero Balarezo 'Odebrecht Scandal Rearranges the Political Landscape in Ecuador and Latin America', *CuencaHighLife* (21 January 2018).

[61] See also e.g. World Bank Group (WBG), Integrity Vice Presidency, 'Curbing Fraud, Collusion and Corruption in the Road Sector' (2011), Table 1 (suggesting the level of collusion in roads projects in developed and developing countries is significant); A. Sánchez Graells, 'Prevention and Deterrence of Bid Rigging: A Look from the New EU Directive on Public Procurement' in G. Racca and C. Yukins (eds), *Integrity and Efficiency in Sustainable Public Contracts* (Bruylant, 2014); Á. Hargita and T. Tóth, 'God Forbid Bid-Riggers: Developments Under the Hungarian Competition Act' (2005) 28 *World Competition* 205, 209; International Consortium of Investigative Journalists, 'Luanda Leaks', available at https://www.icij.org/investigations/luanda-leaks/ (discussing corruption affecting public contracting in Angola); International Competition Network (ICN), 'Anti-Cartel Enforcement Manual: Relationships Between Competition Agencies and Public Procurement Bodies' (April 2015), 37–38 (discussing Spanish Competition Authority decision imposing fines of more than EUR 16 million for price fixing and bid rigging on tenders for asphalt affecting more than 900 projects in Northern Spain—indeed, the Spanish competition authority has uncovered a number of bid rigging arrangements impacting public procurement markets); OECD, 'Fighting Bid Rigging in Public Procurement: Report on Implementing

32 CORRUPTION AND COLLUSION IN PUBLIC PROCUREMENT

in TI's CPI (such as Canada, Singapore, and Sweden; see further examples described in Chapters 5–10[62]) or with stringent laws and satisfactory institutional frameworks. Many of these cases have exposed conduct impacting on the provision of core public services and infrastructure, such as the building of hospitals, regeneration and remediation services, and the provision of bus services for public schools. In addition, the integrity units of a number of multilateral development banks (MDBs) and the European Investment Bank have uncovered numerous incidents of corruption and collusive tendering in MDB-financed public procurement contracts (see further Chapter 3).[63] For example, in 2022, the World Bank Group (WBG) reported on numerous investigations by its Integrity Vice Presidency (INT) which led to a number of firms and individuals being temporarily suspended or sanctioned for corrupt, fraudulent, coercive, collusive, or obstructive practices.[64] Further, a 2011 WBG Report indicated that collusive schemes in relation to road-building contracts are 'significant' across the globe, even if difficult to establish definitively.[65]

D. Harm Caused

The discussion in the preceding sections illustrates that not only are public procurement markets prone to corruption and collusion, but these practices do occur in reality. Cases unveiled also reveal the scale of the incentives that can exist and the significant harm that can result from such practices. For example, the corrupt procurement scheme exposed by OCW in Brazil[66] has been estimated to have caused losses of around USD 15 billion to Brazil[67] (with additional, significant losses in neighbouring Latin American countries) and to have allowed

---

the 2012 Recommendation' (2016) 19, available at https://www.oecd.org/daf/competition/Fighting-bid-rigging-in-public-procurement-2016-implementation-report.pdf; OECD, 'Recommendation of the OECD Council on Fighting Bid Rigging in Public Procurement' (2012), available at https://www.oecd.org/daf/competition/oecdrecommendationonfightingbidrigginginpublicprocurement.htm.

[62] See also e.g. ICN, n. 61, 42 and R. Moldén, 'Public Procurement and Competition Law from a Swedish Perspective – Some Proposals for Better Interaction' (2012) 4 *Europarättslig tidskrift* 562 (discussing in detail five Swedish bid rigging cases from 2009 to 2010) and H. Cassin, 'Wait, does Singapore have a corruption problem?', *The FCPA Blog* (18 July 2023).

[63] A common pattern involves corporations using the same agent to prepare and submit the relevant offers in a public tender, see M. López-Galdos, OECD, Latin American and Caribbean Competition Forum, 'Corruption and Collusion; Two Sides of the Same Coin Against Productivity', DAF/COMP/LACF(2016)32 (30 March 2016), and see *Remonts*, n. 44.

[64] WBG, Sanctions System Annual Report: Fiscal Year 2022 (2022).

[65] WBG, n. 61.

[66] See S.F. Moro, 'Preventing Systemic Corruption in Brazil' (2018) 147(3) *Dædalus* 3 and Chapter 5.

[67] See Brazil's Ministerio Publico General, '*Grandes Casos*', available at http://www.mpf.mp.br/grandes-casos and M.R. Sanchez-Badin and A. Sanchez-Badin, 'Anticorruption in Brazil: From Transnational Legal Order to Disorder' (2019) 113 *American Journal of International Law Unbound* 326, 326.

HARM CAUSED 33

huge benefits to be reaped by public officials, politicians, and private tenderers[68] alike (one senior procuring official agreed, in a plea agreement with the authorities, to return nearly USD 97 million from secret bank accounts abroad[69] and, Petrobras eventually accepted that shareholders had lost approximately USD 1.9 billion as a result of corruption).[70] Further, it is estimated that corrupt activities by defence contractor Leonard Francis led to USD 35 million being lost by the US Navy; the US Department of Justice recovered USD 622 million in relation to bribery impacting on weapon systems procurements; and a retired engineer in Montreal admitted to accepting over CAD 700,000 in payoffs from construction contractors in relation to collusive schemes which had significantly increased the costs of procurement contracts (by 20–100 per cent).[71] The facts emerging from these cases provide support for a body of research outlining both the significant harm that cartels and corruption (as well as inefficiencies) create in the public procurement setting and, in contrast, the benefits that can be reaped from open and transparent contracting, in particular, by contributing to efficiency (higher-quality goods and services at lower prices), reducing corruption, and ensuring higher socialized trust.[72] It is a mistake therefore to consider that these types of conduct—or white-collar crime—should not be taken as seriously as other criminal offences.

i. The costs of corruption

Not only is the incidence of corruption[73] difficult to identify,[74] but its hidden nature makes it difficult to measure its costs, especially given the variety of forms it takes—from petty bribes, to grand corruption affecting huge infrastructure or defence contracts, to other forms of embezzlement.[75] Measurements of corruption

---

[68] See n. 8 and text.

[69] Moro, n. 66.

[70] Moro, n. 66.

[71] See Chapters 6 and 10.

[72] See, e.g., Adam, Hernandez Sanchez, and Fazekas, n. 49; S. Gupta, 'Competition and Collusion in a Government Procurement Auction Market' (2002) 30 *Atlantic Economic Journal* 13; OECD, *Competition and Procurement: Key Findings* (OECD Policy Roundtables, 2011); M. Bauhr, Á. Czibik, J. de Fine Licht, and M. Fazekas, 'Lights on the Shadows of Public Procurement: Transparency as an Antidote to Corruption' (2020) 33 *Governance* 495 (the financial benefits of investing in open and transparent bidding systems undermines corruption risk and decreases single bidding, resulting in savings of EUR 4.5–10.9 billion in the EU); and S. Lewis-Faupel, Y. Neggers, B.A. Olken, and R. Pande, 'Can Electronic Procurement Improve Infrastructure Provision? Evidence from Public Works in India and Indonesia' (2016) 8(3) *American Economic Journal: Economic Policy* 258–83.

[73] OECD, *OECD Business and Finance Outlook* (2017) ('Bribery and corruption are vast global industries'); J. Svensson, 'Eight Questions About Corruption' (2005) 19 *Journal of Economic Perspectives* 19, 24–6 (corruption is driven by a country's wealth, its culture, and whether citizens have a voice in a democratic process and good governance structures, such as freedom of the press).

[74] R. Burguet and Y-K. Che, 'Competitive Procurement with Corruption' (2004) 35 *The RAND Journal of Economics* 50, 51

[75] See Svensson, n. 73, 20–1.

nonetheless tend to be based on either direct methods (measuring actual experiences of corruption based on official statistics and experience-based surveys) or indirect methods (based on perceived levels of corruption).

Corruption has sometimes been defended on the basis that it may be essential for businesses in the short run (as a result of the 'prisoners' dilemma'[76]), it provides an essential mechanism for gaining business in a foreign country, it forms an integral part of a politician's toolkit, it is an inevitable aspect of good politics,[77] it provides a means of greasing the wheels of inadequate laws and rules, and, under specific conditions, it is a way of improving economic outcomes or incentives.[78] The public dialogue about corruption has, however, been transformed over the last 30 years,[79] and these types of arguments have broadly been rejected. Rather, many modern studies draw attention to both the direct economic costs of corruption and its adverse impact on attainment of the UN's Sustainable Development Goals (SDGs);[80] the collection of tax revenue;[81] and the adverse relationship between the level of corruption and a number of variables, including: competitiveness and innovation; economic development and economic growth; poverty reduction or elimination; reduction of inequalities (especially income inequality); foreign direct investment (especially because it leads to political instability and an uncertain business environment); human development (e.g. by reducing social spending on education, health, and safe infrastructure, and the income-earning potential of the poor); environmental programmes; peace, justice, and national security; and strong institutions and democracy (by breeding mistrust in government and allowing powerful business entities to capture public institutions).[82]

---

[76] See nn. 16–17 and text.

[77] B. Bueno de Mesquite and A. Smith, *The Dictator's Handbook: Why Bad Behavior is Almost Always Good Politics* (PublicAffairs, 2011).

[78] See generally Rose-Ackerman and Palifka, n. 1, 32, 83–91.

[79] Heimann and Pieth, n. 17, 13.

[80] See UNODC, Anti-Corruption Module 1, available at https://www.unodc.org/e4j/en/anti-corrupt ion/module-1/key-issues/effects-of-corruption.html,

[81] See IMF, 'Fiscal Monitor: Curbing Corruption' (April 2019), available at https://www.imf.org/en/ Publications/FM/Issues/2019/03/18/fiscal-monitor-april-2019.

[82] Many of these outcomes 'disproportionately affect the poor, since they rely more heavily on government services, which become more costly due to corruption. Moreover, corruption reduces the income-earning potential of the poor as they are less well positioned to take advantage of it. For all these reasons, corruption exacerbates income inequality and poverty', C. Lagarde, 'Addressing Corruption – Openly' in Policy Paper *Against Corruption: A Collection of Essays*, Prime Minister's Office, 10 Downing Street (12 May 2016), relying on S. Gupta, H. Davoodi, and E. Tiongson, 'Corruption and the Provision of Health Care and Education Services' in G. T. Abed and S. Gupta (eds), *Governance, Corruption & Economic Performance* (IMF, 2002) 245–79. See also Rose-Ackerman and Palifka, n. 1, 27–36; H. Marquette, R. Flanary, S. Rao, and D. Morris, 'Supporting Anti-Corruption Reform in Partner Countries: Concepts, Tools and Areas for Action' (October 2011) European Commission, Concept Paper No. 2; Rothstein, n. 55, 35 (the effects of corruption on population health are so profound that people are literally 'dying of corruption'; relying on S. Holmberg and B. Rothstein, 'Dying of Corruption' (2011) 6(4) *Health Economics, Policy and Law* 529); R. Fisman and R. Gatti, 'Bargaining for Bribes: the

Therefore, not only does corruption have significant economic costs, but it contributes to the creation, or maintenance, of unequal societies and higher levels of organized crime; weakens the institutional foundations on which economic growth depends; distorts the rule of law; and undermines citizens' trust in government and erodes its reputation and credibility, so threatening democracy:

> The fallouts are all too clear: higher inequality in political influence, deterioration of public values and, ultimately, a diminution in the overall quality of life. These non-economic costs create a vicious cycle of underperformance in the public sector that is harmful to the economy in the long term. The moral fabric of society is also put at risk.[83]

Although these studies may not be conclusive, especially because cause and consequence may be difficult to disentangle, they do suggest a severely negative impact on multiple factors. Indeed, Rothstein states that corruption is 'one of the most serious social problems we face. Empirical studies have shown that corruption has detrimental effects on almost all standard measures of human well-being, including both "hard" measures of mainly population health, to "softer" measures such as satisfaction with life, support for democracy, and perceptions about political legitimacy.'[84]

Further, and more specifically, research suggests that procurement-related bribery,[85] by increasing the cost of public procurement projects and draining

Role of Institutions' in S. Rose-Ackerman (ed.), *International Handbook on the Economics of Corruption* (Edward Elgar Publishing, 2006); *see also* Svensson, n. 73; R. Wade, *Governing the Market: Economic Theory and the Role of Government in East Asian Industrialization* (Princeton University Press, 1990) 3–7; R.P. Alford, 'A Broken Windows Theory of International Corruption' (2012) 73 *Ohio State Law Journal* 1253, 1255–6; P.M. Emerson, 'Corruption, Competition and Democracy' (2006) 81 *Journal of Development Economics* 193, 208, 211; J.G. Lambsdorff, 'How Corruption Affects Persistent Capital Flows' (2003) 4 *Economics of Governance* 229, 230; S-J. Wei, 'How Taxing Is Corruption on International Investors?' (2000) 82 *The Review of Economics and Statistics* 1, 8; and S. Gupta, H. Davoodi, and E. Tiongson, 'Corruption and the Provision of Health Care and Education Services' in A.K. Jain (ed.), *The Political Economy of Corruption* (Routledge, 2015) 111, 115–19.

[83] Lagarde, n. 82.

[84] B. Rothstein, *Controlling Corruption: The Social Contract Approach* (Oxford University Press, 2020) 1.

[85] See generally e.g. Rose-Ackerman and Palifka, n. 1, 36; OECD, n. 73, 116 (noting that less corrupt countries are likely to invest more abroad and so to benefit via foreign sales and scale economics); Lagarde, n. 82; Søreide, n. 3; Boehm and Olaya, n. 52, 439; Burguet and Che, n. 74; J.G. Lambsdorff, 'Causes and Consequences of Corruption: What Do We Know From a Cross-Section of Countries?' in Rose-Ackerman, n. 82, 3, 4–5 (reviewing investigations suggesting that corruption lowers GDP growth, robust empirical findings that foreign investments are significantly deterred by corruption, and evidence that corruption is also caused by inequality); P. Mauro, 'Corruption and Growth' (1995) 110 *The Quarterly Journal of Economics* 681; OECD, 'Consequences of Corruption at the Sector Level and Implications for Economic Growth and Development' (2015); S. Richey, 'The Impact of Corruption on Social Trust' (2010) 38 *American Politics Research* 676, 687; V. Tanzi, 'Corruption Around the World: Causes, Consequences, Scope, and Cures' (1998) *IMF Staff Papers* 559, 571; General T.N.

36 CORRUPTION AND COLLUSION IN PUBLIC PROCUREMENT

public funds: squanders resources that the government otherwise could invest productively in public goods, services, infrastructure, and social services (especially in education and healthcare); skews public investment (diverting funds to contracts with greater capacity to generate commission rather than by economic justification[86]); undermines the effectiveness of procurement systems in selecting the most qualified or efficient contractor; hinders the efficient allocation of resources and reduces innovation incentives; curbs productivity, economic growth, and development; discourages foreign investment; lowers the quality (and sustainability) of procured goods, services, and infrastructure (including e.g. roads, bridges, and buildings, so causing danger to life[87]); leads to corrupt strategies during contract implementation; leads to the implementation of unnecessary contracts; leads to the capture of state institutions by private firms;[88] and increases the costs of doing business, making it much harder for small and medium-sized enterprises (SMEs) to participate. This had led Borroso to state:

> Corruption kills. It kills patients in public health-service queues, waiting for beds that don't exist and medicines that have not been bought. It kills on badly managed highways. It destroys lives that have not received adequate education due to a paucity of schools, structural deficiencies, and lack of equipment. The fact that the corrupt don't look their victims in the eye as they do their damage does not make them any less dangerous.[89]

McFadden, 'Acting Principal Deputy Assistant Attorney, Remarks Before the American Conference Institute's 7th Brazil Summit on Anti-Corruption' (24 May 2017).

[86] See, e.g., J. Pontes and M. Anselmo, *Operation Car Wash: Brazil's Institutionalized Crime and the Inside Story of the Biggest Corruption Scandal in History* (Bloomsbury, 2022) 150 (noting that contracts are approved for their corruption value, rather than national interest).

[87] See S. Kinzer, 'The Turkish Quake's Secret Accomplice: Corruption', *New York Times* (29 August 1999); UNODC anti-corruption module—citing corruption as a cause for the collapse of a bridge in Genoa in August 2018 which killed at least thirty-nine people (investigations found that a Mafia-controlled construction company appeared to have used weakened cement in the building process) and referring to a 2017 report by Mexicans Against Corruption and Impunity blaming corruption for the collapse of over forty buildings during the September 2017 earthquake in Mexico City (land-use and permit laws appeared to have been bypassed, ostensibly through bribery, cronyism, and influence trading, leading to the presence of fundamentally unsafe buildings around the capital); Transparency International, 'Integrity Pacts – Civil Control Mechanism for Safeguarding EU Funds', available at https://www.transparency.org/en/projects/integritypacts/data/ip-hungary, citing corruption as a cause of poor engineering leading to the collapse of the M6 highway in Hungary; and President Ghani, 'Driving Corruption Out of Public Procurement' in Policy Paper, n. 82, 9.5, available at https://www.gov.uk/government/publications/against-corruption-a-collection-of-essays/against-corruption-a-collection-of-essays#president-ashraf-ghani-driving-corruption-out-of-procurement ('Corrupt practices do not end at contract negotiations. Manipulating procurement so that low-quality goods are delivered rather than the higher-quality supplies that were procured and invoiced is a pervasive practice that leads to collapsed infrastructure, massive overcharging and poor-quality services').

[88] See n. 85 and text.

[89] L.R Barroso, 'Afterword' in Pontes and Anselmo, n. 86. See also Transparency International, 'The ignored pandemic' (19 March 2019), available at http://ti-health.org/content/the-ignored-pandemic/ (corruption in the healthcare sector kills approximately 140,000 children per year).

Some older work estimated that the volume of bribes changing hands for public sector procurement was approximately USD 200 billion per year, amounting to 3 per cent of the world's gross domestic product (GDP) and 3.5 per cent of world procurement spending.[90] Further, that 60 per cent of companies admit to paying bribes.[91] A study from the Organisation for Economic Co-operation and Development (OECD) also documents significant savings (sometimes of up to nearly 50 per cent) in procurement costs in certain countries following the introduction, or improvement, of transparency and procurement procedures,[92] and studies prepared for the European Commission have found substantial savings following implementation of the EU Public Procurement Directives, which contain important anti-corruption elements.[93]

More recently, it has been estimated that 20–30 per cent of the investment in publicly funded construction projects may be lost through mismanagement and corruption,[94] that 10–25 per cent of the money spent by governments ends up in bribes,[95] and that 25 per cent of public procurement funds are lost to corruption each year.[96] In 2016, an International Monetary Fund (IMF) report estimated the cost of bribery to be USD 1.5–2 trillion a year (approximately 2 per cent of global

[90] See, e.g., Auriol, n. 52, 868 ('According to an ongoing research at the World Bank, the total amount of bribery for public procurement can hence be estimated in the vicinity of USD 200 billion per year. That is, approximately 3.5% of the world procurement spending. Assuming this figure is accurate, it represents only one part of the overall cost of corruption because corruption usually involves allocative inefficiency on top of the bribes').

[91] In a study conducted by Transparency International in 2002 to build its second Bribe Payers Index of leading exporting countries, 60 per cent of the respondents claimed that corruption in international business, especially in public works contracts, construction, and arms and defence industries, had either increased or remained the same. See, Press Release, Transparency International, Transparency International Releases New Bribe Payers Index (BPI) (13 May 2002).

[92] See OECD, 'Transparency in Government Procurement: The Benefits of Efficient Governance and Orientations for Achieving It', TD/TC/WP(2002)31/FINAL (5 May 2003) 8 (discussing Colombia, Guatemala, Bangladesh, Nicaragua, and Pakistan).

[93] See generally European Commission, Internal Market Industry, Entrepreneurship, and SMEs, 'Studies and Expert Groups', available at https://ec.europa.eu/growth/single-market/public-procurem ent/studies-networks_en; and Court of Auditors Special Report, 'Efforts to address problems with public procurement in EU cohesion expenditure should be intensified' (16 July 2015) 10 (estimating annual savings by adopting EU legislation to be EUR 6.4–35.5 billion).

[94] See, e.g., J. Wells, 'Corruption and Collusion in Construction: A View from the Industry' in T. Søreide and A. Williams (eds), *Corruption, Grabbing and Development: Real World Challenges* (Edward Elgar Publishing, 2014); Construction Sector Transparency Initiative Press Release, UK Launch of the CoST International Programme (22 October 2012) (stating that annual losses from mismanagement, inefficiency, and corruption in global construction could amount to USD 2.5 trillion annually by 2020).

[95] See E. Bosio, S. Djankov, E. Glaeser, and A. Shleifer, 'Public Procurement in Law and Practice' (2020) PIIE Working Paper 20-14.

[96] United Nations Office on Drugs and Crime, 'Guidebook on Anti-Corruption in Public Procurement and the Management of Public Finances, Good Practices in Ensuring Compliance with Article 9 of the United Nations Convention Against Corruption' (2013), available at https://www.unodc.org/documents/corruption/Publications/2013/Guidebook_on_anti-corruption_in_public_procurement_and_the_management_of_public_finances.pdf. Transparency International stated that the increased cost can be as much as 50 per cent, 'Public Procurement', available at https://www.transparency.org/topic/detail/public_procurement. See also K.V. Thai, 'International Public Procurement: Concepts and Practices' in K.V. Thai (ed.), *International Handbook of Public Procurement* (Routledge, 2009), relying on United Nations Development Programme, 'Capacity Development Practice Note' (2006).

38 CORRUPTION AND COLLUSION IN PUBLIC PROCUREMENT

GDP),[97] and a European Parliamentary Research Service report assessed the cost of corruption risk in public procurement in the EU to be EUR 5 billion.[98] Similarly, an OECD report (2017) estimated that 'individuals and companies pay bribes in the vicinity of the size of France's GDP ... [A]round USD 2 trillion per annum',[99] Transparency International estimated that the annual costs of international corruption is USD 3.6 trillion (in the form of bribes and stolen money),[100] that roughly USD 2 trillion disappears annually from procurement budgets, and that 'few examples of corruption cause greater damage to the public purse and harm public interests to such a grave extent'.[101] Others have calculated that the bribes paid per annum amounts to 'more than half of the global economy's needs for productivity-enhancing infrastructure investment to 2030'.[102] The bribes also do not 'help growth in host countries where foreign investment is concerned, but instead money disappears into shelf companies and foreign bank accounts of corrupt politicians and officials'.[103] Further, in relation to infrastructure procurement, the IMF has estimated that the cost of corruption (combined with incompetence and other causes of inefficiencies) is 15 per cent in advanced economies and 53 per cent in low-income, developing countries[104]; and the United Nations Office on Drugs and Crime (UNODC) has estimated that corruption reduces the value of public contracts by 10–25 per cent.

In addition, the OECD's Foreign Bribery Report for 2014 indicates that nearly 60 per cent of foreign bribery relates to public procurement (especially in the extractive, construction, transportation and storage, and information and communication sectors), and that, in a majority of cases, senior corporate management knew of the bribery,[105] thereby dispelling the idea that the conduct was merely that of a proverbial rogue, low-level employee. This is partly perhaps because of the close interaction between the public and private sectors and the size of the financial flows that public procurement generates. The OECD's Business

---

[97] IMF Staff Discussion Note No. 16/05, 'Corruption: Costs and Mitigating Strategies' (11 May 2016).

[98] See European Parliamentary Research Service, *The Cost of Non-Europe in the Area of Organised Crime and Corruption – Annex II Corruption – Research Paper by RAND Europe* (RAND, 2016) 50–1, 58.

[99] See OECD, n. 73, 96, see also 'The Rationale for Fighting Corruption', *CleanGovBiz.org* (2014).

[100] See Transparency International Corruption Statistics, available at https://www.transparency.org.uk/corruption-statistics.

[101] Transparency International, 'Curbing Corruption in Public Procurement: A Practical Guide' (2014) 8, available at https://www.transparency.org/en/publications/curbing-corruption-in-public-procurement-a-practical-guide.

[102] See OECD, n. 73, 95–6.

[103] See OECD, n. 73, 95–6.

[104] G. Schwartz, M. Fouad, T. Hansen, and G. Verdier, 'How Strong Infrastructure Governance Can End Waste in Public Investment', *IMF Blog* (2020), available at https://blogs.imf.org/2020/09/03/how-strong-infrastructure-governance-can-end-waste-in-public-investment/; and see, Adam, Hernandez Sanchez, and Fazekas, n. 49.

[105] OECD, 'Foreign Bribery Report: An Analysis of the Crime of Bribery of Foreign Public Officials' (2014).

and Finance Outlook for 2017 observes that '[o]btaining and retaining government contracts is, by far, the most common motivation for financial intermediaries' bribes to public officials (it was a motivating factor in 73 per cent of the cases)'.[106] '[T]he desire to obtain or retain government business was the dominant motivation for foreign bribery in all sectors, and even more so in the financial sector.'[107]

ii. The costs of bid rigging

Successful cartels undermine the system of free-market competition, leading to higher prices (contributing to inflation), deadweight loss, productive inefficiency, and dynamic harm (reduced incentives to innovate). The costs of forming and enforcing a cartel also reduce consumer welfare.[108] Further, bid rigging in public procurement wastes public funds; diminishes public confidence in, and the benefits of, the competitive process; and denies citizens, especially the disadvantaged, the benefits of improvements in social services.[109] It may also be 'detrimental for democracy and for sound public governance'.[110] Finally, bid rigging inhibits 'investment and economic development', and these 'deficiencies in public procurement impact ... the wider economy in a way that does not occur with private procurement'.[111]

Although, as with corruption, assessing cartel harm precisely is not easy, a paper focusing on bid rigging in Japan suggests that procurers paid 16–33 per cent more than they would have paid in a competitive bid process,[112] and a paper studying the damage done to Petrobras in Brazil documents empirical evidence that bids won by cartel members had a 17 per cent lower discount than bids won by non-cartel companies.[113] A report published by the WBG in 2011, investigating misconduct in WBG-funded road projects, also provides evidence that bid rigging in procurement markets leads to sharply inflated prices[114] and reductions in quality or safety

---

[106] OECD, n. 73, 100.

[107] OECD, n. 73,100.

[108] M. Monti, 'Cartels Why and How? Why Should We Be Concerned with Cartels and Collusive Behaviour?', *Speech to Third Nordic Competition Policy Conference, Stockholm* (2001).

[109] See OECD, n. 72.

[110] See OECD, n. 72, 31.

[111] See OECD, n. 72, 31.

[112] See J. McMillan, 'Dango: Japan's Price-Fixing Conspiracies' (1991) 3 *Economics and Politics* 201; M. Nihashi, T. Saijo, and M. Une, 'The Outsider and Sunk Cost Effects on 'Dango' in Public Procurement Bidding: An Experimental Analysis 1' (2000) Institute of Social and Economic Research, Osaka University, Discussion Paper No. 514.

[113] J.R. Pereira, R. Terra, A.C. Zoghbi, and R.M Gomes, 'Danos de cartel em contratos com a Petrobras' (2021) 17(2) *Revista Direito GV* e2122.

[114] World Bank, n. 61, 2 ('In the Cambodia Provincial Rural Infrastructure Project, collusion sharply inflated construction costs').

40 CORRUPTION AND COLLUSION IN PUBLIC PROCUREMENT

of products and services provided.[115] Further, it documents examples of bid rigging which reportedly increased prices in Korea, the Netherlands, the Philippines, Romania, Tanzania, Turkey, and the US—by up to 60 per cent in some cases.[116]

More generally, the OECD estimates that eliminating bid rigging could reduce procurement prices by 20 per cent or more,[117] and some competition agencies estimate that cartels charge at least 10 per cent over the competitive price.[118] A number of empirical studies suggest, however, that this figure is conservative, and that cartels 'lead to prices well in excess of 10 per cent, and sometimes in excess of 20 per cent, of competitive levels'.[119] Further, it has been estimated in the EU that a truck cartel inflicted a net welfare loss of up to EUR 15.5 billion on the European economy and an overcharge of up to 7.6 per cent.[120] Although bid rigging conspiracies are, for the reasons described in the preceding text, often considered to be especially harmful, their economic harm resembles that of other cartel activity.[121] It may be, however, that they occur more frequently and have the potential to be more stable and to last for longer periods.[122]

---

[115] World Bank, n. 61 ('In Indonesia, the use of substandard construction materials reduced the useful life of a road and damaged the vehicles using it.... INT also saw contractors fraudulently failing to comply with such essential safety features as lane markings, resulting in a sharply increased risk of accidents').

[116] World Bank, n. 61, 14, Table 3.

[117] See OECD, 'Fighting Bid Rigging in Public Procurement', available at https://www.oecd.org/competition/cartels/fightingbidrigginginpublicprocurement.htm.

[118] See OECD, 'Guide for Helping Competition Authorities Assess the Expected Impact of Their Activities' (2014). Most competition agencies do not provide a formal analysis in their cartel decisions of how much prices increased during the cartel period. However, according to the UK's Competition and Markets Authority, evidence suggests that cartels—including bid rigging—lead to overcharges of up to 20 per cent. See Press Release, Competition and Markets Authority & Crown Commercial Service, Procurement E-Learning Module Targets Bid-Rigging Cheats (June 20, 2016).

[119] L.M. Froeb, R.A. Koyak, and G.J. Werden, 'What Is the Effect of Bid Rigging on Prices?' (1993) 42 Economics Letters 419. See also e.g. Levenstein and Suslow, n. 29, 56; J.M. Connor, 'Price-Fixing Overcharges: Revised 3rd Edition' (February 2014) Unpublished Working Paper 53–4, available at https://papers.ssrn.com/sol3/papers.cfm?abstract_id=2400780 (examining more than 700 economic studies and judicial decisions (and 2041 quantitative estimates of overcharges), and estimating a long-run median overcharge of 23 per cent for all cartels); J.M. Connor and R.H. Lande, 'How High Do Cartels Raise Prices? Implications for Optimal Cartel Fines' (2005) 80 Tulane Law Review 513, 559–60, but contrast M. Boyer and R. Kotchoni, 'How Much Do Cartel Overcharge? (The Working Paper Version)', CIRANO – Scientific Publication (2015) 2015s-37; and M. Boyer and R. Kotchoni, 'How Much Do Cartel Overcharges', CIRANO – Scientific Publication (2011) 2011s-35 (critiquing earlier analysis of Connor and Lande). See more recently, J.M. Connor and R.H. Lande, 'The Prevalence and Injuriousness of Cartels Worldwide' in P. Whelan (ed.), Elgar Research Handbook on Cartels (Edward Elgar Publishing Ltd, 2023).

[120] C. Beyer, K. von Blanckenburg, and E. Kottmann, 'The Welfare Implications of the European Trucks Cartel' (2020) 55(2) Intereconomics 120.

[121] See, e.g., Connor, n. 119, 54.

[122] See, e.g., M. Hellwig and K. Hüschelrath, 'Cartel Cases and the Cartel Enforcement Process in the European Union 2001–2015: A Quantitative Assessment' (2017) 62(2) Antitrust Bulletin 400; J. Zimmerman and J. Connor, 'Determinants of Cartel Duration: A Cross-Sectional Study of Modern Private International Cartels' (2 August 2005) Purdue University Working Paper; and R. Abrantes-Metz, J. Connor, and A. Metz, 'The Determinants of Cartel Duration' (May 2013) Purdue University Working Paper.

E. Conclusions

This chapter stresses the risks that corruption and collusion pose to public procurement processes, as well as the huge costs of these practices to governments, taxpayers, and citizens, as well as to citizens' confidence in governments. It consequently highlights the significant benefits to be reaped from combatting these practices and putting in place a procompetitive public procurement system.

By examining features that are likely to allow corrupt or anti-competitive practices to flourish, this chapter shines a light on the factors to be tackled in order for a fight against them to be successful, both through reducing opportunities for the conduct to occur and by reducing the incentives for wrongdoing. An essential starting point in that battle is a procompetitive public procurement system based on carefully constructed public procurement, anti-corruption, and competition laws which are designed to reduce opportunities and incentives for such conduct to occur. Chapter 3 examines the important features that such a regime should contain. Chapter 4 illustrates, however, that, although a carefully constructed regime is necessary, this is not enough to ensure its success. Great care is required to ensure that it operates effectively and is not undermined by weaknesses in its application, implementation, or enforcement; poor coordination between agencies; or systemic corruption.

3

Basic Elements for Combatting Corruption and Collusion in Public Procurement: Well-Constructed Procurement, Competition, and Anti-Corruption Regimes

A. Introduction   44

B. An Essential Requirement: A Carefully Constructed National Public Procurement Regime   45
   i. The objectives of modern public procurement systems   46
   ii. Shaping an open, competitive bidding system   49
     a. The choice of procurement methods   51
     b. The use of e-procurement tools to enhance transparency, transactional efficiency and accountability   54
     c. Qualification procedures and conditions for participation   55
     d. Description of the subject matter and technical specifications   55
     e. Award criteria and tender evaluation   56
   iii. A vital and often overlooked ingredient: a well-trained and supported procurement workforce   57
   iv. Provisions to reinforce the integrity of the process   58
     a. Debarment   58
     b. Domestic review/appeal procedures (bid protest, remedies, or challenge mechanisms)   59
     c. Certificates of Independent Bid Preparation   60
     d. Integrity pacts and related measures   60
     e. The role of audits and civil society   60

   v. The contribution of trade liberalization to the strengthening of competition and the combatting of corruption   61
     a. Relevant provisions of the WTO GPA   62
     b. Related role of the EU vis-à-vis its Member States   64
     c. Evidence regarding the benefits of trade liberalization   65

C. Further Essential Building Blocks: Robust Competition and Anti-Corruption Laws   67
   i. Anti-corruption instruments   67
     a. The 'War' on corruption   67
     b. Foreign bribery   69
     c. National developments   71
   ii. Competition law   71
     a. The fight against cartels   71
     b. National developments   72
   iii. Effective enforcement   73
     a. Optimal deterrence   73
     b. Enforcement institutions   74
     c. Uncovering infringements: detection techniques and investigative tools   74
     d. Effective judicial protection of the law   77
   iv. Penalties   78
     a. Corporate fines   78
     b. Individual accountability   79
     c. Debarment   79
     d. Recovery of bribes and damages actions   80

D. Conclusions   80

A. Introduction

The discussion in Chapters 1 and 2 highlights the importance of countries having in place effective laws and measures to counter the opportunities and incentives to engage in corruption and supplier collusion during public procurment processes,[1] and provide initial insights into how these rules may be framed. The following elements, in particular, constitute an essential starting point for effective control:

- A well-constructed public procurement regime, designed to achieve good value for money, through relatively open, competitive, and transparent processes, and to minimize corruption and collusion opportunities and incentives;
- The existence of robust competition and anti-corruption laws outlawing anti-competitive and corrupt practices;
- Proactive and independent public agencies to administer the public procurement regime, and enforce the competition and anti-corruption statutes—working together with citizens and business to prevent corruption and collusion, and to root it out when it does occur—using effective investigatory powers and techniques;
- Effective adjudication of the law and the use of effective sanctions, both to punish infringers appropriately and to deter future violations.

This chapter provides further insight into the types of provisions—and some examples of international best practices—that may be helpful to put such a system in place. Its purpose is thus to provide guidance on the basic elements to be addressed in constructing a robust procurement system, which is resilient to corrupt and collusive practices. It recognizes, nonetheless, that any system will need to be tailored to reflect the particular needs and circumstances of an individual jurisdiction.

Although the components noted above comprise essential foundations for countering corruption and supplier collusion in public procurement, it is recognized that they will often not be sufficient on their own to prevent corruption and collusion from occurring. On the contrary, even comprehensive systems may fail to realize their objectives where gaps in the law, or weaknesses in the laws application, implementation, and enforcement, exist. Indeed, many countries in which corruption is widespread have introduced stringent anti-corruption laws, and created institutions to oversee them, which have failed to make a lasting difference. Further, corruption may continue to flourish in countries with inactive institutions or where democratic institutions are weak. Hence, the measures discussed in this chapter are just a starting

---

[1] There is little point in guarding a procurement system internally from corruption threats, if it can be disrupted and distorted by external collusive behaviour (and vice versa).

point. Even the best constructed systems may face difficulties in implementation or may, over time, require adjustment to reflect new practices and developments arising in a particular jurisdiction. Chapter 4, consequently, examines the types of weaknesses that might prevent a system from working effectively and some proposals for addressing them, whilst Chapters 5–10 consider specific difficulties experienced in the identified jurisdictions and proposes solutions to them.

B. An Essential Requirement: A Carefully Constructed National Public Procurement Regime

As we have already noted, effective control/deterrence of corruption and collusive tendering in public procurement begins with public procurement rules themselves—i.e. the laws and regulations that govern public procurement activities and (crucially) the public organizations and people that carry out such activities. It is an illusion to believe that corruption and supplier collusion can be effectively controlled through 'strong' competition and anti-corruption laws, if the procurement system itself limits competition, discourages innovation, is inadequately staffed and managed, and/or is routinely circumvented by political authorities.

To be clear, public procurement regimes are a complex, multifaceted topic in their own right, and a full analysis of the content of such regimes is beyond the scope of this book.[2] Nonetheless, the control and deterrence of corruption and collusion within such regimes also cannot be meaningfully discussed without due attention to their basic elements. In that light, this subsection delves selectively into relevant components of public procurement regimes, giving particular attention to their objectives; the nature of tendering regimes and core elements of their processes; the important role played by domestic review (procurement appeal or remedy) systems in ensuring fair competition in the conduct of individual procurements; and other elements that may be introduced to better ensure the integrity of related processes. Attention is also given to two further dimensions of public procurement systems: (i) the human dimension—i.e. the vital importance of the institutions and (especially) the staff members that conduct procurements within the confines of relevant laws; and (ii) the potential role of international trade policy in reinforcing and sustaining an open public procurement system.

While the details of relevant legislation and practices vary considerably across jurisdictions, there is also a surprising degree of consensus regarding core objectives, elements, and approaches. This is evident, for example, in international

---

[2] For broader studies of the nature, content and problems of public procurement regimes, see, e.g., S. Arrowsmith, J. Linarelli, and D. Wallace Jr., *Regulating Public Procurement: National and International Perspectives* (Kluwer Law International, 2000); S. Arrowsmith, *The Law of Public and Utilities Procurement, Volume 2* (Sweet & Maxwell, 2018) and K.V. Thai (ed.), *International Handbook of Public Procurement* (Routledge, 2009).

instruments such as the United Nations Commission on International Trade Law (UNCITRAL) Model Law on Public Procurement which sets out a menu of options for the design of public procurement laws consistent with international best practices, as perceived and embraced by the broad range of developing and developed countries that participated in the development of the Model Law.[3] Many of the same elements are also reflected in the architecture of the World Trade Organization (WTO) plurilateral Agreement on Government Procurement (GPA),[4] in chapters on public procurement that are found in an increasing number of bilateral and regional trade agreements,[5] in the rules of international financial institutions or multilateral development banks (MDBs)[6] and/or in relevant recommendations of the Organisation for Economic Co-operation and Development (OECD)[7]. Academic commentary provides a further important source of insight and validation for particular models, while also stressing the continuing diversity of approaches that can be found around the world.[8] The following discussion builds on all these sources.

i. The objectives of modern public procurement systems

In a seminal work on contrasting objectives for public procurement systems that has been cited in policy discussions around the globe, Schooner references, without excluding other possible goals, nine objectives that are associated with many such systems: (i) competition; (ii) integrity; (iii) transparency; (iv)

---

[3] See the UNCITRAL Model Law on Public Procurement (2011) and related information, available at https://uncitral.un.org/en/texts/procurement/modellaw/public_procurement, and accompanying Guide to Enactment, available at https://uncitral.un.org/en/texts/procurement/modellaw/public_proc urement/guide.

[4] See WTO, Revised Agreement on Government Procurement (30 March 2012), a plurilateral Agreement covering 48 WTO Members that is designed to promote trade, good governance, and policy reforms in the parties' covered public procurement markets. See, generally, S. Arrowsmith and R.D. Anderson (eds), *The WTO Regime on Government Procurement: Challenge and Reform* (Cambridge University Press and the WTO, 2011).

[5] Which are similar to standards established under the GPA. See R.D. Anderson, A.C. Müller, and P. Pelletier, 'Regional Trade Agreements and Procurement Rules: Facilitators or Hindrances?' in A. Georgopulos, B. Hoekman, and P. Mavroidis (eds), *The Internationalization of Government Procurement Regulation* (Oxford University Press, 2016), and R.D. Anderson, P. Pelletier, and C.R. Yukins, 'Government Procurement in the Comprehensive and Progressive Trans-Pacific Partnership Agreement: A Global Beachhead for Market Access and Good Governance' in D.A. Gantz and J. Huerta Goldman (eds), *The Trans-Pacific Partnership Agreement: Its Substance and Impact on International Trade, NAFTA and Other FTAs* (Cambridge University Press, 2019).

[6] See, e.g., World Bank, 'Procurement Framework and Regulations for Projects', available at https://www.worldbank.org/en/projects-operations/products-and-services/brief/procurement-new-framew ork#framework; and the 'European Bank for Reconstruction and Development, Project Procurement Policies', available at https://www.ebrd.com/work-with-us/procurement/project-procurement.html.

[7] See, e.g., the 'OECD Recommendation of the Council on Public Procurement' (2020), available at https://www.oecd.org/gov/public-procurement/recommendation/.

[8] See references cited in n. 2. See also S.L. Schooner, 'Desiderata: Objectives for a System of Government Contract Law' (2002) 11 *Public Procurement Law Review* 103.

efficiency;[9] (v) customer satisfaction; (vi) best value; (vii) wealth distribution; (viii) risk avoidance; and (ix) uniformity.[10] Three of these (competition, integrity, and transparency) are further characterized by Schooner as 'overarching principles' that underpin the United States (US) and certain other countries' procurement systems. A related approach that appeals to us is to designate 'best value' or 'best value for money' as the overriding goal, with the other objectives serving as instruments for achieving that ultimate goal.[11] Important trade-offs can, nonetheless, arise between the various cited objectives. For example, as we have already noted, while many forms of transparency (e.g. the systematic advertising of procurement opportunities and publication of the procedures for qualification and submitting of related bids) are intrinsically procompetitive, 'too much transparency' (e.g. publication of the full details of losing bids) can facilitate bid rigging.[12] As another important example, too much emphasis on risk aversion can stifle innovation and the introduction of new technologies, undermining both, value for money and customer satisfaction.[13] The same can even be said about 'excessive' zeal with respect to the value of integrity—i.e. an approach that favours regulatory compliance above all else risks deterring appropriate exercises of discretion that could favour competition, innovation, better value for money, and customer satisfaction.[14]

Efficiency, in the narrow sense of lower resource costs in the procurement system itself, may be achieved and is often sought by artificially limiting the size of the procurement work force and/or underinvesting in it. This, nonetheless, is very likely to result in a degradation in the quality of goods, services, and works procured. Schooner identifies this as a pervasive failure of 'acquisition reform' in the US in the 1980s and 1990s.[15] And, an exclusive or undue focus on customer satisfaction relative to costs may cause buyers to 'place inordinate weight on product quality'.[16] Given these trade-offs and the always-evolving context of procurement and governance internationally, no single goal or approach is likely to endure forever.[17]

Beyond the foregoing goals or objectives, many regimes pursue broader policy goals (sometimes referenced as 'horizontal', or 'secondary', objectives or policies), including public or socio-economic policies (e.g. relating to growth, employment, innovation, the promotion of small, medium-sized, or minority enterprises

---

[9] In this context, 'efficiency' principally refers to administrative or transactional efficiency. Schooner, n. 8.

[10] See, generally, Schooner, n. 8.

[11] Arguably, such an approach is reflected in the architecture of both the EU Procurement Directives, see Directive 2014/24/EU (Public Sector), Directive 2014/23/EU (Concessions), and Directive 2014/26/EU (Utilities) and the WTO Agreement on Government Procurement, n. 4.

[12] Recall the discussion in Chapter 1.

[13] Schooner, n. 8.

[14] Schooner, n. 8.

[15] Schooner, n. 8.

[16] W.E. Kovacic, 'Procurement Reform and the Choice of Forum in Bid Protest Disputes' (1995) 9 The Administrative Law Journal 461, 486–7 (also cited by Schooner).

[17] Schooner, n. 8.

(SMEs), economic patriotism, or sustainability).[18] Although the effectiveness of public procurement (as compared with other mechanisms) as a means to achieve these wider objectives can be debated,[19] many governments do use procurement as a means of driving them and supporting certain enterprises (such as SMEs, e.g. the US Small Business Act, local producers, or women-owned businesses, e.g. Chile's Women Supplier Certification Scheme),[20] enhancing national development, employment, and national security, or preventing reliance on foreign suppliers in certain sectors. This approach has become relatively widespread in OECD countries with about 60 per cent of countries having special support for SMEs and/or green procurement,[21] and many countries having policies that favour domestic suppliers in at least some aspects of their public procurement process.[22] These trends have grown since 2000, as challenges to increased globalization have grown, and a growing numbers of populist governments have been re-evaluating the free-market economic model and embracing a more patriotic economic agenda. The proliferation of such goals is not without risks: it greatly complicates the work of procuring agencies and risks diluting their focus on the 'core' concerns of competition, integrity, and value for money, while often facilitating collusion and cronyism.[23]

A policy concern that may be horizontal but is surely, no longer 'secondary' is that of promoting environmental sustainability and climate change adaptation/resilience through public procurement. The promotion of sustainability and the

---

[18] See S. Arrowsmith, 'Horizontal Policies in Public Procurement: A Taxonomy' (2010) 10(2) *Journal of Public Procurement* 149–86. In the EU, an important such objective concerns the free movement of goods and services across borders and between states (as, e.g. in the EU).

[19] See OECD Recommendation of the Council on Public Procurement, n. 7, Recommendation I.V (recommending careful evaluation and balancing of the benefits, e.g., through impact assessments to measure the effectiveness of procurement in achieving secondary policy objectives). Market oriented and populist groups may disagree as to whether these may be appropriate mechanisms, e.g., for safe-guarding national jobs, especially if they increase the cost of government procurement.

[20] See M. Fazekas and J.R. Blum, 'Improving Public Procurement Outcomes: Review of Tools and the State of the Evidence Base' (2021) *World Bank Group Policy Research Working Paper 9690* 15–16.

[21] OECD, *Government at a Glance* (OECD Publishing, 2019).

[22] A description of domestic preferences programmes in regard to public procurement in OECD and non-OECD countries is provided in C. McCrudden, *Buying Social Justice: Equality, Government Procurement and Social Change* (Oxford University Press, 2007). In the US, for example, a 1933 'Buy American' law orders government purchasers to prefer domestic products. Federal policy towards infrastructure projects also requires funds obtained through federal grants to be used on American-made projects, see Chapter 6 and nn. 98-102 and text (discussing the gaps and exceptions to the GPA that impact upon the question of when these rules can be applied to preclude bidding by suppliers based in a country that is party to the GPA). The US approach is sometimes defended on the basis that it provides an essential inducement for countries to seek accession to the GPA or other arrangement providing access to the US market, see C.R. Yukins and S.L. Schooner, 'Incrementalism: Eroding the Impediments to a Global Public Procurement Market' (2007) 38 *Georgetown Journal of Internal Law* 529, 569.

[23] Arrowsmith, n. 18. See also S.L. Schooner, 'Mixed Messages: Heightened Complexity in Social Policies Favoring Small Business Interests' (1999) 8(3) *Public Procurement Law Review* CS78, CS82-3 and R.D. Anderson and W.E. Kovacic, 'Competition Policy and International Trade Liberalisation: Essential Complements to Ensure Good Performance in Public Procurement Markets' (2009) 18(2) *Public Procurement Law Review* 67.

mitigation of climate change are fast becoming defining challenges of our times. Public procurement policy has a vital role to play in responding to the current crises. For example, public procurement is directly and powerfully implicated in many of the actions that are necessary for the world to respond to and (to the extent possible) mitigate climate change and related ecological disasters. Examples would include the purchase of wind turbines to facilitate a transition to green energy sources; public investment in electrical charging facilities for the emerging new generation of automobiles; the construction of sea walls and the improvement of storm sewer systems; the development and deployment of more effective wildfire suppression and control technologies. The manner in which such purchasing is conducted, by itself, will have an appreciable impact on the earth's sustainability.[24] Even so, it must be acknowledged that the magnitude of public funds devoted to supporting the transition to cleaner forms of energy and adaptation to related threats, reinforced by the urgency with which such resources are being deployed, entails major risks of corruption and supplier collusion.[25]

ii. Shaping an open, competitive bidding system

In order to ensure that a public procurement system achieves its objectives, however defined, it will need to be carefully constructed to protect its integrity throughout its process—from needs-assessment, to process design and document preparation, tender evaluation and contract award, and contract execution, implementation, and management—and to minimize the risk of the goals being undermined by inefficiency, incompetence, bribery, or bid rigging.[26] Thus, as

---

[24] See, e.g., S.L. Schooner, 'No Time to Waste: Embracing Sustainable Procurement to Mitigate the Accelerating Climate Crisis' (2021) 61(12) *Contract Management* 24; Mission Possible Partnership, 'Green Public Procurement: Catalysing the Net-Zero Economy' (2022) World Economic Forum, in collaboration with the Boston Consulting Group, White Paper; and R. Baron, 'The Role of Public Procurement in Low-Carbon Innovation' (12–13 April 2016) Background Paper for the 33rd Round Table on Sustainable Development, OECD Headquarters. On the contribution of international coordination and, specifically, the WTO Agreement on Government Procurement in this area, see R.D. Anderson, A. Salgueiro, S.L. Schooner, and M. Steiner, 'Deploying the WTO Agreement on Government Procurement (GPA) as a Tool of Sustainability and Climate Change Mitigation: The GPA Committee's Sustainability Work Programme as a Sleeping Giant and Essential Platform for Progress' (2023) 32 *Public Procurement Law Review* 233

[25] See, for related discussion, Chapter 6.

[26] Two influential documents widely disseminated and relied upon are the 'Recommendation of the OECD Council on Fighting Bid Rigging in Public Procurement' (2012) and the OECD's 'Report on Implementing the OECD Recommendation on Fighting Bid Rigging in Public Procurement' (2016) (the recommendations have helped competition authorities, both to launch advocacy programmes and raise awareness of bid rigging risks, and procurement authorities in designing tenders and detecting bid rigging); see also speech of G. Miralles, Senior Economist, WBG Trade and Competitiveness Global Practice, 'Connecting Public Procurement and Competition Policies: The Challenge of Implementation, Presentation', LEAR Conference (3 July 2017). In addition to calling for appropriate law enforcement activities, these instruments emphasize: the need for procurers to identify markets in which bid rigging is more likely to occur and to adopt methods that maximize the number of bids; best practices for

50   BASIC ELEMENTS FOR COMBATTING CORRUPTION AND COLLUSION

well as being constructed so as to allow its objectives to be pursued proactively, the system must contain mechanisms designed to make it harder for procurers to direct contracts towards preferred bidders, and for firms to arrange and sustain bid rigging schemes. Many systems therefore encompass rules which, for example:

- Guard against corruption, collusion, and single bidding by setting out the procedures that must be used for defined contracts and requiring the use of competitive bidding systems and auction designs which are open and transparent, with minimum barriers to entry (e.g. requiring the publication of tenders, the use of minimum bid periods, and minimum numbers of bidders, and containing provisions designed to widen the pool of bidders).[27] Exemptions from, and exceptions to, these processes should be limited and carefully confined (see further Chapter 4);
- Reinforce the integrity in the process by use of procurer codes of conduct, certificates of independent bidding or 'Integrity Pacts'[28], and by requiring, or allowing, economic operators convicted of corruption or collusion to be excluded, or debarred, from procurement procedures unless and until they have undergone a self-cleaning process;
- Require authorities in setting criteria and evaluating tenders to treat economic operators equally and without favouring or discriminating in favour of certain tenderers, and to act in a transparent and proportionate manner. They should also provide for careful regulation of amendments to concluded contracts;
- Include social-policy provisions in the procurement law to increase gender diversity among actors and, thus, the pool of prospective suppliers;[29]
- Provide for monitoring and auditing of processes (and accountability of decision-takers), as well as complaints and domestic review procedures.

The following provides additional detail on these types of issues.

---

tender specifications requirements and award criteria; procedures that inhibit communication among bidders, and to identify suspicious pricing patterns, statements, documents, and behaviour by firms.

[27] See M. Bauhr, Á. Czibik, J. de Fine Licht, and M. Fazekas, 'Lights on the Shadows of Public Procurement: Transparency as an Antidote to Corruption' (2020) 33 *Governance* 495 (the financial benefits of investing in open and transparent bidding systems undermines corruption risk and decreases single bidding, resulting in significant financial savings) and S. Lewis-Faupel, Y. Neggers, B.A. Olken, and R. Pande, 'Can Electronic Procurement Improve Infrastructure Provision? Evidence from Public Works in India and Indonesia' (2016) 8(3) *American Economic Journal: Economic Policy* 258.

[28] See TI's Integrity Pacts Programme, https://www.transparency.org/programmes/overview/integritypacts.

[29] UNODC, 'The Time Is Now: Addressing the Gender Dimensions of Corruption' (2020) 71.

a. The choice of procurement methods

To drive efficiencies within the system and to limit opportunities for corruption, favouritism, and collusion, competitive procedures should be the norm. Exceptions to competitive tendering should be limited, pre-defined and require justification, with adequate oversight mechanisms.[30] This fundamental principle is recognized in relevant international instruments, for example, in the UNCITRAL Model Law on Public Procurement[31] and the WTO GPA.[32]

The simpler and more streamlined the procedures and institutional frameworks, the easier it will be for a range of suppliers to participate. The more open and transparent the process (at every major stage), the easier it is for a wide range of potential suppliers to participate, and the easier it is for misuses of the process to be identified by a range of stakeholders. 'Evidence suggests, that increased transparency can lead to higher quality implementation ... and stronger competition as measured by the average bidder number.'[33] In constructing such a process, a number of matters need to be considered.

A first point is that the procurement model chosen can help to maximize the opportunity for competition. For example, sealed-bid tender models may diminish the ability and incentive to collude as compared with dynamic open-tender systems where bidders gather in the same place to submit bids.[34] They may also decrease price at the bidding stage (so long as *ex-post* renegotiations do not undermine it). However, individual negotiations with tenderers can also serve as an important tool to upset cartel stability.

Secondly, carefully constructed tender requirements can maximize participation in bidding processes and, where desired, open markets to foreign bidders, for example, by: streamlining requirements for bidders (omitting any unnecessary restrictions); omitting provisions which are likely to limit, artificially or unnecessarily, the number of bidders (e.g. by limiting preferential provisions or prequalification criteria); defining technical specifications by reference to functional performance rather than design or descriptive characteristics; streamlining proof of technical expertise processes; and basing technical specifications on

---

[30] See OECD Recommendation of the Council on Public Procurement, n. 7.

[31] See n. 3.

[32] See GPA, n. 4, Articles IV.4(a) and Article XIII re: the use of limited tendering.

[33] M. Fazekas and B. Tóth, 'Assessing the Potential for Detecting Collusion in Swedish Public Procurement' (2016) 3 *Konkurrensverket Uppdragsforskningsrapport* 19 (relying on Lewis-Faupel, Neggers, Olken, and Pande, n. 27, and Center for Global Development, *Publishing Government Contracts, Addressing Concerns and Easing Implementation* (Washington, 2014)).

[34] See, e.g., F. Boehm and J. Olaya, 'Corruption in Public Contracting Auctions: The Role of Transparency in Bidding Processes' (2006) 77(4) *Annals of Public and Cooperative Economics* 431, 435–6; Y. Lengwiler and E. Wolfstetter, 'Corruption in Procurement Auctions' in N. Dimitri, G. Piga, and G. Spagnolo (eds), *Handbook of Procurement* (Cambridge University Press, 2006) 419; H. Wang and H-M Chen, 'Deterring Bidder Collusion: Auction Design Complements Antitrust Policy' (2016) 12(1) *Journal of Competition Law and Economics* 31, 37 (oral auctions are more vulnerable to collusion than sealed bids, second price sealed-bid auctions are more susceptible than first-price sealed bids, and collusion is easier in ascending than in descending auctions).

52 BASIC ELEMENTS FOR COMBATTING CORRUPTION AND COLLUSION

international standards where they exist (otherwise, on national technical regulations, recognized national standards, or building codes).[35] Such steps will lower barriers to entry and provide clear, objective, and well-defined guidance for the evaluation and award of the tender (with relative weightings where appropriate).

Thirdly, where feasible central (rather than local) purchasing, or collaborative purchasing by two or more procuring agencies, may allow procurers to exercise countervailing market power against suppliers, make bulk purchases, yield economies of scale and process, and put procurers in a better position to prevent, and detect patterns of, collusion.[36] Central purchasing bodies (CPBs) may also use collaborative tools, such as framework agreements,[37] to aggregate needs (especially in relation to homogenous goods or services that are purchased recurrently by contracting authorities), to reduce transaction costs, and so to boost efficiency. Central purchasing may also, in some cases, make it easier to guard against corruption, by facilitating top-level oversight of purchasing.[38] Individual procurers can then purchase from the central agency. Central purchasing may not always be possible or make sense, however. For example, although it may be practicable where standardized products are to be purchased, it may not be able to target local needs sufficiently. Increasing the size of contracts could also deter SMEs from tendering and, increase, corruption incentives. If combined with a provision allowing bids on a portion of a tender, however, the process may increase participation, particularly by local SMEs, which account for a significant percentage of all established businesses worldwide.[39]

Fourthly, it is extremely important to consider how collusion risks are to be minimized. For example, offering contracts less frequently and on long, irregular time cycles, may reduce the incidence of bid rigging[40] by creating powerful incentives for bidders to deviate from any collusive scheme.

In some cases, however, the desire to counter collusion must be carefully balanced against corruption risks. For example, it is seen in Chapter 2 that collusion is more likely to thrive where the market is transparent, and internal and external deviations from a collusive equilibrium can easily be detected. It is possible therefore that steps taken in procurement processes to guard against corruption

---

[35] See discussions of requirements established under the GPA in Chapter 4.

[36] See, e.g., O. Chiappinelli, 'Decentralization and Public Procurement Performance: New Evidence from Italy' (2020) 58(2) *Economic Inquiry* 856 (presenting evidence suggesting that a reorganization of the procurement system, both in terms of partial centralization and increased professionalization of procurement officials, would help improve award stage procurement performance).

[37] These generally involve advertisement of an opportunity by a CPB for the provision of goods, services, or work to a number of different contracting authorities over a specified period and on standardized terms and conditions.

[38] See further Chapter 4, Section C.

[39] See OECD, 'Preventing Corruption in Public Procurement' (2016) 489–91, available at https://www.oecd.org/gov/ethics/Corruption-Public-Procurement-Brochure.pdf.

[40] Wang and Chen, n. 34. Larger contracts may, however, present a greater risk of corruption and, being larger, could reduce the pool of bidders and opportunities for SMEs, see n. 39 and text.

through increasing transparency (e.g. publicizing the details of outcomes, winners, and losers (including prices) to disappointed candidates, in post-award phases, without protecting competition-sensitive information) may have the effect of facilitating collusion by allowing tenderers to monitor a cartel's stability easily and without cost—and so to identify, and rapidly react against and punish, divergences from the arrangement or the entry of new players. Indeed, the rules in some jurisdictions have been criticized for focusing too excessively on market transparency, without taking sufficient account of the collusion risks and ensuring that transparency provisions are targeted at their core objective—fostering accountability.[41]

The foregoing suggests that a one-size-fits-all approach to transparency is not possible or appropriate. Rather, in situations where there is a high risk of collusion which is difficult to mitigate against some lessening of transparency measures might be considered for the sake of preventing collusion—i.e. a 'competition first policy' can be pursued—and other strategies employed to counter corruption, such as the introduction, and use, of negotiation processes.[42] On the other hand, especially in economies where bribery and other 'traditional' forms of corruption are more of a risk, curtailment or elimination of transparency measures could be of greater risk to public funds—in such cases a transparency-first system might be preferable.[43] The OECD recommends that contracting authorities should carefully consider what information is made available when publishing the results of a tender and, in particular should avoid the disclosure of competitively sensitive information.[44] Transparency thus needs to be approached cautiously, ensuring that it is targeted at fostering accountability but without risking competitive distortion, and the reduction of competition between tenderers.[45]

The use of framework agreements[46]—arrangements between the procuring entity and one or more suppliers that provide the terms governing contracts to be established for a certain period of time—while yielding important potential benefits especially in terms of transactional efficiency, also entails potential concerns. In particular, the framework model has been shown to attract more bidders than average at the first stage—and may also incentivize the participation of SMEs,

---

[41] See A. Sanchez-Graells, 'Transparency and Competition in Public Procurement' in K-M. Halonen, R. Caranta, and A. Sanchez-Graells (eds), Transparency in EU Procurements: Disclosure within Public Procurement and during Contract Execution (Edward Elgar, 2019).

[42] See, e.g., R. Klitgaard, *Controlling Corruption* (University of California Press, 1988).

[43] See, e.g., M. Fazekas, S. Mischai, and T. Søreide, 'Public Procurement under and after Emergencies', and B. Baranek and V. Titl, 'Political Connections in Public Contracting' in O. Bandiera, E. Bosio, and G. Spagnolo (eds), *Procurement in Focus: Rules, Discretion, and Emergences* (CEPR Press, 2021), part I.

[44] See OECD, 'Recommendation on Fighting Bid Rigging in Public Procurement', n. 26.

[45] See Sanchez-Graells, n. 41 ('better', rather than just more transparency, is required).

[46] UNCITRAL, Guide to Enactment, n. 3. See also G.L. Albano and C. Nicholas, *The Law and Economics of Framework Agreements: Designing Flexible Solutions for Public Procurement* (Cambridge University Press, 2016).

54 BASIC ELEMENTS FOR COMBATTING CORRUPTION AND COLLUSION

ultimately spurring competition at the second stage. Still, the call-off stage should be carefully designed to avoid issues related to a lack of transparency or flawed advertisement of contract opportunities to the framework awardees.[47]

b. The use of e-procurement tools to enhance transparency, transactional efficiency and accountability

E-procurement, by which contracts are advertised on electronic portals (and preferably a single central platform) and other parts of the procurement process (including bidding) are digitalized (in place of paper-based procedures), enable tenders to be communicated widely to a broad audience, so increasing, as well as facilitating, bidding.[48] E-procurement can extend from e-notification, e-access, e-attestation, e-submission, e-auction, e-evaluation, e-invoicing, e-payment, to e-contract monitoring.[49] It 'can increase transparency, facilitate access to public tenders, reduce direct interaction between procurement officials and companies, increasing outreach and competition, and allow for easier detection of irregularities and corruption, such as bid rigging schemes'.[50]

Indeed, some studies indicate that e-procurement reduces transaction costs and increases the number of bidders, or the prevalence of non-local bidders, so reducing price and improving the quality of procurement.[51] It also has the advantage of facilitating scrutiny and auditing of procurement processes by civil society and the general public, especially where published in accordance with internationally applicable data templates,[52] on (government or independent watchdog[53]) open

---

[47] See, for further discussion, G. Albano and C. Nicholas, 'Promoting effective competition and enhancing outcomes in framework agreements' in Albano and Nicholas, n. 46.

[48] In one case in Slovakia, a EUR 220 million tender was—to ensure that a favoured competitor won—posted only on a bulletin board in a corridor inside a ministry building, see 'Rigging the Bids: Government Contracting is Growing Less Competitive, and Often More Corrupt', *The Economist* (19 November 2016). Non-transparent, paper-based systems in contrast, may therefore facilitate corruption.

[49] Fazekas and Blum, n. 20. See, e.g., the discussion of the ProZorro platform (electronic procurement system) developed in Ukraine by a diverse group of stakeholders to reform public procurement and fight corruption in Chapter 9 and see Transparency International, 'Co-Creation of ProZorro: An Account of the Process and Actors' (4 April 2017), available at https://www.transparency.org/en/publi cations/co-creation-of-prozorro-an-account-of-the-process-and-actors.

[50] OECD, n. 39, 22 ('The digitalisation of procurement processes strengthens internal anti-corruption controls and detection of integrity breaches, and it provides audit services trails that may facilitate investigation activities. The e-procurement system KONEPS in Korea is an example of an integrated online platform for procurement').

[51] See, e.g., Fazekas and Blum, n. 20, 9–12; see also I. Adam, A. Hernandez Sanchez, and M. Fazekas, 'Global Public Procurement Open Competition Index' (2021) *Government Transparency Institute Working Paper GTI-WP/2021:02* 13–15; Lewis-Faupel, Neggers, Olken, and Pande, n. 27; and M. Singer, G. Konstantinidis, E. Roubik, and E. Beffermann, 'Does E-Procurement Save the State Money? (2009) 1 *Journal of Public Procurement* 58.

[52] See, e.g., the Open Contracting Data Standard, available at https://standard.open-contracting.org/ latest/en/ https://standard.open-contracting.org/latest/en/and DIGIWHIST, available at https://digiwh ist.eu/.

[53] Watchdog portals exist in e.g. the Czech Republic, Hungary, Indonesia, Nigeria, Philippines, the Slovak Republic, Ukraine, and Vietnam, see Fazekas and Blum, n. 20, 23.

data portals (such as the EU's open-tender portal, Tender's Electronics Daily,[54] and Ukraine's ProZorro e-procurement system and DoZorro network[55]). This data, if complete and sufficiently disaggregated, can be used to monitor purchasing, identify corruption or collusion risks through, for example, quantitative analysis of bidding patterns, and help to develop performance indicators and collect information on the success of procurement reforms (see further Chapter 4).

The success of e-procurement will, however, depend on both procurement agencies and potential tenderers having appropriate and robust systems (which are expensive and complex to develop) and adequate literacy to operate them, and there being a pool of companies that can tender. Barriers to the development of successful e-procurement regimes must not, therefore, be underestimated.

c. Qualification procedures and conditions for participation

Overly restrictive supplier qualification requirements can limit competition and impede entry by new suppliers. Responding to this problem, the UNCITRAL Model Law sets out an exhaustive list of criteria that the procuring entity may use in the assessment of qualifications of suppliers or contractors at any stage of the procurement proceedings, to regulate other requirements and procedures that it may impose for this assessment, and to list the grounds for disqualification. The provisions are aimed at preventing procuring entities from formulating excessively demanding qualification criteria—that reduce the pool of participants—and from being misused to restrict market access, whether at the domestic or international level.[56] In addition, the principle of public and unrestricted participation is implemented in the Model Law, meaning that even in the case of direct awards, the procuring entity must not simply select its favoured suppliers or contractors and invite them to participate, but requires all suppliers in the market concerned to be invited to participate in the respective tendering proceeding.[57] Similarly, the WTO GPA commits its parties to not adopt or apply any qualification procedure with the purpose, or the effect, of creating unnecessary obstacles to the participation of both domestic and foreign suppliers, in covered procurement.[58]

d. Description of the subject matter and technical specifications

For the purpose of encouraging participation, the UNCITRAL Model Law emphasizes the importance of clarity, sufficient precision, completeness, and objectivity in the description of the subject matter of procurement. Description with those characteristics enables suppliers to forecast the risks and costs of their participation and

---

[54] Tenders Electronics Daily (TED), available at https://ted.europa.eu/TED/browse/browseByMap.do, and Fazekas and Blum, n. 20 and further in Chapter 4.

[55] See Chapter 9 on Ukraine.

[56] UNCITRAL, Guide to Enactment, n. 3, 78.

[57] UNCITRAL, Guide to Enactment, n. 3, 39.

[58] WTO GPA, n. 4, Article IX.3.

offer their most advantageous prices. Also, properly prepared technical specifications contribute to transparency and reduce possibilities of erroneous, arbitrary or abusive actions, or decisions by the procuring entity.[59] This is also reflected in the text of the WTO GPA which sets out that a procuring entity shall not prepare, adopt, or apply any technical specification or prescribe any conformity assessment procedure with the purpose, or the effect, of creating unnecessary obstacles to international trade.[60]

e. Award criteria and tender evaluation

Once tenders have been received, they should be impartially evaluated without discrimination or favouritism, according to established criteria and goals, by a skilled team.[61] One crucial matter to be determined is whether price, quality, or technical factors are to be decisive; which are to be assessed first, and how much weight is to be attributed to each factors. Another consideration is whether past performance (which may favour incumbents) should be relevant.

An intertwined question is how much discretion should be afforded to procurers. The use of price-only criteria, for example, may limit discretion. Like other rule bound approaches, these may safeguard against, and limit opportunities for, corruption, but may not allow procurers to select products which represent the best value for money (particularly those of a higher quality), be creative (and to instead have to conduct a tick-box, rather than a considered, exercise), run contracts efficiently, or to adapt quickly to changing circumstances, especially in emergencies so rigidifying the process.[62] They may also result in bidders reducing costs by cutting quality and facilitate collusion between them. The more discretion that procuring officials have, however, the opaquer the system becomes, and the easier it is for the process to be distorted by corrupt practices.

In determining how much discretion should be conferred on procurers, two factors should therefore be considered: the risk of corruption as compared to the risk of collusion, and the nature of the procurement to be made.

Where the risk of corruption is considered to be relatively low, and the quality of procurement institutions is high, limitations on discretion should be eradicated where increased discretion is likely to improve contracting. For example, more complex procurements, including relating to infrastructure (e.g. dams, ports, or roads) or sophisticated or technically complex goods and services (e.g. military equipment), are likely to demand, and benefit from, the exercise of judgment and

---

[59] UNCITRAL, Guide to Enactment, n. 3, 83.

[60] WTO GPA, n. 4, Article X.1.

[61] See further Chapter 4.

[62] See, e.g., E. Bosio, S. Djankov, E. Glaeser, and A. Shleifer, 'Public Procurement in Law and Practice' (2022) 112 (4) *American Economic Review* 1091 (finding that regulation of procurement improves outcomes only in countries with low public sector capacity. In contrast, regulation is likely to be detrimental in countries with high public sector capacity, because it inhibits socially optimal exercise of discretion).

discretion, and other mechanisms will be required to limit opportunities for corruption. In contrast, where the risk of corruption is real, for certain routine procurement processes of standard products (e.g. stationery) it might be advisable to limit officials' discretion in selecting successful bidders, placing emphasis on price. The key is to match the right approach to the right tenders and contracts.[63]

To reduce the risk of collusion, where further information is required by procurers to make an evaluation, bids should be discussed individually with tenderers rather than jointly, splitting contracts between suppliers with identical bids should be avoided, and joint bids or bids made with the use of industry consultants should be assessed cautiously.[64] Even if the outcome of the process is transparent, or there is a public bid opening, procurers should keep the terms and conditions of each firm's bid, confidential. Records of the design process, decision process, and implementation process should be taken and monitored to ensure processes are carried out according to their letter, bids are allocated fairly, and contracts are not unduly changed or extended during the implementation stage.[65]

iii. A vital and often overlooked ingredient: a well-trained and supported procurement workforce

The success of public procurement laws and related policies depends very significantly upon a skilled, and well-trained, workforce with the capability and administrative capacity to implement the laws and policies. Corruption risks will be significantly reduced if procurement officials are politically neutral and independent, and if employees are reasonably secure (e.g. protected from dismissal for lack of loyalty or failure to conform to superiors' values), well-paid, appointed, promoted, and paid on merit, and required to disclose any possible conflicting personal or business interests. Likewise, if procurement staff are empowered with solid market research skills and the time to employ them, it will be harder for potentially colluding firms to deceive them and to impose higher than competitive prices.

The effectiveness of the public procurement workforce is not solely a function of adequate resourcing, training, and remuneration, though these are all important.

---

[63] See also the section on procurement model and auction design and Fazekas and Blum, n. 20, 23–5.

[64] See, e.g., Case C-542/14, *VM Remonts* EU:C:2016:578, involving a sub-contractor, an independent service provider, which helped to prepare bids on behalf of competitors bidding independently for a public tender. The question which arose before the Court of Justice of the European Union was whether one of the bidding companies, Pārtikas, could be held liable for collusion when the sub-contractor it had engaged to prepare a bid for a public tender had, without its knowledge, used its price information to set the price for tenders made by two of its competitors.

[65] See, e.g., 'Rigging the Bids', n. 48 (reporting on a case where the British Nuclear Decommissioning Authority was found by the High Court to have been fudging the evaluation of tender criteria to favour a particular bidder, and conducting poor record keeping); see also *Nuclear Decommissioning Auth. v EnergySolutions EU Ltd* [2017] UKSC 34.

58   BASIC ELEMENTS FOR COMBATTING CORRUPTION AND COLLUSION

Rather, it is vital, also, that the workforce be appropriately managed and supported by its leaders. And, of course, even a highly professional workforce will prove ineffectual if it is routinely thwarted by unwarranted intervention in particular procurements, by political authorities.[66]

Experience confirms that appropriate investments in human resources, and adequate training for procurement officials in procurement systems and their management,[67] delivers better overall value for taxpayers. According to Schooner and Yukins:[68]

> States must promptly, dramatically, and aggressively invest in their acquisition workforces.... provide these business professionals with the most current, realistic and skills-based training available.... Then, governments should deploy these talented, skilled, incentivized procurement professionals to get the taxpayers the most for their money. No nation can reasonably conclude that additional investments in personnel to improve its performance in any of these disciplines would not pay significant dividends. Rather, most would enjoy dramatically increased return on their procurement investments by strengthening their capacity in each of these critical areas.

As seen in Chapter 4, problems arise if such a workforce does not exist, as there is greater scope for corruption and collusion, as well as mismanagement, to derail processes.

iv. Provisions to reinforce the integrity of the process

A further important element of many procurement systems consists of specific elements to reinforce the integrity of the procurement process.

a. Debarment

The integrity of procurement processes can be protected by ensuring that economic operators involved in corrupt or collusive processes are excluded, or debarred, from procurement procedures unless they have undergone a self-cleaning process. Such integrity regimes should be approached with care, however. If the approach is

---

[66] See discussion of related experience in Canada in Chapter 10.

[67] See further Section C.iii.c. See also F. Decaolis, L. Giuffrida, E. Iossa, and V. Mollisi, 'The Role of Buyer Competence' in *Procurement in Focus: Rules, Discretion, and Emergencies*, n. 43.

[68] S.L. Schooner and C.R. Yukins, 'Public Procurement: Focus on People, Value for Money and Systemic Integrity, Not Protectionism' in R. Baldwin and S. Everett (eds), *The Collapse of Global Trade, Murky Protectionism, and the Crisis: Recommendations for the G20* (Centre for Economic Policy Research, VoxEU.org, 2009) 87, 91.

CAREFULLY CONSTRUCTED NATIONAL PUBLIC PROCUREMENT REGIME   59

too draconian and inflexible, they may have the reverse effect—weakening the procurement system and failing to protect taxpayers' money.[69]

b. Domestic review/appeal procedures (bid protest, remedies, or challenge mechanisms)

An accessible, user-friendly, timely, and rigorously operated complaints and/or domestic review procedure for disappointed, or dissatisfied, bidders before an independent review body (such as a specialized procurement tribunal or ordinary court) is essential to facilitate detection of irregularities and breaches of public procurement rules and to build bidders' confidence in the integrity and fairness of the system.[70] Indeed the GPA, and other international conventions, recognizes the importance of such systems and their compliance with baseline standards.[71]

A challenge in designing a review process is to ensure that a proper process is in place, which is timely, effective, transparent, and non-discriminatory, but which does not unduly restrain and delay procurement processes, or place an undue burden on relevant authorities by encouraging an excessive number of demands for review.[72] This will require careful consideration of a number of questions, such as who should have standing to request review (perhaps limited to persons with an interest in obtaining the relevant contract and who has been, or risks being, harmed by an alleged infringement), permissible grounds for review, and the standard, and nature, of the review. Such systems should also provide for time-sensitive procedures—short limitation periods running from the time of knowledge (or constructive knowledge) of the grounds for proceedings, and for their rapid determination prior to the awarded contract being concluded. Indeed, to be effective, meaningful remedies must be available to rectify violations committed, including by setting aside tainted procurement awards and providing for processes to be rerun, and possibly even for the payment of damages. Review bodies should also have the power to impose interim measures to suspend commencement of an award pending resolution of the review proceedings. To deter unjustified or ill-founded claims, review systems could provide for summary dismissal of claims that do not set out legally sufficient grounds of protest, require fees for the filing of demands, or require losing claimants to pay for a successful procurer's costs. To ensure integrity within the process and encourage compliance with it, oversight

---

[69] See, for further discussion, Section C.iv.c below, Chapter 4 and Chapter 10 (discussing the Canadian regime).

[70] Some jurisdictions also allow bidders to request reconsideration by the procuring entity. Indeed, some require such requests to be made prior to the launch of review procedures, see Arrowsmith, Linarelli, and Wallace, n. 2, Chapter 12; Arrowsmith, n. 2, Chapter 22; and S. Williams-Elegbe, *Fighting Corruption in Public Procurement: A Comparative Analysis of Disqualification or Debarment Procedures* (Hart Publishing, 2012).

[71] See GPA, Article XVIII, n. 4 and, e.g., UNCITRAL's Model Procurement Law, Chapter VIII, n. 3.

[72] See, e.g., D.I. Gordon, 'Constructing a Bid Protest Process: Choices Every Procurement Challenge System Must Make' (2006) 35(3) *Public Contract Law Journal* 427.

60 BASIC ELEMENTS FOR COMBATTING CORRUPTION AND COLLUSION

mechanisms are required to be conducted both by auditors and through review procedures.

c. Certificates of Independent Bid Preparation

The integrity of a public procurement process can be bolstered in a number of different ways (including through close oversight of them, see further Section D). One particular tool that has been found to be helpful in many jurisdictions concerns the use of Certificates of Independent Bid Preparation or Independent Bidding, also known as 'Certificates of Independent Bidding' or 'Independent Price Determination' in some jurisdictions.[73] Such requirements can have an important deterrent effect and may also facilitate successful prosecution where suppliers do, in fact, collude.[74]

d. Integrity pacts and related measures

In situations where there is a high risk of corruption, an 'Integrity Pact'[75] may be considered. This is a collaborative mechanism to establish a level playing field in which public entities and tendering parties commit not to accept, demand, pay, or offer a bribe, and which involve a civil society organization that monitors compliance with the commitments.[76] It may also, specifically, set out the sanctions that will follow violations for the individuals and companies involved. Likewise, procurement officials should be subject to civil-service regulation or codes of conduct designed to prevent private interests from creating conflicts of interest (conflicting with performance of public duties).[77]

e. The role of audits and civil society

Auditing should be carried out by a range of stakeholders,[78] including, for example, internal counter-corruption officers dedicated to encouraging adherence

---

[73] See OECD, 'Guidelines for Fighting Bid Rigging in Public Procurement' (2009), available at https://www.oecd.org/competition/cartels/42851044.pdf.

[74] Firms may be uncomfortable about signing such clauses when engaged in bid rigging, see, e.g., in the UK, 'Design, Construction and Fit-Out Services' (1 March 2019), paras [3.129]–[3.135]. If firms have signed, and breached such a clause, subsequent proceedings for criminal law violations may also be facilitated. For non-collusion clauses, see, e.g., Hong Kong Competition Commission, 'Model Non-Collusion Clauses and Non-Collusive Tendering Certificate' (December 2017), available at https://www.compcomm.hk/en/media/press/files/Model_Non_Collusion_Clauses_and_Non_Collusive_Tendering_Certificate_Eng.pdf. Tenders could also clarify that procurement agencies will be vigilant for bribery and bid rigging and take action if corruption or collusion is detected, explaining penalties that may result for these practices, reserving the right not to award a contract if suspicion of bid rigging arises, and requiring bidders to disclose upfront any subcontracting plans.

[75] See 'TI's Integrity Pacts', n. 28.

[76] See, e.g., the discussion of DoZorro network in Ukraine in Chapter 9.

[77] Training programmes to raise awareness about integrity risks should also be conducted routinely and compliance backed up by internally or externally conducted audits, see further Chapter 4.

[78] Care will need to be taken to ensure that audit rules do not distort incentives, for example, by encouraging a shift away from transparent auctions towards direct awards; see M.P. Gerardino, S. Litschig, and D. Pomeranz, 'Traditional Audit Design May Distort Incentives' in *Procurement in Focus: Rules, Discretion, and Emergencies*, n. 43.

CAREFULLY CONSTRUCTED NATIONAL PUBLIC PROCUREMENT REGIME   61

to policies and procedures, analysing spending, and overseeing corruption risk assessments (e.g. through reporting on corruption and procurement risks, and liaising with law enforcement authorities); independent state auditors; and external auditors who might be able to identify trends and risk. Civil society groups and international organizations of watchdogs, such as 'Integrity Watch', may also play important roles in monitoring public procurement processes and identifying wrongdoing.[79]

v. The contribution of trade liberalization to the strengthening of competition and the combatting of corruption

Preferential treatment policies, such as those favouring domestic firms and SMEs, can be designed to increase competition from the preferred group and lead to reduced prices (e.g. where higher production costs are offset by enhanced competition).[80] Nonetheless, in so far as these strategies increase barriers to entry, reduce the pool of potential bidders, or favour bidders that are less productive or produce products of a lower value/price ratio,[81] it is likely that they will have the effect of *reducing* the number and diversity of potential bidders and raising prices. Not only does this mean that (as a conscious choice) public purchasing is not achieving best value for money,[82] but such policies may also contribute in some scenarios to the creation of a protected procurement environment for corrupt and collusive schemes to thrive, and for close relationships between public officials and private companies to be cemented.

Indeed, it seems likely that the 'Buy Brazilian' policy pursued by the Brazilian government contributed to the stability of the corrupt procurement scheme unveiled by Operation Car Wash (OCW, introduced in Chapter 2), especially in relation to larger construction, engineering, and infrastructure projects (see further Chapter 7).[83] Even though foreign participants can also be corrupt (OCW itself uncovered involvement of some multinationals), and there is some evidence that companies may select countries to do business on the basis of their perceived

---

[79] See further Section C.iii.c and discussion of domestic review procedures, Section B.iv.b.

[80] See Adam, Hernandez Sanchez, and Fazekas, n. 51, 17–18 (identifying research of such policies favouring SMEs in Japan, Canada, Hungary, and Italy).

[81] Fazekas and Blum, n. 20, 15.

[82] See, e.g., P. Rossetti, J. Varas, and B. Fernadez, 'Buy America Regulations May Raise Cost of Subsidized Infrastructure', *American Action Forum Research* (2021), available at https://www.amer icanactionforum.org/research/buy-america-regulations-may-raise-cost-subsidized-infrastructure/ (finding the price of US metro cars, subject to Buy American regulations, to be 34 per cent more expensive than their foreign counterparts, and concluding that Buy American policies 'almost certainly contribute to higher infrastructure costs in the U.S.').

[83] It is unlikely to be a coincidence that preferential treatment in Brazil was especially strong in the oil and gas sector and in the naval industry, procurement markets significantly affected by the corrupt scheme uncovered by OCW, see Chapter 7.

62 BASIC ELEMENTS FOR COMBATTING CORRUPTION AND COLLUSION

corruptibility,[84] it is also the case that new players may increase competition for tenders and, in some circumstances, shake up stable arrangements and 'have stronger incentives and fewer inhibitions ... to report collusion and/or corruption [than domestic players], as they are less subject to ongoing scrutiny and social pressures'.[85]

In order to dilute these relationships and to reap the benefits of more open procedures, a number of countries have sought to enhance competition in the home market through trade liberalization. This may also provide the opportunity for specialization, exchange, and access to technology that is not available in that home market.[86] Liberalization of trade in relation to government procurement markets can, in principle, be undertaken unilaterally. In practice, however, it almost always occurs through participation in the WTO plurilateral GPA,[87] membership of a regional trade agreement or the European Union (EU) (EU Member States are also members of the GPA), or participation in bilateral agreements embodying rules and commitments similar to those of the GPA.[88]

a. Relevant provisions of the WTO GPA

The GPA's provisions promote an open approach to procurement in a number of ways, for example, by: requiring procurement to be conducted 'in a transparent and impartial manner';[89] requiring non-discriminatory treatment ('national treatment') of other GPA parties' goods, services, and suppliers;[90] incorporating provisions that discourage 'wiring' of technical specifications to favour particular brands or suppliers;[91] prohibiting procuring entities from taking advice on procurement

---

[84] See further discussion of foreign bribery in Section C.i.b and C. Wahrman, 'Competing to be Corrupt' in P.F. Lagunes and J. Svejnar (eds), *Corruption and the Lava Jato Scandal in Latin America* (Routledge, 2020). Participation by foreign companies can therefore contribute to supply-side corruption, and corrupt governments may make deals with foreign companies, giving the latter privileged access to their markets and concessions from compliance with domestic economic regulations, see Transparency International's Bribe Payer Index 2011, available at https://www.transparency.org/en/publications/bribe-payers-index-2011.

[85] R.D. Anderson, W.E. Kovacic, and A.C. Müller, 'Ensuring Integrity and Competition in Public Procurement Markets: A Dual Challenge for Good Governance', in *The WTO Regime on Government Procurement: Challenge and Reform*, n. 4, 92.

[86] See Anderson, Kovacic, and Müller, n. 85, 90; WTO, 'Parties, Observers and Accessions', available at https://www.wto.org/english/tratop_e/gproc_e/memobs_e.htm.

[87] See GPA, n. 4 and discussion in Chapter 3. The GPA consists of 22 parties covering 49 WTO members (counting the European Union and its 27 member states as one party. Another 35 WTO members/observers and several international organizations participate in the Committee on Government Procurement as observers. Several WTO members have initiated accession negotiations, 'Parties, Observers and Accessions', n. 86.

[88] For further analysis, see Anderson, Müller, and Pelletier, n. 5.

[89] GPA, n. 4, Article IV, para. 4, so ensuring that information necessary to participate in and to prepare tenders is disseminated beyond 'the usual suspects' (a procuring entity's preferred suppliers), Anderson, Kovacic, and Müller, n. 85, 91.

[90] GPA, n. 4, Article IV, paras 1–2.

[91] For example, the GPA articulates a clear preference for technical specifications that are framed in terms of performance and functional requirements, rather than design or descriptive characteristics,

CAREFULLY CONSTRUCTED NATIONAL PUBLIC PROCUREMENT REGIME 63

specifications from a person that may have a commercial interest in the procurement;[92] and requiring procurement to be conducted in a transparent and impartial way that avoids conflicts of interest.[93]

To encourage compliance, the GPA provides for external oversight of national procurement systems by the WTO Committee on Government Procurement[94] and GPA parties are required to establish national bid protest or remedy systems (domestic review procedures) through which suppliers can challenge questionable contract awards or other decisions by national procurement authorities' before impartial and independent bodies.[95] GPA parties may also invoke the WTO's Dispute Settlement Understanding (DSU) where they believe that international competition has been thwarted through measures taken in breach of GPA commitments.[96] These avenues of recourse are crucial to ensure supplier confidence that contracts will be awarded on the basis of product quality and competitive pricing, and to encourage participation from a broader pool of potential suppliers.[97]

The principal limitation on the GPA's effectiveness as a tool for the promotion of competition, innovation, integrity, and value for money in public procurement lies in the gaps and exceptions that are embodied in the Parties' market access commitments (formally known as their 'Appendix I Annexes to the Agreement'). The key here is that the GPA's rules—including the all-important requirement for non-discriminatory treatment of other Parties' goods, services, and suppliers and the related procedural and other norms—are legally binding only with respect to procurements that are 'covered' by the Agreement.[98] In addition to excluding procurements covered by specific limitations that are built into the Agreement's text (e.g. relating to measures that are necessary for the protection of Parties' essential security interests relating to the procurement of arms, ammunition, or war materials), this principally refers to procurements that are referenced in the individual Parties' Appendix I Annexes. As well as 'thresholds' that exclude lower-value procurements of all Parties from the ambit of the Agreement, the latter (i.e. the

---

GPA, Article X, para. 4. In this and multiple other respects, the GPA aims simply to codify and enforce good procurement practice as it is understood by the parties to the agreement.

[92] GPA, n. 4, Article X, para. 5.

[93] GPA, n. 4, Article IV, para. 4. The preamble and recitals indicate that the provisions are designed to ensure accord with international instruments and reflect the view 'that the integrity and predictability of government procurement systems are integral to the efficient and effective management of public resources [and] the performance of the Parties' economies'.

[94] GPA, n. 4, Article XXI.

[95] GPA, n. 4, Article XVIII.

[96] GPA, n. 4, Article XX, para. 2. Although only employed relatively infrequently, in this context, its existence is important to ensure that governments honour their commitments and do not arbitrarily exclude potential competitors from other GPA countries. Anderson, Kovacic, and Müller, n. 85, 91.

[97] Anderson, Kovacic, and Müller, n. 85, 91.

[98] GPA, n. 4, Article II(1).

64 BASIC ELEMENTS FOR COMBATTING CORRUPTION AND COLLUSION

Appendix I Annexes) embody multiple explicit or implicit limitations on, or derogations from, Parties' coverage.[99]

To cite a prominent example relevant to current international policy tensions and debates, the GPA market access schedules of the US incorporate an important exclusion for restrictions (e.g. Buy American requirements) attached to federal funds for mass transit and highway projects.[100] Furthermore, a general note to the US schedules excludes from the country's GPA coverage 'any set aside on behalf of a small- or minority-owned business'.[101] A set-aside may include any form of preference, such as the exclusive right to provide a good or service, or any price preference.

The above-mentioned derogations explain how, particularly in the case of the US and to some extent also in other GPA Parties, Parties' obligations under the GPA can co-exist with buy-national requirements that, on their face, would appear inconsistent with the GPA's rules. Specifically, where US procurements are covered by the US GPA commitments, they are subject to a waiver system that displaces the application of Buy American requirements in favour of preserving the rights of GPA Parties under the GPA (or other relevant international agreements, e.g. US Free Trade Agreements incorporating commitments on government procurement).[102] Where this is not the case (i.e. US procurements are not covered in the GPA's schedules or otherwise excluded from the Agreement), Buy American rules apply. In effect, Buy American requirements apply within established (and deliberate) gaps in coverage that are written into the GPA schedules. As we shall see in Chapter 6, this is a continuing concern for US trade partners (notably the EU).

b. Related role of the EU vis-à-vis its Member States

The EU also takes a keen interest in ensuring that Member States have procompetitive procurement regimes in place. Efficient public procurement contributes to its core objectives of creating an internal market, growth, jobs, investment, and undistorted competition within it, and helps to ensure the efficient use of EU funds in Member State government contracting and the protection of these funds from corrupt and anti-competitive practices. It has consequently taken steps to harmonize public procurement laws in the Member States through an EU framework, deriving both from the Treaty on the Functioning of the European

---

[99] GPA, n. 4, Article II(2) and for clarifying discussion, S. Arrowsmith, *Government Procurement in the WTO, Volume 16—Studies in Transnational Economic Law* (Kluwer Law International, 2003), Chapter 5.

[100] GPA, n. 4, Appendix I, 'United States of America', Sub-Central Government Entities, Annex 2, note 5. This note, by itself, excludes a significant portion of procurements associated with US federal infrastructure construction programmes.

[101] GPA, n. 4, Appendix I, 'United States of America', Sub-Central Government Entities, Annex 7, note 1.

[102] See, for thoughtful discussion and clarification, J.H. Grier, *The International Procurement System: Liberalization & Protectionism* (Dalston Press of Djaghe LLC, 2022), especially Chapter 7.

Union (TFEU) itself (as interpreted by the Court of Justice of the European Union (CJEU))[103] and, more specifically for higher value and EU-funded contracts, EU Directives[104] (which themselves reflect the transnational architecture established by GPA).[105]

The foregoing directives are designed to ensure good use of public funds in the Member States through transposing legislation and rules providing for well-regulated procurement, which will facilitate free movement of goods and services between the states and, by ensuring equal access of all EU operators to procurement opportunities across the EU, contribute to the creation of an internal market.[106] The rules guard against corruption and collusion and contain provisions to protect its integrity, including a mandatory and discretionary exclusion system,[107] and provisions requiring Member States to put in place effective remedies regimes.[108] These rules, their part within the EU order, and their significance for the effective control of corruption in potentially 'backsliding' Member States are discussed further in Chapter 8.

c. Evidence regarding the benefits of trade liberalization

In has already been noted that trade liberalization entails its own set of political and other challenges, and that many countries are reluctant to embrace, or are re-trenching from, market opening both generally and in the procurement sector.[109] A growing number of governments are supporting domestic preference, or purchasing policies, as a means of nurturing domestic businesses and enhancing national development, employment, export strategies, and as a mechanism for safeguarding national security and critical infrastructure. Liberalization is thus not universally embraced, and a considerable backlash against it has been experienced

---

[103] The CJEU includes the Court of Justice (CJ), the General Court (GC), and specialized courts. The Member States are committed to the internal market 'an area without internal frontiers win which the free movement of goods, persons, services and capital is ensured' (TFEU, Article 26). The CJEU has interpreted the rules governing these freedoms in a pro-integrationist way and general principles developed—including non-discrimination and equal treatment, transparency, proportionality, mutual recognition, free movement of goods, right of establishment, and freedom to provide services—apply to procurement falling below the thresholds set out in the public procurement directives or otherwise falling outside of their scope, see further n. 11 and text.

[104] See, especially Directive 2014/24/EU, n. 11 and, for example, specific directives governing utilities and concession contracts, Directives 2014/25 and 2014/23. A separate body of legislation governs procurement by the EU institutions, which is subject to Financial Regs, see Regulation 2018/1046 on the financial rules applicable to the general budget of the Union [2018] OJ L193/1, and Rules of Application.

[105] See GPA, n. 4, designed to open up competition in public procurement markets amongst signatories.

[106] See Court of Auditors Special Report, 'Efforts to Address Problems with Public Procurement in EU Cohesion Expenditure Should Be Intensified' (16 July 2015) 10 (estimating annual saving from having EU legislation to be between EUR 6.4 and 35.5 billion, and additional annual savings to be EUR 36.5 and 66.5 billion if the single market in public procurement were completed).

[107] See, e.g., Directive 2014/24/EU, Article 57, n. 11.

[108] See, e.g., Directive 89/665/EEC (as amended by Directive 2007/66/EC).

[109] See Chief Economist Note, Z. Kutlina-Dimitrova, 'Government Procurement: Data, Trends and Protectionist Tendencies' (2018) *DG TRADE Chief Economist Notes* 2018-3.

in many countries in the last two decades. Further, it seems possible that the war in Ukraine and resulting sanctions on Russia may 'speed up the corrosion of globalization'.[110]

Nonetheless, the potential benefits which can be achieved through trade liberalization in terms of the efficiency of public procurement, and the control of collusion and corruption affecting it, are identified in relevant literature.[111] For example, an empirical analysis conducted in 2018 using new data sources and sophisticated econometric techniques affirmed that GPA participation strengthens competition in at least three measurable ways: (i) it increases the number and diversity of firms bidding for particular procurements, including by allowing foreign firms to bid; (ii) it decreases the number of contracts with single bidders; and (iii) it decreases the total number of contracts awarded to individual firms.[112] The assessment also found that, in doing so, the GPA fosters cost-effective public procurement by lowering the probability that the procurement price is higher than estimated cost.[113] These findings build upon data sources that may eventually yield an even better understanding of the respective costs and benefits of protectionism and liberalization in the public procurement sector.[114]

Further, an important report prepared for the European Parliament employs advanced statistical methods to test the major hypotheses arising from the modern literature on the causality of corruption, using time-series data covering a sample of 113 countries. According to its principal author, 'The results show that power discretion and dependency on fuel-export determine poor control of corruption. By contrast, economic openness, consisting in lower trade and financial barriers, and social openness as well as press freedom, positively influence control of corruption.'[115]

There is, therefore, concern in some quarters that the trend against globalization, the move away from risky global supply chains, and the onshoring of manufacturing may result in increased costs, lower growth, and greater corruption and collusion risks.[116] 'Domestic incumbent companies and industries will

---

[110] See A.S. Posen, 'The End of Globalization? What Russia's War in Ukraine Means for the World Economy', *Foreign Affairs* (17 March 2022), available at https://www.foreignaffairs.com/articles/world/2022-03-17/end-globalization.

[111] See Kutlina-Dimitrova, n. 109, 18–20. See also Schooner and Yukins, n. 68; R.D. Anderson, P. Pelletier, K. Osei-Lah, and A.C. Müller, 'Assessing the Value of Future Accessions to the WTO Agreement on Government Procurement (GPA): Some New Data Sources, Provisional Estimates, and an Evaluative Framework for Individual WTO Members Considering Accession' (2011) *WTO Staff Working Paper ERSD* 2011-15.

[112] See B.K. Onur Taş, K. Dawar, P. Holmes, and S. Togan., 'Does the World Trade Organization Government Procurement Agreement Deliver What It Promises?' (2018) *World Trade Review* 5–7.

[113] Onur Taş et al., n. 112, 9.

[114] Kutlina-Dimitrova, n. 109.

[115] See A. Mungiu-Pippidi, 'Fostering Good Governance Through Trade Agreements: An Evidence-Based Review' in *Anti-Corruption Provisions in EU Free Trade and Investment Agreements: Delivering on Clean Trade* (European Parliament, 2018) 11.

[116] See also the discussion of current developments in the US in Chapter 6.

have more power to demand special protections' and, unconstrained by competition from outside their economic block, 'they are more likely to be inefficient, and consumers are less likely to get as much variety and reliability as they currently do. When that consumer is the government, protected domestic firms are even more likely to engage in waste and fraud, because there will be less competition for government procurement contracts. Throw in nationalism and fears of national security threats, and it will be easy for such companies to cloak themselves in patriotism and take it all the way to the bank knowing that they are politically too big to fail. There is a reason why closed economies are more likely to experience corruption.'[117] There is also concern that protectionist developments will negatively impact innovation, which will be diminished without the global pool of scientific talent, and the exchange of ideas.

It seems clear, therefore, that trade liberalization should at least be considered as a possible tool in the fight to improve public procurement processes and to protect them from being undermined by bid rigging and bribery.

C. Further Essential Building Blocks: Robust Competition and Anti-Corruption Laws

Procurement systems can help to minimize the opportunities for corruption and collusion to arise. Many also incorporate their own mechanisms for dealing with breaches of those rules and irregularities. In most jurisdictions, however, distinct anti-corruption and competition law regimes also exist.

i. Anti-corruption instruments

a. The 'War' on corruption
In some jurisdictions, bestowing gifts on public officials in return for a benefit or other practices considered corrupt in other nations is, or has been, a way or life, normal, or considered to be acceptable and an integral part of the culture, a politician's toolkit, and good politics. Indeed, for many years corruption was not a major concern or a priority in national or international agendas.[118] It was not a topic widely covered by politicians, or researchers, especially in political science,[119] and few attempts to evaluate the cost of corruption were made. In the last thirty

---

[117] Posen, n. 110 (arguing that in the US national security and pride is being used to justify policies that short-change both national defence and the 85 per cent of US workers not employed in heavy industry).

[118] See further Chapter 2, D.i.

[119] B. Rothstein, *Controlling Corruption: The Social Contract Approach* (Oxford University Press, 2021) 1.

68 BASIC ELEMENTS FOR COMBATTING CORRUPTION AND COLLUSION

years, however, efforts of international, and non-governmental, organizations such as the United Nations (UN),[120] the OECD,[121] the Council of Europe,[122] and Transparency International (TI)[123] have sought to reverse this mentality, to promote a more uniform understanding and concept of corruption across the world and, following assessments of its costs to a nation, an orchestrated fight against it.[124] The media and individual citizens have also played an important role in changing perspectives on corruption through revealing scandals, seeking to hold governments to account, political movements, and even uprising and the overthrow of corrupt governments. This has resulted in a 'war' against, and a significant shift in thinking towards, corruption.[125] There is now broad consensus that corruption causes economic and other harm (including to international trade), and constitutes 'a cancer' to be rooted out[126] through a multipronged strategy including preventative techniques, a reshaping of many national anti-corruption laws through harmonization processes, and tying conditions to external aid and MDB infrastructure loans.[127]

This has resulted partly from the adoption of a number of anti-corruption conventions. In particular, the United Nations Convention against Corruption (UNCAC), spearheaded by United Nations Office on Drugs and Crime (UNODC), seeks to prevent and combat corruption and develop a harmonized approach towards corruption across its numerous signatories and ratifying jurisdictions.[128]

---

[120] Through its UN Office on Drugs and Crime (UNODC). Created in 1997, its remit was expanded from dealing with illicit drugs to cover organized crime and corruption.

[121] The OECD has been instrumental in developing rules to create a level playing field for global trade through its Working Group on Bribery.

[122] The Group of States against Corruption (GRECO) was established in 1999 to monitor compliance with the organization's anti-corruption standards set out in its Twenty Guiding Principles (Resolution (97)24) and its Criminal Law, and Civil Law, Conventions on Corruption (ETS 173 and ETS 174, respectively).

[123] TI was launched in 1993 as a global NGO to combat corruption, see https://www.transparency.org/en/our-story, and has been publishing an index ranking levels of corruption in countries since 1995.

[124] See, e.g., the Inter-American Convention against Corruption (1996); the EU Convention on anti-Corruption (1997); the OECD Convention on Combating Bribery of Foreign Public Officials in International Business transactions (1997); the Council of Europe Criminal Law Convention on Corruption (1998); the Council of Europe Civil Law Convention on Corruption (1999); the African Union Convention on Preventing and Combating Corruption (2003); and the global instrument, United Nations Convention against Corruption, UNCAC (2003).

[125] B. Rothstein, 'Fighting Systemic Corruption: The Indirect Strategy' (2018) 147(3) *Dædalus* 35 (noting that although many nations have put the weapons in place to fight this war, few have been successful on the ground—in short these new regimes have failed to deliver positive results, see further Chapter 4).

[126] World Bank, 'Voice of the World's Poor: Selected Speeches and the Writings of World Bank President James D. Wofensohn, 1995–2005' (2005) 45.

[127] See, e.g., I. Carr and O. Outhwaite, 'Investigating the Impact of Anti-Corruption Strategies on International Business: An Interim Report' (2009) available at, https://papers.ssrn.com/sol3/papers.cfm?abstract_id=1410642

[128] The UN General Assembly adopted the resolution on 31 October 2003—G.A. Res. 58/4, United Nations Convention against Corruption (UNCAC) (31 October 2003). UNCAC has been ratified by a huge proportion of UN members, more than 180 governments from industrialized, emerging, developing, and least-developed economies.

UNCAC tackles demand- and supply-side corruption issues, bribery of foreign public officials, and specifically applies to corruption within procurement (see Article 9), by requiring procurement systems to be based on 'transparency, competition and objective criteria in decision-making, that are effective, inter alia, in preventing corruption'.[129] It also contains provisions on: law enforcement and liability of persons, obliging Party States to adopt such legislative, and other measures as may be necessary to establish certain corrupt practices as criminal offences, including domestic and foreign bribery, and embezzlement of public funds in certain circumstances;[130] consequences of corruption, including annulment or rescinding of contracts, withdrawing concessions, and compensation for damages; international cooperation; asset recovery; and preventive policies, including the establishment of anti-corruption bodies, introduction of transparent recruitment processes, codes of conduct for public servants, and promotion of transparency and accountability in public finance.[131] Implementation is monitored through the Conference of States Parties, a peer-review process, and a country-based database that is kept on the UNODC website. Although crucial to the Convention's success, maintaining an effective monitoring and review process of over 180 countries is challenging.[132] Implementation reviews do reveal nonetheless that nearly all of the State parties have criminalized at least some acts of corruption as defined in the Convention.

Subsequently, the OECD has promulgated a set of 'Principles for Integrity in Public Procurement', designed to enhance integrity throughout the procurement process.[133] Many international trade instruments also require signatories to ensure their procurement processes are free of corruption and conflicts of interest[134] and the G20 has become an important voice in the fight against corruption.

b. Foreign bribery

Foreign bribery can perpetuate problems in countries struggling to fight corruption. Indeed, there have been indications that bribes paid to public officials in countries ranked most corrupt in country rankings (such as TI's Corruption Perceptions

---

[129] G.A. Res. 58/4, n. 128, Article 9, para. 1.

[130] G.A. Res. 58/4, n. 128, Articles 15–42.

[131] G.A. Res. 58/4, n. 128, Articles 5–14, 43–59.

[132] Experience establishes that follow-up monitoring is essential to ensure anti-corruption conventions work. See F. Heimann and M. Pieth, *Confronting Corruption: Past Concerns, Present Challenges, and Future Strategies* (Oxford University Press, 2018) 115; United Nations Office on Drugs and Crime (UNODC), 'Guidebook on Anti-Corruption in Public Procurement and the Management of Public Finances: Good Practices in Ensuring Compliance with Article 9 of the United Nations Convention against Corruption 3' (2013); and E. Bao and K. Hall, 'Peer Review and Global Anti-Corruption Conventions: Context, Theory, and Practice' (2017), available at https://ssrn.com/abstract=3025230.

[133] See OECD, 'OECD Principles for Integrity in Public Procurement' (2009) 10, available at https://www.oecd.org/gov/ethics/48994520.pdf.

[134] See, e.g., GPA, n. 4.

70 BASIC ELEMENTS FOR COMBATTING CORRUPTION AND COLLUSION

Index) are frequently made by multinational companies coming from, or based in, top ranked countries.[135] In spite of early initiatives to fight it, for many years relatively few national laws have actively targeted, or precluded, foreign bribery, so exacerbating the practice, especially in countries where anti-corruption systems and enforcement institutions are weaker or non-existent. Indeed, for some time, bribery of foreign officials was the standard operating practice for some corporations[136] and countenanced on national security grounds or to smooth state foreign relations.

In the US, however, in 1977, following a number of scandals,[137] President Jimmy Carter, acknowledging the need to restore the reputation of US businesses and institutions and to strengthen its foreign relations,[138] signed the Foreign Corrupt Practices Act (FCPA) into law. This legislation now makes it unlawful for a person—whether an issuer, a US concern, *or* a foreign national or business acting in the US—to make payments to an official of a foreign government, or public international organization, to assist in obtaining or retaining business.[139] Although for a number of years other governments were reluctant to follow suit (with many exporting countries believing foreign bribery to be a necessary evil and that the FCPA hampered US exporters' ability to compete abroad),[140] US efforts to create a level playing field and to internationalize the FCPA have gained momentum.

In 1997, the OECD adopted the 'Convention on Bribery of Foreign Officials', promoting the adoption of anti-bribery laws criminalizing foreign bribery (and incitement of, aiding, or abetting acts of bribery) by member nations.[141] The

---

[135] See, e.g., from the top ten cases that resulted in settlements and fines under the US's Foreign Corruption Practices Act (FCPA) as of March 2019, eight involved companies based in the bracket of the least corrupt countries according to the CPI; R.L. Cassin, 'With MTS in the New Top Ten, Just One US Company Remains', *The FCPA Blog* (11 March 2019), available at https://fcpablog.com/2019/3/11/with-mts-in-the-new-top-ten-just-one-us-company-remains/.

[136] See L.O. Youngman, 'Deterring Compliance: The Effect of Mandatory Debarment under the European Union Procurement Directives on Domestic Foreign Corrupt Practices Act Prosecutions' (2013) 42(2) *Public Contract Law Journal* 411.

[137] Following Watergate, it was discovered that as well as making unlawful payments to President Nixon's re-election campaign, a number of US corporations were also making questionable payments to foreign government officials. Further, following a US Securities and Exchange Commission (SEC) investigation into payment of bribes by US Defence company, Lockheed Martin, to the Japanese Prime Minister, almost 400 companies sought exemption from sanctions from the SEC. The scale of these voluntary admissions shocked the US legislator into drafting foreign bribery laws.

[138] See, e.g., E. Acorn, 'Law and Politics in FCPA Prosecutions of Foreign Corporations' (2021) 17(2) *Revista Direito GV*.

[139] 15 U.S.C. §§ 78dd-1 (1998). Petrobras agreed to pay USD 853.2 million to settle charges relating to bribing politicians and seeking to conceal payments in breach of the Act, see 'Brazil's Petrobras to Pay $853 Million Fine in U.S. Car Wash Probe', *Reuters* (27 September 2018) and Chapter 7.

[140] Rather, many governments continued to allow their companies to make foreign bribe payments (and to treat them as a tax-deductible business expense) and considered the US Act to be 'a quixotic step depriving US exporters of a powerful competitive tool', Heimann and Pieth, n. 132, 72 (The 'attitude *"when in Rome do as the Romans do"* prevailed. Even companies based in countries culturally averse to bribery ... rarely saw a problem when bribing in the Third World ... Overall, this attitude was very much embedded in (post) colonial thinking', 75). Partly to deal with this perceived disadvantage to US companies, US authorities also enforce the FCPA against foreign corporations (not just US ones), see further Chapters 4 and 6.

[141] See OECD, 'Convention on Combating Bribery of Foreign Public Officials in International Business Transactions' (the Anti-Bribery Convention), 47 (entered into force 15 February 1999),

Convention entered into force in 1999, and implementation is actively and rigorously monitored by an OECD Working Group on Bribery through four phases.[142] The Working Group also organizes regular meetings of law enforcement officials to share enforcement experience. A 2021 recommendation of the Working Group recognizes that more still needs to be done to detect and fight foreign bribery.[143]

c. National developments

As a result of these international initiatives, numerous jurisdictions have now enacted or revamped bribery or anti-corruption laws to meet their obligations under them and have made the receipt of a bribe (passive bribery), and bribery of a domestic government, or a foreign,[144] official (active bribery), a criminal or civil offence, or both. Although such legislation may not capture, or easily capture, all of the forms of corrupt conduct described in Chapter 1 (e.g. cronyism and favouritism), it frequently seeks to hold corporates, as well as individuals, liable for the payment, or receipt, of bribes, holds aiders, abettors, or those encouraging bribery liable, and provides for extraterritorial application of the laws.[145] Despite different legal, social, and political traditions, diverse jurisdictions across the world are thus now fighting anti-democratic and harmful public corruption in similar ways and through a consistent approach.

ii. Competition law

a. The fight against cartels

During the 1990s, international consensus over the economic harm caused by cartels also began to emerge, and it has become widely accepted that cartels—including bid rigging schemes—constitute 'the supreme evil of antitrust',[146] the

---

available at https://www.oecd.org/corruption/oecdantibriberyconvention.htm. There are now forty-four parties to the Convention, all of which have now criminalized bribery and strengthened or created corporate liability laws.

[142] It has conducted four phases of monitoring and made thousands of recommendations for improving anti-bribery laws and their enforcement, see OECD, 'Fighting the Crime of Foreign Bribery: The Anti-Bribery Convention and the OECD Working Group on Bribery' (2018), available at https://www.oecd.org/daf/anti-bribery/Fighting-the-crime-of-foreign-bribery.pdf.

[143] See OECD 'Recommendation of the Council for Further Combating Bribery of Foreign Public Officials in International Business Transactions', available at https://legalinstruments.oecd.org/en/instruments/OECD-LEGAL-0378.

[144] As attitudes towards corruption have hardened, the conduct has been prohibited in many jurisdictions by national criminal justice rules, legislation on ethics in public office, public procurement regulations, or bespoke anti-corruption laws.

[145] See generally T. Markus Funk and A.S. Butros (eds), *From Backsheesh to Bribery: Understanding the Global Fight Against Corruption and Graft* (Oxford University Press, 2019) (surveying the global fight against corruption).

[146] *Verizon Communications v Law Offices of Curtis V. Trinko*, 540 US 398, 408 (2004)

72   BASIC ELEMENTS FOR COMBATTING CORRUPTION AND COLLUSION

most 'egregious' violation of competition law,[147] and 'cancers on the open market economy'.[148] International initiatives[149] and greater multilateral and bilateral co-operation between competition authorities has contributed significantly to the dramatic shift in perceptions of, and attitudes towards, cartels and also to the development of an international fight against them.[150] A 'truly global effort against hard core cartels' has emerged.[151]

b. National developments

As a result of international developments, most modern antitrust systems clearly prohibit cartels, summarily condemning them through the use of clear *per se* prohibitions or strong (and difficult to rebut) presumptions of illegality.[152] Rather than the question of how substantive analysis should be conducted, therefore, the debate in the cartel context has shifted to the question of how hidden or more amorphous forms of cartel conduct can be identified and how such activity is to be combatted; how it can best be prevented, detected, deterred, and sanctioned. In particular, important issues to be determined include what detection techniques should be available to competition agencies to uncover such conduct, should civil or criminal offences be used and what sanctions—civil or criminal—should attach to persons—legal or natural—found to have engaged in illegal cartel activity. A diversity of approaches is adopted. Although in a majority of jurisdictions, cartel offences are civil in nature, a growing number have introduced criminal regimes for cartel behaviour, or certain forms of it, such as bid rigging.[153]

---

[147] OECD, 'Recommendation of the Council Concerning Effective action Against Hard Core Cartels' (1998), OECD Publication C(98)35/FINAL and updated in 2019, see OECD/LEGAL/0452.

[148] M. Monti, 'Fighting Cartels Why and How? Why Should We Be Concerned with Cartels and Collusive Behaviour?' (11–12 September 2000) 3rd Nordic Competition Policy Conference, Stockholm.

[149] See, e.g., OECD, 'Fighting Hard-Core Cartels: Harm, Effective Sanctions and Leniency Programmes' (2002); OECD, 'Hard Core Cartels: Third Report on the Implementation of the 1998 Recommendation' (2005). The GPA also promotes competition (and the eradication of collusion) in procurement markets in a number of ways.

[150] See International Competition Network (ICN), 'Defining Hard Core Cartel Conduct: Effective Institutions; Effective Penalties' (2005).

[151] ICN, n. 150, 5.

[152] For example, in the US, cartel arrangements are considered to be illegal per se under Section 1 of the Sherman Act of 1890, see *Northern Pacific Railroads. V United States*, 356 U.S. 1, 5 (1958). Similarly, in the EU, cartels generally violate Article 101 TFEU—they automatically infringe Article 101(1) (restrict competition by object)—and, being naked, are incapable of satisfying the conditions for the legal exception set out in Article 101(3), see A. Jones and W.E. Kovacic, 'Identifying Anticompetitive Agreements in the US and the European Union: Developing a Coherent Antitrust Analytical Framework' (2017) 62 *Antitrust Bulletin* 254 and discussion in Chapters 5–10.

[153] See A. Stephan, 'Lessons from the UK's Experience of Criminalising Cartels' (24 September 2012) presentation at The Antitrust Enforcement Symposium, Pembroke College, Oxford; and G.C. Shaffer and N.H. Nesbitt, 'Criminalizing Cartels: A Global Trend?' University of Minnesota Law School Legal Studies Research Paper Series, Research Paper No. 11–26 ('More than thirty countries have criminalized cartel conduct, in some form. All but five have done so since 1995 and over twenty since 2000, and the list is growing').

iii. Effective enforcement

a. Optimal deterrence

Anti-corruption and competition laws will only matter, and compliance with the rules encouraged, if they are effectively enforced. Indeed, evidence suggests that although some people will never act corruptly on moral grounds, and others will act corruptly out of habit, in a majority of cases, people will weigh the costs and benefits of so acting (they are opportunistic).[154] Corruption is thus not a crime committed on impulse, but an economic one, where givers and takers of bribes respond to incentives and punishments. In the competition sphere, firms and individuals may similarly weigh the costs and benefits of anti-competitive conduct and respond to incentives and punishments.

Theory suggests that infringements of the law will occur if it is estimated *ex ante* that the gain (from a bribe or cartel) will be greater than the cost. Consequently, anti-corruption, and competition laws are only likely to achieve their objectives, and deter prohibited behaviour, if actors cannot act with impunity, and the anticipated costs of the conduct exceed the illegal gain—there is a high risk of *both* (i) the illegal conduct being uncovered and prosecuted[155] and (ii) effective sanctions being imposed (this can include legal sanctions but also, e.g. shame and loss to reputation). Deterrence is dependent on expected punishment, measured by multiplying the probability of apprehension by the punishment imposed. Sanctions are thus important not only to punish *ex post* those who are caught, but also to send a credible message of general deterrence *ex ante* to firms that might otherwise be tempted to engage in cartel or corrupt practices. Further, levels of enforcement are crucial. If an enforcement agency, to minimize public expenditure (or because it is captured by corrupt players), sets detection close to zero, a

---

[154] See S. Rose-Ackerman and B.J. Palifka, *Corruption and Government: Causes, Consequences, and Reform* (Cambridge University Press, 2nd edn, 2016) 52; Heimann and Pieth, n. 132, 231; J. Tirole, 'Heirarchies and Bureaucracies: On the Role of Collusion in Organizations' (1996) 2 *Journal of Law, Economics, and Organization* 181 and W. Landes, 'Optimal Sanctions for Antitrust Violations' (1983) 50(2) *University of Chicago Law Review* 652.

[155] Given the huge costs of successful enforcement, the optimal level of corruption and collusion is not zero. Rather the level of deterrence expenditures has to be set where net benefits will be maximized, see Rose-Ackerman and Palifka, n. 154, 205–6. Becker's research on major felonies in the US suggests that the probability of detection had a greater impact on the commission of such offences than the level of punishment, see G.S. Becker, 'Crime and Punishment: An Economic Approach' (1968) 76 *Journal of Political Economy* 169. Arguably, competition agencies could prioritize further resources on detecting collusive tendering, see also A. Stephan, 'An Empirical Evaluation of the Normative Justifications for Cartel Criminalization' (2017) 37(4) *Legal Studies* 621. Some jurisdictions are taking steps to increase enforcement in this area, see the DOJ's creation of a procurement collusion strike force, available at https://www.justice.gov/opa/pr/justice-department-announces-procurement-collusion-strike-force-coordinated-national-response and the remarks of Makan Delrahim, then Assistant Attorney General (US DOJ) at the American Bar Association Antitrust Section Fall Forum (15 November, 2018) (confirming the Antitrust Division's commitment to effective antitrust enforcement against bid rigging which cheats the US Government and American taxpayer), available at https://www.justice.gov/opa/speech/assistant-attorney-general-makan-delrahim-remarks-american-bar-association-antitrust.

74 BASIC ELEMENTS FOR COMBATTING CORRUPTION AND COLLUSION

perception will be created that that enforcement will not occur, leading to incentives for law-breaking.[156]

b. Enforcement institutions

Effective enforcement is dependent upon the existence of politically supported (but politically neutral) enforcement institutions (anti-corruption and competition agencies), which are independent from a budget and operational perspective, sufficiently resourced, and have a mandate and administrative support that is sufficient to allow them to carry out their tasks (politically supported but isolated from political influence). Such agencies should, therefore, ideally have leaders appointed for fixed terms, and leaders and staff appointed on the basis of meritocratic criteria, have sources of funding sufficient to provide necessary human and technical resources, and have the power to set their own enforcement priorities, which is not dependent on the discretion of a head of state, the executive, or legislators.[157] In contrast, if law enforcement agencies are not independent, but are political appointees, they may be powerless to act against illegal practices engaged in by, or involving, the political elite or their cronies.

In the competition sphere, in particular, private enforcement may also play an important supplemental role in the enforcement of the rules and in ensuring compensation for victims.

c. Uncovering infringements: detection techniques and investigative tools

Serious offences like collusion and corruption are usually committed in secret (bid rigging, e.g. tends to be designed to mask collusion and is arranged to simulate and create illusions of a genuine competitive bidding process)[158] and often by sophisticated, powerful, and well-resourced businesses and people. Given the hidden nature of the conduct, and that the victims are generally unaware that an offence has taken place, enforcement agencies must have the tools to allow them to find out about and adduce evidence of an offence. Competition and anti-corruption enforcement agencies should therefore use a variety of detection techniques (reactive and proactive) to obtain information or evidence of infringements (see further Chapter 4), including from self-reports, leniency, or amnesty applicants.

For example, more than eighty jurisdictions now encourage undertakings to cooperate with them prior to or during cartel investigations through the operation

---

[156] See, e.g., E. Combe and C. Monnier, 'Fighting Cartels: The Interaction between Detection, Sanction, and Compliance' in A. Riley, A. Stephan, and A. Tubbs (eds), *Perspectives on Antitrust Compliance* (Concurrences, 2022), Chapter 8.

[157] See, e.g., W.E. Kovacic and M. Winerman, 'The Federal Trade Commission as an Independent Agency: Autonomy, Legitimacy, and Effectiveness' (2010) 76 *Antitrust Law Journal* 929, IV; and W.E. Kovacic and D.A Hyman, 'Competition Agency Design: What's on the Menu?' (2012) *The George Washington University Law School Public Law and Legal Theory Paper No. 2012-135, Legal Studies Research Paper No. 2012-135*, B.1.

[158] See Chapter 2.

of 'leniency' regimes, offering immunity from, or reduction in, penalties for those self-reporting cartel infringements and meeting specified conditions.[159] In some jurisdictions, competition authorities also use 'Leniency Plus' programme, offering applicants an additional credit in one cartel investigation, in return for self-reporting involvement in another. The latter can be especially effective in cases where repeated infringements have been committed (highly possible in the bid rigging context). In the Brazilian OCW case, for example, contractors that were not eligible for leniency in one investigation brought new cases to the attention of the authorities in order to obtain leniency in the new cases as well as a discount in the original investigation.[160] These led to several new bid rigging investigations being launched and the snowballing of the OCW investigation. Authorities operating leniency programmes believe that the public interest in eliminating cartels outweighs the public interest in punishing the violators that are granted full or partial amnesty. Although, it is accepted that high penalties are ordinarily necessary to deter the unlawful conduct, it is also recognized that the success of a cartel programme depends upon a high probability of detection which may only be possible with the grant to some of a reduced, or even no, penalty.

The leniency regime in the US, for example, seems to have initially been successful because it makes a genuinely good offer—complete immunity from a significant penalty (both fines and/or imprisonment) for the first cartel member to come forward[161]—and it generates and exploits the insecure nature of cartels, and a nervousness that other cartel members may well be tempted by the same offer, and win the race to obtain leniency. This ploy is reinforced by the knowledge that only the *first* to report gets the big prize.

> [The US regime] is thus reminiscent of the classical 'Prisoner's Dilemma'— whether to play ball now, and quickly, or risk losing altogether. The strategy thus promotes within the cartel the sense of a higher risk, first, that somebody will blow the whistle and, secondly and consequently, of the other members being convicted. This serves to outweigh the previous benefits of solidarity, that is, of big profit from the offence plus a low risk of detection and conviction.[162]

In conjunction with leniency, many competition authorities also use settlement procedures in administrative proceedings—for example, discounts in fines in return for a party not contesting the case and agreeing to streamlined procedures

---

[159] See C. Beaton-Wells and C. Tran (eds), *Anti-Cartel Enforcement in a Contemporary Age: Leniency Religion* (Hart Publishing, 2015).

[160] See A. Jones and C. Mario da Silva Pereira Neto, 'Combatting Corruption and Collusion in Public Procurement: Lessons From Operation Car Wash' (2021) 71(Supplement 1) *University of Toronto Law Journal* 103 and Chapter 7.

[161] See, e.g., OECD, 'OECD Competition Trends' (2020); C. Harding and J. Joshua, *Regulating Cartels in Europe* (Oxford University Press, 2nd edn, 2010) 235.

[162] Harding and Joshua, n. 161.

76 BASIC ELEMENTS FOR COMBATTING CORRUPTION AND COLLUSION

(these proceedings also reduce the risk of appeal from the agency's decision). As proceeding to final decision, or judgment, is time-consuming, these mechanisms, where feasible, shorten and facilitate proceedings. Through shifting from an adversarial process to cooperative or negotiated ones, which reward cooperation, a greater number of cases can be decided upon.

Anti-corruption prosecutors also frequently offer leniency, plea bargains, immunity, or protection from prosecution (e.g. through use of no-action letters or deferred prosecution agreements (DPAs)—deferring prosecution in return for compliance with certain requirements, for example payment of a penalty, compensation of victims, or disgorgement of profits, and/or implementation of, or changes to, a compliance programme), to those that self-report.[163] In some jurisdictions, penalties may also be imposed on those who fail to report or prevent a corrupt scheme so aiming, like leniency regimes, to create a race to confess and additional incentives for compliance. Self-reporting schemes may work best where they operate transparently and when combined with steps to encourage businesses to introduce corrective measures, including competition and anti-corruption compliance programmes or, for example, the use of compliance monitors. They have also been used successfully where cross-border investigations have taken place—and facilitate the reaching of coordinated responses.

These types of programmes have obvious attractions for both those investigated (including for companies, the significant advantage that debarment might be avoided), and prosecutors, especially given the complexities, costs and risks involved in establishing violations. Nonetheless, they are unlikely to be attractive where wrongdoing is stable and profitable and there is not a good track record of enforcement following use of other detection techniques (see further Chapter 4). Enforcement agencies should therefore also have a range of other mechanisms for uncovering infringements, including through encouraging complaints, whistleblowing, direct referrals from other agencies (e.g. competition, anti-corruption or procurement agencies), or through their own ex officio investigations (monitoring, intelligence, and screening), which allow them subsequently, to use their investigative powers to uncover evidence. The latter might include, subject to applicable rights of defence, powers to interview individuals; make document requests; enter premises to search for information; directed surveillance (monitoring the movement of people and vehicles); use of covert human intelligence sources (e.g. informants); and or more intrusive surveillance, such as property interference and access to communications data. At the beginning of an investigation, agencies may prefer to use covert tools which do not alert wrongdoing to the investigation, and provide them with the opportunity to hide, or to destroy, evidence. These powers (especially where informants are involved) may

---

[163] Not self-reporting may be an aggravating factor in some jurisdictions—meaning that the corporate is likely to pay a heavy price if the conduct is discovered.

help law enforcement agencies to uncover both direct 'smoking gun' evidence of an infringement and circumstantial evidence, which may help them to piece together evidence of a violation from a variety of sources. In criminal trials in particular, direct evidence is likely to be essential or, at least, highly desirable.

Reporting via complaints and whistleblowing (such as disgruntled employees, ideally with financial rewards for those who offer information about infringements)[164] may also constitute rich sources of information on infringements. Steps to educate the public may facilitate public support for policies to counter bid rigging and bribery and create a wider group of stakeholders vigilant for illegal conduct.[165] Transparency International, for example, stresses the importance of social accountability and the engagement of communities, social groups, and professional associations affected by public contracts.[166] These mechanisms build trust in public procurement processes, encourage monitoring of processes by those affected, and reflect the public interest,[167] and encourage civil society groups to act as independent monitors (see, e.g. 'Social Witness' in Mexico and the Philippines).[168]

The media and work of independent journalists can also play an important role in the identification of wrongdoing, especially corruption. For example, the OECD's 2018 study on foreign bribery enforcement,[169] notes the central role that the media plays in international information flow. It found that '[t]he media were the most important source of detection for the demand-side authorities, having been a source in 14 cases. Other sources of detection on the demand side were: reports by government institutions (4 cases); self-reporting by the offender (2 cases) and whistle-blowers (2 cases)'.[170]

d. Effective judicial protection of the law

The rule of law is essential to ensure accountability within a system and that violations of the rules are prevented, punished, and deterred. Effective judicial protection under the control of independent and impartial courts is thus central to the success of a system and to constrain improper exercise of public powers, ensure that the law is upheld, and effective legal protection of rights conferred by the law.

---

[164] See further Chapter 4.

[165] See G.A. Res. 58/4, n. 128, Article 13.

[166] See S. Kühn and L.B. Sherman, *Curbing Corruption in Public Procurement: A Practical Guide* (Transparency International, 2014) 12–13.

[167] See Transparency International, 'Integrity Pacts Programme–Safeguarding EU Funds in Europe' (2018), available at https://www.transparency.org/programmes/overview/integritypacts and Adam, Hernandez Sanchez, and Fazekas, n. 51, 16–17.

[168] See Kühn and Sherman, n. 166, 29.

[169] OECD, 'Foreign Bribery Enforcement: What Happens to the Public Officials on the Receiving End?' (2018), available at https://www.oecd.org/corruption/foreign-bribery-enforcement-what-happens-to-the-public-officials-on-the-receiving-end.htm.

[170] OECD, n. 169, 9.

78 BASIC ELEMENTS FOR COMBATTING CORRUPTION AND COLLUSION

iv. Penalties

a. Corporate fines

A range of penalties may follow a finding of an infringement of anti-corruption and competition laws. In many countries, a core response is to impose corporate fines on legal persons found to have engaged in unlawful cartel activity or bribery. In some jurisdictions (such as the US), corporate fines are ordinarily imposed in the course of criminal cartel or corruption proceedings. In others, however, fines can be, and are regularly, imposed on persons or corporations, that have committed infringements of civil cartel or anti-corruption rules (this is the case, e.g. in Brazil, the EU (at the EU level), and the UK).

These differences in approach (civil or criminal) reflect disparate views about the appropriateness, or wisdom, of criminalizing corporate behaviour. Some countries are wary about doing so. This is not just because it raises the burden and standard of proof beyond that required in civil proceedings, making prosecution (arguably, unnecessarily) more complex, but because it may be considered that criminalization is inappropriate, given that corporations are not human (so cannot have moral obligations), feel no shame or guilt, cannot be imprisoned and could in any event be subject to the same sanctions for committing civil offences.

Others, in contrast, believe that criminalization of the conduct of corporations can be intelligible and desirable in appropriate circumstances. In particular, as corporations are systems with a culture that exists independently of the specific personnel in the company, corporate policy can be regarded as the corporation's 'purpose', containing a synthesis and compromise of the views of the individuals involved.[171] Consequently, the intentionality which can be said to lie behind a policy, can be attributed to a blameworthy corporation. Indeed, as bid rigging and bribery offences may result in the award of highly lucrative contracts, in some cases such conduct may, rather than resulting from the conduct of rogue individuals, be condoned and even incentivized (e.g. by career, pay, and bonus systems),[172] or encouraged, as part of an extremely profitable business strategy. Where this is the case, corporate criminal liability may be seen as reflective of the fact that the conduct has not only a human dimension but also a collective corporate one. Criminal liability may be considered necessary to express 'the community's condemnation of the wrongdoer's conduct by emphasizing the standards for appropriate behaviour',[173] to ensure that management takes a personal interest in facilitating compliance with

---

[171] See E. Colvin, 'Corporate Personality and Criminal Liability' (1995) 6 *Criminal Law Forum* 1 and, e.g., J. Gobert, 'Corporate Criminality: Four Models of Fault' (1994) 14 *Legal Studies* 393; B. Fisse and J. Braithwaite, 'The Allocation of Responsibility for Corporate Crime: Individualism, Collectivism and Accountability' (1986–1988) 11 *Sydney Law Review* 468, 478; and J. Ohlin, 'Group Think: The Law of Conspiracy and Collective Reason' (2008) 98(1) *Journal of Criminal Law and Criminology* 147, 173.

[172] OECD, *Business and Finance Outlook 2017* (OECD Publishing, 2017) 22 and see Chapter 2.

[173] L. Friedman, 'In Defense of Corporate Criminal Liability' (2000) 23 *Harvard Journal of Law and Public Policy* 833.

the company's legal obligations, and in recognition of the fact that deterrence requires that corporates should also bear responsibility for, and the costs of, infringement. The stigma caused by the criminal conviction, and the expression of the community's condemnation of the behaviour, thus, justifies criminalization and the higher standard of proof.

Where corporate conduct is criminalized, an important question to be determined is what needs to be demonstrated to establish liability and whether, for example, the controlling corporate mind needs to know of the offending behaviour before it is held culpable and, if so, how this is to be proven. In some jurisdictions, separate 'failure to prevent' offences help to circumvent these types of difficulty, holding a corporation strictly liable for failing to prevent an offence by its agents, subject to certain defences (e.g. that the company had adequate procedures in place to prevent such actions).[174]

b. Individual accountability

Evidence implies that a number of personal factors may encourage procurement officials to receive bribes.[175] Further, that even if bribery, or collusion with competitors, forms part of corporate policy, individual actors involved may receive incentives for performance enhanced by such conduct. As a result, an important question is whether the law should recognize that, to counterbalance the effects of these individual incentives, liability, and sanctions (e.g. fines, director disqualification, prison sentences, or the confiscation of bribes or the proceeds of crime)[176] for such offences should also be attached to responsible individuals. Numerous jurisdictions do hold individuals (including those offering and receiving bribes) either civilly and/or criminally liable for bribery. In addition, a number of jurisdictions have criminalized bid rigging practices or provided for individual sanctions in the context of civil proceedings. Indeed, one view is that, to increase deterrents to cartel activity, custodial sentences, fines, or other consequences for individuals (whether criminal or civil), are required to focus the mind of those involved.[177]

c. Debarment

It has been seen that debarment processes help to preserve the integrity of the public procurement processes both by mitigating against the risk of, and by deterring,

---

[174] See, e.g., discussion of position in the UK, Chapter 5.

[175] See OECD, 'Bribery in Public Procurement: Methods, Actors and Counter-Measures' (2007) 50–1 (describing greed, financial difficulties, public administration politics, frustration with compensation, and private connections as reasons that officials accept bribes).

[176] In addition to incentives to report or refuse bribes.

[177] See further Chapter 4 and, e.g., G.J. Werden, 'Sanctioning Cartel Activity: Let the Punishment Fit the Crime' (2009) 5(1) *European Competition Journal* 19; A. Hoel, 'Crime Does Not Pay but Hard-Core Cartel Conduct May: Why it Should Be Criminalised' (2008) 16 *Trade Practices Law Journal* 102; and A. Khan, 'Rethinking Sanctions for Breaching EU Competition Law: Is Director Disqualification the Answer?' (2012) 35(1) *World Competition* 77.

80 BASIC ELEMENTS FOR COMBATTING CORRUPTION AND COLLUSION

violations of anti-corruption and competition laws. The risk of losing the chance to secure public contracts for a period of time in the future is designed to act as an incentive for firms to comply with the rules. A jurisdiction should therefore consider providing for the possibility of debarring those involved in an infringement of anti-corruption or competition laws from participating in public tenders (mandatory or discretionary debarment),[178] subject to the possibility of self-cleaning (e.g. by infringers providing compensation to those harmed as a result of the wrongdoing and adopting measures—including compliance programmes—to prevent future violations). Debarment, including debarment with conditional release, is a core sanction used by MDBs against firms that engaged in bribery or collusion. In some jurisdictions, it may also be possible to prohibit individuals that have played a particularly active role in the wrongdoing, from participating directly, or indirectly, in legal entities that have contracts with public administration or, through disqualification orders, from acting as a director of a company in the future.[179]

d. Recovery of bribes and damages actions

Asset recovery and damages actions are also important tools that may not only increase deterrence, but also ensure that wrongdoers do not profit from their wrongs, or that those who have suffered in consequence of the breach are compensated.

Many anti-corruption systems allow enforcement agencies to recover illicit bribes (or the proceeds of corruption) both from natural and legal persons; damages may also be available to the treasury. Further, many antitrust systems allow victims of competition law infringements (including bid rigging offences) to seek damages in respect of loss suffered in consequence of the breach.[180]

D. Conclusions

To ensure the integrity of its public procurement processes, a state needs not only good public procurement laws but also laws to tackle anti-competitive and

---

[178] See, e.g., Office of Federal Procurement Policy Act of 1974, 41 U.S.C. §§ 401–38 (2012) (instituting the US Federal Acquisitions Regulations providing for the suspension and debarment (by a debarment official) of those committing crimes, including violation of federal or state antitrust laws); Directive 2014/24/EU, n. 11, Article 54 (providing that contracting authorities may be required by EU Member States to exclude undertakings from procurement procedures where there are plausible grounds to conclude that they entered into agreements infringing Article 101; the implementing conditions are to be provided by the Member States); Case C-470/13, *Generali-Providencia Biztosító Zrt v Közbeszerzési Hatóság Közbeszerzési Döntőbizottság*, EU:C:2014:2469 (an undertaking may be excluded by public authorities from tendering for public contracts where it has committed an infringement of competition law, for which it was fined, even if the procurement procedure is not covered by the EU procurement directive).

[179] See, e.g., the position in, Brazil, discussed in Chapter 7.

[180] See also Case No. 14-CV-9662 *In re Petrobras Securities Litigation* (SDNY 2018) (involving a USD 2.95 billion settlement following a class action securities fraud lawsuit brought in the US by investors). Actions for the tort of bribery may also be available in some jurisdictions.

corrupt practices, and effective mechanisms for enforcement of the laws. Each of these sets of rules needs to be prepared carefully and to focus on prevention, as well as punishment, and deterrence of corrupt and anti-competitive practices. Public procurement laws should be constructed so as to minimize corruption and collusion opportunities in the first place. These rules should be backed up, and reinforced, by monitoring and auditing of compliance, and robust competition and anti-corruption laws enforced by proactive and independent agencies with powers to ensure that wrongdoing is deterred and punished.

Although these foundations are vital, as we have already noted, a statutory framework alone cannot guarantee the success of the system, especially in countries where corruption and particularism are embedded in the culture. Chapter 4 thus examines a variety of factors which may undermine the effectiveness of the public procurement system and considers how further steps may be taken to safeguard the integrity of public procurement processes and embed a procompetitive regime into the system.

4

Towards a More Comprehensive Approach: Strengthening Anti-Corruption and Anti-Collusion Systems, Dealing with Systemic Corruption and the Contribution of Multi-Level Governance

A.	Introduction	83		d. Effective penalties or remedies	111
B.	Weaknesses in Relevant Laws, or their Application, Enforcement and Coordination	84		e. Separation of powers and independence of enforcement agencies, monitoring agencies, and the judiciary	118
	i. Honing the public procurement regime	84		iii. Siloed regimes	119
	a. Exceptions to open, competitive bidding systems and emergency purchasing	85		a. Policy coordination—national and international cooperation and coordination	119
	b. Professionalization and training of the procurement workforce	85		b. Laws acknowledging the interaction between corruption and bid rigging	121
	c. Bidding by separate companies in the same corporate group	91	C.	Combatting Endemic, or Systemic, Corruption	122
	d. Evaluation and reform of public procurement processes	92	D.	Anti-Money-Laundering Regimes and Other Anti-Corruption Measures	130
	ii. Honing the anti-corruption and competition law regimes	92			
	a. Gaps in the law	93	E.	Impetus for Reform: Domestic, International, and EU Initiatives	131
	b. Insufficient or under-enforcement of the laws	95			
	c. Encouraging greater compliance through educating businesses	109	F.	Conclusions	137

A. Introduction

This chapter considers why, even in countries with comprehensive public procurement, anti-corruption, and competition law systems in place, corrupt practices and supplier collusion may continue to occur. Further, it considers how such systems

84 TOWARDS A MORE COMPREHENSIVE APPROACH

may be bolstered to address shortcomings, or limitations, and to help these laws to achieve their objectives.

Section B commences by considering why public procurement, anti-corruption, and competition laws might not protect the integrity of the systems sufficiently. It stresses not only the need for possible refinements in the design, application, and enforcement of the three areas of law, but also the need for a joined-up and coordinated approach to the laws in this sphere. If the three areas of law become more closely united around a unified public procurement strategy, they stand a better chance of achieving their objectives and good results for citizens, in particular, by ensuring that the respective agencies and enforcers have an expanded understanding of each other's remits, powers, and procedures, and work cooperatively together to prevent, prohibit, and deter bid rigging and bribery, and to encourage compliance.

Section C acknowledges that the efforts described in Section B are likely to require supplementing in certain jurisdictions, especially those where ethical universalism is not the norm, where corruption is widespread, or a culture of particularism pervades. In such countries, a broader set of reforms may be required to fight corruption, to change norms, and to promote procompetitive procurement. Sections D and E also consider other laws which might be required to fight corruption and collusion successfully and how effective pressure for reform might be achieved, whether as a result of domestic, international, or European Union (EU) initiatives.

Section F concludes that, given the persistent and enduring nature of the problem presented by corruption and collusion in public procurement, every nation needs to think periodically how to bolster their systems to ensure they achieve their goals, whether through incremental changes to adapt to developments in markets or practices, or via more radical changes to it. Reform efforts are however only likely to be successful if there is political will at the domestic level to implement the changes needed. In jurisdictions where that will is lacking, concerted domestic and international pressure may be required to encourage it.

B. Weaknesses in Relevant Laws, or their Application, Enforcement and Coordination

i. Honing the public procurement regime

The sections below discuss a range of problems which can arise, and which may mean that, even a well-designed public procurement regime, may falter.

a. Exceptions to open, competitive bidding systems and emergency purchasing

A first cause of difficulty could be that default, competitive bidding systems are too easily sidestepped through overriding legislation, the application of high jurisdictional thresholds, or through provision for simplified procedures, or direct awards, in special, but indistinctly, defined circumstances, such as extreme urgency or emergency. These types of exceptions, increase the risk of conflict of interest and corruption arising, and make control of public purchasing more difficult. Indeed, experience suggests that where ministers or other top officials are in a position to take charge of procurement activities that could, in fact, be managed through normal bureaucratic processes, the chances of abuse can increase (see, e.g., the discussion of Canadian experience in Chapter 10). Indeed, the COVID-19 pandemic and the war in Ukraine have highlighted the need for many jurisdictions to improve procurement outcomes in emergency and crisis situations by, for example, providing greater clarity on the circumstances in which contract awards can be made without prior publication, ensuring adherence to certain standard processes, preparing the procurement workforce better through the use of crisis-ready contracting procedures,[1] and increasing the transparency of such processes, so they can be monitored to ensure that the wider discretion conferred by simplified procedures is not abused.

b. Professionalization and training of the procurement workforce

As noted in Chapter 3, the capacity, training, and adequacy of resourcing, management, and remuneration of the public procurement workforce is a consideration of fundamental importance, not just to achieving value for money in public procurement, but also to preventing corrupt practices and supplier collusion. Diverse dimensions of this challenge are discussed in this section.

Capacity, capability, and independence. The Organisation for Economic Cooperation and Development (OECD) has noted that, in many countries, the public procurement workforce lacks 'both capability (defined as skills-based ability for an individual, group o[r] organisation to meet obligations and objectives) and capacity (defined as the ability to meet obligations and objectives based on existing administrative, financial, human, and infrastructure resources). Only ten countries (Canada, Chile, France, Iceland, Japan, the Netherlands, New Zealand, Peru, Portugal, and Slovakia) indicated in the 2018 Survey that they have competency models. A lack of competency models makes it difficult to identify exactly where the gaps are and to design a strategy (including training) to fill those gaps.'[2]

---

[1] See, e.g., O. Bandiera, E. Bosio, and G. Spagnolo (eds), *Procurement in Focus: Rules, Discretion, and Emergencies* (CEPR Press, 2021).

[2] See OECD, 'Reforming Public Procurement: Progress in Implementing the OECD 2015 Recommendation' (2019) C(2019)94/FINAL, para. 251, available at https://www.oecd.org/gov/public-procurement/reforming-public-procurement-1de41738-en.htm.

86 TOWARDS A MORE COMPREHENSIVE APPROACH

Given that, as seen in Chapter 3, the nature of the professional civil service impacts dramatically the quality of procurement and, in particular, ensuring its integrity, this picture is obviously of concern. Indeed, corruption risks will be increased if procurement officials are not politically neutral and not secure, well-paid, appointed on merit, or required to disclose possible conflicting personal or business interests. 'If public-sector pay is very low, corruption is a survival strategy.'[3] Low pay is also liable to reduce the number of skilled applicants willing to work, or remain, in the public rather than the private sector. It will consequently affect the ability to recruit, and retain, competent and quality professional staff on the basis of merit. In contrast, appointing staff, and providing remuneration that is meritocratic,[4] will increase the independence of officials and decrease the risk of corruption.[5] Professionalization of the procurement workforce should therefore form a central and important plank of public procurement reform.[6]

Other problems which may arise where an anti-corruption organizational culture is not sufficiently developed within procurement authorities, or where procurement officials are not sufficiently aware of collusion risks, or willing to report suspicions of bid rigging. Training on these issues can help to bolster the professionalization process.

Anti-corruption training. Although codes of conduct and rules on conflicts of interest are important to the protection of the integrity of public procurement, in many jurisdictions these measures need to be strengthened to ensure that they are more successful in countering temptations to accept, or solicit, bribes or other kickbacks from tenderers or bid riggers. Training programmes may help to ensure that procurers are clear about their duty to conduct procurement procedures in a fair, ethical, and impartial way, and that they understand anti-corruption laws, standards, and expectations of good conduct, as well as the consequences of infringement (including infringement of criminal laws). These should reinforce the

---

[3] S. Rose-Ackerman and B.J. Palifka, *Corruption and Government: Causes, Consequences, and Reform* (Cambridge University Press, 2nd edn, 2016) 169. See also C. Lagarde, 'Addressing Corruption – Openly', in Policy Paper, *Against Corruption: A Collection of Essays*, Prime Minister's Office, 10 Downing Street (12 May 2016) 13.3.

[4] Studies indicate nonetheless that caution needs to be exercised. For example, an increase in remuneration is unlikely to be effective unless accompanied by clear signals that employment is dependent upon compliance with ethical standards and anti-corruption laws, Lagarde, n. 3, 13.3.

[5] See V. Tanzi, 'Corruption around the World: Causes, Consequences, Scope, and Cures' (1998) *IMF Staff Papers* 559, 572–3 (discussing literature on the link between wages and corruption); C. Van Rijckeghem and B. Weder, 'Bureaucratic Corruption and the Rate of Temptation: Do Wages in the Civil Service Affect Corruption and by How Much?' in G.T. Abed and S. Gupta (eds), *Governance, Corruption & Economic Performance* (International Monetary Fund, 2002) 59; and M. Fazekas and J.R. Blum, 'Improving Public Procurement Outcomes: Review of Tools and the State of the Evidence Base' (2021) *World Bank Group Policy Research Working Paper 9690* 26–7 (noting that there is little theoretical and empirical research on the impact of performance pay and other incentives).

[6] I. Adam, A. Hernandez Sanchez, and M. Fazekas, 'Global Public Procurement Open Competition Index' (2021) *Government Transparency Institute Working Paper GTI-WP/2021:02* 18, available at https://www.govtransparency.eu/wp-content/uploads/2021/09/Adam-et-al_Evidence-paper_procurement-competition_210902_formatted_2.pdf.

point that officials' private interests must not improperly influence performance of their public duties and make it clear why public officials are obliged to disclose information or make asset declarations, for example, on electronic registers of conflicts of interest, gifts, and hospitality, that may reveal public and private conflicts. Developing this type of organizational culture is central to preventing, detecting, and responding to corruption. Procurement codes of conduct and training exist in a number of countries, for example, Canada, Austria, and France.[7] In addition to increasing the integrity of the procurement process, ethical codes and conflicts registers more generally promote good governance. Steps which go beyond formal training, and which permeate societal culture more generally, can also help 'to develop a cadre of public officials who are—and are perceived to be—independent from both private influence and political interference'.[8] To bolster compliance, failure to comply with procurement laws,[9] integrity standards, and ethical codes should also be met with real consequences (e.g. including disciplinary proceedings or loss of job).[10]

An acute difficulty, nonetheless, is that these codes of conduct and anti-corruption laws may not always be able to counteract the incentive to accept bribes and so to act as an effective deterrent—they may simply serve to increase the size of the acceptable bribe (see further Section B. iv). An additional tool to consider, therefore, is positive reinforcement—the reward of strong and ethical performance and achievement of a set of measurable goals[11] through pay structures and promotion. In this way the pay increase, or promotion, incentivizes the official's performance (to the benefit of the public), rather than a bribe (which acts to the detriment to the public).[12] As performance evaluation can be difficult and complex to complete well, care and thought is required to construct an appropriate system.[13] Other mechanisms—such as, rotation of civil servants (to prevent officials from creating

---

[7] See, e.g., Public Services and Procurement Canada, 'Code of Conduct for Procurement', available at https://www.tpsgc-pwgsc.gc.ca/app-acq/cndt-cndct/cca-ccp-eng.html and OECD, 'Preventing Corruption in Public Procurement' (2016) 6, available at https://www.oecd.org/gov/ethics/Corruption-Public-Procurement-Brochure.pdf.

[8] Lagarde, n. 3, 13.6.

[9] That all procurements are operated, as required by law, for example that they are publicized and operated as they should be at all stages of the process.

[10] See M. Wakui, 'Bid Rigging Initiated by Government Officials: The Conjuncture of Collusion and Corruption in Japan' in T. Cheng, S. Marco Colino, and B. Ong (eds), *Cartels in Asia: Law and Practice* (Wolters Kluwer, 2015) 42–3 (discussing the Japanese competition authority's role of enforcing anti–bid rigging legislation in Japan). In Brazil, the Public Spending Observatory scrutinizes procurement expenditures, see further Chapter 7.

[11] For example, providing valuable public service, by bringing down the price of public purchases, and increasing the efficiency of the purchasing process.

[12] See, e.g., Rose-Ackerman and Palifka, n. 3, 178–84. Also, reviewing much of the relevant literature on these points, see, especially, R. Klitgaard, *Controlling Corruption* (University of California Press, 1988) 19 (incentive payments based on performance are more likely to be successful if additional effort actually produces substantial gains, employees are not too risk averse, effort and results can be measured, and officials have sufficient discretion to respond to incentives).

[13] See also, e.g., Tanzi, n. 5.

88   TOWARDS A MORE COMPREHENSIVE APPROACH

strong ties with industries with which they routinely work), or sequential as opposed to one-stop-shop systems (e.g. ensuring that the officer that issues the call for bids is different to the one that selects the winning bidder, and yet another officer oversees delivery)[14]—may also make corruption more difficult.

In Section C, it is seen that reducing corruption incentives is more complex and may require different solutions where corruption is not simply the result of a rogue public official but is more broadly institutionalized—whether or not it starts with low-level officials collecting bribes and sharing them with superiors (bottom-up schemes), or with corrupt superiors who enlist lower-level officials into their scheme (top-down ones). In such cases, solutions proposed to counteract individual corruption incentives, for example rotation of the work force, may actually facilitate corruption by allowing those that do not buy into the scheme to be punished, for example, by means of transfer to less favourable locations or positions. Further, if superiors are involved, they may cover up corruption of subordinates making it difficult to evaluate performance effectively. Where this is the case, broader mechanisms may be required to improve the accountability of governments and public officials more generally.

Training of procurement officials in the basics of competition law and economics. Procurers may be able to take better steps to prevent and detect unlawful bid rigging practices if they had a good understanding of when they are likely to occur and how, and the harm they cause. Training in competition law and economics can facilitate this by underlining the benefits to be reaped from open approaches to procurement design and procompetitive procurement practices, highlighting the factors that are likely to enable tenderers to collude effectively, the importance of careful market research at the outset of the tender process to the success of the tender (especially through tailoring it to reduce collusion risks), how collusive practices might undermine the process and be identified through careful bid evaluation, and how suspicions of collusion should be dealt with.

For example, with modern electronic search tools and increased transparency, procurement officials can be encouraged to familiarize themselves, prior to the opening of a tender and the receipt of tenders, with the goods and services that are potentially available, and, in many cases, with the prices that have been paid in similar procurements in their own, and in adjoining, jurisdictions. Such a survey will also allow it to be determined whether the market is likely to support collusion,[15] the potential bidders (their costs, prices, and previous tender history), and how possibilities for soliciting innovative, competitive solutions can be maximized. In markets where there is a high risk of collusion, this information will aid the construction of processes that will not enhance, but will rather offset, the risk especially by allowing consideration of how to: draw up appropriate prequalification

---

[14] See Rose-Ackerman and Palifka, n. 3.
[15] See discussion of factors likely to facilitate collusion in Chapter 2.

criteria and tender specifications, structure the auction so as to reduce barriers to entry, and encourage the maximum number of qualified bidders; reduce opportunities for bidders to meet or coordinate conduct during the tender process (e.g. avoiding the organization of pre-bid meetings or site visits where possible, managing any meetings carefully, making procurement patterns less predictable, and avoiding presenting similar size contracts regularly); and design the process so as to ensure reduced communication and flow of competitively sensitive information among the bidders, and between bidders and the tendering authorities. It can also help procurers to recognize the benefits of anti-collusion tender clauses, and other techniques to make bid rigging less attractive, and to react quickly when, for example, likely bidders do not participate, or where bids seem to exceed anticipated pricing levels.

Given their knowledge of the market and their capacity to spot patterns in bidding processes, to interact with bidders, to observe behaviour, and to intercept documents, public officials are also in a unique position to detect bid rigging arrangements when they arise. Competition training can also help to ensure that procurers are vigilant for signs of bid rigging, and are encouraged to report suspicions of actual collusion to competition enforcers and to collect and pass on key data for screening and monitoring compliance with the competition law rules.[16]

A reality nonetheless is that, even with better training, procurers are likely to be reluctant or unwilling to derail or delay the procurement process they are employed to carry out, if their performance is evaluated not on how many cartels they discover, but on the basis of their ability to set up and complete the procurement process successfully and conclude contracts.[17] Consequently, as well as training, it is imperative that procurers be provided with incentives to monitor for, and report, suspected bid rigging. For example, '[t]he money saved from a cartel that an administration helped discover [could] at least in part remain with the administration itself, and the official who helped discover a cartel [could] gain some career benefits'.[18] Commending letters or 'rewards' for uncovering collusion (positive reinforcement) could also be considered along with the introduction of negative

[16] See International Competition Network (ICN), 'Anti-Cartel Enforcement Manual: Relationships Between Competition Agencies and Public Procurement Bodies' (April 2015) 25–7 (discussing activities in Australia, Botswana, Canada, Colombia, Cyprus, the EU, and Finland). In the US, the DOJ routinely engages in training of procurement officials, aiming to teach them how to evaluate bids like an antitrust expert, ICN, 32–3. The ICN-WBG Competition Policy Advocacy Awards have revealed a number of examples of successful collaboration between procurers and competition agencies, which have led to significant savings in public money. See T. Goodwin and M. Martinez Licetti, 'Transforming Markets Through Competition: New Developments and Recent Trends in Competition Advocacy' (2016) 51, available at http://documents.worldbank.org/curated/en/640191467990945906/pdf/104 806-REPF-Transforming-Markets-Through-Competition.pdf.

[17] See A. Heimler, 'Cartels in Public Procurement' (2012) 8 *Journal of Competition Law and Economics* 849, 860.

[18] Heimler, n. 17, 862.

repercussions or disciplinary instruments to enhance accountability for not following relevant monitoring or reporting laws or guidelines.

Training in market research, negotiation, and related skills. The building of capacity in procurement systems is often approached principally as a matter of training in ethics and legal compliance, including how to ensure compliance, with the anti-corruption and competition regimes. While, as highlighted in the discussion above, these matters are *all* important, a central plank of the training that procurement officials need both to perform their functions and, particularly, to prevent and deter supplier collusion, is training in skill areas that are intrinsic to their jobs—e.g. market research, bid evaluation, and (where appropriate) negotiation and project management. Increasingly, these functions will also require solid expertise in the use of electronic search and related tools.

When we look beyond the routine procurement of relatively simple goods and services, for example to the procurement of defence hardware and major infrastructure construction projects, a much deeper and broader set of skills and knowledge is likely to be required. For example, specialized training and experience in aeronautical engineering or related disciplines will be a critical element of preparation for at least some of the officials involved in the procurement of military aircraft. Similarly, procurement of public infrastructure systems or other major public works, which increasingly take the form of public–private partnerships (PPPs), requires a particular skillset including attention to issues of risk management—i.e. the assessment of which aspects of the risks associated with major projects are best borne by public and private actors.[19]

The connection between these skills and the prevention of bid rigging and corrupt practices is clear: the better equipped that purchasers are to evaluate bids and proposals, and to search for alternatives, the less likely they are to be duped, or grifted, by suppliers.[20] Likewise, the more aware they are of the possibilities that are potentially available in the market, the more likely they will be able to see through corrupt efforts, for example, to convince them that only a certain technology is suitable or that only a particular firm or firms can do the job. Of course, these skills also greatly increase the chances that procurement officials will achieve what should be their overall guiding goal, namely attaining best value for money for the citizens they are employed to serve.

---

[19] See A. Deep, J. Kim, and M. Lee, *Realizing the Potential of Public–Private Partnerships to Advance Asia's Infrastructure Development* (Asian Development Bank and Korean Development Institute, 2019).

[20] See R.D. Anderson and W.E. Kovacic, 'Competition Policy and International Trade Liberalisation: Essential Complements to Ensure Good Performance in Public Procurement Markets' (2009) 18(2) *Public Procurement Law Review* 67. See also S.L. Schooner and C.R. Yukins, 'Public Procurement: Focus on People, Value for Money and Systemic Integrity, Not Protectionism' in R. Baldwin and S. Everett (eds), *The Collapse of Global Trade, Murky Protectionism, and the Crisis: Recommendations for the G20* (Centre for Economic Policy Research, VoxEU.org, 2009) 87, 91.

c. Bidding by separate companies in the same corporate group

A problem arising in some jurisdictions is that the benefits of competitive bidding processes may be undermined if bids can be submitted by companies within the same corporate group, without disclosure of the fact that they form part of a single economic unit or entity. In the EU, for example, the Court of Justice confirmed in *Ecoservices projektai in the 'Specializuotas transportas'*[21] that EU Public Procurement Directives (EU Directives) did not preclude companies forming part of the same economic unit from bidding and making separate offers in the same procurement procedure (rather such a policy would run counter to the policy of ensuring the widest possible participation in tendering procedures). Further that tenderers could not, in the absence of express legislative provision or specific conditions in the call for tenders, be obliged to disclose links between them to the contracting authority. Although the EU Directives require tenderers to submit autonomous and independent tenders,[22] it may be difficult to detect coordinated bids by companies within the same economic unit if separate tenders can be submitted without disclosure of corporate links. Coordinated bids by companies within the same economic unit also fall outside the scope of the competition cartel rules in the EU (they do not apply to agreements concluded between companies forming part of the same economic entity).

The effectiveness of debarment or exclusion regimes may also be undermined, if they do not also exclude parents, subsidiaries, or sibling companies within the same economic unit of the excluded company. The World Bank Group (WBG) sanction regime, for example, applies not only to culpable individuals and firms, but affiliates that control respondents[23] and affiliates controlled by sanctioned parties. An entity is an affiliate of another if: '(i) either entity controls or has the power to control the other, or (ii) a third party controls or has the power to control both entities'.[24] The choice and level of sanctions applied to affiliates is a matter

---

[21] Case C-531/16 *Ecoservices projektai in the 'Specializuotas transportas'* ECLI:EU:C:2018:324, para. 28. But see also Case C-416/21 *J. Sch. Omnibusunternehmen and K. Reisen* EU:C:2022:689 (finding that the exclusion grounds set out in Directive 2014/24/EU of the European Parliament and of the Council of 26 February 2014 on Public Procurement [2014] OJ L 94/65, Article 57(4) covers cases in which economic operators enter into any anti-competitive agreement, and is not limited to agreements between undertakings referred to in Article 101 TFEU).

[22] Article 2 of Directive 2004/18/EC, now repealed by Directive 2014/24/EU, n. 21, precluded the award of a contract to a tenderer who had submitted a coordinated or concerted, rather than an independent and autonomous, tender. Consequently, a contracting authority, with evidence calling into question the autonomous and independent character of submitted tenders, is obliged to verify whether tenderers' offers are in fact autonomous and independent. See also Case C-538/07 *Assitur v Camera di Commercio, Industria, Artigianato e Agricoltura di Milano* EU:C:2009:317.

[23] World Bank Group, 'The World Bank Group Sanction Regime: Information Note', available at https://www.worldbank.org/content/dam/documents/sanctions/other-documents/osd/The_World_Bank_Group_Sanctions_Regime.pdf, 20 ('because they have a degree of responsibility for the sanctionable practice, for example, due to a failure to supervise or to maintain adequate controls, or an ethical culture within the corporate group').

[24] World Bank Group, n. 23, 22 ('Control' means the ability to direct or to dominate the direction of the policies or operations of another entity, whether through the ownership of voting securities, by contract, or otherwise).

92 TOWARDS A MORE COMPREHENSIVE APPROACH

of discretion decided on the merits of each case, to ensure that is both, commensurate with the degree of culpability or responsibility, but also prevents evasion of the sanctions.

Jurisdictions may consequently need to consider how their rules apply to firms within a corporate group. For example, whether tendering firms should be obliged to disclose links between them and another bidding company and how sanctions imposed on one firm should affect bidding by another company within the group.

d. Evaluation and reform of public procurement processes

In many countries, procurement outcomes are not systematically evaluated against key performance indicators. Evaluation is, however, crucial to ensure that weaknesses in the system are identified, and that reforms can be instituted to ensure that the law is able to keep up with new practices and market developments. While the effectiveness of procurement review and reform processes should be a concern for all actors involved in public financial management, including Treasury or Finance Ministry bodies and officials, auditors, and Legislative or Parliamentary Committees, two additional innovations can be helpful. First, peer reviews organized by relevant international organizations can be a very helpful tool for enabling procurement agency executives and other leaders to visualize ways in which their organizations can improve performance.[25] Second, a growing body of experience has highlighted the central importance of involving civil society and other user organizations in procurement policy reviews and reform efforts, especially in countries where corruption is more prevalent.[26]

ii. Honing the anti-corruption and competition law regimes

Although global initiatives have encouraged the adoption of anti-corruption, foreign bribery, and competition laws, supported by active enforcement by independent enforcement institutions, it has been seen that fighting bid rigging and bribery is a complex task and that even these efforts may not be sufficient to guarantee reductions in the targeted behaviour. Rather, as already highlighted, the effectiveness of any regime is highly dependent upon not only on good laws, but political commitment to it, the existence of independent institutions (which have not been captured) able to enforce it,[27] enforcers choosing to prioritize

---

[25] For instance, the OECD undertakes hands-on peer reviews that assess public procurement systems at both the national and sub-national levels and provide proposals for improvements, see https://www.oecd.org/gov/public-procurement/publications/.

[26] See, generally, A. Mungiu-Pippidi, *The Quest for Good Governance* (Cambridge University Press, 2015); A. Mungiu-Pippidi, *Rethinking Corruption* (Edward Elgar, 2023); and discussion of steps taken in Ukraine in Chapter 9.

[27] For a discussion of the challenges faced by police in Brazil when courts dismissed cases on dubious or incomprehensible grounds, see J. Pontes and M. Anselmo, *Operation Car Wash: Brazil's Institutionalized Crime and the Inside Story of the Biggest Corruption Scandal in History* (Bloomsbury, 2022).

enforcement, an independent judiciary, companies being committed to compliance, and a real risk of penalties sufficient to punish and deter infringements and to offset the benefits of the conduct.[28] Indeed, in each of the countries examined in greater detail in this book, it is seen that the core problem is not the lack of sound laws, but ensuring compliance with them. For example, although the United Kingdom (UK) has one of the most (theoretically) stringent anti-corruption statutes that exist, the Bribery Act 2010[29] (it has been described by a House of Lords Select Committee as the gold standard for bribery legislation and a lodestar for other countries),[30] Chapter 5 notes that it does not seem to have been as successful as it should in rooting out, and deterring, cases of domestic bribery in public procurement processes.

Anti-corruption and competition laws will thus only matter, if they are effectively enforced—whether publicly or privately[31]—and if the costs of acting corruptly or anti-competitively outweigh the benefits. The rule of law and effective enforcement[32] is essential to ensure accountability.

a. Gaps in the law

Difficulties may arise if gaps in relevant laws exist. For example, in Chapter 1 *corruption* was defined broadly in the public procurement context to encompass not only bribery (active and passive) but also cronyism and favouritism. In many jurisdictions, nonetheless, anti-corruption laws may find it difficult to reach some of this conduct, where it is of a less overt or more intangible nature, for example,

---

[28] See OECD, 'Fighting the Crime of Foreign Bribery, The Anti-Bribery Convention and the OECD Working Group on Bribery' (2018), available at https://www.oecd.org/daf/anti-bribery/Fighting-the-crime-of-foreign-bribery.pdf (noting, in 2018, that although foreign bribery enforcement actions have increased since the adoption of the OECD Convention, and individuals and corporations had been sanctioned in twenty-three party states, twenty-one countries are yet to conclude a foreign bribery enforcement action) and Section B.ii.c.

[29] It overhauled a patchwork of anti-corruption laws following the UK's participation in anti-corruption conventions, including UNCAC and the OECD Convention on Combating Bribery of Foreign Public Officials in International Business Transactions and considerable domestic and international pressure to do so (including from the OECD), especially following the intervention by the UK Government suggesting that an investigation into British Aerospace's payment of bribers to secure a contract to supply Taifun planes to Saudi Arabia should be closed (the 'Al Yamamah' contract); see F. Heimann and M. Pieth, *Confronting Corruption: Past Concerns, Present Challenges, and Future Strategies* (Oxford University Press, 2018) 84–99 and further Chapter 5. See also generally M. Raphael, *Bribery: Law and Practice* (Oxford University Press, 2016).

[30] See House of Lords Select Committee on the Bribery Act 2010, 'The Bribery Act 2010: Post-Legislative Scrutiny' (March 2019) 14.

[31] In addition to enforcement by effective law enforcement institutions, private parties play an additional role in monitoring compliance, reporting infringements and, in some circumstances, bringing private proceedings in relation to violations.

[32] The significance of effective enforcement is reflected in the OECD 'Recommendation of the Council for Further Combating Bribery of Foreign Public Officials in International Business Transactions' (the 2021 OECD Anti-Bribery Recommendation), which emphasizes the importance of members promoting a holistic approach to fighting foreign bribery through enhancing awareness of bribery laws, detection and investigation of this conduct, and more effective international cooperation among enforcement authorities, available at https://www.oecd.org/daf/anti-bribery/2021-oecd-anti-bribery-recommendation.htm.

conduct that does not manifest itself in clear payoffs but results from more subtle conferral of other monetary or preferential benefits which make bribery more complex to establish (e.g. as a reward for (past or anticipated future) political donations), or where contracts are awarded, not in return for specific bribes, but as a favour to family or friends.[33] An important additional question therefore may be whether other laws can reach this conduct, such as public procurement laws, or criminal laws which extend beyond bribery, for example, to misconduct in public office, or whether new laws need to be created.

Another important debate is whether more needs to be done in some jurisdictions to tackle the demand side of bribery. In the United States (US), for example, domestic bribery laws criminalize both active and passive bribery, but the Foreign Corrupt Practices Act (FCPA) only applies to bribery of foreign officials, not the soliciting or receiving of bribes by foreign officials.[34] This has led to concerns that an uneven approach has been created; whilst companies face a credible enforcement risk and high sanctions for bribery of foreign officials, foreign public officials themselves are able to extract bribes from firms doing business in their jurisdictions and act with impunity.[35] In many cases, they do not face enforcement by either US or domestic authorities and so remain free to operate and demand further bribes in future transactions. Indeed, an OECD 2018 study,[36] reports that credible enforcement risks do not exist for public officials in many member nations of the OECD Anti-Bribery Convention. Rather, it found that of fifty-five cases between 2008 and 2013 in which sanctions had been imposed on a supply-side participant in a foreign bribery cases (so bribery was known to have been committed), a public official had been sanctioned in only one-fifth of the cases. Further that, despite opportunities and OECD Working Group meetings, cooperation between enforcement authorities in the demand-side and supply-side jurisdictions did not play a material role in the cases. The OECD has consequently acknowledged that further steps are required to address the demand side of foreign bribery, and to better

---

[33] See discussion on the Anti-Oligarch Law in Ukraine in Chapter 9 (one aim of which is to seek to limit the role of big business in politics).

[34] Some states' foreign bribery laws do also criminalize demand-side foreign bribery, see e.g. Transparency International, US Office, 'Civil Society Letter of Support for the Foreign Extortion Prevention Act' (2 November 2021). Further, it may be possible to recover assets purchased with the proceeds of bribes through civil forfeiture orders. For example, in 2018 the UK's Serious Fraud Office recovered, under their mutual legal assistance agreement with the US, GBP 4.4 million from two Chad diplomats that had received bribes from Canadian oil company, Griffiths Energy, in the US and Canada to secure oil development rights in Chad. These funds were eventually returned oversees to invest in projects designed to benefit the poorest people in Chad, see H. Cassin, 'Recovered Corruption Money Provides "Life-Saving Support" to 150,000 Vulnerable People', *The FCPA Blog* (2022), available at https://fcpablog.com/2022/06/27/recovered-corruption-money-provides-life-saving-support-to-150 000-vulnerable-people/.

[35] See Section B.ii.

[36] OECD, 'Foreign Bribery Enforcement: What Happens to the Public Officials on the Receiving End?' (2018), available at https://doi.org/10.1787/5f738e0d-en.

support companies facing bribe solicitation risks.[37] These findings have fuelled calls by some for new laws to deal with these demand-side issues.[38]

b. Insufficient or under-enforcement of the laws

Insufficient or under-enforcement of bribery or competition rules may occur for a number of reasons, for example, because agencies are inadequately staffed (including where staff are not selected or promoted on the basis of merit) or re-sourced,[39] have not prioritized enforcement in this area, or have inadequate detection techniques or powers.[40] Difficulties may also arise if enforcement institutions, including enforcers and the judiciary, are not sufficiently independent or impartial[41] (or are subject to political interference or have become compromised[42]), or if politicians sabotage investigations (see further Section E).[43]

Capability, capacity, and prioritization. Law enforcements agencies may not be able to enforce the rules effectively if they lack the resources, or human capacity—the volume of experienced and skilled staff—they need to bring proceedings against, often well-resourced, corporations or individuals.[44] Indeed, enforcers of criminal bribery laws may have to choose between investigating complex white-collar crime cases, or focusing their limited resources on violent crimes such as terrorism, homicide, or other violations of the person or property offences.[45]

A particular challenge faced in many countries is how to provide checks against corruption and collusion in certain spheres—e.g. conduct which distorts public

---

[37] See 2021 OECD Anti-Bribery Recommendation, n. 32, Recommendations XII–XIV.

[38] See, e.g., H.R.4737, S.3137, available at https://www.congress.gov/bill/117th-congress/senate-bill/3137/text?q=%7B%22search%22%3A%5B%22S3137%22%2C%22S3137%22%5D%7D&r=1&s=5, a bill introduced in the US into Congress for a Foreign Extortion Prevention Act (FEPA) in spite of the jurisdictional and enforcement challenges and complications that such legislation entails (see the companion bill in the Senate, available at https://www.congress.gov/bill/117th-congress/senate-bill/3137). Had it been enacted, the Act would have made it a crime for a foreign official to demand or accept a bribe from a US person or company, or in any way that substantially impacts interstate commerce in the US. 'This law could have been used, for example, to punish the officials in the Russian Attorney General's office who used their positions to accept bribes from Hewlett Packard in exchange for a valuable contract', see Transparency International, US Office, 'Seven Measures Congress Can Adopt to Address Russia's Corruptly Financed Military Aggression' (3 February 2022), available at https://us.transparency.org/resource/seven-measures-congress-can-adopt-to-address-russias-corruptly-financed-military-aggression/. See also H.R. 5209 (a bill on counter-kleptocracy).

[39] See, 2021 OECD Anti-Bribery Recommendation, n. 32, Recommendation VII (recommending that member countries provide adequate resources to law enforcement authorities so as to permit effective investigation and prosecution of bribery).

[40] See discussion in Section B.iii.d below and 2021 OECD Anti-Bribery Recommendation, n. 32, Recommendation VI and VIII.

[41] See Pontes and Anselmo, n. 27.

[42] See further discussion in Section C below.

[43] See R.L. Cassin, 'Five Ways Politicians Sabotage Anti-Corruption Agencies' (28 July 2022) *The FCPA Blog.*

[44] See further Chapter 3, C.iii.b.

[45] See Pontes and Anselmo, n. 27 (complaining that police were pushed to focus on drug crime, so meaning that they did not have sufficient resources to prioritize investigation of 'gargantuan frauds being committed against public funds', 41).

96 TOWARDS A MORE COMPREHENSIVE APPROACH

procurement at the local or municipal level. Such purchasing, because of its smaller scale than central government purchasing, often attracts less scrutiny from auditors and journalists,[46] and enforcement agencies may not think it worthwhile to pursue it given its complexity, but low-level and relatively low value. It nonetheless provides rich opportunities for cronyism, wrongdoing, and petty corruption and can, cumulatively, result in significant harm to citizens. In 2019, a UK House of Lords Select Committee drew attention to this problem in the UK:[47]

> The case of John Poulson provides an example of how small-scale bribery can, if unchecked, build up into a multi-million pound industry. Over 30 years Poulson, though not a qualified architect, starting with a £50 loan, built up the largest architectural practice in Europe through the corrupt purchase of local government contracts in northern England, and of contracts for the re-development of major railway termini through bribery of a British Rail employee, Graham Tunbridge. The bribes involved were not always large. When Tunbridge became Estates and Rating Surveyor for BR Southern Region, he gave Poulson contracts for the re-development of London Waterloo, Cannon Street and East Croydon stations–all in return for £25 a week and the loan of a Rover car.
>
> Such corruption breeds more corruption; it was estimated at Poulson's trial that 23 local authorities and over 300 individuals were involved. But the corruption had other deleterious effects. Taxpayers' money was misused in paying more than the contracts might have cost on an open public tender. The businesses which genuinely deserved to be awarded such contracts suffered. The public, who might have had buildings to admire, instead saw their city centres blighted by some of the worst examples of sixties brutalist architecture. Mercifully, most of the city centres of Newcastle and Leeds have since again been redeveloped, as has Cannon Street station; but some examples remain.[48]

It may be important therefore for enforcers to target resources on some of these cases, to signal that this conduct is prohibited and to create a deterrent to its occurrence in the future. For example, in 2019, the UK's Competition and Markets Authority (CMA) found that local estate agents (in the Berkshire area) had breached competition laws by concluding a cartel.[49] The decision led to three firms being fined more than GBP 600,000 and two directors being disqualified for their roles in the cartel. As this was not the first case involving estate agents breaking

---

[46] But see, e.g., M. Fazekas and Á. Czibik, 'Measuring Regional Quality of Government: The Public Spending Quality Index Based on Government Contracting Data' (2021) 55(8) *Regional Studies* 1459 (reviewing regional quality of public spending in EU Member States, noting within-country regional variations in performance, and a steady deterioration of performance in old Member States).

[47] House of Lords Select Committee on the Bribery Act 2010, n. 30.

[48] House of Lords Select Committee on the Bribery Act 2010, n. 30.

[49] See residential estate agency services in Berkshire (17 December 2019), available at https://www.gov.uk/cma-cases/provision-of-residential-estate-agency-services#infringement-decision.

competition law uncovered, the CMA sought to reinforce its message that they expected the sector to clean up its act—to comply and to understand the consequences of non-compliance. 'The industry needs to take note: this kind of behaviour will not be tolerated. If you break the law, you risk similar consequences.'[50]

Scrutiny of defence procurement is also frequently challenging for enforcers, given its sensitive nature and secrecy in the sector, leading to a relative paucity of publicly available information. Nonetheless, most countries spend vast sums on defence contracts (approximately EUR 205 billion in the EU in 2016[51] and USD 250 billion, half of Federal Government procurement spending, in the US[52]) creating significant corruption and collusion risks that are exacerbated by the close contacts between government procurers and the small numbers of potential suppliers that generally tend to exist.[53] This has led many NGOs to call on governments to develop better anti-corruption action plans for the defence area, to reduce secrecy to the minimum, to ensure open and fair contracting, and to allow for greater involvement of civil society in procurement.

Special measures designed to increase oversight in these more difficult areas and other pervasive corruption trouble spots—such as infrastructure and construction, and the pharmaceuticals sector—are therefore desirable. In the US, for example, the Department of Justice (DOJ) Antitrust Division has set up a Procurement Collusion Strike Force to prioritize enforcement in this sphere across the US and leading it to open more than seventy investigations (involving fifty different industries) impacting on government purchasing, between its creation in 2019 and the end of 2022.[54]

Foreign bribery. In Chapter 3 it has been seen that to fight corruption globally, the OECD Convention on Foreign Bribery has, with the help of monitoring by an active working group, led many states to adopt or improve foreign bribery laws. Although these rules have led to an increase in action against foreign bribery, concerns that there is not yet a true level playing field across countries, means that in many jurisdictions there is an unwillingness to pursue, what are frequently key national corporations for foreign bribery, especially if perceived to be required to secure contracts abroad—government's do not want their own companies to be disadvantaged.[55] Indeed, in some cases enforcement agencies may face political pressure not to investigate cases of foreign bribery involving leading national

---

[50] M. Grenfell, Executive Director of Enforcement, Press Release available at https://www.gov.uk/government/news/estate-agents-fined-over-half-a-million-pounds-for-price-fixing.

[51] See European Defence Agency, 'Defence Data 2016–2017: Key Findings and Analysis' (2018).

[52] C.R. Yukins, 'US Government Contracting in the Context of Global Public Procurement' in A.C. Georgopulos, B. Hoekman, and P.C. Mavroidis (eds), *The Internationalization of Government Procurement Regulation* (Oxford University Press, 2017), figure 9.1.

[53] Yukins, n. 52, noting that the top five companies accounted for USD 73 billion of US federal defence contracts in 2014.

[54] See further Chapter 6.

[55] Heimann and Pieth, n. 29, 208–10.

corporations[56] and according to Transparency International in 2022, enforcement of foreign bribery has now dropped to an historic low.[57] Thus although no country is immune from exporting foreign bribery, active enforcement of foreign bribery laws only occurs in four countries (the US, the UK, Switzerland, and Israel), moderate enforcement in nine (Germany, France, Italy, Spain, Australia, Brazil, Sweden, Norway, and Portugal) and limited, little, or no enforcement in the remainder—under-enforcement of the rules is therefore common.[58] In particular, non-OCED Convention exporters, such as China, Hong Kong SAR, and India, still fail to enforce foreign bribery laws, even though tackling foreign bribery in exporting countries is a crucial way of supplementing domestic corruption control measures.

The continuing role of international bodies—such as the OECD Working Group on Bribery and Transparency International— is consequently crucial in maintaining pressure on states to adhere to their international commitments, or to join international conventions, and to take steps to ensure that foreign bribery laws are both introduced and enforced. The OECD's 2021 recommendation urges members to reinvigorate their fight against foreign bribery through the adoption of new measures to tackle it and the strengthening of enforcement. It also recommends addressing the demand side of foreign bribery, enhancing international cooperation, introducing principles on the use of non-trial resolutions in foreign bribery cases, incentivizing anti-corruption compliance by companies, and providing comprehensive and effective protection for reporting persons.[59] For example, Recommendation XIII urges member countries to raise awareness of their public officials on their domestic bribery and solicitation laws with a view to stopping the solicitation and acceptance of bribes and to publish on a publicly available website, rules and regulations governing gifts, hospitality, entertainment, and expenses for domestic public officials.[60]

The US policy of enforcing the FCPA against *foreign* (as well as US) corporations, appears to be designed to help level the playing field for companies engaging in foreign bribery, to change the incentives of both US and foreign corporations, and to ensure that US firms are not disadvantaged, as compared to their foreign

---

[56] See, e.g., the 'Al Yamamah' crisis, when the then UK prime minister (Tony Blair) suggested to the attorney general, and indirectly to the Serious Fraud Office, that an investigation into British Aerospace's payment to secure a large arms deal with Saudi Arabia, might be closed. The case led to widespread criticism of the UK, including from the OECD's Working Group on Bribery, see Heimann and Pieth, n. 29, 84–99.

[57] Transparency International, 'Exporting Corruption, Progress Report 2022: Assessing Enforcement of the OECD Convention on Combatting Foreign Bribery' (11 October 2022), available at https://www.transparency.org/en/publications/exporting-corruption-2022

[58] Transparency International, n. 57 But see, e.g., OECD, 'Implementing the OECD Anti-Bribery Convention in Brazil Phase 4 report' (19 October 2023) (concluding that Brazil could better detect and enforce its foreign bribery offence).

[59] See, the 2021 OECD Anti-Bribery Recommendation, n. 32.

[60] See Section B.i.e.

competitors, by enforcement of the FCPA against them.[61] It has also been seen that consideration is being given by some to the question on how to ensure that foreign officials in jurisdictions in which their corrupt practices are not challenged, are not able to act with impunity in the future.[62]

Detection techniques: overuse of self-reporting schemes? In many jurisdictions, there is scope to improve or supplement detection methods used by enforcement agencies.

Although leniency and self-reporting schemes have become important mechanisms for inducing the provision of evidence, especially first evidence of an offence, there is a growing view in the antitrust community that leniency systems have their limits and authorities should not overly rely on them.[63] In particular, some evidence suggests that they may be most successful where a cartel is close to being discovered or breaking up,[64] and are less able to be effective in contexts (such as public procurement) where a cartel is especially profitable and stable.[65] Other literature suggests that these programmes may be used by some larger multiproduct firms operating a number of cartels as a technique to prevent cheating and deviant conduct by smaller cartel members.[66] The increasing risk of multiple enforcement fora attracting possible individual sanctions, criminal prosecution, and private damages actions in many jurisdictions, may also be making firms more wary of leniency applications which may apply only to certain areas of legal exposure. Indeed, some evidence indicates that leniency applications have been decreasing in some jurisdictions.[67] Further and crucially, it is self-evident that for a self-reporting programme to be successful, there must be a good track record of enforcement following use of other detection techniques (without which, there will be no incentive to seek amnesty).[68] Thus 'theory and practical experience seem to suggest that reliance on amnesty/leniency programmes alone may produce a

---

[61] See, e.g., E. Acorn, 'Law and Politics in FCPA Prosecutions of Foreign Corporations' (2021) 17(2) *Revista Direito GV* 2021.

[62] See n. 38 and text.

[63] See C. Mena-Labarthe, 'Mexican Experience in Screens for Bid-Rigging' (2012) 3 *CPI Antitrust Chronicle* 2.

[64] See, e.g., J.E. Harrington, 'Detecting Cartels' in P. Buccirossi (ed.), *Handbook of Antitrust Economics* (MIT Press, 2008).

[65] See A. Heimler, 'Cartels in Public Procurement' (2012) 8(4) *Journal of Competition Law & Economics* 11 ('Public procurement markets differ from all others because quantities do not adjust with prices but are fixed by the bidding authority. As a result, there is a high incentive for organizing cartels ... that are quite stable because there are no lasting benefits for cheaters and few incentives to apply for leniency').

[66] See R.C. Marshall, 'Unobserved Collusion: Warning Signs and Concerns' (2017) 5(3) *Journal of Antitrust Enforcement* 329.

[67] See OECD Competition Trends 2022 (2022), available at https://www.oecd.org/daf/competition/oecd-competition-trends-2022.pdf.

[68] See D.C. Klawiter, 'Conspiracy Screens: Practical Defense Perspective', *CPI Antitrust Chronicle* (13 March 2012) 2; D.C. Klawiter, 'Enhancing International Cartel Enforcement: Some Modest Suggestions', *CPI Antitrust Chronicle* (28 September 2011) 4; K. Hüschelrath, 'How Are Cartels Detected? The Increasing Use of Proactive Methods to Establish Antitrust Infringements' (2010) 1 *Journal of European Competition Law and Practice* 522–3.

sub-optimal probability of cartel detection, which in turn may have a negative effect on deterrence'.[69]

Similarly, in the anti-corruption context, there is concern about the overuse of non-prosecution or deferred prosecution agreements (DPAs)—meaning that in some jurisdictions few actual prosecutions are brought in practice. Such arrangements have the potential to produce procedural efficiencies, speed up processes, reduce costs, and increase the quantity of cases dealt with, whilst ensuring that the defendant makes reparation for its alleged offence. Care must be exercised, however, to ensure that they do not reduce the punitive and deterrent effect of relevant laws (e.g. by shielding companies from debarment from procurement processes (without a conviction, debarment rules may not apply in some jurisdictions)), and do not hinder the development of the law or extinguish societal condemnation of the conduct. As with leniency regimes, they may also, by limiting prosecutions, in the end discourage firms from self-reporting, cooperating and entering DPAs.

It is important, therefore, that investigators should not be overly reliant on self-reporting programmes, but should apply principled criteria for their use, and should ensure that they continue to bring some prosecutions and collect evidence from a broad range of sources, including from procurement officials, employees, and other informants capable of delivering credible evidence, and through ex officio investigations and the use of their own proactive detection techniques. A well as producing 'positive externalities' in terms of improving the efficacy of self-reporting programmes, each of these mechanisms will help uncover evidence of conduct that would otherwise remain hidden or remain stablish under a standalone amnesty or leniency regime.[70]

Detection techniques: complaints, whistleblowing and direct referrals. Although a number of competition enforcement and anti-corruption agencies do seek to gather information about possible infringements from a broad range of complainants, including competitors, customers, disgruntled employees, citizens, disappointed bidders, victims, and other public agencies, in many jurisdictions their use could be further encouraged. For example, it has been seen, that procurement officials could be better incentivized to report suspicions of collusion, in particular through competition law training and building good relations between procurement and competition agencies.[71] Closer relationships between anti-corruption and competition agencies may also encourage direct referrals of cases between them where infringements are suspected.[72]

---

[69] OECD Policy Roundtables 'Ex Officio Cartel Investigations and the Use of Screens to Detect Cartels', DAF/COMP(2013)27 (7 July 2014), 16.

[70] OECD Policy Roundtable, n. 69, 17.

[71] See Section B.i above.

[72] On the importance of coordination more generally between agencies see Section B.iii.a below.

Further, whistleblowing tools may benefit from development to encourage reporting[73] through ensuring the careful protection of whistleblowers from reprisal, allowing them to remain anonymous (where possible),[74] and providing them with financial rewards (such as a share of penalties imposed or damages recovered) which can offset the, frequently significant, adverse consequences that flow from whistleblowing. Indeed, it will not be encouraged if it attracts negative repercussions beyond its benefits.[75] The OECD's 2021 Anti-bribery Recommendation thus proposes that members protect and provide remedies against retaliatory action to persons who report suspected acts of bribery.[76] Although financial rewards are available in some jurisdictions (the UK's Competition and Markets Authority offers in exceptional circumstances financial rewards of up to GBP 100,000 to those, especially insiders, who offer information about cartel activity[77] and the US Federal Civil False Claims Act, known as the *qui tam* statute, offers monetary rewards for exposure of any fraud affecting the government[78]), this is not the case in all jurisdictions and even where they exist, rewards may not be sufficient.

Detection techniques: red flags, monitoring, and screening tools. An interesting development is the increasing interest in the possible use of screens, both structural (identifying markets which are more prone to collusion and based e.g. on a list of factors that influence the likelihood of collusion (such as the number of rivals, the homogeneity of the product, stability of the product, etc.[79])) and behavioural (focusing on firms' behaviour) to provide first prima facie evidence of an infringement, so reducing the need to rely on self-reports or whistleblowers to trigger investigation.[80]

---

[73] See, e.g., European Commission, 'Whistleblower Communication Tools', available at https://ec.eur opa.eu/competition-policy/cartels/whistleblower_en.

[74] See Case 145/83, *Stanley George Adams v Commission* EU:C:1985:323 (concerning a case in which the European Commission was found to have enabled Stanley Adams to be identified as the source of information which led the Commission to impose a fine on Adam's former employer, the Swiss company, Hoffmann-La Roche, for cartel conduct. As a result, Adams was arrested and sent to prison in Switzerland for industrial espionage and his wife committed suicide).

[75] See the Criminal Antitrust Anti-Retaliation Act of 2019 in the US (recently expanded to cover employees who provide information relating to criminal antitrust infringements) and the EU's new Directive setting out whistleblower protection in the EU, Council Directive 2019/1937, [2019] OJ L305/17.

[76] 2021 OECD Anti-Bribery Recommendation, n. 32, Recommendation XXII.

[77] See Competition and Markets Authority, 'Rewards for Information About Cartels' (2014), and Chapter 5.

[78] See A. Dyck, A. Morse, and L. Zingales, 'Who Blows the Whistle on Corporate Fraud?' (2010) LXV *Journal of Finance* 2213.

[79] See discussion of the factors that are likely to facilitate collusion on a market in Chapter 2.

[80] See, e.g., Harrington, n. 64; P. Bajari and G. Summers, 'Detecting Collusion in Procurement Auctions' (2002) 70 *Antitrust Law Journal* 143; K. Hüschelrath and T. Veith, 'Cartel Detection in Procurement Markets' (2013) 35 *Managerial and Decision Economics* 404–5 ('[M]onitoring procurement markets through screening tools has the potential of substantial cost reductions'); K. Hüschelrath, 'Economic Approaches to Fight Bid Rigging' (2013) 4 *Journal of European Competition Law and Practice* 185; OECD, n. 69, 6.

102 TOWARDS A MORE COMPREHENSIVE APPROACH

Public contract tenders are particularly suitable for the application of screening tools as the identification of a public tender market facilitates structural assessment (e.g. identification of concentrated market structures, and whether concentration is increasing, and (artificially) stable market structures) and the data generated by the process facilitates subsequent behavioural assessments.

In the competition sphere, examination of susceptible markets on the basis of structural factors,[81] or bids, bidding patterns, suspicious behavioural patterns, and a periodic review of past tender information may therefore be helpful. In particular, the following are recognized as 'red flag', indicators of possible collusion, which procurement officials can be vigilant for:[82]

- Fewer firms than anticipated bid, bidders unexpectedly withdraw from bidding, bidding in a particular territory or to a particular customer.
- The same suppliers submit bids, and each company seems to take a turn being the successful bidder, or the same company always wins a particular procurement.
- Different bidders have the same contact details.
- There are indications that bids were prepared together—for example, two or more proposals are submitted at the same time or with similar handwriting, typeface, paper, calculations, or amendments or with identical errors, or emanate from a common web or IP address.[83]
- Unusual or suspicious bidding patterns,[84] when viewed over time or when compared with other bids[85] or prior bids on different tenders, or where they involve identical line-item prices, similar pricing trends, discounts, or costs or persistently or suddenly high prices, significantly above list prices or internal agency cost estimates.
- Refusal among competitors to negotiate pricing.
- Sharing of pricing or commercially sensitive information among tenderers.
- Bid prices drop whenever a new or infrequent bidder submits a bid.
- A winner does not take the contract, or winners routinely subcontract part of the tender to another (losing) bidder.

---

[81] See, e.g., P. Grout and S. Sonderegger, 'Predicting Cartels' (March 2005) Office of Fair Trading Economic Discussion Paper.

[82] See Malaysian Competition Commission, 'Detecting Bid Rigging in Public Procurement' (28 August 2014).

[83] For example, in a storm damage repair case in the US (Guam), identical typos were spotted in cover letters and, in an ice cream case, identical mistakes were made in bid forms; it was noted that the bids had been mailed at the same time from the same post office and the postage stamps had been ripped from the same roll, see 'Detecting Bid Rigging in Public Procurement' n. 82.

[84] For example, where there appears to be rotation or allocation of winning bids by time, geography, job description, or product line.

[85] For example, when identical, too close or far apart, or where bids are exact percentages apart.

- There is evidence of communication between bidders, especially shortly before the tender deadline, or of statements indicating knowledge of competitors pricing, price schedules, or other bid rigging activity.

In addition, a burgeoning literature now explores how data analytics, data on market structure, and data collected in the course of the bidding process (on tenders and bidders) can be used to devise and run electronic tests to screen for possible cartel behaviour.[86] These involve empirical analysis, based on economic and statistical assessment of variable data[87] including price variance analysis, which can be applied to flag possible unlawful cartel behaviour (looking for collusive markers, abrupt changes, or anomalies, in the data),[88] and a need for further investigation.[89] In the bid rigging context, they seek to identify whether collusion or cheating may exist, who might be involved, and how long the conduct may have lasted. Some data-driven detection tools being developed adopt machine learning, for example, using informative patterns extracted from data from past scenarios

---

[86] R.M. Abrantes-Metz, 'Proactive *vs* Reactive Anti-Cartel Policy: The Role of Empirical Screens' (2013), available at https://papers.ssrn.com/sol3/papers.cfm?abstract_id=2284740, 2–3 ('A screen is a statistical test based on an econometric model and a theory of the alleged illegal behaviour designed to identify whether manipulation, collusion, fraud, or any other type of cheating may exist in a particular market, who may be involved, and how long it may have lasted. Screens use commonly available data such as prices, bids, quotes, spreads, market shares, volumes, and other data to identify patterns that are anomalous or highly improbable'). See also Hüschelrath and Veith, n. 80; R.M. Abrantes-Metz, L. Froeb, J. Geweke, and C.T. Taylor, 'A Variance Screen for Collusion' (2006) 4(3) *International Journal of Industrial Organization* 467–86; A. Deng, 'Cartel Detection and Monitoring: A Look Forward' (2017) 5 *Journal of Antitrust Enforcement* 488; D. Imhof, 'Detecting Bid-Rigging with Descriptive Statistics' (2020) 15(4) *Journal of Competition Law & Economics* 427; J.E. Harrington and J. Chen, 'Cartel Pricing Dynamics with Cost Variability and Endogenous Buyer Detection' (2006) 24 *International Journal of Industrial Economics* 1185; Harrington, n. 64; D. Imhof, Y. Karagök, and S. Rutz, 'Screening for Bid-Rigging: Does It Work?' (2018) 14(2) *Journal of Competition Law & Economics* 235; OECD Roundtable on ex officio Cartel Investigations and the use of screens to detect cartels, n. 69, 12; R.H. Porter and J.D. Zona, 'Detection of Bid Rigging in Procurement Auctions' (1993) *Journal of Political Economy* 101; and R.H. Porter and J.D. Zona, 'Ohio School Milk Markets: An Analysis of Bidding' (1999) 30 *RAND Journal of Economics* 263. Screens can also help firms to improve their corporate governance and find out about potentially infringing behaviour. Firms that suspect they are affected by anti-competitive behaviour may also use screens to collate evidence and potentially file a complaint, see Oxera, 'Hide and Seek: The Effective Use of Cartel Screens' (19 September 2013).

[87] Including prices, volumes, and market shares.

[88] See, e.g., J.E. Harrington and D. Imhof, 'Cartel Screening and Machine Learning' (2022) II *Stanford Computational Antitrust* 134; Abrantes-Metz, n. 86, 2–3 (noting that use of screens have become increasingly popular in the antitrust context and were successfully used to identify the LIBOR conspiracy and manipulation); R.M. Abrantes-Metz and P. Bajari, 'The Use and Spread of Screens: Screens for Conspiracies and their Multiple Applications' (2012) 8 *Competition Policy International* 177, 187; Hüschelrath, n. 80; Hüschelrath, n. 68, 528; and Imhof, n. 86. Screens can also be used as means to strengthen compliance and audit programs, as a helpful tool for due diligence in M&A activities, during litigation, and in quantifying damage claims in private actions. See, e.g. Klawiter, 'Conspiracy Screens', n. 68, 3–4.

[89] See, e.g., OECD, 'Summary of the Workshop on Cartel Screening in the Digital Era', DAF/COMP/M(2018) (30 January 2018), 3, available at https://one.oecd.org/document/DAF/COMP/M(2018)3/en/pdf.

(of bid rigging or competition), to create models that will then be able to operate as more effective screens.[90]

The reliability of screens based on quantitative analysis of procurement data are, however, dependent on the availability of reliable and unbiased data sets. Indeed, some commentators suggest that to support higher level collusion risk assessments, the following information should be made available by governments: bidder and bid price-related information (including bidders' addresses, beneficial owners, and excluded bidders); price information and final contract values (including final and estimated prices and timing of bid submissions); data on contract award phase and contract implementation; the purchased products; the use of joint-bidding schemes and subcontracting; and details of consortium bidders and subcontractors.[91] This will be facilitated by the use of: a central public procurement platform publishing all tender notices regulated by the national public procurement law; a uniform data capture system with processes for safeguarding its quality; and use of standard forms defining expected publication content to include the systematic collection of key data.[92]

The construction and maintenance of national databases providing easily reviewable data is however costly and time-consuming, so despite current initiatives for open procurement data,[93] relatively few countries have sophisticated systems

[90] See, e.g., Harrington and Imhof, n. 88 (Guidance is also provided for competition authorities to deploy machine learning algorithms, including deep learning, to make cartel screening more effective). Three different machine learning approaches have been defined—supervised, unsupervised, and reinforced learning, see OECD, 'Data Screening Tools in Competition Investigations', *OECD Competition Policy Roundtable Background Note* (2022), available at https://www.oecd.org/competition/data-screening-tools-for-competition-investigations.htm. See also M. Huber and D. Imhof, 'Machine Learning with Screens for Detecting Bid-Rigging Cartels' (2019) 65 *International Journal of Industrial Organization* 277.

[91] See M. Fazekas and B. Tóth, 'Assessing the Potential for Detecting Collusion in Swedish Public Procurement' (2016) 3 *Konkurrensverket Uppdragsforskningsrapport* 42–4. See Harrington and Imhof, n. 88 and discussion of Swiss competition authority approach, nn. 115–120 and text. In addition, evidence of conflicts of interest, or the existence of political connections, may be required to assess corruption risks fully.

[92] Fazekas and Tóth, n. 91.

[93] A. Sanchez-Graells, 'Procurement Corruption and Artificial Intelligence: Between the Potential of Enabling Data Architectures and the Constraints of Due Process Requirements' in S. Williams-Elegbe and J. Tillipman (eds), *Routledge Handbook of Public Procurement Corruption* (Routledge, Forthcoming). Open data may, however, if not carefully approached, create other difficulties, for example, from public over-exposure, creating data-protection issues, concerns about the protection of commercially sensitive information, and collusion risks. Some consequently suggest that there should be a decoupling of data availability from transparency (in the sense of general accessibility or publication for everyone to see), with access to data being developed on a 'need to know' basis. See also, e.g., the OECD Public Governance Committee's, *Recommendation of the Council on Public Procurement* (OECD, 2015); D. Berliner and K. Dupuy, 'The Promise and Perils of Data for Anti-Corruption Efforts in International Development Work' (2018), available at https://www.u4.no/publications/theprom ise-and-perils-of-data-for-anti-corruption-efforts-in-international-development-work). See also A. Sanchez-Graells, 'The UK's Green Paper on Post-Brexit Public Procurement Reform: Transformation or Overcomplication?' (2021) 16(1) *European Procurement and Public Private Partnership Law Review* 4.

in place.[94] Rather, data gaps may exist because of, for example, errors in reporting, high mandatory reporting thresholds, because only certain information (such as the bidding and bid evaluation phases) is captured, with other key information missing (e.g. relating to estimated prices of tenders, subcontracting, geographical location of bidders, contract implementation, modifications and completion, including overruns and costs, or historical data),[95] or because it is not stored in line with internationally applicable data templates or is not machine-readable.[96] 'If some of the key variables are missing from a procurement data system it can rule-out the possibility for qualitative collusion risk analysis altogether.'[97] This suggests that further steps need to be taken in many jurisdictions to ensure more comprehensive and consistent reporting of high-quality procurement data.

As a result, some commentators warn that data screens should be approached with caution. Further, because they are extremely costly and difficult to operate accurately,[98] they cannot distinguish explicit from tacit collusion[99] and cannot prove collusion (but only identify collusion risks—they ordinarily provide just one piece of evidence which might be relied on to trigger a deeper investigation[100]), they are limited in what they can achieve.[101] Nonetheless, screens remain of considerable interest as a mechanism for detecting first signs of law contraventions, especially as technological developments improve and competition agencies are keen to keep pace and catch-up with market players. Screens have played a part in revealing first evidence in some of the largest conspiracies, manipulations, and frauds uncovered to date, including Bernie Madoff's Ponzi scheme[102] and the LIBOR conspiracy,[103]

---

[94] Data on procurements falling within the scope of EU Public Procurement Directives are stored on Tenders Electronic Daily, available at https://ted.europa.eu/TED/main/HomePage.do. See discussion of digitalization of public procurement in Ukraine, in Chapter 9.

[95] See Fazekas and Tóth, n. 91, 19–23.

[96] See, e.g., the Open Contracting Data Standard, available at https://standard.open-contracting.org/latest/en/and DIGIWHIST, available at https://digiwhist.eu/.

[97] See Fazekas and Tóth, n. 91, 23.

[98] Not only are they difficult to create and set up, but in human resources terms they require specialist staff (e.g. IT specialists and data scientists) to ensure that they are operated and updated as necessary.

[99] Explicit collusion occurs where firms reach a mutual understanding as to the strategies that they will pursue through express communications amongst themselves. Tacit collusion occurs where the mutual understanding occurs without express communication.

[100] Screens thus merely isolate outcomes that are improbable to occur under a competitive environment and which consequently merit closer scrutiny. Standing alone, they cannot serve as the ultimate proof of the existence or absence of a cartel, though they can provide valuable assistance when combined with other such evidence. No purely empirical or statistical approach can be used as the *single* proof of collusion. See also Hüschelrath, n. 68, 526; Heimler n. 17; Hüschelrath and Veith, n. 80, 407; Porter and Zona, 'Ohio School Milk Markets', n. 86, 522.

[101] See Mena-Labarthe, n. 63, 3 (screens can be good but also can be costly wasting 'resources and never ending work to find a needle in a haystack where ultimately there is none').

[102] See H. Markopolos, *No One Would Listen: A True Financial Thriller* (Wiley, 2010) 192.

[103] See C. Mollenkamp and L. Norman, 'British Bankers Group Steps up Review of Widely Used Libor', *Wall Street Journal* (17 April 2008); C. Mollenkamp and M. Whitehouse, 'Study Casts Doubt on Key Rate: WSJ Analysis Suggests Banks May Have Reported Flawed Interest Data for Libor', *Wall Street Journal* (29 May 2008). Investigations then extended to Euribor, Yen LIBOR and TIBOR.

106 TOWARDS A MORE COMPREHENSIVE APPROACH

and a number of competition authorities[104] are now actively exploring their use in the bid rigging context, including in Brazil, Colombia, Chile, Korea, Mexico, Romania, and Switzerland (although the extent and success of their use is not entirely easy to estimate given that some initiatives, to prevent cartelists being able to adapt their behaviour to them, are shrouded in secrecy).[105]

In the Republic of Korea, for example, the Korea Fair Trade Commission (KFTC) systematically monitors public procurement through a Bid Rigging Indicator Analysis System (BRIAS).[106] BRIAS automatically receives online public procurement data (which public procuring authorities are required to submit within thirty days of the tender award through the e-procurement system KONEPS—Korea Online E-Procurement System[107]) and quantifies the likelihood of bid rigging, by assigning a score representing the statistical likelihood of collusion based on factors including: the tendering method; the number of bidders, successful and failed bids; bid prices of failed bids; and the price of the winning bid. Although the initial system (2006) had difficulties and has been subject to criticism (in particular for flagging too many cases, few of which were actually investigated by the KFTC[108]),

---

[104] See generally R. Abrantes-Metz, 'A Note on Screens' Worldwide Adoption and Successes' (2020) *OECD Regional Centre for Competition in Latin America Newsletter No. 2*.

[105] See, e.g., T. Schrepel and T. Groza (eds), *The Adoption of Computational Antitrust by Agencies: 2nd Annual Report* (Stanford Computational Antitrust, 2023) (discussing use, or development, of screening by agencies in e.g. Australia, Brazil, Bulgaria, Chile, Finland, Greece, Mexico, Romania, and Spain); OECD, 'Data Screening Tools in Competition Investigations', n. 90; Note by Brazil, DAF/COMP/WP3/WD(2022)36; Note by Columbia, DAF/COMP/WP3/WD(2022)28; Note by Korea, DAF/COMP/WP3/WD(2022)31; Note by Mexico, DAF/COMP/WP3/WD(2022)32; and Note by Romania, DAF/COMP/WP.3/WD(2022)37 (discussing the importance of competition agencies using tech driven investigative tools to access/use data for initiation and development of cases, cartel screening, and bid rigging detection); D. Pachnou and D. Westrik, 'Developments in Cartel Screening', *CPI Columns* (January 2023); and 'Spanish Bid Riggers set to see Collusion Caught by Improved AI Tool, Regulator Says', *MLex* (20 October 2023). The Mexican competition authority, following an informal complaint from the Mexican Social Security Institute (IMSS) which had observed strange patterns in the procurement processes of various generic drugs, used empirical and behavioural screening of procurement databases before targeting and launching an investigation, and collecting evidence that supported its hypothesis of collusion. Eventually, it issued a decision (which also relied on the screens) and fined four pharmaceutical laboratories for eliminating competition through bid rigging in the market for human insulin and three other laboratories for coordinating bids in IMSS's public procurement of serums, see Mena-Labarthe, n. 63, 3–4 and RA-019-2010, *Resolución Recurso de reconsideración Fresenius Kabi México, S.A. de C.V. y otros*, Diario Oficial de la Federación 10-06-2010. The Mexican Supreme Court of Justice affirmed and accepted the empirical and economic evidence provided by the screens, see 'Resuelve la SCJN caso sobre colusión en licitaciones del IMSS', COFECE-009-2015, available at https://www.cofece.mx/imagenes/comunicados/Boletines_2015/COFECE-009-2015.pdf. Colombia has devised a computer programme, and in Chile the competition authority uses procurement data acquired in part through a cooperation agreement with central purchasing body, ChileCompra, to monitor tenders and perform screening exercises. Although the UK's CMA introduced a screening tool for procurers, which was made available to the public in July 2017, this was withdrawn in 2020 after problems with its operation, see Chapter 5.

[106] The Korean Electric Power Corporation has also developed an AI-based machine learning bid rigging detection scheme. See, e.g., Korea Fair Trade Commission (KFTC), available at https://www.ftc.go.kr/www/cop/bbs/selectBoardArticle.do?key=267&nttId=85556&bbsId=BBSMSTR_000000002363&bbsTyCode=BBST05.

[107] See the Korean Online E-Procurement System, available at http://www.g2b.go.kr/index.jsp.

[108] From 2006–2017, the KFTC flagged over 10,000 bids but only seven were investigated. See https://www.sisafocus.co.kr/news/articleView.html?idxno=168195.

WEAKNESSES IN RELEVANT LAWS, OR THEIR APPLICATION   107

upgrades have sought to enable BRIAS to become a more sophisticated mechanism for identifying procurements for further investigation.[109] Even if some concerns about the system remain, the analysis by BRIAS was relied on to uncover bid rigging for manholes and sewer pipes.[110]

In Brazil, Brain Project is an artificial intelligence (AI) system which develops programmed algorithms to detect suspicious behaviour—e.g. using the government procurement e-system, by comparing prices expected in a competitive market and actual market behaviour.[111] The system has been used in a number of public investigations. For example, in Operation Meeting Point, the Brazilian competition authority, CADE, following a complaint and in partnership with the Federal Police, was able to use the Brain Project system to identify 4,779 procurements in which companies involved in the alleged cartel participated, and to screen for signs of bid rotation and cover bidding (through statistical tests). As a result, sixteen companies were selected for further investigation through search and seizures authorized through warrants (carried out on 31 October 2018).[112] This led to consideration of how the Brain Project could be expanded, for example, through open government initiatives or integrating databases (such as ComprasNet) for real-time application.[113] The project illustrates some of the challenges that may be involved in running such systems, including the need for access to relevant data, the need for trained specialists to operate the system, the need to embed the system within the institutional framework and to keep it updated, and the need for good inter-institutional cooperation (given its reliance on data mining, access to a multiplicity of datasets, and the sharing of information and data).[114]

Also interesting are developments in Switzerland, where the Swiss Competition Commission (ComCo) has initiated a screening policy, relying exclusively on publicly available procurement authorities' tender data, to strengthen its fight

---

[109] See Presentation by Sunmi Lee, Director of Bid Rigging Investigation Division KFTC, 'Alternative Tools to Detect Cartels: Bid-Rigging Indicator Analysis System' (November 2018), and OECD, 'Summary of the Workshop on Cartel Screening', n. 89, 3.

[110] Kolon Industries, Hankuk Fiber, Hankuk Polytech, and Finetec Composite were fined a total of USD 20.8 million for bid rigging manholes and sewer pipes, KFTC Communication (9 March 2021), available at https://www.ftc.go.kr/www/selectReportUserView.do?key=10&rpttype=1&report_data_no=8988.

[111] See A. Cordeiro Macedo and R. Mazzuco Sant'Ana, 'Brazil: New Investigation Techniques to Fighting Cartels–the "Brain Project"' (2020) *OECD Regional Centre for Competition in Latin America Newsletter No. 2* and Presentation at the OECD Workshop on Cartel Screening in the Digital Era, 'Screening and Data Mining Tools to Detect Cartels: Brazilian Experience' (30 January 2018). Brazilian and US authorities have also relied on screens to identify potential anti-competitive behaviour in gasoline markets, see, e.g., C.E. Joppert Ragazzo, 'Screens in the Gas Retail Market: The Brazilian Experience' (2012) *CPI Antitrust Chronicle* 3 and FTC Working Paper, available at https://www.ftc.gov/reports/variance-screen-collusion.

[112] See also CADE's Press Release, 'CADE's General Superintendence Initiates Administrative Proceeding to Investigate a Cartel in the Market of Orthoses, Prostheses and Special Medical Supplies' (4 August 2017), case opened following use of algorithms as an investigation device.

[113] Cordeiro Macedo and Mazzuco Sant'Ana, n. 111.

[114] Cordeiro Macedo and Mazzuco Sant'Ana, n. 111.

108 TOWARDS A MORE COMPREHENSIVE APPROACH

against bid rigging and to help it to select appropriate cases for *ex officio* investigation. Despite difficulties relating to the availability and quality of data, it has been working on the development of simple screens, which are easy to implement and flexible, and which are based on experience from previous cases. Indeed, one study relied on procurement data relating to a case in which ComCo found bid rigging by regional road construction companies in the canton of Ticino,[115] to conclude that the use of simple screens, which are relatively easy to apply with available data relating to bids (a relatively low data requirement), would have revealed striking irregularities in the cartelized market and could have been used by ComCo (or procurement bodies as large customers) to justify the opening of an investigation.[116] Subsequently ComCo has relied on statistical analysis of tender data (based on variance[117] and relative distance[118] screens[119]) to launch investigations. The first such investigation was commenced in 2013 into bid rigging in the See-Gaster region of the canton St Gallen. It led to eight firms being fined for rigging bids for contracts awarded between 2002 and 2009.[120]

Screens may also be utilized in the anti-corruption context. Red flags may be raised where evidence indicates tendering risk: use of non-open procedure types, calls for tenders not published, short-period advertising tenders, steps taken to narrow the pool of bidders,[121] bidders have been arbitrarily excluded or disqualified at the assessment stage,[122] or single bidding (only one contractor bids); or long delays in contract negotiations or post-award order changes that modify or lengthen the contract or increase the contract price.[123] Evidence that a group of suppliers' share in a buyer's total spending is high or that contracts are frequently awarded to tenderers registered in tax havens may also be suggestive of corrupt networks.

Technology and data tools have the potential of advancing the working of screens and corruption control by automatically analysing, and cross-checking,

---

[115] See Strassenbelage Tessin (LPC 2008-1).

[116] Imhof, n. 86. See also D. Imhof and H. Wallimann, 'Detecting Bid-Rigging Coalitions in Different Countries and Auction Formats' (2021) *Papers 2105.00337*, available at arXiv.org.

[117] On the basis of its finding that in tenders where bids are set collusively, the variance is lower than in non-collusive tenders.

[118] Measuring the difference between the two lowest bids compared, and the mean of the differences between the losing bids. This is selected on the basis that bid riggers manipulate the tender award by creating a difference between the bid of the designated winner and cover bids.

[119] They also take account of the fact that there may only be partial collusion (bid rigging affecting only a subset of contracts).

[120] See OECD, 'Annual Report on Competition Policy Developments in Switzerland: 2018', DAF/COMP/AR(2019)33 (3 May 2019), para. 30.

[121] For example, inadequate advertising of the tender process, not operating an open-tender process, and the application of unreasonable procedures or tender criteria. See M. Fazekas, I.J. Tóth, and L.P. King, 'An Objective Corruption Risk Index Using Public Procurement Data' (2006) 22 *European Journal on Criminal Policy and Research* 369, 372–3.

[122] Guide to Combating Corruption and Fraud in Dev. Projects, 'Excluding Qualified Bidders', available at https://guide.iacrc.org/potential-scheme-excluding-qualified-bidders/.

[123] Fazekas, Tóth, and King, n. 121.

large bodies of information and data for anomalies and identifying these types of 'corruption risk indicators', such as use of exceptionally short bidding periods, many tenders with single bidders, or other suspicious patterns (e.g. no competition for the winning bid, or bids repeatedly won by the same company).[124] There is consequently also considerable interest in the development of data analytics to enable counter-fraud and anti-corruption agencies to identify corruption and fraud risks.[125] Indeed, some agencies are seeking to build capacity for use of machine learning tools to identify fraud and corruption affecting public funds.[126] Further, some public agencies crosscheck, through computer-assisted audits, procurement expenditure with other government databases to identify atypical situations, such as conflicts of interest or personal relations between suppliers and public officials, inappropriate use of exemptions and waivers, substantial contractual amendments, or suspicious patterns of bidding which warrant further investigation.[127] The Government Transparency Institute also examines significant volumes of data sets of public procurement procedures from a number of countries and search for abnormal patterns.[128]

Nonetheless, as with bid rigging screens, the success of AI, or machine-based systems, is highly dependent on the availability of good-quality, and unbiased, procurement data. As, it may be difficult to ensure the availability of such data, some have cautioned against placing too much hope in, and emphasis on, these types of solutions and from their attracting attention away from use of, and building capacity for, more traditional mechanisms of corruption control.[129] Further, as already highlighted, screens are only likely to be able to 'flag' cases for closer examination by investigators, rather than providing concrete evidence of wrongdoing. Current screens—whether for bid rigging or corruption—only identify risks and cannot rule out the possibility of false positives or negatives.

c. Encouraging greater compliance through educating businesses
Throughout this book it is stressed that the success of any anti-corruption and anti-cartel policy depends not only on the ability to detect and sanction infractions

---

[124] L. Silveira, '4 Technologies Helping Us to Fight Corruption', *World Economic Forum* (18 April 2016), available at https://www.weforum.org/agenda/2016/04/4-technologies-helping-us-to-fight-corruption/.

[125] I. Adam and M. Fazekas, 'Big Data Analytics as a Tool for Auditors to Identify and Prevent Fraud and Corruption in Public Procurement' (2019) 2 *European Court of Auditors Journal* 172–9; European Parliament, 'Proceedings of the Workshop on Use of Big Data and AI in Fighting Corruption and Misuse of Public Funds – Good Practice, Ways Forward and How to Integrate New Technology into Contemporary Control Framework' (2021).

[126] See, e.g., OECD Public Governance Reviews, *Countering Public Grant Fraud in Spain: Machine Learning for Assessing Risks and Targeting Control Activities* (OECD Publishing, 2021).

[127] OECD, n. 126 and see OECD, 'Integrity Review of Brazil—Managing Risks for a Cleaner Public Service' (2012), available at http://dx.doi.org/10.1787/9789264119321-en.

[128] See, The Government Transparency Institute, available at http://www.govtransparency.eu/.

[129] Sanchez-Graells, n. 93.

optimally, but also on its ability to prevent it. It has been seen that a wide range of policies, including ethical rules, rules on conflicts and asset disclosure, the building of a culture of integrity within organizations from the top, and effective internal and external control mechanisms, may contribute to the success of a system. Further, outreach by law enforcement agencies to businesses and the wider community will also contribute to the successful creation of a procompetitive procurement system if it encourages greater compliance with the rules.[130] Agencies should therefore play more prominent roles in informing and educating businesses about the laws, the immoral nature of the conduct they seek to prevent, the consequences of infringing them, and the benefits of compliance. Indeed, it seems clear that many companies still need to protect themselves much better from high-profile scandals, and consequent loss of reputation from employees breaching the rules (especially where the breach results because they are ignorant of laws or do not understand them fully).[131]

Many systems could also consider increasing incentives for firms to be proactive both about complying with the law and seeking out contraventions, through the introduction of strong and comprehensive competition and anti-corruption compliance programmes[132] backed by audits, monitoring, reviews, risk assessments, and consequences for non-compliance to create a culture of compliance.[133] For example, in some jurisdictions the existence of compliance programmes may be taken into account by prosecutors when making charging decisions[134] or may impact on penalties.[135] Their existence may also be especially relevant in countries where

---

[130] On competition compliance generally, see A. Riley, A. Stephan, and A. Tubbs (eds), *Perspectives on Antitrust Compliance* (Concurrences, 2022).

[131] See, e.g., Ernst & Young, 'Integrity in the spotlight: the future of compliance', *15th Global Fraud Survey* (2018).

[132] For example, these could be required as a condition for public contracting. See, e.g., the 2021 OECD Anti-Bribery Recommendation, n. 32, Appendix II; the OECD, 'Good Practice Guidance on Internal Controls, Ethics, and Compliance' (adopted on 18 February 2010), available at https://www.oecd.org/daf/anti-bribery/44884389.pdf; and J. Murphy, 'Promoting Compliance with Competition Law: Do Compliance and Ethics Programs Have a Role to Play?' (2011) OECD Paper DAF/ COMP(2011).

[133] See 2021 OECD Anti-Bribery Recommendation, n. 32, Recommendation XXIII (accounting requirements, external audit, and internal controls, ethics, and compliance) and Annex 2.

[134] For example, in the US the DOJ offers incentives for compliance programmes, which are taken into account by prosecutors as part of every corporate charge recommendation, see Remarks of (then) Assistant Attorney General Makan Delrahim, New York University School of Law Program on Corporate Compliance and Enforcement, New York (11 July 2019), available at www.justice.gov/opa/speech/assistant-attorney-general-makan-delrahim-delivers-remarks-new-york-university-school-l-0; DOJ Antitrust Division, 'Evaluation of Corporate Compliance Programs in Criminal Antitrust Investigations' (July 2019) and US Sentencing Guidelines for Organizations.

[135] See, e.g., the position in Brazil where compliance programmes may be taken into account as a mitigating factor in enforcement of the Anti-Corruption Laws and where the competition authority, has issued Guidelines on Competition Compliance Programme which recognize that compliance programmes may lead to a reduction in monetary contributions imposed. See P.F. de Azevedo Silveira and P. de Andrade Baqueiro, 'Practical Perspectives from the Brazilian Competition Authority: Building an Institutional Framework for the Adoption of Antitrust Compliance' in Riley, Stephan, and Tubbs, n. 130 and Administrative Council for Economic Defense (CADE), 'Guidelines Competition Compliance Programs', available at http://en.cade.gov.br/topics/publications/guidelines/compliance-guidelines-final-version.pdf. For the view that to encourage a corruption-free corporate culture, prosecutors

offences exist for persons that fail to prevent infringements of anti-corruption or competition laws. Steps to increase compliance can also be imposed in settlement arrangements or as part of an exclusion or debarment arrangement.

Compliance tools cannot make an entity immune from misconduct but can help to prevent, detect, and mitigate violations. Like competition agencies and procurers, companies can use screens to identify the risk of malfeasance and to allow for targeted audits, more efficient monitoring of their own compliance regimes, and self-reporting of wrongdoing.[136] Firms can also consider how to counteract the range of factors that may motivate bribery or bid rigging by employees, for example, by changing how employees view this conduct, or by eliminating commission-based compensation structures or rigidly aggressive sale goals that might incentivize bribery.[137]

d. Effective penalties or remedies

Although repressive measures alone are insufficient to tackle corruption and collusion, the ability of a system to impose dissuasive penalties, sufficient to punish and deter infringements and to combat corruption incentives at whatever level they exist, is vital. A difficulty experienced in many countries is that the consequences of infringing anti-corruption and competition laws are not sufficiently severe to deter this highly profitable conduct, so relevant players act with relative impunity. In addition, therefore, to ensuring greater enforcement of anti-corruption and competition laws, it is also necessary that there is a threat of sanctions being imposed which would produce sufficient disutility to outweigh the benefits participants expect to gain from the prohibited activity. Sanctions need to be enough to account for the fact that they may not be imposed at all and, even if imposed, that they bite only after the gains had been realized.[138] Because the chance of detection and conviction of competition or bribery offences is normally well below one, sanctions imposed should therefore constitute a multiple of individual gains from the corrupt or collusive conduct.[139]

---

should give credit to companies that conduct rigorous compliance and that self-report violations and that this should be made clear in, for example, sentencing guidelines, see Heimann and Pieth, n. 29, 233.

[136] See Hüschelrath, n. 68, 524 and R.M Abrantes-Metz and A.D. Metz, 'Why Screening Is a "Must Have" Tool for Antitrust Compliance Programmes' in Riley, Stephan, and Tubbs, n. 130, Chapter 5 (noting that the DOJ's Antitrust Division explicitly considers whether screens and statistical analyses are elements of the corporation's antitrust compliance programme, see also US Sentencing Guidelines, § 8B2.1(b)(5)(A)) and, e.g., Chilean competition authority, FNE, 'Competition, Compliance Programs: Complying with Competition Law' (June 2012).

[137] See, e.g., A. Wrage, 'The Psychologies of Corruption', *The FCPA Blog* (8 May 2023).

[138] G.J. Werden, 'Sanctioning Cartel Activity: Let the Punishment Fit the Crime' (2009) 5(1) *European Competition Journal* 19; see also J.M. Connor, 'Recidivism Revealed: Private International Cartels 1999–2009' (2010) 6 *Competition Policy International* 101; C. Veljanovski, 'Cartel Fines in Europe: Law, Practice and Deterrence' (2007) 30 *World Competition* 65, 65.

[139] Rose-Ackerman and Palifka, n. 3, 209 and 213 ('If expected penalties do not increase along with the benefits of corruption for bribers and bribes, governments may be caught in a trap where high corruption levels beget high corruption levels').

112 TOWARDS A MORE COMPREHENSIVE APPROACH

Adversarial vs cooperative procedures. In Section C, the importance of agencies not overly relying on self-reporting regimes to detect illegal activity was discussed. Overuse of self-reporting, combined with settlement programmes, also risks reducing the punitive and deterrent effect of the law (as well as hindering its development),[140] extinguishing societal condemnation of the conduct and shielding companies from effective sanctions and debarment from procurement processes. They should therefore be used selectively, and sparingly.

Moving beyond corporate fines. Many jurisdictions are heavily reliant on corporate fines—ether civil or criminal—to sanction infringements of competition and even anti-corruption laws. Although high penalties may lower the incidence of the conduct (by reducing conduct which produces lower rewards), they are unlikely to have a deterrent effect on highly profitable conduct (it has been seen that a US court in FCPA proceedings found that USD 788 million of corrupt payments made by Odebrecht had secured procurement contracts leading to USD 3.3 billion profits). Rather, because the legal criteria for setting corporate fines in these situations frequently does not relate to the likely gain,[141] or the likelihood of detection, and is normally capped by the law—they may not be set at the optimal level.[142] There is a danger therefore that corporate fines are simply viewed by firms as a cost of doing business. Indeed, some studies reinforce the view that corporate fines for cartels are not the highest concern to companies[143] and may not deter recidivism.[144] In the EU, for example, where corporate fines are the European Commission's main weapon against cartels, a number of firms operating in chemical and electronics markets have been found to be involved in three or more commission cartel decisions (and some as many as nine).[145] This latter evidence has been argued to indicate that these cartels, rather than resulting from individual behaviour operated without the knowledge or help of senior management, may

---

[140] For example, in the US, there has been concern about the use of DPAs as they 'limit the punitive and deterrent value of the government's law enforcement efforts and extinguish the societal condemnation that should accompany criminal prosecution', D.M. Uhlmann, 'Deferred Prosecution and Non-Prosecution Agreements and the Erosion of Corporate Criminal Liability' (2013) 72(4) *Maryland Law Review* 1295, 1302.

[141] But see the discussion in Chapter 11 of the position in the US where fines may relate to the gain or losses resulting from the infringement.

[142] See 2021 OECD Anti-Bribery Recommendation, n. 32, Recommendation XV (recommending that sanctions against natural and legal persons for foreign bribery are transparent, effective, proportionate, and dissuasive in practice, including by taking into account the amounts of the bribe paid and the value of the profits or other benefits derived, and other mitigating or aggravating factors).

[143] See, e.g., Office of Fair Trading, 'Drivers of Compliance and Non-Compliance with Competition Law' (May 2010), available at https://assets.publishing.service.gov.uk/government/uploads/system/uploads/attachment_data/file/284405/oft1227.pdf.

[144] See, e.g., Connor, n. 138, 108–9; J.M. Connor and R.H. Lande, 'How High Do Cartels Raise Prices? Implications for Optimal Cartel Fines' (2005) 80 *Tulane Law Review* 513, 559–60 (but see M. Boyer and R. Kotchoni, 'How Much Do Cartel Overcharge?' *CIRANO* 2015-37); and J.M. Connor and R.H. Lande, 'The Prevalence and Injuriousness of Cartels Worldwide' in P. Whelan (ed.), *Elgar Research Handbook on Cartels* (Edward Elgar Publishing Ltd, 2023). See also W.P.J. Wils, 'Recidivism in EU Antitrust Enforcement: A Legal and Economic Analysis' (2012) 35 *World Competition* 5.

[145] See Marshall, n. 66, 331.

WEAKNESSES IN RELEVANT LAWS, OR THEIR APPLICATION   113

sometimes be embraced as part of the business model and profitmaking strategy of multiproduct and multinational firms.[146]

Consequently, it may be necessary to ensure or bolster additional controls, including sanctions for individuals that play a role in instigating, or even not preventing, infringements (such as fines, disqualification, or imprisonment);[147] and non-monetary sanctions for corporations, such as debarment or exclusion.

Individual accountability. As with corporate fines, there is concern as to whether individual fines may be sufficient to deter, and whether they can be made truly unindemnifiable and unshiftable. In the corruption context, for example, the different scenarios surrounding corrupt behaviour, involving recipients of bribes (who may have instigated the payment or being drawn into others' illegal schemes) and payers of bribes (who may have paid to get favourable treatment or only paid to be treated fairly), means that the question of which individuals should be sanctioned, and by how much, to ensure optimal deterrence is complex. Ideally penalties should be able to connect to the benefits each individual receives. 'To deter bribery, at least one side of the corrupt transaction must face penalties that reflect its own gains.'[148] The reality is, however, that in most jurisdictions legal penalties bear only a weak relationship to deterrence priorities, providing for symmetric penalties which are not linked to either the social harm of corruption (or supplier collusion) or the private benefits obtained by those who engage in it, meaning that large-scale corrupt deals may only be slightly deterred.[149] It follows from the above that even if sanctions are significant, they are likely to remain below their 'optimal' level.

An equilibrium with low corruption therefore requires an active law enforcement strategy, penalties to be tied to expected gains and, ideally, the threat of non-monetary penalties such as director disqualification or imprisonment. Indeed, bribery is a criminal offence in many jurisdictions and, US enforcers—working with and through organizations such as the OECD and the ICN—have not been shy about advocating their view that imprisonment of individuals is the most effective deterrent to cartel behaviour.[150]

---

[146] Marshall, n. 66, 331.

[147] See, e.g., Office of Fair Trading, n. 143, 6; A. Hoel, 'Crime Does Not Pay but Hard-Core Cartel Conduct May: Why it Should be Criminalised' (2008) 16 *Trade Practices Law Journal* 102. Individual sanctions do not necessarily have to be criminal in nature, A. Khan, 'Rethinking Sanctions for Breaching EU Competition Law: Is Director Disqualification the Answer?' (2012) 35(1) *World Competition* 77

[148] Rose-Ackerman and Palifka, n. 3, 209. In the US, for example, maximum penalties for corruption are symmetric (for those who make and accept corrupt payments), judges are, under Federal Sentencing Guidelines, able to incorporate the benefits attained into their calculation of the fine, Rose-Ackerman and Palifka, n. 3, 211.

[149] Rose-Ackerman and Palifka, n. 3, 212–13, see n. 139.

[150] OECD, 'Roundtable on Promoting Compliance with Competition Law', DAF/COMP/WD(2011)38 (21 June 2011), 5–6.

114   TOWARDS A MORE COMPREHENSIVE APPROACH

In the cartel sphere, an acute problem is that even though more than thirty jurisdictions have introduced criminal offences for those involved in cartels or bid rigging, significant obstacles to successful criminalization have arisen. Not only are criminal cartel cases—because of the higher standard of proof—more difficult to establish, but in many countries it has proved difficult to persuade juries to convict persons or to persuade courts to imprison offenders.[151] Criminalization has not generally proved fruitful where introduced principally as a mechanism for creating deterrence, but without a concerted attempt to build or shape attitudes or an understanding of why criminalization is justified—in particular, what is morally reprehensible about cartel conduct. In the US, in contrast, the DOJ generated support for its cartel enforcement program by targeting bid rigging cases for prosecution,[152] the subset of cartel activity where a lack of good faith is perhaps most evident—especially if a Certificate of Independent Bid Determination (CIBD)[153] has been required and signed. Further, many successful criminal convictions have ensued in Germany where the criminal offence is reserved exclusively for bid rigging activity (and does not extend to other cartels).[154] It seems therefore that a competition authority struggling with this predicament could try to generate support for a criminal programme by bringing carefully selected bid rigging cases which have a particularly acute impact on the procurement of important public goods and services. Alternatively, or additionally, to criminal liability, however, civil liability might provide a less complex mechanism for increasing individual deterrence, by providing not only for fines but also, for example, the imposition of disqualification orders[155] on responsible individuals.

Another solution could be to expand the category of actors to be held responsible for corruption and competition offences, to encompass not only individuals directly involved but also others, such as financial intermediaries and banks that act as accomplices (e.g. frequently used in grand corruption schemes by corporations), or managers, lawyers, underwriters, outside directors, or accountants who have the capacity to influence firm behaviour and to ensure compliance with the law.[156]

---

[151] See A. Jones and R. Williams, 'The UK Response to the Global Effort Against Cartels: Is Criminalization Really the Solution?' (2014) *Journal of Antitrust Enforcement* 100.

[152] See Chapter 6.

[153] OECD, 'Tool: Certificate of Independent Bid Determination' (2009) 2, available at https://www.oecd.org/governance/procurement/toolbox/search/certificate-independent-bid-determination.pdf.

[154] F. Wagner-von Papp, 'What If All Bid Riggers Went to Prison and Nobody Noticed? Criminal Antitrust Law Enforcement in Germany' in C. Beaton-Wells and A. Ezrachi (eds), *Criminalising Cartels: Critical Studies of an International Regulatory Movement* (Hart Publishing, 2011) 157, 167, 172.

[155] See Khan, n. 147, 78, and see, e.g., discussion of the position in the UK (Chapter 5) and Brazil (Chapter 7). One difficulty is that disqualification orders generally only take effect in the jurisdiction in which they are imposed.

[156] See, e.g., one US bill stated to be designed to address the endemic corruption that has helped to fuel Russia's authoritarian regime and military aggression, is the Enablers Act (H.R. 5525). If enacted, this Act would require professional service providers who serve as gatekeepers to the US financial system to perform full anti-money-laundering due diligence on prospective clients.

Debarment or exclusion. These regimes may operate both to prevent those that have committed infringements of anti-corruption or competition laws from participating in public tender exercises and to deter firms from engaging in prohibited activity. Despite their laudable aims, it is not clear that many debarment regimes achieve their objectives, as in many states enforcement tends to be unpredictable and relatively few corporations are debarred in practice.[157] This could be because accessible registers for recording debarred companies are not kept, because guidance indicating how debarment provisions are to be implemented and complexities overcome is unavailable or limited, or because relevant authorities are reluctant to exercise debarment powers, perhaps because they are fearful of exacerbating procurement difficulties that already exist in concentrated markets or they believe that conviction under bribery or competition laws is already punishment enough.

Indeed, there is some concern that certain mandatory debarment regimes may be too blunt, especially if they do not allow the sanction to be tailored appropriately and proportionately to the offence committed—e.g. if they impose lengthy, mandatory debarment periods on contractors regardless of cooperation or the nature.[158] Such regimes may compromise the viability of the debarred company, have a chilling effect on self-reporting, cooperation and future compliance, and encourage prosecutors to pursue lesser offences or, in lieu of prosecution, to resolve cases through DPAs or other settlements in order to ensure that the debarment regime does not get triggered. The system could thus harm the debarred company (and its employees) as well as the taxpayer, especially through reducing competition in affected markets and undermining the goals of the procurement system. Some thus consider that it is 'unworkable to permanently debar large contract firms', that inflexible, mandatory debarment systems are counterproductive to the goal of decreasing corruption and increasing corporate compliance, and advocate that, as in the US, a flexible, non-punitive regime should be available—debarment sanctions should be imposed 'only in the public interest for the Government's protection and not for the purposes of punishment'.[159]

To be successful, therefore, an effective debarment regime would seem to require: (i) flexibility to suspend or debar contractors which may threaten the integrity of procurement process, whilst preventing overly draconian and unnecessary debarments; (ii) a register of debarred companies to be instated and easily

---

[157] E. Auriol and T. Søreide, 'An Economic Analysis of Debarment' (2017) 50 *International Review of Law and Economics* 36–7. See also example S. Hawley, 'Excluding Corrupt Bidders from Public Procurement: Real Threat or Pipe Dream? The UK Experience', Conference Paper (June 2017), available at https://drive.google.com/file/d/12-nQ10zHtSm3WiZ0FLLhlw_G7HPt_l0l/view.

[158] See, e.g., J. Tillipman and S. Block, 'Canada's Integrity Regime: The Corporate Grim Reaper' (2022) 53 *George Washington International Law Review* 475 and L.O. Youngman, 'Deterring Compliance: The Effect of Mandatory Debarment under the European Union Procurement Directives on Domestic Foreign Corrupt Practices Act Prosecutions' (2013) 42(2) *Public Contract Law Journal* 411.

[159] US Federal Acquisition System Regulation, 9.402, see also n. 158 and Chapter 6.

116 TOWARDS A MORE COMPREHENSIVE APPROACH

accessible to all procurement officials; and (iii) the publication of clear policy guidance for procurers addressing implementation issues and how complications are to be managed (e.g. what the scope and length of debarment should be, how debarment should be managed in concentrated markets, how self-cleaning is to be established, and when discretionary debarment powers should be exercised—and by whom[160]). Although the multilateral development banks (MDBs), for example, have developed relatively sophisticated sanction systems with differentiating sanction scales and conditional as well as permanent debarment, not all national regimes have done so. Greater, and principled, use of debarment powers would, however, protect the integrity of procurement processes and send a clear message that access to public procurement markets requires full compliance with the law.

Damages and recovery of bribes and the proceeds of bribery. Damages and recovery mechanisms may increase deterrents to illegal activity whilst also ensuring compensation of victims or recovery of unlawfully paid sums. Many anti-corruption systems allow enforcement agencies to ensure that illicit bribes (or the proceedings of corruption) are recovered both from natural and legal persons;[161] damages may also be available to the Treasury.

Further, many antitrust systems allow victims of infringements (including bid rigging offences) to bring actions for damages. Nonetheless, in the competition law sphere at least, there are relatively few jurisdictions in which private actions for damages are routinely lodged in relation to bid rigging that has been exposed or which result in final judgments.[162] Such actions may be unattractive as not only are damages actions lengthy, expensive, and complex to bring and win, but procurers may have few incentives to seek recovery of lost public money and may be unwilling to sour relations with contractors they may have to continue to conduct business with.[163] If brought regularly, however, it is clear that actions for damages would allow a government to both claw back taxpayer money lost due to inflated contract prices and raise the stakes for those breaching competition law. Claims may be facilitated by, for example, giving standing to public prosecutors (this is the case in Brazil, see Chapter 7), or by other features of the system. In Japan, where private litigation has formed 'part of the enforcement arsenal from the very beginning of Japanese antitrust law', a preponderance of private lawsuits have been brought against bid riggers, including some by residents on behalf of their local government.[164] In the US, where a sophisticated system of private antitrust enforcement

---

[160] For example, where infringers provide compensation to those harmed as a result of the wrong-doing and adopt measures to prevent future violations.

[161] See also 2021 OECD Anti-Bribery Recommendation, n. 32, Recommendation XVI.

[162] Even if final judgments are low, however, this would not reflect cases that are settled.

[163] Such proceedings may also be complicated if a member of the public authority was involved in, or facilitated, the cartel.

[164] S. Vande Walle, 'Private Enforcement of Antitrust Law in Japan: An Empirical Analysis' (2011) 8 *Competition Law Review* 7, 7.

WEAKNESSES IN RELEVANT LAWS, OR THEIR APPLICATION 117

exists,[165] the Clayton Act specifically allows the government (and states) to recover treble damages in cases of harm caused to it as a result of antitrust infringements, including collusive bidding (Sections 4A and 4). Between 1980 and 2009, however, only five cases were filed under Section 4A, leading to concern that taxpayer money is being left on the table.[166] As a result, the DOJ pledged to revitalize Section 4A's use: 'Going forward, the Division will exercise 4A authority to seek compensation for taxpayers when the government has been the victim of an antitrust violation. We hope that these efforts will also deter future violations.'[167]

In the EU, full compensation must, in principle, also be available to victims of antitrust violations.[168] Although private damages actions were initially slow to develop, such actions are beginning to play an increasingly important part in the EU enforcement framework, and an EU directive sets out rules designed to facilitate such claims in the national courts.[169] Studies conducted of cartel damages claims in EU Member States between 2017 and 2021 indicate that private actions are growing, noting that some entities now bringing damages claims are local authorities or municipality procurers, such as those in Hungary, Denmark, and France.[170] The 2018 edition finds that in nearly two-thirds of the claims analysed 'the allegedly affected purchases resulted from tendering processes' (and that 57 per cent of the claims were brought by local authorities, publicly owned companies, or central governments) and provides examples of cases where damages have been awarded to victims of bid rigging. In one Danish case, a municipality was awarded compensation from bid riggers (calculated by reference to the payments made to a losing tenderer by a bid winner as compensation).

The European Commission itself also sought damages against members of the Elevators and Escalators cartel for losses suffered as a result of the bid rigging in relation to the installation of elevators and escalators in Commission buildings.[171] Although the action before the Belgian courts was rejected on the grounds that the Commission had failed to produce sufficient evidence of loss, in the future,

---

[165] See, e.g., A. Jones, 'Private Enforcement of EU Competition Law: A Comparison with, and Lessons from, the US' in M. Bergström, M. Iacovides, and M. Strand (eds), *Harmonising EU Competition Litigation: The New Directive and Beyond* (Hart Publishing, 2016).

[166] See H. First, 'Lost in Conversation: The Compensatory Function of Antitrust Law' (2010) New York University Center for Law, Economics, and Organization Law & Economics Research Paper Series, Working Paper No. 10-14.

[167] See Delrahim, n. 134.

[168] Case C-453/99, *Courage Ltd v Crehan* EU:C:2001:465 and Cases C-295/04 to 298/04, *Manfredi v Lloyd Adriatico Assicurazioni SpA* EU:C:2006:461.

[169] Council Directive 2014/104 on certain rules governing actions for damages under national law for infringements of the competition law provisions of the Member States of the EU, Article 1, [2014] OJ L349/1.

[170] J-F. Laborde, 'Cartel Damages Claims in Europe: How Courts Have Assessed Overcharges' (2021) 3 *Concurrences* 232–42; (2018 edn), *Concurrences Review* 2 (February 2019); and *Concurrences Review* 36 (February 2017). In 2023, a regional Spanish healthcare provider also lodged an action claiming EUR 500 million as a result of price fixing by adult diaper manufacturers, see 'Public Health Service Lodges Spain's Largest-ever Antitrust Damages Claim', *Global Competition Review* (10 February 2023).

[171] COMP/38.823, *PO/Elevators and Escalators*, Commission Decision of 21 February 2007, on appeal see, e.g., C-557/12, *Kone AG v ÖBB-Infrastruktur AG* EU:C:2014:1317.

118 TOWARDS A MORE COMPREHENSIVE APPROACH

this type of action might be facilitated by provisions set out in the Damages Directive,[172] especially on disclosure, which have now been implemented within Belgian Law.[173]

In Germany, a number of damages actions have also been brought by state authorities hurt by bid rigging or other anti-competitive conduct.[174] For example, the local transportation undertaking of the city of Darmstadt and Deutsche Bahn, relying on a competition law infringement finding by the Bunderskartellamt, successfully sued members of a rail manufacturer cartel (Schienenkartell) for damages resulting from overpriced rails and track switches.[175] In addition, Deutsche Bahn[176] and the Cities of Essen, Nürnberg, Dortmund, Bielefeld, and Köln, relying on the EU Commission's elevators and escalators cartel decision,[177] successfully sought damages from cartel members.[178]

e. Separation of powers and independence of enforcement agencies, monitoring agencies, and the judiciary

Separation of powers, the presence of independent monitoring and enforcement organizations, and an independent and impartial judiciary are of central importance if constraints are to be imposed on the public procurement activity of politicians, government bodies, and powerful entities.[179] In contrast, weaker institutions are unlikely to be able to provide the control required. Difficulties thus arise if, for example, politicians impose pressure on law enforcement agencies not to investigate cases or if leaders dismantle, or weaken, checks and balances in a democratic system (e.g. through backsliding on adherence to rule-of-law principles).

Where this is the case, steps may be required to ensure the impartiality of agencies and judges, their independence in relation to the legislature and executive, and their ability to exercise their functions autonomously, unconstrained by external, especially political, interventions. Where strong and independent law enforcement agencies and

---

[172] Directive 2014/104/EU [2014] OJ L349/1, see n. 169 and text.

[173] See J. Marcos Ramos and D. Muheme, 'The Brussels Court Judgment in *Commission v Elevators Manufacturers*, or the Story of How the Commission Lost an Action for Damages Based on Its Own Infringement Decision' (2015) 36 *ECLR* 384, 384.

[174] See, e.g., OECD, 'Relationship between Public and Private Antitrust Enforcement' (2015), DAF/COMP/WP3/WD(2015).

[175] See Case No. 2-06 O 464/14, Landgericht District Court 30 March, 2016, Frankfurt am Main.

[176] See Case No. 16 O 193/11, Landgericht District Court 6 August 2013, Berlin.

[177] See Marcos Ramos and Muheme, n. 173.

[178] See Press Release, Bundeskartellamt, 'Bundeskartellamt Imposes Multi-Million Euro Fines Against Manufacturers of Fire-Fighting Vehicles' (10 February 2011)—explaining that manufacturers of fire-fighting vehicles were found to have infringed competition law.

[179] Rose-Ackerman and Palifka, n. 3, 374. In developed democracies, strong and independent enforcement institutions and separation of powers may better provide 'checks and balances' capable of curbing wrongdoing by other government institutions or powerful elites or private corporations. For a critique of the assumption that checks and balances are effective in curbing corruption, see L. Da Ros and M.M. Taylor, 'Checks and Balances: The Concept and Its Implications for Corruption' (2021) 17(2) *Revista Direito GV*, available at https://doi.org/10.1590/2317-6172202120.

judges are not in place, and checks and balances are limited, competition and anti-corruption strategies are of course unlikely to succeed (see further Section C). In such cases, domestic and international pressure may be essential to encourage meaningful political and institutional reform, commitment to the rule of law and the curbing of wrongdoing by government institutions and powerful corporations.

iii. Siloed regimes

a. Policy coordination—national and international cooperation and coordination

The distinct but complementary nature of bid rigging and bribery in public procurement has already been flagged. The interlinked nature of these problems highlights the importance of agencies working together to achieve their unified objective. At the public procurement stage, negative coordination[180] is required to ensure, for example, that measures designed to ensure the internal integrity of the system (such as transparency provisions) do not inadvertently increase the risk of external threats to it from collusion. Further, positive coordination[181] ensures that procurers and agencies work better in pursuit of their interrelated remits and achieve greater mutual understanding and can assist one another.

In many jurisdictions, however, public procurement, competition, and anti-corruption law operate as fairly siloed regimes, with limited interaction between relevant agencies. Greater collaboration may therefore ensure negative and positive coordination through, for example, memorandums of understanding, networks, advocacy,[182] training, outreach, placements, and exchange of staff, collaboration, cooperation, and the creation of knowledge sharing systems, which allow, subject to confidentiality rules, information uncovered or gathered by one authority to be shared or brought to the attention of another. Indeed, legislation or interagency agreements providing for transfer of lawfully obtained evidence could ensure that important evidence uncovered by one agency is not discarded simply because it does not fit with its powers, remit, or enforcement priorities.[183]

---

[180] Negative coordination occurs 'when decisions made in one program or organization consider those made in others and attempt to avoid conflict', see, e.g., B.G. Peters, 'The Challenge of Policy Coordination' (2018) 1(1) *Policy Design and Practice* 1, 2.

[181] Aiming to find ways to cooperate on solutions that can benefit all involved, Peters, n. 180.

[182] More advanced and sophisticated approaches to competition advocacy will also help to ensure that procurers are trained in the operation of tender processes that are likely to be prone to collusion and that competition agencies can also warn procurers when processes are not so drawn up, for example, where they are presented too regularly or incorporate inappropriately tailored transparency requirements.

[183] See, e.g., M. Jenkins, 'Interagency Coordination Mechanisms: Improving the Effectiveness of National Anti-Corruption Efforts', *Transparency International* (18 January 2019). This is important as evidence of corrupt payments may come to light in an antitrust investigation or vice versa, see, e.g., S. Braga, C.P. Conniff, and M.S. Popofsky, 'The Anticorruption and Antitrust Interface', *CPI Antitrust Chronicle* (1 February 2012).

120 TOWARDS A MORE COMPREHENSIVE APPROACH

Further, the creation of a special task force to investigate unlawful distortions to public procurement processes could be considered and beneficial, for example, a specialized police unit targeting corruption in the public sector or a specialized unit focusing on bid rigging (such as the US Department of Justice's Procurement Collusion Strike Force discussed in Chapter 6). In some jurisdictions, competition agencies, in addition to training public procurement bodies, have a procurement remit.[184] Indeed, it has been seen that greater oversight of procurement, especially that occurring at the local level, is highly desirable.

In addition, and particularly as markets have become more globalized and multinational entities have proliferated, international cooperation between competition and anti-corruption agencies may facilitate investigations. This could be achieved through the conclusion of treaties (including mutual legal assistance treaties (MLATs)) or other arrangements governing mutual cooperation (for investigations, prosecution, sanctions, and settlements[185]) in relation to transnational cases.[186] These may facilitate obtaining of foreign evidence and other assistance (e.g. serving documents, sharing of information, taking testimony, requesting searches, provision of evidence, extradition, and the identification, freezing, seizure, confiscation, and recovery of the proceeds of bribery of public officials)[187] and facilitate coordinated responses.

Indeed, the United Nations Convention against Corruption (UNCAC), recognizing the strictly territorial nature of law enforcement, sets out extensive and detailed provisions relating to international cooperation in criminal matters and requires states to combat convention offences through mutual legal assistance in investigations, prosecutions, and judicial proceedings.[188] The OECD also facilitates bi-annual meetings between enforcers, and both international agencies provide superstructures to aid national enforcement systems and help governments to build capacity and strengthen democratic institutions. Although these developments are significant, in 2021 the OECD has recommended that member countries take further steps to ensure cooperation and coordination sufficient to combat bribery of foreign officials through the development of international and regional law enforcement networks (involving member and non-member countries).[189] They should thus ensure that they have measures in place allowing them to make

---

[184] See the position in Ukraine, Chapter 9. This is also the case in Germany, Sweden, Denmark, and the Czech Republic, see A. Sanchez-Graells, *Public Procurement* (Hart Publishing, 2nd edn, 2015) 447.

[185] See discussion of Odebrecht settlement with US, Brazilian, and Swiss authorities in Chapter 7.

[186] Competition authorities also habitually work together, through the ICN and other formal and informal bilateral and multilateral arrangements, to combat cartels and to coordinate searches and investigations across jurisdictions.

[187] During 'Operation Car Wash', many legal assistance requests were made by Brazilian authorities, to Swiss and US authorities which were instrumental in advancing the investigation, see Chapter 7.

[188] G.A. Res. 58/4, United Nations Convention against Corruption (31 October 2003).

[189] See 2021 OECD Anti-Bribery Recommendation, n. 32, Recommendations XIX.

full use of MLATs, and the conclusion of new MLATs, or bilateral agreements or arrangements.

In both the spheres of anti-corruption and antitrust law, the cross-border challenges create a demand for greater collective action across nations.

b. Laws acknowledging the interaction between corruption and bid rigging

Many jurisdictions do not have legislation that explicitly acknowledges the interaction between corruption and bid rigging. Rather, these types of conduct are frequently treated as distinct offences (civil and/or criminal competition offences and civil and/or criminal bribery offences) governed by different regimes and enforced by different agencies. Where the conduct occurs together in the public procurement context, this will mean that separate investigations involving different agencies and prosecutors are likely to be required, and that coordination issues arise. In later chapters of this book, it is seen that this can cause considerable complexity and difficulties in some countries, both for agencies and firms, and may mean that not all of the elements of the conduct get probed. For example, a competition authority may investigate bid rigging between the tenderers but may not have the power to investigate any evidence of corruption.[190] Similarly, not all enforcers of anti-corruption laws can proceed against bid rigging (unless the conduct is covered by anti-corruption laws, or it involves fraud or a criminal cartel offence).[191]

Complexities are likely to be reduced and enforcement facilitated where the same agency can probe both offences (in the US, the DOJ can investigate infringements of antitrust, bribery, and other criminal laws) or where law enforcement agencies have advanced mechanisms for sharing evidence[192] or have formal co-operation mechanisms in place.[193] These formal cooperation devices can achieve synergies, ensure that operational intelligence exposed in one investigation can be

---

[190] In some jurisdictions, it is theoretically possible for competition agencies that uncover bid rigging involving procurement officials to find the procurer or procurement agency to have infringed competition laws by acting as a facilitator to the cartel, see, e.g., Case C-194/14 P, *AC-Treuhand AG v Commission* EU:C:2015:717. But in the EU, the procurer will only be caught by the competition law rules if it is an 'undertaking'—an entity engaged in economic activity, which most individuals are not, see Case C-205/03 P, *FENIN v Commission* EU:C:2006:453.

[191] MDBs adopt a more holistic approach to bid rigging, inquiring into both vertical and horizontal elements and sanctioning both, but they lack the investigative powers and techniques of competition and anti-corruption agencies. Even if MDBs are more willing to impose sanctions for both corruption and collusion, they are therefore less able to expose it.

[192] For example, where enforcers or anti-corruption law aid competition agencies that (1) may not have access to the information to trigger an initial investigation and (2) tend to have more limited evidence-gathering powers than criminal justice agencies.

[193] See, e.g., J. Pecman, 'Cooperation between Anti-Corruption and Competition Authorities', *Government of Canada* (14 June 2016), available at http://www.competitionbureau.gc.ca/eic/site/cb-bc.nsf/eng/04114.html (discussing Canada's increasing cooperation with law enforcement agencies and procurement authorities on corruption and bid rigging investigations); and OECD Roundtable on Collusion and Corruption in Public Procurement, DAF/COMP/GF(2010)6 (15 October 2010).

122 TOWARDS A MORE COMPREHENSIVE APPROACH

used in the other, and improve the chance that all misconduct in public procurement is uncovered and prosecuted.[194]

In some jurisdictions, the link between bid rigging and corruption is explicitly recognized in legislation. For example, in Japan 'dango', or bid rigging in public tendering, has for a long time been a core focus of criminal competition law enforcement.[195] However, growing concern arose that the laws did not reach facilitators or procurement officials, who were regularly found to have been involved, or even to have played a central role, in such arrangements.[196] In 2002, therefore, legislation was adopted specifically outlawing conduct that promotes and aides bid rigging (e.g. through determining the winner or disclosing information).[197] This legislation is enforced by the Japan Fair Trade Commission (JFTC), which has the power to demand procuring departments to investigate the issue, publish the outcome of the investigation, and take action against officials found guilty (e.g. through claims for damages or disciplinary action).[198] Where involvement by officials is found, procuring departments must also implement improvement measures that will eliminate the illegal activity.[199] The law has been argued to have established 'a unique system under which the government procuring offices introduce measures to make public tendering system more competitive under the scrutiny of the [JFTC]'.[200] Indeed, the 2002 law has been enforced in a number of cases in the construction and engineering industries.[201] In these cases, bidders and public officials were found to have worked closely together and interacted frequently, especially in tight-knit local communities or where ex-officials moved to work for bidding companies.

C. Combatting Endemic, or Systemic, Corruption

The discussion above proposes mechanisms designed not only to prevent corruption and collusion, but also to detect and punish it when it does occur and to deter future infringements. Evidence suggests that these mechanisms, including more

---

[194] See OECD, n. 193, 31–2 and speech of R. Alford, Deputy Assistant Attorney General, Antitrust Division, US DOJ, 'Antitrust Enforcement and the Fight against Corruption' (3 October 2017), 8.

[195] The legislation was adopted in recognition of the lacuna, and of the especially strong temptation that exists in Japan for procurement officials to become involved in bid rigging, see Wakui, n. 10, 42–3 (noting that almost half of the JFTC's 134 cases in the fiscal years 2006–2012 were related to bid rigging in public procurement).

[196] In 2000, for example, government officials were found to have played a central role in bid rigging in construction contracts procured by the Hokkaido prefecture government, but the JFTC was powerless to sanction their conduct, Japanese Fair Trade Commission, 'Annual Report' (2000), 6.

[197] Act on Elimination and Prevention of Involvement in Bid Rigging, etc. and Punishments for Acts by Employees that Harm Fairness of Bidding, Law No. 101 of 2002 (Japan).

[198] See Wakui, n. 10, 46.

[199] Wakui, n. 10, 46, see also Law No. 101 of 2002, n. 197, Article 3, § 4.

[200] Wakui, n. 10, 43.

[201] See OECD, 'Competition Law and Policy in Japan' (2002) 8–9.

and better law enforcement (a big enforcement push), have merit and can work to control corruption in some countries, especially where the problems are individualistic, ethical universality is the norm, and strong democratic institutions are in place which are led by determined political leaders with the will to challenge corruption. In other situations, however, it can be difficult to make them occur, 'take root and achieve real change',[202] even where reforms are based on international best practices.[203] This may be the case where the behaviour is institutionalized, particularism is embedded in the culture, executive, and legislative branches, and where it affects legislative activities and appointments in, and the operation of, the civil service, ministries, the judiciary, and public or state-owned entities. In these scenarios, a government may fail to deliver public integrity and politics and institutional resistance are likely to block or manipulate new rules that would undermine the advantages to the political and business elite of the prevailing system and the informal power they hold. 'Both empirical and theoretical analyses have cast doubt on whether the standard elements of anti-corruption law, namely, explicit legal prohibitions on corrupt activity enforced by impartial law enforcement agencies and courts, are effective responses to systemic corruption.'[204]

A core problem thus stems from the fact that an approach centred on prevention, deterrence including through invigorated law enforcement, is predicated on the fact that the corruption results from a principal–agent problem, where an agent, entrusted to act on behalf of a principal, acts unlawfully and against established norms by abusing or misusing its public office for private gain. Under this model, corruption, like supplier collusion, is primarily combatted through minimizing opportunities for wrongdoing, changing incentives, facing corrupt actors to ensure that staying away from corruption is in their self-interest (by adopting stringent laws and using law enforcement to detect, punish, and deter the conduct), and by better aligning their interests with those of their principals. This approach—relying on acting against persons motivated by, for example, greed or need, and behaving as a rational self-interested utility maximizer—may be rendered impossible or thwarted by players that are not independent, or otherwise ineffective where corruption is widespread, persistent, self-reinforcing, and part of the system itself and where a 'collective action' problem exists.[205] Indeed, the policy solutions described in the sections above depend on an ethical principal, whilst 'in most systemically corrupt systems, it is the agents at the top—the presumed

---

[202] See generally, R.I. Roberg (ed.), 'Anticorruption: How to Beat Back Political & Corporate Graft' (2018) 147(3) *Dædalus*, Summer 2018 edition.

[203] For example, in the 1990s, Japan introduced changes to its public procurement system, to make it more open and competitive, while boosting law enforcement against collusion, but bid rigging persisted, See Rose-Ackerman and Palifka, n. 3, 155–6.

[204] K.E. Davis, 'Anti-Corruption Law and Systemic Corruption: The Role of Direct Responses' (2021) 17(2) *Revista Direito GV* e2129, 2 and Mungiu-Pipiidi, *Rethinking Corruption*, n. 26, Chapter 2.

[205] See B. Rothstein, 'Anti-Corruption: The Indirect "Big Bang" Approach' (2011) 18(2) *Review of International Political Economy* 228, 234–6.

124 TOWARDS A MORE COMPREHENSIVE APPROACH

principals—who earn most of the rents from corruption. Obviously, such principals will have little motivation to change the incentives for their opportunistic agents who are engaged in corruption.'[206]

Thus, in societies where corruption is a norm, or the standard operating procedure, where a legitimate social contract between citizens and the state[207] does not exist, and where actors hold deeply engrained beliefs that others will act corruptly, actors will be disincentivized from acting in a principled manner, especially if they also believe that corruption will not be investigated or sanctioned—citizens simply accept that they will have to pay bribes and that there is no point in reporting corruption or acting otherwise.[208] Corrupt behaviour patterns may consequently be sustained by all key players, including enforcement officials, and corruption may be perceived by actors to be persistent and necessary to compete and operate. In such situations, corruption is not entirely motivated by utility maximization, but by what actors perceive will be the most likely behaviour or strategy of others, and what is expected or required. As a result, initiatives which have been successful in some jurisdictions by incentivizing changes in behaviour may be impossible— because the government systems that should prevent corruption are the ones used to enable it—or ineffective because they tend to focus on a small number of corrupt actors, are dependent on the initiative of incorruptible legal officials or independent enforcement agents and judges, and are designed to shape incentives not norms. Indeed, 'despite a number of large-scale "attacks" … corruption has proved itself to be a very resilient, often well-organized, and -entrenched enemy'.[209] Core questions, therefore, are how can corruption, which is institutionalized, highly persistent, and highly profitable for those involved, be controlled and how can beliefs that bribes must be paid be changed in a way which will break the cycle and set in train a virtuous spiral of change through a more fundamental or revolutionary alteration of incentives and expectations?[210]

In these circumstances, some are wary about direct legal responses (based closely on principal–agent theory and attacking corrupt behaviour head on with increased control, stricter punishments (especially for big fish)) as a mechanism

---

[206] B. Rothstein, 'Fighting Systemic Corruption: The Indirect Strategy' (2018) 147(3) *Dædalus* 35, 36.

[207] A set of agreements on mutual roles and responsibilities, see World Bank Report, *Social Contracts for Development: Bargaining, Contention, and Social Inclusion in Sub-Saharan Africa* (World Bank Group, 2021), or where a mutual understanding exists, based on principles of meritocracy and impartiality, as to what the state can expect from citizens and citizens can expect from the state; see B. Rothstein, *Controlling Corruption: The Social Contract Approach* (Oxford University Press, 2021), referring to J. Rawls, *A Theory of Justice* (Harvard University Press, 1971).

[208] See, e.g., L.D. Carson and M. Mota Prado, 'Using Institutional Multiplicity to Address Corruption as a Collective Action Problem: Lessons from the Brazilian Case' (2016) 62 *Quarterly Review of Economics and Finance* 56–8.

[209] Rothstein, n. 206, 36.

[210] See A. Mungiu-Pippidi, 'Seven Steps to Control of Corruption: The Road Map' (2018) 147(3) *Dædalus* 20, 23. See also the '*We Continue the Change Alliance*', which has been seeking to change norms and fight corruption in Bulgaria, K. Petkov, 'Bulgaria's Window of Opportunity to Break Systemic Corruption', *The FCPA Blog* (21 July 2022).

COMBATTING ENDEMIC, OR SYSTEMIC, CORRUPTION   125

for solving the problem.[211] Rather, it is feared that such an approach may be over-whelmed, subverted, or paralysed by corruption,[212] suggesting that an indirect approach aimed at disrupting the moral equilibrium and building a new social contract—through systems directed at taxation, expenditure on public goods, the welfare state, equality, and meritocracy—is required.

> The point is that policies such as these do not attack corruption directly. Instead, they are likely to undermine systemic corruption by creating an implicit contract between citizens and the state to produce common goods.[213]

Donors such as the World Bank are increasingly looking at their development activities through a social lens, with rebuilding the social contract being at the core of them.[214] Social contract diagnostics—helping to understand what citizens expect from the state and vice versa—can help it to identify disequilibrium between the two and understand development challenges in a country, such as entrenched inequalities, weak institutions, and why, for example, past attempts to prevent corruption may not have been working.

This change in moral equilibrium can be attempted in a variety of different ways, whether through a 'big bang' approach requiring multiple measures aimed in this direction (encompassing a comprehensive, and jurisdiction-specific, reform package changing the institutional environment and creating a wholesale change in culture and political, economic, and social reform);[215] a more rapid and aggressive reform process; or through a more gradual approach. Each is likely to necessitate, with the support of the government, a coalition of national actors, and international institutions (where welcome), measures to reform institutions and to rebuild a social contract between the state and its citizens (based on the principle of impartiality in the exercise of public power) and develop corruption control from the ground up. This may require steps to increase engagement by citizens, the freedom of the press, transparency, accountability, the independence of the judiciary, anti-corruption enforcement agencies, and civil service based on a system of meritocracy, measures to address weaknesses in these institutions, and entrenched inequalities, and improvements in governance and the introduction of political reform, including, for example, changes to the party or electoral system

---

[211] Rothstein, n. 206, 36.

[212] See, e.g., A. Mungiu-Pippidi, 'Corruption: Diagnosis and Treatment' (2006) 17(3) *Journal of Democracy* 86.

[213] Rothstein, n. 207, 153.

[214] See Independent Evaluation Group, 'Social Contracts and World Bank Country Engagements: Lessons from Emerging Practices' (2019) *World Bank Group Report*.

[215] Rothstein, n. 206, 44 (including for example a functioning system of taxation, gender equality in the public sector, and free universal public education). For a critique, see M. Stephenson, 'Corruption as a Self-Reinforcing "Trap": Implications for Reform Strategy' (2019) University of Gothenburg Working Paper.

126 TOWARDS A MORE COMPREHENSIVE APPROACH

and campaign finance rules.[216] Indeed, research indicates that constitutional structure, the electoral process, the strength of political parties and the party system, methods of campaign finance, the relationship between political structure and private wealth, security (or insecurity) of tenure, and state capacity can all have a significant impact on corruption risk.[217]

These types of indirect and wholesale responses are not, of course, easy to implement and in many circumstances may be unrealistic, unachievable, and may not be successful even if tried (see further Chapter 9 discussing the reform efforts involving extensive coalition building in Ukraine following the departure of President Yanukovych in 2014[218]). Further, some argue that the literature does not contain a close scrutiny of problems arising in middle-income economies, that have built capacity to detect and punish corruption and does not sufficiently engage with the possibility that more direct reforms can encompass a wide range of self-reinforcing changes beyond anti-corruption law and its enforcement, including, the range of preventative and deterrent measures discussed in Section B. In addition, not all agree with the assessment that (relatively easy to implement) direct legal responses based on anti-corruption laws and a big law enforcement push by anti-corruption agencies should be discounted. Rather, there is some past evidence of successful strategies with components of reform focused on anti-corruption law and policy or increased law enforcement by newly created, or invigorated, anti-corruption agencies,[219] and such initiatives are still tried (see, especially, discussion of Operation Car Wash (OCW) in Chapter 7). Many thus consider that even in cases of systemic corruption, criminal law remains one important, powerful

---

[216] See Rose-Ackerman and Palifka, n. 3.

[217] See, e.g., Rose-Ackerman and Palifka, n. 3, 372 (arguing that although all democratic systems may be prone to corruption, proportional representative (PR) electoral systems are more susceptible to it than plurality—or first past the post—ones as party leaders have more control over individual legislators in PR systems and voters have less ability to hold them to account (especially where there are closed party lists). Further, that parliamentary systems (where the prime minister is chosen by the political party controlling parliament) are less vulnerable to corruption than presidential ones (where the President is popularly elected and may be in a different party to that which controls the legislature), as the President can extract payoffs to overcome political roadblocks). See also E. Dávid-Barrett et al., 'Controlling Corruption in Development Aid: New Evidence from Contract-Level Data' (2020) 55 *Studies in Comparative International Development* 481. Campaign finance rules may also, by introducing opportunities and incentives for politicians to favour those supporting their campaigns, encourage corruption, for example: if they are so restrictive that they encourage illegal campaign contributions and bribery in return for legislative, regulatory, or other benefits, or, even where permissive, if they lead to expectations of political favours and returns on such investments. All of these issues highlight the importance of processes which eliminate corrupt incentives and control the impact of private wealth on public power, and, crucially, public oversight mechanisms which hold governments to account. Indeed, as elections are inevitably imperfect tools for restraining corruption, other means of ensuring public accountability must be available, through independent monitoring and enforcement organizations, including judicial institutions, anti-corruption agencies, and the public (citizens, groups of citizens, private associations, and watchdog groups, such as Transparency International, and the media). The latter however depends on sufficient information being provided by a government or independent auditors, such as the GAO in the US or the Audit Commission in the UK.

[218] See also Section E (and e.g. discussion of failed reform attempts in Bulgaria).

[219] Davis, n. 204.

COMBATTING ENDEMIC, OR SYSTEMIC, CORRUPTION   127

(and perhaps in some scenarios the most realistic) tool available to deal with these problems. It can, and is necessary to, challenge the sense of impunity felt by those targeted, can result in severe sanctions being imposed on those found to have violated the law, and can play an important role in the collection of key information, informing the public and winning popular support, and in the development of a norm of honest behaviour.[220] Anti-corruption law can thus be refashioned to address collective action problems and the 'Prisoner's Dilemma',[221] for example, through enhancing the scale and efficiency of law enforcement, expanding the agencies (including foreign agencies) able to monitor and prosecute corrupt acts (through institutional multiplicity), and using apolitical law enforcement, as well as other mechanisms, to challenge and influence norms around corruption.[222]

This alternative, advocated view is, therefore, that dismissing law enforcement as a tool to achieve systemic transformation is misguided, and that anti-corruption law enforcement can be reinvigorated and repurposed to deal with concerns about systemic corruption through political engagement, a big enforcement push by better resourced or reinvigorated law enforcement agencies, or through institutional multiplicity—the creation of new and impartial enforcement institutions that are more difficult for corrupt actors to subvert and which are able to change incentives and to deliver incremental, but transformative change.[223] 'For instance, in many legal systems, the same corrupt act may be subject to administrative, civil, or criminal sanctions, and several distinct institutions, both local and foreign, may enforce those sanctions.'[224]

Although these types of steps, in which reforms are introduced, tested, and become part of the civic culture progressively over time, may be more attainable than more dramatic systemic changes,[225] they will be challenging to achieve in the absence of policies for ensuring good governance and building strong democratic institutions,[226] and the existence of structures for combatting corruption and collusion, such as robust legal systems, transparent and clear processes, free access

---

[220] Of course, if enforcement agencies have been entirely corrupted, then a big enforcement push may not be feasible at all, see Rothstein, n. 206, (2018) 35.

[221] For example, firms dealing with a corrupt procurement official would collectively benefit from not paying a bribe, but each firm individually has an incentive to pay the bribe to gain preferential treatment.

[222] Davis, n. 204.

[223] See Carson and Mota Prado, n. 208 and Davis, n. 204.

[224] K.E. Davis, M.R. de Assis, R. de M. Pimenta, and M.M Prado, 'Legal and Political Responses to Systemic Corruption' (2021) 17(2) *Revista Direito GV* Editorial, 5.

[225] See, e.g., M. Andrews, *The Limits of Institutional Reform in Development: Changing Rules for Realistic Solutions* (Cambridge University Press, 2013).

[226] Although there may be less opportunity in democracies where politicians are constrained by the need to get re-elected, and where civil liberties, free speech, and freedom of the press are more likely to be protected, these factors do not always check corruption. Rather, many examples exist of democracies which have bred well-established corruption, whether at the federal, state, or local level. The nature of corruption and its ability to thrive is likely to depend on the organization and power of governments and private actors, respectively, see Rose-Ackerman and Palifko, n. 3, 276.

128 TOWARDS A MORE COMPREHENSIVE APPROACH

to information, independent and effective enforcement agencies and judicial systems, a free press and active civil associations. Success will also be dependent on the effective design and creation of new law enforcement institutions, which become legitimized and do not themselves becoming impregnated with the dominant culture,[227] hijacked to carry out a political agenda, or, for example, used to allow unelected law enforcement officers to repress political opponents and engage in over-zealous enforcement.[228]

As seen in later chapters, care must also be taken to ensure that institutional multiplicity, if introduced, does not lead to complex coordination issues where laws and enforcement agencies have overlapping remits and create a risk of double—or even multiple—jeopardy and, potentially, an infringement of the *ne bis in idem* principle.[229] These difficulties may be exacerbated where foreign institutions also become embroiled in investigations, whether through parallel domestic investigations or foreign bribery proceedings. Some of these types of problem were experienced in Brazil, where it seems clear that OCW, enhanced by institutional multiplicity, challenged the sense of impunity felt by leading politicians and businesspeople, but has not proved to be successful in breaking the cycle of corruption exposed (see further Chapter 7). To be effective, therefore, it seems that incremental reforms, encompassing (apolitical) law enforcement, need to be carefully planned, as well as being complemented, enhanced, and supported by other measures targeted at the structural drivers of the corruption and aimed at shifting norms. This will require a mapping out of the landscape of corruption. Where corruption pervades public procurement, these steps are likely to require measures: to weaken close ties between procurers, politicians, and businesses (which may include political reforms, e.g. changes to campaign finance rules);[230] to improve public procurement processes (e.g. by controlling corruption through centralizing procurement and allowing top-level oversight[231] or as discussed in Section B.i, through investment in, and performance based pay for, independent bureaucrats (appointed on merit), limiting bureaucratic discretion and increasing the transparency and auditing of their decision taking[232]); and by continuing to address the sense of impunity felt by the leading players involved (through carefully

---

[227] See, e.g., R. Nizhnikau, 'Love the Tender: ProZorro and Anti-Corruption Reforms after the Euromaidan Revolution, Problems of Post-Communism' (2022) 69(2) *Problems of Post-Communism* 192.

[228] This might serve to increase cynicism about a reform culture and reinforce belief in the need to act corruptly. Law enforcement must not therefore become a hunt for opponents or those poorly connected who cannot bail themselves out, Report 4/2011 prepared by A. Mungiu-Pippidi et al., *Contextual Choices in Fighting Corruption: Lessons Learned* (Norad, 2011), xvii. See further Chapter 7.

[229] Broadly, protecting a person from being tried or punished again for an offence of which they have already been acquitted or convicted.

[230] See, e.g., the discussion in Chapter 9 on the 2021 Anti-Oligarch Law in Ukraine.

[231] See, e.g., President Ashraf Ghani, 'Driving corruption out of public procurement' in Policy Paper, n. 3, 9.5.

[232] See, e.g., Ghani, n. 231, 9.6–9.7.

targeted and apolitical law enforcement or justice sector reform). Although each of these reforms individually may not be sufficient, their unifying and self-reinforcing nature may augment their effect in combatting, destabilizing, and reversing a corrupt cycle and building a momentum towards meaningful change. Further, even if some of these steps may require commitment from top political leadership (e.g. following leadership change[233]), others may be achievable without significant legislative or institutional change. In some jurisdictions international institutions and MDBs may be well-situated to play a role in diagnosing causes of corruption and to facilitate the fight against it by, for example, providing technical assistance, reviewing procurement decisions, and conditioning receipt of aid or loans on compliance with steps to prevent and deter corruption (e.g. through steps to improve governance, public administration, and to aid capacity building for law anti-corruption agencies and judicial authorities and the building of sound audit frameworks and systems).[234] In addition, the threat and risk of extraterritorial enforcement of foreign bribery laws against foreign officials may create incentives both for compliance, and for action against those officials at the national level.

It is clear, therefore, that where corruption is widespread in a country, serious attempts need to be made to challenge social norms, change expectations, and to deal with the collective action problem, in addition to measures designed to prevent and deter corruption, such as those described in Section B. This is likely to require a combination of 'political signalling, managerial reforms, technical oversight, and increasing engagement with an aware citizenry to fundamentally change a culture and systems that are facilitating corruption'.[235] Anti-corruption agencies or police may themselves seek to build public support, for change. Further institutional changes and procurement reform backed by national leadership and tools such as integrity pacts, collective action and/or industry sector initiatives—such as the Extractive Industries Transparency Initiative (EITI) designed to promote collective compliance and make sectors more transparent and accountable[236], the use of foreign bribery laws and the entry into trade agreements, may also help to create systemic change and send a signal from a government to the population that it intends to tackle corruption, and set 'new rules of the game'. For example, an Integrity Pact (see Chapter 3), involving commitments by relevant officials and businesses not to accept, or give, bribes or to collude, and overseen by a civil society group, may help to address Prisoner's Dilemma through the provision of assurances to each bidder that competitors will refrain from bribery and that procurers will commit to preventing corruption by their officials and by establishing a level

---

[233] See, e.g., Ghani, n 231 (especially important where corruption results from fragmented regimes that lack accountability).

[234] See Mungiu-Pippidi, n. 210, 33.

[235] Ghani, n. 231, 9.8

[236] See, e.g., http:eiti.org/our-mission.

130 TOWARDS A MORE COMPREHENSIVE APPROACH

playing field.[237] 'Anti-corruption collective action' agreements by firms to create a commitment not to bribe may also help to ensure a level playing field between themselves.[238]

Some countries have sought to use accession to the GPA (discussed in Chapter 3) precisely to help to build belief that there is commitment to change; participation can signal 'to both domestic suppliers and the outside world that an acceding country is intent on conforming to international best practices ... [and] challenging entrenched expectations ... with regard to collusion and corruption'.[239] This reasoning undeniably formed part of the motivation for Ukraine's accession to the GPA (see Chapter 9). Similarly if Brazil had decided to push on with its application to join the GPA, this could have been used to send a powerful message that it was determined to grapple with corruption and collusion which has plagued its public procurement system over many years (see Chapter 7).[240] For other countries, accession to the GPA or participation in related bilateral or regional trading arrangements can similarly be considered as an important possible tool to increase corruption and collusion-resilience and lock in related reforms.

D. Anti-Money-Laundering Regimes and Other Anti-Corruption Measures

The discussion in this chapter illustrates that corruption control requires a multifaceted approach. This is likely to include measures which extend beyond the scope of matters discussed in this book. For example, political systems, the independence of the media, rules governing the financing of political parties, and anti-money-laundering frameworks, all impact on the ability to fight corruption successfully. Anti-money-laundering rules in particular are crucial to prevent individuals and firms benefiting from the proceeds of their crimes. To deter such criminal activity,

---

[237] Transparency International, 'The Integrity Pact: A Powerful Tool for Clean Bidding' (2009). See also discussion of such measures in Chapter 8 (Hungary and Poland) and Chapter 9 (Ukraine).

[238] See, e.g., G. Aiolfi and C. Müller Torbrand, 'Is Collective Action Against Corruption a Competition Risk for Companies' in Riley, Stephan, and Tubbs, n. 130.

[239] R.D. Anderson, A.C. Müller, and W.E. Kovacic, 'Promoting Competition and Deterring Corruption in Public Procurement Markets: Synergies with Trade Liberalisation' (2017) 18 *Public Procurement Law Review* 67, 69.

[240] Although Brazil applied to join under President Bolsonaro (see 'Application for Accession of Brazil to the Agreement on Government Procurement', WTO Communication, GPA/152 GPA/ACC/BRA/1 (19 May 2020)), President Lula announced in May 2023 that he was withdrawing the application, see https://www.gov.br/mre/en/contact-us/press-area/press-releases/brazil-withdraws-offer-to-accede-to-the-wto-government-procurement-agreement#:~:text=As%20a%20plurilateral%20instrument%2C%20the,to%20its%20public%20procurement%20market, see further Chapter 7 (negotiations are, however, continuing with the EU in relation to the EU-Mercosur Trade Agreement). See also, e.g., R.D. Anderson and N. Sporysheva, 'The Revised WTO Agreement on Government Procurement: Evolving Global Footprint, Economic Impact and Policy Significance' (2019) 3 *Public Procurement Law Review* 71.

these provisions, should require banks, and a range of other gatekeepers,[241] to report suspicious transactions and to scrutinize closely transactions by politically exposed persons. Investigators—and police forces—should also have specialized units capable of investigating large-scale, financial irregularities to ensure that wrongdoing in public tendering is detected and that assets transferred abroad can be traced and recovered.

E. Impetus for Reform: Domestic, International, and EU Initiatives

Where a procompetitive procurement system is not in place, and especially where corruption is prevalent, it may be hard to achieve meaningful reforms along the lines discussed in the sections above—particularly because such reforms are likely to be actively opposed by those that have captured the prevailing system and have been able to take advantage of its weaknesses. Domestic or international pressure, or a change in political leadership, may however lead to a genuine desire to reform public procurement processes for the better.[242]

The poor state of a public procurement system and concerns about misuse of public money may make it a target for anti-corruption activities by members of the government opposition, or citizens and civil society actors calling for reform or building new political parties to pursue an anticorruption agenda. Ultimately, of course, and despite the fight against corruption being a global phenomenon 'the battlefield where this war is lost or won remains national'.[243] Nonetheless, it can be challenging to achieve reform, even following a change of government. For example, although in Bulgaria in 2022, Kiril Petkov's pro-EU government, establishing the 'We Continue to Change' Alliance sought to reverse the trend of corruption by those in high positions,[244] ideological differences and, arguably resistance by the status quo to the anti-corruption efforts, led to the government losing a vote of no confidence, and the collapse of the coalition government, after just six months in power.[245] In Polish elections in October 2023 the Law and Justice party, which had made illiberal changes in democracy and the economy in Poland,

---

[241] In the US, a Bill to adopt an Enablers Act sought to require professional service providers who serve as 'gatekeepers' to the US financial system to perform full anti-money-laundering due diligence on prospective clients. The concern is that enablers are able to provide corrupt foreign officials access to the US financial system, see also n. 156 and text.

[242] For a discussion of how a bottom-up reform process initiated by volunteers and created through a process of broad dialogue between a varied group of creators, led to procurement reform and the adoption of a new e-procurement regime, see discussion of ProZorro platform, in Chapter 9.

[243] Mungiu-Pippidi, n. 228, xiv.

[244] See, e.g., Petkov, n. 210.

[245] Petkov, n. 210 and see 'Bulgarian Prime Minister Petkov Resigns after Losing Confidence Vote', *Euronews* (27 June 2022), available at https://www.euronews.com/2022/06/27/bulgarian-prime-minis ter-petkov-resigns-after-losing-confidence-vote.

132 TOWARDS A MORE COMPREHENSIVE APPROACH

failed to win a majority, paving the way for a coalition government including Donald Tusk's Civic Platform party.[246] It is anticipated that the new Government will start to reverse some of the illiberal trends, which have been increasing corruption risks in Poland, see Chapter 8.

Beyond steps at the domestic level, it has been seen that international conventions and initiatives have also helped to shape anti-corruption and competition law policies in many states and that monitoring exercises encourage signatories, or members, to adhere to the principles they have agreed to. International observers and external actors can thus seek to have an impact on a domestic procurement and anti-corruption regimes, through imposing pressure on politicians and policymakers to create new institutions and rules which will enable them to comply with international obligations. To be successful, this pressure must convince national governments to make changes or to take steps to change norms, or highlight malfeasance, which may encourage domestic pro-change actors. Thus, fighting corruption in societies where particularism is the norm is likely to require a coalition of national actors and the main role of the international community should be to support them. 'No country can change without domestic collective action which is both representative and sustainable over time.'[247] International institutions, such as UNCAC and OECD can help to galvanize national support and collective action through their work—not only by setting standards, but by drawing attention in their reviews to countries' failure to comply with them.

International financial institutions are also seeking to play a role in driving change, especially as MDB loans are frequently used to fund public procurement projects. For many years, some MDBs focused only on economic issues (e.g. for some time the World Bank adhered to the view that it was tasked with making loans and was not empowered to deal with political issues, including corruption[248]). This led to concern that many loans did not achieve their socio-economic objectives in some of the poorest areas of the world but were instead spent irresponsibly or siphoned off by corrupt politicians, officials, and corporations. Consequently, resources intended to address basic development needs of poor people were being diverted or misallocated through corrupt practices. These kinds of concerns led, over time, to an acceptance that corruption is as much an economic as a political matter,[249] which can prevent the realization of development goals. MDBs are consequently under increasing pressure, and are taking steps, to ensure that their money is spent well and not wrongly diverted by corrupt officials or politicians. Thus, even though corruption (and collusion) may constitute offences in the individual states involved and MDBs can prepare reports and provide information

---

[246] See Poland election result confirms victory for coalition led by Donald Tusk, *Financial Times* (17 October 2023).

[247] Mungiu-Pippidi, n. 228, xv.

[248] Heimann and Pieth, n. 29, 12–13, 21.

[249] Heimann and Pieth, n. 29, 21.

to national law enforcement authorities in the country (or countries) where mis-conduct occurs,[250] MDBs now also take their own actions to safeguard their loans. For example, many MDBs seek to work with recipient states to build capacity and anti-corruption initiatives and to reshape social contracts,[251] have reformed their procurement rules to improve oversight of the spending of their funds, and seek to ensure wider access to, and competition for, these public tenders.[252] Further, they have developed their own legal structures and sanction processes with the aim of enabling them to fulfil their fiduciary duties, to control their spending and to en-sure that loans are used only for the purposes for which they are granted.

To achieve these objectives, most MDBs now have integrity units (INTs), such as the WBG's Integrity Vice Presidency or the European Bank for Reconstruction and Development's ('EBRD') Office of the Chief Compliance Officer.[253] In addition to providing advice to borrower countries on institutional and procurement reform and corruption prevention, these units also investigate misconduct, and operate sanctions systems allowing them to debar entities found to have engaged in mis-conduct from bidding on future MDB-financed contracts. Indeed, clauses relating to sanctionable practices and procurement policies now form part of the standard financing and transaction arrangements executed; typically such documents re-quire local procurement offices to include equivalent terms in their procurement documents.[254]

The WBG was one of the first MDBs to take action to counter corruption[255] and it now operates a two-tiered administrative system of investigation and

---

[250] See, e.g., The World Bank office of suspension and debarment, 'Report on functions, data, and les-sons learned 2007–2013, available at http://documents.worldbank.org/curated/en/353781468320949 616/The-World-Bank-office-of-suspension-and-debarment-report-on-functions-data-and-lessons-learned-2007-2013. In some states there may be weak governance arrangements and enforcement of the rules, however.

[251] See n. 214 and text (the WBG emphasizes the importance of social contracts in eliminating pov-erty and creating the conditions for growth and meeting development challenges in client countries. It thus seeks to use social contract diagnostics to understand development challenges, why despite past efforts development paths have not altered, and to help countries reshape their social contracts. These could also be used to develop its approach to lending so as to ensure it does not prolong or exacerbate broken social contracts).

[252] The International Monetary Fund (IMF) also has a policy of helping members to design and im-plement anti-corruption strategies, and sometimes withholds support until a credible reform strategy is in place.

[253] INTs are independent units within the Bank that investigate sanctionable practices in rela-tion to Bank-financed projects and monitor compliance by sanctioned entities. See, e.g., Integrity Vice Presidency, World Bank (2019); T. Dickinson, C. Lammers, and M. Heavener, 'The Increasing Prominence of World Bank Sanctions', Law (1 December 2014) 360; and European Bank for Reconstruction and Development, Integrity, and Compliance, available at https://www.ebrd.com/integrity-and-compliance.html.

[254] See, e.g., World Bank Borrowers, 'Guidelines: Procurement of Goods, Works, and Non-Consulting Services Under IBRD Loans and IDA Credits and Grants' (2014).

[255] Committees and investigation units created in 1998 were replaced in 2001 by the establishment of the INT (elevated to vice presidency in 2009) following recommendations of a review panel, see D. Thornburgh, R.L. Gainer, and C.H. Walker, 'Report Concerning the Debarment Process of the World Bank' (2002) 15–16.

134 TOWARDS A MORE COMPREHENSIVE APPROACH

decision-making with an expansive ambit of sanctionable practices and sanctionable entities.[256] The sanctions system plays a key part of the WBG's anti-corruption efforts and seeks to ensure that fraud and corruption impacting on its operations are addressed efficiently and fairly and that a strong deterrence message is complemented with a focus on prevention and integrity compliance programmes.[257] Many other MDBs also operate similar systems, with decision-making bodies embedded within them making decisions based on the preponderance of evidence standard,[258] with appeals to an appellate authority, and with harmonized sanctioning procedures and policies.[259] In particular, the Uniform Framework for Preventing and Combating Fraud and Corruption[260] sets out common guidelines for the conduct of sanction investigations and establishes a portfolio of sanctions available to MDBs, including permanent or conditional debarment, reprimand, restitution, and a requirement that the borrower repay tainted loans.[261] Further, the Agreement for Mutual Enforcement of Debarment Decision ('AMEDD'), concluded by the African Development Bank, the Asian Development Bank, EBRD, the Inter-American Development Bank Group (IADB), and WBG in 2010, allows for a sanction imposed by one MDB to be recognized by, and added to the sanctions list of, other MDBs, even if they were not directly affected by the sanctionable practice.[262] For example, in July 2022, the IADB debarred a Brazilian construction company, Construcap, for 18 months. Construcap admitted to paying around USD 1million in bribes to a Brazilian public official supervising and managing an IADB financed project in Brazil. As part of the settlement, the company agreed to report on its compliance programme through an independent monitor and to pay fines and restitution. The debarment qualified for cross-debarment under the

---

[256] For a detailed history of the evolution of the Bank's Sanction System, see A-M. Leroy and F. Fariello, 'The World Bank Group Sanctions Process and its Recent Reforms' (2012) 9–11.

[257] See WGB, 'Twenty Milestones from Combatting Corruption: The World Bank Group Integrity Vice Presidency's 20th Anniversary' and World Bank Office of Suspension and Debarment, n. 250, 15–25. Further its road investigations, for example, revealed evidence of 'inflated highway construction costs', bribery, and 'siphoning of funds during contract execution'. WBG, Integrity Vice Presidency, 'Curbing Fraud, Collusion and Corruption in the Road Sector' (2011) 1.

[258] Typically, once the investigating authority concludes that there is sufficient evidence to show that a sanctionable practice has been committed in the context of a MDB-financed project, it presents the case for evaluation at the first tier of the adjudication phase.

[259] For example, the Joint International Financial Institution Anti-Corruption Task Force focuses on the standardization of sanctions investigation procedures, defining sanctionable practices, and fostering cooperation, see Inter-American Development Bank, 'Harmonization Efforts with Other International Financial Institutions', available at https://www.iadb.org/en/transparency/transparency-accountability-and-anti-corruption.

[260] See, African Development Bank Group et al., 'International Financial Institutions Anti-Corruption Task Force–Uniform Framework for Preventing and Combating Fraud and Corruption' (2006).

[261] See, African Development Bank Group, 'General Principles and Guidelines for Sanctions' (2006).

[262] See, African Development Bank Group et al., 'Agreement for Mutual Enforcement of Debarment Decision' (2010), para. 4. MDBs may, however, decide not to enforce a sanction imposed by another MDB when such enforcement would be inconsistent with its legal or other institutional considerations, African Development Bank Group, n. 261, para. 7.

AMEDD.[263] On 18 March 2022, the IADB also debarred twenty-seven firms for corruption and collusion in relation to projects in Brazil.[264]

Fighting corruption also forms an important part of many jurisdictions' international development and external (as well as internal) policies.[265] New Zealand, for example, works closely with Pacific Island countries to build stronger governance frameworks and to promote sustainable economic and social development through promoting transparency, accountability, and justice system reform. In addition, the EU, the biggest donor of international aid, pursues external anti-corruption policies. These seek to address corruption as part of its strategy for supporting third countries to which it provides financial assistance. It thus tries to protect its financial assistance from corruption and to benefit development in the recipient state through, for example, advocating improvements to governance in the recipient state, encouraging public administration reform, aiding capacity building for law enforcement, judicial authorities, and anti-corruption agencies, and the development of sound audit frameworks and systems. Indeed, the European Anti-Fraud Office (OLAF, an acronym for its French name, *l'Office europe'en de lutte anti-fraude*, part of the Commission), created to ensure the better functioning of criminal justice, is tasked[266] with conducting administrative investigations for the purposes of fighting corruption and other illegal activities affecting the EU's financial interest (e.g. fraud against the budget and spending of structural funds), including in third countries. Where it finds that EU money has been used by recipients for procurement procedures which have been fraudulently manipulated, OLAF can recommend the recovery of any affected funds from the project.[267] The European Investment Bank (EIB), the lending arm of the EU, also uses 'exclusion' decisions in a similar way in which MDBs use debarment decisions, to protect the EU's financial interests. For example, in 2021 the EIB reached a settlement with GE Steam Power, in relation to prohibited behaviour carried out by some of its companies in Slovenia, by which the offending companies agreed not to participate in any EIB funded projects during specified exclusion periods, to bolster their compliance procedures, and to contribute to the financing of anti-corruption, integrity, sustainability, climate change, and/or environmental projects. The companies also settled civil proceedings in Slovenia. The EIB also conducts proactive integrity reviews (PIRs) to identify corruption risks early and prior to allegations of misconduct being reported.

---

[263] A list of IDB sanctioned companies and individuals is available at https://www.iadb.org/en/trans parency/sanctioned-firms-and-individuals.

[264] List of IDB debarred companies and individuals, n. 263.

[265] See Prime Minister John Key, 'New Zealand: A Culture of Fair Play' in Policy Paper, n. 3.

[266] See, European Anti-Fraud Office (OLAF), available at https://anti-fraud.ec.europa.eu/index_en.

[267] See discussion of African water treatment case, available at https://ec.europa.eu/anti-fraud/inv estigations/success-stories_en#eu-expenditure.

136 TOWARDS A MORE COMPREHENSIVE APPROACH

The EU has also taken steps to bolster its fight against anti-corruption internally in EU institutions and its Member States.[268] With regard to the latter, it has developed a strict and wide-set of conditions for those wishing to accede to the EU, which include commitment to democracy, rule of law, stable institutions, a functioning market economy, and robust anti-corruption strategies,[269] and developed mechanisms to measure national efforts on corruption control, and to support national authorities in the better implementation of laws and policies against corruption through a constructive dialogue.[270] OLAF, and the European Public Prosecutor's Office (EPPO), the independent public prosecution office of the EU which has been responsible since 2021 for prosecuting crimes (including corruption) against the financial interests of the EU and the EU budget, also investigate fraud against the budget both at the EU level,[271] and in the Member States. The Commission considers corruption control to be a key element contributing to growth, jobs, and investment in the EU, and seeks to ensure that all Member States have the means to ensure that EU funds are not misused and adhere to its fundamental values of 'respect for human dignity, freedom, democracy, equality, the rule of law, and respect for human rights, including the rights of persons belonging to minorities' (Article 2 Treaty on European Union, TEU). The EU also has tools which can be used to challenge individual cases of suspected corruption and collusion in the Members States, and violations of EU law by the Member States themselves (e.g. for not having mechanisms in place to ensure that EU funds are not misused), see Chapter 8.

Pressure for reforms affecting the public procurement sphere may therefore come from a variety of different stakeholders and institutions, domestic, regional, and international. The difficulty is to build paths for reform and, through inclusive political processes and participation in policy coalitions,[272] to make them stick. Opposition and roadblocks generally need to be navigated and careful measures are required to ensure that there is no backsliding from reforms that are introduced. Reform of public procurement process can, nonetheless, provide an important and powerful tool for tackling widespread corruption in a country. In particular, in so far as such reforms focus partly at least on the *prevention* of corruption (and collusion), it may be less threatening to those who might otherwise oppose change, than reforms focused principally on enforcement by anti-corruption agencies of punitive anti-corruption laws.

---

[268] See further Chapter 8.

[269] See further discussion in Chapters 8 and 9 (dealing with Hungary and Poland, and Ukraine, respectively).

[270] See, e.g., Report from the Commission to the Council and the European Parliament—EU Anti-Corruption Report (the Anti-Corruption Report 2014), COM(2014) 38 final.

[271] Good administrations and transparency are also reviewed by the European Court of Auditors and the European Ombudsman.

[272] See Nizhnikau, n. 227.

F. Conclusions

Corruption and supplier collusion in public procurement markets impact negatively on consumer welfare, economic growth, and the provision of vital infrastructure that citizens rely on. The inherent nature and features of public procurement make procurement particularly prone to distortion by these practices. Despite increasingly vigorous efforts over the past two to three decades to fight these practices, such conduct continues to undermine public procurement systems around the globe.

This chapter argues that, given this relentless problem, the traditional tools applied to the problems of corruption and supplier collusion in public procurement markets, which focus on transparency and effective enforcement of anti-corruption and competition laws, are likely to require enhancement in most states, whether through incremental or (where necessary) more radical change.

Fundamental to any reform is a political commitment to implement them—ensuring that appropriate foundations are laid, and appropriate systems are put in place to strengthen procurement, competition, and anti-corruption laws and systems. This in turn depends upon a recognition that: (i) these provisions are central to the welfare of citizens and to the effectiveness and credibility of states; (ii) there is an extremely close connection between the three spheres of law, and no individual set of rules is likely to achieve its full objectives in the absence of the others; and (iii) a joined-up approach and dialogue between enforcers is required at both the national and international level.

Although unique jurisdictional problems will demand different solutions, it seems clear that both preventative techniques and criminal law are likely to form part of the solution—without legal risk of prosecution for corruption at least, self-regulation and preventative techniques are unlikely to work—along with other measures to supplement them. The proposals made in this chapter are likely in many jurisdictions to require modifications to laws, enforcement techniques, sanctioning practices, design of procurement systems, working practices of staff within procurement entities, or even changes to law enforcement and procurement agencies and the judiciary. In addition, a shift in the incentives affecting, and a change in the mindsets of, procurers, enforcers, businesses, and the public may be required. If each of these stakeholder categories can be incentivized to play a role in achieving the overall benefits of procompetitive procurement and to recognize that significant consequences will follow from transgression of these rules, changes may materialize through, for example: a greater ability and willingness of procurers to combat bid rigging, to comply with ethical codes, and to recover public money lost; encouraging firms to comply with anti-corruption and competition laws and to monitor for, and self-report, transgressions; enhancing the ability of enforcers to detect, act against, and sanction unlawful bid rigging and bribery; building public

138 TOWARDS A MORE COMPREHENSIVE APPROACH

support for procompetitive procurement; and allowing the public to play a greater role in monitoring compliance with the law.

Different overall approaches and techniques are likely to be required in jurisdictions where problems are more systemic, than in jurisdictions where problems derive principally as a result of individualist behaviour, driven by a range of factors such as greed, peer pressure, or opportunism.[273] Although in the latter scenario, leaders committed to combatting corruption may be able to create rules, organizations and a culture to curb it, in the former circumstances[274] leaders may enable corruption to breed throughout the system, meaning that more wide-ranging measures will be required to promote change, for example, to the state, its institutions and their relationship with society. To reduce corruption in these scenarios a number of steps may need to be taken to improve institutions, combat corruption incentives, and to challenge customs or personal ethics.

This chapter also recognizes that measures beyond procurement, anti-corruption, and competition law may be required to achieve the objective of protecting the integrity and efficiency of a procurement system. In particular, trade liberalization can play a significant role in helping to address corruption and competition concerns by facilitating progressive market opening and limiting the scope for protectionism in the public procurement sector. Money-laundering regimes are also crucial to prevent the conversion of illegally achieved gains into funds available to the criminal from seemingly legitimate sources.

---

[273] A principal–agent problem.

[274] E. Dávid-Barrett and M. Fazekas, 'Grand Corruption and Government Change: An Analysis of Partisan Favouritism in Public Procurement' (2020) 26 *European Journal on Criminal Policy and Research* 411.

5

Corruption and Supplier Collusion under the Waterline? Combatting Risks to Public Procurement in the United Kingdom

A. Introduction	139		ii. Weaknesses in procurement processes	158
B. The System in England and Wales	140		iii. Weaknesses in corruption and competition laws	160
i. Public Procurement Law	140		iv. Siloed regimes	164
ii. Competition and anti-corruption law	143	D.	Proposals for the Future	165
a. Bid rigging	143		i. Fact finding	166
b. Corruption	145		ii. Improving public procurement processes	167
c. Detection and outcomes	147		iii. Improving anti-corruption and competition laws	169
iii. Cases finding supplier collusion, or corruption, in domestic public procurement processes	150		iv. More effective enforcement of anti-corruption and competition laws	170
iv. Foreign bribery	153		a. Increasing enforcement	170
C. Is There a Corruption or Collusion Problem in the Public Procurement Sector in England and Wales?	155		b. Using the full range of penalties	172
			v. Increased policy coordination	176
i. Perceptions and survey evidence	155	E.	Conclusions	177

A. Introduction

The United Kingdom (UK) spends billions of pounds, and a substantial portion of government expenditure, on public procurement.[1] In the years just preceding the COVID-19 pandemic, this amounted to approximately GBP 290 billion per year.[2]

---

[1] This chapter is based on, and develops, an article written by A. Jones, 'Combatting Corruption and Collusion in UK Public Procurement: Proposal for Post-Brexit Reform' (2021) 84(4) *Modern Law Review* 667.

[2] See Cabinet Office Minister, Lord Agnew, Press Release, 'Procurement Teams Must Consider Wider Benefits of Public Spending' (3 June 2021) ('The public sector across the UK, from hospitals and schools to central government, police forces and universities, spend about GBP 290 billion a year through public procurement'); Cabinet Office, 'Green Paper: Transforming Public Procurement'

A commonly held view is that there is no need to be concerned about corruption, or collusion, impacting on public procurement in the UK. It is a relatively clean economy[3] where the spending is protected by comprehensive procurement, anti-corruption, and competition laws, and where relatively few instances of corruption and collusion in domestic public procurement processes have been revealed. This chapter challenges that assumption. Indeed, after putting the system as a whole under the microscope (focusing on England and Wales),[4] it concludes that as a result of weaknesses in that system, there are reasons to be concerned that corruption or collusion may in fact be occurring, undetected and unchecked.

Although the Government has reviewed and sought to improve public procurement and competition laws post-Brexit, this chapter suggests that further improvements to the framework could help to ensure that corruption and collusion in public procurement are prevented and deterred. In particular, it highlights the need for the adoption of a more joined-up approach to the problem and that, even beyond adjustments to procurement, competition and anti-corruption laws, procurers, and anti-corruption and competition enforcement agencies need to work more closely together to achieve synergies and to ensure that their policies do not contradict one another. The three currently siloed regimes need to be more closely united around a single public procurement strategy.

B. The System in England and Wales

i. Public Procurement Law

In England and Wales, a sophisticated regime regulates public procurement—from needs assessment to bid design and award, to post-contract implementation. For many years, the rules were principally set out in Regulations[5] derived

---

(December 2020) (recording GBP 290 billion of government spending every year); and Institute for Government, 'Government Procurement: The Scale and Nature of Contracting in the UK' (December 2018), 2–5 (noting government procurement expenditure of GBP 284 billion (around GBP 300 billion if academies are included), representing approximately one-third of its total expenditure (28 per cent and 47 per cent of central government and local government spending, respectively)).

[3] In 2022, the UK dropped significantly from 11th in 2021 to 18th most clean country out of 180 according to Transparency International's (TI's) 2022 Corruption Perceptions Index (CPI) (between 2013 and 2015 it was the 7th most clean), see further Chapter 2. See 'UK Is Not a Corrupt Country, Says Boris Johnson', *BBC News* (10 November 2021), available at https://www.bbc.co.uk/news/uk-politics-59238 464, and 'Boris Johnson Says the UK Is Not "Remotely a Corrupt Country". Is it?', *The Guardian* (11 November 2021), available at https://www.theguardian.com/politics/2021/nov/11/boris-johnson-says-the-uk-is-not-remotely-a-corrupt-country-is-it.

[4] Some rules discussed apply only in England and Wales and Northern Ireland (with separate regimes applying in Scotland, see, e.g., n. 11 and text). National court systems apply in each constituent nation.

[5] See especially the Public Contracts Regulations 2015, SI 2015/12 (PCR), available at https://www.legislation.gov.uk/uksi/2015/102/contents/made, which applied to public sector procurements (but

from European Union (EU) law, which reflect the transnational architecture established by the World Trade Organisation Revised Agreement on Government Procurement (WTO GPA).[6]

Post Brexit, however, the Government took the opportunity to overhaul and reform the rules,[7] albeit subject to their continued need to comply with the requirements of the GPA. Indeed, although prior to the UK's departure from the EU—on 31 January 2020—the UK only participated in the GPA by virtue of its status as an EU Member State,[8] it subsequently acceded to the GPA as a party 'in its own right',[9] so preventing the UK from falling out of it.[10] The new Procurement Act (PA23)[11] received royal assent on 26 October 2023 and is expected to take effect in 2024. The aim of the PA23 is to ensure that the procurement delivers value for money and maximizes public benefits.[12] However, other horizontal objectives are also relevant, such as encouraging participation by small and medium-sized enterprises (SMEs) and sustainability.[13]

---

separate Regulations existed e.g. for regulated utilities, defence and security contracts, and the procurement of works and services concession contracts).

[6] See e.g. Directive 2014/24/EU on Public Procurement (2014) OJ L94/65. The rules reflect the transnational architecture established by the World Trade Organisation Revised Agreement on Government Procurement (30 March 2012) (WTO GPA), see further discussion in Chapters 3 and 4. The UK rules based on EU law were initially retained post-Brexit.

[7] A particular aim was to speed up and simplify processes, and improve their flexibility and overcome perceived rigidities, see, 'Green Paper: Transforming Public Procurement', n. 2; see, e.g., S. Arrowsmith, 'Transforming Public Procurement Law after Brexit: Early Reflections on the Government's Green Paper' (15 December 2020), available at https://ssrn.com/abstract=3749359, S. Arrowsmith, 'Reimagining Public Procurement Law after Brexit: Seven Core Principles for Reform and Their Practical Implementation, Part 1' (10 January 2020), available at https://ssrn.com/abstract=3523 172 and S. Arrowsmith, 'Reimagining Public Procurement Law after Brexit: Seven Core Principles for Reform and Their Practical Implementation: Part 2' (12 August 2020), available at https://ssrn.com/abstract=3672421.

[8] Although the UK had signed the GPA, in its individual capacity, at the 1994 Marrakesh Conference establishing the WTO (see WTO, The Status of the WTO Legal Instruments (2015)), it never in fact submitted the required instrument of ratification, see R.D. Anderson, 'The UK's New Role in the WTO Agreement on Government Procurement: Understanding the Story and Seizing the Opportunity' (2021) 30(3) Public Procurement Law Review 159.

[9] See WTO, 'UK and Switzerland confirm participation in revised government procurement pact', news item (2 December 2021), available at: https://www.wto.org/nglish/news_e/news20_e/gpro_02 dec20_e.htm.

[10] This turned a potential commercial catastrophe (which would have disrupted essential supply chains and imposed heavy costs on UK suppliers, procuring entities, and other GPA parties) into a major negotiating success (now providing the UK with the opportunity to exercise leadership and influence future outcomes regarding the GPA and other accessions to the Agreement), see Anderson, n 8.

[11] Procurement Act 2023 (PA23), https://www.legislation.gov.uk/ukpga/2023/54/enacted. See also Procurement Bill [HL], 'A Bill to Make Provision about Procurement', which originated in the House of Lords, Session 2022–23, available at https://bills.parliament.uk/Bills/3159. The new rules do not apply in Scotland. The Act is to be accompanied by secondary legislation, in the form of implementing regulations, and guidance, etc.

[12] See PA23, n. 11, s 12(1). PCR, reg 67 referred to the need to ensure that contracts are awarded to the 'most economically advantageous' tender, determined by reference to price or cost, cost-effectiveness, or price-quality ratio.

[13] PA23, n. 11, ss 12(4) and 13 and the Public Services (Social Value) Act 2012, available at https://www.legislation.gov.uk/ukpga/2012/3/enacted.

In order to achieve their goals, both the PA23 and the previous regime have provided for competitive tendering procedures for public contracts (except in special cases where a direct award may be possible or warranted),[14] and contain provisions which guard against corruption and collusion through the use of open or competitive, flexible procedures. For example, the PA23 provides for: preliminary market engagement;[15] competitive tendering procedures to be carried out in accordance with a tender notice and associated tender documents (to be published via the Contracts Finder online portal[16] (prior to Brexit, they also had to be published in the Official Journal of the EU where EU thresholds were exceeded));[17] and the disregarding of tenders from excluded or excludable suppliers.[18] It also seeks to ensure a wide pool of bidders; regulates modifications to public contracts;[19] requires authorities to treat suppliers the same and not to put a supplier, without justification, at an unfair advantage or disadvantage,[20] including as a result of a conflict of interest;[21] and seeks to ensure procurement transparency.[22] The importance of the integrity in the process is reinforced by procurer codes of conduct—whether civil service[23] or local authority[24] created—and broad mandatory exclusion grounds for suppliers posing an unacceptable risk, including situations where a supplier, or a connected person, has been convicted of one or more specified offences (including bribery, the cartel offence, or a competition law infringement[25]) and has not undergone a self-cleaning process (a relevant factor is whether the circumstances giving rise to the exclusion ground are likely to arise again).[26]

The detection of irregularities, and bidders' confidence in the process, is also facilitated by provisions allowing disappointed tenderers to bring civil proceedings

---

[14] PA23, n. 11, Part 3, Chapters 2 and 3.

[15] See e.g., PA23, n. 11, Part 3, Chapter 1.

[16] See Government UK, 'Contracts Finder', available at https://www.gov.uk/contracts-finder.

[17] See e.g., PA23, n. 11, Part 3, Chapter 2.

[18] PA23, n. 11, Part 3, Chapters 2 and 6 and see n. 26 and text.

[19] PA23, n. 11, Part 4.

[20] PA23, n. 11, s 12.

[21] PA23, n. 11, Part 5.

[22] See Government UK Policy Paper, 'Transforming Public Procurement – Our Transparency Vision' (30 June 2022).

[23] See Government UK, Statutory Guidance, 'Civil Service: Values and Standards of Behaviour' (published on 30 November 2010, last updated on 16 March 2015), available at https://www.gov.uk/government/publications/civil-service-code.

[24] Local authorities are responsible for maintaining their own Code of Conduct (incorporating the seven principles of public life), a register of disposable pecuniary interests, and for dealing with allegations that the Code or registration requirements have been breached, see the Localism Act 2011, s 28, available at https://www.legislation.gov.uk/ukpga/2011/20/contents/enacted.

[25] It is not entirely clear, however, how bribery, cartel and competition law offence convictions will be collected and investigated under these provisions, see further Section D.ii.

[26] See PA23, n. 11, s 57 and Schedule 6 (and previously PCR, n. 5 regs 56–57) and discussion in Section D below.

THE SYSTEM IN ENGLAND AND WALES   143

for breach of statutory duty.[27] Other interested parties may also bring judicial review proceedings.[28] For example, a number of challenges were brought in relation to some procurement processes which occurred during the COVID-19 pandemic under emergency power rules (allowing contract award without competition), including on the grounds of apparent bias.[29] These challenges have illustrated, however, the difficulty of succeeding in these types of cases and, even where successful, of ensuring that meaningful consequences follow from a breach.[30]

ii. Competition and anti-corruption law

In line with international norms,[31] the UK has also reformed both competition and bribery laws in the past 25 years to ensure that draconian sanctions exist for those who engage in bid rigging and bribery (see summary in Table 5.1 below).

a. Bid rigging

Cartel activity—including bid rigging—is prohibited by both a civil offence set out in Chapter I of the Competition Act 1998 (CA98)[32] (modelled on Article 101 of the Treaty on the Functioning of the European Union (TFEU)[33]) and a criminal cartel offence set out in the Enterprise Act 2002 (EA02).[34] The former prohibits cartel agreements concluded between *undertakings*—that is, corporations,

---

[27] PA23, n. 11, Part 9. In exceptional circumstances concluded contracts can be cancelled and damages may be available, see *Nuclear Decommissioning Authority v EnergySolutions EU Ltd* [2017] UKSC 34. See also e.g. UNCTAD, Implementation Review Group, 'Review of Implementation of the United Nations Convention against Corruption', CAC/COSP/IRG/II/2/1/Add.4 (20 March 2019), available at https://assets.publishing.service.gov.uk/government/uploads/system/uploads/attachment_data/file/802272/Executive_Summary_of_the_United_Kingdom_-_Review_cycle_2__Chapter_II_and_V_.pdf. Although informal complaints could previously be lodged with the Cabinet Office Public Procurement Review Services (PPRS), as well as with the procuring authorities, the new regime and informal complaints are to be overseen by a Procurement Review Unit.

[28] *R (on the application of the Law Society) v Legal Services Commission* [2007] EWHC 1848). These rules are difficult to use in practice, see, e.g., S. Arrowsmith and R. Craven, 'Public Procurement and Access to Justice: A Legal and Empirical Study of the UK System' (2016) 25 *Public Procurement Law Review* 227 and see Arrowsmith, 'Reimagining Public Procurement Law after Brexit, Part 1' n. 7, 4.7.

[29] See discussion of concerns arising as a result of the use of a VIP fast lane at nn. 129–133 and text.

[30] See especially *R (Good Law Project) v Minister for the Cabinet Office* [2022] EWCA 21 (overturning a first instance decision finding apparent bias in relation to a contract award), *R (Good Law Project and Every Doctor) v Secretary of State for Health and Social Care* [2022] EWHC 2648 and *R (Good Law Project and others) v Secretary of State for Health and Social Care* [2021] EWHC 346 (finding breach of transparency policy and principles).

[31] See Chapter 3.

[32] Competition Act 1998 (CA98), available at https://www.legislation.gov.uk/ukpga/1998/41/contents. See also e.g. Case 1032/1/1/04, *Apex Asphalt and Paving Co Ltd v OFT* [2005] CAT 4.

[33] Article 101 was directly applicable in the UK until 1 January 2021 but is now not enforceable as part of UK law.

[34] Enterprise Act 2002 (EA02), available at https://www.legislation.gov.uk/ukpga/2002/40/contents.

partnerships, or other entities engaged in economic activity.[35] It is enforced publicly—by the Competition and Markets Authority (CMA) and certain sectoral regulators (in relation to conduct occurring within their sector)[36] pursuant to an administrative model—and privately, by private litigants before the civil courts (e.g. by a claimant that has suffered loss in consequence of the infringement).[37] The CMA, which acts as an integrated decision-taker[38] when enforcing the CA98, has the power to impose fines on undertakings that it finds to have infringed the rules of up to 10 per cent of their worldwide turnover.[39] It is also able to apply for a disqualification order against directors of companies found to have committed a CA98 infringement and to be unfit to be involved in the management of a company.[40]

A criminal cartel offence operates alongside the CA98 civil regime and applies to *individuals* engaged in cartel agreements. It was introduced to increase deterrents to cartel activity after the Government concluded that custodial sentences for individuals were required to 'focus the mind of potential cartelists'.[41] An individual convicted of an offence may receive a sentence of up to five years' imprisonment and/or an unlimited fine.[42] Investigations and prosecutions in England and Wales may be brought by the CMA,[43] or the Serious Fraud Office (SFO).[44]

---

[35] Case C-41/90, *Höfner and Elser v Macrotron GmbH* EU:C:1991:161.

[36] Several sector-specific regulators share concurrent powers with the CMA, see, e.g., CMA10, 'Concurrent Application of Competition Law to Regulated Industries' (12 March 2014), available at https://www.gov.uk/government/publications/guidance-on-concurrent-application-of-competition-law-to-regulated-industries.

[37] Litigants may bring follow-on actions (following on from a prior finding of infringement by a competition agency), see, especially, CA98, n. 32, ss 47A and 58A) or their own standalone actions.

[38] Investigating, prosecuting, and adopting its own decisions.

[39] Of up to 10 per cent of the undertaking's worldwide turnover, in the business year preceding the CMA's decision, CA98, n. 32, s 36. Appeals against such decisions, and private actions, are heard by the Competition Appeals Tribunal (CAT) or the ordinary courts.

[40] EA02, n. 34, s 204, amending the Company Directors Disqualification Act of 1986. Although this was only used for the first time to disqualify the director of a company involved in a cartel infringement in online sales of posters and frames (Trod Ltd: posters and frames, 12 August 2016), the CMA now routinely seeks to use this power, see n. 185 and text.

[41] See Joint Treasury/DTI Report, 'The UK's Competition Regime 2001'; Department of Trade and Industry White Paper, 'A World Class Competition Regime' (Cm 5233); and OFT365, 'Proposed criminalisation of cartels in the UK', A report prepared for the OFT by Sir Anthony Hammond KCB QC and Roy Penrose OBE QPM (November 2001), 1.4. It was thought that individual liability would censure those involved and be fairer than corporate fines, which may be insufficient to deter cartels.

[42] When convicted before a jury in the Crown Court.

[43] The CMA has published guidance on how it exercises its prosecutorial discretion (taking an account both of available evidence and the public interest), see 'Cartel Offence Prosecution Guidance' (CMA9) (March 2014), available at https://assets.publishing.service.gov.uk/government/uploads/system/uploads/attachment_data/file/288648/CMA9__Cartel_Offence_Prosecution_Guidance.pdf.

[44] EA02, n. 34, s 190(2). In cases of serious or complex fraud, the CMA can request the SFO, created by the Criminal Justice Act 1987 (CJA87), to accept the matter. See SFO and CMA Memorandum of Understanding (MOU), available at https://assets.publishing.service.gov.uk/government/uploads/system/uploads/attachment_data/file/307038/MoU_CMAandSFO.PDF. Third parties can also bring prosecutions with the consent of the CMA.

b. Corruption

In 2010, the Government overhauled a patchwork of anti-corruption laws[45] and adopted one of the world's most stringent anti-corruption statutes, the Bribery Act 2010 (BA10).[46] This Act, a consequence of domestic and international pressure[47] to revamp UK laws following the UK's participation in a variety of international anti-corruption conventions,[48] criminalizes: (i) bribery (active *and* passive) committed by individuals and corporations to induce or reward the performance of a relevant function or activity improperly in both the public and private sector (Sections 1 and 2); (ii) bribery concerning foreign public officials and officials of public international organizations (Section 6); and (iii) failure to prevent bribes from being paid on an organization's behalf (Section 7). Section 7 was introduced partly to sidestep the general complexities involved in England and Wales in establishing criminal liability of corporations (including under Sections 1 and 6[49]) where, in particular, it must be established that the controlling corporate mind (usually the board of directors) knew of the offending behaviour (the 'identification principle').[50] Section 7 holds corporations strictly liable for failing to prevent bribery anywhere in the world by an employee or agent of the commercial organization—which includes another corporate person or subsidiary[51]—unless they can show they have adequate procedures in place to prevent it.[52]

---

[45] See e.g. the common law(s) of bribery, the Public Bodies Corrupt Practices Act 1889, the Prevention of Corruption Acts of 1906 and 1916, the Criminal Law Act 1977, and the Anti-Terrorism, Crime and Security Act 2001. See also M. Raphael QC, *Bribery: Law and Practice* (Oxford University Press, 2016) and N. Lord et al, 'Implementing a Divergent Response? The UK Approach to Bribery in International and Domestic Contexts' (2020) 40 *Public Money and Management* 1.

[46] Bribery Act 2020 (BA10). Described as the gold standard for bribery legislation and a lodestar for other countries by the House of Lords, Select Committee on the Bribery Act 2010, *The Bribery Act 2010: Post-Legislative Scrutiny* (HL Paper 3030, 2019) 14.

[47] In 2008, the OECD criticized the UK's failure to upgrade its anti-corruption laws, in line with international obligations, see OECD Working Group on Bribery, 'Phase 2bis Report' (2008), available at http://www.oecd.org/daf/anti-bribery/oecdgroupdemandsrapidukactiontoenactadequateanti-briberylaws.htm and Ministry of Justice, 'Bribery Act 2010 Guidelines' (March 2011). The evaluation was sparked by the UK's controversial decision (following intervention by then prime minster, Tony Blair) to close an investigation into allegations that BAE paid bribes to members of the Saudi royal family to secure contracts to supply Taifun planes to Saudi Arabia (the Al Yamamah crisis), see further Chapter 4, nn. 29 and 56.

[48] Especially the United Nations Convention against Corruption (UNCAC) and the OECD Convention on Bribery of Foreign Officials, see Chapter 3. The UK is also a member of the Group of States Against Corruption (GRECO) and launched the 'United Kingdom Anti-Corruption Strategy 2017–2022' in December 2017.

[49] In November 2022, however, Glencore Energy UK pleaded guilty to both substantive and failure to prevent offences under the BA 10 and was ordered by Mr Justice Fraser, in the Southwark Crown Court, to pay a penalty of GBP 281 million (which included a fine, a confiscation order for the proceeds of the bribe, and the SFO's costs).

[50] See e.g. J. Horder, *Ashworth's Principles of Criminal Law* (Oxford University Press, 9th edn, 2019), Chapter 6, 6.3. It is frequently complained that this principle is inequitable (it is far easier to attribute the requisite knowledge to smaller owner-managed companies than larger ones) and it should be replaced for example by a principle of vicarious liability. In June 2022, the Law Commission published options for improvements and ensuring companies are effectively held to account for committing serious crimes, see https://www.lawcom.gov.uk/project/corporate-criminal-liability/.

[51] BA10, n. 46, s 8. This avoids the problem in England and Wales that acts of a subsidiary are not generally attributable to its parent, see, e.g., *Prest v Petrodel* [2013] UKSC 34.

[52] BA10, n. 46, s 7(2). This puts pressure on corporations to have compliance systems in place.

146 CORRUPTION AND SUPPLIER COLLUSION UNDER THE WATERLINE?

Individuals convicted of bribery offences may be sentenced to up to 10 years in prison. Both individuals and corporations may also be required to pay an unlimited fine, and further, to have proceeds of crimes confiscated.[53] Successful prosecutions—which can be brought only with the consent of either the Director of Public Prosecutions (DPP) or the Director of the SFO[54] following investigation by local police, the City of London Police, the Ministry of Defence Police, the National Crime Agency (NCA),[55] or the SFO—thus punish infringers and seek to ensure that they, and others, are deterred from committing future infringements and do not benefit from the proceeds of their crime. Wrongdoers may also be liable to pay damages following civil proceedings for the tort of bribery.[56]

A number of other criminal offences also catch some forms of bribery[57] or related conduct (e.g. conspiracy to commit an offence,[58] aiding, abetting, procuring or encouraging an offence,[59] false accounting,[60] or money laundering[61]). Of particular relevance to the public procurement context is the common law offence of misconduct in public office, which holds public officials to account for misconduct committed in connection with their public duties (and which carries a maximum sentence of life imprisonment). This offence applies beyond bribery to breaches of duty giving rise to a risk of serious harm (e.g. because of conflicts of interest that exist), where a public officer acting as such wilfully neglects to perform his or her duty, and/or wilfully misconducts himself or herself, to such a degree as to amount to an abuse of the public's trust in the office-holder, without reasonable excuse or justification.[62]

---

[53] The Proceeds of Crime Act 2002 (POCA), Part 2 provides for the making of confiscation orders, through Civil Recovery Orders (CROs), following conviction in criminal cases. The state claims property obtained through crime—the proceeds do not go to victims, available at https://www.legislation.gov.uk/ukpga/2002/29/contents.

[54] The consent of the Attorney General is not required, BA10, n. 46, s 10. The SFO leads responses for international cases, tackles serious or complex fraud, bribery and corruption, recovers the proceeds of those crimes, and assists other agencies in their equivalent investigations. The International Corruption Unit (ICU) of the National Crime Agency (NCA) also investigates allegations of bribery of foreign officials. Although bribery may be detected by police forces or other agencies, no agency has been conferred with responsibility for coordination of domestic anti-corruption work, see further nn. 176–177 and Section C.iii.

[55] Set up in 2013 to lead response to serious and organized crime, including economic crime. The National Economic Crime Centre (NECC) operates within it and includes officers from a number of agencies, including the NCA, City of London Police, and SFO.

[56] See Raphael, n. 45, 171.

[57] See e.g. the Fraud Act 2006 and Theft Act 1968, available at https://www.legislation.gov.uk/ukpga/2006/35/contents and https://www.legislation.gov.uk/ukpga/1968/60/contents, respectively.

[58] Criminal Law Act 1977, available at https://www.legislation.gov.uk/ukpga/1977/45/contents.

[59] See Accessories and Abettors Act 1861 and Serious Crime Act 2007, Part II (creating a separate criminal offence for aiding and encouraging a criminal offence to be committed—even if the crime did not take place), available at https://www.legislation.gov.uk/ukpga/Vict/24-25/94/section/8 and https://www.legislation.gov.uk/ukpga/2007/27/contents, respectively.

[60] For example, under Companies Acts (1985 and 2006) for failure to keep adequate accounting records, available at https://www.legislation.gov.uk/ukpga/1985/6/contents and https://www.legislation.gov.uk/ukpga/2006/46/contents, respectively.

[61] For example, the Proceeds of Crime Act 2002 (POCA), n. 53.

[62] There is a general consensus, however, that the offence requires reform, see Law Commission, 'Misconduct in Public Office', available at https://www.lawcom.gov.uk/project/misconduct-in-public-office/.

c. Detection and outcomes

UK agencies, like many of their counterparts, employ a combination of reactive and proactive detection techniques to gather evidence and rely on mechanisms, where feasible, to shorten and facilitate proceedings.

The CMA, for example, offers immunity from, or reductions in,[63] fines to leniency applicants meeting specified criteria in CA98 cases,[64] as well as immunity from criminal prosecution to certain applicants, through no-action letters.[65] Even if leniency is not available to an undertaking, CMA also seeks to streamline administrative procedures and reduce the risk of appeals,[66] by settling cases with firms that cooperate through early adoption of infringement decisions and the imposition of reduced penalties.

In corruption cases, the criminal penalty to be imposed is determined by the courts, which will not necessarily approve and affirm any arrangement made with the prosecutor (e.g. a reduction in penalty in return for cooperation or a guilty plea).[67] However, criminal prosecution can be forgone against those that self-report infringements or cooperate extensively with investigators.[68] For example, individuals can be offered conditional immunity from prosecution, following consultation with the Attorney General.[69] Further, prosecutors may seek a civil recovery order (CRO)[70] or conclude a deferred prosecution agreement (DPA)[71] with legal persons instead of criminal prosecution. DPAs allow—subject to the Crown Court being satisfied that it is in the interests of justice and that its terms

---

[63] See OFT413, 'Guidance as to the appropriate amount of a penalty' (September 2012) and OFT1495, 'Applications for leniency and no-action in cartel cases' (July 2013).

[64] Whether or not immunity or fine reductions are available is dependent on a number of factors, see OFT1495, n. 63. Like other leniency programmes it is designed to exploit the insecure nature of cartels and to provide greatest rewards for those that confess first.

[65] The CMA has power to confer immunity from prosecution in England and Wales, through the grant of a no-action letter to individuals, see OFT1495, n. 63.

[66] Although leniency is principally a tool to increase detection and deterrence and facilitate investigations, cooperation by leniency applicants may also create procedural efficiencies during the investigation and minimize the risk of appeals.

[67] See e.g. judgment of Thomas LJ in *Innospec Ltd* [2010] Crim LR 665 (where a guilty plea followed a plea agreement arranged with the DOJ in the US and the SFO in the UK).

[68] It is a factor that tends towards, but does not guarantee, non-prosecution.

[69] See Serious Organised Crime and Police Act 2005, s 71, available at https://www.legislation.gov.uk/ukpga/2005/15/contents.

[70] CROs have been possible since 24 February 2003, see SI 2003/130, the Proceeds of Crime Act 2002 (Commencement No. 4 Transitional Provisions and Savings) Order 2003 and available to the SRO since 2008. Until 2012, SFO policy was to deal with self-reporting of foreign bribery by CRO where possible. See e.g. CRO under POCA against Mabey Engineering (Holding) Ltd, in recognition of sums received through share dividends derived from contracts won by subsidiary (Maybey and Johnson) from foreign bribery.

[71] Introduced by the Government to supplement criminal prosecution and CRO tools, see Crime and Courts Act 2013, s 45, available at https://www.legislation.gov.uk/ukpga/2013/22/contents/enacted and DPA Code of Practice, available at https://www.cps.gov.uk/sites/default/files/documents/publications/DPA-COP.pdf. If a DPA is not complied with, the prosecutor may apply to the Crown Court for its variation or termination, in which case prosecution may follow.

148   CORRUPTION AND SUPPLIER COLLUSION UNDER THE WATERLINE?

are fair, reasonable, and proportionate[72]—prosecutions for bribery and other economic crime against bodies corporate and partnerships[73] to be deferred in return for the company's compliance with certain requirements, for example:[74] payment of a financial penalty (broadly in line with that which would have been imposed in the case of conviction following a guilty plea); compensation of victims; making a charity donation; disgorgement of profits; implementation of, or changes to, a compliance programme; cooperation in an investigation (self-reporting is beneficial but not a requirement and there is no obligation to admit guilt); or, the payment of reasonable costs of the prosecutor. DPAs were introduced to build confidence in the justice system and to allow economic crime to be tackled better, particularly by encouraging self-reporting, cooperation, and future compliance.[75] DPAs have obvious attractions for companies, including the significant advantage that mandatory debarment will not follow (as no conviction of a relevant offence has occurred).[76] They are also appealing to prosecutors, especially given the complexities, costs, and risks involved in establishing corporate criminal liability in England and Wales.

Because self-reporting is unlikely to be attractive where wrongdoing is stable and profitable and where there is not a good track record of enforcement following use of other detection techniques,[77] both the CMA and SFO, in addition to using their own monitoring and search powers, also encourage reporting via complaints and whistleblowing. For example, the CMA encourages complaints from customers, employees, or the general public,[78] and whistleblowing (it offers financial rewards of up to GBP 100,000 to those who offer information about cartel activity[79]) (whistleblowers in the UK are protected from reprisal by the Public Interest Disclosure Act 1998 (see Section 47B)).[80] In addition, UK competition and anti-corruption agencies possess their own distinct powers to gather evidence proactively, subject to applicable rights of defence,[81] through for example: interviewing

---

[72] See Crime and Courts Act 2013, n. 71, Schedule 17, paras. 7–8.

[73] Corporations do not have the right to a DPA but may be invited to negotiate one.

[74] Criminal Procedure Rules 2015, para. 5(5), available at https://www.legislation.gov.uk/uksi/2015/1490/contents/made.

[75] DPAs provide 'a way of holding companies to account without punishing innocent employees, and are an important tool in changing corporate culture for the better', Lisa Osofsky, (then) Director of the SFO, Press Release, 'UK's first Deferred Prosecution Agreement, between the SFO and Standard Bank, Successfully Ends' (30 November 2018), available at https://www.sfo.gov.uk/2018/11/30/uks-first-deferred-prosecution-agreement-between-the-sfo-and-standard-bank-successfully-ends/.

[76] The ability of the SFO to conclude DPAs has also facilitated joint investigations and cooperation with other jurisdictions, where plea arrangements or DPAs are possible (such as the US).

[77] See Chapters 2 and 3.

[78] See e.g., CMA, 'Guidance on the CMA's Investigation Procedures in Competition Act 1998 cases' (CMA8) (March 2014).

[79] See CMA, 'Rewards for Information about Cartels' (31 March 2014).

[80] It has sought to raise awareness of cartel laws and to prompt reporting by whistleblowers and leniency applicants through a CMA's 'Cheating or Competing Campaign', available at https://cheatingorcompeting.campaign.gov.uk/.

[81] Such as the principles of legal privilege, self-incrimination, and confidentiality in civil cases.

THE SYSTEM IN ENGLAND AND WALES   149

individuals; requiring documents; entering premises to search for information;[82] directed surveillance (monitoring the movement of people and vehicles); power to use covert human intelligence sources (e.g. informants);[83] and, in criminal cases, even more extensive Regulation of Investigatory Powers Act 2000 (RIPA) powers, including intrusive surveillance, property interference, and access to communications data.[84]

In addition, the CMA created a tool, which it made available to procurers and the general public, designed to screen for warning signs or red flags revealing first evidence of bid rigging in public procurement. Unfortunately, it was withdrawn following concerns about its effectiveness and flaws in its design and implementation (partly stemming from a lack of relevant data).[85] It was, therefore, proving to be a blunt tool that was not achieving its objective.

Table 5.1 Summary of core cartel and corruption offences

	CA98 (civil offence for cartel agreements)	EA02 (criminal cartel offence)	BA10 (criminal bribery offences)[86]
Individuals	× (unless an undertaking)[87]	√	√
Corporations and Partnerships	√	×	√
Enforcement	Public (e.g. CMA) and private	Prosecuted by CMA or SFO	Prosecuted by SFO or DPP

(continued)

---

[82] See CA98, n. 32, ss 25–29; EA02, n. 34, ss 192–197, and s 201; and CJA87, n. 44, s 2 and 2A.

[83] These powers are regulated by the Regulation of Investigatory Powers Act 2000 (RIPA), see ss 28 and 29 and the Regulation of Investigatory Powers (Directed Surveillance and Covert Human Intelligence Sources) Order 2010, SI 2010/521. In certain circumstances penalties (civil and criminal) may be imposed on firms, and their officers, that do not comply with powers of investigation or requirements, see, e.g., CA98, n. 32, ss 40A and B, 59, 72.

[84] See e.g. EA02, n. 34, s 199, RIPA, the Regulation of Investigatory Powers (Directed Surveillance Sources) Order 2010 and the Regulation of Investigatory Powers (Communications Data) Order 2010.

[85] The CMA launched a bid rigging awareness campaign and a free e-learning tool in June 2016. In July 2017, it produced a data analysis tool, see CMA, 'About the Cartel Screening Tool' (15 December 2017), available at https://www.gov.uk/government/publications/screening-for-cartels-tool-for-procurers/about-the-cartel-screening-tool. The tool was withdrawn from use on 19 February 2020, following extensive criticism of it, see, e.g., A. Sanchez Graels, '"Screening for Cartels" in Public Procurement: Cheating at Solitaire or Fool's Gold' (2019) 10(4) *Journal of Competition Law and Economics* 199.

[86] See also offences outlined in nn. 57–62.

[87] Such as a sole trader, see n. 35 and text.

150 CORRUPTION AND SUPPLIER COLLUSION UNDER THE WATERLINE?

Table 5.1 Continued

	CA98 (civil offence for cartel agreements)	EA02 (criminal cartel offence)	BA10 (criminal bribery offences)[86]
Sanctions for, or other consequences of, Infringement	Fines Director Disqualification Order Note leniency and settlement Exclusion/Debarment Damages	Up to 5 years imprisonment Unlimited fines Exclusion/ Debarment Note no-action letters	Up to 10 years imprisonment Fines (Corporate and Individual) Exclusion/ Debarment Note deferred prosecution agreements and civil recovery orders Note civil proceedings for tort of bribery

iii. Cases finding supplier collusion, or corruption, in domestic public procurement processes

Although the CMA is becoming increasingly interested in rooting out bid rigging impacting on public procurement, relatively few instances of either bid rigging or corruption, affecting public procurement in the UK, have been uncovered by enforcement agencies in recent years and, in no case, have corruption and collusion been found to operate together. This section summarizes some of the key cases investigated by the CMA (or its predecessor, the Office of Fair Trading (the OFT)),[88] the SFO, or the police, respectively. Essentially, they amount to a handful of competition cases—mainly civil, not criminal proceedings—and some bribery cases. The most recent higher-profile bribery cases have, however, focused on foreign bribery affecting procurements outside of the UK.

A noteworthy competition case is *Construction*,[89] where the OFT uncovered 'endemic' bid rigging in the English construction industry, which had occurred between 2000 and 2006. Bid rigging was established on 199 tenders,[90] affecting

---

[88] Although bid rigging affecting public procurement in the UK could, prior to Brexit, also be investigated by the European Commission under EU competition laws, in fact, relatively few such cases exist, see M. Hellwig and K. Hüschelrath, 'Cartel Cases and the Cartel Enforcement Process in the European Union 2001–2015: A Quantitative Assessment' (2017) 62 *Antitrust Bulletin* 400). *Marine Hoses*, however, affected UK markets, nn. 94–96.

[89] See, Case No. CE/4327-04, Decision of the Office of Fair Trading No. CA98/02/2009, 'Bid Rigging in the Construction Industry in England' (21 September 2009).

[90] The collusion occurred predominantly through cover pricing and compensatory payments made from successful bidders to unsuccessful ones. Although the OFT received evidence of cover pricing in relation to thousands of tenders, it focused its investigation on a more limited and manageable, but

THE SYSTEM IN ENGLAND AND WALES   151

building projects for schools, universities, hospitals, and private sector projects, worth more than GBP 200 million, leading to the imposition of fines totalling GBP 129.2 million on 103 companies.[91] Although the OFT considered whether, as an additional deterrent, it should recommend to procurers that they exclude infringing firms from public procurement auctions, it ultimately considered this would be inappropriate given the pervasive nature of the problem, its ability to pursue only a small proportion of the likely infringements involved,[92] and that many of the parties were taking competition law compliance seriously and steps to help avoid future breaches of competition law.

Prior to *Construction*, the OFT also issued a series of CA98 decisions finding bid rigging in the roofing industry across the UK[93] and obtained its first criminal convictions under the EA02 in relation to a global marine hoses bid rigging cartel.[94] The latter cartel divided markets and affected both public contracts emanating from the Ministry of Defence and private tenders. The three individuals involved pleaded guilty to dishonestly participating in the cartel following their arrest, and concluded plea agreements in the United States (US).[95] They were sentenced to prison, disqualified from acting as company directors, and had over GBP 1 million of assets confiscated. The companies involved were subsequently fined in administrative proceedings brought by the European Commission.[96]

Since *Construction* and *Marine Hoses*, only two individuals (both of whom also pleaded guilty) have been convicted under the criminal cartel offence[97], and

representative, number, where evidence was greatest and strongest so allowing it to reach a decision comparative swiftly, see OECD 'Policy Roundtables, Collusion and Corruption in Public Procurement', DAF/COMP/GF (2010)6 (15 October 2010), UK contribution, available at https://www.oecd.org/comp etition/cartels/46235884.pdf.

[91] The offer of penalty reductions in return for admissions led to significant procedural efficiencies and resource savings, allowing the OFT to conclude the investigation more efficiently and comparatively quickly.

[92] See n. 90.

[93] See *West Midland Roofing Contractors* (17 March 2004); *Collusive tendering for Mastic Asphalt Flat-roofing Contracts in Scotland* (8 April 2005); *Collusive tendering for felt and single ply flat-roofing contracts in the North East of England* (8 April 2005); *Collusive tendering for felt and single ply roofing contracts in Western Central Scotland* (12 July 2005); *Flat Roof and Car Park Surfacing Contracts in England and Scotland* (23 February 2006).

[94] See OFT Press Release, 'Three Imprisoned in first OFT Criminal Prosecution for Bid-Rigging' (11 June, 2008); *R v Whittle, Brammar and Allison* [2008] EWCA Crim 2560.

[95] The defendants had already pleaded guilty in the US and were returned to the UK on condition that they also plead guilty in the English courts, see further discussion of antitrust and foreign corrupt proceedings in Chapter 6.

[96] Case COMP/39406, *Marine Hoses*, Commission Decision of 28 January 2009, affirmed but fines reduced; see Case T-146/09 RENV, EU:T:2016:411.

[97] These convictions were against Nigel Snee and Barry Kenneth Cooper in relation to two separate cases, *Supply of Galvanised steel tanks: criminal investigation* (two defendants who did not plead guilty in this case were subsequently acquitted) and *Supply of precast concrete draining products: criminal investigation*, respectively, available at www.gov.uk/cma. The latter involved market sharing and price fixing, including on contracts that had been put out for tender. In both cases, the undertakings were

the CMA has only uncovered collusive tendering in breach of the CA98 in a few instances, including by office fit-out firms (cover bidding, including to one client in the public sector—Newham College of Further Education),[98] in relation to the supply and installation of certain access control and alarm systems,[99] and in 2023 again, in relation to construction, this time relating to demolition and asbestos removal contracts.[100] With regard to the latter, the CMA found that ten suppliers of demolition and removal of asbestos services had engaged in cover bidding (and, in some cases, had made side payments) in relation to contracts worth over GBP 150 million (including contracts for the development of the Bow Street Magistrate Court and Police Station, the Met Police Training College, and Oxford University). Eight of the firms received reduced fines after settling with the CMA and admitting their participation (two also benefited from discounts under the CMA's leniency policy). This case illustrates the CMA's more recent prioritization of action in the public procurement sphere, and also its willingness to conduct investigations where suspicions of bid rigging arise.[101]

The SFO has concluded a number of investigations involving bribery in procurement processes (some under the BA10 and some under the pre-existing laws[102]). However, perhaps because it is tasked with leading responses in international cases and because it focuses only on cases of serious and complex fraud involving a high value,[103] its principal focus of attention in relation to corruption and procurement has been on cases of *foreign* bribery.[104] In contrast, only one case between 2014-2022, *FH Bertling* (Project Jasmine), appears to relate to bribery in a domestic procurement process, and it did not involve public procurement or bribery of a public official.[105]

---

subsequently found to have infringed CA98 Chapter 1; see *Galvanised steel tanks for water storage main cartel decision*, 19 December 2016 and *Galvanised steel tanks for water storage information exchange decision*, 19 December 2016 and *Supply or precast concrete draining products*, 23 October 2019, affirmed Case 1337/1/12/19, *FP McCann v CMA* [2020] CAT 28.

[98] 'Design, Construction and Fit-Out Services' (12 April 2019).

[99] 'Collusive Tendering in Relation to the Supply and Installation of Certain Access Control and Alarm Systems' (6 December 2013).

[100] See '*Supply of Construction Services*' (21 March 2023).

[101] See CMA Press release, 'CMA Provisionally Finds Illegal Cartels in Construction Industry' (24 June 2022) and J. Enser, G. Laverack, and V. Siguan-Cevera, 'UK Public Procurement: Increasing Risks for Cartel Participants' *CPI Antitrust Chronicle* (August 2022). In December 2022, however, the CMA dropped a probe into procurement processes run by the Home Office in relation to immigration removal centres.

[102] See n. 45.

[103] See n. 54 (it deals with a small number of large economic crime cases which rarely involve sums of less than GBP 50 million).

[104] See Section B.v below.

[105] See SFO's public record of archived cases, Lord et al., n. 45 and M. Sognnes Andresen and M. Button, 'The Profile and Detection of Bribery in Norway and England and Wales: A Comparative Study' (2019) 16(1) *European Journal of Criminology* 18.

THE SYSTEM IN ENGLAND AND WALES   153

Cases involving domestic bribery thus tend to be prosecuted by the Crown Prosecution Service (CPS) following non-SFO investigations, see for example *R v Ozakpinar* (Adam Osman),[106] *Skansen Interior Ltd,*[107] and *R v Brian Chant.*[108] Only the former concerned public procurement. In this case, Mr Osman, the chief procurement officer for the CPS, received concurrent sentences of two-and-a-half years' imprisonment for corruption and false accounting after he sidestepped normal procedures and awarded, in return for lump sum payments, contracts to two friends.

iv. Foreign bribery

The UK has been one of the more active enforcers of foreign bribery laws, or corruption involving foreign procurements.[109] For example, the SFO[110] has concluded DPAs with Airbus SE,[111] Amec Foster Wheeler,[112] Anonymous SME,[113] Gulrap

---

[106] [2008] EWCA Crim 875. See also e.g., *R v Ford* [2011] EWCA Crim 473; *R v Bush* [2003] EWCA Crim 480; *R v Bennett & Wilson* [1996] 2 Cr App R(S) 879; *R v Foxley* [1995] 2 Cr App R 523.

[107] February 2018, proceedings under BA10, n. 46, against the company and its previous manager, Banks, in relation to bribes paid (totalling GBP 10,000) to Deakin to secure private refurbishment contracts. Even though the case was self-reported by new management, which had put a compliance programme in place and cooperated with the investigation, the corporation was convicted under s 7 (and its adequate procedures defence was rejected by the jury). Banks and Deakin also pleaded guilty to offences under ss 1 and 2 and were sentenced to imprisonment and disqualified from acting as a director for a period of years.

[108] This case involved a conviction for bribery, following an investigation by City of London Police's Fraud Operations Team. Chant was found to have abused his position in a company to secure multimillion pound contracts for an IT company he had previous connections with, in return for payments totalling GBP 474,069.60. See also discussion of challenges to public procurement processes based on apparent bias, n. 29 and text.

[109] The total number of SFO cases relative to the UK economy nonetheless remains low, see further Chapter 4, and in 2022 Transparency International noted that it dropped from an active to only a moderate enforcer of the laws, see https://www.transparency.org/en/press/exporting-corruption-2022-enfo rcement-against-foreign-bribery-hits-historic-low; Lord et al., n. 45, and OECD, 'Implementing the OECD Anti-Bribery Convention – Phase 4 Two-Year Follow-Up Report: United Kingdom' (2019), available at https://www.oecd.org/corruption/united-kingdom-phase-4-follow-up-report-eng.pdf.

[110] Further details of the cases discussed below are available at https://www.sfo.gov.uk/our-cases/case-archive/#azk. Some cases have also been prosecuted by the CPS, see, e.g., in 2013 Andrew Capelson, following an investigation by the City of London Police, was convicted of corruption for paying a bribe to secure a loan from the European Bank of Reconstruction and Development and imprisoned.

[111] In 2020, a DPA was concluded which included payment of EUR 990,963,712 (comprising disgorgement of profit of EUR 585,939,740, a penalty of EUR 398,034,571 and costs). The case concerned an investigation in cooperation with French and US authorities into failure to prevent bribery in Malaysia, Sri Lanka, Taiwan, Indonesia, and Ghana.

[112] The company concluded a GBP 103 million DPA agreement with the SFO on 1 July 2021, but the SFO did not pursue prosecutions against individuals, despite widespread bribery in multiple countries, available at https://www.sfo.gov.uk/cases/amec-foster-wheeler-plc/.

[113] In 2016, following an investigation into conspiracy to corrupt and bribe to win contracts in foreign jurisdictions and failure to prevent bribery (payment of GBP 6.55 million (disgorgement of profits plus a penalty)).

Systems,[114] Rolls-Royce Plc,[115] Sarclad Ltd,[116] and Standard Bank.[117] A number of criminal individual[118] and corporate convictions have also been obtained, for example, against Alstom Network UK,[119] Sweet Group Plc,[120] Innospec Ltd[121], and Smith and Ouzman.[122] On some occasions, it has been sought to reinvest the proceeds of crime in the jurisdiction in which the bribes were paid.[123] A number of criminal proceedings brought have, however, been unsuccessful, and the SFO has been criticized for its poor record in prosecuting cases.[124]

[114] Concluded in 2019 in relation to bribery of a Korean public official. However, two individuals were acquitted following criminal proceedings, available at https://www.sfo.gov.uk/2019/12/20/three-individuals-acquitted-as-sfo-confirms-dpa-with-guralp-systems-ltd/.

[115] Payment of GBP 497.25 million (plus GBP 13 million prosecution costs) in 2017 following investigations involving bribery and conspiracy to corrupt to win business in Indonesia, Thailand, India, Russia, Nigeria, China, and Malaysia, false accounting and failure to prevent bribery. Although the DPA involved an agreement to assist in prosecution of individuals, no prosecution of individuals associated with the company occurred, available at https://www.sfo.gov.uk/cases/rolls-royce-plc/.

[116] Concluded in 2016 following investigations into a conspiracy to corrupt in relation to twenty-seven separate overseas contracts, and a failure to prevent the systematic use of bribes. The terms of the DPA included: GBP 6,201,085 (disgorgement of gross profits), GBP 352,000 financial penalty (reduced substantially because of the inability of the corporate to pay). Sarclad's US registered parent company paid GBP 1,953,085 as repayment of a significant proportion of the dividends that it received from the company over the indictment period, available at https://www.sfo.gov.uk/cases/sarclad-ltd/. In subsequent criminal proceedings three individuals (Michael Sorby, Adrian Leek, and David Justice) were acquitted.

[117] Approved in 2016 following investigation of a corrupt payment made by a sister company in Tanzania in an attempt to win a contract there (including payment of compensation (USD 6 million), disgorgement of profit (USD 8.4 million), penalty (USD 16.8 million), and payment of SFO costs). No individuals were prosecuted in the UK.

[118] See e.g., convictions of Basil Al Jarah (payments related to the award of contracts to Unaoil), 15 July 2019, and Carole Ann Hodson (bribery scheme to secure contracts for ALCA Fasteners Ltd), June 2019. On 11 January 2019, Stephen Emler, Giuseppe Morreale, Christopher Lane, and Colin Bagwell were sentenced in relation to the SFO's Angola investigation into FH Bertling (Angola), available at https://www.sfo.gov.uk/2019/01/11/four-more-sentenced-in-fh-bertling-trial/. Peter Michael Chapman was also convicted in relation to corrupt payment to secure contracts for his company, Securency, and four individuals were sentenced in relation to bribery to secure contracts from the governments of Indonesia and Iraq for the supply of products produced by Innospec, see n. 121.

[119] Both individuals and the corporation, Alstom Network, were convicted in proceedings relating to conspiracy to corrupt in relation to a contract to supply trams in Tunisia, 25 November 2019.

[120] Sweet Group pleaded guilty in relation to failure to prevent bribery by its Middle Eastern subsidiary and was ordered to pay GBP 2.25 million, 19 February 2016.

[121] Innospec Ltd pleaded guilty and was fined (USD 12.7 million) after cooperation with the SFO and US authorities.

[122] This was the first SFO trial resulting in conviction of a corporate (Smith and Ouzman Ltd) for foreign bribery (to secure business contracts in Kenya and Mauritania), 22 December 2014. Two individuals were also convicted (Nicholas Smith and Christopher Smith).

[123] See e.g., the SFO's confiscation order relating to the Smith and Ouzman case, n. 122, paid for seven new ambulances in Kenya, GTDT, *Anticorruption Laws*, 2020, 180 and Chapter 3, Section C.ii.b.

[124] For example, it has been criticized for failure to charge individuals at Amec Foster Wheeler Energy following widespread bribery in multiple countries and conclusion of a GBP 103 million DPA with the company. The failure is argued to highlight the lack of UK action against executives. The SFO is also being investigated for its handling of the prosecution of Unaoil executive, Ziad Akle, and for disclosure failings, after the Court of Appeal found the defendant's conviction to be unsafe. The investigation by former High Court judge and director of public prosecutions, Sir David Calvert-Smith, was announced by the (then) attorney general, Suella Braverman QC, on 9 February 2022

C. Is There a Corruption or Collusion Problem in the Public Procurement Sector in England and Wales?

Section B notes that relatively few cases of supplier collusion or corruption in domestic public procurement processes have been uncovered or sanctioned. Although a greater number of cases of foreign bribery have been highlighted, the number is low relative to the UK economy.[125] This section examines a range of factors suggesting that the scarcity of cases may not be because the rules are having their desired effect (preventing and deterring corruption and collusion), but because these practices are simply not being exposed. Indeed, not only do a number of reports and surveys suggest that these practices may be occurring undetected, but the foreign bribery cases indicate that firms have been willing to engage in unethical and unlawful behaviour overseas. It seems conceivable therefore that they might also do so in the UK.[126] Further, a closer examination of the system indicates that the cause of this mismatch between revealed cases and perceptions could be that: (i) weaknesses in the public procurement system may not be preventing corruption and collusion from occurring; and (ii) anti-corruption and competition law enforcement agencies have not (until recently at least in the competition sphere) prioritized enforcement in this area, so reducing the deterrent effect of the law and allowing such conduct to operate below the surface. Finally, difficulties result from the fact that the three distinct regimes are not working together to produce synergies.

i. Perceptions and survey evidence

A number of surveys and Government reports suggest that concerns (including Government concerns) about unlawful behaviour in this sphere do exist and that deeper diagnosis in the UK is required. For example: the Cabinet Office Cross-Government Fraud Landscape Annual Reports 2019 and 2022 estimate that significant sums are lost to procurement fraud each year;[127] the Cabinet Office recognizes the inherently high risk of fraud and corruption undermining government responses to emergency or disaster recovery situations;[128] the House of Commons Public

---

[125] See n. 109.

[126] The 2019 Report of the Fraud Advisory Panel, available at https://www.fraudadvisorypanel.org/wp-content/uploads/2019/07/Hidden-in-plain-sight-Jul19-WEB.pdf.

[127] Cabinet Office, 'Cross-Government Fraud Landscape Annual Report 2019' (2020), available at https://assets.publishing.service.gov.uk/government/uploads/system/uploads/attachment_data/file/864268/Cross-Government_Fraud_Landscape_Annual_Report_2019_WA__1_.pdf and Public Sector Authority, 'Cross-Government Fraud Landscape, Annual Report 2022 report, available at https://www.gov.uk/government/publications/cross-government-fraud-landscape-annual-report-2022.

[128] See International Public Sector Fraud Forum, 'Fraud in Emergency Management and Recovery: Principles for Effective Fraud Control' (2020) (published in collaboration with the Cabinet

Accounts Committee found that, of GBP 12 billion spent on personal protection equipment (PPE) in the first year of the COVID-19 pandemic, 75 per cent was lost (GBP 6.6 billion worth of the PPE did not meet standards or was not of a standard preferred by the national health service (NHS), GBP 673 million was spent on defective equipment, and GBP 4.7 billion was lost in overpayments) and concern has been expressed that the use of a 'VIP' fast lane by the Government and NHS bodies during the pandemic may have contributed to GBP billions being misspent;[129] the Chartered Institution of Public Finance and Accountancy's Counter Fraud and Corruption Tracker (CFacT) survey[130] states that 23 per cent of respondents reported experiencing fraud, bribery, or corruption relating to procurement in the 2017/18 financial year and that procurement is one of the greatest areas of perceived fraud risk; and a 2020 Ministry of Housing, Communities and Local Government review into the risks of fraud and corruption in local government procurement[131] records a number of case studies involving corruption or collusion in council public procurement. In addition, the latter review expresses fear that, as with an iceberg, these constitute only the visible portion above the waterline and a small fraction of the total problem, with the unknown majority of incidents hidden below the surface.[132] The details emerging of the Government's use of the VIP lane to fast-track offers of PPE from companies with political links (a process which arguably seemed systemically biased) is one of the factors, along with concerns about persistent, unaddressed breaches of ministerial codes, that has led to the UK's sharp descent in 2022 in Transparency International's Corruption Perceptions Index (CPI).[133]

Office and the Commonwealth Fraud Prevention Centre), available at https://assets.publishing.service. gov.uk/government/uploads/system/uploads/attachment_data/file/864310/Fraud_in_Emergency_Ma nagement_and_Recovery_10Feb.pdf.

[129] See UK Parliament, '£4 billion of unusable PPE bought in first year of pandemic will be burnt "to generate power"', *Public Accounts Committee*, News Article (10 June 2022), available at https://committ ees.parliament.uk/committee/127/public-accounts-committee/news/171306/4-billion-of-unusable-ppe-bought-in-first-year-of-pandemic-will-be-burnt-to-generate-power/ (some of the defective PPE is yet to be disposed of) and for example, the national crime agency is investigating potential fraud by PPE Medpro, a company that received more than GBP 200 million of PPE contracts weeks after Baroness Mone used a Government 'VIP' lane procedure for prioritization of contracts towards suppliers recommended by members of parliament and the House of Lords, and the politically connected, during the pandemic. Baroness Mone and her husband are alleged to have benefited from the contract, and most of the supplies were rejected by the health department, see 'Revealed: The Full Inside Story of the Michelle Mone PPE Scandal', *The Guardian* (9 December 2022), available at https://www.theguardian.com/uk-news/2022/dec/09/revealed-the-full-inside-story-of-the-michelle-mone-ppe-scandal.
[130] See CIPFA, 'CIPFA Fraud and Corruption Tracker', available at https://www.cipfa.org/services/ cipfa-solutions/fraud-and-corruption/fraud-and-corruption-tracker.
[131] Ministry of Housing, Communities & Local Government, 'Review into the Risks of Fraud and Corruption in Local Government Procurement—A Commitment from the UK Anti-Corruption Strategy 2017 to 2022' (June 2020), available at https://assets.publishing.service.gov.uk/government/ uploads/system/uploads/attachment_data/file/890748/Fraud_and_corruption_risks_in_local_gover nment_procurement_FINAL.pdf.
[132] 'Review into the Risks of Fraud and Corruption in Local Government Procurement—A Commitment from the UK Anti-Corruption Strategy 2017 to 2022', n. 131, 8.
[133] See n. 3 and text.

Further, the Chartered Institute of Building in 2013[134], while exploring corruption (which it defines to include bid rigging) in the construction industry, reported that nearly half of the professionals surveyed (49 per cent) believed that corruption is common in UK construction (most commonly at the prequalification and tendering stages) and 10 per cent thought that corruption cost their organization more than GBP 1 million in a year.[135] These findings are especially concerning when combined with: the large proportion of public procurement spending on construction (45 per cent between 2009 and 2013[136]); reports estimating that a significant percentage of investment in publicly funded construction projects may be lost through mismanagement, cronyism, or corruption;[137] the OFT's 2009 finding that bid rigging was endemic in UK construction; and current CMA research suggesting that 77 per cent of businesses still do not understand competition law well and that only six per cent run any competition law training.[138]

These reviews reinforce the less than rosy pictures painted by other, more general surveys, for example:[139] an EU survey estimating GBP 3 billion of losses each year through UK procurement fraud;[140] and a 2017 Special Eurobarometer[141] recording that, of 1382 UK interviewees, 55 per cent thought that corruption was widespread, 45 per cent thought that corruption had increased in the previous three years, 14 per cent had been affected by corruption, and 25 per cent thought that the taking of bribes for personal gain by officials awarding public tenders was

---

[134] The Chartered Institute of Building (CIOB), 'A Report Exploring Corruption in the UK Construction Industry' (2013), available at https://www.ciob.org/sites/default/files/CIOB%20resea rch%20-%20Corruption%20in%20the%20UK%20Construction%20Industry%20September%202 013.pdf.

[135] 20 per cent also thought that cover pricing was not corrupt, see Government UK, 'UK Businesses' Understanding of Competition Law', available at https://www.gov.uk/government/publications/uk-bus inesses-understanding-of-competition-law.

[136] M. Fazekas and E. Dávid-Barrett, 'Corruption Risks in UK Public Procurement and New Anti-Corruption Tools' (2015) Government Transparency Institute Research Paper, relying on OJEU (TED) data.

[137] See e.g., Construction Sector Transparency Initiative, 'UK Launch of the Construction Sector Transparency Initiative International Programme' (22 October 2012) (stating annual losses from mismanagement, inefficiency, and corruption in global construction could amount to USD 2.5 trillion annually by 2020); reports of breach of procurement laws in the Grenfell Tower Procurement Process, 'Grenfell Tower Landlord Had "Secret" Meeting on Cost Cutting, Inquiry Told', *The Guardian* (15 October 2020), available at https://www.theguardian.com/uk-news/2020/oct/15/grenfell-tower-landlord-had-secret-meeting-on-cost-cutting-inquiry-told; J. Wells, 'Corruption, Grabbing and Development: Real World Challenges' in T. Søreide and A. Williams (eds), *Corruption and Collusion in Construction: A View from the Industry* (Edward Elgar Publishing, 2014) 23.

[138] See 'UK Businesses' Understanding of Competition Law', n. 135.

[139] Fraud Advisory Panel, n. 126 ('Does the UK have a corruption problem? Officially, no. In reality we just don't know').

[140] See 'Public Procurement—Study on Administrative Capacity in the EU United Kingdom Country Profile', available at https://ec.europa.eu/regional_policy/sources/policy/how/improving-investment/ public-procurement/study/country_profile/uk.pdf.

[141] Special Eurobarometer 470 (December 2017). See also Eurobarometer (2017), Flash Eurobarometer 375 and Eurobarometer (2014), Businesses' Attitudes towards Corruption in the EU, Flash Eurobarometer 374 (February 2014).

158 CORRUPTION AND SUPPLIER COLLUSION UNDER THE WATERLINE?

widespread.[142] Even if these surveys reflect the fact that businesses and individuals may now be better informed as spending on ethics and compliance increases, the core indication that corruption and collusion might be relatively common in public procurement cannot be ignored.

ii. Weaknesses in procurement processes

Although UK procurement rules are designed to ensure open and transparent government contracting, there has been concern that opportunities for both corruption and collusion arose under the pre-PA23 regime as a result of weaknesses in the design of the rules or in implementation or monitoring of processes. Corruption or collusion may have been occurring, for example, where:

(i) Weaknesses in the procurement laws have existed. One difficulty has been that UK rules have allowed for negotiated procedure without prior publication in specific circumstances (e.g. in cases of extreme urgency).[143] A concern exists that it has been relatively easy for justifications for such awards to be proffered, whilst at the same time it has been difficult to monitor for conflicts of interest and for the breaches of the rules to be challenged (as the COVID-19 experience demonstrates);[144]

(ii) Procuring bodies do not sufficiently promote an anti-corruption organizational culture (actively highlighting and tackling corruption risks by using conflicts of interest and gifts and hospitality registers[145]), or take steps to ensure officials have a sufficient understanding of the objectives of the procurement processes. Indeed, neither anti-corruption nor competition law training[146] is conducted systematically within procuring bodies, general use is not made of counter-fraud models, and procurers do not

---

[142] See also e.g., RAND Europe, Eur. Parliamentary Res. Serv. PE 579.319: The Cost of Non-Europe in the Area of Organised Crime and Corruption: Annex II Corruption (2016) 9 (corruption risks during public procurement could cost Europe around EUR 5 billion a year).

[143] PCR, n. 5, reg 32, especially 32(2)(c). These powers were used during the COVID-19 pandemic, Procurement Policy Note, 'Responding to COVID-19 Information Note', PPN 01/20 (March 2020), see n. 129 and text.

[144] See Section B.i.

[145] This is especially problematic as increased commercialization is creating a greater number of conflicts of interests in government contracting and corruption incentives. See also Transparency International UK, 'Permission Accomplished—Assessing Corruption Risks in Local Government Planning' (2020), available at https://www.transparency.org.uk/sites/default/files/pdf/publications/Per mission%20Accomplished%20-%20TIUK.pdf (noting that thirty-two councillors across twenty-four councils held critical decision-making positions in their local planning system whilst also working for developers that might be applying for planning permission to them).

[146] See e.g., the Cheating or Competing Campaign, Advice for Public Procurers, available at https://cheatingorcompeting.campaign.gov.uk/#advice_for_public_procurers.

routinely work closely with law enforcement agencies.[147] There is also some concern that the UK Ministerial Code of Conduct, which includes a duty to ensure that no conflict arises, or appears to arise, between ministers' public duties and private interests, lacks teeth and effectiveness;[148]

(iii) Procurers are able to reduce a pool of bidders artificially by, for example, failing to publicize tenders in advance, as required, or providing too short advertising periods;

(iv) Tenders only attract a single bidder;[149]

(v) Post-award contract modifications occur as a result of weak post-contract award management;

(vi) Electronic systems are not used consistently to record registers or to conduct e-procurement;

(vii) There is insufficient oversight of procurement decisions via internal or external controls;

(viii) Insufficient data is available (although there are requirements to publish data, there is great variation in the quality of data that is published, mandatory data is often missing, and no procedure for sanctioning noncompliance exists[150]);

(ix) Pressure exists to ensure that procurement decisions reflect not only value for money, but also other public policy goals including social and environmental ones.[151] These objectives inevitably inject a greater degree of subjectivity into the selection process, making it more difficult to monitor for tender awards affected by improper motives;

(x) The legal complexity surrounding the use of exclusion grounds, and their lack of use, have created a risk to the integrity of the procurement processes.

Particular problems thus appear to lie in culture, training, and monitoring of public procurement processes and adherence to rules. Indeed, a Government report draws attention to the fact that, following the abolition of the Audit Commission

---

[147] See 'Review into the Risks of Fraud and Corruption in Local Government Procurement— A Commitment from the UK Anti-Corruption Strategy 2017 to 2022', n. 131 and Transparency International Report, 'Corruption in UK Local Government: The Mounting Risks?' (October 2013), available at https://www.transparency.org.uk/sites/default/files/pdf/publications/Corruption_in_UK_Local_Government-_The_Mounting_Risks.pdf (identifying 16 corruption risks arising from legislative change, including e.g. the abolition of the Audit Commission (which provided an independent source of public audit and powers to collect and analyse nationwide fraud and corruption data), Standards for England and the abandonment of a universal code of conduct).

[148] Whether and how it is investigated is entirely at the Prime Minister's discretion. Contrast e.g. the Canadian Conflicts of Interests Act discussed in Chapter 10.

[149] See, e.g., the Opentender UK website, available at https://opentender.eu/uk/dashboards/integrity; Fazekas and Dávid-Barrett, n. 136.

[150] Fazekas and Dávid-Barrett, n. 136.

[151] See n. 13.

160 CORRUPTION AND SUPPLIER COLLUSION UNDER THE WATERLINE?

and the handing back of responsibility for ethical standards to local authorities, monitoring and scrutiny of local spending has become especially hard in spite of the large sums of money they spend[152] and the close connections that often exist between officials and businesses.[153] Further, it notes that there is no longer any clear record of how many detected procurement fraud cases exist as this information does not have to be published under the Local Government Transparency Code.[154] Council auditors have also identified red flags, weaknesses in governance, and in construction of public procurement processes.[155] For example,[156] a public interest report into Newham Council in 2015 identified irregularities (including failure to obtain cost reports or revised contracts from contractors, no consultation on changes to the scope of the project and price increases, and the allocation of work without following procurement rules and member approval) in relation to Newham Council projects to build a new Sixth Form Centre, extend the Town Hall, and improve the Council Chambers.[157]

Although Section D notes that the PA23 seeks to address some of these weaknesses, not all of the matters highlighted are dealt with.

iii. Weaknesses in corruption and competition laws

One difficulty with the Bribery Act is that it does not capture, or easily capture, all forms of corrupt conduct, as broadly described in this book (especially, cronyism and favouritism[158]). In addition, it appears that enforcement in this sphere may be insufficient to deter bribery or bid rigging. Indeed, although it is seen in the earlier chapters of this book that the probability of detection has a significant impact on

---

[152] Councils in England spend approximately GBP 55 billion a year on goods, and works and services, Local Government Association, 'National Procurement Strategy for Local Government in England 2018' (June 2018) 5, available at https://www.local.gov.uk/sites/default/files/documents/11.122%20-%20National%20Procurement%20Strategy%202018_main%20report_V7.pdf. See also *Permission Accomplished*, n. 145.

[153] See e.g., 'Review into the Risks of Fraud and Corruption in Local Government Procurement—A Commitment from the UK Anti-Corruption Strategy 2017 to 2022', n. 131 and Fazekas and Dávid-Barrett, n. 136.

[154] In contrast, when in existence, the Audit Commission reported on detected procurement fraud cases (e.g. cases with a value of GBP 4.4 million in the year 2013/14 and GBP 15.3 million in the year 2010/11).

[155] Further, the National Audit Office has expressed concern that red flags, and anxieties about weaknesses in governance arrangements suggesting that certain councils may not be securing value for money, National Audit Office. 'Local auditor reporting in England 2018' (January 2019), available at https://www.nao.org.uk/wp-content/uploads/2019/01/Local-auditor-reporting-in-England-2018.pdf.

[156] See also June 2012 Public Interest Report on Wirral Council (raising concerns about conflicts of interest at Wirral Council in relation to contracts for the provision of highway and engineering services).

[157] June 2015 Public Interest Report on Newham Council, see also n. 98 and text.

[158] But see discussion of public procurement challenges based on apparent bias, n. 29 and text.

the commission of serious offences,[159] there is a picture of limited enforcement in both the bid rigging and bribery spheres.

In the competition sphere, this problem has been well known for some time. In 2011, the Government set out its view that the competition regime was not having its desired deterrent effect in relation to anti-competitive agreements because of: insufficient public decisions under the CA98 (and/or Article 101 TFEU)[160] and the weak record of enforcement under the cartel offence.[161] Although a number of reforms were implemented to rectify this problem, the low volume of enforcement continued to receive criticism.[162] When still a member of the European Competition Network (ECN), the CMA (and its predecessor, the OFT) adopted less than sixty infringement decisions under the CA98 and/or Articles 101 and 102 TFEU[163] between the Act's coming into force and December 2019 (a low rate of activity compared to other competition agencies in the EU).[164] Only just over half of these cases involved cartels,[165] meaning the UK competition agency has adopted less than two cartel decisions on average per year since the CA98 came into force. Further, since *Construction* in 2009, few decisions have, until recently at least, focused on collusive tendering involving public procurement.

In addition, in spite of (i) the importance attached by the Government to the deterrent effect of the criminal cartel offence, and (ii) fundamental reforms introduced to increase its effectiveness (in particular through increasing funding, enhancing enforcement personnel, and removing the dishonesty requirement from the offence[166]), only five individuals have to date been convicted under it in

---

[159] See Chapters 3 and 4.

[160] For example, in 2011 the Government noted that only 27 infringement decisions had been adopted since 2004, the UK had only notified 12 intended Article101/102 TFEU decisions to the European Commission (compared to the 71 reported by France, 66 by Germany, 62 by Italy, and 42 by Spain: Department for Business Innovation and Skills, 'A Competition Regime for Growth: A Consultation on Options for Reform' (March 2011), available at https://www.regulation.org.uk/library/2011-competition-regime-for-growth-consultation.pdf.

[161] And concern that the criminal offence might not be viable, in particular because of the competition agency's insufficient expertise in running a criminal investigation successfully, see 'A Competition Regime for Growth', nn. 160 and 170.

[162] See e.g., National Audit Office Report of 2016, available at https://www.nao.org.uk/report/the-uk-competition-regime/.

[163] See Competition and Markets Authority Cases, available at https://www.gov.uk/cma-cases. See also B.J. Rodger, 'Application of the Domestic and EU Antitrust Prohibitions: An Analysis of the UK Competition Authority's Enforcement Practice' (2020) 8(1) *Journal of Antitrust Enforcement* 86 (identifying 55 CA98 infringement decisions by the OFT/CMA).

[164] For example, the UK notified 41 envisaged Articles 101 and 102 decisions to the European Commission between 1 May 2004 and 31 December 2019, compared with 159, 124, 160, and 127 envisaged decisions notified by France, Germany, Italy, and Spain, respectively, available at https://ec.europa.eu/competition/ecn/statistics.html.

[165] See Rodger, n. 163, identifying 35 cartel cases. The sectoral regulators have only adopted three infringement decisions in total (they have adopted a number of non-infringement decisions in contrast).

[166] See A. Jones and R. Williams, 'The UK Response to the Global Effort Against Cartels' (2014) 2(1) *Journal of Antitrust Enforcement* 100.

162 CORRUPTION AND SUPPLIER COLLUSION UNDER THE WATERLINE?

seventeen years, all following guilty pleas.[167] Although the CMA now routinely seeks director disqualification orders in civil cases,[168] the record in the criminal sphere is a far cry from the six–ten annual prosecutions predicted.[169] In contrast, a number of criminal investigations have been closed; all other criminal prosecutions under the Act have failed; and in 2019, the then Chairman of the CMA requested that the CMA be relieved of its primary responsibility for criminal prosecutions, especially as it does not have the specialist expertise or the scale of cases to warrant the cost, and the complexity of tackling criminal cases.[170]

Although collecting data on prosecutions and convictions under the BA10 is not straightforward,[171] a similar picture of limited enforcement exists.[172] Relatively few investigations into bribery have ensued;[173] those that take place are often of a long duration; and, the SFO has focused on foreign bribery[174] and cases of higher value and made extensive use of DPAs.[175] Further, no single institution has been tasked with responsibility for coordination of domestic anti-corruption work; there is no central register of bribery investigations or judgments; and enforcement against corrupt activity within the UK does not appear to have been prioritized[176]—such cases have not been significant 'numerically or in terms of the status'.[177] Rather, the spotlight has not fallen on domestic bribery because of the lack of a clear or central approach and a mechanism for reporting and responding to domestic bribery;

[167] See nn. 95–97 and text.

[168] See n. 185 and text.

[169] OFT365, n. 41, 3.6.

[170] See Chairman of the CMA, Andrew Tyrie's letter to the Secretary of State for Business Enterprise, Industry and Skills, available at https://www.gov.uk/government/publications/letter-from-andrew-tyrie-to-the-secretary-of-state-for-business-energy-and-industrial-strategy. Although the SFO has power to accept cases, it is not responsible for the grant of no-action letters (however, it will not bring fraud proceedings where the CMA has granted immunity, see MOU, n. 44, para. 10) and has not to date undertaken its own cartel offence prosecution.

[171] House of Lords, Select Committee, n. 46, 16.

[172] Tony Blair's legacy on anti-corruption is to have provided the UK with the toughest anti-corruption law worldwide, if applied (however, arguably in breach of the separation of powers, he was able to encourage the closing of a corruption investigation into BAE, see n. 47); F. Heimann and M. Pieth, *Confronting Corruption: Past Concerns, Present Challenges, and Future Strategies* (Oxford University Press, 2018) 94.

[173] House of Lords, Select Committee, n. 46, 16.

[174] But, the number of these cases remains low relatively, see n. 109.

[175] The UK enforcement authorities have been less active than for example their US or German counterparts, see T. M. Funk and A.S. Butros (eds), *From Backsheesh to Bribery: Understanding the Global Fight Against Corruption and Graft* (Oxford University Press, 2019) xxxiii; House of Lords, Select Committee, n. 46, 7–9.

[176] See House of Lords Bribery Act Committee, 2018, 108 and Lord et al., n. 45. See also Her Majesty's Inspectorate of Constabulary and Fire and Rescue Services, 'Time to Choose: An Inspection of the Police Response to Fraud' (April 2019), available at https://www.justiceinspectorates.gov.uk/hmicfrs/publications/an-inspection-of-the-police-response-to-fraud/ (finding disjointed and ineffective law enforcement against fraud, that fraud was not the highest of enforcement priorities, and the need for a national policing fraud strategy).

[177] Lord et al., n. 45, 6–7 ('The UK approach, whether strategic or institutional, has focused on the international context, in part because of the drivers for reform and in part because of the UK's very public commitment to taking a proactive role in addressing international bribery').

its smaller scale;[178] its less overt nature in some cases;[179] the inherent difficulties in detecting a crime that the victim is unaware of and in convicting corporations; the lack of comprehensive training on the BA10 in many police forces;[180] the lack of interagency cooperation and coordination;[181] and the abolition of monitoring agencies such as the Audit Commission.[182]

All of this suggests that the risk of collusive tendering or bribery being detected, prosecuted, and prohibited is low.[183] Consequently, it is especially important that any sanctions actually imposed for these infringements are sufficient to ensure deterrence and to compensate for the fact that the sanctions may not be imposed at all (and even if imposed will bite well after the gains had been realized).[184] In criminal cases, penalties must also be sufficient to punish the offender and to reflect societal condemnation of the conduct. The record under both the competition and bribery laws, however, suggests that penalties are unlikely to be having these effects.

In relation to cartels, the main outcome of cases has been the imposition of corporate sanctions for breach of the CA98. Although the CMA has started to make greater use of its power to seek disqualification of directors involved in CA98 infringements,[185] criminal sanctions for individuals have been rare, even though a core aim of the criminal cartel regime was to increase deterrence.[186]

---

[178] Small-scale bribery can, 'if left unchecked, build up into a multi-million pound industry', see House of Lords, Select Committee, n. 46, 5 and Chapter 4, nn. 47-48 and text.

[179] See Chapter 4 and discussion of the misconduct in public office offence, n. 62 and text.

[180] Police forces and the CPS already find it difficult to cope with their normal caseload of for example rape, robbery, and murder, without having to deal with lengthy and complex corruption investigations and prosecutors.

[181] House of Lords, Select Committee, n. 46, Chapter 3.

[182] Prosecution of white-collar crime may also have fallen as a result of government targets pressurizing police forces to concentrate on cases with high clear up statistics, businesses becoming more sophisticated, and austerity hitting resources of investigating authorities, including the SFO, and fraud squads within police forces. For example, the SFO's core funding was reduced from GBP 52 million to GBP 33 million between 2008 and 2016 (it was able to apply for 'blockbuster funding' from the Treasury to deal with specific cases, but this resulted in the SFO having to rely on temporary staff and prevented it from building capacity and expertise, see, e.g., The HM Crown Prosecution Services Inspectorate, available at https://www.justiceinspectorates.gov.uk/hmcpsi/inspections/sfo-governance-arrangements/). Although its funding increased again to GBP 52.7 million in April 2018, relatively few defendants have been convicted following prosecution by it, see Lord Garnier statement before House of Lords Select Committee, n. 46, 69.

[183] CIOB, n. 134 ('The distinct lack of prosecutions under the act has raised questions from some industry figures about how it is enforced by the [SFO]. Interestingly, in a poll of over 2,000 individuals from various industries by Deloitte LLP, 57 per cent of respondents were not worried about the possibility of enforcement action against their company. In addition, one third of respondents lacked any knowledge of the act').

[184] See Chapter 4.

[185] This power has existed since 2002. Although it was only first used in 2016, the CMA has now started to use it more routinely; P. Whelan, 'The Emerging Contribution of Director Disqualification in the UK' in B. Rodger, P. Whelan, and A. MacCulloch (eds), *The UK Competition Regime: A Twenty-Year Retrospective* (Oxford University Press, 2021).

[186] See e.g., OFT, 'Drivers of Compliance and Non-Compliance with Competition Law – An OFT Report' (2010), available at https://www.gov.uk/government/uploads/system/uploads/attachment_data/file/284405/oft1227.pdf; J.M. Connor, 'Recidivism Revealed: Private International Cartels

164 CORRUPTION AND SUPPLIER COLLUSION UNDER THE WATERLINE?

In relation to bribery, the force of the law has also arguably been weakened by the difficulties involved in convicting corporations (leading to the lack of a credible threat of criminal prosecution in many cases), the SFO's tendency to favour CROs or DPAs over criminal prosecutions, and its lack of success in prosecuting company officers or employees even where DPAs have been approved in return for a corporation's cooperation.[187] Although DPAs have the potential to produce procedural efficiencies, speed up processes, reduce costs, and increase the quantity of cases dealt with, whilst ensuring that the company makes reparation for alleged criminal behaviour, there is concern that they are being over-used and so are reducing the punitive and deterrent effect of the law (as well as hindering its development),[188] extinguishing societal condemnation of the conduct and shielding companies from debarment from procurement processes (without a conviction, the mandatory debarment rules do not apply). Their frequent use may also, by limiting prosecutions, in the end, discourage firms from self-reporting, cooperating, and entering DPAs. 'Serious questions are now being raised about whether the DPA regime can be effective in a context where corporate may face better outcomes in court rather than through cooperation, or by refusing cooperation with an investigation and thereby making a prosecution virtually impossible.'[189] Indeed, there are now grave concerns about the ability of relevant law enforcement authorities to fight economic crime effectively, especially corruption and fraud.[190]

iv. Siloed regimes

A final point is that policy coordination and cooperation between the relevant institutions seems to be lacking or insufficient. There is a need for greater attention to be paid to corruption and collusion risks in constructing procurement processes, and for closer cooperation between agencies to facilitate investigations and enforcement. For example, evidence of collusion could come to light in a procurement process or bribery investigation, or evidence of corruption may emerge in a competition investigation or procurement review. However, were a suspicion or

---

1999–2009' (2010) 6(2) *Competition Policy International* 3 and W.P.J. Wils, 'Recidivism in EU Antitrust Enforcement: A Legal and Economic Analysis' (2012) 35(1) *World Competition* 5.

[187] See C. King and N. Lord, 'Deferred Prosecution Agreements in England and Wales: Cases Made of Sand?' (2020) 2 *Public Law* 307 and Section B.v above.

[188] See Chapter 4.

[189] S. Hawley, C. King, and N. Lord, 'Justice for Whom? The Need for a Principled Approach to Deferred Prosecution in England and Wales' in T. Søreide and A. Makingwa (eds), *Negotiated Settlements in Bribery Cases: A Principled Approach* (Edward Elgar, 2020).

[190] See e.g., The Law and Politics Podcast with K. Macdonald and T. Owen, Double Jeopardy, Episode 17 with Clare Montgomery KC, 'Getting Away with Fraud' and T. McClements, 'UK's New Strategy to Fight Fraud Grabs Headlines but Leaves Police Outgunned', *The FCPA Blog* (22 May 2023).

allegation of both bribery and bid rigging in a procurement tender to arise, several separate lines of investigation may be demanded, respectively, under the CA98, the criminal cartel offence, and criminal bribery laws in relation to active and passive bribery offences. These would involve different enforcement models,[191] and a number of distinct proceedings against companies and individuals, involving different investigative powers, cooperation and self-reporting regimes, rights of defence, standards of proof, and investigating and enforcement agencies (the CMA (or sectoral regulators), SFO, the police, and DPP). Particular care, cooperation and coordination, would be required to ensure that any civil process did not compromise a criminal one, or vice versa.[192] Although some mechanisms for coordination and cooperation exist, these are not sufficient to resolve the multiple issues potentially arising.

D. Proposals for the Future

The discussion above indicates that corruption and/or collusion in the public procurement sector may be occurring unchallenged and 'under the water-line'. This section, consequently, makes proposals for the development of a more procompetitive procurement system. Although some of the problems diagnosed within the current system are challenging to tackle, the Government's and relevant agencies' post-Brexit reviews of relevant laws and procedures have provided for reforms in this area to be debated. It has been seen that the Government has sought to improve, streamline, simplify, and reshape UK Public Procurement Law post-Brexit.[193] A Digital Markets, Competition and Consumer Bill is also being brought forward (although its impact on the issues discussed in this chapter is minimal).[194] It appears nonetheless that the reforms, when implemented, will not tackle all of the problems identified in this chapter. Some further proposals for change are consequently set out below.

---

[191] The rationale for treating undertakings and individuals differently resulted from the Government's desire to maintain consistency with EU law (for undertakings) whilst at the same time seeking to separate the criminal offence from the civil regime with the objective of ensuring that its enforcement would not be compromised by virtue of it being characterized as 'national competition law' within the meaning of Regulation 1/2003, Article 3, see Jones and Williams, n. 166.

[192] See e.g., Case 1337/1/12/19, *FP McCann Ltd v CMA* [2020] CAT 28, rejecting the argument that the civil proceedings concerning a cartel for concrete drainage products, which followed criminal proceedings against Barry Kenneth Cooper, took an unreasonably long period of time to complete, see n. 97. See also *Galvanised Steel Tanks* (criminal proceedings preceded the CMA civil decision), n. 97, and *Marine Hoses* (administrative proceedings in this case by the Commission under Article 101), nn. 94–96.

[193] See Section B.i.

[194] Following two consultations on proposed reform. The Bill seeks to enhance the CMA's ability to enforce UK consumer protection laws, establish an *ex ante* regulatory regime for digital markets,

166 CORRUPTION AND SUPPLIER COLLUSION UNDER THE WATERLINE?

i. Fact finding

A first preliminary step should be for some broad reviews to be conducted to look for 'red flags' or 'indicators' of hidden corruption and collusion.[195] These could be conducted by the Government, especially in the context of its Anti-Corruption Strategy, the CMA, and through the use of intuitive risk indicators.[196]

For example, the Government's yearly updates of its Anti-Corruption Strategy 2017–2022 (due to be developed with a new strategy) recognized the need for better identification and mitigation of corruption risks, including in the context of public procurement.[197] In these documents, the Government states that it is seeking to increase transparency and participation in public procurement, and is exploring ways to reduce fraud and corruption in the defence industry and to reduce corruption in public procurement. A comprehensive review of procurement in local government also highlights significant corruption and collusion risks and proposes measures that councils could implement to strengthen their resilience to them.[198] Particular issues may thus be arising in defined sectors and at local levels, so suggesting a need to strengthen awareness and capabilities within contracting authorities and in these areas. More generally, growing concerns about increased corruption in the UK suggest a need for active attempts to fight corruption and the need to appoint an influential Anti-Corruption Champion to develop an anti-corruption strategy following the resignation of John Penrose MP in 2022.

The CMA also has broad tools for identifying risks to competition and investigating possible breaches of competition law (see Section B.ii). Not only has it the power to conduct market studies to see if a market is working well for consumers and to commission reports,[199] but it did also develop a procurement data analysis tool. Although the latter was withdrawn in the light of acute and significant concerns raised about its efficacy,[200] it is seen in Chapter 4 that, if developed, honed, and used systematically, this type of tool could reap huge benefits by allowing the CMA (and other interested stakeholders, such as reporters, academics,

---

introduce a new merger threshold, and enhance the CMA's investigative and enforcement powers (including enhanced information gathering and enforcement power to facilitate swifter investigations).

[195] Although surveys and reports suggest that such conduct exists, more research could be completed to better understand the scale of the problem.

[196] Fazekas and Dávid-Barrett, n. 136, 5.2.

[197] See HM Government, 'UK Anti-Corruption Strategy 2017 to 2022', Policy Paper (2017), available at https://www.gov.uk/government/publications/uk-anti-corruption-strategy-2017-to-2022. Development of a new anti-corruption strategy has been stated to be underway. See also the Government's 'Fraud Strategy: stopping scams and protecting the public', Policy Paper (May 2023).

[198] See n. 131.

[199] See EA02, n. 34, Part 4 (the Government is proposing reforms to the markets regime powers); e.g. OFT commissioned report (assessing the impact of public sector procurement on competition in 2004), 'Local Authority Waste Contracts: CMA Analysis' (November 2017), available at https://assets.publishing.service.gov.uk/government/uploads/system/uploads/attachment_data/file/657858/local-authority-waste-contracts-cma-analysis.pdf; and OFT, 'More Competition, Less Waste' (May 2006), available at https://webarchive.nationalarchives.gov.uk/ukgwa/20140525130048/http://www.oft.gov.uk/shared_oft/reports/comp_policy/oft841.pdf.

[200] See n. 85.

PROPOSALS FOR THE FUTURE   167

consultants, market experts, or procurers) to analyse procurement data for indicators of unlawful collusive tendering. These tools, however, are dependent on better data and analysis systems. If the Government is successful in ensuring greater procurement transparency and if open data availability is extended across the public procurement system, and linked to other data sets, data analytics could be developed to identify first indicators of corruption as well.[201]

ii. Improving public procurement processes

It has been seen that shortcomings in the system, and its operation, may mean that it has not been guarding sufficiently against corruption or bid rigging risks throughout the procurement cycles. Some improvements are being introduced by the Government following its review of Public Procurement Laws,[202] including through elaborating on the circumstances of where direct awards can be made and providing for the pre-publication of a transparency notice when such procedures are used.[203] It remains to be seen, however, if these changes will increase the effectiveness of conflict rules and guard against improper transfer of contracts to favourites, or whether more will need to be done to ensure proper scrutiny of government emergency contracting. Indeed, it is arguable that further steps are required to restore integrity in public life and to enable effective enforcement of standards against government ministers.[204]

Training for public procurement officials could also be improved. Although the Government is enhancing training on good procurement practices,[205] mandatory competition training programmes for procurers would increase their understanding of the benefits flowing from procompetitive procurement design, improve procurement design, and increase their ability to detect bid rigging and the likelihood that they will report suspected collusion to the CMA. It is true that the CMA has published advice to procurers, provides a free e-learning tool,[206] and is committed to training public procurers across the country. Such training could, however, be rolled into a programme to be provided more systematically and on a regular basis, perhaps via Civil Service Learning. Anti-corruption law training

---

[201] See Chapter 4.

[202] The Government considered amongst other things: the process governing tendering in the case of crisis or extreme urgency; whether authorities should be required to implement open contracting data standards (OCDS) and to publish contract amendment notices; and how best to create a workable debarment system and to create an effective and balanced public procurement review process, see also Section B.i.

[203] PA23, n. 11, ss 41–43, Sched. 5.

[204] See e.g., the Public Service (Integrity and Ethics) Bill introduced into the House of Lords in September 2022. See also proposals in C. Bryant, *Code of Conduct: Why We Need to Fix Parliament - and How to Do It* (Bloomsbury, 2023), Chapter 7.

[205] See 'Getting Ready for the New Procurement Act: Update on the Official Learning and Development Offer for Contracting Authorities' (February 2023).

[206] See e.g., the Cheating or Competing Campaign, Advice for Public Procurers, n. 146.

would also draw attention to codes of conduct designed to prevent private interests from creating conflicts with the performance of public duties. Electronic registers of conflicts of interest, gifts, and hospitality should be kept, rules on the revolving door tightened, and an organizational culture of zero tolerance to violations created.[207] As well as sanctions for violations, further positive incentives can be created for strong performance or reporting bid rigging suspicions.[208] For example, although the CMA's scheme of offering financial rewards for information about cartel activity[209] is intended to apply principally to those with 'inside' information of cartels, and does not generally apply to their victims or co-contractors, greater thought could be given to the question of how procurers can be better incentivized to report cartel suspicions (perhaps through extending a similar scheme for the benefit of procurers or imposing reporting obligations on them[210]).

So that the benefits of transparency are reaped, it should be ensured, in accordance with the goals of the PA23 regime, that: all procurements are, as required by law, publicized (e.g. on Find a Tender, which replaces the EU's Tender Electronic Daily for contracts over GPA thresholds[211]) with consequences for not doing so; e-procurement is used routinely; procurement data is collected systematically, recorded, and made publicly available (open contracting), including through publication of procurement notices at all major stages of the process; and that contract implementation is carefully managed and scrutinized.[212] The Government's aim is for a digital platform to display all of this information publicly. More effective auditing is also required to develop a better 'counter fraud and anti-corruption culture' in government, particularly at local government level.[213] Development of internal mechanisms would encourage adherence to policies and procedures, and could improve systems and processes, identify and quantify losses from corruption, analyse spending more carefully (including through data analytics), encourage whistleblowing by staff members, and encourage the building of effective relationships with law enforcement and other agencies (e.g. local authorities could be required to have an audit committee, with a specific remit to oversee corruption risk assessments and corruption investigations, and a dedicated officer(s) responsible

---

[207] 'Review into the Risks of Fraud and Corruption in Local Government Procurement—A Commitment from the UK Anti-Corruption Strategy 2017 to 2022', n. 131, 34. See also 'Permission Accomplished', n. 145. It can, however, be difficult to avoid conflicts entirely in very specialized areas where there is a limited pool of experts capable of appraising the tenders adequately.

[208] See Chapter 4.

[209] See n. 79 and text.

[210] See e.g. discussion of the obligations on contracting personnel in the US in Chapter 6.

[211] See also e.g. Contracts Finder and data.gov.uk.

[212] 'Review into the Risks of Fraud and Corruption in Local Government Procurement—A Commitment from the UK Anti-Corruption Strategy 2017 to 2022', n. 131, 37; Fazekas and Dávid-Barrett, n. 136.

[213] For example, at the central government level, the National Fraud Initiative seeks to identify and quantify fraud losses, available at https://www.gov.uk/government/collections/national-fraud-initiative.

PROPOSALS FOR THE FUTURE   169

for counter-corruption, reporting of corruption and procurement risks, and liaising with law enforcement authorities).[214] An obligation could also be imposed on external auditors to report suspected violations of the law to authorities and to identify sector trends and risk (e.g. in a similar manner to Public Interest Reports).[215] Some commentators proposed the creation of an 'Office for Public Procurement' to collect, publish, and analyse data, and so to increase transparency and accountability, and facilitate the identification of trends.[216] However, the Government decided instead to create a new 'Procurement Review Unit' to monitor processes and with power to address more systematic and institutional breaches of procurement regulations. Although post-Brexit, the Minister for the Cabinet Office has assumed powers relating to compliance with procurement rules, a difficulty is the lack of separation between the Cabinet Office and central Government.

Anti-collusion tender clauses and anti-corruption provisions could also be built as a matter of routine into procurement processes and contract templates, including through requiring bidders to sign a Certificate of Independent Bid Determination (CIBD),[217] to operate audited competition and anti-corruption compliance programs, and to disclose upfront subcontracting plans if they wish to bid for public contracts. Other techniques could also be considered to make cover bidding less attractive. For example, as tenderers that engage in cover bidding are usually unwilling to spend significant time or money preparing their tender response, requirements (without overly increasing the costs for SMEs) for tenderers to make site visits and give presentations in person could help to guard against it and increase its visibility to procurers. The remedies regime could also be improved to make it more effective and less costly[218] and debarment processes could be strengthened (see further Section D.iv.b).

iii. Improving anti-corruption and competition laws

Changes to anti-corruption and competition laws could improve the working of the regimes in the public procurement sphere. For example, anti-corruption laws

---

[214] 'Review into the Risks of Fraud and Corruption in Local Government Procurement—A Commitment from the UK Anti-Corruption Strategy 2017 to 2022', n. 131, s 8 and Transparency International, n. 147.

[215] See Tyrie, n. 170, Sir Donald Brydon's report on the quality and effectiveness of audit (18 December 2019) and Transparency International, n. 147.

[216] Fazekas and Dávid-Barrett, n. 136, 5.4.

[217] Firms may be uncomfortable about signing such clauses, see, e.g., 'Design, Construction and Fit-Out Services', n. 98, paras. 3.129–3.135, and their existence could make successful prosecutions of offence easier.

[218] To correct non-compliance and incentivize compliance, see Arrowsmith, 'Reimagining Public Procurement Law', n. 7, X. Zhang, 'Supplier Review as a Mechanism for Securing Compliance with Public Procurement Rules: A Critical Perspective' (2007) 16 *Public Procurement Law Review* 325 and D.I. Gordon, 'Constructing a Bid Protest Process: Choices Every Procurement Challenge System Must Make' (2016) 35(3) *Public Contract Law Journal* 427.

could be reformed to ensure that they better cover conduct which is less overt than bribery, including cronyism and favouritism, perhaps by reforming the misconduct in public office offence.[219] Section D.iv.b below also discusses possible ways of reinvigorating, or reforming, the (almost defunct) criminal cartel regime.

iv. More effective enforcement of anti-corruption and competition laws

To increase the deterrent effect of the bribery and competition laws, there needs to be, both, a greater number of cases brought and more effective penalties imposed. This will require public enforcement agencies to be adequately resourced,[220] to prioritize enforcement in the public procurement area, to be better able to respond to criminal bid rigging and bribery offences, and to work cooperatively with each other. In particular, as the SFO does not concentrate on smaller cases or domestic bribery, it is vital that the awareness of other BA10 investigators is raised through training. In addition to greater cooperation and coordination between anti-corruption investigators and prosecutors, police forces in England and Wales could consider creating a specialized unit to target corruption in the public sector.[221]

a. Increasing enforcement

Because of the difficulty of uncovering bid rigging and bribery, relatively heavy reliance is currently placed on the collection of information from those involved in infringements, in return for leniency (in competition cases) or deferred prosecution (in bribery cases).[222] These programmes reinforce steps taken, including in the Bribery Act and by the CMA, to encourage businesses to introduce compliance programmes[223] and to be proactive about preventing, seeking out, and reporting

---

[219] See n. 62 and text.

[220] See n. 182.

[221] See e.g., the unit created in Scotland in 2013, 'Police Scotland Target Corruption in Public Sector', *BBC News* (19 September 2013), available at https://www.bbc.co.uk/news/uk-scotland-24149483. Indeed, the UK Government proposed the creation of a new national fraud squad, see Policy Paper, 'Fraud Strategy', n. 197, has created a Public Sector Fraud Authority (August 2022) to increase scrutiny of activity and to reduce fraud and economic crime and adopted Guidance, 'A Standard for the Counter Bribery and Corruption Professional' (19 May 2023). It remains to be seen whether the Government's successor to the Anti-corruption Strategy 2017–2022, which may also address broader economic crime, will incorporate a similar proposal for a new specific anti-corruption squad.

[222] But see n. 240.

[223] See n. 52 and text, and e.g. Financial Conduct Authority's (FCA) Principles for Business, Principle 3 (requiring firms to organize their affairs responsibly and to have adequate risk assessments in place and providing fines for breach, see, e.g., GBP 1.8 million fine imposed by FCA on JLT Specialty Limited for failing to have appropriate checks and controls in place to guard against the risk of bribery when making overseas payments, FCA Press Release, 'Firm fined GBP 1.8 million for "unacceptable" approach to bribery & corruption risks from overseas payments' (19 December 2013), available at https://www.fca.org.uk/news/press-releases/firm-fined-%C2%A318million-unacceptable-approach-bribery-corruption-risks-overseas.)

any illegal conduct. They could be bolstered, however, by imposing more onerous obligations on companies[224] (e.g. to appoint a board member tasked with responsibility for assessing and reporting competition law and bribery risks[225]). Further, as seen in Chapter 4, their limits must be recognized as they are unlikely to be effective in the absence of a healthy, independent enforcement record.

Investigators should, therefore, prioritize (or, in the CMA's case, continue to prioritize) enforcement in this sphere and ensure that evidence is also collected using a range of other reactive and proactive detection techniques. In addition to continuing to work with public officials to monitor for bid rigging and introducing improved data screening tools,[226] further steps could be taken to incentivize whistleblowers to provide evidence on corrupt or anti-competitive practices. For example, even though the CMA offers financial rewards of up to GBP 100,000 to those who offer information about cartel activity,[227] higher rewards are likely to be required to provide a stronger motive for reporting and to reinforce the Government's message that it takes infringements seriously (the current sum has been argued to be nugatory compared to the consequences that are likely to flow for the whistleblower).[228] Greater efforts also need to be made by the UK authorities to raise awareness of the importance of whistleblowers as a source of information on bribery.[229] The development of data tools would also help the wider public, including communities and professional associations affected by public contracts, to monitor public procurement for signs of illegal practices.

Information from these wider sources could then provide the foundation for competition and anti-corruption agencies to use their powers of search, interview, and surveillance to uncover further direct or indirect evidence sufficient to support a criminal trial or a civil infringement finding. As well as encouraging greater use of self-reporting programmes, each of these other mechanisms will help to uncover evidence of conduct which would otherwise remain hidden. A particular challenge, nonetheless, will be to incentivize investigators to probe low-level and low-value local cases, particularly where proof may be difficult in the absence of a leniency applicant or self-reporter.

---

[224] Screens can also help firms to uncover infringing behaviour, see Oxera, 'Hide and Seek: the Effective Use of Cartel Screens' (19 September 2013), available at https://www.oxera.com/wp-content/uploads/2018/07/Cartel-screens-1.pdf-1.pdf and Chapter 4.

[225] See Tyrie, n. 170 (see also e.g. 'Design, Construction and Fit-Out Services', n. 98, on whether disqualified directors should be granted limited leave to continue to act as directors following a company director disqualification order, see also *Stamatis and Davies v CMA* [2019] EWHC 3318 (Ch)).

[226] See nn. 200–201 and text.

[227] See CMA Rewards for Information about Cartels (2014). In the years 2017–2022, ninety-three disclosures were made under this scheme, with fifty-four leading to further investigation or action being taken, see www.gov.uk/government/collections/cma-whistleblower-statistics.

[228] Tyrie, n. 170.

[229] See OECD Working Group on Bribery, 'Implementing the OECD Anti-Bribery Convention – Phase 4 Report: United Kingdom' (2017), available at https://www.oecd.org/corruption/anti-bribery/UK-Phase-4-Report-ENG.pdf.

b. Using the full range of penalties

It has been seen that in the UK, financial penalties may be, and are, imposed on corporations involved in cartel or bribery law violations. However, a concern may be that, although the UK has deliberately sought to ensure that other controls are available to deter such conduct, including criminal, or civil, sanctions for both natural and legal persons, asset recovery, and damages' actions, it has (until recently at least) been relatively rare for these to be used in practice. Rather, the system incentivizes criminal prosecutors to sidestep complex and risky criminal proceedings, by pursuing civil alternatives, or DPAs, instead. If the laws are to have their intended deterrent and punitive effect, the full range of sanctions should be used, when appropriate.

Breathing new life into the criminal cartel offence. The CMA has not had, to date, success in enforcing the criminal cartel offence and has mainly relied on its administrative process instead. There are a number of possible explanations for this, including that: a moral case for criminalization has not yet been sufficiently built[230] it is difficult to define and identify *criminal cartel behaviour* and to distinguish it from legitimate horizontal collaboration;[231] procedural difficulties result from the co-existence of the civil and criminal regimes; and the CMA lacks criminal law expertise.[232] These kinds of difficulties have led to suggestions that it may be better to abandon the criminal offence entirely and, instead, to increase deterrents for individuals through continued routine use of CDOs in CA98 cases and enhancing civil sanctions[233]—e.g. a provision could be made in the CA98 for the imposition of fines on responsible individuals.

If the offence is to be retained, however, one option for generating support for it, and building the moral case for criminalization, could be, as discussed in the chapter on the US (Chapter 6), to target prosecutions on bid rigging that negatively affects the purchase of vital public goods, services, and works. Such cases are likely to prove especially difficult for those prosecuted to defend, especially if the conduct has been hidden, operated to simulate ordinary competitive behaviour, and where CIBDs have been required and signed.

---

[230] No sustained attempt has been made to build public support for the moral condemnation of cartel conduct in the UK and this omission has been compounded by: the requirement in the original offence that the jury and judge had to believe that the individual cartelists had acted 'dishonestly'; the CMA's decisions to use leniency applicants as core prosecution witnesses in criminal cases (such as *British Airways*, see OFT withdraws criminal proceedings against current and former BA executives, press release 47/10 (10 May 2010) and *Galvanised Steel*, n. 97); and, perhaps, the failure to extend the criminal offence to corporations as well as individuals, see, e.g., Jones and Williams, n. 166.

[231] The new criminal cartel offence contains no mens rea requirement but applies to horizontal price fixing and other cartel activity, unless a statutory exclusion (EA02, n. 34, Section 188A) or defence (EA02, n. 34, Section 188B) applies.

[232] See n. 170 and text.

[233] See, e.g., A. Khan, 'Rethinking Sanctions for Breaching EU Competition Law: Is Director Disqualification the Answer?' (2012) 35(1) *World Competition* 77, 82.

Another option could be to introduce additional changes to the offence. It has been seen that were corruption and collusion do occur together, a number of different investigators and prosecutors would need to be involved. In the US, in contrast, the Department of Justice (DOJ), the main law enforcement agency and part of the executive branch, has broad powers to prosecute violations of criminal law, including fraud, corruption, and antitrust laws, and to deal with leniency and plea bargains. Synergies in the UK would clearly be unlocked if all horizontal and vertical elements of bid rigging and bribery, in relation to both corporations and individuals, could be probed together. One way of enabling this would be to expand the criminal cartel offence to legal persons, as well as individuals, and those promoting or aiding bid rigging.[234]

Although criminalizing corporate cartel behaviour would raise the evidential bar for prosecutors (especially because of the higher standard of proof applicable in criminal cases and the difficulties presented by the identification principle),[235] without substantially changing the available sanctions (corporate fines already being a core sanction for breach of the CA98), such a change would allow *all* competition cartel proceedings against individuals and corporations to be brought together under the umbrella of the criminal offence. It might also bolster the moral case for criminalization of cartels[236] and reinforce community condemnation of such conduct where corporate culture has contributed to the commission of a cartel offence.[237] Concerns about complexities raised by the identification principle could be met by creating, as in the case of bribery, additionally or alternatively, a separate 'failure to prevent' offence for corporations, a strict liability corporate offence of failing to prevent the conclusion of an unlawful cartel agreement by an officer, employee, or agent of the company, subject to a defence that the company had adequate procedures in place to prevent such actions.[238] In addition, if the legislation were to recognize explicitly the link between bid rigging and corruption by creating a promoting or aiding offence, the prosecutor would be able to bring criminal proceedings against corporations, individuals, and corrupt procurement officials under the same Act, were such conduct to occur together.[239]

---

[234] Alternatively, in some jurisdictions anti-corruption laws apply to bid rigging in relation to public tenders.

[235] Arguably reform is required in England and Wales as the difficulties inherent in establishing corporate liability for economic crime mean that corporate prosecutions are rare, see King and Lord, n. 187 and text.

[236] See n. 230.

[237] Post-Brexit, the risk of the criminal offence being emasculated on account of it being found to constitute national competition law has been removed, see n. 191.

[238] See nn. 50–52 and e.g. C. Wells, 'Corporate Failure to Prevent Economic Crime—A Proposal' (2017) 6 *Criminal Law Review* 426 and Ministry of Justice, *Corporate Liability for Economic Crime, Call for Evidence* (TSO, 2017) Cm 9370.

[239] Even without such a change, however, the SFO could bring proceedings against a person that had assisted or encouraged the commission of the cartel offence, see n. 59.

If the criminal offence was expanded in this way, consideration would need to be given to who would have lead responsibility for enforcing the offence. As, currently, neither the CMA nor the SFO are displaying much appetite for its enforcement, it may be that another entity, such as the NCA or a newly created police corruption unit, would have to be entrusted with the task.

Raising the stakes for those involved in bribery. Consideration also needs to be given as to how more domestic bribery prosecutions can be brought and how these should be balanced with the use of DPAs.[240] Although the SFO has increasingly used DPAs to handle corporate bribery cases,[241] concern has been expressed that these breach mandatory debarment obligations, and undermine their effectiveness and the effectiveness of the criminal bribery laws, more generally.[242] Further, even where DPAs are agreed, the condemnatory and deterrent effect of the law will be dependent upon greater success with prosecuting senior executives (the cooperation expected of a company should include provision of all relevant evidence implicating individuals),[243] and ensuring that the corporate sanctions imposed strike a careful balance between the need to ensure that bribery does not pay, the need to provide incentives for self-reporting and cooperation,[244] and the need to prevent reoffending—e.g. through commitments to reform corporate practices, culture, and policies and to introduce compliance programmes and an independent monitoring process.[245] Prosecutors could also consider insisting that voluntary director disqualification undertakings are offered as a condition for agreeing a DPA. This would be facilitated if, as with the CA98, the BA10 explicitly allowed disqualification orders to be imposed on directors of companies convicted of bribery.

Exclusion. In Chapter 4, it is seen that exclusion (or debarment) of corporations or contractors involved in bid rigging or corrupt conduct helps to preserve the integrity of the public procurement process by both mitigating against the risk of, and deterring, future violations. Further, an effective regime is likely to require a central register of excluded companies and central policy guidance.[246]

---

[240] For example, the SFO received considerable criticism for concluding a DPA with, rather than prosecuting, Rolls-Royce, even though it had not self-reported its 'egregious criminality' and the vast corrupt sums paid out over decades (despite initial concerns Lord Justice Leveson, presiding judge, eventually went on to approve the DPA, Rolls-Royce unreported 17 January 2017).

[241] House of Lords, Select Committee, n. 46, 91.

[242] See S. Arrowsmith, 'Constructing Rules on Exclusions (Debarment) Under a Post-Brexit Regime on Public Procurement: A Preliminary Analysis' (24 July 2020), available at https://ssrn.com/abstract=3659909.

[243] Arrowsmith, n. 242, para. 317.

[244] Hawley, King, and Lord, n. 189.

[245] Hawley, King, and Lord, n. 189.

[246] See e.g. Arrowsmith, n. 242 and S. Hawley, 'What Makes a Good Debarment Regime? Keeping Corrupt and Fraudulent Companies Out of Public Procurement' (2020) *University of Sussex, Centre for the Study of Corruption Working Paper No. 7.*

PROPOSALS FOR THE FUTURE   175

Although procurers have always had obligations and powers to exclude corporations convicted of bribery and competition offences from public contracting until self-cleaning has occurred,[247] data is limited as to how the process has been used in practice.[248] Indeed, there has been concern that, under the pre-PA23 regime, these powers were not being exercised perhaps because of the relatively frequent use of DPAs, because there was no central register for recording excluded companies or adequate central policy guidance indicating how debarment provisions are to be implemented and complexities overcome, because procurers are fearful of exacerbating procurement difficulties that already exist in concentrated markets, or because procurers believe that conviction under bribery or competition laws is already punishment enough.[249]

The PA23 seeks to improve exclusion processes, for example, by extending mandatory grounds to suppliers, and persons connected to them, that have committed cartel or competition law offences,[250] and by requiring the keeping of a 'debarment list' of excluded suppliers on a digital platform, so allowing public sector organizations to see who should be excluded.[251] As recognized in Chapter 4, care needs to be exercised to ensure that debarment processes are flexible and that exclusion sanctions can be tailored appropriately and proportionately so that they do not have a chilling effect on self-reporting, cooperation, and future compliance. The PA23 system contains some flexibility as, a supplier is only excludable under the mandatory grounds if the circumstances giving rise to the application of the exclusion ground are likely to occur again, so creating incentives for self-cleaning. Further, it provides for investigations to be conducted prior to a supplier being added to the debarment list.[252] An important issue, nonetheless, and which remains unclear, is how the accuracy of the list of excluded suppliers is to be ensured; in particular, how breaches of laws that trigger mandatory debarment will be reported or be brought to the attention of the relevant minister. One solution could be to impose an obligation on the CMA, and anti-corruption prosecutors, to report relevant convictions.

Greater use of recovery powers and damages' actions. Bribery proceedings have, in some cases, led to confiscation orders and the recovery of profits from bribery (especially through CROs and DPAs).

---

[247] The prosecutor could also apply for a Serious Crime Order, if there is evidence of a risk of reoffending.

[248] See Hawley, n. 246.

[249] But see, e.g., 'Applying Exclusions in Public Procurement, Managing Conflicts of Interest and Whistleblowing – A Guide for Commercial and Procurement Professionals', available at https://assets.publishing.service.gov.uk/government/uploads/system/uploads/attachment_data/file/780802/A_Guide_for_Commercial_and_Procurement_Professionals.pdf.

[250] PA23, n. 11, s 57 and Sched. 6.

[251] PA23, n. 11, ss 62–65. See further Chapter 4, B.ii.d.

[252] PA23, n. 11, ss 62–65.

176 CORRUPTION AND SUPPLIER COLLUSION UNDER THE WATERLINE?

In contrast, it appears that no civil action for damages has been lodged by a public procurer in England and Wales that has been a victim of bid rigging.[253] It is seen in Chapter 4 that competition damages actions may be deterred by their complex and expensive nature, the fact that procurers have reduced incentives to bring such cases, and may be unwilling to sour relations with contractors. However, if routinely brought, these actions would allow the Government both to claw back taxpayer money lost and raise the costs for those breaching competition law. Such a programme could be developed in the UK, for example, by entrusting responsibility for recovery of damages on behalf of public procurers to a central body, such as the Department for Business, Energy and Industrial Strategy (BEIS).[254] BEIS could then liaise with CMA to make a workable system. Further, the CMA could make immunity or reductions in fine dependent on a payment into voluntary redress systems or on the parties' willingness to settle damages actions.[255]

v. Increased policy coordination

The procurement, competition, and anti-corruption agencies in the UK can do more to expand understanding of each other's remit, powers, and procedures, so that they can work better together to prevent, detect, and prosecute violations of the relevant laws. Although it is true that the CMA and SFO have a Memorandum of Understanding,[256] this relates only to cooperation in relation to the investigation and/or prosecution of individuals in respect of the criminal cartel offence where serious or complex fraud is suspected. In the absence of any further legislative reform, the distinct agencies could thus still do much more to achieve greater mutual understanding and assistance through networks, advocacy, training, outreach, placements and exchange of staff, collaboration, cooperation, and the creation of knowledge sharing systems, which allow, subject to confidentiality rules, information uncovered or gathered by one authority to be shared or brought to the attention of another.[257] Indeed, legislation or interagency agreements providing for transfer of lawfully obtained evidence could ensure that important evidence uncovered by one agency is not discarded simply because it does not fit with its

---

[253] It has also been seen that it is difficult for private parties to challenge breaches of public procurement laws and to seek compensation, see Section B.

[254] For example, the NHS has a unit which focuses on recovery of damages in relation to infringements committed by pharmaceutical companies.

[255] See, e.g., payments made, in connection with settlement, to the Department of Health and Social Care (which agreed they would offset the payment against any potential future damages action), following the CMA's fludrocortisone investigation, Case 50455, 9 July 2020, and Case CA98/05/2006, *Private Schools*, 20 November 2006.

[256] See n. 44.

[257] For example, there is no statutory rule in the CA98 that says evidence obtained under the CA98 cannot be used for other purposes, but see also EA02, n. 34, part 9.

CONCLUSIONS   177

powers, remit, or enforcement priorities. The creation of a special task force to investigate unlawful distortions to public procurement processes would also be beneficial, whether within the CMA or between the CMA and a specialized police unit, targeting corruption in the public sector.[258] Another possibility could be for the CMA, in addition to training public procurement bodies, to be given a procurement remit or a role in providing greater oversight of procurement or review of public procurement decisions.[259]

E. Conclusions

This chapter concludes that, even though the UK is perceived to be a relatively clean economy, there are reasons to be concerned that undetected corruption and bid rigging may be operating to undermine public procurement processes in England and Wales. It consequently recommends specific steps to combat the weaknesses in the current system diagnosed.

In particular, the chapter proposes a number of interlinked reforms aimed to raise awareness of the likely problem and to ensure that the distinct procurement, anti-corruption, and competition regimes work together to achieve a robust and harmonious procompetitive procurement strategy. This policy coordination will help to ensure that procuring bodies are informed of, and better able to guard against, corruption and collusion opportunities and risks and that law enforcement agencies work together to identify, root out, punish, and deter corruption and anti-competitive practices affecting public procurement. It also proposes that civil litigation can play a more effective role in the enforcement process.

The Government's Anti-Corruption Strategy and processes to reform public procurement and competition laws have provided fora for some of the identified problems to be debated, and the PA23 seeks to address some of them. A number of the additional proposals made could be implemented relatively easily by procuring authorities and anti-corruption or competition agencies. For example, procuring authorities could immediately act to improve internal counter-fraud, auditing, and monitoring of processes, to introduce routine training programmes in collaboration with anti-corruption and competition agencies, to forge closer relationships with these enforcement authorities, and, to find a mechanism to centralize actions for recovery of damages on behalf of public procurers. Anti-corruption and competition enforcers can also work to improve detection techniques, to improve their cooperation and coordination in investigations and with procurers, to develop a national strategy to combat criminal conduct impacting on the public sector (even

---

[258] See n. 221 and text and e.g. the creation of the US Procurement Collusion Strike Force (PCSF), referred to in Chapter 4 and discussed in Chapter 6.

[259] See also e.g. A. Sanchez-Graells, *Public Procurement* (Hart Publishing, 2nd edn, 2015) 477–8.

offences involving relatively small sums of money), and to augment the effectiveness of their enforcement actions and resulting penalties, whether criminal or civil.

The measures proposed are designed to combine together to lower the cost, and improve the quality and quantity, of essential public goods, services, and infrastructure; to protect public money; and to increase confidence in the Government and its institutions. These steps are acutely important today, as the UK seeks to develop its own procurement policy and reputation as an engaged global citizen post-Brexit and to grapple with the demands that a number of recent crises has placed both on public purchasing and the public purse.

6

Persistent Corruption and Supplier Collusion in an Advanced Industrialized Country: The Case of the United States

A. Introduction	179	ix. Boeing's bribery of Darlene Druyen	193
B. Historical Perspective: Prominent Examples of Corruption and/ or Collusion in US Public Procurement and Their Significance for the Regulatory Regime	182	x. 'Fat Leonard' corruption scandal	193
		xi. Marine hoses	194
		xii. COVID-19, the Federal Government response, and corruption	194
		xiii. Trump era scandals and challenges to the Rule of Law	195
i. Naval build-up at the end of the nineteenth century and in the early twentieth century	183	xiv. Summary: Some notable lessons from US experience	197
ii. Early applications of the Sherman Act	184	C. The Regulatory Framework	199
		i. Substantive requirements	199
iii. Wartime mobilization: the example of World War II	186	a. Antitrust statutes	199
		b. Public Procurement Law	200
iv. Expanded global reach of US foreign policy after the World War II era	189	c. Anti-Corruption and Public Integrity Laws	201
v. 'The Gentlemen Conspirators': The Tennessee Valley Authority and the electrical equipment conspiracy cases	189	d. Foreign Corrupt Practices Act	202
		ii. Enforcement mechanism	202
		a. Antitrust Laws	203
		b. Public Procurement Law	204
vi. Expansion of Criminal Antitrust Enforcement in the 1970s and 1980s: the construction cartels and other supplier collusion for public projects	190	c. Anti-Corruption and Public Integrity Laws	205
		d. Foreign Corrupt Practices Act	206
		e. Interagency collaboration	206
		f. Qui Tam actions	207
vii. Watergate-related scandals and the revelation of Foreign Bribery Schemes	191	iii. Exceptions to pro-competition procurement policy	208
		D. Vulnerabilities of the Existing Regime and Suggested Improvements	209
viii. Operation Ill Wind	192		

A. Introduction

The United States (US) has developed the world's most comprehensive regulatory controls to challenge and deter supplier collusion and various forms of corrupt

180 PERSISTENT CORRUPTION AND SUPPLIER COLLUSION

behaviour that undermine effective competition in public procurement. Firms doing business with the government bodies in the US are subject to an array of measures—adopted at the national, state, and local levels—that are unequalled in their volume and complexity and in the power of sanctions available to punish wrongdoers.[1] Over time, an elaborate regulatory and prosecutorial bureaucracy has emerged to implement these commands.

Despite the development of seemingly formidable regulatory mechanisms, collusion and corruption remain vexing problems in the US public procurement system. With distressing regularity, scandals involving corrupt attempts by private firms and public officials to subvert competition in public procurement have come to light. As the following sample of cases from the past twenty years indicates, cartels and various forms of corruption undermine programmes that seek to address a range of serious economic and social needs:

Demolition Services in Detroit. Since the late 1990s, the City of Detroit has undertaken a programme to demolish abandoned houses and other derelict structures that blighted the municipality.[2] The initiative was an important element of a programme to reverse decades of economic decline that had seen the once-prosperous hub of the automobile industry in North America ('the Motor City'), descend into abject poverty. In 2019, the Department of Justice (DOJ) prosecuted a conspiracy by which firms bid collusively on demolition contracts and bribed city officials to channel contracts to the demolition services cartel members.[3]

New Jersey Superfund Site Remediation. Since the early 1980s, federal and state environmental protection bodies have cooperated in projects, authorized by the federal Superfund Act, to clean up areas contaminated by industrial waste. Many of these efforts have focused on New Jersey, whose large petrochemical sector generated a major concentration of contaminated sites. In New Jersey and in other states, remediation contracting and subcontracting have provided frequent targets for collusive bidding and corruption.[4] Since 2010, the DOJ has prosecuted a

---

[1] W.E. Kovacic, 'The Sorcerer's Apprentice: Public Regulation of the Weapons Acquisition Process' in R. Higgs (ed.), *Arms, Politics, and the Economy: Historical and Contemporary Perspectives* (Independent Institute, 1990) 104; W.E. Kovacic, *The Antitrust-Government Contracts Handbook* (American Bar Association, Section of Antitrust Law, 1990); W.E. Kovacic, 'Illegal Agreements with Competitors' (1988) 57(2) *Antitrust Law Journal* 517.

[2] Detroit's population has fallen from 1.9 million in 1950 to under 700,000 in 2023. The exodus has left behind thousands of vacant homes and abandoned shops that became targets for arsonists and vandals. The disintegration of the city's economy and the collapse of its governance institutions is recounted in C. LeDuff, *Detroit: An American Autopsy* (Penguin Books, 2013).

[3] *United States v Aradondo Haskins et al.* (April 2019). As an official working for the City of Detroit's Building Authority, Aradondo Haskins accepted bribes from contractors who had rigged bids on the demolition contracts. In an earlier case, filed in December 2010, federal prosecutors had charged the former mayor of Detroit (Kwame Kirkpatrick), the mayor's father, and several other individuals for conspiracy to rig bids on demolition contracts.

[4] Unites States Environmental Protection Agency, Office of the Inspector General, 'When Good Money Goes Bad – True Stories of Fraud in the EPA Superfund Program' (2009), available at www.epa. gov/oig.

number of bid rigging and kickback schemes involving tenders for remediation services.[5]

Puerto Rico School Bus Services. The US Department of Education funds school bus services in a large number of localities across the country. These services provide an essential transportation network for the operation of public schools. In Puerto Rico, a small number of transportation firms serve the island's school districts. The small number of commercial players, coupled with the frequent issuance of public tenders by school districts, creates conditions highly conducive to effective supplier collusion in the US, and globally, regarding contracts for transportation services and various types of school supplies.[6] In 2018, the DOJ filed antitrust and mail fraud charges against four individuals who had conspired to rig bids on Puerto Rico's busing contracts.[7]

As noted in Chapters 1 and 2, transgressions of the type sketched above have especially destructive effects. Procurement failures stemming from collusion and corruption shake confidence in the government's ability to deliver essential services to the public, and they undermine respect for public institutions generally.[8] Repeated abuse of the procurement system is a grave affliction in an economy where procurement outlays account for roughly 17 per cent of a gross domestic product (GDP) of over USD 16 trillion, and public expenditures support vital public services.[9]

This chapter examines the problem of collusion and corruption in the US in three parts. It begins in Section B with a historical perspective that illuminates recurring scenarios of misconduct and identifies enduring weaknesses in the public procurement system. This historically oriented overview highlights formative events that have shaped the regulatory regime. The second part of the chapter sets out the framework of legal controls that seek to detect, punish, and deter misconduct by

---

[5] 'DOJ Wins Ninth Conviction of Individuals from New Jersey EPA Superfund Site Probe', *Bloomberg* (2 October 2013) (challenging a scheme involving bid rigging, kickbacks, and fraud); 'Company to Pay $2.7 Million to Resolve Claims of Bid Rigging at Superfund Site', *Bloomberg* (18 November 2014).

[6] See, e.g., P. Schmidt, 'Bid Rigging Among School Suppliers is "Pervasive", Experts Fear', *Education Week* (22 September 1993), available at https://www.edweek.org/education/bid-rigging-among-sch ool-suppliers-is-pervasive-experts-fear/1993/09; and 'Fourteen Charged after Inquiry into School Bus "Cartel"', *The Times* (28 June 2022), available at https://www.thetimes.co.uk/article/fourteen-charged-after-inquiry-into-school-bus-cartel-t865t9kph.

[7] *United States v Ganino Rivera Herrera et al.* (6 February 2018); Department of Justice, Antitrust Division, 'Four School Bus Company Owners Convicted for Bid Rigging and Mail Fraud Conspiracies Involving Puerto Rico Public School Bus Services', *Press Release* (26 January 2017).

[8] As noted in Chapter 1, the Biden Administration has described the broad harm that corruption inflicts on the nation and the world in similar terms. See, 'Memorandum on Establishing the Fight against Corruption as a Core United States National Security Interest', *The White House Briefing Room* (3 June 2021), available at https://www.whitehouse.gov/briefing-room/presidential-actions/2021/06/03/mem orandum-on-establishing-the-fight-against-corruption-as-a-core-united-states-national-security-interest.

[9] On the magnitude of public expenditures channelled through public contracts and grants, see OECD, 'Director Disqualification and Bidder Exclusion in Competition Enforcement' (2022) OECD Competition Policy Roundtable Background Note 6, available at https://www.oecd.org/daf/competit ion/director-disqualification-and-bidder-exclusion-in-competition-enforcement-2022.pdf.

private suppliers and by public officials responsible for procurement (see Section C). The final part, Section D, highlights contemporary weaknesses in the public procurement regime and suggests possible paths for improvement.

Our policy recommendations emphasize the possibilities for improved performance with the application of existing statutory and regulatory tools. Perhaps the greatest challenge is for antitrust agencies and public procurement bodies to deepen cooperative programmes, already underway, that would strengthen the government's ability to identify, prosecute, and deter misconduct. Our suggested strategies include better data analytics, intensified study of past experience in the prosecution of cartels, and measures to reduce barriers to entry by prospective government tenderers.

In examining the US procurement regime, we acknowledge a degree of perplexity and dismay at the persistence of supplier collusion and related conduct that undermines effective competition. We do not expect that the attainment of perfect compliance is feasible, or that the benefit from seeking to extract the last increment of fraud from the procurement process would be worth the cost. Perhaps, the sheer volume of procurement activity in the US to some degree defies effective human control. Nonetheless, given the urgent social interest in gaining fuller value for public expenditures, we remain confident that the pursuit of improvements is a worthwhile and necessary endeavour. Even small advances promise to generate significant benefits in terms of goods and services delivered and in the growth of public confidence in the proper functioning of their government.

B. Historical Perspective: Prominent Examples of Corruption and/or Collusion in US Public Procurement and Their Significance for the Regulatory Regime

Policies related to competition law, corruption, and public procurement have crossed paths many times since the creation of the federal antitrust regime in the late nineteenth century. This section discusses a number of formative developments that have shaped the evolution of public programmes to challenge supplier collusion and to attack illicit agreements by which private firms and government insiders suppress rivalry among actual or potential contractors. The episodes recounted here do not constitute a comprehensive history of the field.[10] Instead, they underscore the seriousness of collusion and corruption as impediments to good performance in government procurement and illuminate the strengths and weaknesses of public programmes to address misconduct.

---

[10] More comprehensive accounts of the history of the US public procurement system include J.F. Nagle, *A History of Government Contracting* (George Washington University, 1992).

i. Naval build-up at the end of the nineteenth century and in the early twentieth century

In the late nineteenth and early twentieth centuries, no public procurement issue commanded greater attention in the US than the conversion of the Navy's antiquated fleet of Civil War-vintage wooden vessels into one of the world's paramount naval forces.[11] The naval build-up entailed an unprecedented programme of peacetime defence expenditures. Among other technical disciplines, the effort to build a modern fleet of warships required the development of new domestic steel-making capability to construct armour plate and forge large diameter guns. To organize, execute, and fund the naval improvement program, the Department of the Navy, industry, and the Congress established new relationships that formed the early foundations of the institutional arrangements—what Robert Higgs has called a 'military–industrial–congressional–complex'[12]—through which the acquisition of major weapon systems takes place today.[13]

The procurement of the new US fleet encountered many difficulties. Along with claims that contractors had fraudulently concealed product defects and had used retired naval officers to influence Navy Department officials improperly, congressional critics charged that expanded defence appropriations merely had enabled cartels of armour plate and explosives producers to extract inflated prices from the government.[14] As construction boomed in the years before World War I, Congressman Augustus Stanley of Kentucky captured a common sentiment in warning that 'it is time for this Government, [which] can make its own armor plate and [which] should make it, if necessary, shall say that it will not become ... the maintainer of an illicit, illegal, and lawless combination in restraint of trade'.[15]

---

[11] So feeble was the condition of the American fleet that the Secretary of the Navy, William C. Whitney, wrote in 1885: 'At the present moment it must be conceded that we have nothing which deserves to be called a navy.... [I]t is questionable whether we have a single vessel finished and afloat at the present time that could be trusted to encounter the ships of any important power...'. L.D. White, *The Republican Era—A Study in Administrative History 1899–1901* (The Macmillan Company, 1958) 159. In 1883, the US Congress had begun to correct this condition by authorizing construction of four steam-powered, steel-hulled cruisers. This initiated an improvement programme that by 1909 had elevated the United States from twelfth to second among the world's navies. See also, S. Hayes, *The Response to Industrialism 1885–1914* (University of Chicago Press, 1st edn, 1957) 165.

[12] R. Higgs, *Crisis and Leviathan* (Oxford University Press, 1st edn, 1987) 211–15, 230–3.

[13] The importance of the turn-of-the-twentieth-century naval build-up in shaping the modern US weapons acquisition process is examined in B.F. Cooling, *Gray Steel and Blue Water Navy—The Formative Years of America's Military-Industrial Complex, 1881–1917* (Archon Books, 1st edn, 1979).

[14] A. Chandler Jr. and S. Salsbury, *Pierre S. duPont and the Making of the Modern Corporation* (Harper and Row, 1st edn, 1971) 259–300; Cooling, n. 13, 120–37; W.H.S. Stevens, 'The Powder Trust, 1872–1912' (1912) 26 *Quarterly Journal of Economics* 444; M. Urofsky, 'Joseph us Daniels and the Armor Trust' (1968) 45 *North Carolina Historical Review* 237.

[15] Cooling, n.13, 181. Evidence of persistently uniform bidding on armour contracts created substantial congressional support for establishing government-owned factories to produce armour, shells, and guns. In 1916, Congress authorized the Secretary of the Navy to build or purchase an armour factory to be owned and operated by the Navy Department. The Navy eventually oversaw the construction of the 'Great Naval Plant and Projectile Factory' in Charleston, West Virginia. The Charleston facility operated during World War I and fell into disuse in the 1920s. Cooling, n. 13, 202–12.

184   PERSISTENT CORRUPTION AND SUPPLIER COLLUSION

Concern with bid rigging regarding armour and munitions for the Navy created strong political pressure for antitrust scrutiny that culminated in suits by the DOJ to dissolve US Steel and DuPont.[16]

Crucial to the development of a modern navy was a switch from coal to petroleum as the fuel source for marine propulsion systems. During the presidency of William Howard Taft, the Congress began designating certain potential oil production regions for the sole use of the US Navy. The most important of the government's petroleum reserves were Teapot Dome in Wyoming and Elk Hills in California. The development of the naval petroleum reserves soon provided the setting for one of the nation's greatest political scandals.[17] During Warren Harding's presidency, the Department of the Interior secretly granted exclusive licences, without competitive bidding, for the development of Teapot Dome and Elk Hills. The recipients of the exclusive rights were two cronies (Harry Sinclair and Edward Doheny) of the Interior Secretary, Albert Fall, and President Harding. Tipped off by newspaper stories that uncovered the exclusive licences, Congress in the 1920s conducted investigations that documented how Doheny and Sinclair had bribed Fall to gain the concessions. Albert Fall and the oil company executives subsequently were prosecuted and convicted for their role in the bribery scheme. The Interior Department voided the exclusive leases and used competitive bidding to reissue the concession development rights.

ii. Early applications of the Sherman Act

As the discussion above indicates, the adoption of national antitrust legislation in the late nineteenth century provided a tool for addressing apparent instances of supplier collusion on public procurement contracts. In 1890, Congress enacted the Sherman Act, which became and remains the central pillar of the US antitrust regime.[18] The Sherman Act was the first federal white-collar crime statute; it forbade restraints of trade (such as cartels), monopolization, and attempted monopolization, as crimes.[19] Early judicial interpretations of the statute established a principle that, with occasional refinement, remains a foundation of

---

[16] *United States v United States Steel Corp.*, 251 U.S. 417 (1920) (dismissing complaint); *United States v E.I. duPont de Nemours & Co.*, 188 F. 127 (CCD Del. 1911) (finding liability and ordering divestiture).

[17] The naval petroleum reserves scandal is examined extensively in L. McCartney, *The Teapot Dome Scandal: How Big Oil Bought the Harding White House and Tried to Steal the Country* (Random House, 2009); and J.L. Bates, *The Origins of Teapot Dome: Progressives, Parties, and Petroleum, 1909–1921* (University of Illinois Press, 1963).

[18] For a brief history of the Sherman Act and the implementation of antitrust policy in the first century after the Act's adoption, see W.E. Kovacic and C. Shapiro, 'Antitrust Policy: A Century of Economic and Legal Thinking' (2000) 14 *Journal of Economic Perspectives* 23.

[19] 15 U.S.C. §§ 1–2. The mechanism currently employed to enforce these provisions is discussed in Section C, below.

modern US antitrust jurisprudence: agreements among competitors to set the terms of trade by fixing prices and output levels or allocating customers or geographic territories ordinarily will be treated as serious offences and punished as crimes.[20]

Within a decade of the adoption of the Sherman Act, it was apparent that courts would invoke the new federal antitrust statute and notions of sound procurement policy to strike down bid rigging arrangements. In 1897, in *United States v Trans-Missouri Freight Ass'n*,[21] the Supreme Court established an important foundation for this approach by ruling that agreements by direct rivals to eliminate price competition among themselves were subject to summary condemnation under the Sherman Act. A striking number of cases in the Sherman Act's early, formative decades involved the prosecution of bid rigging schemes that targeted public purchasing authorities.[22]

Two years later, in *McMullen v Hoffman*,[23] the Court refused, on grounds of sound public procurement policy, to enforce an agreement between two construction companies to rig the award of various public contracts. The belief that bid rigging posed a grave danger to the public procurement process is evident in Justice Rufus Peckham's opinion for the Court in *McMullen*:

> Upon general principles it must be apparent that biddings for contracts for public works cannot be surrounded with too many precautions for the purpose of obtaining perfectly fair and bona fide bids. Such precautions are absolutely necessary in order to prevent the successful perpetration of fraud in the way of combinations among those who are ostensible rivals, but who in truth are secretly banded together for the purpose of obtaining contracts from public bodies such as municipal and other corporations at a higher figure than they otherwise would.[24]

To Justice Peckham, who wrote for the Court in *Trans-Missouri Freight*, those who seek public contract awards must be held to an especially high standard: 'It is not too much to say that the most perfect good faith is called for on the part of bidders in these public lettings ... '.[25]

---

[20] A. Jones and W.E. Kovacic, 'Identifying Anticompetitive Agreements in the United States and the European Union: A Coherent Antitrust Analytical Framework' (2017) 62 *Antitrust Bulletin* 254, 266–77.

[21] 165 U.S. 290 (1897).

[22] See *United States v Addyston Pipe & Steel Co.*, 85 F. 271 (6th Cir. 1898), aff'd, 175 U.S. 211 (1899) (market allocation scheme involving sales of iron pipe to municipal governments); see also *United States v Trenton Potteries Co.*, 273 U.S. 392 (1927) (bid rigging scheme involving sales of bathroom fixtures to municipalities).

[23] *McMullen v Hoffman*, 174 U.S. 639 (1899).

[24] *McMullen*, n. 23, 651.

[25] *McMullen*, n. 23 at 652–3.

186   PERSISTENT CORRUPTION AND SUPPLIER COLLUSION

iii. Wartime mobilization: the example of World War II

Wartime mobilization efforts have catalysed major changes in the relationship of the government to its suppliers. The urgency to acquire arms and other materials to support military forces as quickly as possible has elevated speed as a procurement objective and has tended to subordinate the application of strict safeguards against collusion and corruption. This condition has created opportunities for suppliers to exploit imperfections in the wartime monitoring and oversight regime. In some cases, the drive to meet demanding timetables for weapons programmes has created pressure on government antitrust agencies to be cautious in investigating or prosecuting suppliers which are providing essential inputs to the war effort.[26] In times of crisis, defence procurement authorities stand in the awkward position of coaxing contractors to accelerate deliveries but also demanding that they comply with the antitrust laws and other legal mandates.

The experience in the run-up to US participation in World War II highlighted a variety of methods that major firms had used to cartelize sectors vital to the national defence. Many schemes involved the use of patent licensing to execute collective schemes to fix prices, allocate customers, or allocate geographic sales territories.[27] From the earliest decades of antitrust law, antitrust policy has viewed the patent system warily and has given careful attention to the possibility that patent licensing and patent pools could facilitate collusion and the monopolization of entire industries.[28] Perhaps more than at any time in American history, these concerns crystalized during the proceedings, in the late 1930s and early 1940s, of the Temporary National Economic Committee (TNEC) and its 'Investigation of Concentration of Economic Power'.[29] The final TNEC report described the patent system and its operation in scathing terms:

---

[26] From the time of the Japanese attack on Pearl Harbor in December 1941 until the end of World War II, the DOJ often clashed with war production officials about the filing and prosecution of antitrust cases against a number of the country's leading defence contractors. See, W. Wells, *Antitrust and the Formation of the Postwar World* (Columbia University Press, 2002) 43–89; M.B. Stoff, J.F. Fanton, and H. Williams, *The Manhattan Project: A Documentary Introduction to the Atomic Age* (McGraw-Hill, 2000) 55–7.

[27] W.E. Kovacic, R.C. Marshall, and M.J. Meurer, 'Patents and Price Fixing by Serial Colluders' (2021) 10 *New York University Journal of Intellectual Property & Entertainment Law* 152.

[28] See, W. Hamilton, 'Patents and Free Enterprise' (1941) *Monograph No. 31* (prepared for the Temporary National Economic Committee's Investigation of Concentration of Economic Power). Walton Hamilton's monograph recounts the longstanding concern among antitrust specialists that patent rights, unless properly constrained, would undermine competition. In a section titled 'The Peril to Free Enterprise', Hamilton observed that 'In their concern with trade practices, the Federal Trade Commission and the Department of Justice have been plagued with a legalistic conception of a patent as a sacrosanct area in the economic realm', 159. Hamilton cautioned that a rebalancing of the interests of the patent system and the antitrust regime was necessary: 'If presently the patent is not brought into accord, free enterprise can survive only on the fringes of a closed economy', 163.

[29] Temporary National Economic Committee, Final Report and Recommendations of the Temporary National Economic Committee on the Investigation of Concentration of Economic Power (31 March 1941) (hereinafter TNEC Final Report).

No one can read the testimony developed before this committee on patents without coming to a realization that in many important segments of our economy the privilege accorded by the patent monopoly has been shamefully abused.... It [patenting] has been used as a device to control whole industries to suppress competition, to restrict output to enhance prices, to suppress innovation, and to discourage inventiveness.[30]

The TNEC report reflected the work of researchers who had documented how patent licensing arrangements had facilitated the cartelization of global markets.[31] The acute suspicion with which US antitrust policy sometimes has treated patent arrangements almost surely flows out of findings in this era that patent licensing helped to cartelize sectors critical to the World War II mobilization effort.[32] The TNEC proceedings also bolstered existing efforts by Thurman Arnold, then the Assistant Attorney General for Antitrust, to challenge domestic and international cartels that used patent licences as coordination mechanisms.[33] Much of what we know about the use of patent licensing as a collusive device comes from government cases and studies inspired by the TNEC proceedings.

One of the most striking allegations of collusive behaviour appeared in the DOJ's prosecution of Alcoa for illegal monopolization.[34] Ultimately resolved in an influential interpretation of Section 2 of the Sherman Act,[35] the government's case focused, in part, on the relationship among Alcoa, one of its foreign affiliates (Aluminum Limited), and various European producers. Aluminum Limited was created in the late 1920s to assume the ownership of most of Alcoa's properties located outside the US.[36]

---

[30] TNEC Final Report, n. 29, 36.

[31] See Hamilton, n. 28, 165 ('At peace, or at war, the international cartel poses its problem. A corporation barricades its monopoly by securing grants in all the dominant nations. If concerns here and abroad lay claim to rival technologies, the conflict is usually resolved by a private understanding.... The consumer is denied the protection of competition; and an agreement between gentlemen which vaults over frontiers becomes the actual regulation of commerce with foreign nations').

[32] Wells, n. 26, 96–107.

[33] Wells, n. 26, 83–9. Arnold testified on behalf of the DOJ Antitrust Division before the TNEC body at the close of its proceedings. TNEC Final Report, n. 29, 98–138. At several points he emphasized how the DOJ was working to prosecute cartels in sectors that supplied vital means for the wartime mobilization. TNEC Final Report, n. 29, 99 (testimony of Thurman Arnold; stating that 'expenditures for national defence have imposed the immediate task on the Antitrust Division of breaking up combinations which are restricting production in national defence industries or which are causing the Government to pay artificial prices for its defence materials').

[34] M. Winerman and W.E. Kovacic, 'Learned Hand, Alcoa, and the Reluctant Application of the Sherman Act' (2013) 79 *Antitrust Law Journal* 295, 330–45; S.W. Waller, 'The Story of *Alcoa*: The Enduring Questions of Market Power, Conduct and Remedy in Monopolization Cases' in E.M. Fox and D.A. Crane (eds), *Antitrust Stories* (Foundation Press, 1st edn, 2007) 121.

[35] *United States v Aluminum Co. of America (Alcoa)*, 148 F.2d 416 (2d Cir. 1945).

[36] S.N. Whitney, *Antitrust Policies, Volume II* (Twentieth Century Fund, 1958) 93–5. The presidents of Alcoa and Limited were brothers, and the shareholders of the two concerns were largely the same.

188 PERSISTENT CORRUPTION AND SUPPLIER COLLUSION

The DOJ argued that Alcoa, through the 1930s, had taken steps to restrict supply by delaying needed increases in production capacity and thus to raise the price of aluminium.[37] Alcoa's failure to boost capacity in a timely manner, coupled with what the DOJ portrayed as nearly treasonous collusive behaviour by the company's affiliates abroad, placed the mobilization efforts of the US in peril:

> The indifference displayed since 1935 to the ominous signal of their aims given by the Nazis is difficult to understand. The expansion of Germany's productive capacity at an unprecedented rate, though not widely publicized, was surely known to Alcoa through its representation (via Limited) in the Alliance, which had removed German restrictions. While Germany was expanding its capacity, Alcoa and Limited sat by, complacently cooperating, through the Alliance, in the policy of restricting production capacity outside of Germany. As a result, America's productive capacity for aluminum at the outbreak of the war was grossly deficient.[38]

No US antitrust case, before or since, has accused a defendant of creating such dangers by its collusive and exclusionary conduct. Alcoa bitterly disputed the DOJ's hypothesis. The US Court of Appeals for the Second Circuit, which sat as the court of last resort in the case against Alcoa, ruled that Aluminum Limited (though not Alcoa) had violated Section 1 of the Sherman Act by participating in an international cartel with 'the Alliance', a cartel consisting mainly of foreign aluminium producers.[39]

The TNEC proceedings mentioned above also drew attention to serious weaknesses in the public procurement system and documented disturbing levels of 'identical bidding' on public tenders at the national, state, and local levels.[40] TNEC's procurement research reported promising efforts by the DOJ and the Federal Trade Commission (FTC) to collaborate with procurement officials to identify instances of collusion and to formulate enforcement strategies.[41] The TNEC procurement study recommended an expansion of efforts by the antitrust agencies and procurement authorities to detect and prosecute collusion and noted that funds spent on anti-collusion programmes tended to yield significant returns to government buyers in the form of reduced prices for goods and services.[42]

---

[37] Brief for the United States at 327, Alcoa, n. 35, No. 144 ('Alcoa's failure to expand its capacity in the early 1930s is readily understandable; but the tardiness of its response to the growing market demand after 1935 is clearly attributable to the monopolistic urge to restrict supply').

[38] Alcoa, n. 36.

[39] Alcoa, n. 36, 439–45.

[40] C.C. Linnenberg Jr. and D.M. Barbour, *Monograph No. 19: Government Purchasing—An Economic Commentary* (US Government Print Office, 1940) 31-1 (prepared for the Temporary National Economic Committee investigation of concentration of economic power).

[41] Linnenberg and Barbour, n. 40, 99–115.

[42] Linnenberg and Barbour, n. 40, 115.

iv. Expanded global reach of US foreign policy after the World War II era

With the end of World War II came a fundamental adjustment in US foreign policy. To contain communism and accomplish other objectives, the US developed a large permanent presence across the globe in the form of military installations and the establishment of an infrastructure, to provide nonmilitary aid and technical assistance. This foreign policy re-orientation stimulated the development of a new network of locally based contractors which, for example, could provide logistical services to support the operation of US military bases.

The procurement apparatus that supported US operations abroad was no less vulnerable to manipulation than its domestic counterpart. Patterns of misconduct that undermined domestic procurement programmes emerged in many locations abroad. Local suppliers were as adroit as their domestic US counterparts in forming cartels to raise the price of products and services for US government buyers.[43] As the discussion below of the 'Fat Leonard' scandal indicates, bribery of individual US officials likewise has figured prominently in corrupt schemes. These phenomena made clear that an effective programme to counteract cartels and corruption necessarily required a strong international dimension.[44]

v. 'The Gentlemen Conspirators': the Tennessee Valley Authority and the electrical equipment conspiracy cases

Throughout the 1950s, the three principal US manufacturers of turbine generators and heavy electrical equipment—Allis Chalmers, General Electric, and Westinghouse—and a variety of other equipment producers operated cartels targeting electric utilities.[45] Among the principal purchasers were

---

[43] See more recently, e.g., the Korea Fuel Supply Investigation, which resulted in South Korean companies agreeing to plead guilty and to enter civil settlements for rigging bids on US Department of Defense Fuel Supply contracts for military installations in South Korea, available at https://www.justice.gov/opa/pr/three-south-korean-companies-agree-plead-guilty-and-enter-civil-settlements-rigging-bids and https://www.justice.gov/opa/pr/more-charges-announced-ongoing-investigation-bid-rigging-and-fraud-targeting-defense.

[44] In 2021, the DOJ obtained indictments against a Belgian company and three executives for their roles in rigging bids and allocating customers for security services provided by the Belgian government to the US Department of Defense in Belgium, *United States v Series Security NV, Danny Vandormael, Peter Verpoort, and Jean Paul Van Avermaet* (29 June 2021), available at https://www.justice.atr/case/us-v-seris-security-nv-et-al.

[45] The 'gentlemen conspirators' phrase comes from John Fuller's account of the equipment producers' cartel. See, J.G. Fuller, *The Gentlemen Conspirators: The Story of Price-Fixers in the Electrical Industry* (Grove Press, Inc, 1st edn, 1962).

190 PERSISTENT CORRUPTION AND SUPPLIER COLLUSION

government-owned power systems such as the Tennessee Valley Authority (TVA). A crucial step in the detection of the cartel was the discovery by TVA purchasing officials in 1958 that the leading producers had submitted seemingly incomprehensible bids to supply equipment for a new generation facility.[46] The TVA procurement team noticed a striking uniformity in submitted bids; many tenders contained identical prices—down to the penny—for expensive, complex machinery where differences in production techniques and shipping costs ordinarily could be expected to yield varied bids.[47]

Acting on information provided by the TVA, the DOJ undertook what, at the time, was the most significant cartel prosecution in the Sherman Act's history.[48] The DOJ obtained twenty separate indictments in which a total of forty-five individuals and twenty-nine corporations were charged. A total of seven company officials received thirty-day prison sentences. The judicial proceedings in the criminal cases attracted extensive media coverage and highlighted for the public the cravenness of the defendants' behaviour and the economic cost of the misconduct. The prosecution also demonstrated the crucial role that procurement officials could play in alerting the DOJ to suspicious tendering.

vi. Expansion of criminal antitrust enforcement in the 1970s and 1980s: The construction cartels and other supplier collusion for public projects

Bid ridding on public procurement projects provided the context for another major expansion of US efforts to challenge supplier collusion and corruption. The prosecution of the electrical equipment conspiracies in the late 1950s and early 1960s was a crucial step in building awareness of the economic harms caused by cartels. The electrical equipment cases also exposed grave weaknesses in the anticartel programme. As determined by the then existing statutes, antitrust crimes could be prosecuted only as misdemeanours, and the maximum criminal fine for the corporate defendants charged in the electrical equipment cases was USD 50,000. In 1974, Congress adopted a much-needed upgrade in sanctions. The Antitrust Procedures and Penalties Act raised the status of the criminal offence to a

---

[46] Fuller, n. 45; J. Herling, *The Great Price Conspiracy: The Story of the Antitrust Violations in the Electrical Industry* (Greenwood Press, 1962).

[47] C.C. Walton and F.W. Cleveland Jr., *Corporations on Trial: The Electrical Cases* (Wadsworth Publishing Company, Inc, 1964) 24–9.

[48] K.G. Elzinga and W. Breit, *The Antitrust Penalties: A Study in Law and Economics* (Yale University Press, 2nd edn, 1976) 32 (observing that 1960 'witnessed the most dramatic episode in the history of the Sherman Act, the advent of the electrical equipment cases, which involved every major corporation in that industry').

felony, boosted the maximum incarceration sentence for individuals from one year to three years, and lifted the maximum fine for corporations from USD 50,000 to USD 1 million.[49]

From the mid-1970s through the 1980s, the DOJ undertook a major campaign to urge judges to impose the enhanced sanctions and to seek the imprisonment of culpable individuals.[50] A vital element of this strategy was to bring cases involving public procurement, which had the appeal of addressing serious misconduct and providing juries with episodes of behaviour that robbed taxpayers of full value in the provision of essential public services.[51] The DOJ soon uncovered widespread conspiracies—sometimes involving most or all of the service providers in a single state—to rig bids for the construction or improvement of infrastructure assets, such as airports, roads, and port facilities.[52] An expanded programme of cooperation with public procurement authorities soon identified numerous instances in which cartels had imposed inflated prices in contacts for the supply of milk to public school districts and the supply of food and uniforms to the Department of Defence (DOD). From 1972 through 1992, the DOJ obtained 1159 indictments for Sherman Act violations; 625 (54 per cent of the total) involved collusion against government buyers.[53]

vii. Watergate-related scandals and the revelation of Foreign Bribery Schemes

The Watergate investigations that ultimately toppled the presidency of Richard M. Nixon drew attention to questionable campaign financing practices by major corporations. The Watergate inquiries triggered a broader examination of corporate behaviour, including inquiries by the Securities and Exchange Commission (SEC) and Congress into alleged schemes to obtain public contracts and commercial concessions from foreign governments.[54] As described in Chapter 3, these proceedings inspired the enactment in 1977 of the Foreign Corrupt Practices Act (FCPA), which now bans US firms and foreign firms acting in the US[55] from paying

---

[49] Public Law No. 93-528, 88 Statutes at Large 1706 (1974) (codified as amended in various sections of 15 U.S.C.).

[50] D.L. Baker, 'The Use of Criminal Law Remedies to Deter and Punish Cartels and Bid-Rigging' (2001) 69 *George Washington Law Review* 693 (describing the evolution of US criminal enforcement in antitrust cases).

[51] W.E. Kovacic, 'The Modern Evolution of U.S. Competition Policy Enforcement Norms' (2004) 71 *Antitrust Law Journal* 377, 418-23.

[52] D.H. Ginsburg, 'Rationalizing Antitrust: A Rejoinder to Professor Armentano' (1990) 35(2) *The Antitrust Bulletin* 329.

[53] W.E. Kovacic, 'Is Uncle Sam Too Easy a Mark?', *Legal Times* (2 November 1998) S42.

[54] J. Goodman, 'The Anti-Corruption and Antitrust Connection', *The Antitrust Source* (April 2013), available at https://silo.tips/download/the-anti-corruption-and-antitrust-connection.

[55] Indeed, some of the largest sanctions have been imposed on foreign firms, see E. Acorn, 'Law and Politics in FCPA Prosecutions of Foreign Corporations' (2021) 17(2) *Revista Direito GV*.

192 PERSISTENT CORRUPTION AND SUPPLIER COLLUSION

bribes to officials of foreign governments for the purpose of gaining contracts or other commercial favours.[56]

Revelations of commercial bribery also led the FTC to bring cases against three leading US aerospace firms under the commercial bribery provision of the Robinson-Patman Act.[57] The FCPA soon became the instrument of choice for government efforts to attack the bribery of foreign government officials; yet the FTC prosecutions demonstrated the availability of antitrust theories of liability to address certain forms of commercial bribery abroad.[58]

viii. Operation Ill Wind

During the eight years of his presidency, Ronald Reagan accomplished the largest programme of peacetime expenditures for defence in the history of the US—a total of over USD 2.02 trillion for fiscal years 1981 through 1988.[59] The massive build-up inspired close scrutiny of the DOD purchasing procedures. A series of well-publicized scandals raised fundamental questions about the capability of the federal contracting regime and the vulnerability of defence procurement to manipulation by its major suppliers.

The most spectacular and influential episode was the DOJ's 'Operation Ill Wind' investigation, which focused on the use by defence contractors of consultants to gather inside information about the DOD's purchasing intentions.[60] The inquiry revealed that various Defence Department officials had accepted bribes in return for bidding information that enabled major contractors to gain an advantage in weapon system procurements. The DOJ prosecuted more than sixty contractors, consultants, and government officials, including a DOD assistant secretary and deputy assistant secretary of the Navy.[61] The DOJ cases yielded USD 622 million in monetary recoveries and spurred Congress to enact new ethics safeguards.[62]

---

[56] See, Section B.x, below.

[57] 15 U.S.C. §13(c). The FTC obtained consent agreements that enjoined the forbidden practices. Lockheed Corp., 92 FTC 968 (1978); Boeing Co., 92 FTC 972 (1978); McDonnell Douglas Corp., 92 FTC 976 (1978). The FTC cases challenged behaviour that took place before the FCPA took effect.

[58] F.A. Gevurtz, 'Using the Antitrust Laws to Combat Overseas Bribery by Foreign Companies: A Step to Even the Odds in International Trade' (1987) 27 *Virginia Journal of International Law* 211; J.F. Rill and R.L. Frank, 'Antitrust Consequences of United States Corporate Payments to Foreign Officials' (1977) 30 *Vanderbilt Law Review* 131.

[59] W.W. Kaufmann and L.J. Korb, *The 1990 Defense Budget* (Brookings Institution, 1989) 8–19.

[60] For the pre-eminent account of the 'Ill Wind scandal', see A. Pasztor, *When the Pentagon Was For Sale: Inside America's Biggest Defense Scandal* (Scribner, 1st edn, 1995). Many of the consultants involved in the bribery schemes were former government officials who used friendships with former government colleagues to gain access to the Defense Department.

[61] Operation Ill Wind, available at https://www.fbi.gov/history/famous-cases/operation-illwind.

[62] The most notable legislative measure was the Procurement Integrity Act.

HISTORICAL PERSPECTIVE   193

ix. Boeing's bribery of Darlene Druyen

From 1992 to 2002, Darlene Druyen served as the leading civilian acquisition official for the US Air Force. During her tenure, Boeing Co. was one of the main suppliers of major weapon systems to the Air Force. An investigation carried out by
the DOD and the DOJ found that Druyen had given Boeing preferential treatment
on contracts for some of DOD's most important defence programmes, including a
multi-billion-dollar procurement award to supply the Air Force with a next generation aerial refuelling tanker and a USD 4 billion contract to upgrade the avi-
onics on various cargo aircraft.[63] In return, Boeing provided Druyen with a senior
executive position with Boeing upon her retirement and gave assurances that the
firm would secure employment for her daughter and son-in-law.[64] Druyen pled
guilty to several criminal offences and served nine months in prison. The Air Force
voided the tainted contracts with Boeing, and the DOJ obtained guilty pleas from
senior Boeing officials who had orchestrated the bribes.

x. 'Fat Leonard' corruption scandal

The US Navy relies on a wide network of contractors to supply its fleet operations
around the globe. Among these was Leonard Francis (known as 'Fat Leonard'),
whose company (Glen Defense Marine Asia) provided logistical support services
at various Navy facilities in Asia. For several decades,[65] Francis cultivated corrupt
relationships with Navy personnel (including high-ranking admirals) through
which he provided hotel stays, meals, concert tickets, and sex workers in exchange
for classified information about Navy logistics needs and to obtain contracts at inflated prices.[66] Between 2006 and 2013, Francis is estimated to have swindled at
least USD 35 million from the Navy.[67]

From 2010 through 2013, the Navy and the DOJ undertook an investigation
that, to date, has yielded over sixty indictments of individuals and twenty-two
guilty pleas. Among those who have pleaded guilty and been sentenced to prison
are senior Navy officers responsible for managing the Navy's logistics system in

---

[63] Among other corrupt acts, Druyen gave Boeing information about the bid that Boeing's rival, the
European Aeronautic Defense and Space Company, had submitted for the tanker replacement contract.
Druyen also negotiated a leasing arrangement with Boeing for the tanker contract that gave the com-
pany a better deal than the firm might have obtained in a properly-conducted procurement.

[64] 'Druyen's Downfall' *Air Force Magazine* (November 2004).

[65] J. Greene, 'The Glenn Defense Marine Asia Problem: The Role of Ethics in Procurement Reform'
(2018) 48 *Public Contract Law Journal* 15.

[66] Among other information, Francis received highly classified data about Navy ship movements
across Asia.

[67] B. Herzinger, 'Fat Leonard Cost the U.S. Navy More Than Money', *Foreign Policy* (24 October
2022), available at https://foreignpolicy.com/2022/10/24/fat-leonard-us-navy-corruption-scandal.

Asia.[68] In 2015, Leonard and his firm pleaded guilty to many corruption-based offences.[69] Leonard's corruption scheme is feared to have done lasting damage to the Navy's readiness in the Asia Pacific Region, an area of acute foreign policy concern for the US and its allies.[70]

xi. Marine hoses

In 2007 and 2008 a number of marine hose manufacturers, and their executives, pled guilty to participating in a conspiracy to rig bids, fix prices, and allocate market shares of marine hoses sold in the US and abroad.[71] These antitrust investigations also led to discovery of foreign corrupt payments, which culminated in Misao Hioki pleading guilty to both FCPA and Sherman Act offences[72] (Hioki was one of eight foreign executives arrested in May 2007 following participation in a cartel meeting in Houston). Bridgestone, the company for which he worked, also concluded a plea agreement admitting FCPA and Sherman Act violations.[73]

xii. COVID-19, the Federal Government response, and corruption

In the US and many other jurisdictions, governments have spent massive sums to respond to the COVID-19 healthcare crisis and to fund programmes designed to spur economic recovery and increase the resilience of supply chains. US crisis expenditures have included outlays for medical supplies and services, financial support for distressed businesses, infrastructure projects, and the

---

[68] G. Fuentes, 'Former 7th Fleet Logistics Chief Sentenced to 30-Months in "Fat Leonard" Bribery Case', *U.S. Naval Institute News* (25 February 2023), available at https://news.usni.org/2023/02/25/for mer-7th-fleet-logistics-chief-sentenced-to-30-months-in-fat-leonard-bribery-case.

[69] Weeks before he was due to be sentenced in US district court in San Diego, Francis fled home-detention. He subsequently was detained in Venezuela when he attempted to board a plane bound for Russia, see Fuentes, n. 68. Pursuant to an agreement between Venezuela and the US, Leonard was extra-dited to the US in December 2023.

[70] Herzinger, n. 67.

[71] See, e.g., Department of Justice, 'British Marine Hose Manufacturer Agrees to Plead Guilty and Pay $4.5 Million for Participating in Worldwide Bid-Rigging Conspiracy', *Press Release* (1 December 2008), available at https://www.justice.gov/archive/opa/pr/2008/December/08-at-1055.html and further discussion of the proceedings in the UK and in the EU in Chapter 5.

[72] See Department of Justice, 'Japanese Executive Pleads Guilty, Sentenced to Two Years in Jail for Participating in Conspiracies to Rig Bids and Bribe Foreign Officials to Purchase Marine Hose and Related Products', *Press Release* (10 December 2008), available at https://www.justice.gov/archive/opa/pr/2008/December/08-at-1084.html.

[73] Department of Justice, 'Bridgestone Corporation Agrees to Plead Guilty to Participating in Conspiracies to Rig Bids and Bribe Foreign Government Officials', *Press Release* (15 September 2011), available at https://www.justice.gov/opa/pr/bridgestone-corporation-agrees-plead-guilty-participat ing-conspiracies-rig-bids-and-bribe.

expansion of domestic production capacity in strategically important sectors, such as semiconductors.

As the dire effects of the pandemic became apparent, the first priority of public relief programmes was speed. Government-funded programmes, in the form of procurements and transfer payments, spent massive sums of money in a great hurry. To dispense assistance expeditiously, public authorities did not initially deploy the full complement of auditing and monitoring controls that ordinarily precede outlays of this magnitude. The urgency to alleviate medical and financial distress, understandably, subordinated concerns that huge expenditures would attract fraud.

The postponed or attenuated auditing and monitoring processes are now unfolding, and investigations are revealing that corruption, including supplier misconduct, tainted a number of government expenditure programmes. The exact dimensions of fraud remain to be determined, but episodes of serious corruption affecting billions of dollars of funds have come to light.[74] More dispiriting revelations are likely to emerge as public agency investigations examine the dispersal of contracts, grants, and subsidies through a multitude of federal, state, and local programmes.

xiii. Trump era scandals and challenges to the Rule of Law

Immediately before and during his presidency, Donald Trump engaged in conduct that appeared, in the eyes of many government contracts experts, to violate federal rules and norms designed to prevent public officials from taking action in matters that pose a conflict of interest or create the appearance of such conflicts. The foremost example was a lease agreement that Trump's business organization signed with the US General Services Administration (GSA) in the years before his presidency. Trump's company leased a Washington, DC landmark, the Old Post Office, and renovated it to serve as a luxury hotel. The possibility that Trump or his family would continue to operate the hotel appeared to contradict a lease provision that forbade him from holding a proprietary interest while serving as head of state (as president, Donald Trump would exercise direct supervisory authority over the GSA, which was responsible for overseeing the lease). The GSA issued an ethics decision that allowed the Trump family to continue to administer the hotel, subject to the President's withdrawal from direct involvement in its operations. This outcome stunned public procurement experts who interpreted the lease terms and their ethics safeguards to require President Trump to surrender the lease back to

---

[74] 'Biggest Fraud in a Generation: The Looting of the COVID Relief Plan known as PPP', *NBC News* (28 March 2022), available at https://www.nbcnews.com/politics/justice-department/biggest-fraud-generation-looting-covid-relief-program-known-ppp-n1279664.

196 PERSISTENT CORRUPTION AND SUPPLIER COLLUSION

the GSA upon assuming office.[75] Among other clients, the Trump International Hotel became a favoured destination for foreign diplomats on official visits and lobbyists doing business with government agencies—arguably providing a direct route for interested parties to funnel funds to the former President.[76] The hotel episode was one of a number of instances in which former President Trump or his closest advisors raised concerns for public procurement experts and public administration ethicists.[77]

The more serious threat to the institutional integrity of the US and the nation's stature globally emerged in the aftermath of the November 2020 general elections, in which Joseph Biden defeated Donald Trump for the presidency. In the run-up to the official certification of the election results, as documented in an expansive report prepared by a select committee of the US House of Representatives,[78] President Trump actively sought to persuade state government officials to invalidate the results of the November balloting, and he appears to have attempted to press the DOJ to take steps to overturn the 2020 election results.[79] The House select committee report also recounted the violent attack on the US Capitol building on 6 January 2021. A mob entered the Capitol building as the US Senate, presided over by Vice-President Michael Pence, was convened to certify the November election results. The mob entered the Senate chamber soon after the members of the Senate and Vice-President Pence had fled the room, proceeded to the House of Representatives and, among other acts, occupied the office of House Speaker Nancy Pelosi.

Before the mob descended on the Capitol building, President Trump gave an impromptu address to many of its participants near the White House. In his spoken

---

[75] D.L. Gordon and S.L. Schooner, 'GSA's Trump Hotel Decision Debacle', *Government Executive* (28 November 2016), available at https://www.govexec.com/management/2016/11/gsas-trump-hotel-lease-debacle/133424.

[76] The Trump organization sold its rights in the property in May 2022. See, E. Lipton, 'Trump Completes Sale of Washington Hotel to Investor Group', *New York Times* (11 May 2022), available at https://www.nytimes.com/2022/05/11/us/politics/trump-hotel-sale-washington.html.

[77] On additional procurement irregularities linked to the White House, see D.J. Figuenick III, 'Billions and Billions, and Billions: Recent Administrations, Cronyism, and the Need for Greater Independence in Contract Awards' (2022) 51 *Public Contract Law Journal* 599.

[78] U.S. House of Representatives, Final Report of the Select Committee to Investigate the January 6th Attack on the US. Capitol, Rep. 117-663, 117th Cong., 2d Sess. (22 December 2022), available at https://www.govinfo.gov/content/pkg/GPO-J6-REPORT/pdf/GPO-J6-REPORT.pdf.

[79] According to one report, 'Donald Trump's extraordinary effort to overturn his 2020 election defeat brought the DOJ to the brink of chaos, and prompted top officials there and at the White House to threaten to resign.' See 'Report Details Trump's All-Out Bid to Undo Election Results', *Associated Press* (7 October 2021), available at https://apnews.com/article/donald-trump-election-2020-judiciary-presidential-elections-elections-2fec942d0c09bc31858190afbb5d8e42. In two cases, one prosecuted by the DOJ and one prosecuted by state officials in Georgia, Trump has been indicted on the ground that he sought to subvert the 2020 presidential election. Trump also faces a variety of criminal and civil charges, including charges that accuse him of mishandling confidential government documents after leaving the presidency and of engaging in fraud in the management of his business interests. See D. A. Graham, 'The Cases Against Trump: A Guide', *The Atlantic* (30 October 2023), available at https://www.theatlantic.com/ideas/archive/2023/10/donald-trump-legal-cases-charges/675531/.

HISTORICAL PERSPECTIVE   197

comments and in various tweets, he addressed the gathering in ways that suggested he supported the efforts of the crowd to march on the Capitol and confront the legislators who were about to verify the election of Joseph Biden. During the mob's assault on the Capitol, President Trump watched the rampage on television and, despite urging from his aides to intervene, took no immediate steps to urge his supporters to leave the Capitol. The January 6 mayhem has created what promise to be enduring doubts about the quality of the institutions that govern the US.[80]

xiv. Summary: Some notable lessons from US experience

The events recounted above illuminate several important themes regarding public policy initiatives to curtail supplier collusion and related forms of behaviour that suppress competition in government procurement.

The Arms Race Between Public Agencies and Violators. The interaction between public authorities and participants in schemes that subvert the integrity and effectiveness of public procurement in important respects resembles an arms race. This is a dynamic context in which public authorities develop new techniques for suppressing misconduct (e.g. the enactment and periodic enhancement of a federal antitrust regime) and firms devise countermeasures to thwart them. The volume of public procurement expenditures is so immense, and the rewards from successful collusion and corruption are so great, that firms will not simply surrender in the face of new government measures to address misconduct; they adapt. Policymakers must assume that some contractors will persist in efforts to exploit weaknesses in the procurement regime and find new ways to achieve their collusive ends. Government agencies must anticipate this inevitable process of adaptation and continually refine existing mechanisms to address it.

Massive Increases in Expenditures Intensify Misconduct. Some of the most serious scandals sketched above have followed in the wake of massive increases in procurement outlays. Examples here include the naval rearmament programme of the late nineteenth and early twentieth centuries, the mobilization to prepare for the possible entry of the US into World War II, the Reagan-era military build-up, and the emergency expenditures to combat the effects of the COVID-19 pandemic. The potential for supplier misconduct is greatest when the increase in public outlays, as with the COVID pandemic, responds to crisis, and government agencies place the highest priority upon dispensing funds quickly.

Public Procurement Personnel as Arsonists and Firefighters. The government's procurement officials feature prominently, for good and for bad, in many of the episodes recited above. In some instances, they serve as valuable 'coast watchers'

---

[80] Many of the insurgents have been prosecuted, and the DOJ has obtained a large number of guilty pleas and convictions.

198 PERSISTENT CORRUPTION AND SUPPLIER COLLUSION

for antitrust authorities and other government prosecutors, alerting law enforcers to the apparent presence of illegal collusion. This showcases the value of close co-operation between law enforcement agencies (such as DOJ's Antitrust Division) and procurement offices to develop techniques for identifying suspicious supplier conduct. The gloomy theme of the story is that government insiders sometimes facilitate supplier misconduct. Government procurement officials enabled wrong-doers in the naval rearmament case, the Operation Ill Wind scandal, Boeing's bribery of Darlene Druyen, and the Fat Leonard logistics scandal. Thus, a compre-hensive programme to address supplier collusion must include safeguards to pre-vent public employees from misusing their office to abet misconduct.

Importance of Investments in Institutional Quality. Building effective systems to detect and deter supplier collusion and related misconduct, requires significant in-vestments in human capital (in law enforcement and procurement departments) and in physical assets (such as electronic systems that facilitate the use of analytics to examine patterns in procurement tenders). A number of studies over time have documented a gradual decline in the government's ability to build capable teams of procurement officials, especially to design and manage programmes involving large outlays or complex systems, or both.[81] The gaps are especially evident when episodes of scandal drive the adoption of new regulatory measures without com-mensurate increases in funding for agencies to implement them. As remedial measures, investments in training, professionalization, and adequate remuner-ation for the procurement workforce are all relevant.[82]

Mismatches Between Expectations and the Actual Performance of Government. Gaps in government procurement (and law enforcement) capabilities are part of a larger tension that one observes in the US public contracting experience. As sug-gested above in the discussion of early implementation of the federal antitrust laws, one element of the tension is the view that governments should spare no expense to ensure complete integrity in the procurement process. Thus, the Supreme Court in 1899 states in *McMullen v Hoffman* 'it must be apparent that biddings for contracts for public works cannot be surrounded with too many precautions for the purpose of obtaining perfectly fair and bona fide bids.'[83] Yet, for generations, legislators and the taxpayers who elect them have shown no evident desire to provide the funds needed to attain the requisite 'precautions'. Nor is it self-evident that absolutely perfect compliance is an attainable or desirable goal in light of what it might cost to achieve such a state of affairs. Perhaps a more realistic aim for a procurement system is to minimize the occurrence of serious fraud, to mitigate harm as quickly as possible, and to build systems to seek to avoid the recurrence of known failures.

---

[81] A long succession of government reports has documented weaknesses in procurement personnel as a cause of performance lapses and vulnerability to corrupt behaviour by suppliers. See, W.E. Kovacic, 'Blue Ribbon Defense Commissions: The Acquisition of Major Weapon Systems' in Higgs, n. 1.

[82] See also relevant comments in Chapters 3 and 4.

[83] *McMullen*, 174 U.S. at 651, n. 23.

C. The Regulatory Framework

For the most part, the legal regimes of antitrust law, public procurement law, and anti-corruption law share a mutual and abiding suspicion towards conduct that suppresses rivalry among suppliers and regard competition as a valuable mechanism to ensure good purchasing outcomes. There are, to be sure, also glaring exceptions to this general principle. As described below, the US procurement system embraces policies that sometimes restrict, rather than seek to stimulate, competition among suppliers. The most significant of these are measures that require purchasing officials to give preference to goods or services sourced within the US or, in the case of state and local purchasing, from regional or local suppliers.

This section of the chapter describes the regulatory framework with respect to these three bodies of law. The section first sets out the principal substantive commands and then presents the enforcement mechanism for implementing them.

i. Substantive requirements

a. Antitrust statutes

The federal antitrust regime for combatting supplier collusion rests chiefly upon Section 1 of the Sherman Act, which prohibits contracts, combinations, or conspiracies in restraint of trade.[84] This measure is the tool that supports most antitrust challenges to bid rigging and other collusive schemes aimed at public procurement tenders. Courts routinely condemn agreements between competitors to submit collusive bids and allocate contracts among themselves.[85] Courts also have sustained criminal convictions for firms and individuals engaged in bid rotation schemes, or arrangements to allocation procurement customers or geographic regions.[86]

Section 2 of the Sherman contains a ban upon conspiracies to monopolize which also can serve the same end when the participants in the scheme collectively could exercise substantial market power.[87] Invitations by one company to induce a rival to engage in a collusive scheme, even if rejected by the rival, can result in liability under the attempted monopolization prohibition of Section 2 of the Sherman

---

[84] 15 U.S.C. §1.

[85] See, e.g., *United States v W.F. Brinkley & Son Construction Co.*, 783 F.2d 1157 (4th Cir. 1986); *United States v Koppers Co.*, 652 F.2d 290 (2d Cir. 1981); *United States v David E. Thompson, Inc.*, 621 F.3d 1147 (1st Cir. 1980).

[86] See, e.g., *United States v Champion Int'l Corp.*, 557 F.2d 1270 (9th Cir. 1977).

[87] 15 U.S.C. §2; see *United States v National Led Co.*, 63 F. Supp. 513, 522-25 (SDNY 1945), aff'd, 332 U.S. 319 (1947).

200 PERSISTENT CORRUPTION AND SUPPLIER COLLUSION

Act[88] or the prohibition against unfair methods of competition in Section 5 of the Federal Trade Commission Act.[89]

Most states in the US have adopted replicas of Sections 1 and 2 of the Sherman Act.[90] State attorneys general have applied these statutes to challenge, among other conduct, bid rigging schemes aimed at state and local government procurement authorities. States also have standing as plaintiffs to enforce the Sherman Act.

b. Public Procurement Law

The federal procurement laws generally embrace the competition philosophy of the antitrust laws, although some policies favour US-based businesses and domestic products.[91] The Competition in Contracting Act of 1984 (CICA) establishes a presumption that federal purchasing authorities should use competitive procurement techniques.[92] The Federal Acquisition Regulations (FAR) also contain specific provisions, sketched below, to prevent antitrust violations and other behaviour that compromises the effectiveness and integrity of the procurement process.

Certification Obligations. US Procurement Law relies extensively on requirements that its contractors certify that they have fulfilled statutory and regulatory duties concerning, among other matters, the fulfilment of procompetition requirements of the federal procurement regime. Failures to meet certification obligations can be prosecuted as procurement fraud.

The most significant certification obligation relating to supplier collusion requires that competitors certify that they have not colluded with rival firms in preparing bids on certain government contracts. Solicitations involving firm-fixed-price contracts must include a 'Certificate of Independent Price Determination' (CIPD).[93] The CIPD states that the contractor have set its prices 'independently, without, for the purpose of restricting competition, any consultation, communication, or agreement with any other offeror or competitor relating to (i) those prices, (ii) the intention to submit an offer, or (iii) the methods or factors used to calculate the prices offered'.[94]

---

[88] 15 U.S.C. §2; see *United States v American Airlines, Inc.,* 743 F.2d 1114 (5th Cir. 1984). In *United States v Nathan Nephi Zito,* Case No. 22-cr-00113 (D. Mt. Sept. 19, 2022), the DOJ brought a criminal attempted monopolization case and obtained a guilty plea against a construction company for inviting its rival to collude on bids for publicly funded road repair contracts in Montana and Wyoming.

[89] 15 U.S.C. §45; see also, A.I. Gavil, W.E. Kovacic, J.B. Baker, and J.D. Wright, *Antitrust Law in Perspective: Cases, Concepts and Problems in Competition Policy* (West Academic Publishing, 4th edn, 2022) 426–7 (describing FTC invitation to collude cases).

[90] Gavil et al., n. 89, 1348–50.

[91] See Section C.iii, below.

[92] 10 U.S.C. §2304(a)(1) and 41 U.S.C. §253(a)(1). CICA specifies two main competitive acquisition procedures: sealed bids and competitive proposals.

[93] FAR §3.103-3. The CIPD appears in FAR §52.203-2.

[94] FAR, n. 93. The CIPD also attests that the contractor has not knowingly disclosed its prices to other offerors before the purchasing authority has opened the bids or awarded the contract. The certificate further states that the contractor has not attempted to induce other firms to submit or withhold bids for the purpose of restricting competition.

THE REGULATORY FRAMEWORK 201

In 1988, the DOD imposed additional competition-oriented certification requirements upon companies implicated in the Operation Ill Wind inquiry, discussed above. Affected firms must submit a 'Competitive Information Certificate' before the award of all competitively awarded new contracts valued at over USD 100,000.[95] The certificate requires the contractor to attest that it has set its prices independently and has neither disclosed its prices to other offerors nor sought to induce other firms to submit or withhold a bid for the purpose of suppressing competition.[96]

Prime Contractor Restrictions on Subcontractors. Federal procurement policy bars prime contractors from obstructing efforts by their subcontractors to sell directly to government buyers. Federal contracts must include a clause that forbids a prime contractor from entering agreements with its subcontractors that unreasonably restricts direct sales by the subcontractors to the government.[97]

Conflicts of Interest. Federal procurement law and policy establish a number of safeguards to ensure that government officials do not take decisions or participate in decision-making that would create conflicts, or the appearance of conflicts, between their interests as individuals and the larger interests of the government.[98] The application, or nonapplication, of these requirements has provided a source of continuing controversy. As noted above, perhaps the most dramatic recent illustration of the sometimes problematic implementation of this regime has involved the lease agreement that Donald Trump signed with the GSA in the years before his presidency began.[99]

c. Anti-Corruption and Public Integrity Laws

As suggested above, episodes of bid rigging on government contracts often involve other illegal behaviour, including bribery of procurement officials and the signing of false CIPD certificates. Wrongdoers also may execute collusive schemes by using the federal postal system and using communications networks to transmit messages across state borders. These and related actions may violate a variety of anti-corruption statutes that serve to ensure the integrity of the public procurement process, to ensure truthful dealing with the government, and prevent the obstruction of law enforcement.

Noteworthy anti-corruption measures include federal statutes that prohibit bribery of government officials,[100] the giving of certain gratuities to public employees,[101] the payment of kickbacks to public officials,[102] conspiracy to defraud the

---

[95] 32 CFR §173.2(a).
[96] 32 CFR §173.2(f).
[97] 48 CFR §§3.503-2 and 52.203-6.
[98] FAR §§3.11 and 9.5.
[99] See, subsection B.xiii, above. On recent procurement irregularities linked to the White House, see Figuenick III et al., n. 77.
[100] 18 U.S.C. §201(b).
[101] 18 U.S.C. §201(f).
[102] 41 U.S.C. §8707.

202 PERSISTENT CORRUPTION AND SUPPLIER COLLUSION

government,[103] mail and wire fraud,[104] false statements to public agencies,[105] false claims for payment by the government,[106] major procurement fraud,[107] racketeer-influenced and corrupt organizations activity,[108] obstruction of justice,[109] and perjury.[110] When it prosecutes bid rigging arrangements, the DOJ frequently alleges violations of one or more of these anti-corruption statutes when it files charges under the federal antitrust laws.[111]

d. Foreign Corrupt Practices Act

In 1977, in the Foreign Corrupt Practices Act, Congress forbade firms from paying bribes or similar forms of consideration to foreign officials involved in the purchase of goods or services. The statute was a pathbreaking effort to prevent business from paying foreign governments to provide favourable treatment in public tendering or other contracting devices.[112] The law does not apply to the foreign officials who solicit improper payments, yet it seeks to discourage such behaviour by barring firms from responding favourably to such requests.[113]

Enactment of the law met with severe disapproval from US firms which argued that the measure tied their hands but allowed companies from other nations to continue to offer illicit compensation. Over time, US enforcement of the FCPA and advocacy before international fora, such as the Organisation for Economic Co-operation and Development (OECD), have fostered increasing acceptance of an international norm that forbids bribery of public officials to obtain contracts and other important commercial concessions.

ii. Enforcement mechanism

The US has developed a formidable enforcement mechanism to implement the substantive commands described above. Principal responsibility for enforcement resides with the DOJ, with significant contributions from the government

---

[103] 18 U.S.C. §371.
[104] 18 U.S.C. §§1341, 1343.
[105] 18 U.S.C. §1001.
[106] 18 U.S.C. §287.
[107] 18 U.S.C. §1031.
[108] 18 U.S.C. §1962.
[109] 18 U.S.C. §§1503, 1505, 1510, and 1512.
[110] 18 U.S.C. §§1621, 1623.
[111] See, e.g., *United States v Dynalectric Co.*, 859 F.2d 1559 (11th Cir. 1989) (bid rigging conspirators charged with antitrust and mail fraud violations); *United States v Portac, Inc.*, 869 F.2d 1288 (9th Cir. 1989) (antitrust conspirator charged with making false statements to grand jury).
[112] See further Chapter 3, this book.
[113] Many commentators have noted the weakness in an anti-corruption tool that focuses only on the party that pays the bribe and does not address the party who solicits the bribe. See, e.g., L.B. Arrieta, 'Attacking Bribery at Its Core: Shifting Focus to the Demand Side of the Bribery Equation' (2016) 45 *Public Contract Law Journal* 587, and Chapter 4.

purchasing agencies. As noted below, an important frontier for improvement in policy implementation is deeper cooperation across these public institutions.

a. Antitrust laws

The DOJ is the dominant federal enforcement agency for matters involving public procurement. Most notably, the DOJ has exclusive power to seek criminal sanctions for bid rigging and related offences. Since the 1980s, state governments have played an increasingly important role in policing federal and state antitrust statutes that forbid supplier collusion that distorts public contract awards.[114]

Conduct forbidden by the Sherman Act may be prosecuted as a civil offence or a criminal violation. The DOJ typically prosecutes bid rigging as a crime and uses a wide array of information gathering techniques—including wire taps, electronic surveillance, and search warrants—to collect evidence of misconduct.[115]

One of the most important tools for detecting and deterring collusion is the DOJ's leniency program, which gives strong incentives to companies and individual employees to reveal misconduct.[116] The latest iteration of the leniency programme gives complete dispensation from criminal prosecution to a firm that is the first to reveal the existence of a cartel. Even where a firm is not the first to inform, it can receive reductions in the sanctions imposed in sentencing. The most recent reforms to the leniency programme make eligibility dependent on the firm's commitment to establish compliance safeguards that will prevent future infractions. The DOJ also encourages procurement officials to look for indicators of collusion and to report any suspicion to the Department.[117]

Sanctions for criminal antitrust violations have become progressively more severe since the early 1970s.[118] A formative step in this process was the adoption of the Antitrust Procedures and Penalties Act in 1974, which, among other steps, raised the status of the criminal offence from a misdemeanour to a felony.[119] All Sherman Act offences are punishable by a fine of USD 100 million, regardless of the actual economic harm suffered by the government. In the 1980s, Congress adopted an alternative criminal fine calculation methodology that allows the government to recover twice the pecuniary loss suffered by victims or twice the pecuniary gain

---

[114] See, e.g., *Colorado v Western Paving Construction Co.*, 833 F. 2d 867 (10th Cir. 1987) (Sherman Act suit by state of Colorado challenging bid rigging on state highway construction contracts).

[115] The development of the DOJ's cartel enforcement programme is examined in V. Ghosal and D. Sokol, 'The Evolution of U.S. Cartel Enforcement' (2014) 57(S3) *Journal of Law & Economics* 51.

[116] See, for further details, https://www.justice.gov/atr/leniency-program.

[117] See, e.g., additional information on the Department of Justice's Leniency Program, available at https://www.justice.gov/atr/preventing-and-detecting-bid-rigging-price-fixing-and-market-allocation-post-disaster-rebuilding.

[118] This progression is documented in Ghosal and Sokol, n. 115; W.E. Kovacic, 'Criminal Enforcement Norms in Competition Policy: Insights from US Experience' in C. Beaton-Wells and A. Ezrachi (eds), *Criminalising Cartels: Critical Studies of an International Regulatory Movement* (Hart Publishing, 2011).

[119] Pub. Law 93-528, 88 Stat. 1706 (21 December 1974).

realized by wrongdoers. The alternative fining formula can yield criminal fines well above the USD 100 million level specified in the Sherman Act.

Individuals found guilty of bid rigging face harsh penalties, as well. Individual defendants may be sentenced for up to ten years in prison, fined up to USD 1 million, and are subject to an alternative fining mechanism that parallels the 'double the loss, double the gain' formula applied to corporate defendants. Since the 1980s, sentencing practice applied pursuant to the US Sentencing Guidelines, dictates that individuals serve a minimum prison sentence of eighteen months, whether an individual is convicted at trial or enters a guilty plea.

The Federal Government also can bring civil suits to challenge bid rigging. The DOJ can obtain an injunction, structural relief, or three times the damages that the Federal Government has suffered in its capacity as a purchaser.

State governments injured in their capacity as buyers have standing to seek treble damages and injunctions for federal antitrust violations. State antitrust laws also have been interpreted to give state prosecutors ability to sue as indirect purchasers.[120]

b. Public Procurement Law

Suspension and Debarment. Government purchasing authorities may suspend or debar government contractors when doing so serves the public interest.[121] Due to the severe consequences for affected firms, the government purchaser must satisfy strict evidentiary and procedural requirements before imposing suspension and debarment remedies. Firms suspended, debarred, or proposed for debarment are excluded from receiving contracts, performing subcontracts, or conducting business with the government as agents or representatives of other contractors.

Within this general framework, antitrust violations involving bid rigging ordinarily result in the contractor's suspension or debarment. An indictment for antitrust violations constitutes adequate evidence for a suspension, and the entry of a criminal conviction or civil judgment for antitrust violations (such as bid rigging) creates grounds for debarment. The framework for suspension and debarment at the state level is less completely elaborated than the federal regime, but states increasingly impose these sanctions to firms convicted of bid rigging.

---

[120] Several states have enacted so-called 'Illinois Brick repealer' statues that expressly permit indirect purchasers to maintain a claim for damages under the state's Antitrust Act. See, C.R. Price, E.J. McCarthy, and G.S. Seador (eds), *Indirect Purchaser Lawsuits: A State-by-State Survey* (ABA Book Publishing, 2010).

[121] C. Garlick, 'Putting Federal Suspension and Debarment Officials in the Driver's Seat: Empowering S&D Programs to Efficiently Save Taxpayer Dollars' (2019) 48 Public Contract Law Journal 315; J. Berrada, 'Suspension and Debarment in Federal Government Contracting: A Call for Pre-Exclusion Notice and Opportunity to Respond' (2018) 48 *Public Contract Law Journal* 165; D.E. Schoeni, 'Personal Debarment for Non-Distributive Corporate Misconduct: On the Efficacy of Debarring the Individual from Government Contracts for Collective Wrongdoing' (2016) 46 *Public Contract Law Journal* 51.

Bid Protests. Bidders and potential offerors on government contracts sometimes seek to use alleged episodes of anti-competitive behaviour or apparent corruption to support bid protests.[122] The invocation of apparent antitrust violations generally does not support a successful bid protest, but proof that favouritism (e.g. a contractor's effort to bribe a public official or otherwise exert undue influence over procurement decisions) has distorted the design of a tender or the evaluation of bids can sustain a protest.

c. Anti-Corruption and Public Integrity Laws

As mentioned above, indictments accusing contractors of antitrust violations often include additional claims based on violations of anti-corruption statutes. Criminal indictments frequently include counts challenging the formation of the bid rigging conspiracy, the bribery of government officials, the submission of certificates that falsely assert compliance with independent pricing requirements, the use of the mail or telecommunications systems to transmit tainted bids or requests for payments, and the obstruction of law enforcement inquiries. Virtually every episode of bid rigging on public contracts gives the DOJ a wide array of theories, beyond antitrust law, to prosecute the participants criminally.

One focus of US anti-corruption enforcement efforts has been conduct that takes place in a shadowy realm between lobbying—that the law regards as acceptable (if not edifying)—and influence peddling that involves the illegal act of soliciting action from government officials in return for financial or other consideration. An important anti-corruption tool has been the Federal Wire Fraud Act and its application to any 'scheme or artifice to deprive another of the intangible right of honest services'.[123]

In its recent decision in *Percoco v United States*,[124] the Supreme Court narrowed the use of the 'honest services' theory of liability in public corruption cases. In this case, a real estate development company paid USD 35,000 to Joseph Percoco, a former aide to the governor of New York (Andrew Cuomo), to assist in gaining the State's support for a major real estate development project. Percoco had left the governor's office by the time of the payment but while he was serving on Cuomo's re-election campaign. His intervention with the relevant state agency assisted in receiving the requisite approval. Relying on the fact that Percoco had not been a public official at the time he received the payment, the Court overturned his conviction for honest services fraud. Though refusing to rule that the honest services obligation applies only to public officials, the Court concluded that the jury was

---

[122] The potential contributions of an effective bid protest system to good outcomes in the US public procurement regime are discussed in D.L. Gordon, 'Bid Protests: The Costs Are Real, But the Benefits Outweigh Them' (2013) 42 *Public Contract Law Journal* 489.

[123] 18 U.S.C. §1346.

[124] 598 U.S. ___, 143 S.Ct. 1130 (2023).

given a vague instruction to account for the fact that Percoco, though a private citizen, had a 'special relationship' with the government.

d. Foreign Corrupt Practices Act

The FCPA is another important component of the US anti-corruption regime. The Act can be enforced in either criminal or civil proceedings by the DOJ and the SEC. The DOJ's FCPA Unit frequently accompanies FCPA charges with non-FCPA crimes, for example, money-laundering violations. Enforcement of the Act has increased in the last twenty years, and the US is now one of the few active enforcers of foreign bribery laws, opening forty-eight investigations, commencing 163 cases, and concluding 145 cases with sanctions between 2018 and 2021.[125]

e. Interagency collaboration

Since the early twentieth century, US competition authorities and public procurement departments have recognized that cooperation among them would increase the effectiveness of anti-collusion policy.[126] Over the past four decades, the DOJ has strengthened its public procurement efforts by working more extensively with government purchasing officials at the federal, state, and local levels. Liaison programmes with procurement offices and training programmes for contracting officers have yielded increasingly effective methods for detecting bid rigging and alerting DOJ to possible misconduct.

The most significant recent enhancement of these collaborative arrangements took shape in November 2020 with the DOJ's creation of the Procurement Collusion Strike Force (PCSF).[127] Through late 2022, the PCSF comprised a total of thirty-four agencies and offices 'committed to deterring, detecting, investigating, and prosecuting antitrust crimes and related schemes that target government procurement grants and programme funding at all levels of government'.[128] The PCSF has expanded the DOJ's existing training programmes for procurement personnel and updated earlier guidance that the Department had provided on the identification of antitrust misconduct. The expanded cooperation facilitated by the network has increased the effectiveness of the government's anti-collusion and anti-corruption programmes and has supported the successful prosecution of a wide range of illicit schemes.[129]

---

[125] See, Transparency International, 'Exporting Corruption, Progress Report 2022: Assessing Enforcement of the OECD Convention on Combatting Foreign Bribery' (11 October 2020), available at https://www.transparency.org/en/publications/exporting-corruption-2022.

[126] Linnenberg and Barbour, n. 40, 99–115.

[127] For additional details, see Department of Justice, Antitrust Division, 'Procurement Collusion Strike Force', available at https://www.justice.gov/procurement-collusion-strike-force.

[128] 'Procurement Collusion Strike Force', n. 127.

[129] A leading priority of the PCSF is to ensure that a variety of new, major federal expenditure programmes fulfil their ambitions. Relevant measures include the Infrastructure and Jobs Act, the Inflation Reduction Act of 2022, the Creating Helpful Incentives to Promote Semiconductors and Science Act of 2022. See J. Kantor, Assistant Attorney General for Antitrust, Department of Justice, 'Justice

THE REGULATORY FRAMEWORK   207

The voluntary forms of interagency cooperation supplement mandatory duties imposed by law or regulation. The federal procurement statutes and the FAR require executive agencies to notify the Attorney General about bids or proposals that indicate possible antitrust violations.[130] FAR 3.301(b) observes: 'Contracting personnel are an important potential source of investigative leads for antitrust enforcement and should therefore be sensitive to indications of unlawful behaviour by offerors and contractors.'[131] To assist government purchasing officials spot evidence of possible bid rigging, the FAR provides a roster of 'practices or events' that may indicate collusive bidding and directs contract personnel to watch for apparent signs of misconduct.[132]

f. Qui Tam Actions

In a series of measures beginning in the mid-1980s, Congress has increased the ability and incentives of private citizens (including employees of contractors) to bring 'qui tam' suits under the Civil False Claims Act on behalf of the US to attack conduct that defrauds government purchasers.[133] Conduct, such as bid rigging, that violates the antitrust laws, has figured in a number of successful qui tam suits.[134] An individual (the 'relator') who is the original source of evidence of contractor false claims is entitled to a substantial share of the funds (ordinarily 15–25 per cent) ultimately recovered by the government. Successful qui tam plaintiffs can recover reasonable attorney's fees, court costs, and expenses. The attorney's fees

---

Department's Procurement Collusion Strike Force Announces Four New National Law Enforcement Partners as It Enters Its Fourth Year', *Press Release* (15 November 2022), available at https://www.just ice.gov/opa/pr/justice-department-s-procurement-collusion-strike-force-announces-four-new-natio nal-law ('Recent legislation will finance billions of dollars for government procurement and grants').

[130] The statutory command to report suspicious bids and proposals to the Attorney General appears in 10 U.S.C. §2305(b)(5) and 41 U.S.C. §253(b)e. FAR 3.303(a) directs agencies to notify the Attorney General of evidence of collusive bidding. FAR 3.301(b) requires agency contracting personnel to refer instances of identical bids in advertised acquisitions to the Attorney General and to supply evidence of suspected antitrust violations to the agency office responsible for contractor suspension and debarment.

[131] 48 CFR §3.301(b).

[132] 48 CFR §3.303(c). These indicators include (1) the existence of an industry price list or price agreement to which contractors refer in formulating their offers; (2) a sudden change from competitive bidding to identical bidding; (3) simultaneous price increases or follow-the-leader pricing; (4) rotation or bids or proposals; (5) market division arrangements; (6) establishment by competitors of a collusive price estimating scheme; (7) the submission of joint bids where at least one of the firms appears to have the capability to bid independently; (8) behavioural patterns that suggest coordination among competitors, including the submission of bids with identical typographical errors or the submission by a single firm of bids for all offerors; and (9) assertions by firms or their employees that an agreement to restrain trade exists.

[133] W.E. Kovacic, 'Whistleblower Bounty Lawsuits as Monitoring Devices in Government Procurement' (1995) 29 *Loyola of Los Angeles Law Review* 1799. The economic rationale for enlisting whistleblowers to detect and report on illegal collusive behaviour is set out in C. Aubert, P. Rey, and W. Kovacic, 'The Impact of Leniency and Whistle-Blowing Programs on Cartels' (2006) 24 *International Journal of Industrial Organization* 1241.

[134] D. O'Neill, 'Resolving the Confusion: Granting the Government Unfettered Discretion to Dismiss Qui Tam Actions' (2020) 49 *Public Contract Law Journal* 403, 407–11.

mechanism has inspired the development of a highly specialized and effective bar of practitioners who represent potential qui tam relators. Since the enhancement of the qui tam mechanism in the 1980s through September 2022, qui tam recoveries by the Federal Government have totalled nearly USD 39 billion.[135]

iii. Exceptions to pro-competition procurement policy

US public procurement policy is not single-minded in its support for competition. In a number of instances, the procurement system subordinates competition to the attainment of other public policy goals. Perhaps the most important deviation from a competition ethic takes the form of statutes, at the federal, state, and local levels that give preferences to domestically or locally sourced goods and services. In Chapter 3, it is seen that economic analysis confirms the potentially high costs associated with such policies.[136]

The most significant federal measure is the 'Buy American Act',[137] expanded by the Federal Acquisition Regulatory Council in 2022, and, more recently, massive public spending bills that seek to promote recovery from the COVID-19 pandemic. As a group, these provisions narrow the pool of potential bidders—a condition that can facilitate effective collusion. Entry by firms outside the cartel can be a powerful disruptive force that undermines the discipline needed to operate a successful collusion scheme. The 'Buy American Act' and related measures run the risk of dampening this disruptive threat, thereby actively facilitating bid rigging in relevant markets.[138] As explained in Chapter 3, the US is able to maintain its Buy American and related policies notwithstanding its participation in the WTO Agreement on Government Procurement (GPA) and related regional and bilateral trade agreements due, in part, to gaps in its coverage commitments under those agreements and exceptions embodied in the text of the agreements.

---

[135] Civil Division, Department of Justice, Fraud Statistics—Overview, available at https://www.just ice.gov/org/press-release/file/1567691/download.

[136] See G.C. Hufbauer and E. Jung, ' "Buy American" and similar domestic purchase policies impose high costs on taxpayers' (6 August 2020), available at https://www.piie.com/research/piie-charts/buy-american-and-similar-domestic-purchase-policies-impose-high-costs. See also G.C. Hufbauer and M. Hogan, 'Why eliminating "junk fees" and imposing "Buy American" on spending are not the solutions they seem to be', Peterson Institute for International Economics (14 March 2023) and A.A. Millsap, '"Buy American" Rules Hurt More Than They Help', *Forbes* (23 March 2022), available at https://www.forbes.com/sites/adammillsap/2022/03/23/buy-american-rules-hurt-more-than-they-help/?sh=49ad400d65f6.

[137] See, e.g., 41 U.S.C, Sections 10 a-d.

[138] See, for elaboration of the mechanisms involved, R.D. Anderson and W.E. Kovacic, 'Competition Policy and International Trade Liberalisation: Essential Complements to Ensure Good Performance in Public Procurement Markets' (2009) 18(2) *Public Procurement Law Review* 67, preliminary version available at https://www.ftc.gov/sites/default/files/documents/public_statements/competition-policy-and-international-trade-liberalisation-essential-complements-ensure-good.anderson/2009procurem entmkts.pdf.

We recognize that those gaps and exceptions have a historical basis and represent an effort to achieve an overall balance of commitments across the participating Parties that is fair, reasonable, and politically sustainable. Still, given the costs that such policies entail for the US and other countries (including by facilitating bid rigging and related practices), it is hoped that future negotiations can expand the coverage of relevant agreements and reduce the scope of related derogations beyond what has already been achieved.[139] At a minimum, those commitments should not be abandoned.

D. Vulnerabilities of the Existing Regime and Suggested Improvements

In the modern era, US policymakers have strengthened safeguards against collusion and corruption in public procurement. Major steps in this direction include the adoption of a more powerful framework of laws and sanctions, the development of better procurement techniques, and improved cooperation among public bodies with mandates to protect the integrity and effectiveness of government contracting. These are notable achievements, and we do not underestimate them.

Despite these admirable efforts, the US procurement system remains prone to serious misconduct. Corruption and collusion reduce the ability of public bodies to provide vital services, repair the harm caused by caused by calamities such as COVID-19 and natural disasters, and address the needs of the most disadvantaged. Visible instances of misconduct not only undermine the effectiveness of public expenditures but also drain the reservoir of civic trust on which democracy depends.

Several conditions create dangerous vulnerabilities. First, the demands of the procurement regime exceed the capacity of procurement personnel to operate effectively. The mismatch between the system's nominal commitment to superior performance and its actual capacity to deliver grows more worrisome as new expenditure programmes seek to accomplish the aims of economic recovery, infrastructure renewal, and the green agenda.

Second, the resources devoted to enforcement of anti-collusion and related anti-corruption measures are deficient. The scope of the enforcement responsibility at home and abroad greatly exceeds the number of personnel—investigators, forensic specialists, prosecutors—available to apply the government's nominally powerful tools.

---

[139] It is noteworthy that the WTO GPA contains a 'built-in' commitment to future negotiations to expand the scope and coverage of the Agreement. See WTO, 'Agreement on Government Procurement 2012 and related WTO legal texts', available at https://www.wto.org/english/docs_e/legal_e/rev-gpr-94_01_e.pdf, Article XXII:7. Hence, this suggestion is not without basis in the Agreement itself.

210 PERSISTENT CORRUPTION AND SUPPLIER COLLUSION

Third, contemporary policy commands contain a number of features that can tend to increase the effectiveness of collusion and corruption. We are aware of the economic policy ends that domestic content and sourcing restrictions seek to achieve. These can have adverse side effects by creating entry barriers that facilitate cartel discipline and stabilize bribery schemes. A careful examination of the side effects of domestic content restrictions could be part of a larger initiative through which competition and procurement authorities cooperate to identify procurement system features that tend to reduce competition without offsetting benefits. This inquiry could suggest how other procurement system goals might be achieved through measures that impede competition less severely. A full-scale competitive effects analysis of the US procurement system also would be an opportunity to consider techniques that the modern literature on public procurement has identified as helpful in discouraging collusion and improving procurement performance.[140]

Several measures can serve to reduce the vulnerabilities noted above. Some involve spending more money; others involve making better use of the public resources at hand. One of the most urgent measures is to increase the capability of the procurement workforce. This necessarily involves greater expenditures for hiring additional staff and training for procurement officials. Perhaps the best way to build political support for these outlays is to develop awareness of how even small improvements in the performance of the procurement system can boost the return from contract expenditures.

A second needed step is to enhance the capability of law enforcement units responsible for implementing anti-collusion and anti-corruption laws. Capacity improvements can come in the form of increased staff, broader application of existing and new artificial intelligence tools to identify instances of misconduct, and deeper collaboration that joins up public agencies in the US. DOJ's PCSF is a very encouraging development and is worthy of continued expansion. It provides a useful model for cross-border cooperation, as well. Fuller cooperation also would engage enforcement and procurement bodies across jurisdictions.

A third measure is to improve the ability of public agencies to learn from past experience and apply that learning to strengthen existing programmes. Deeper historical awareness could benefit procurement policy in several respects. First, greater historical awareness can help the procurement system anticipate and respond to the intense demands that arise in times of crisis and massive increased expenditures. In these circumstances, the procurement process is most vulnerable

---

[140] The content of this type of competitive effects assessment of a public procurement system is suggested in G. Spagnolo, G-L. Albano, P. Buccirossi, and M. Zanza, 'Preventing Collusion in Procurement: A Primer' in N. Dimitri, G. Pigo, and G. Spagnola (eds) *Handbook of Procurement* (Cambridge University Press, 2006) 347; W. Kovacic, R. Marshall, L. Marx, and M. Raiff, 'Bidding Rings and the Design of Anti-Collusive Measures' in N. Dimitri, G. Pigo, and G. Spagnolo (eds) *Handbook of Procurement* (Cambridge University Press, 2006) 381; W. Kovacic, 'An Integrated Policy to Deter and Defeat Cartels' (2006) 51 *Antitrust Bulletin* 813, 830–34.

to supplier misconduct. The study of past experience would also drive home an important lesson from the history of US procurement policy. Firms are ingenious and adaptive, and some suppliers will respond to new enforcement techniques with countermeasures that enable them to create and sustain cartels.

An additional benefit would be to make policymakers more attentive to the adverse consequences of policies that shield domestic suppliers from foreign competition. Entry or expansion by non-cartel members is one of the greatest threats to effective collusion. An important side effect of procurement measures that restrict participation to domestic or local firms is to forestall an important source of entry that destabilizes cartels.[141]

A third application of knowledge regarding past experience would be to build data sets that comprehensively record previous enforcement efforts and reconstruct the creation of corrupt schemes.[142] Superior data sets and related analytics can support the application of fast-evolving and more effective screening tools.[143] Case reconstructions help identify the techniques that wrongdoers use to form and executive collusive arrangements, including plans that engage government officials as participants. The reconstructions would give enforcement officials insights into behaviours and organizational arrangements that indicate the presence of illegal behaviour.[144] These studies would also help guide firms in devising more effective compliance regimes.[145]

Finally, better historical awareness also can inform future reforms to the procurement system—e.g. by identifying how crisis-driven reforms establish exceedingly elaborate regulatory commands that defy effective implementation and serve as barriers to entry and desirable innovation in public procurement. The sheer complexity of the regulatory process can obstruct participation in procurement markets by smaller firms that lack the resources to engage lawyers and other advisors to guide them through the increasingly complex body of regulatory controls.

---

[141] Anderson and Kovacic, n. 138.

[142] W.E. Kovacic, R.C. Marshall, and M.J. Meurer, 'Cartel Issues in Plain Sight' (2023) 11(2) *Journal of Antitrust Enforcement* 215.

[143] Modern developments in the design and application of screening tools are examined in J. Harrington, Jr. and D. Imhoff, 'Cartel Screening and Machine Learning' (2022) 11 *Stanford Computational Antitrust* 133, see further Chapter 4.

[144] W.E. Kovacic, 'Regulatory Controls as Barriers to Entry in Government Procurement' (1992) 25 *Policy Sciences* 29.

[145] On the possibilities for significant upgrades in modern compliance practice, see B. Kouroupas, 'Corrupts Absolutely: How Power, Unhappiness, and the Need for Recognition Can Be Mitigated by Implementing Psychology into Public Procurement' (2022) 51 *Public Contract Law Journal* 623.

7

Brazil: Lessons from Operation Car Wash

A. Introduction	213	i. The need for, and feasibility of, reform	228
B. Combatting Corruption and Collusion and the Operation Car Wash Experience	215	ii. Weakening links between business, procurement officials, and politicians	229
i. Anatomy of Operation Car Wash	215	iii. Making public procurement a less protected environment for wrongdoing	230
a. The multiple fronts of investigation	215		
b. Political sanctions	221	iv. Ensuring that players cannot act with impunity	232
c. A multi-layered anti-corruption and competition investigation	221	a. A concentrated cleanup campaign	232
ii. Was Operation Car Wash a success?	223	b. A good track record of enforcement and fine-tuning institutional coordination	232
C. Beyond Operation Car Wash: Lessons and Challenges Ahead	228	c. More effective sanctions	236
		D. Conclusions	237

A. Introduction

The question of how a nation can combat corruption and collusion and prevent these practices from plaguing and undermining public procurement processes, is especially important to Brazil[1] where the government spends approximately BRL 35.5 billion on procurement[2] and Operation Car Wash (*Operação Lava Jato*) (OCW)[3]

---

[1] This chapter draws on, and develops, a paper by A. Jones and C.M.S. Pereira Neto, 'Combatting Corruption and Collusion in Public Procurement: Lessons from Operation Car Wash' (2021) 71(Supplement 1) *University of Toronto Law Journal* 103–50.

[2] See OECD Report, 'Fighting Bid Rigging in Brazil: A Review of Federal Public Procurement' (2021), available at https://www.oecd.org/daf/competition/Fighting-Bid-Rigging-in-Brazil-A-Review-of-Fede ral-Public-Procurement-2021.pdf; and C. Pereira and R. Wallbach Schwind, 'Public Procurement in Brazil' in A.C. Georgopulos, B. Hoekman, and P.C. Mavroidis (eds), *The Internationalization of Government Procurement Regulation* (Oxford University Press, 2017).

[3] It commenced in 2014 in Curitiba, State of Paraná, focusing on criminal organizations believed to be using gas stations and car washes to launder money and commit foreign exchange crimes, hence its name.

unveiled a widespread, and entrenched, corrupt procurement[4] scheme estimated to have caused Brazil around USD 15 billion of losses.[5]

According to the Federal Public Prosecutors' Office (*Ministério Público Federal*) (FPO),[6] OCW exposed an arrangement involving large Brazilian companies,[7] organized in cartels, paying bribes of between 1 per cent and 5 per cent of the value of the contracts won[8] to high-level executives of state-owned enterprises (SOEs), including the oil and gas exploration giant Petrobras—Petróleo Brasileiro S/A.[9] These executives took a cut of the bribes, before passing the remainder to senior politicians responsible for their appointment, and their political parties, so enriching politicians and helping to finance their electoral campaigns.[10] OCW thus uncovered material evidence of institutionalized wrongdoing involving many different 'elite' players in Brazil, despite a publicly stated effort to tackle corruption, particularly through new laws, the strengthening of accountability institutions and enhancing institutional multiplicity.[11]

This chapter examines OCW and charts the breath-taking number of criminal, civil, and administrative proceedings it spawned against corporations, well-known businesspeople, politicians, and financial operators.[12] As it notes that, in spite of the dramatic scale of actions, the cycle of corruption in Brazil has not been broken, it also explores why this might be the case and how Brazil might try to escape from this 'high-corruption' equilibrium in the future. In so doing, it engages

[4] In Brazil, public administration shall obey the principles of legality, impersonality, morality, publicity, and efficiency and public procurement should be contracted through public bidding, *Federal Constitution of Brazil 1988*, Article 37, XXI, available at https://www.oas.org/es/sla/ddi/docs/acceso_informacion_base_dc_leyes_pais_b_1_en.pdf.

[5] See 'Grandes Casos', *Ministério Público Federal*, available at http://www.mpf.mp.br/grandes-casos; M.R. Sanchez-Badin and A. Sanchez-Badin, 'Anticorruption in Brazil: From Transnational Legal Order to Disorder' (2019) 113 *American Journal of International Law Unbound* 326, 326; it also caused significant losses in neighbouring Latin American countries.

[6] See 'Entenda o Caso—Caso Lava Jato', *Ministério Público Federal*, available at http://www.mpf.mp.br/grandes-casos/lava-jato/entenda-o-caso; and discussion by a judge in the case, S.F. Moro, 'Preventing Systemic Corruption in Brazil' (2018) 147(3) *Dædalus* 157.

[7] Although principally Brazilian, including Brazilian's largest construction company Odebrecht, multinational companies were also involved in some cases, see below n. 44.

[8] Moro, n. 6, 160.

[9] In return for the bribes, the SOE employees helped to secure the success of the bid rigging scheme by, for example, sharing confidential information, limiting other participation, and favouring the colluding companies.

[10] See W. Connors, 'How Brazil's "Nine Horsemen" Cracked a Bribery Scandal', *The Wall Street Journal* (6 April 2015); J. Pontes and M. Anselmo, *Operation Car Wash: Brazil's Institutionalized Crime and the Inside Story of the Biggest Corruption Scandal in History* (Bloomsbury, 2022); Moro, n. 6, 163; and E. Mello and M. Spektor, 'Brazil: The Costs of Multiparty Presidentialism' (2018) 29(2) *Journal of Democracy* 113, 124. Three political parties found to be directly involved in the appointment and support of Petrobras directors were PP (*Partido Popular*), PT (*Partido dos Trabalhadores*), and MDB (*Movimento Democrático Brasileiro*).

[11] See further Section B.i.c and, e.g., L.D. Carson and M. Mota Prado, 'Using Institutional Multiplicity to Address Corruption as a Collective Action Problem: Lessons from the Brazilian Case' (2016) 62 *The Quarterly Review of Economics and Finance* 56, and V. Pereira Ferreira, 'When Institutional Multiplicity Backfires: The Battle Over the Jurisdiction to Prosecute Politicians for Administrative Improbity in Brazil' (2021) 17(2) *Revista Direito GV* e2130.

[12] For a discussion of the obstacles faced by police in acting effectively on the evidence amassed during their investigations, see Pontes and Anselmo, n. 10.

with the debate, discussed in Chapter 4, as to how systemic corruption, and resistance to reform, can be combatted. Although Brazilian experience provides support for the view, that an invigorated law enforcement push may be insufficient on its own to create a lasting difference, the chapter proposes a multipronged, and self-reinforcing, set of reforms designed to trigger change, concentrated on weaknesses diagnosed in the system. In particular, it suggests adjustments to procurement, competition and anti-corruption laws or policies, closer institutional cooperation to coordinate strategies, achieve synergies, and combat incentives, and broader measures to tackle the roots of the corrupt system revealed.

B. Combatting Corruption and Collusion and the Operation Car Wash Experience

i. Anatomy of Operation Car Wash

a. The multiple fronts of investigation

The investigations unleashed by OCW unfolded across six main fronts: (i) criminal; (ii) administrative anti-corruption; (iii) competition; (iv) federal accounting; (v) damages lawsuits, and (vi) investigations against politicians. The OCW special task forces also engaged in significant international collaboration with over sixty different counties. Table 7.1 summarizes these main fronts—the laws under which they were acting, the possible subjects of enforcement in each case (corporations or individuals), and the agencies responsible for each type of investigation. The subsequent discussion seeks to provide a flavour of the scope and scale of unlawful scheme, the huge volume and variety of legal challenges to it, and the complex issues, enforcement challenges, and coordination difficulties arising from them.

Table 7.1 OCW's main fronts of investigations

Investigation under	Subjects	Core possible sanctions	Enforcement agencies
Criminal Law – including for bribery (passive and active[13]) affecting the public interest, and bid rigging[14]	Individuals	Fines Imprisonment (between 2 and 12 years (with potential increase of 1/3) for bribery and 4–8 years for bid rigging)	Federal Prosecutors Office (FPO) / State Prosecutors' Office & Federal and State Police

(continued)

[13] See Criminal Code, Article 317 (passive corruption), Article 333 (active corruption). There is also a prohibition of active bribery of foreign officials, Article 337-B. This chapter does not deal with money-laundering or other related criminal offences.

[14] Federal Law No. 8,137/1990, Article 4 (bid rigging). See also Criminal Code, Article 337-F. Subsequently, in 2021, a new Public Bid Law was introduced with the aim of ensuring fairness of public bids and seeking to reinforce controls on public procurement and to create stronger incentives for compliance with them, Federal Law No. 13,133/21 (some of the provisions only come fully into force in 2023).

216 BRAZIL: LESSONS FROM OPERATION CAR WASH

Table 7.1 Continued

Investigation under	Subjects	Core possible sanctions	Enforcement agencies
		Plea deals apply to individuals subject to criminal investigations	Actions against 'high-level' serving officers of the Federal Government with 'privileged jurisdiction'[15] (*foro privilegiado*) have to be prosecuted in Brasília before the Supreme Court[16] or the Superior Court of Justice[17]
Anti-corruption Law (ACL or Clean Company Act/ Corporate Liability Act)[18] – which contains a number of strict liability administrative offences regarding: (i) active bribery;[19] (ii) bid rigging, fraud and manipulation of public tenders; (iii) obstruction of anti-corruption investigations; and (iv) bribery concerning public officials abroad[20]	Corporations	Fines (of up to 20 per cent of gross revenues)[21] Disgorgement of profits, Debarment from public tenders[22] In addition, the FPO and the *Federal Attorney General's Office* (*Advocacia Geral da União*) (FAGO) have authority to file lawsuits and to seek judicial sanctions, including: (i) expropriation of the benefits of the infringing conduct; (ii) suspension or partial prohibition of activities of the legal entity; (iii) dissolution of the legal entity, and (iv) a prohibition on the receipt of subsidies, grants, and loans from public entities and public financial institutions for 1 to 5 years[23]	Office of the Comptroller General (OCG) / FAGO / FPO The Act aims to enhance detection, enforcement, and the gathering of evidence by permitting enforcers to enter leniency agreements with investigated entities (offering the possibility of up to two-thirds reductions in fines in exchange for cooperation), see ACL, Articles 16 and 17

[15] Special jurisdiction based on the function excised by a certain individual (or *foro por prerrogativa de função*) is not governed by the general rule that criminal lawsuits start at courts of first instance.

[16] Federal Constitution, n. 4, Article 102, I, b) and c) (referring to the President, the Vice-President, members of Congress, and cabinet members).

[17] Federal Constitution, n. 4, Article 105, I, a). As, these latter procedures usually take a very long time, convictions of politicians have generally occurred after they left office (either at the end of their mandate, or, as in the case of Senator Delcídio do Amaral and Representative Eduardo Cunha, following its revocation by Congress, see below n. 54 and text) and following the transfer of the case to the lower courts.

[18] Law No. 12,846/2013 ('Anti- Corruption Law' or ACL), 'establishing the rules that discipline the civil and administrative liability of legal entities that carry out acts against national or foreign governments, and lays down other provisions'.

[19] See ACL, n. 18, Articles 1 and 5.

[20] ACL, n. 18, Articles 4 and 28. Brazil also signed and ratified the 'OECD Convention on Combating Bribery of Foreign Public Officials in International Business Transactions' (the Anti-Bribery Convention), which establishes standards to criminalize bribery of foreign public officials in international business transactions.

[21] ACL, n. 18, Article 6.

[22] Debarment sanctions, which may also be imposed by the FAC, CADE, the contracting entity of the Public Administration and/or through administrative improbity lawsuits, must be recorded on the National Register of Sanctioned Companies, which is available to the entire public administration, ACL, n. 18, Article 22.

[23] ACL, n. 18, Article 19.

COMBATTING CORRUPTION AND COLLUSION 217

Table 7.1 Continued

Investigation under	Subjects	Core possible sanctions	Enforcement agencies
Competition Law[24] – which prohibits cartels and bid rigging, as well as other collusive practices	Corporations and individuals	Fines (for corporations, from 0.1 to 20 per cent of the gross revenues in the year prior to the beginning of the procedure; for individuals, from BRL 50,000 to BRL 2 billion or, in case of an executive, a percentage of the fine applied to the company[25]) Debarment of infringing entities from bidding for public sector contracts and prohibition of exercise of commercial activity, on natural persons	Administrative Council for Economic Defense (CADE) The Competition Law allows firms and individuals to take part in CADE's leniency, Leniency Plus, or settlement regimes[26]
Federal Accounting Rules	Corporations, political parties, and individuals	Correction of illegalities and irregularities in public acts and contracts Sanctions, including the return of illicit gains, fines (fixed or of up to 100 per cent of the damage caused to the Treasury)[27] Debarment of individuals from occupying senior public positions or debarment of companies from contracting with the public entities[28]	The *Tribunal de Contas da União* or Federal Accounting Court (FAC) has constitutional power to control public administration and the Federal Government.[29] It establishes norms applicable to the federal budget, supervises federal public spending, audits central government and state-owned enterprises (SOEs).

(continued)

[24] Article 36 of Law No. 12,529/2011 ('the Competition Law'), which 'structures the Brazilian System for Protection of Competition; sets forth preventive measures and sanctions for violations against the economic order; amends Law No. 8,137 of December 27th 1990; Decree-Law No. 3,689 of October 3rd 1941 – Code of Criminal Procedure; and Law No. 7,347 of July 24th 1985; revokes provisions of Law No. 8,884 of June 11th 1994 and Law No. 9,781 of January 19th 1999; and sets forth other measures'.

[25] Brazil's Competition Law, n. 24, Article 37.

[26] Brazil's Competition Law, n. 24, Articles 85 (settlements), 86, and 87 (leniency and Leniency Plus programmes). Leniency offers the possibility of full immunity from fines to companies and individuals and immunity for individuals from criminal prosecution regarding cartels and related behaviour (companies do not obtain immunity from independent private actions for damages, and individuals do not obtain immunity from other criminal prosecution for unrelated crimes like corruption or money laundering); while settlements offer reductions in fines to companies and individuals. Leniency plus offers the possibility of an increased discount in an existing case and full immunity in relation to another disclosed offence, which was previously unknown to CADE, Brazil's Competition Law, n. 24, Article 86(7).

[27] Federal Law 8,443/1992 ('establishing the Organic Law of the Federal Court of Accounts'), Articles 57 and 58; the value of the damage to the Treasury is based on the 'overprice' calculated by the Court according to a variety of methods, see Ordinance No. 33/2012 of the General External Control Secretariat of the Court.

[28] Federal Law 8,443/1992, n. 27, Article 46; the latter sanction is applied in cases where the court finds fraud in public tenders or any irregular behaviour that hinders the competition for public contracts, such as cartels and bid rigging.

[29] See Federal Constitution, n. 4, Articles 33(2), 70, 71, 72(1), 74(2) and 161 (single paragraph).

218   BRAZIL: LESSONS FROM OPERATION CAR WASH

Table 7.1 Continued

Investigation under	Subjects	Core possible sanctions	Enforcement agencies
The Administrative improbity law[30] – which holds public and private agents accountable for acts committed against the public administration that: (i) lead to illegal enrichment; (ii) cause damage to the Treasury; or (iii) violate public administration principles. These laws were reformed in October 2021 with the alleged objective of making them clearer and less open-ended[31]	Corporations and individuals	Damages Debarment of companies from contracting with the public entities Debarment of individuals from occupying public positions Fines	FPO / FAGO
Political consequences	Individual politicians	Revocation of mandate Debarment from standing in elections[32]	Congress / Electoral courts

The early criminal investigations which made extensive use of powers derived from the 2013 Criminal Organization Act[33] to negotiate 'cooperation agreements' with wrongdoers (through non-prosecution agreements or plea bargains),[34] were key drivers of OCW. In March 2020, the FPO reported[35] that these proceedings had led to 226 lawsuits, 1,054 individuals being prosecuted, 210 convictions (upheld by an appellate court), and the conclusion of 279 cooperation agreements. Proceedings were brought against private employees, financial operators, public employees, business executives (including construction magnate, Marcelo Odebrecht), a number of politicians (including former and now re-elected President Luís Inácio

---

[30] Federal Law No. 8,429/1992 ('on Administrative Improbity'). For a discussion of the law and its limitations, see Pereira Ferreira, n. 11.

[31] See, Law No. 14,239/21.

[32] Complementary Law No. 135/2010 ('Clean Record Act').

[33] Federal Law No. 12,850/2013 ('Criminal Organization Act'), Articles 3-A, 3-B, 3-C and 4, as amended by Federal Law No. 13,964/2019.

[34] And so to prevent trial or to obtain reductions in sanctions, see Law No. 12,850/13, n. 33, Article 4.

[35] See now 'Resultados—Caso Lava Jato', *Ministério Público Federal*, available at http://www.mpf.mp.br/grandes-casos/lava-jato/resultados.

Lula da Silva,[36] former Speaker of the House Eduardo Cunha, and former Governor of Rio de Janeiro Sérgio Cabral), and other individuals.[37] Although President Lula was convicted at trial, he was released after serving 580 days in prison to await the result of his appeal to the Supreme Court out of custody (the Supreme Court held that the Constitution, and the presumption of innocence, requires all appeals to higher courts to have been exhausted, before a defendant serves jail time[38]). In the end this appeal was successful as the Supreme Court annulled his conviction on procedural grounds (finding the trial court lacked territorial jurisdiction).[39] The judgment, and a subsequent judgment finding that the proceedings had been tainted by bias,[40] paved the way for President Lula to stand in, and win, the 2022 presidential election and to take office in 2023.[41]

The multiple lawsuits and the evidence gathered in the criminal sphere fuelled cooperation with, and investigations by, other authorities. Indeed:[42]

- As criminal bribery charges can only be brought against individuals, the OCG commenced administrative ACL proceedings into suspected corrupt practices of eight construction companies. Between then and 2019, OCG and the FAGO executed nine leniency agreements,[43] including with some of the largest construction and oil and gas companies in Brazil,[44] which resulted in the

[36] The (then) former President was convicted in a lower court, in Curitiba, after he left office and so did not benefit from privileged jurisdiction, see n. 15 and 17 and text; see Criminal Appeal No. 5046512-94.2016.4.04.7000 (Electronic Process – E-Proc V2 – TRF) and Criminal Appeal No. 5021365-32.2017.4.04.7000 (Electronic Process – E-Proc V2 – TRF) (judgments 2018 and 2019, respectively).

[37] The FPO also accused then President, Michel Temer, of involvement in OCW. Although following the end of his tenure he was temporarily imprisoned as a result of a preventive injunction, this was eventually set aside by the appellate court, Redação Jota, 'Leia a íntegra da decisão que determinou a prisão de Michel Temer', *JOTA Info* (21 March 2019). See F. Bächtold, 'Um ano após prisão, Temer se beneficia de decisões na Justiça e de ações travadas', *Folha de S.Paulo* (22 March 2020). Former president Dilma Rousseff, although not convicted in any OCW procedure, was impeached for breach of budget rules and lost political support because of the involvement of her Labour Party (PT) in the scheme uncovered, 'Cercada pela Lava Jato, Dilma reforça ataques a conduta de Sérgio Moro', *El País* (8 March 2016), available at https://brasil.elpais.com/brasil/2016/03/04/politica/1457115590_947838.html.

[38] ADCs No. 43, No. 44 and No. 54, *Supremo Tribunal Federal*, 7 November 2019 (except in cases of pre-trial arrest, no defendant shall be imprisoned for conviction before the final appeal at the higher courts). This decision overturned the decision previously set in HC No. 126,290, *Supremo Tribunal Federal*, 17 February 2016.

[39] 'Lula: Brazil Ex-President's Corruption Convictions Annulled', *BBC News* (9 March 2021), available at https://www.bbc.co.uk/news/world-latin-america-56326389.

[40] STF, HC 164.493/PR. See 'Brazil Supreme Court Confirms Ruling that Judge was Biased against Lula', *Reuters* (24 June 2021), available at https://www.reuters.com/world/americas/brazil-supreme-court-confi rms-ruling-that-judge-was-biased-against-lula-2021-06-23/ and UN Communication, No. 2841/2016. See also 'Brazil Judge Annuls Evidence from Odebrecht Confessions in Operation Car Wash Case', *Brazil Reports* (7 September 2023) (reporting that a Justice in Brazil's Supreme Court called the arrest of now-President Lula, as one of the biggest legal mistakes in the history of the country), see further Section B.ii.

[41] See Section B.i.b below.

[42] For greater detail of these cases, see Jones and Pereira Neto, n. 1.

[43] ACL, n. 18, Articles 16 and 17; Brazil, Presidential Decree No. 8,420, Articles 28–40; Brazil, CGU Ordinance No. 910, and CGU and AGU Inter-ministerial Ordinance No. 2,278.

[44] See 'Acordo de Leniência', *A Controladoria-Geral da União* (June 2020); in addition, a leniency agreement related to corruption with Petrobras was also executed with the Dutch company SBM Offshore.

payment of fines, the recovery of damages, and illegal enrichment totalling approximately BRL 12.375 billion (no debarment of the companies followed). OCG also found a number of infringements, which resulted in the imposition of fines or debarment.[45] The sums recovered in these latter proceedings were small compared to those secured through leniency agreements;

- CADE started competition investigations following a leniency agreement executed with Setal Engenharia Group, in March 2015.[46] The information collected from this, and other subsequent leniency applications, led CADE to open numerous investigations against both legal entities and individuals, including many large construction companies and the conclusion of a number of leniency agreements. In 2023, CADE adopted its first formal OCW decision imposing fines on companies that engaged in bid rigging;[47]

- The FAC has issued more than 100 substantive decisions related to the investigation and ordered a number of entities and/or individuals to return illegally obtained assets to the Public Treasury or to pay fines.[48] It has also used debarment sanctions[49] and in some cases adopted interim, precautionary measures freezing assets of companies and individuals pending its final decision;[50] and

- FPO task forces and the FAGP commenced a number of administrative improbity lawsuits against public officials, political parties, politicians, private companies, and their employees, to recover damages caused to the Treasury and to impose other sanctions, claiming more than BRL 50 billion.[51] Administrative improbity cases, however, take a long time to come to trial (more than six years on average). Combined with weaknesses in legal design in the system, this has meant that serious obstacles have been experienced in bringing these proceedings and recovering any sums actually awarded.[52]

---

[45] OCG reported to Congress ('Prestação de Contas Do Presidente Da República 2019', *Controladoria-Geral da União (CGU)*, available at https://www.gov.br/cgu/pt-br/assuntos/auditoria-e-fiscalizacao/avaliacao-da-gestao-dos-administradores/prestacao-de-contas-do-presidente-da-republica/arquivos/2019-1/pcpr-2019-livro.pdf) that the 692 investigations opened between 2016 and 2019 led to 92 fines, totalling BRL 21.1 million and, for example, Queiroz Galvão Engenharia S/A was debarred for bid rigging from contracting with the public administration at all levels (federal, state and municipal) for two years, Administrative Procedure No. 00190.025830/2014-63.

[46] See further, the Petrobras onshore cartel case, https://www.gov.br/cade/en/matters/news/cade-opens-administrative-proceeding-on-petrobras-public-bid-cartel-investigation.

[47] See CADE, PAC Favelas, Administrative Proceeding nº 08700.007776/2016-41, Reporting Commissioner Sérgio Costa Ravagnani (known as the 'PAC Favelas case'). See also CADE's decision imposing fines on construction companies for bid rigging affecting contracting engineering work and services in public schools, 8 March 2023. The companies were also prohibited from contracting with the government for five years.

[48] For example, in relation to Petrobras contracts involving the construction of three refineries, FAC ordered companies and individuals to return approximately BRL 4.864 billion to the public coffers.

[49] See, e.g., FAC Decisions 930/2019, Reporting Judge Benjamin Zymler, 24 April 2019.

[50] See, e.g., Construction of North-South Railway (Decisions 296/2018, 2504/2019, 930/2019, 2305/2017, and 2310/2017).

[51] See 'Resultados—Caso Lava Jato', *Ministério Público Federal*, available at http://www.mpf.mp.br/grandes-casos/lava-jato/resultados.

[52] See Pereira Ferreira, n. 11.

b. Political sanctions

OCW also had profound implications for a number of politicians in Brazil. For example, Congress itself has imposed sanctions for lack of parliamentary decorum,[53] revoking the mandate of at least one senator[54] and two representatives.[55] Prior to OCW, such steps were rare.[56] Further, the Clean Record Law[57] provides that individuals subject to certain criminal convictions confirmed by an appellate court[58] cannot stand in elections. In particular, this led the Superior Electoral Court to bar President Lula[59] from standing as a candidate for the 2018 presidential campaign.[60] Following annulment of his conviction in 2021, however, President Lula stood in, and won, the 2022 election. Finally, more than half of the politicians under investigation in OCW were not re-elected in 2018 and many have been subjected to lawsuits in the lower criminal courts (having left office, they no longer benefited from privileged jurisdiction).[61]

c. A multi-layered anti-corruption and competition investigation

OCW thus led to a complex web of actions with severe consequences for individuals and corporations resulting from criminal or civil law enforcement actions. The system of 'institutional multiplicity' existing in Brazil creates checks and balances among institutions and a healthy competition for enforcement, reducing the possibility of institutional capture and increasing the probability of detection of wrongdoers.[62] However, it also creates overlapping enforcement regimes, generating potential for conflicts and wasteful duplication of resources, and a risk of double (or multiple) jeopardy for defendants that collaborate, making it difficult for them to bring proceedings to an end and to start afresh.[63]

---

[53] Federal Constitution, n. 4, Article 55.

[54] Senator Delcídio do Amaral had his mandate revoked in 2016; 'Delcídio do Amaral tem mandato cassado no Senado', *Bom Dia Brasil* (11 May 2016).

[55] Representatives Eduardo Cunha (MDB) and André Vargas (PT) had their mandates revoked in 2014 and 2016, respectively.

[56] G. Hirabahasi, 'Apenas 7 Deputados Foram Cassados Pela Câmara Desde 2002', *Poder 360* (3 March 2017) (stating only seven representatives had mandates revoked between 2002 and 2017).

[57] Complementary Law No. 135/2010 (Clean Record Law, or Lei da Ficha Limpa).

[58] Complementary Law No. 135/2010, n. 57, Article 2 (providing for ineligibility due to certain criminal convictions).

[59] See nn. 38–40 and text.

[60] Superior Electoral Court, Registro de Candidatura 0600903-50.2018.6.00.0000, 1 September 2018, but see, e.g., D. Phillips, 'Brazilian Court Bars Lula from Presidential Election', *The Guardian* (1 September 2018).

[61] 40 politicians who were candidates in the 2018 elections and investigated as part of OCW were not elected. M. Lara, 'Mais da metade dos candidatos alvo da Lava Jato não consegue se eleger', *O Estado de S. Paulo* (8 October 2018). Further many lost their right to stand as a result of the Clean Record Law, n. 57 and text.

[62] See Carson and Mota Prado, n. 11.

[63] M. Jenkins, 'Interagency Coordination Mechanisms: Improving the Effectiveness of National Anti-Corruption Efforts', *Transparency International* (18 January 2019).

222 BRAZIL: LESSONS FROM OPERATION CAR WASH

Indeed, OCW exposed weak institutional cooperation and led to investigations and the imposition of sanctions and penalties by different agencies in relation to what, in some cases at least, was, essentially, the same conduct. Agencies were also criticized for relying on cooperation agreements concluded by one authority to bring prosecutions and impose sanctions, in disregard of the safeguards agreed with the original authority. This led to complaints that the objectives of these policies (especially to encourage firms to introduce anti-corruption compliance measures, to self-report infringements in return for a reward and to provide evidence, which might allow successful prosecution of those that do not self-report) were undermined[64] and 'vitiated by the inability of Brazil and its agencies to provide legal certainty for its whistleblowers'.[65] For example, although Odebrecht may have hoped that a 2016 settlement of criminal proceedings with the United States (US), Swiss and Brazilian authorities[66] would end Brazilian proceedings against it, it remained embroiled in multiple other procedures at federal and state level, including with FAGO (under administrative probity laws), OCG (based on the ACL), CADE (for bid rigging), and in proceedings before the FAC.[67]

The unprecedented breadth and scope of these investigations also generated coordination challenges for the agencies themselves. The agencies (federal and state) thus strived to find new mechanisms for coordinating their investigations, cooperating, negotiating parallel leniency and collaboration agreements, sharing information and managing potential overlaps (e.g. in sanctions) and conflicts through the execution of formal cooperation agreements.[68] Although important, these arrangements have not resolved all of the difficulties arising from their overlapping mandates.

---

[64] See Sanchez-Badin and Sanchez-Badin, n. 5, 327.

[65] See Sanchez-Badin and Sanchez-Badin, n. 5, 329.

[66] But see 'Brazil Judge Annuls Evidence from Odebrecht Confessions in Operation Car Wash Case', n. 40. For a discussion of the other international investigations it provoked, in R.M. Pimenta and O. Venturini, 'Cooperation and Negotiated Settlements for Transnational Bribery: A Study of the Odebrecht Case' (2021) 17(2) *Revista Direito GV* e2131.

[67] In the end, Odebrecht concluded a leniency agreement in which it agreed to pay BRL 2.7 billion in exchange for withdrawal of the administrative improbity and ACL lawsuits (the settlement provided for the reduction of this value from the settlement of December 2016), 'Acordo de leniência com a Odebrecht prevê ressarcimento de 2,7 bilhões', *A Controladoria-Geral da União* (27 July 2018), available at https://www.gov.br/cgu/pt-br/assuntos/noticias/2018/07/acordo-de-leniencia-com-a-odebre cht-preve-ressarcimento-de-2-7-bilhoes; 'Em disputa com AGU, TCU decide se suspende acordo da Odebrecht', *Exame* (11 July 2018). It also agreed to pay BRL 578 million in fines and participated in three publicly known leniency agreements with CADE, 'Cade fecha acordos de R$ 898 mi com empreiteiras investigadas na Lava Jato', *Poder 360* (21 November 2018), available at https://www.poder360.com.br/economia/cade-fecha-acordos-de-r-898-mi-com-empreiteiras-investigadas-na-lava-jato/.

[68] Multiple bilateral agreements were executed between institutions such as FPO, CADE, OCG, FAC, BNDES, COAF, and others, see Jones and Pereira Neto, n. 1.

ii. Was Operation Car Wash a success?

OCW revealed, and shined a light on a large-scale, long-lasting corruption scheme deeply engrained within Brazilian institutions and facilitated by a number of features, both general to public procurement and specific to the Brazilian system, which enabled it to take root, grow, and blossom, including:

- The large value of the procurement contracts which, combined with 'Buy Brazilian' policies,[69] and opaque[70] procurement processes for SOEs[71] provided an ideal and sheltered environment for the scheme to be implemented and hidden. These factors combined to narrow the pool of tenderers (especially in procurement involving engineering, oil, gas, the naval industry, or infrastructure (such as subway tunnels), where tendering by foreign entities was difficult and complex[72]), allowed Brazilian companies to cement close relationships with public officials and politicians, and made it easier for officials to manipulate procurement processes without detection and to keep 'outsiders', without political connections, from disrupting tenders and away from these larger projects.
- The widespread involvement of politicians[73] who appointed officials at the procuring entities in return for personal bribes and political donations that helped fund expensive electoral campaigns and to keep them, and their complex coalitions, in power.[74]

---

[69] Although general public procurement rules are based on traditional principles such as efficiency, equality, transparency and administrative probity, Brazilian rules also promote sustainable national development (a 'Buy Brazilian' policy (see, e.g., Law No. 8,666/1993, Law No. 12.3492010 and Brazil Constitution, n. 4)).

[70] The conduct was facilitated by the fact that procurement by SOEs was largely opaque and SOEs, such as Petrobras, were at the time exempted from the general procurement rules, see Georgopulos et al., n. 2. There was also limited transparency post-contract award during the implementation period of projects allowing corruption opportunities to arise through contractual amendments or the adding of payments, see, e.g., J.S.S. Cristóvam and J.C.L. Bergamini, 'Governança orporative na Lei das Estatais: aspectos destacados sobre transparência, gestão de riscos e compliance' (2019) 278(2) *Revista de Direito Administrativo* 179, 183–4; but see Federal Constitution, n. 4.

[71] See Decree No. 2,745/1998 which establishes a simplified procurement process for Petrobras.

[72] For example, foreign companies were required to have a local subsidiary or authorization to operate in Brazil, see Federal Law No. 8,666/93 Article 28 (V); Brazil, Civil Code, Article 1.134 and other regulatory and technical requirements imposed significant barriers to foreign companies seeking to tender, especially in certain sectors. See also, C.M.S. Pereira Neto and M.P. Adami, 'Mercado de obras públicas, corrupção e investimentos', *JOTA* (2 March 2018). In early 2020, the Federal Government signalled that it would eliminate requirements for foreign companies to establish local presence in order to participate in public tenders, and the new Public Procurement Law (Law No. 14,133/2021), allows foreign bidders to participate in national procurement proceedings without discrimination (Article 9, II). However, further regulation by the Federal Government is still pending regarding the conditions under which foreign documents are to be considered as equivalent to national requirements (Article 70).

[73] According to former Senator Amaral, who was arrested for obstructing justice and executed a plea agreement, the scheme was masterminded by politicians, including President Lula when he was in power, see J. Watts, 'Operation Car Wash: Is this the Biggest Corruption Scandal in History?', *The Guardian* (1 June 2017).

[74] Necessitated, for example, by the fragmented party structure, and multiparty presidential structure, Mello and Spektor, n. 10, 113. The multiparty system encourages horse-trading and politicians

224 BRAZIL: LESSONS FROM OPERATION CAR WASH

- The sense of impunity felt by individuals and firms, who did not appear to have believed that their corrupt and collusive conduct would be uncovered, punished, or sanctioned. On the contrary, Brazil was still perceived to be a country where the risk of anti-corruption enforcement was low or minimal,[75] and where the federal and state police lacked the resources, the expertise, and the support it needed to conduct complex investigations regarding sophisticated criminal activities. Consequently, despite a Code of Conduct for Federal Employees[76] and the enactment of new anti-corruption laws in 2013,[77] public ethics did not take root. Rather, '[d]ecades of weak law enforcement against crimes committed by high politicians and powerful businessmen ... generated a breeding ground for bribery, kickbacks, and corruption'.[78]

OCW led to a significant number of convictions, some of the largest fines ever imposed in Brazil for bribery and bid rigging, a number of powerful individuals and corporations being held to account, and some investigations are still ongoing. It seems likely, therefore, that it has contributed to a significant shift in compliance culture and that individuals and companies are now more wary of the costs, as well as the benefits, of breaking anti-corruption and competition laws in the future.[79]

Nonetheless, and despite these developments, it appears that OCW has not been sufficient to alter entrenched practices, to strike at the heart of the cronyism that occurred, or to challenge sufficiently the sense of impunity felt. Rather, a number of factors have combined to undermine OCW's powerful anti-corruption message.

First, allegations have been made, and are gaining momentum, that OCW was politically, or improperly, motivated. For example, journalists exposed leaked private exchanges between Sérgio Moro, the lead judge of OCW in Curitiba, and public prosecutors, suggesting that the judge advised and instructed prosecutors during the investigation and may have been biased. Although the accuracy of the reports has not been confirmed, and the alleged illegal access to the exchanges through hacking of mobile phones led to criminal charges against individuals who

---

from small parties surviving, by helping major parties form coalitions in exchange for patronage posts and other perks, including the power to appoint senior executives in SOEs and obtain the opportunity to receive payments into campaign coffers, C. Barros, 'The Twilight of Brazil's Anti-Corruption Movement', *The Atlantic* (28 July 2017), and Connors, n. 10; Watts, n. 73.

[75] See Moro, n. 6, 158, Connors, n. 10, and Watts, n. 73 (investigations that did occur 'faded away ... There was a popular expression for this: *acabou em pizza* (to end up with pizza), which suggested that there was no political row that could not be settled over a meal and a few beers').

[76] See the Public Servants Act, Federal Law No. 8,112/1990.

[77] See Section B.i.c., also n. 18.

[78] Moro, n. 6, 165; further, the enactment of new competition laws in 2011 and the consolidation of the enforcement function into the single competition agency, CADE, meant that, while the new system bedded in, competition law enforcement did not tackle large-scale domestic bid rigging until OCW took off.

[79] See OECD, *Integrity Review of Brazil: Managing Risks for a Cleaner Public Service* (OECD Publishing, 2012) 90.

COMBATTING CORRUPTION AND COLLUSION   225

accessed the information, the leaked information, and following accusations, inevitably weakened confidence in OCW's legitimacy.[80] Indeed, a narrative has been building that OCW disrespected due legal process and was politically biased against President Lula and his political party.[81]

Secondly, OCW left deep scars in sectors of the Brazilian economy. Some of the largest construction companies in the country—including Odebrecht, OAS, Galvão, UTC, and others—went through a process of corporate reorganization under bankruptcy protection.[82] These processes significantly reduced their size and capability, and affected both their ability to perform ongoing contracts, and to participate in new bids. Since these companies were involved in numerous large infrastructure projects (e.g. roads, airports, railways), many of these projects suffered delays, setbacks, or collapse.[83] The problem became so acute that Congress had to pass a new law allowing the early termination of infrastructure concession contracts and their retendering.[84] Some politicians and critics sought to blame these catastrophic consequences on the 'dubious' OCW.

Thirdly, government support for the anti-corruption message waned significantly during President Jair Bolsonaro's tenure, even though OCW may have contributed to his election following a campaign which included a strong discourse about commitment to corruption control, through government transparency, dismissal of team members accused of corruption, and bolstering accountability institutions.[85] Evidence indicates that he failed on this mandate and, rather, weakened transparency and the accountability of institutions.[86] For example, in 2020, only a year after taking office, President Bolsonaro, changed the leadership of the Federal Police, so challenging the independence and autonomy of the institution, leading to criticism of undue political interference,[87] and causing the then Minister of Justice,

[80] See 'Leak Reveals Ethics Failures in Brazil's Operation Car Wash', *The Intercept* (9 June 2019); Ministério Público Federal, 'Operação Spoofing: MPF denuncia sete por crimes envolvendo invasões de celulares de autoridades brasileiras' (21 January 2020); and n. 40 and text.

[81] See 'Brazil Judge Annuls Evidence from Odebrecht Confessions in Operation Car Wash Case', n. 40; 'Brazil is Taking Worrying Steps Away from Clean Politics', *Financial Times* (21 October 2023); and nn. 39 and 40 and text.

[82] See, e.g., 'Brazil's Odebrecht Files for Bankruptcy Protection after Years of Graft Probes', *Reuters* (17 June 2019).

[83] See, e.g., 'Brazil's Viracopos Airport Operator Files for Bankruptcy Protection', *Reuters* (17 May 2018).

[84] Federal Law No. 13,448/2017; *See also* 'Brazil Moves to Retender Concessions' *Latin Finance* (19 August 2019).

[85] See V.A. de Carvalho, 'One Year After Bolsonaro's Election, How Well Is His Administration Fighting Corruption in Brazil?', The Global Anticorruption Blog (28 October 2019) (stressing the importance of Car Wash for Bolsonaro's election) and P. Lagunes, G. Michener, F. Odilla, and B. Pires, 'Unkept Promises? Taking Stock of President Jair Bolsonaro's Actions on Corruption Control' (2021) 17(2) *Revista Direito GV* e2121.

[86] de Carvalho, n. 85; Lagunes et al., n. 85.

[87] Lagunes et al., n. 85. He also weakened the financial intelligence unit, COAF, that was investigating allegations against his son.

Sérgio Moro (former lead judge of OCW), to resign.[88] As Moro's appointment represented a symbol of OCW—even if the Judge showing partiality and political engagement in this way made some uncomfortable—his resignation was interpreted as a signal of retreat from the President's commitment to fight corruption. In addition, during President Bolsonaro's term in office, Congress approved, either with his explicit support or at least without his opposition, a series of laws considered to setback the anti-corruption agenda.[89] President Bolsonaro also attempted (albeit unsuccessfully) to change the law to restrict access to governmental information[90] and nominated Augusto Aras, an individual aligned with the President's agenda,[91] as the Chief Federal Prosecutor (the highest official at the FPO, which was designed to be autonomous and independent of the three branches of government), in a departure from the established tradition of nominating the Chief from a list of names chosen by the Association of National Prosecutors. Aras, supported by President Bolsonaro, disbanded the OCW task force at the end of January 2021.[92] Concerns also grew during his tenure, that the FPO might be hindering politically sensitive investigations and about the independence of CADE.[93] Anxieties about transparency, accountability, and independence of institutions in Brazil persist following the election of President Lula.[94]

Fourthly, there are now concerns as to whether enforcers would be able to be as effective in the future, especially as high-profile investigations have tailed off.[95] Not only may political developments have affected the independence of key investigators and prosecutors, but a 2019 law now allows public officials who abuse

---

[88] He was the 8th minister to resign within 15 months of President Bolsonaro taking office, see E. Londoño, L. Casado, and M. Andreoni, 'Turmoil in Brazil: Bolsonaro Fires Police Chief and Justice Minister Quits', *The New York Times* (24 April 2020).

[89] See the Transparency International report 'Brazil: Setbacks in the legal and institutional anti-corruption frameworks – 2020 update', available at https://www.transparency.org/en/publications/brazil-setbacks-in-the-legal-and-institutional-anti-corruption-frameworks.

[90] An executive order restricting responses to freedom of information requests during the COVID-19 pandemic was struck down by the Supreme Court, see A. de Moraes, 'STF Suspende Alterações Da Lei de Acesso à Informação', *Portal Dos Jornalistas* (26 March 2020), and Lagunes et al., n. 85.

[91] See 'Brazil's Senate Approves Nomination of Augusto Aras as Chief Prosecutor', *Reuters* (25 September 2019); A. Krüger, G. Mazui, and M. Oliveira 'Bolsonaro indica Augusto Aras para novo procurador-geral; aprovação depende do Senado', *G1* (5 September 2019). This step jeopardized the OCW task force, Lagunes et al., n. 85.

[92] Lagunes et al., n. 85, 19.

[93] See R.F. Taffarello and F. Guimarães Leardini, 'Bribery & Corruption, Brazil' (2022) *Global Legal Insights (GLI)*. For example, in 2022, shortly before the Brazilian election, Brazil's Superior Electoral Court annulled the decision of CADE's President asking his agency to open an investigation into possible collusion among (polling) research institutes to manipulate the market and consumers with misleading presidential election data. At the same time, it also annulled a decision of the Minister of Justice, asking the Federal Police to investigate the matter, see A.P. Candil, 'Brazil Superior Electoral Court Annuls CADE President, Justice Minister Requests to Investigate Possible Manipulation of Presidential Election Sata', *MLex* (17 October 2022).

[94] See also 'Brazil is Taking Worrying Steps Away from Clean Politics', n. 81 and OECD, 'Implementing the OECD Anti-Bribery Convention in Brazil Phase 4 report' (19 October 2023).

[95] See 'Brazil is Taking Worrying Steps Away from Clean Politics', n. 81 and Taffarello and Guimarães Leardinin, *GLI*, n. 93.

their powers to be punished[96] and 2021 law reforms[97] make it harder to impose civil liability on individuals and companies. There is concern that the 2019 law will 'have a cooling effect on the independence of the judiciary and the autonomy of prosecutors and the police to pursue criminal corruption as they see fit'.[98] In turn, a reduction in this enforcement threat is also likely to decrease the incentive for individuals and legal entities to cooperate with enforcers (these programmes were already likely less attractive given that many of the companies that decided to co-operate with OCW have already paid or committed to pay billions, but remain entangled in multiple, overlapping procedures[99]).

Fifthly, although the ultimate sanctions following OCW have been significant, and unprecedented, they may still not have been optimal or sufficient to have the deterrent effect desired. For example: the deterrent and punitive effective of the laws may have been diminished by the numerous leniency, settlements, cooperation, and plea arrangements;[100] the decision of the Supreme Court to allow defendants to wait for trial out of prison until all appeals have been exhausted,[101] arguably enables elite individuals to avoid prison by launching ongoing appeals and running down limitation periods;[102] the complicated and time-consuming nature of certain cases, including for administrative improbity or before the Supreme Court for those with privileged jurisdiction, has resulted in under-enforcement of the law, especially against high-ranking serving politicians; congressional censure or removal from office of corrupt politicians is still too exceptional;[103] only a fraction of the benefits of wrongdoing has been recovered to date.

Finally, it is clear that an enduring perception of widespread corruption remains in Brazil. Indeed, Brazil has fallen significantly in the Transparency International's

---

[96] Federal Law No. 13,869/2019, seemingly adopted in reaction to the expanded enforcement powers that enabled OCW to happen, see A. Shalders, 'Três casos da Lava Jato em que investigadores seriam punidos por nova lei do abuso de autoridade', *BBC News Brasil* (5 September 2019) (illustrating actions by OCW investigators that could be punished under the new law).

[97] See Federal Law No. 14,230/2021.

[98] Moro, n. 6, 165. See also 'Brazil is Taking Worrying Steps Away from Clean Politics', n. 81.

[99] See example of Odebrecht in Section B.i.c.

[100] Although these programmes may have been central to the uncovering of direct evidence of infringements against key players and allowing a large quantity of cases to be dealt with, the frequency of their use may have reduced the deterrent effect of the law and they may have been used unnecessarily in some cases where clear evidence of an infringement had already been amassed, see Pontes and Anselmo, n. 10 (noting that the Police were against arrangements concluded with Odebrecht as they already had evidence in hand). In the administrative anti-corruption context, only a few fines have been imposed by the OCG outside of leniency arrangements. Similarly, CADE has, to date, principally adopted leniency and settlement agreements relating to OCW. Further the number of plea agreements, exceed the number of individual criminal convictions.

[101] See n. 38 and text.

[102] See Moro, n. 6, 158 (due to the heavy caseload of Brazilian Superior Courts, powerful defendants may be able 'to manipulate the judicial process to prevent their cases from ever reaching a conclusion and effectively avoiding accountability').

[103] Mello and Spektor, n. 10, 123 and Section B.i.b.

(TI) Corruption Perceptions Index (CPI)[104] table since 2014 when OCW began—from forty-three to thirty-eight points and from 69th to 94th (out of 180) most clean. Although, this drop could reflect an increased perception of corruption following OCW, it may also reflect the fact that businesses and citizens believe that, in spite of the promises of reform, this is just another Brazilian scandal which will not be met by meaningful change in the future.[105]

C. Beyond Operation Car Wash: Lessons and Challenges Ahead

i. The need for, and feasibility of, reform

The setbacks and difficulties described in the preceding section, make it clear that, in spite of the existence of strong public procurement, competition and anti-corruption laws in Brazil and the large scale of OCW, and its unique successes, more still needs to be done to tackle corruption and collusion in Brazilian public procurement processes. This section argues that, even if wholesale change to the political culture is unrealistic, it is possible to capitalize on the invigorated fight against corruption started by OCW by developing a more overarching approach to the problem. In line with the approach set out in Chapter 4, a three-pronged set of mutually reinforcing reforms is proposed to augment the battle against, and reverse the cycle of, corruption focusing on: (i) weakening the illicit ties between businesses, public officials, and politicians and to strike at the heart of the developed culture in which businesses expect to pay, and officials and politicians expect to receive, bribes;[106] (ii) adjustments to public procurement to make it more difficult for corruption and collusion to occur during the process; (iii) challenging the sense of impunity felt by the powerful by ensuring that corruption and collusion occurring will be detected quickly and sanctioned effectively.[107] It also highlights the need to fine tune the enforcement system with the aim of: minimizing the overlaps in the work the distinct institutions conduct, especially where they create conflicts; enhancing and streamlining cooperation between relevant institutions to capture synergies and ensure more effective enforcement; and enhancing and integrating multiple leniency and collaboration programs by creating a one-stop-shop, self-reporting mechanism for bid rigging and corruption

---

[104] Transparency International, CPI 2022, available at https://www.transparency.org/en/cpi/2022/. National surveys also reflected widespread perceptions of corruption after the election of President Bolsonaro, see Lagunes et al., n. 85.

[105] Barros, n. 74.

[106] See A. Persson, B. Rothstein, and J. Teorell, 'Why Anticorruption Reforms Fail—Systemic Corruption as a Collective Action Problem' (2013) 26 *Governance* 449, 465.

[107] See also Jones and Pereira Neto, n. 1.

designed to strengthen safeguards and opportunities for resolving all proceedings for those self-reporting.

At the core of these proposals is the need to tackle the cultural norms that helped to reinforce the scheme revealed by OCW and led to the alignment of incentives among powerful actors and firms to accept that the payment of bribes in return for preferential treatment by state officials was 'a rule of the game'[108] and an ordinary cost of doing business (with lucrative results); politicians becoming reliant on bribes to fund their parties and electoral campaigns and to lock in the support of coalitions; and individual politicians, public servants, and employees of SOEs becoming accustomed to the receipt of bribes and kickbacks for private purposes.

It is recognized that implementation of these proposals depends on sufficient support and that not all, especially the more ambitious political or legislative reforms, will be achievable in the shorter term. Nonetheless, some of the recommendations could be adopted by relevant institutions keen to build on the momentum created by OCW.

ii. Weakening links between business, procurement officials, and politicians

The scheme uncovered by OCW flourished because politicians were able to work with a relatively small group of hand-selected procurement officials and powerful businesses to extract bribes to fund their political campaigns and support fragile political coalitions as well as their privileged lifestyles. A number of steps could help to weaken links between these people, creating an institutional environment less favourable to systemic corruption.

For example, the close link between serving politicians and the appointment of procurement officials within SOEs or the central government could be severed,[109] ensuring that officials are appointed on the basis of merit through open and professional hiring processes without the influence of party politicians.[110] Further, some limited adjustments to political processes could help to dilute the 'interface between corruption and political structure'[111] and protect against some of the vulnerabilities exposed. Indeed, the decision of the Supreme Court to ban corporate donations to electoral campaigns,[112] combined with new legislation to limit the

---

[108] Moro, n. 6, 161.

[109] Law No. 13,303/2016, 'establishing a new framework for the governance of SOEs', is an important step in this direction, providing some objective criteria for the appointment of high-level executives, and creating additional governance layers. However, the goal of further reducing the links of SOEs' officials and politicians remains important.

[110] Moro, n. 6, 163.

[111] B. Winter, 'Brazil's Never-Ending Corruption Crisis Why Radical Transparency Is the Only Fix' (2017) 96(3) *Foreign Affairs* 87. But see 'Brazil is Taking Worrying Steps Away from Clean Politics', n. 81.

[112] See Brazil Supreme Court, ADI 4.650, 17 September 2015. The ten measures against corruption, proposed by the FPO included proposals to curtail irregular campaign financing, but these were not included in the crime bill that passed. See, Bill No. 3,855/2019 known as '10 measures against corruption'.

230 BRAZIL: LESSONS FROM OPERATION CAR WASH

number of political parties,[113] could provide the foundation for improved mechanisms aimed at reducing the extraction of bribes for partisan purposes. Of course, any such measures would need to be calibrated in order to avoid negative side effects in the democratic process, such as a reduction in pluralism.

In addition, measures could be adopted to weaken the close relationship between procurers/politicians and the small pool of companies that have dominated many areas of Brazilian public procurement for so long. As this close relationship has been cemented by procurement conditions, especially within larger construction, engineering, and infrastructure projects, which impose significant obstacles to other bidders, especially foreign bidders, liberalizing trade and reducing bureaucratic barriers for technical qualification would increase the number and diversity of bidders, products and services, dilute existing cosy relationships and destabilize existing corrupt schemes.[114] Although Brazil's application to accede to the World Trade Organization Agreement on Government Procurement (WTO GPA) has been withdrawn, negotiations for an EU-Mercosur Trade Agreement are ongoing.[115] Further, irrespective of accession, the preferential treatment policies currently applied could be reduced and used only exceptionally where robust justifications for it apply.

iii. Making public procurement a less protected environment for wrongdoing

The features of the Brazilian public procurement system, which made it especially prone to corrupt and collusive practices at the time of OCW, have been exacerbated by the financial distress of corporations embroiled in OCW which increased concentration on some markets. As described in Chapter 4, a number of adjustments to the public procurement system[116] could, however, help to preserve its integrity by minimizing opportunities for bid rigging or bribery. For example, measures

---

These measures were not supported by President Bolsonaro. See also the discussion of the Anti-Oligarch Law in Chapter 9 (Ukraine).

[113] Constitutional Amendment 97/2017 took an initial step in the latter direction by limits access to public funds and free radio and TV time during election for parties with low voting percentages, see the so-called 'performance clause'.

[114] See Chapter 4.

[115] Brazil applied to accede to the WTO GPA in May 2020, see 'Application for Accession Of Brazil To The Agreement On Government Procurement', WTO Communication, GPA/152 GPA/ACC/BRA/1 (19 May 2020) but President Lula announced in May 2023 that he was withdrawing the application, see https://www.gov.br/mre/en/contact-us/press-area/press-releases/brazil-withdraws-offer-to-accede-to-the-wto-government-procurement-agreement#:~:text=As%20a%20plurilateral%20instrument%2C%20the,to%20its%20public%20procurement%20market.

[116] Law No. 14,133, approved by Congress in 2021, establishes new general procurement rules at the federal level, consolidating and detailing other public procurement laws. However, the recent reform does not substantially address the main points made in this section. More importantly, it does not change the relevance, nor the feasibility, of the proposed reforms.

for lowering barriers to entry, disciplining and controlling procurer discretion, professionalizing the procurement workforce through meritocratic recruitment processes, and training, could be considered. Further an anti-corruption culture and compliance incentives could be built through routine use of Certificates of Independent Bid Determination (CIBDs),[117] use of 'Integrity Pacts'[118] in appropriate circumstances, and increasing transparency,[119] monitoring and auditing of compliance with the rules. These could build on steps already taken by the Federal Government to make procurement data available for public access and research, through the use of application programming interfaces (APIs) that facilitate automated collection and processing of data,[120] and the FAC and the OCG (and its Public Spending Observatory) monitoring procurement processes for irregularities and misconduct.

A particular challenge in Brazil may be to control procurer discretion, which is likely to be required in larger, more complex procurements especially those relating to, for example, infrastructure and construction. Although, limiting the discretion of government officials in relation to routine purchases of standardized products and services[121] may help to reduce corruption, other measures may be required to tackle corruption in relation to procurement of these large, one-of-a-kind projects, for example, through rotation of civil servants, sequential as opposed to one-stop-shop systems, and careful overseeing and monitoring of procurement processes *ex post*.[122]

---

[117] Although some of these requirements are already being used in federal bids and in states like São Paulo, they should be routine, and included in the general federal rules of procurement. See, for additional information, OECD, 'Tool: Certificated of Independent Bid Determination', available at https://www.oecd.org/governance/procurement/toolbox/search/certificate-independent-bid-determination.pdf.

[118] Transparency International, 'Integrity Pacts', available at https://www.transparency.org/en/tool-integrity-pacts.

[119] Law No. 14,133, approved by Congress in 2021, establishing new general procurement rules, takes a step in this direction, determining that all tender rules must be published in a National Portal of Public Procurement on the Internet (Articles 53 and 174). It is yet to be seen how this ambitious programme will work and whether it will be sufficient to provide transparency.

[120] See the ComprasNet project, part of the Open Government Partnership, which makes raw data from the federal buying system available for third-party access: 'Dados Abertos – Compras Governamentais', *API de Compras Govermentais* (July 2020), available at http://compras.dados.gov.br/docs/home.html. Although the Congress considered an FPO proposal to oblige government entities, including SOEs, to dedicate a percentage of their advertising budgets to educating the public about the dangers of corruption and publicizing outlets for whistleblowers, see Bill No. 3,855/2019, n. 112, Article 63, these measures were not supported by President Bolsonaro. The Bill also included proposals to end some of the legal privileges that make it difficult to prosecute elected officials, and increased penalties for those convicted.

[121] See centralized systems developed in São Paulo (electronic bidding for common goods and services called 'Electronic Buying Exchange' ('Bolsa Eletrônica de Compras do Estado de São Paulo') and by the Federal Government (electronic tenders applied to goods and common services using federal funding, see Brazil, Federal Decree No. 10,024, of 20 September 2019).

[122] See Chapter 4.

232 BRAZIL: LESSONS FROM OPERATION CAR WASH

iv. Ensuring that players cannot act with impunity

a. A concentrated cleanup campaign

It is seen in Chapter 4 that enforcement of anti-corruption and competition laws is generally important to fight these practices, even if it is not a sufficient one. Backlashes to OCW mean that if a concentrated cleanup campaign is to be continued, further measures will be required to ensure that anti-corruption enforcement continues, is seen as impartial and respects due process, and that there is a real threat of effective sanctions in cases of infringement. As a starting point, this requires adequate resources to be channelled to investigative and enforcement agencies, especially the Federal Police, CADE, and OCG, and for such institutions and key appointments within them,[123] to be free of political interference and intervention by the President and other high-ranked politicians.

Indeed, two former Federal Police officers who played a central role in the OCW investigation, have stressed that Federal Police chiefs should be appointed for a non-renewable four-year period from a shortlist supplied by a superior college of Federal Police chiefs.[124] They have also called for the creation of a specialized unit within the police focusing on the investigation of large-scale, high-level embezzlements of public funds and with the tools to analyse federal expenditure, to detect fraud in public tenders and to trace and recover assets transferred abroad. 'The harder it becomes to enjoy the fruits of corruption, the less interesting an option it becomes. Achieving more agility and efficiency in rooting out money-laundering schemes and beefing up our means of prevention are therefore the utmost importance if we are to ensure that crime does not pay.'[125] They also propose that Brazilian police forces be protected from continued expansion of their remit—so enabling them to focus resources on high-level corruption, and the introduction of a new criminal law taking a harder line against crimes of corruption involving the occupants of public positions.[126]

b. A good track record of enforcement and fine-tuning institutional coordination

During OCW, many individuals sought to cooperate with, or obtain leniency from, relevant agencies. The ability for agencies to rely on self-reporting in the future will be dependent both on a good track record of enforcement using other, independent detection techniques (including through use of screens[127] and monitoring for red

---

[123] See Section B.ii. But see 'Brazil is Taking Worrying Steps Away from Clean Politics', n. 81 and OECD, n. 94.

[124] Pontes and Anselmo, n. 10, Chapter 12.

[125] Pontes and Anselmo, n. 10, 155.

[126] Pontes and Anselmo, n. 10, Chapter 12.

[127] See discussion of Project Brain in Chapter 4, which has challenges but has led to some investigations being opened following the use of algorithms to analyse procurement data.

BEYOND OPERATION CAR WASH   233

flags by procurement officials and enforcement agencies and computer-assisted audit tracks[128]) and improved coordination between agencies—especially through informing each other of possible wrongdoing,[129] eliminating overlaps, enhancing cooperation, and coordination of self-reporting and leniency programs. Indeed, it has been seen that OCW presented major coordination challenges to both defendants and enforcement institutions (with e.g. the FPO, CADE, OCG, and FAC all seeking sanctions against individuals or corporations for corruption and/or collusion under criminal, ACL, competition, federal auditing, and administrative improbity laws).[130]

Although the modular system and institutional multiplicity has benefits,[131] the size and scope of the Brazilian investigation tested the respective agencies' limits, as well as their coordination capacity. It has been noted that it also led to conflicts and multiple jeopardy for defendants.[132] The fragilities exposed imply a need for change and collaboration which will facilitate sharing of information and expertise, build a joint view of common problems, create relationships of trust, and open space for more positive cooperation which helps to increase detection and enhance deterrence.

One solution could be to accept that even though multiple enforcement institutions exist, not all of them should necessarily act in parallel. Rather, it would be preferable for the agencies to coordinate their action either *ex ante* or on an *ad hoc* basis, in order to decide which agency is best placed to lead each investigation, or the best way of grouping different investigations together. The institutional framework could thus be adjusted by allowing authority and functions to be allocated to the institution best positioned to implement it, or granting certain agencies the prerogative to lead proceedings relating to a particular issue or type of sanction. For example, at the federal level, proceedings for corruption against corporations could be concentrated at the OCG, while fighting bid rigging, could be concentrated at CADE.[133] In contrast, general courts or the FAC might be better placed

[128] In Brazil the Public Spending Observatory, created by the OCG, has computer-assisted audit tracks which could be used more proactively to crosscheck procurement expenditure with other government databases and to identify atypical situations warranting further investigation, OECD Integrity Review, n. 79, 313.

[129] Evidence of wrongdoing has materialized in the criminal sphere in bid rigging cases, not only those arising from OCW itself by subsequently, see, e.g., Administrative Proceeding No. 08012.009732/2008-01 (known as the 'Leech cartel').

[130] Further, both OCG and CADE investigations and improbity lawsuits have led to damages actions.

[131] See K.E. Davis, M. Machado, and G. Jorge, 'Coordinating the Enforcement of Anti-Corruption Law: South American Experiences' (2021) 54 *Verfassung in Recht und Übersee* 160 (discussing modularity in the Brazilian System).

[132] C.A. Sundfeld, 'Controle sabotando controle', *JOTA Info* (22 March 2017) (describing how the multiple layers of enforcement may conflict and undermine one another, and providing an example of 'control sabotaging control').

[133] Although the ACL recognizes the power of CADE to investigate and convict a competition law infringement (see Article 29), it does not prevent the possibility of both the OCG and CADE investigating and sanctioning the conduct.

234 BRAZIL: LESSONS FROM OPERATION CAR WASH

to deal with actions for the recovery of damages.[134] Although these measures could be implemented through agreements among agencies, legislative changes could clarify the position by allocating leadership to a certain agency in a given area. These types of steps would preserve the benefits of institutional competition, while avoiding some of its pitfalls. Although the possibility of overlaps would not be eliminated, the proposal is to make overlaps a conscious choice and not an erratic by-product of multiple actions.

Even if allocation of functions is improved, better fora for coordination among the multiple agencies also needs to be created. Indeed, overlapping investigations will remain necessary in certain circumstances, for example, where both criminal investigations against individuals and civil/administrative proceedings against corporations are being pursued. Enhancing and streamlining cooperation among these institutions will thus remain an essential part of building more efficient enforcement.[135]

Although cooperation agreements between agencies do exist, they proved insufficient to ensure effective cooperation in OCW.[136] Further institutional coordination—negative and positive—thus seems crucial to build trust and better communication and to ensure, for example, that leniency granted by one agency is not undermined by prosecution initiated in another agency, reducing incentives for self-reporting. This would seem to require better formal inter-institutional arrangements for coordination of enforcement strategies, sharing information, pooling information in common databases, and discussing findings through, for example, permanent joint committees or councils, where agency representatives may sit,[137] or other bilateral arrangements. One option might be to develop the National Strategy for Combatting Corruption and Money Laundering (*Estratégia Nacional de Combate à Corrupção e à Lavagem de Dinheiro (ENCCLA)*),[138] as such a forum.

Agencies could also work together to enhance and integrate their cooperation and leniency programmes, perhaps building a one-stop-shop for collaboration. For example, implementation difficulties arose in OCW, which relied on three distinct collaboration programmes implemented by the FPO, CADE, and OCG/FAGO, respectively. For individuals and legal entities, this involved complex negotiations with the different agencies, including distinct requirements and outcomes, varied timings, and complications because obtaining immunity or

---

[134] An exception could apply where damages are arbitrated as part of a negotiation of leniency or settlement.

[135] For a detailed discussion of the inherent necessity of coordination among integrity agencies, with a survey of the literature, see Jenkins, n. 63.

[136] Jenkins, n. 63, 10 ('institutional design appears to be less important than de facto collaboration').

[137] Jenkins, n. 63, 15.

[138] ENNCLA, available at http://enccla.camara.leg.br, created as a forum for coordination of anti-corruption actions, see Jenkins, n. 63, 18 and OECD Integrity Review, n. 79, 71–2.

penalty reductions in one enforcement sphere did not guarantee them in another. For enforcers, this also meant a multiplication of time and energy, delays to accessing valuable information, the creation of conflicts and the inability to calculate sanctions in an integrated manner.[139] Both parties and agencies would thus have benefited from a more streamlined negotiation process across the distinct spheres. In the future, such a procedure could be achieved by either (i) the creation of a permanent committee of the responsible authorities to deal with corruption and collusion in public procurement; or (ii) the delegation of powers to one authority to function as the administrator of an integrated collaboration/leniency agreement.[140] A new institutional framework could then create a single entry point/marker system for leniency/collaboration and a joint negotiation system applicable to all legal entities in the same economic group, and related individuals, and relating to all three enforcement spheres (i.e. criminal, competition, and anti-corruption). It could thus expand on the system of 'competition' leniency, operated by CADE.[141]

Further, enforcement agencies and procurers could work more closely together. Although some agencies have issued guidelines designed to promote competition and the combatting of bid rigging and corruption in public procurement (see, e.g. CADE guidelines,[142] SEAE, a competition advocacy agency within the Ministry of Economy, proposals for procompetitive rules in tenders for new infrastructure projects[143] and OCG guidelines[144]), enforcers could develop routine training programmes for procurement agents, prosecutors, and staff of the auditing court,[145] and enhance their own collective expertise by developing joint and cross-training programs or allowing secondments to help build cooperation channels.[146]

---

[139] See, e.g., R. Canetti, *Acordo De Leniência: Fundamentos Do Instituto E Os Problemas De Seu Transplante Ao Ordenamento Jurídico Brasileiro* (Fórum, 2019) 217–35.

[140] Some provision for bilateral collaboration already exists, see Jones and Pereira Neto, n. 1. See also, e.g., R. Luz and G. Spagnolo, 'Leniency, Collusion, Corruption, and Whistleblowing', *SSRN Scholarly Paper* (April 18, 2016) (proposing a 'one-stop' integrated leniency program) and Law No. 12,529/2011, Article 86, paragraph 60; 'Guidelines to CADE's Antitrust Leniency Program', *Conselho Administrativo de Defesa Econômica* (June 2016) 20–1; and OECD, 'OECD Peer Reviews of Competition Law and Policy, Brazil' (2019) 58, available at https://www.oecd.org/daf/competition/oecd-peer-reviews-of-competition-law-and-policy-brazil-ENG-web.pdf.

[141] See further Jones and Pereira Neto, n. 1.

[142] See 'Guia: Combate a Cartéis em Licitações', *Conselho Administrativo de Defesa Econômica* (December 2019), and 'Medidas para Estimular o Ambiente Concorrencial dos Processos Licitatórios: Contribuição do CADE', *Conselho Administrativo de Defesa Econômica*.

[143] C.M.S. Pereira Neto et al., *Advocacia da Concorrência: propostas com base nas experiências brasileira e internacional* (Editora Singular, 2016).

[144] 'Integridade', *A Controladoria-Geral da União*.

[145] B.E. Hawk, *International Antitrust Law & Policy: Fordham Competition Law 2010* (Juris Publishing, Inc., 2011) 79 (referring to SDE, a former Brazilian competition authority, training of 1700 public procurement officers and prosecutors to identify bid-rigging). SDE and CADE have also issued guidelines regarding bid rigging.

[146] See Jenkins, n. 63, 16 (discussing training and secondment as informal strategies to achieve institutional cooperation).

236   BRAZIL: LESSONS FROM OPERATION CAR WASH

Finally, agencies could cooperate more closely in relation to penalties—to ensure that they have some deterrent effect, but do not infringe the *ne bis in idem* principle and are not beyond the economic capacity of the investigated parties, thereby leading to bankruptcy, and the reduction of competition. In a first step in this direction, CADE issued a resolution allowing for the reduction of fines for parties that can demonstrate that they have paid damages in association with the same conduct, a provision that was applied for the first time in OCW settlements.[147]

c. More effective sanctions

Another concern is that penalties beyond corporate fines were not used in OCW as widely as required to ensure deterrence, especially because of the difficulty of convicting high-level politicians and, arguably, the overuse of cooperation procedures. Further steps thus seem necessary to increase the costs of infringement, especially through greater use of the sanctions that can be imposed on individuals. In particular, to prevent individuals from being able to evade justice through long-winded appeals processes (following the Supreme Court's decision to allow defendants to avoid prison until all appeals have been exhausted[148]) and to reduce the perception of impunity, it could be considered whether the Constitution or criminal code should be amended to require individuals convicted of a criminal offence to serve jail time once an appellate court confirms a conviction ('second-instance' imprisonment). Another step to reduce impunity would be, given the constraints on the Supreme Court's time, to limit or eliminate privileged jurisdiction for serving politicians through constitutional amendment, so allowing more proceedings to be brought before lower courts and for politicians to be treated as other citizens when facing criminal proceedings.[149] This might require other measures to ensure that trials of politicians are removed from local political pressures, that the rules on privileged jurisdiction are designed to prevent, for example by removing cases from their natural territorial jurisdiction where there is a risk of bias.[150] Although these kinds of measures were supported by Jair Bolsonaro during his presidential campaign, these were not adopted during his tenure.[151]

In addition, debarment remedies could be used more consistently and transparently, than is currently the case. Further, to counteract cronyism, individuals playing a particularly active role in the wrongdoing could also be prohibited from participating directly or indirectly in legal entities that have contracts with public administration.[152] In extreme cases, self-cleaning rules could demand an overhaul

---

[147] Brazil, CADE Resolution 21/2018, Article 12 and see Section B.i.b.

[148] See n. 22 and text.

[149] See '10 Measures against Corruption', n. 112 and Lagunes et al., n. 85, 25–6.

[150] See Pereira Ferreira, n. 11.

[151] Lagunes et al., n. 85.

[152] The Law of Administrative Improbity provides for this possible sanction of prohibition to contract with the public administration, see, Law 8,429/1992, n. 30, Article 12. Competition, anti-corruption and federal accounting laws also provide for debarment sanctions, see Section B. However, change of corporate control would require legislative change to be implemented.

of management or change in corporate control over a legal entity involved in the wrongdoing. These steps would also help to weaken ties between business and the political establishment.

D. Conclusions

The discussion in this chapter indicates that despite the vigorous law enforcement campaign provoked by OCW, corruption (and collusion) risks remain real in Brazil. In accordance with the discussion in Chapter 4, a broader approach is thus proposed using political, legal, procurement, and other reforms as a supplement to a sustained law enforcement effort. Although each of these reforms individually may be insufficient to drive change, it is argued that their unifying and self-reinforcing nature could ultimately augment their effect, decreasing opportunities for, and increasing the cost of, wrongdoing, and operating to destabilize the corrupt system.

Some of the reform proposals made in this paper could be implemented relatively rapidly by procuring authorities or enforcement agencies, without the need for extensive legislative change. For example, links between businesspeople, procurers, and politicians might be diluted by adjustments to the procurement processes that widen the pool of bidders to outsiders who might be less willing to engage in established practices and more likely to avail themselves of review procedures. These ties can be further weakened by the use of sanctions that require debarment or change in management of companies involved in corrupt or anti-competitive activities. The procurement process could also be made a less protected environment for traditional contractors through simple adjustments to tender criteria, limitations on the exercise of procurers' discretion where feasible, and the routine use of CIBDs and targeted use of Integrity Pacts. Moreover, anti-corruption and competition agencies could play a more active role in training procurement officials and in ensuring the integrity of procurement processes. Further, the independence of law enforcers could be strengthened, and law enforcement agencies can also take steps to improve detection techniques (including through the use of screens and so increasing incentives for self-reporting and the effectiveness of leniency programs), to improve cooperation and coordination of their activities, and to augment the effectiveness of remedies, in particular, through seeking to use the full range of sanctions including imprisonment and debarment.

It is acknowledged, nonetheless, that the reforms proposed require some change of mindset within institutions, and that a number of the proposals, which require political support, broad political agreement, or even constitutional change, are likely to be more challenging to achieve, for example: the prevention of politicians interfering in the appointment of procurement officials; greater independence and resourcing of key investigative bodies; constitutional amendments governing the serving of jail time pending appeal or reducing privileged jurisdiction; and any political reform dealing with the party system and campaign finance rules. Nonetheless, in the longer term, domestic and international pressure (arising from e.g. public frustration about recurrent corruption scandals, increased pressure on the public purse flowing from current global crises, the WTO and other countries adversely impacted by OCW) may combine to persuade the political establishment of the importance of these types of proposals and how they can improve the institutional environment and the welfare of individual citizens.

OCW's accomplishments and limitations provide powerful lessons for other jurisdictions seeking to combat corruption and collusion in public procurement. The Brazilian experience supports the view that a strong enforcement push *alone* is unlikely to carry the day where corruption is embedded in a system, and that such enforcement is likely to be strongly resisted and contested by those accused. However, the focused, multipronged approach to reform proposed in this paper, including a mapping exercise of measures that are easier to implement, may be helpful to any jurisdiction suffering endemic corruption. Indeed, a series of self-reinforcing incremental changes in paths of least resistance may be the most effective way forward—and, in reality perhaps, the most realistic option.

8

Addressing Democratic Backsliding and Increasing Corruption and Supplier Collusion Risks in Hungary and Poland: The Impact of EU Membership

A. Introduction	239	D. Mechanisms for Reform	254
B. The Influential Role of the EU in Establishing a Liberal Framework for its Member States' Procurement Systems	240	i. Initiatives at the national level	254
		ii. Compliance with EU law	255
		a. Backsliding and breaches of EU Law	255
C. The Illiberal Influence of Populist Governments in Hungary and Poland	245	b. Acting against individual cases of suspected corruption and bid rigging	257
i. Transformation of the post-communist Central European countries and populism as a driver of illiberal change in Hungary and Poland	245	c. Procedures against Member States for infringement of EU law and values	258
		d. Enforcement, penalties, and financial mechanisms	261
a. Illiberal change in democracy in Hungary and Poland	246	e. Proposals for more proactive steps to prevent breaches: increased oversight of public procurement processes and cooperation mechanisms	264
b. Illiberal change in the economy in Hungary and Poland	247	
ii. The impact on public procurement: increasing corruption and collusion risks	248	E. Conclusions	266

A. Introduction

This chapter examines how illiberal changes, both in the political system and the economy, introduced by populist governments in Hungary and Poland have been increasing the risk of corruption and collusion in public procurement processes in those countries.[1] It notes that these developments are having serious consequences not only for Hungary and Poland, but also for the European Union (EU) in terms of their impact on EU law, fundamental values, and finances. It thus considers what role Hungary, Poland, and crucially EU law, can play in reducing, mitigating, or reversing these risks and ensuring that these Member States have procompetitive public procurement systems in place.

The chapter starts, in Section B, by examining how EU law has shaped public procurement, competition and anti-corruption laws in its Members States, including Hungary and Poland. It establishes that the EU has played an essential role in putting in place a common and (in broad terms) liberal and transparent framework for public procurement policy across the Union and its Member States. It then goes on in Section C, to consider how illiberal developments that have occurred in Hungary and Poland may be breaching EU law and values and threatening the effectiveness of these carefully constructed systems. In particular, it examines how liberal market and democratic regression may be creating opportunities for public procurement processes to be manipulated, unchecked, in a way that favours public officials, state-owned enterprises (SOEs), government cronies, or other national firms or cartels. Even if, therefore, relatively few significant instances of corruption and collusion in domestic public procurement processes have actually been proven, the weaknesses in relevant laws, processes, and their enforcement that have developed may have allowed opportunities for such conduct to occur, without risk of exposure or challenge.

Recognizing that a purely national programme for reform is unlikely in the near future, in Hungary at least, Section D focuses on the toolkit that the EU possesses to challenge both individual cases of suspected corruption and collusion in a Member State and systematic and serious violations of EU law by a Member State, which create corruption and collusion risks in public procurement processes (including those involving the use of EU funds). It also considers whether further steps can be taken to protect EU funds better from misuse in national public procurement processes, for example, through closer cooperation between EU and national agencies, more proactive, real-time monitoring of processes, the use of integrity pacts, and the development of the EU's early detection and exclusion and remedies systems.

B. The Influential Role of the EU in Establishing a Liberal Framework for its Member States' Procurement Systems

Every year, over 250,000 public authorities across the EU spend approximately EUR 2 trillion, deriving both from national and EU funds (the latter, predominantly

---

[1] This chapter is based, and draws, on the paper written by M. Bernatt and A. Jones, 'Populism and Public Procurement: An EU Response to Increased Corruption and Collusion Risks in Hungary and Poland' (2022) 41 *Yearbook of European Law* 11.

European Structural and Investment (ESI) funds), on public procurement.[2] The EU consequently has a keen interest in ensuring that Member States have comprehensive public procurement systems in place. Not only is this necessary to ensure the proper spending of EU funds, but transparent and competitive bidding processes contribute to EU objectives, including growth, jobs, investment, and undistorted competition. Further, by requiring equal access of all EU operators to procurement opportunities across the EU (any company, organization, or institution in the EU has the right to compete for a public tender in the EU without discrimination[3]), public procurement contributes to the establishment of the internal market.

In Chapter 3, it is seen that public procurement laws in the EU Member States have been harmonized by an EU framework deriving both from the Treaty on the Functioning of the European Union (TFEU) and, more specifically, for higher value and ESI funded contracts, EU Directives.[4] The latter, which were estimated by the Commission in 2017 to apply to approximately EUR 545 billion worth of contracts,[5] require tenders worth more than specified amounts[6] to comply with core principles of transparency, equal treatment (non-discrimination), proportionality, mutual recognition, open competition, and sound procedural management. The rules are designed to guard against corruption and collusion through, for example: providing for standard use of competitive tendering processes (such as open, restricted, or competitive negotiated procedures, competitive dialogue, or innovation partnerships) with minimum bid periods and minimum number of bidders; requiring publication of contract opportunities in the Official Journal of the EU (tenders electronic daily, TED[7]) at the outset of the procedure; and by requiring authorities in setting criteria and evaluating tenders to treat economic operators equally and without favouring or discriminating in favour of certain tenderers, and to act in a transparent and proportionate manner. The regime also provides both mandatory and discretionary grounds for exclusion of bidders engaged

---

[2] See DG GROW, B, 'Public Procurement Indicators, 2018' (17 May 2021) (estimating total EU general government expenditure to be EUR 2,163 billion in 2018, accounting for approximately 14 per cent of total gross domestic product (GDP) in the EU), available at https://ec.europa.eu/docsroom/docume nts/48156.

[3] See further Section B.

[4] See, especially, Directive 2014/24/EU on Public Procurement [2014] OJ L94/65 and e.g. specific directives governing utilities and concession contracts, Directives 2014/25 and 2014/23. A separate body or legislation governs procurement by the EU institutions, which is subject to Financial Regulations; see Regulation 2018/1046 on the financial rules applicable to the general budget of the Union [2018] OJ L193/1 and Rules of Application.

[5] DG GROW G4—Innovative and e-Procurement, 'Public Procurement Indicators' (9 July 2019).

[6] Currently, EUR 140,000 for most types of services and supplies purchased by central government authorities, and EUR 5,382,000 for construction contracts.

[7] See further Chapter 4 and Tenders Electronic Daily, available at https://ted.europa.eu/TED/main/ HomePage.do.

242 THE IMPACT OF EU MEMBERSHIP

in corrupt or collusive practice.[8] Further, EU Remedies Directives[9] seek to ensure that EU companies, which have an interest in a public procurement procedure and believe that it has been run without proper application of the EU Directives, have access to rapid and effective review, and adequate remedies, at the national level, according to minimum national review standards.

In addition, EU competition laws protect the process of competition in the internal market.[10] In particular, Article 101 TFEU, which has direct effect in the Member States, prohibits anti-competitive bid rigging arrangements affecting trade between Member States and is enforced both at the EU level, by the European Commission, and at the Member State level by designated national competition authorities (NCAs)[11] and national courts, which also enforce national competition laws.[12] EU law requires NCAs to have the necessary independence, resources, and enforcement and fining powers to be able to enforce Article 101 effectively,[13] and national courts to ensure effective judicial protection of rights conferred by Article 101.[14]

Although the EU has no criminal code, anti-corruption laws in most Member States have been shaped by their participation in international anti-corruption conventions (now generally a requirement for states when acceding to the EU), including the United Nations Convention against Corruption (UNCAC), the OECD Convention on Combatting Bribery of Foreign Public Officials, and the Council of Europe's Group of States against Corruption (GRECO).[15] Further, even though EU law does not provide for rules governing the organization of justice in the Member States, it does impact national criminal law in different ways,[16] for example, through: (i) European organizations, such as the European Anti-Fraud Office (OLAF, *l'Office européen de lutte anti-fraude,* part of the Commission), created to ensure the better functioning of criminal justice and with power to investigate fraud impacting on EU funds, and the European Public Prosecutor's Office (EPPO), the independent public prosecution office of the EU which has been responsible since 2021 for investigating and prosecuting crimes (including corruption) against the

---

[8] See, e.g., Directive 2014/24/EU, Article 57.

[9] See, e.g., Directive 89/665/EEC (as amended by Directive 2007/66/EC).

[10] TFEU, Article 3(1)(b).

[11] Regulation 1/2003 [2003] L1/1.

[12] Regulation 1/2003, n. 11, Article 3.

[13] See now Directive (EU) 2019/1 of the European Parliament and of the Council of 11 December 2018 to empower the competition authorities of the Member States to be more effective enforcers and to ensure the proper functioning of the internal market [2019] OJ C11/3, especially Article 1(1).

[14] See, e.g., Case 14/68, *Walt Wilhelm v Bundeskartellamt* EU:C:1969:4 and Case C-453/99, *Courage Ltd v Crehan* EU:C:2001:465.

[15] See Chapter 3. Hungary and Poland ratified: UNCAC on 19 April 2005 and 15 September 2006, respectively, the OECD Convention on 4 December 1998 and 8 December 2000, respectively; and have been members of the European Council's GRECO (Group of States against Corruption) since 9 July 1999 and 20 May 1999, respectively.

[16] See J. Spencer, 'EU Criminal Law – the Present and the Future?' in A. Arnull, C. Barnard, M. Dougan, and E. Spaventa (eds), *A Constitutional Order of States? Essays in EU Law in Honour of Alan Dashwood* (Hart Publishing, 2011).

THE INFLUENTIAL ROLE OF THE EU   243

financial interests of the EU and the EU budget;[17] (ii) EU instruments which prescribe rules of substantive criminal law, or criminal procedure, which the Member States are required to adopt; (iii) EU laws—including public procurement laws—which contain important anti-corruption elements (iv) accession processes;[18] and (v) requiring Member States to comply with their obligations deriving from EU law. In the anti-corruption sphere, a 1997 Convention on fighting corruption involving officials of the EU or officials of Member States requires ratifying Member States to take necessary steps to criminalize active or passive bribery involving EU or national officials (whether or not impacting the Union's financial interests),[19] Article 325 TFEU requires Member States to counter fraud and other illegal activities affecting the financial interests of the Union,[20] and Article 83(1) TFEU recognizes corruption as a 'euro-crime', a particularly serious crime with a cross-border dimension for which minimum rules on the definition of *criminal offences* and *sanctions* may be established. Indeed since the end of the 1990s, the EU has sought to strengthen its internal EU policy towards corruption, to reduce corruption within EU institutions and Member States (as well as outside the EU), and to develop mechanisms to measure national efforts on corruption control, and to support national authorities in the better implementation of laws and policies against corruption through a constructive dialogue.[21] The Commission considers anti-corruption to be a key element contributing to growth, jobs, and investment in the EU, meaning that European Semester reports,[22] a tool for economic policy recommendations, include analysis of corruption risks and associated challenges.

Finally, because the EU is based on the rule of law which is essential to the protection of its fundamental values of 'respect for human dignity, freedom, democracy, equality, the rule of law and respect for human rights, including the rights of persons belonging to minorities' (Article 2 of the Treaty on European Union, TEU), Member States must be able to ensure effective judicial protection of EU laws and rights.[23] The independence and impartiality of law enforcement institutions and the judicial system in particular is central to constraining improper

---

[17] See further Chapter 4, n. 267 and Council Regulation (EU) 2017/1939 of 12 October 2017, implementing enhanced cooperation on the establishment of the European Public Prosecutor's Office [2017] OJ L283/1, Directive (EU) 2017/1371 of the European Parliament and of the Council of 5 July 2017 on the fight against fraud to the Union's financial interests by means of criminal law [2017] OJ L198/29.

[18] See further Section D below.

[19] Council Act 97/C 195/01 of 26 May 1997, drawn up on the basis of Article K.3 (2) (c) of the TEU, the Convention on the fight against corruption involving officials of the European Communities or officials of Member States of the EU, [1997] OJ C195/1 (entered into force 28 September 2005).

[20] See also, e.g., the Convention, drawn up on the basis of Article K.3 of the TEU, on the protection of the European Communities' financial interests [1995] OJ C316/48 requiring Member states to take necessary measures to ensure that fraud affecting the EU's financial interests are punishable by effective proportionate and dissuasive criminal penalties (Articles 1 and 2).

[21] See, e.g., the Anticorruption Report 2014, COM(2014) 38 final.

[22] Council of the European Union, 'The European Semester Explained', available at https://www.consilium.europa.eu/en/policies/european-semester/

[23] See further Section D.ii.

244 THE IMPACT OF EU MEMBERSHIP

exercise of public powers, ensuring that EU law is upheld, that national law is compatible with EU law, mutual trust between the courts, and effective legal protection of rights conferred by EU law.[24] The rule of law is thus essential to the upholding of the public procurement system and to protecting it from corrupt[25] and anti-competitive practices.

As a result of these developments, all EU Member States have comprehensive—and relatively consistent—public procurement, anti-corruption and competition laws in place. They are obliged to have independent institutions to enforce them and to protect EU rights, values, and funds. Indeed, when preparing to accede to the EU, both Hungary and Poland introduced competition laws which mirrored Articles 101–102 TFEU and their competition authorities enforce both EU and national rules.[26] 1990s public procurement and anti-corruption laws were also amended, or replaced by new acts, in 2003 and in 2004 on the eve of accession to the EU.[27]

Notwithstanding the many positive contributions of the EU framework that are outlined above, the efficacy and integrity of EU Member States' public procurement systems depends upon their application, implementation, and enforcement at the national level. The acute concern with regard to Hungary and Poland, is that illiberal changes by populist governments,[28] regarding both the political system and the economy, are increasing the risk of corruption and collusion in public contracting, which may cause substantial harm to EU citizens, and misuse of EU funds. These developments may therefore be thwarting achievement of the high-minded goals and values of the EU framework.[29]

---

[24] See further Section D.

[25] Cases C-357 etc/19, *Criminal Proceedings Against PM and others* EU:C:2021:1034, para. 223.

[26] See T. Skoczny, 'Polish Competition Law in the 1990s – On the Way to Higher Effectiveness and Deeper Conformity with EC Competition Rules' (2001) 2(3–4) *European Business Organization Law Review* 777.

[27] See now in Poland, the Public Procurement Law of 11 September 2019 (in force since 1 January 2021), and in Hungary Act CXLIII of 2015 on Public Procurement and Polish Penal Code, Articles 228–230a and Hungarian Criminal Code, see, e.g., Articles 293 and 294.

[28] These processes have been referred to as democratic backsliding (the 'process through which elected public authorities deliberately implement governmental blueprints which aim to systematic-ally weaken, annihilate, or capture internal checks on power with the view of dismantling the liberal democratic state and entrenching the long-term rule of the dominant party', L. Pech and K.L. Scheppele, 'Illiberalism within: Rule of Law Backsliding in the EU' (2017) 19 *Cambridge Yearbook of European Legal Studies* 3, 8) and liberal-market backsliding (the processes 'marking a departure from the ideas of economic liberalism, since they undermine the principal role of market competition, the dominant role of private ownership in the economy, market openness across borders, and the principle of competitive neutrality', M. Bernatt, *Populism and Antitrust. The Illiberal Influence of Populist Government on the Competition Law* (Cambridge University Press, 2022) 43). See further Section B.

[29] See, for a complementary perspective, A. Mungiu-Pippidi, *Europe's Burden: Promoting Good Governance Across Borders* (Cambridge University Press, 2019).

C. The Illiberal Influence of Populist Governments in Hungary and Poland

i. Transformation of the post-communist Central European countries and populism as a driver of illiberal change in Hungary and Poland

Until 1989, Hungary and Poland made up part of the Soviet bloc of satellite states. Their economies were centrally planned, with little space for private economic initiative and market competition. Their political system, while nominally called (popular) 'democracy', was in practice a one-party regime. Civil liberties, which were enshrined in constitutions, were not fully respected. Judicial independence was limited.

The change to this economic and political model came about in 1989 when communism came to an end in Hungary and Poland. Both countries then embarked on reforms, introducing a system of liberal democracy and a free-market economy, and a process of de-monopolization of the economy and privatization of SOEs in major industries. They also signed Association Agreements (AA) and sought accession to the EU. EU accession processes required both countries to meet stringent 'Copenhagen' criteria designed to ensure that that their political, economic, and regulatory developments converged with EU values and norms.[30] Amongst other things, these required Hungary and Poland to embrace democracy and the rule of law, to have stable institutions, and to have in place a functioning market economy, protected by robust competition and anti-corruption systems, with the capacity to cope with competitive pressure and market forces within the Union. Corruption control was an especially important condition given concerns about the capacity for corruption to permeate Central and Eastern Europe (CEE) candidate countries when transitioning from communism to democracy and a market economy.

Accession thus led to a process of approximation of Hungarian and Polish law to the EU legal framework, including, as seen in Section B above, in the spheres of public procurement, anti-corruption and competition law. Accession was finalized in 2004 when, reflecting the fact that both countries had been recognized as rule of law-based democracies and market economies, Hungary and Poland joined the EU.

From the end of the first decade of the 2000s, however, a re-orientation of the political and economic model started to occur. Following parliamentary elections, in 2010 the populist government of the Fidesz party was formed in Hungary and in 2015 the Law and Justice (PiS) government was formed in Poland. Both

---

[30] C. Hillion, 'The Copenhagen Criteria and Their Progeny' in C. Hillion (ed.), *EU Enlargement: A Legal Approach* (Hart Publishing, 2004).

246 THE IMPACT OF EU MEMBERSHIP

parties were headed by strong leaders who publicly questioned the safeguards of the liberal democratic order and the overall positive perception of the countries' transformations. The changes that followed in both countries constitute a representation of populist governments' influence on the liberal democratic and economic order.[31] Even if the reasons behind the rise of populism may be diverse,[32] illiberal changes introduced by populist governments tend to be justified by the same claim—that the will of ordinary people needs to be implemented without constraint.[33] Therefore, central to it are a rejection of pluralism (including institutional pluralism), a willingness to consolidate power,[34] and reforms undermining checks and balances as well as the rule of law.[35] Further, as far as the economy is concerned, ruling populist governments frequently opt for a re-evaluation of the existing free-market economic model and embrace a statist and patriotic economic agenda.[36]

The sections below examine more closely how these processes, complemented with new widespread and generous social-distribution programmes, as well as nation-centred patriotic rhetoric, including with respect to migration and the economy (i.e. economic patriotism), have played out in Hungary and Poland. Although the new coalition government in Poland formed following the election in October 2023 has stated that it will work to restore the rule of law and so to reverse some of these developments, at the time of writing it is too early to predict what will happen or how rapidly any changes will be implemented.

a. Illiberal change in democracy in Hungary and Poland

In both countries, important checks and balances in the system have been dismantled, in particular through a weakening and capture of constitutional courts.[37] These steps have severely limited the ability of their constitutional courts to carry out their role as guardians of the Constitution and to ensure conformity of lower rank legislation with it, so enabling the ruling populist majority to pass laws without an effective check of whether they are within constitutional limits.[38] The

---

[31] See Bernatt, n. 28, Chapter 2, 24–53 and the literature discussed there.

[32] They are commonly seen to include anger against ruling elites, hostility towards minorities, fear of immigration, rising economic inequalities, globalization, economic insecurity, disillusionment with the transformation processes, and a feeling of 'being left behind'.

[33] Bernatt, n. 28, 22–3.

[34] Bernatt, n. 28, 22–3.

[35] Bernatt, n. 28, 53. As a result, Hungary has now been categorized as an electoral autocracy, and Poland an electoral democracy, by the Varieties of Government (V-Dem) Institute, available at https://www.v-dem.net/.

[36] Bernatt, n. 28, 53.

[37] M. Bernatt and M. Ziółkowski, 'Statutory Anti-Constitutionalism' (2019) 28 *Washington International Law Journal* 485.

[38] See Bernatt and Ziółkowski, n. 37 and Bernatt, n. 28, 31; European Commission, 2021 Rule of Law Report—Country Chapters Hungary and Poland, available at https://commission.europa.eu/publications/2021-rule-law-report-communication-and-country-chapters_en; and N. Chronowski and M. Varju, 'Two Eras of Hungarian Constitutionalism: From the Rule of Law to Rule by Law' (2016) 8 *Hague Journal on the Rule of Law* 271, 278–80.

rule of law has also been weakened through steps to reduce the independence of the broader judiciary and to increase the influence of the executive and the legislature over the justice system, for example, through imposing political pressure on judges by the introduction of new regimes governing their appointment, dismissal or discipline (see further Section D.ii.c).[39]

Further, the working of the regulatory state has changed in both countries as a result, for example, of the politicization of the civil service, the erosion of the independence of core law enforcement agencies (including public prosecutors, public procurement supervision agencies, and competition agencies), and the limitation of media freedom.[40] Political influence and favouritism in the civil service in Hungary is growing,[41] the independence of institutions responsible for the prevention and fight against corruption in both Hungary and Poland has been weakened (e.g. through the subordination of the Central Anti-Corruption Bureau (CBA) in Poland to the executive and through the appointment of the Minister of Justice as the Prosecutor General[42]) and media pluralism has been limited, especially in Hungary.[43] The PiS government's attempts to deter political opponents (e.g. by seeking to block politicians for alleged pro-Russia activities) and to control the media in the run up to the October 2023 election also caused significant concern.[44]

b. Illiberal change in the economy in Hungary and Poland

The weakening of liberal democracy and the rule of law has occurred alongside processes leading to illiberal changes in the economy in both countries, signalling the concentration of both political, and economic, power by ruling governments.[45] This has occurred through a number of processes.

One method concerns the re-definition of the role of the state, through increasing the role of state-owned and state-controlled enterprises and halting

---

[39] 2021 Rule of Law Report—Hungary, n. 38. See also Z. Fleck, 'A Comparative Analysis of Judicial Power, Organisational Issues in Judicature and the Administration of Courts' in A. Bado (ed.), *Fair Trial and Judicial Independence Hungarian Perspectives* (Springer, 2014) 19–20, and Z. Fleck, 'Judges under Attack in Hungary', *Verfassungsblog on Matters Constitutional* (14 May 2018), available at https://verfassungsblog.de/judges-under-attack-in-hungary/.

[40] See, more in detail, Bernatt, n. 28, 34–8.

[41] European Commission, 2020 European Semester Report, available at https://commission.europa.eu/publications/2020-european-semester-country-reports_en.

[42] 2021 Rule of Law Report—Poland, n. 38, and see nn. 74–76 and text.

[43] 2021 Rule of Law Report—Hungary, n. 38.

[44] A proposed law, seeking to block allegedly pro-Russian politicians from public office (referred to as 'Lex Tusk'), led to significant public demonstrations and caused the EU to commence infringement proceedings against Poland for unduly interfering with the democratic process, see 'Brussels Takes Legal Action against Warsaw's "Lex Tusk"', *Financial Times* (8 June 2023). See also M. Bernatt, 'Market Power, Democracy and (Un)Fair Elections', *Verfassungsblog on Matters Constitutional* (16 October 2023). In December 2023, the new administration asserted control over state media, see 'Tusk take Polish state TV news channel off air', Financial Times (20 December 2023)

[45] Bernatt, n. 28, 42–3.

248 THE IMPACT OF EU MEMBERSHIP

privatization processes, characteristic of the liberalization period.[46] The result has been re-nationalization, i.e. the return of the state as an owner, including in the banking and public utilities sectors,[47] especially through acquisitions in Poland and new laws in Hungary (e.g. granting exclusive rights).[48] Another is economic patriotism,[49] a governmental agenda which considers economic policies as a platform for building national identity and pride through state support for, or outright favouritism of, national businesses.[50] Finally, legal safeguards against the abuse of state power vis-à-vis private firms have also been weakened perceptibly. This has resulted especially as a result of the weakening of constitutionality and judicial review discussed earlier.

ii. The impact on public procurement: increasing corruption and collusion risks

These illiberal developments collectively create risks of departure from fundamental principles of EU law and that public procurement contracts may be misallocated as a result or unchecked corruption or collusion. For example, that:

a. Derogations from application of normal public procurement procedures will be created and political appointees in the civil service and procurement agencies will divert contracts according to the political agenda rather than in strict accordance with public procurement laws;

b. National entities, SOEs, and crony companies (possibly operating in cartels) will be favoured (over other companies from other EU Member States or other non-favoured companies), in breach of EU public procurement, internal market and competition rules, and principles of non-discrimination, or national anti-corruption laws;

c. Weakened oversight of public procurement processes will result because public prosecutors, auditors, and competition agencies are less independent, and may be pressurized not to investigate cases where they suspect public procurement contracts may have been wrongly diverted to firms in breach

---

[46] P. Kozarzewski and M. Bałtowski, 'Return of State-Owned Enterprises in Poland' (2019), available at https://www.researchgate.net/publication/333480750_Return_of_State-owned_Enterprises_in _Poland.

[47] Bernatt, n. 28, 44–5.

[48] See, e.g., Act 2011:CXCVI, and Lendület-HPOPs Research Group, 'The Legal and Regulatory Environment for Economic Activity in Hungary: Market Access and Level Playing-Field in the Single Market' (2017) Hungarian Academy of Sciences, Centre for Social Sciences, Lendület-HPOPs Research Group, available at https://hpops.tk.mta.hu/uploads/files/HLEE_HPOPs_2017_final-1.pdf, 47–9.

[49] M. Papp and M. Varju, 'The Crisis, Economic Patriotism in Central Europe and EU Law' in L. Antoniolli, L. Bonatti, and C. Ruzza (eds), *Highs and Lows of European Integration: Sixty Years After the Treaty of Rome* (Springer, 2018) and Bernatt, n. 28, 48.

[50] See, e.g., Bernatt, n. 28, 49–50.

THE ILLIBERAL INFLUENCE OF POPULIST GOVERNMENTS   249

of the law. Scrutiny by rivals, third parties, and the media may also be reduced as a result of more limited access to information, media freedom,[51] or independent judicial review. As the rule of law is essential to ensure accountability and deterrence, these developments open the door for collusion, corruption, and breaches of public procurement laws to operate unchallenged.

Finally, it also possible that corruption risks in Hungary and Poland have been augmented as a result of the provision of increased EU funding (on top of national spending) for public procurement processes. Additional funding for public investment increases the pool of potential rents to earn and research indicates that grand corruption thrives on public resources, whose allocation can be influenced to benefit a small circle of businessmen and politicians.

In Hungary, a variety of sources, including EU Semester Country and Rule of Law[52] Reports confirm these concerns and record:

a. A decrease in the protected status, and protection from undue influence, of the civil service with the abolition of the career-based advancement system (creating a risk to public procurement control and the management of the national wealth of SOEs[53]);
b. Risks of clientelism, favouritism, and nepotism in high-level public administration, and risks arising from links between businesses and political actors;
c. A high percentage of public contracts awarded in procedures where there was just one bidder (around 40 per cent in 2018–2020 (one of the highest percentages in the EU));
d. Insufficient control mechanisms for detecting corruption and oversight of assets and interest declarations;
e. A poor track record for investigations of corruption allegations concerning high-level offices and their immediate circle. There thus 'still has not been enough determined action to prosecute corruption in high-level cases'[54] and is a 'perception of impunity among the business community';[55]
f. Limited enforcement of the antitrust laws, other than with regard to small cases, and a drop off in cases involving bid rigging in the construction sector,

---

[51] Independent journalists in particular can play an important role in the identification of wrongdoing, see further Chapters 3 and 4.

[52] The 'Rule of Law' reports examine developments across the Member States, both positive and negative, in four key areas for the rule of law: the justice system, the anti-corruption framework, media pluralism, and other institutional issues related to checks and balances. They involve an annual dialogue, involving the Commission, the Council, the European Parliament, Member States national parliaments, civil society, and other stakeholders, on the rule of law.

[53] See 2020 European Semester Report, n. 41 and text.

[54] 2020 European Semester Country Report—Hungary, n. 41, 42.

[55] 2020 European Semester Country Report—Hungary, n. 41, relying on European Commission, 'Flash Eurobarometer 482 – Businesses' Attitudes towards Corruption' (2019), dataset available at https://data.europa.eu/data/datasets/s2248_482_eng?locale=en.

despite increased EU funding for construction projects.[56] This has created suspicion that the competition authority is failing to investigate politically sensitive or controversial cases, such as the award of public tenders to Hungarian firms which have links with the ruling Fidesz government;[57]

g. Weakened independence of the judiciary, with the appointment and discipline of judges, now tightly controlled by the ruling party;

h. Restrictions on access to information,[58] which are hindering corruption prevention.

These concerns are supported by the Corruption Research Center (CRC) Budapest's research. For example, its analysis of Hungarian public procurement data from more than 250,000 contracts between 2005 and 2021[59] finds a high corruption risk and in particular: a high share of contracts awarded with a single bidder (without competition) (34.6 per cent in 2021), especially for Hungarian taxpayer-funded tenders (more than 40 per cent in 2021); that the share of public procurements won by 'crony companies' (companies of so-called 'Fidesz-affiliated' business owners with close relations with Viktor Orbán and his inner circle) within the total public procurement value has increased significantly since 2011, including in relation to EU-funded contracts;[60] and that during the COVID-19 pandemic, the share of non-competitive contracts from among all contracts won by crony companies increased from an already-high percentage. It also identifies higher corruption risks for EU funded, as compared to nationally funded, processes, arguably resulting from an increase in funds without sufficient counterbalancing corruption controls.[61] Thus, even though these transactions attract close scrutiny at the EU level, irregularities still seem to occur. Indeed, failures in public procurement have been exposed in Commission audits of public procurement in Hungary financed by

---

[56] Bernatt, n. 28, 127–9.

[57] Bernatt, n. 28, 127–9. See also, e.g., OECD, 'OECD Economic Surveys: Hungary 2021' (2021), available at https://doi.org/10.1787/1d39d866-en and 'Monitoring Public Contracting: Experiences from 18 Integrity Pacts in the EU', *Integrity Pacts – Civil Control Mechanism for Safeguarding EU Funds* (7 April 2022) 28, available at https://images.transparencycdn.org/images/IP_monitoring-public-contr acting_ENG_20220406.pdf (noting that the Hungarian competition authority decided not to investigate suspicions of bid rigging reported to it by Transparency International Hungary in relation to a public procurement for a Hungarian motorway construction).

[58] Dissuasive practices for accessing public information have been adopted, 2020 European Semester Report – Hungary, n. 41.

[59] See CRC Budapest, 'New Trends in Corruption Risks and Intensity of Competition in the Hungarian Public Procurement from January 2005 to April 2020', *Flash Report 2020:1* (26 May 2020), and I.J. Tóth, 'Two Tendencies in the Hungarian Public Procurement' (2022) *CRCB Research Notes 2022:2*, available at https://www.crcb.eu/wp-content/uploads/2022/02/2022_research_notes_01_22 0209_01.pdf.

[60] See also CRC Budapest, 'Corruption Risk and the Crony System in Hungary: A Brief Analysis of EU Funded Contracts in Hungarian Public Procurement 2005–2021' (2022) *CRCB Research Notes: 2022:3*, available at https://www.crcb.eu/wp-content/uploads/2022/03/2022_research_notes_0 3_220307_02.pdf.

[61] CRC Budapest, n. 59. See also M. Fazekas, L.P King, and I.J. Tóth, 'Hidden Depths. The Case of Hungary' (2013) ERCAS Working Paper 36.

EU funds, including through discriminatory or restrictive exclusion, selection or award criteria, and unequal treatment of bidders. For example: OLAF found significant irregularities (including collusion, conflicts of interest and conspiracy to commit budget fraud) in EU-funded contracts for public lighting projects won by Elios Innovatív Zrt, then co-owned and managed by Viktor Orbán's son-in-law;[62] in 2019, OLAF recommended the recovery of 3.93 per cent of payments made to Hungary (about EUR 1 billion financial corrections, roughly ten times the EU average);[63] and the 2020 Semester report noted that Hungary topped OLAF's list of countries where the agency made a financial recommendation to recover EU funds due in part to deficiencies observed in public procurement.[64] Despite OLAF's recommendations, however, the will of the Prosecutor General's Office in Hungary to prosecute high-level corruption seems to be lacking.

These developments have all contributed to 'a continuous decline in Hungary's performance on controlling corruption' and performance in worldwide corruption and perception indices.[65] The Corruption Risk Forecast reports a loss of procurement competitiveness and transparency, and weak conflict of interest regulation,[66] and Transparency International (TI) notes the descent of Hungary, once a forerunner among CEE countries, on its Corruption Perceptions Index (CPI), which was accelerated during the coronavirus pandemic. Hungary is now amongst the worst performers in Europe, with a CPI score of just 42 in 2022. Indeed, in the EU's 2021 Rule of Law Report, Hungary was urged to take further measures: to ensure regulatory predictability and increased competition in services, including in public procurement; to reinforce the anti-corruption framework, including by improving prosecutorial efforts and access to public information; and to strengthen judicial independence.[67]

---

[62] See 'Hungary Launches Fraud Probe into EU-Funded Projects', *Politico* (8 February 2018) (reporting that the Hungarian authorities dropped the procedure against Elios (concluding no crime had been committed) but declined to claim EU funds in respect of the contracts (the burden consequently fell on Hungarian taxpayers)).

[63] The OLAF Report 2019, available at https://ec.europa.eu/anti-fraud/sites/default/fi les/olaf_report_2019_en.pdf (the highest financial correction in the EU in the 2014–2020 period); see also K.L. Scheppele, R.D. Keleman, and J. Morijn, 'The EU Commission Has to Cut Funding to Hungary: The Legal Case' (2021) Greens/EFA Group in the European Parliament, available at https://www.greens-efa.eu/files/assets/docs/220707_rolcr_report_digital.pdf.

[64] Between 2016 and 2020, Hungary's financial recommendations in the areas of regional development and agriculture were 'almost eight times the EU average', Commission Letter to Hungary 20 November 2021, see also K.L. Scheppele, G. Mészáros, and P. Bárd, 'Hungary's Proposed Judicial Review of the Prosecutorial Decisions: Useless and Maybe Unconstitutional', *Vergassungsblog.de* (26 October 2022).

[65] 2020 European Semester Country Report – Hungary, n. 41.

[66] See Corruptionrisk.org, 'Hungary', available at https://corruptionrisk.org/country/?country=HUN#forecast.

[67] GRECO has also subjected Hungary to its non-compliance procedure and made recommendations for reform on key institutional and organizational aspects of the prosecution service which 'remain only partly implemented', Relying on Council of Europe, 'Group of States Against Corruption – Fourth Evaluation Round, Interim Compliance Report on Hungary' (2018) *GrecoRC4* 16.

252 THE IMPACT OF EU MEMBERSHIP

In relation to Poland, there has also been concern, prior to the formation of the new coalition government at the end of 2023, about the robustness of its procurement processes and the effectiveness of its fight against corruption and collusion, in particular around:

a. The PiS ruling majority bypassing public procurement laws when in its political interest;[68]

b. Non-compliance with relevant public procurement regulations, strategic contract value manipulation around EU public procurement thresholds, and significantly fewer bidders and higher rates of single bidding where contracts are manipulated.[69] 'These can be considered as tentative evidence for strategic bundling around the threshold being partly motivated by restricting competition for corrupt purposes ... while most certainly simply cutting regulatory costs without corrupt motives also plays a role';[70]

c. The high number of auctions with only a single bidder (in 2021, 40 per cent of public procurement cases below the EU threshold[71] and 34 per cent of auctions above it);[72]

d. Scandals suggesting an increase in corrupt behaviour by high-ranking officials;[73]

e. Weakened independence of the Financial Supervision Commission (following serious allegations against its head, Marek Chrzanowski),[74] the

---

[68] For example, in response to the migration crisis at the Polish-Belarussian border, the Government determined to construct a 187-kilometres long wall at the border and introduced a special law that exempted the process (worth EUR 350 million) from public procurement laws, see https://www.gov.pl/web/mswia-en/completion-of-the-physical-part-of-the-barrier-on-the-polish-belarusian-border---an-event-with-the-participation-of-the-leadership-of-the-ministry-of-the-interior-and-adminis tration.

[69] B. Tóth and M. Fazekas, 'Compliance and Strategic Contract Manipulation Around Single Market Regulatory Thresholds – The Case of Poland' (2017) GTI-WP/2017:01, available at https://www.govt ransparency.eu/compliance-and-strategic-contract-manipulation-around-single-market-regulatory-thresholds-the-case-of-poland/.

[70] Tóth and Fazekas, n. 69, 21.

[71] Tóth and Fazekas, n. 69, 33.

[72] Tóth and Fazekas, n. 69, 33.

[73] For example, the respiratory device procurement scandal, which related to the purchase of 1241 respiratory devices from a weapons dealer (only 200 of which arrived) by the Ministry of Health in April 2020 as part of the government's emergency response to the COVID-19 health crisis; see, e.g., A. Koper, 'Need a Ventilator? Polish Arms Dealer Has Plenty', *Reuters* (17 December 2020), available at https://www.reuters.com/article/health-coronavirus-poland-ventilators-in-idUSKBN28R0OI; Z. Wanat, 'Poland's Health Minister Resigns Amid Coronavirus Second Wave Fears' *Politico* (18 August 2020), available at https://www.politico.eu/article/polands-health-minister-resigns-amid-coronavirus-sec ond-wave-fears/; G. Makowski and M. Waszak, 'Polish Legislation during the Pandemic vs. Corruption Anti-Crisis Shields: Completing the Law and Justice State Project?' (2021) Stefan Batory Foundation, available at https://www.batory.org.pl/wp-content/uploads/2021/01/Tarcze_ENG.pdf.

[74] G. Makowski, 'Laying the Groundwork for "Grand Corruption": The Polish Government's (Anti-) Corruption Activities in 2015–2019' (2020) Stefan Batory Foundation, available at https://www.batory. org.pl/wp-content/uploads/2020/12/Laying-the-groundwork-for-Grand-Corruption_ENG.pdf, 24. See also M. Broniatowski, 'Banking Corruption Scandal Throws Polish Politics into Turmoil', *Politico* (13 November 2018), available at https://www.politico.eu/article/banking-corruption-scandal-throws-polish-politics-into-turmoil/.

Supreme Audit Office (the President of which, Marian Banaś, was appointed by the Parliament's ruling majority despite controversies relating to his financial affairs and property holdings which had been exposed by investigative journalists)[75] and the CBA (supervised, by Mariusz Kamiński, who was sentenced for abuse of power when previously in charge of it (between 2006 and 2009), before controversially being pardoned by President Andrzej Duda in 2015);[76]

f. The lack of effectiveness and impartiality of the prosecution service given that the Minister of Justice is the Prosecutor General. It has also been reported that Poland had refused to cooperate in European proceedings regarding abuses of spending EU money and cross-border VAT crimes[77] and that the overall number of investigations concerning the EU financial interest launched was low; only 33 per cent of cases delegated by the OLAF to Polish prosecutors over the years 2016–2020 resulted in criminal charges.[78] More broadly, there is a concern that a growing number of allegations of corruption, approximately 89,359 between 2014 and 2017, has only resulted in a low, flat level of final convictions over the same period (approximately 9,450);[79]

g. Limited scrutiny by the Office of Competition and Consumer Protection (UOKiK) of the big investment projects financed from EU funds (most bid rigging investigations have focused on local markets).[80] In 2020, however, the UOKiK Warsaw central office created a bid rigging sub-unit and UOKiK reports for 2020 and 2021 suggest increased activity. Particularly notable is the wooden railway sleepers decision (decision DOK-2/2020), in which the fine of nearly PLN 13.5 million (around EUR 2.8 million) was imposed on six manufacturers involved;

h. The lack of independence of judges, creating concerns about the effectiveness and impartiality of judicial proceedings on cases related to the irregularities in procurement processes;

---

[75] Makowski, n. 74, 25.

[76] K. Sobczak, 'SN: prezydent nie mógł ułaskawić b. szefów CBA', *Prawo.pl* (31 May 2017), available at https://www.prawo.pl/prawnicy-sady/sn-prezydent-nie-mogl-ulaskawic-b-szefow-cba,70752.html.

[77] T. Wahl, 'European Chief Prosecutor: Poland Systematically Refuses Cooperation with EPPO', *EUCRIM* (6 April 2022), available at https://eucrim.eu/news/european-chief-prosecutor-poland-systematically-refuses-cooperation-with-eppo/. Poland justifies its unwillingness to cooperate by its lack of a legal basis in the criminal procedure code to do so, see, e.g., M. Pankowska, 'Ziobro ma kontrolować kontakty polskich śledczych z Prokuraturą Europejską. Zapłacimy za to w euro?', *Oko Press* (30 June 2022), available at https://oko.press/ziobro-ma-kontrolowac-kontakty-polskich-sledczych-z-prokuratura-europejska-zaplacimy-za-to-w-euro/.

[78] A. Łukaszewicz, 'Prokuratorzy mało skuteczni w sprawach unijnych nadużyć', *Prawo* (18 August 2022), available at https://www.rp.pl/zawody-prawnicze/art36890611-prokuratorzy-malo-skuteczni-w-sprawach-unijnych-naduzy.

[79] Makowski, n. 74, 17.

[80] Bernatt, n. 28, 131. For example, in 2021 the UOKiK issued a decision concerning bid rigging scheme of five firms related to a tender for keeping the town of Tychy clean in the years 2015–2018 (decision RKT-5/2021).

i. The reduction in the overall transparency of the activity of public administration.[81]

These developments have impacted on Poland's performance in perception indices. TI records Poland's declining performance in its CPI since 2015,[82] laying responsibility for this change on: the politicization of the Constitutional Tribunal and the drastic reduction in the independence of the common judiciary; the changes to the appointment of government officials in the public administration (and the demotion and driving out of those appointed prior to 2016); and the takeover of public service media. 'The systematic breach of the rule of law ... is directly linked to corruption, as it invariably leads to monopoly of power, opacity in public decisions and the impunity of politicians and officials.'[83] Further, in 2023 Corruption Risk Forecast[84] commented on a notable regression in Poland, formerly one of the most successful post-Community countries in creating a governance based on public integrity, and a policy of reducing corruption through privatization and administrative simplification. It records a deterioration of press freedom and judicial independence, and the growth of non-competitive procurement and a return to politicization and government favouritism practices (perhaps exacerbated by an abundance of EU funds).

D. Mechanisms for Reform

i. Initiatives at the national level

The developments described in Section C paint a concerning picture for the integrity of public procurement processes in Hungary and Poland. To reverse the growing corruption and collusion risks in public procurement in these countries, a broad range of measures, tailored to the specific problems arising in each country, is required to further efforts both to prevent opportunities for corruption and collusion arising and to increase the deterrent effect of the laws. These are likely to include (as a minimum starting point):

- Reintroducing a professional, politically neutral, and independent, civil service and procurement workforce which has the capability and capacity to

---

[81] See, e.g., P. Bogdanowicz and P. Buras, ' "Wielka korupcja" za unijne pieniądze? Jak ograniczyć ryzyko dla Polski i UE', Fundacja im. Stefana Batorego (9 July 2021) 9–10.

[82] G. Makowski, 'Corruption Thrives as Rule of Law and Democratic Oversight Weaken in Poland', *Transparency International Blog* (4 February 2021).

[83] Makowski, n. 74.

[84] Corruptionrisk.org, 'Poland', available at https://corruptionrisk.org/country/?country=POL#forecast.

carry out their functions and which complies with to ethical codes of conduct and rules governing conflicts of interest and is well-trained in competition law;

- Ensuring full compliance with EU Public Procurement Directives and principles (and reversing unjustified exemptions from them), especially through rigorous monitoring and auditing of the processes by independent bodies, and ensuring real opportunities for challenge and effective review in cases of breach;
- Taking measures to weaken ties between procurers, politicians, and businesses, where concerns about cronyism and favouritism are rife;
- Addressing any sense of impunity felt by the leading players involved especially through carefully targeted and apolitical law enforcement and justice sector reform. This requires immunities from prosecution to be appropriately confined, the independence of the public prosecutors, competition agencies and the judiciary to be restored so ensuring that decisions on enforcement of anti-corruption and competition laws are taken free from undue political influence and impartial adjudication on anti-corruption and antitrust cases. Freedom of access to information, a free media and active non-governmental or civil society groups will also help to root out corrupt and anti-competitive practices;
- Ensuring policy coordination between procuring, anti-corruption and competition agencies.

The steps required to achieve these changes are, however, dependent upon political will and a conscious decision to reverse some of the illiberal developments that have occurred. Despite considerable domestic, EU, and international pressure for reform, that will has largely been lacking, although the result of the October 2023 Polish election has provided the opportunity for a change of course in Poland and steps to reverse these trends. An important question, nonetheless, is whether EU law can play a role in encouraging and driving change at the national level.

ii. Compliance with EU law

a. Backsliding and breaches of EU law
As well as creating opportunities for public procurement processes in Hungary and Poland to be undermined by corrupt or collusive practices, the backsliding described in Section C has the potential to lead Hungary and Poland to commit infringements of EU law. First, the illiberal changes to the economy, and the process of favouring or protecting national champions or crony companies in procurement processes, could lead to violations of fundamental principles of the Treaty and EU public procurement and competition rules, including where the State's public

256 THE IMPACT OF EU MEMBERSHIP

procurement processes fail to comply with core EU principles of transparency, non-discrimination, and open competition.

Secondly, the illiberal changes resulting in the dismantling of checks and balances within the national systems—especially through interfering with the independence of the civil service, law enforcement agencies, and the judiciary—also mean that compliance with EU public procurement and competition laws cannot be ensured, that the disbursement of EU funds is not sufficiently protected from fraud or corrupt practices, and that EU values are not adhered to. Indeed, in a body of case-law,[85] the Court of Justice of the European Union (CJEU) has stressed the centrality of the rule of law to the Union and the fundamental values on which it is founded (Article 2 TEU).[86] These cases hold that effective judicial protection, under the control of independent and impartial courts at the EU and national level, is essential to ensure rule of law in the EU legal order (see Article 19(1) TEU).[87] The rule of law has thus been held to be an enforceable principle of EU law which requires national judicial systems to adhere to standards sufficient to enable them to meet their EU obligations. Member States cannot, therefore, undermine the independence of their judiciary, for example, through the adoption of retirement, disciplinary, or other rules, designed to dismiss, pressure, or intimidate judges or affect the content of their judicial decisions, or through national appointment procedures. Nor can they undermine the independence of their law enforcement, regulatory, and supervision agencies, such as prosecutors, competition authorities, and public procurement supervision agencies.[88]

The important question that follows is what can be done to prevent and deter such breaches of EU law and to encourage compliance with them. The Commission, under the control of the CJEU, is entrusted with responsibility for promoting the general interest of the Union (it is guardian of the Treaties),[89] and responding to non-compliance with EU law, and the TFEU provides for various resolution and enforcement mechanisms by the Commission, Member States, and private parties.[90] Although the Commission and other EU institutions have been criticized by some for dragging their feet and responding too slowly to serious violations, especially Hungary's and Poland's backsliding on the rule of law,[91] the sections below

[85] See, especially, Case C-64/16, *ASJP (Portuguese Judges)* EU:C:2018:117 and Cases 585, 624, and 625/18, *A.K.* and Cases C-558 and 563/18, *Miasto Lowicz and Prokurator Generalny*, EU:C:2020:234.

[86] See European Commission Press Release IP/21/1770, 'Rule of Law: Commission Launches Infringement Procedure against Poland for Violations of EU Law by its Constitutional Tribunal', (22 December 2021), available at https://ec.europa.eu/commission/presscorner/detail/e%20n/ip_21_7070.

[87] See generally, e.g., P. Craig and G. de Burca, *EU Law: Text, Cases, and Materials* (Oxford University Press, 2019), Chapters 2 and 13.

[88] M. Bernatt, 'The Double Helix of Rule of Law and EU Competition Law: An Appraisal' (2022) 27 *European Law Journal* 1, 4. See, especially, Case T-791/19, *Sped-Pro S.A. v Commission*, EU:T:2022:67.

[89] TEU, Article 17.

[90] See, e.g., Articles 258–260 TFEU and through enforcement of directly effective EU law at the national level.

[91] See, e.g., P. Bárd and D.V. Kochenov, 'War as a Pretext to Wave the Rule of Law Goodbye? The Case for an EU Constitutional Awakening' (2021) 27 *European Law Journal* 39.

MECHANISMS FOR REFORM   257

discuss the variety of legal, political, and financial tools that are available to prevent, halt, and deter infringements; how they can be used more effectively in the future; and whether new mechanisms should be considered.[92]

b. Acting against individual cases of suspected corruption and bid rigging

Although enforcement of criminal anti-corruption laws is a matter for national law, for some time the EU has had in place a range of measures designed to protect EU funds and the EU budget[93] from fraud and corruption, through both preventative techniques and mechanisms to detect and correct infringements. It thus seeks to prevent improper use of funds, for example, through the application of strict rules on conflicts of interest (national authorities involved in budget implementation, audit, or control must not take any action which may bring their own interests into conflict with those of the Union and must take measures to prevent a conflict of interests from arising in the functions under their responsibility),[94] and by interrupting or suspending payments of EU funds where problems are detected but are unresolved (see further Section D).

OLAF,[95] and, since 2021, the EPPO are also able to conduct administrative investigations into fraud against the budget which has affected the spending of structural funds, at the Member State (as well as the Union)[96] level.[97] Although OLAF does not have power to prosecute fraud it discovers, and neither Hungary nor Poland participates in the EPPO,[98] OLAF can make recommendations to EU institutions and relevant authorities in the Member States, for example, that EU funds should be recovered or that potentially criminal conduct should be investigated. The Commission can thus work to recover all or some of the affected EU funds from the Member State and encourage appropriate actions by the relevant Member State authorities. However, if those national authorities fail to investigate and prosecute

[92] See also, e.g., Communication from the Commission to the European Parliament, the Council, the European Economic and Social Committee, and the Committee of the Regions, 'Enforcing EU law for a Europe that delivers', COM(2022) 518 final.

[93] See, e.g., nn. 17 and 20 and text, and discussion of the Recovery and Resilience Funding and the Conditionality Regulation, in Section D.

[94] These rules are provided for in the Financial Regulations, n. 4, Article 61. See also 'Guidance on the avoidance and management of conflicts of interest under the Financial Regulation' [2021] OJ C121/ 1 emphasizing the complementarity with the Regulation on a general regime of conditionality for the protection of the EU budget under which the failing of public authorities to ensure the absence of conflicts of interest may be indicative of breaches of the principles of the rule of law, as well as with effective monitoring of the implementation of Recovery and Resilience Plans, and further compliance efforts in respect of the implementation of the EU budget under direct, indirect, and shared management, available at https://ec.europa.eu/info/strategy/eu-budget/protection-eu-budget/conflict-interest_en.

[95] Established in 1999, available at https://anti-fraud.ec.europa.eu/index_en.

[96] Good administration and transparency are also reviewed by the European Court of Auditors and the European Ombudsman.

[97] It also tries to protect its external financial assistance from corruption and to benefit development in the recipient state.

[98] This accords with the notion that populist governments seek to avoid checks on the way they exercise power, see Section C; see also Scheppele, Mészáros, and Bárd, n. 64 (noting that 71 per cent of Hungarians want the country to join).

the misuse of public funds,[99] the EU cannot take over; it is for the national authorities to decide whether to act on the recommendation.[100] The Commission does nonetheless operate an Early Detection and Exclusion System,[101] allowing it to impose a penalty on persons representing a risk to the Union's financial interest (including those engaged in fraud or corruption) and to exclude them from processes involving the implementation of EU funds.

In the competition sphere, in contrast, the Commission is able to investigate suspected cases of bid rigging in Hungary and Poland affecting public procurement processes and to sanction undertakings found to be in breach of Article 101.[102] Indeed, in *Sped-Pro*,[103] the GC made it clear that it may be obliged to investigate complaints relating to such practices, if there is a risk that they may not be impartially investigated by authorities at the national level. The Commission has a range of proactive and reactive detection tools to help it discover infringements and could seek to use public tender data available in Hungary and Poland—via TED[104]—to screen for red flags, suspicious bidding patterns that may warrant further investigation. It may also seek to use screens in the anti-corruption context,[105] to check for signs of possible misuse of EU funds (see further Section E).

These approaches are important but case specific, and corrections (or recommendations of corrections) in single cases do not deal with systemic or structural problems occurring in Hungary and Poland.

c. Procedures against Member States for infringement of EU law and values

The general Treaty mechanism empowering the Commission to bring proceedings against infringing Member States and to seek States' compliance with—and uniform observance of—EU law is set out in Article 258 TFEU.[106] The Commission

---

[99] As may be feared in Hungary and Poland, see Section C.ii above.

[100] Spencer, n. 16 ('The tendency of national prosecutors to ignore reports which OLAF believes to be well founded is, of course, a source of deep frustration within OLAF').

[101] European Commission, 'Early Detection and Exclusion System (EDES)', available at https://ec.eur opa.eu/info/strategy/eu-budget/how-it-works/annual-lifecycle/implementation/anti-fraud-measures/ edes_en.

[102] On 14 June 2022, the Commission confirmed that it was conducting inspections into suspected bid rigging in tenders involving EU funds for the construction of networks and treatment plants for drinking water and wastewater, see European Commission Press Release IP 22/ 3706, 'Antitrust: Commission Carries Out Unannounced Inspections in the Water Infrastructure Sector Over Alleged Bid-Rigging', available at https://ec.europa.eu/commission/presscorner/detail/en/ip_22_3706.

[103] See Case T-791/19, *Sped-Pro S.A. v Commission*, EU:T:2022:67.

[104] See n. 7 and text.

[105] See, e.g., I. Adam and M. Fazekas, 'Big Data Analytics as a Tool for Auditors to Identify and Prevent Fraud and Corruption in Public Procurement' (2019) 2 *ECA Journal* 172, available at https://www. govtransparency.eu/wp-content/uploads/2019/05/ECA-JOURNAL19_02.pdf; European Parliament, 'Proceedings of the Workshop on Use of Big Data and AI in Fighting Corruption and Misuse of Public Funds – Good Practice, Ways Forward and How to Integrate New Technology into Contemporary Control Framework' (2021).

[106] Broadly, this Article allows the Commission to bring Member States which fail to fulfil their Treaty obligations—or those imposed by secondary legislation, or the general principles of law—before the CJEU, following (i) the issue of a letter of formal notice, setting out the subject matter of the dispute,

MECHANISMS FOR REFORM   259

makes it clear that it will act firmly against infringements obstructing important EU policy objectives, such as the internal market[107] and the four fundamental freedoms, and it has brought some proceedings in relation to breaches of public procurement laws by Member States, for example, for non-communication of the transposition of, or non-conformity of legislation with, certain directives.[108]

More difficult, however, has been to know what to do when Member States do not adhere to EU values (inherent in, and necessary to qualify for, EU membership). Initially the EU used Reports, such as EU Semester Reports (a tool for economic policy recommendations) and more specific Rule of Law Reports,[109] as a means to identify rule of law weaknesses and to make specific recommendations for reform. When these recommendations are not followed, one response has been for the Commission to use Article 258 to bring proceedings for breach of Article 19(1) TEU, in conjunction with Article 47 of the EU Charter on Fundamental Rights (the right to an effective remedy and a fair trial). This procedure has now been used on several occasions in relation to infringements that reveal systemic weaknesses which undermine the functioning of the EU's institutional framework,[110] including in a series of proceedings against Poland.[111] In particular, in three judgments given between 2019 and 2021, the CJEU held, rejecting Poland's claims that the Court lacked jurisdiction to review reforms to national justice systems, that certain Polish rules governing retirement rules and disciplinary procedures for Polish judges violated the rule-of-law principle.[112] The CJEU, although recognizing the competence of Member States to organize justice and adopt their own constitutional model in their jurisdictions, held that when exercising that competence states had to comply with their EU law obligations, including the ability to provide effective judicial protection and the right to a fair trial. This requires courts to be 'independent', in particular in relation to the legislature and the executive, as a guarantee that EU rights will be protected and that EU values safeguarded.[113] Consequently, rules incompatible with the

and giving the Member State in question a reasonable time to respond, and if not resolved, (ii) a reasoned opinion, describing the infringement and giving the Member State a reasonable time to comply.

[107] See Communication from the Commission, n. 92, 3.

[108] See, e.g., INFR(2019)0140, INFR(2018)2310 (see further https://ec.europa.eu/commission/pres scorner/detail/EN/INF_22_1769) and INFR(2018)2276).

[109] See, n. 52.

[110] Commission Communication, 'Better Results through Better Application' [2017] OJ C18/02.

[111] See also, e.g., Case C–288/12, *Commission v Hungary*, EU:C:2014:237 and Case C–286/12, *Commission v Hungary*, EU:2012:687 (compulsory retirement of judges).

[112] See, e.g., Case C-619/18, *Commission v Poland (Independence of Supreme Court)*, EU:C:2019:531, interim order Case C-619/18 R, EU:C:2018:1021, Commission infringement procedure, INFR(2017)2121 (involving a challenge to Polish law affecting the terms of working, and retroactively lowering the retirement age, for Supreme Court judges and vesting wide, discretionary powers in the President).

[113] Cases C-357 etc/19, *Criminal Proceedings Against PM and Others*, EU:C:2021:1034, paras 222–8. The concept of independence has an external and internal aspect to it. The former requires the court to

260 THE IMPACT OF EU MEMBERSHIP

principles of irremovability of judges and of judicial independence breach EU law.[114]

In addition to these Court proceedings, the Commission's Rule of Law Framework has been used to raise concerns about systemic threats and to issue Rule of Law Opinions and, Article 7 TEU (which provides for suspension of Treaty rights for Member States that breach Article 2 TEU values[115]) has been invoked against both Hungary and Poland.[116]

The use of these tools against Hungary and Poland, however, had limited practical impact[117] and did not deter the general trend of constitutional and economic regression. Both Article 258 and Article 7 appear therefore to lack sufficient teeth; Article 258 because it relies principally on dialogue, cooperation, and naming and shaming to resolve infractions;[118] and Article 7 because its inherent difficulties make it difficult to use. Not only does the ultimate sanction, suspension of EU rights, make it problematic, but a finding of a 'persistent and serious' breach of

---

exercise its functions wholly autonomously and protected from external interventions. The latter requires judges to be impartial, objective, and without any interest in the outcome of the proceeding, Case C-610/18, *Commission v Poland (Independence of Supreme Court)* EU:C:2019:531, para. 224.

[114] Case C-791/19, *Commission v Poland*, EU:C:2021:596, see interim order EU:C:2020:277 and INFR(2019)2076. See also Case C-204/21, judgment pending and Cases C-357 etc/19, *Criminal Proceedings Against PM and Others*, para. 227. Other proceedings against Poland are still ongoing, for example, in relation to: the independence of the judiciary and Constitutional Tribunal (Case C-204/21, *Commission v Poland* (judgment pending, interim order EU:C:2021:593) and European Commission, n. 86); the independence of the national regulatory authority (NRA), the Office of Electronic Communications (European Commission Press release IP/ 21/ 4611, 'Commission refers Poland to the Court of Justice of the European Union for undermining the independence of the national telecommunications regulator', *Press release IP/21/4611* (23 September 2021), available at https://ec.eur opa.eu/commission/presscorner/detail/en/ip_21_4611); and (along with a number of other Member States (Germany, Italy, Netherlands, and Portugal)) Poland's failure to apply EU rules on public procurement in defence and security markets, European Commission Press Release IP/ 18/ 357, 'Defence Procurement: Commission Opens Infringement Procedures Against 5 Member State', (25 January 2018), available at https://ec.europa.eu/commission/presscorner/detail/en/IP_18_357. In 2021, the Commission also referred Poland to the CJEU as it considered that Polish legislation exempting two categories of contracts from the application of public procurement laws and competitive tender requirements failed to comply with the Public Procurement directives, Case C-601/21, *Commission v Poland* EU:C:2023:61.

[115] TEU, Article 7(1) sets out a procedure to declare the existence of a clear risk of serious breach of Article 2 values. Article 7(2) provides a procedure to state the existence of a serious and persistent breach of those values and a sanctioning mechanism for established serious and persistent breaches is set out in Article 7(3).

[116] On 20 December 2017; see European Commission, Reasoned Proposal in Accordance with Article 7(1) of the TEU Regarding the Rule of Law in Poland—Proposal for a Council Decision on the Determination of a Clear Risk of a Serious Breach by the Republic of Poland of the Rule of Law, [2017] COM(2017) 835 final and European Parliament resolution of 12 September 2018 on a proposal calling on the Council to determine, pursuant to Article 7(1) of the TEU, the existence of a clear risk of a serious breach by Hungary of the values on which the Union is founded (2017/2131 (INL)).

[117] For an in-depth study, see K.L. Scheppele, D.V. Kochenov, and B. Grabowska-Moroz, 'EU Values Are Law, after All: Enforcing EU Values through Systemic Infringement Actions by the European Commission and the Member States of the European Union' (2020) 39 *Yearbook of European Law* 3–121, but see also discussion in Section D.ii.d.

[118] For the view that these dialogues and compromises do not work with regimes that are not constitutional democracies, see Bárd and Kochenov, n. 91, 49.

MECHANISMS FOR REFORM   261

Article 2 TEU values must be found by the Council acting unanimously, except for the Member State against which suspension is being sought (Article 7(2)), so allowing Hungary to veto its use against Poland, and vice versa.[119]

This raises the question of what other options might be available to secure compliance with EU law. For example, whether (i) as with 'individuals' and 'corporations', Member States require incentivization through ensuring that the costs of breaching the rules are more significant[120] and if so, whether EU law can provide them; or (ii) more proactive steps can be taken to prevent violations of public procurement, anti-corruption and competition laws and to encourage compliance with the rules through working more closely with national procurement agencies and civil society groups and ensuring more active monitoring of processes.

d. Enforcement, penalties, and financial mechanisms

The focus of the EU institutions is now shifting to the use of financial mechanisms—either through the imposition of penalties or the withholding of EU funds—to encourage compliance.

Although no financial penalties[121] can be imposed directly in Article 258 proceedings, they can follow from them in two ways. First, where an interim order, sought in conjunction with Article 258 proceedings, to suspend application of the contested act[122] is breached—daily penalty payments can be imposed.[123] Such interim measures have been sought and granted in some of the Polish rule-of-law cases pending their resolution,[124] and in one case,[125] the CJEU imposed a EUR 1 million daily penalty on Poland until the time it complied with the interim order (or the proceedings were closed).[126]

Fines may also be imposed under Article 260 TFEU, where the Court finds, following proceedings by the Commission (and after giving the State the opportunity

---

[119] Although a finding of a risk of infringement can be found by the Council acting by a four-fifths majority (Article 7(1)).

[120] See, e.g., G.S. Becker, 'Crime and Punishment: An Economic Approach' (1968) 76 *Journal of Political Economy* 169 and W. Landes, 'Optimal Sanctions for Antitrust Violations' (1983) 50(2) *University of Chicago Law Review* 652.

[121] See, e.g., Case C-70/06, *Commission v Portuguese Republic*, EU:C:2008:3.

[122] TFEU, Articles 278 and 279.

[123] See Case C-441/17R, *Commission v Poland (Bialowieza forest)*, EU:C:2017:877 and Case C-121/21, *Czech Republic v Poland*, EU:CL:2021:752 and discusion in Chapters 3 and 4.

[124] See Case C-204/21 R, *Commission v Poland*, EU:C:2021:593 (concerning the legality of legislative acts governing the function of the justice system in Poland, see also European Commission Press Release IP/ 21/ 1524, 'Rule of Law: European Commission Refers Poland to the European Court of Justice to Protect Independence of Polish Judges and Asks for Interim Measures', (31 March 2021), available at https://ec.europa.eu/commission/presscorner/detail/CS/IP_21_1524, and INFR(2020)2182).

[125] Case C-204/21, *Commission v Poland*, EU:C:2021:878 (for breaching interim order Case C-204/21R, n. 124).

[126] By October 2022 these fines amounted to over EUR 325 million, see 'EU Withholding Billions in Cohesion Funds from Poland Over Rule-of-Law Concerns', *Notes from Poland* (17 October 2022), available at https://notesfrompoland.com/2022/10/17/eu-withholding-billions-in-cohesion-funds-from-poland-over-rule-of-law-concerns/.

to submit observations), that a Member State has not complied with a judgment finding it to have failed to fulfil its obligations.[127] In 2021, the Commission started formal procedures under Article 260(2) for the imposition of a penalty on Poland in relation to its failure to comply with an Article 258 ruling.[128] This emphasizes the importance of the Commission continuing to bring enforcement actions under Article 258—not only relating to the rule of law but in relation to specific and repeated infringements of the public procurement directives. Although it has been seen that Article 258 proceedings themselves lack teeth, their effectiveness can be bolstered by combining them with proceedings for interim orders and following them up with Article 260 proceedings in case of failure to comply.

At the same time the EU institutions are becoming more willing to take steps to protect the Union's financial interest. For example, the Recovery and Resilience Facility (RRF)[129] provides built in *ex ante* controls to ensure that Member States come up with investment plans which will support the funds' goals and effectively address challenges identified in the European Semester and Country Specific Recommendations prior to their approval by the Council. Thus, although in June 2022 the Commission proposed that the Council should adopt an implementing decision approving Poland's plan, and disbursement of EUR 35.5 billion in grants and loans under the RRF, no disbursements can actually be made until Poland fulfils prearranged milestones, especially through improving the investment climate, and improving audit and control measures both by strengthening the independence of the judiciary and adopting Arachne,[130] a data-mining IT tool that supports Member States in their anti-fraud activities.[131] The Commission has still not approved Hungary's RRF plan and request for EUR 7.2 billion in grants, because of rule-of-law concerns.[132] These steps have been marked by controversy, however. Some believe that the Commission should never have approved Poland's plan, whilst Poland has threatened legal action, and both Poland and Hungary have threatened the veto of EU initiatives, if the funds are not released.[133]

---

[127] Or where it has failed to fulfil its obligation of notifying measures transposing a directive.

[128] European Commission Press Release IP/ 21/ 4587, 'Independence of Polish Judges: Commission Asks European Court of Justice for Financial Penalties against Poland on the Activity of the Disciplinary Chamber', (7 September 2021), available at https://ec.europa.eu/commission/presscorner/detail/en/IP_21_4587.

[129] Part of the EU response to the COVID-19 crisis, and designed to address common challenges.

[130] Developed by the Commission and rolled out from 2014, Arachne enables Member States to collect data on final recipients of funds, contractors, subcontractors, and beneficial owners and make this available upon request.

[131] The Commission also, reportedly, considered freezing cohesion funds to Poland (regional aid worth EUR 76.5 billion between 2021 and 2027) until rule of law concerns are addressed, see 'Rule of Law Stand-Off Threatens New EU Funding to Poland', *Financial Times* (16 October 2022).

[132] See, e.g., 'Hungary Accelerates Talks with EU to Unlock Billions in Funding', *Financial Times* (23 May 2023) and 'Hungary Makes Changes to Judiciary to Comply with EU Demands', *Financial Times* (4 May 2023).

[133] See, e.g., 'Hungary Blocks €18 bn Worth of EU Aid for Ukraine', *Financial Times* (7 December 2022); 'Brussels to Unfreeze Hungary Funds as it Seeks Help for Ukraine', *Financial Times* (3 October 2023); and 'EU's Battle to Maintain Support for Ukraine', *Brussels Playbook from Politico* (4 October 2023).

Crucially, the 2020 Conditionality Regulation is specifically designed to protect the EU budget from rule-of-law deficiencies in Member States.[134] Broadly it allows the Council, acting on a qualified majority on the initiation of the Commission, to take proportionate measures, including suspension of payments or specific programmes under the Union budget, where (i) breaches of the principles of the rule of law (ii) which concern conduct of relevant public authorities or attributable to such authorities, (iii) affect, or seriously risk affecting, the sound financial management of the Union budget, or the protection of the financial interests of the Union in a sufficiently direct way.[135]

Although no decisions have yet been adopted under the Regulation, the CJEU has upheld its validity[136] and these judgments, together with Commission guidance, suggest that it will be a possible tool to guard against corruption and collusion risks impacting on EU-funded public procurement. It has been seen that a number of the illiberal changes described in Section C constitute breaches of the principles of the rule of law.[137] Further, it appears that these developments seriously risk affecting the sound financial management of the Union budget in a sufficiently direct way (creating a real risk of public procurement contracts financed by EU funds being awarded in breach of EU procurement law at inflated prices to SOEs, crony or favoured companies, or members of a cartel, and that such wrongdoings or irregularities will not be detected, investigated, or sanctioned).[138] Indeed, on 19 November 2021, the Commission took a first, informal step towards a possible trigger of the Regulation against both Hungary and Poland—the sending of letters requesting information on possible rule of law breaking, especially the independence of courts and prosecution services, and their implications for the protection of EU money.[139] Further, on 27 April 2022, the Commission actually triggered the start of formal processes under the Regulation against Hungary,[140] reiterating its concerns about what is happening with EU funds in Hungary as a result, in particular, of irregularities, deficiencies, and weaknesses in public procurement procedures, the high percentage of single-bidder-awarded contracts, the funnelling of contracts to specific companies, limitations in effective auditing and monitoring

---

[134] Commission Guidelines on the application of Regulation (EU, EURATOM) 2020/2092 on a general regime of conditionality for the protection of the Union budget C(2022) 1382 final (Guidelines), para. 16 relying on Case C-156/21, *Hungary v Parliament and Council*, EU:C:2022:97, para. 131 and Case C-157/21, *Poland v Parliament and Council*, EU:C:2022:98, para. 149.

[135] Regulation 2020/2092, Articles 3–6, and see Guidelines, n. 134 and Cases C-156/21 and C-157/21, n. 134.

[136] Cases C-156/21 and C-157/21, n. 134.

[137] See Section 4.ii.a and see Case C-156/21, n. 134.

[138] Guidelines, n. 134, para. 31.

[139] See 'European Commission Presses Poland and Hungary on Rule of Law', *Financial Times* (20 November 2021).

[140] The reasons for launching formal proceedings against Hungary, but not yet Poland, are not clear. Explanations could be: the slightly less evident link between backsliding and EU funds in Poland; that it is less clear whether particularism is being promoted as a social norm in Poland; and that Poland engaged earlier in dialogue with the Commission on rule-of-law reforms in the context of its RRF Plan.

264   THE IMPACT OF EU MEMBERSHIP

of processes, and investigation and prosecution of criminal activity (including a lack of an anti-corruption strategy). Although Hungary is taking a number of steps to demonstrate that it can properly handle EU funds, including by setting up an Integrity Authority and Anti-Corruption Task Force, allowing the general public to challenge decisions of Hungarian public prosecutors to drop corruption cases,[141] and proposing judicial reforms,[142] concerns still remain about the strength and likely effectiveness of these measures.

e. Proposals for more proactive steps to prevent breaches: increased
   oversight of public procurement processes and cooperation mechanisms

An additional important issue is whether more can be done at the EU level to ensure greater supervision and oversight of public procurement processes carried out in Member States using EU funds.[143] Such steps, taken in conjunction with national authorities and civil society, could help to anticipate and avoid infringements, to prevent the misuse of EU funds, and to bolster a core aim of the public procurement directives—to protect the integrity of the processes and to minimize opportunities for them to be undermined by either corruption or collusion.

One possibility could be the creation of a body—made up of the Commission and the national procurement agencies of the Member States tasked with overseeing government contracting and publishing contracting information—to foster discussion, cooperation, and exchange of information in public procurement matters, especially those involving EU funds.[144] This would provide a mechanism for agencies and EU authorities to discuss best practices, mechanisms for combatting corruption and collusion, challenges in preventing them, and for authorities to support each another. It could also provide a forum for discussion of how Member States are ensuring compliance with particular EU rules, for example on conflicts of interest which apply when conducting procurement processes involving EU funds,[145] and how to react rapidly where those rules are not being complied with.

The Commission could also intensify its proactive integrity reviews with the aim of identifying fraud and corruption risks sooner, and detecting prohibited conduct which might otherwise remain undetected through the usual monitoring processes. For example, the Prevention and Detection Unit of the European Investment Bank (EIB), the lending arm of the EU, uses innovative technologies and big data analytics to identify Fraud and Integrity Risks (the Fraud and Integrity Risk Scoring Tool) in real time and to assess the risk of corruption and irregularities

---

[141] See Scheppele, Mészáros, and Bárd, n. 64.

[142] See 'Hungary Vows to Overhaul its Judiciary, Hoping to Unlock EU Funds', *Politico* (7 November 2022).

[143] See Communication from the Commission, n. 92.

[144] In the competition sphere, for example, the Commission and national competition authorities of the Member States cooperate through the European Competition Network (ECN).

[145] See n. 94 and text.

(through the development of a Corruption Risk in Procurement (CRIP) Robot, using data from the EU TED) to identify fraud and as part of its standard monitoring processes in EIB-financed projects.[146] These allow it to monitor and complete on-site review of selected projects and help to ensure that its funds are used for their intended purpose. These processes may also identify gaps in weaknesses in processes and procedures, and shape recommendations for improvements to policies, procedures, and controls to reduce opportunities for prohibited conduct in the future.

Where significant corruption risks are identified in relation to an EU-funded procurement project, an obligation to use an 'Integrity Pact'[147] could be imposed. The Commission, in collaboration with TI, has been piloting, with positive results,[148] the use of such pacts in several Member States,[149] including during a public contracting procedure for the construction of a highway in Hungary.

Another important step could be to develop a more transparent and quicker sanctions system to prevent corrupt actors from participating in future public procurement processes involving EU funds, in line with those used by multilateral development banks (MDBs) and the EIB. Although the power exists in the EU to exclude persons representing a risk to its financial interest through its Early Detection and Exclusion System, it is unclear how frequently or effectively this system is used. Indeed, even though a number of OLAF investigations have found irregularities in public procurement processes, and Article 136(1) of the Financial Regulation provides that the grounds for exclusion include corruption and that information on early detection or exclusion may derive from facts and findings of OLAF, there are only five companies included in the public list of economic operators excluded or subject to financial penalty.[150]

It could also be considered whether EU Directives could be amended to expand the persons granted standing to participate in domestic review procedures, beyond those having an interest in obtaining a particular public supply or works contract, to include the European Commission or civil society groups participating in integrity pacts.[151] This would allow these bodies to step in and prevent irregular processes from being carried out and implemented.

---

[146] See, e.g., EIB Investigations Activity Report 2021, available at https://www.eib.org/attachments/lucalli/investigations_activity_report_2021_en.pdf.

[147] See TI's Integrity Pacts Programme, available at https://www.transparency.org/programmes/overview/integritypacts.

[148] 'Monitoring Public Contracting: Experiences from 18 Integrity Pacts in the EU', n. 57, 5.

[149] See European Commission, 'Integrity Pacts', available at https://ec.europa.eu/regional_policy/en/policy/how/improving-investment/integrity-pacts/.

[150] See EDES database, available at https://ec.europa.eu/info/strategy/eu-budget/how-it-works/annual-lifecycle/implementation/anti-fraud-measures/edes/database_en.

[151] See n. 9 and text.

E. Conclusions

As outlined in this chapter, the procurement systems of all EU Member States, including Hungary and Poland, have been shaped by the EU Treaty, the EU Procurement Directives and the values embodied in those instruments. Still, most states, including EU Member States, find it challenging to protect their public procurement processes from corrupt and collusive practices (as well as from mismanagement).

In the cases of Hungary and Poland, illiberal developments in both the political and economic spheres under the Fidesz and PiS governments have been increasing the risks of these practices undermining the integrity of the countries' public procurement systems. Although calls for reform have been falling on deaf ears during the tenure of these governments, Hungary's and Poland's memberships of the EU make a material difference, as it is predicated on respect for fundamental values safeguarded by the EU Treaties, including democracy, equality, the rule of law, and compliance with, and the upholding of, EU law. The changes that have occurred in Hungary and Poland are not only likely to be resulting in violations of core EU goals (internal market integration), principles and laws (including public procurement and competition laws) but are also violating foundational EU values, especially the rule of law, which would disqualify them from membership were they to apply. They also create a risk of negative impact on EU funds, distributed through public procurement processes in Hungary and Poland. The consequences of these developments thus extend beyond Hungary's and Poland's borders and into the EU more broadly.

Despite the politically sensitive nature of the situation, the EU has a range of tools to try to prevent, deter, and reverse these violations. Not only can the Commission be more vigilant with respect to individual cases of collusion or corruption in public procurement processes in Member States, but action can be taken to deal with the more systemic issues, the undermining of EU law and values and their negative impact on the spending of EU funds. Indeed, it is arguable that the duty of the EU to act should be augmented where alternative, national, routes of action are weakened. Although, many of the softer or general techniques, such as reports, recommendations, or Article 258 proceedings proved too weak to divert the Hungarian and Polish government from conscious paths being trodden there, and Article 7 TEU has so far proved to be an impotent weapon against their serious infringements of EU laws and values, enforcement actions provide the springboard both for requests for interim measures, and for the imposition of penalties in case of breach of interim rulings or a failure to comply with an Article 258 ruling. Collectively, these steps can enhance the effectiveness of EU law. The EU has also become more willing to condition payments on closely monitored investment plans, and to suspend the payment of EU funds where rule-of-law regressions occur. However, the possibility of affected countries vetoing important EU initiatives, if funds are not released, creates difficulties.

Consequently, this chapter also proposes the development of supplementary mechanisms to protect the integrity of public procurement processes and to prevent breaches from arising, and the misuse of EU funds, when they do go ahead, for example, through: closer cooperation between the Commission and national procurement agencies; more proactive real-time monitoring of procurement processes; the use of 'Integrity Pacts' in procurements identified as high risk by corruption or integrity risk scoring tools; the development of a more principled and transparent Early Detection and Exclusion System to exclude persons representing a risk to the EU's financial interest; and by granting standing to the Commission or certain civil society groups in domestic review procedures.

Although these steps may not outweigh the complex and diverse array of benefits to a government and its associates from illiberal changes, the hope is that cumulatively, they will increase the cost of non-compliance with EU laws and fundamental values, make misuse of EU funds more difficult, and halt the distribution of EU funds where the rule of law cannot be ensured, so requiring Member States to think hard about the trade-offs involved. Further, by highlighting the magnitude of the non-compliance in a Member State, such steps may also increase domestic and international pressure for political change or reform (indeed, in October 2023, the PiS party in Poland failed to win a majority in the elections, so creating the opportunity for change under the new coalition government). At the same time these proposals provide a possible template for more effective enforcement of, and greater compliance with, EU rules governing public procurement processes across the entire EU.

9

Ukraine: Ukraine's Ongoing Fight Against Corruption and Supplier Collusion in Public Procurement: Relation to the Country's Broader Existential Struggle

A. Introduction   270

B. The Struggle to Establish Legitimate (Non-Corrupt) Public Procurement and Other Institutions in Ukraine, the Legacy of the Soviet Union, Post-2014 Reform Efforts, and Implications of the Current War   275

C. Specific Measures Taken to Combat Corruption in Public Procurement in Ukraine: Progress to Date and Current Challenges   280

   i. The legislative reforms of 2014: revamping public procurement in Ukraine   280

   ii. Digital transformation to enhance transparency and deter corruption in public procurement: implementation of the ProZorro platform   281

   iii. The engagement of civil society in monitoring outcomes and fighting corruption in public procurement activities in Ukraine   283

   iv. The related (and successful) campaign by Ukraine to join the WTO Agreement on Government Procurement   285

   v. Corruption control in the war context   286

   vi. A mid-war reality check   287

D. The Internationally Supported Quest to Strengthen Competition Policy in Ukraine   289

   i. Competition law and policy in Ukraine: origins, institutional basis, and pre-2014 history   290

   ii. Pursuing bid rigging and related conduct in public procurement   291

   iii. The AMCU's role in the debarment of infringing suppliers: a further innovation   295

   iv. An additional role: the AMCU as the independent review body for public procurement complaints   296

   v. Competition enforcement in the current war context   297

   vi. International support for strengthening of the competition regime in Ukraine, with a specific focus on public procurement   298

E. Ukraine's Anticipated Post-War Reconstruction: Major Challenges Ahead   300

   i. General measures to restore confidence in the Rule of Law and the integrity of related institutions   301

   ii. Strengthened measures to deter corruption in the public procurement sphere   303

   iii. Measures to ensure the effective enforcement of competition law, including with respect to public procurement markets   305

   iv. The transcendent importance of international support   306

F. Concluding Remarks   306

A. Introduction

In Ukraine, the ongoing fight against corruption in its many forms—including, very much, bribery, kickbacks, and other forms of malfeasance in public procurement—is an essential element of the country's broader ongoing struggle for national survival, security, democratic governance, and a decent way of life. Widespread corruption and supplier collusion—including, but not limited to the public procurement sphere—has been a barrier to the country's development for decades. A classic analysis is that of the international scholar, Anders Aslund, writing in 2015, who observed as follows:

> A root cause of Ukraine's problems is pervasive corruption.... Ukraine's funda-mental problem is that it did not experience any clear break from the communist system. Its tardy transition to a market economy bred pervasive corruption by giving the old elite ample opportunities to transform their power into personal wealth. Ukraine's economy has consistently underperformed because of perva-sive corruption since independence.[1]

It is important to appreciate that corruption in Ukraine is not a matter of just an exceptionally large number of isolated instances of rule-breaking; rather, it is sys-temic in nature and is deeply embedded in the country's fabric. As De Waal re-marked in 2016:

> Since the country achieved independence in 1991, the problem is not that a well-functioning state has been corrupted by certain illegal practices; rather, those corrupt practices have constituted the rules by which the state has been run. Ukraine's political system is best described as [one of] state capture.[2]

Ukraine's challenges thus provide a compelling example of the problem of 'sys-temic corruption' as outlined in Chapter 4, offering insights as to both the persist-ence of related tendencies and their ability to frustrate the aims of a wide array of policy interventions/corrective measures. Ukraine also offers an intriguing con-trast with the situations of Hungary and Poland (discussed in Chapter 8) in the sense that, while all three jurisdictions were formerly members of the 'Eastern Bloc'

---

[1] A. Aslund, 'Ukraine: What Went Wrong and How to Fix It' (2015) *Peterson Institute for International Economics*.

[2] See T. De Waal, 'Fighting a Culture of Corruption in Ukraine', *Carnegie Europe* (18 April 2016), available at https://carnegieeurope.eu/2016/04/18/fighting-culture-of-corruption-in-ukraine-pub-63364. 'State capture' has been defined as '... efforts of firms to shape the laws, policies, and regulations of the state to their own advantage by providing illicit private gains to public officials'. See J. Hellman and D. Kaufmann, 'Confronting the Challenge of State Capture in Transition Economies' (2001) 38(3) *Finance and Development*. See also M.R. Tregle, Jr., 'Corruption and Conflict: Public Procurement Reform and International Integration in Ukraine and Georgia' (2023) 52(4) *Public Contract Law Journal* 601, and Aslund, n. 1.

INTRODUCTION 271

of countries dominated by Russia/the former Soviet Union, since the latter's fall, Hungary and Poland have benefited from substantially closer ties with the West (including, since 2004, European Union (EU) Membership).[3] As we have seen, EU membership has certainly not solved all of Hungary and Poland's governance challenges; still it has been an important source of institutional support and, perhaps, helped the two EU Member States to avoid the worst possible outcomes. The situation in Ukraine is emblematic of the even more limited progress that is likely to be made without such support for countries suffering from systemic corruption.

Recent surveys, analysis, and events confirm the continuing impact of corruption and related practices on Ukraine's economic and national prospects.[4] For example, in 2022, Ukraine scored 33 out of 100 on Transparency International's Index of Perceived Corruption (with zero standing for the highest possible level of corruption).[5] Similarly, it ranked fifth on the Economist's Crony-capitalism Index (implying a pervasive problem).[6] Ukraine's public procurement sector is repeatedly cited as a key locus of concerns in relevant analysis and reports.[7] In early 2023, four deputy ministers and five regional governors were required to leave their posts, in connection with high-level corruption allegations centring on public procurement in the context of Ukraine's war effort.[8] In an apparent illustration of

[3] See, for a multi-layered institutional and historical analysis, A. Aslund, *How Capitalism Was Built: The Transformation of Central and Eastern Europe, Russia, the Caucasus, and Central Asia* (Cambridge University Press, 2nd edn, 2012).

[4] See, for a summary of pertinent indicators and incisive related commentary, A. Mungiu-Pippidi, 'For a Clean and Sustainable Reconstruction of Ukraine', *European Research Centre for Anticorruption and State Building (ERCAS)* (2022), available at https://www.againstcorruption.eu/articles/for-a-clean-and-sustainable-reconstruction-of-ukraine/. See also N. Fenton and A. Lohsen, 'Corruption and Private Sector Investment in Ukraine's Reconstruction', *Center for Strategic and International Studies (CSIS)* (2022), available at https://www.csis.org/analysis/corruption-and-private-sector-investment-ukraines-reconstruction.

[5] Transparency International, 'Corruption Perceptions Index 2022: Ukraine', available at https://www.transparency.org/en/cpi/2022/index/ukr. See also related discussion in this book, Chapter 4.

[6] See 'Our Crony-Capitalism Index Offers a Window into Russia's Billionaire Wealth', *The Economist* (12 March 2022), available at https://www.economist.com/finance-and-economics/2022/03/12/our-crony-capitalism-index-offers-a-window-into-russias-billionaire-wealth.

[7] See, e.g., Mungiu-Pippidi, n. 4; D. Skidmore, D. Wessel, and E. Asdourian, 'Financing and Governing the Recovery, Reconstruction, and Modernization of Ukraine', *Brookings* (3 November 2022), available at https://www.brookings.edu/blog/up-front/2022/11/03/financing-and-governing-the-recovery-reconstruction-and-modernization-of-ukraine/; and L. Blumenthal, C. Seamon, N. Eisen, and R.J. Lewis, 'History Reveals How to Get Ukraine Reconstruction Right: Anti-Corruption', *Brookings* (20 October 2022), available at https://www.brookings.edu/blog/up-front/2022/10/20/history-reveals-how-to-get-ukraine-reconstruction-right-anti-corruption/; and 'In High-Profile Raids, Zelensky Showcases Will to Tackle Corruption', *New York Times* (2 February 2023), available at https://www.nytimes.com/2023/02/02/world/europe/ukraine-corruption-probe.html.

[8] See 'Ukraine's Zelensky Removes Top Officials in Bid to Contain Corruption Scandals: Graft Allegations Shake-Up Could Threaten Western Confidence in Kyiv', *Wall Street Journal* (24 January 2023), available at https://www.wsj.com/articles/ukraines-president-zelensky-removes-top-officials-in-bid-to-contain-corruption-scandal-11674560046; 'Zelensky Shakes Up Ukrainian Government Amid Growing Corruption Scandal', *CNN* (24 January 2023), available at https://www.cnn.com/2023/01/24/europe/ukraine-anti-corruption-zelensky-intl/index.html; 'Defense Minister Reznikov under Fire as Corruption Probes Rock Ukraine', *Politico* (23 January 2023), available at https://www.politico.eu/article/defense-minister-reznikov-ukraine-corruption-probe-war-russia-zelenskyy/; 'Senior

broader problems with the rule of law in Ukraine, in May 2023, the Chief Justice of Ukraine's Supreme Court was arrested by officers of the National Anti-Corruption Bureau of Ukraine who searched his home and office, and reportedly found large sums of cash.[9] Most recently, President Zelensky has replaced Ukraine's Minister of Defence, Oleksii Reznikov, amid continuing concerns relating to alleged overpayments and graft relating to food and other supplies in the context of the war effort.[10] The causes, extent, and possible solutions to Ukraine's challenges with respect to corruption and supplier collusion in the public procurement sector cannot be meaningfully assessed in isolation from these current developments and broader context.

The ongoing war prompted by Russia's invasion of Ukraine has made the nexus of national viability with good governance and corruption control more salient, not less so. The possibility and hope of Ukraine establishing itself as a stable and relatively well-governed (corruption-free) society is not just a key factor underpinning the support it has received from the West; it is itself a part of the threat that Ukraine poses to Russia. In the words of two prominent Ukrainian anti-corruption activists, Daria Kaleniuk and Olena Halushka:

> Despite the challenges Ukraine faces, it is a real electoral democracy that has experienced a peaceful transition of power and has genuine political competition, and ... is closer than ever before to becoming a role model of successful democracy in action.
>
> This is exactly what Russian President Vladimir Putin's autocratic regime fears. Having tried to undermine Ukraine through military and hybrid aggression, Putin now [has undertaken] a large-scale invasion to destroy the country – not only because it is successfully undergoing comprehensive domestic

---

Ukrainian Officials Ousted in Corruption Crackdown', *NBC News* (24 January 2023), available at https://www.nbcnews.com/news/world/senior-ukrainian-officials-depart-corruption-crackdown-rcna67130; and M. Minakov, 'Fighting Corruption in Wartime Ukraine', *Wilson Center* (13 February 2023), available at https://www.wilsoncenter.org/blog-post/fighting-corruption-wartime-ukraine. Additional details are discussed in Section C.v, below.

[9] See 'Ukraine Arrests a Top Judge as Crackdown on Corruption Expands', *New York Times* (18 May 2023), available at https://www.nytimes.com/2023/05/18/world/europe/ukraine-bribery-supreme-court.html.

[10] 'Zelensky replaces defense minister, citing need for "new approaches"', *New York Times* (3 September 2023), available at https://www.nytimes.com/2023/09/03/world/europe/zelensky-ukraine-defense-minister.html#:~:text=President%20Volodymyr%20Zelensky%20said%20on,than%2018%20months%20of%20conflict; see also 'Removal of defense Minister shows wartime Ukraine is changing', *Atlantic Council* (5 September 2023), available at https://www.atlanticcouncil.org/blogs/ukrainealert/removal-of-defense-minister-shows-wartime-ukraine-is-changing/#:~:text=Removal%20of%20defense%20minister%20shows%20wartime%20Ukraine%20is%20changing,-By%20Melinda%20Haring&text=Ukraine's%20outgoing%20Defense%20Minister%20Oleksii,with%20the%20country's%20Western%20partners.

INTRODUCTION   273

transformation but, more importantly, because it has the potential to trigger similar democratic reforms in Russia.[11]

These fault lines admittedly go beyond public procurement per se; nevertheless, the public procurement sector has (rightly) been a pre-eminent focus of anti-corruption measures and efforts to promote competition and good governance in Ukraine, including on the part of the international community.[12] Indeed, it is abundantly clear that comprehensive corruption control will be essential not only to the success of reconstruction efforts, but to securing and maintaining the necessary international funding for such efforts (and even the continuing war effort). This connection is now being made explicit in contemporaneous reporting and analysis.[13]

To his credit, the current President, Volodymyr Zelensky, has declared his firm intention to eradicate the plague of corruption in Ukraine, emphasizing that 'there will be no return to what used to be in the past'.[14] The recent flurry of firings of senior government officials and the arrest of the Chief Justice of the country's Supreme Court are intended to reinforce this message. Nonetheless, a clean break with the past will not be easily achieved. The challenge for President Zelensky, for Ukraine itself and for the allied international community will be to ensure that the President's brave words are fulfilled.[15]

Efforts to prevent and deter corruption and supplier collusion in public procurement in Ukraine are *not* starting from zero. In fact, both problems have been the subject of extensive targeted efforts at the national level, with significant international support, over an extended period. These have included not only general efforts to strengthen the rule of law but also the development of an internationally recognized and highly transparent platform for public procurement activities, 'ProZorro'; a successful campaign to join the World Trade Organization (WTO) Agreement on Government Procurement (GPA), as a means of reinforcing and

---

[11] D. Kaleniuk and O. Halushka, 'Why Ukraine's Fight against Corruption Scares Russia', *Foreign Policy* (17 December 2021), available at https://foreignpolicy.com/2021/12/17/ukraine-russia-corruption-putin-democracy-oligarchs/#.

[12] See, for pertinent details, Sections C and D, below.

[13] See 'Ukraine's Zelensky Removes Top Officials in Bid to Contain Corruption Scandals: Graft allegations shake-up could threaten Western confidence in Kyiv', n. 8. See also C.M. Savoy, 'To Keep Western Assistance Flowing, Ukraine Must Engage Corruption Concerns Head-On', *Center for Strategic and International Studies (CSIS)* (30 June 2022), available at https://www.csis.org/analysis/keep-west ern-assistance-flowing-ukraine-must-engage-corruption-concerns-head. See also J. Rudolph and N.L. Eisen, 'Ukraine's Anti-Corruption Fight Can Overcome US Skeptics', *JustSecurity.org* (10 November 10 2022), available at https://www.justsecurity.org/84076/ukraines-anti-corruption-fight-can-overcome-us-skeptics/; 'Ukraine Ambassador: Every Dollar from US Is Going to Good Use', *The Hill* (8 January 2023), available at https://thehill.com/homenews/3804507-ukraine-ambassador-every-dollar-from-us-is-going-to-good-use/; and F. Stockman, 'Corruption is an existential threat to Ukraine, and the Ukrainians know it', *New York Times* (10 September 2023), available at https://www.nytimes.com/2023/09/10/opinion/ukraine-war-corruption.html.

[14] 'Senior Ukrainian Officials Ousted in Corruption Crackdown', *NBC News*, n. 8.

[15] See also Sections C and E, below.

gaining recognition for adherence to best practices internationally in the public procurement field; related efforts to engage civil society in the monitoring of public procurement activities, including through the establishment of the 'DoZorro' network; and significant efforts, over an extended period, to nurture the development of effective competition law enforcement in the country, including in but not limited to the public procurement sphere.[16] These efforts are of considerable interest in their own right and have much to contribute to international understanding regarding related issues, due in part to Ukraine's situation of having to implement the relevant measures under significant time pressures and close international scrutiny.

In fact, the ongoing experience of Ukraine with respect to corruption and supplier collusion in public procurement and related contextual developments discussed in this chapter illustrates and buttresses multiple themes of this book. These include:

- The challenges involved in transitioning from a society where corruption is the norm to one where corruption is controlled and a better moral equilibrium established, and the complexity and interdependence of the measures needed to achieve such an outcome;[17]
- The centrality of issues concerning the public procurement sector, to efforts to eradicate corruption and foster good governance and effective competition in many countries;
- The importance of the wider political and institutional context (including the independence, impartiality, and integrity of courts, prosecutors, and other relevant bodies, and politicians' respect for the rule of law) for the success of reform efforts centred on the public procurement sector;
- The important potential contribution of digital tools and 'open' contracting systems to the deterrence and prevention of corruption;
- The overriding importance of engaging civil society in the struggle for good governance;[18] and
- The importance of international support and multilateral arrangements (including international trade and related agreements) for the struggle against corruption and supplier collusion at the national level.[19]

The chapter is organized as follows: Section B reflects on the 'big picture'—i.e. the ongoing struggle to establish legitimate and non-corrupt (democratic) public institutions in Ukraine, the continuing legacy of the Soviet Union as it pertains to

---

[16] See, for details of these and other initiatives, Sections B and C below, and references cited therein.
[17] See, for in-depth analysis, this book, Chapter 4.
[18] See, for elaboration, Section C. iii. below.
[19] See, for additional reflections, Section F, below.

those efforts, the clear need for general measures to strengthen the rule of law in addition to public procurement-specific measures, the recent history of attempts to implement such measures in the aftermath of the 2014 'Revolution of Dignity' or 'Maidan Revolution', and the exceptional (and severe) related challenges posed by the current war with Russia. Section C delves into the significant measures taken to combat corrupt practices in public procurement in Ukraine since 2014, including far-reaching transparency measures, a successful campaign to join the WTO GPA, significant efforts to engage civil society, and related measures. Section D examines, in parallel, the efforts that have been made to strengthen competition policy in Ukraine over time, including with respect to public procurement and with substantial support from the international community. Section E reflects on the major challenges that lie ahead, if Ukraine is to be successfully rebuilt as a modern, rule-of-law economy and society in the aftermath of the current war. Section F provides concluding remarks.

B. The Struggle to Establish Legitimate (Non-Corrupt) Public Procurement and Other Institutions in Ukraine, the Legacy of the Soviet Union, Post-2014 Reform Efforts, and Implications of the Current War

As we have already seen, Ukraine has a long and deep history of corruption in governance, including but not limited to the public procurement sphere.[20] The challenge of corruption has, moreover, intimate links with Ukraine's past membership in the former Soviet Union. As observed by Kaleniuk and Halushka:

> Ukraine's corruption-related problems go back to the fall of the Soviet Union in 1991. When the state-planned economy collapsed, state enterprises went bankrupt and were privatized on the principle of 'first come, first serve' amid lawlessness and chaos. This gave birth to oligarchy, which remains a [key] roadblock to Ukraine's progress.[21]

Ukraine's problems in the period immediately following the collapse of the USSR, however, went beyond those of oligarchy; rather, they consisted also in a near-total breakdown of governance institutions. According to Kaleniuk and Halushka:

> Simultaneously, the country's judiciary and law enforcement institutions were broken. They often carried out political orders. In cases with no political sensitivity, investigators or judges were free to take bribes and make decisions at their

---

[20] Aslund, n. 1; see also De Waal, n. 2 and N. Fenton and A. Lohsen, n. 4.
[21] Kaleniuk and Halushka, n. 11.

discretion. *Millions of dollars were embezzled on public procurements annually, including in such sectors as healthcare, infrastructure, and the military. The secrecy of ownership data (such as real estate, land, and company ownership) enabled corruption schemes by providing anonymity and shielding wrongdoings.*[22] [Emphasis added.]

The breadth and depth of corruption in Ukraine in the period between the breakup of the Soviet Union and the 2014 'Revolution of Dignity' was staggering. It consisted not merely of isolated instances of rule-breaking: rather, it was systemic and touched the highest levels of Ukraine's body politic. In 2015, Aslund observed as follows:

The fundamental insight is that not only the Ukrainian economy but also Ukrainian politics are pervasively corrupt. The old system hardly allowed anybody to come to power unless they were prepared to play the corruption game. Cynical Ukrainians do not ask whether corruption will decline but who will benefit under the new rule. In September 2014, the popular view was that the post-Yanukovich regime was as corrupt as the Yanukovich regime. [In such a circumstance, it] is vital to oust corrupt politicians, but the whole political system needs to be reformed....[23]

Through the 1990s and into the 2010s, sporadic efforts were made by the national authorities, with international support, to implement meaningful reforms. These were, however, largely or entirely nullified by adverse political developments. For example, initial hopes generated by the Orange Revolution of 2004 were followed by an extended period of political chaos and a failure of efforts to reprivatize former state assets in a more egalitarian and structurally competitive manner. Subsequently, oligarchy was restored and economic and political powers were increasingly consolidated under the Yanukovych Regime and the Yanukovych family itself, which Aslund terms a state of 'Ultimate Predation'. In his words:

The regime of President Yanukovych, 2010–2014, was a nightmare for Ukrainians. It was a predatory regime despite the fact that Yanukovych was democratically elected. To begin with, he appeared to [be principally interested in re-establishing the oligarchy], but within a year he started concentrating power and wealth to his own family circle, upsetting not only the populace but also the big businessmen.[24]

Furthermore, the Yanukovych family was alleged to have:

[22] Kaleniuk and Halushka, n. 11.
[23] Aslund, n. 1, 122.
[24] Aslund, n. 1, 4.

STRUGGLE TO ESTABLISH LEGITIMATE PUBLIC PROCUREMENT 277

.... enriched itself during its four-year reign through energy subsidies, discretionary public procurement, embezzlement from the state, privileged privatization, fraudulent refunds of value-added tax to exporters, extortion, and corporate raiding [forcing business owners to sell their enterprises at unduly low prices].[25]

Citizen outrage over these and related matters culminated in the 2014 'Revolution of Dignity' and the ouster of Yanukovych.[26]

The 2014 Revolution ushered in important changes in Ukraine's political system, including the formation of an interim government, the restoration of the pre-existing (democratic) Constitution, a demand for new presidential elections to be held within months and important efforts at 'decommunization'.[27] Far-reaching efforts were made by Ukrainian governmental reformers, civil society groups, and international partners to grapple with the above-noted problems and strengthen Ukraine's anti-corruption architecture.[28]

Anti-corruption reforms subsequent to the 'Revolution of Dignity' were inspired partly by earlier experiences of Romania and Georgia, and had two principal thrusts.[29] The first consisted in the opening to the public of as much state-controlled information as deemed possible, to make corrupt practices more difficult. As we will see, a major focus of this effort concerned the public procurement sector. The second focused on establishing independent anti-corruption institutions. According to Kaleniuk and Halushka:

These measures significantly empowered civil society experts and investigative journalists to reveal and expose corruption, thus elevating the risk for corrupt officials, who are sensitive to any public exposure of their wrongdoings. Also, these measures [were aimed at improving] the country's business climate, particularly via better protection of property rights.[30]

As central elements of these efforts, four important and interrelated measures relevant to public procurement were successfully put in place:

---

[25] Aslund, n. 1, 92.

[26] An important related factor was the desire of a broad segment of Ukraine's population for closer links with the EU and (more broadly) the West, which Yanukovych initially championed and subsequently (under pressure from Moscow) renounced. See related discussion, below.

[27] Aslund, n. 1, Chapter 7; Kaleniuk and Halushka, n. 11.

[28] Kaleniuk and Halushka, n. 11.

[29] Kaleniuk and Halushka, n. 11.

[30] Kaleniuk and Halushka, n. 11. As observed by those authors: 'in 2015–16 the Ukrainian government opened state databases, including real estate, vehicle, land, and company registries. Public procurement was transferred to the online system ProZorro (which means "transparent" [or transparently] in English), which now saves up to 10 percent of the funds budgeted for each purchase due to the site's auction approach, transparency, and competitiveness.'

- First, a new Law on Public Procurement (PPL) was adopted in April 2014;[31]
- Second, Ukraine initiated the development of the ProZorro e-procurement system (see related discussion, below). Both the new procurement law and ProZorro built upon, and were influenced by, the transparency standards of the United Nations Commission on International Trade Law (UNCITRAL), Model Law on Public Procurement,[32] and the Open Contracting Data Standard (OCDS);[33]
- Thirdly, Ukraine initiated its application for accession to the WTO GPA and officially joined the Agreement in May 2016 (following further revisions to its procurement law to ensure compliance with the GPA's requirements); and
- As a fourth key thrust of relevant reforms, Ukraine made a conscious decision to engage civil society and ordinary citizens in the policing of the public procurement process. A key step in this effort was the establishment of the DoZorro network, a dedicated platform for the monitoring of public procurement activities.[34]

At the same time, significant attempts were made, with support from organizations such as the Organisation for Economic Co-operation and Development (OECD), the United Nations Conference on Trade and Development (UNCTAD), the European Union (EU) Commission, and the United States' (US) competition authorities (in addition to prominent international scholars), to strengthen the enforcement of competition law in Ukraine, including with respect to public procurement markets.[35]

Beyond these measures that focused to a significant degree on the public procurement sector and the strengthening of competition law enforcement, more general efforts have periodically been made to strengthen the rule of law and the independence and integrity of related institutions generally. For example, even in the time of the Yanukovych regime, Parliament adopted a law aimed at limiting the power and discretion of prosecutors. However, these measures had (at best) mixed success and, as of 2015, Aslund did not hesitate to say that 'Ukraine's judicial system, including the prosecutor's office, is in dire need of reform'.[36]

The current regime led by President Zelensky came into office in May 2019. In addition to other reform efforts, in September 2021, a new 'Anti-Oligarch Law' was

---

[31] Law No. 1197-VII 'on Public Procurement' of 10 April 2014 (PPL). See, for pertinent details, Section C, below.

[32] United Nations Commission on International Trade Law (UNCITRAL), 'The 2011 UNCITRAL Model Law on Public Procurement', available at https://uncitral.un.org/en/texts/procurement/model law/public_procurement.

[33] See, Open Contracting Partnership, 'The Open Contracting Data Standard', available at https://www.open-contracting.org/data-standard/.

[34] See, Section C, below.

[35] See Section D, below, and references cited therein.

[36] Aslund, n. 1, 144.

enacted.[37] The Law's official title refers to 'Preventing Threats to National Security Associated With Excessive Influence by Persons Who Wield Significant Economic and Political Weight in Public Life (Oligarchs)'. Its avowed aim is to free Ukraine's national politics and economy from the oligarchs' influence, by bringing them under the regulatory umbrella of the Law 'On the Prevention of Corruption', and requiring compliance with various anti-corruption limitations and requirements, similar to the ones applied to Ukrainian public servants.[38]

Throughout this period, Ukraine's anti-corruption struggles have been extensively intertwined with the country's endeavours to extricate itself from excessive dependence on Russia, to better align itself with western European institutions, and thereby to ensure its viability as a sovereign state and polity.[39] Indeed, a key factor leading ultimately to the fall of President Yanukovych was Russian President Putin's opposition to an effort, initially (and perhaps surprisingly) led by Yanukovych, to establish an Association Agreement between Ukraine and the EU. This generated significant retaliatory actions by Russia, including imposition of arbitrary restrictions on Ukraine's exports to Russia.[40]

Clearly, while Russia's occupation of various eastern territories of Ukraine beginning in 2014 already placed the country's anti-corruption and reform efforts under stress, its full-scale invasion of the country beginning in early 2022 has made continued progress dramatically more difficult. As observed trenchantly by Mungiu-Pippidi:

> Nothing creates more opportunities for corruption than war. But a war where foreign money pours in is bound to multiply exponentially such opportunities, especially in an already enabling environment.[41]

Nonetheless, it is striking that, even in the context of the war, Ukraine's efforts to fight corruption and implement structural economic reforms have not ceased. In the public procurement sector, both the ProZorro system and the DoZorro network continue to function, and to receive international support.[42] Most recently, as already noted, as of January 2023, President Zelensky has initiated a major shakeup of top-level officials in response to allegations of corruption regarding public procurement and related activities concerning (in substantial part) the war effort,

---

[37] Law No. 1780-IX adopted by the Verkhovna Rada 'On Prevention of Threats to National Security Related to Excessive Influence of Persons Who Have Significant Economic and Political Weight in Public Life (Oligarchs)' (Anti-Oligarch Law).

[38] 'Explainer – Ukraine's Anti-Oligarch Law', *Civil Georgia* (5 October 2022) available at https://civil.ge/archives/510674.

[39] De Waal, n. 2.

[40] Aslund, n. 1, 94–7.

[41] Mungiu-Pippidi, n. 4.

[42] S. Kelman and C.R. Yukins, 'Overcoming Corruption and War – Lessons from Ukraine's ProZorro Procurement System' (2022) GWU Legal Studies Research Paper No. 2022-60, 22–7, available at https://scholarship.law.gwu.edu/cgi/viewcontent.cgi?article=2887&context=faculty_publications.

acknowledging that this is vital to its retaining international support.[43] These developments manifest clearly the dire importance of Ukraine's fight against corruption for its survival as a nation state.[44]

C. Specific Measures Taken to Combat Corruption in Public Procurement in Ukraine: Progress to Date and Current Challenges

Efforts to combat corruption and improve the governance of public procurement markets have been under way in Ukraine for more than two decades,[45] and intensified significantly following the 2014 'Revolution of Dignity'. The following reviews key developments since then:

i. The legislative reforms of 2014: revamping public procurement in Ukraine

As already noted, multiple elements of Ukraine's broader anti-corruption program were targeted specifically at the public procurement sector. The first of these was a new Public Procurement Law adopted in April 2014[46] and further revised prior to the completion of Ukraine's accession to the WTO GPA.[47] The legislation built extensively on elements of the UNCITRAL Model Law on Public Procurement and other international standards, including the GPA.

The public procurement legal framework is complemented by Law No. 4851-VI 'on Peculiarities of Public Procurement in Certain Spheres of Entrepreneurial Activities' of 24 May 2012 relating to the procurement of utilities. Also, the Parliament (Verkhovna Rada) adopted legislation to implement e-procurement in 2015, complying with legal commitments under Ukraine's GPA accession.[48]

Although the pre-existing 2010 procurement Law was considered to be generally consistent with international standards, it had been amended frequently to exempt particular sets of contracts from its scope (thereby diluting its effectiveness).[49] In comparison, the 2014 procurement law significantly reduced the extent

---

[43] See references cited in n. 13, above, and accompanying text. See also further discussion in Section C, below.

[44] See also Minakov, n. 8.

[45] See, for the history of earlier reform efforts, Aslund, n. 1, especially Chapters 4 and 5.

[46] The 2014 law repealed Law No. 2289-VI 'On Public Procurement' of 1 June 2010, a law on government contracts from 1996, and a 1996 resolution of the Verkhovna Rada concerning the supply of goods for state needs.

[47] See below, Section C.iv.

[48] World Trade Organization, 'Trade Policy Review: Ukraine' (2016) WT/TPR/S/334, available at https://www.wto.org/english/tratop_e/tpr_e/s334_e.pdf.

[49] See Tregle, n. 2.

of exemptions from the Law's scope. Further important changes relate to the availability of information and access to data. Under the new procurement framework, procuring entities must provide free access to the information required by the law to all bidders, allowing both domestic and foreign bidders to participate in the procedures on an equal basis. The 2014 Law also paved the way for the digital transformation of public procurement in Ukraine.[50]

ii. Digital transformation to enhance transparency and deter corruption in public procurement: implementation of the ProZorro platform

Of possibly even greater significance in the reform process was the introduction of ProZorro, an open-source e-procurement platform developed for the Government of Ukraine with the support of various non-governmental and intergovernmental bodies, including the European Bank for Reconstruction and Development (EBRD), the World Bank (WB), the US Agency for International Development (USAID), and the Open Contracting Partnership (OCP).[51]

ProZorro was born from intense civilian frustration with a closed and corrupt system of procurement.[52] As outlined on the website of the OCP:

> The ProZorro project was initiated in Kiev in May 2014 by a group of anti-corruption social activists. The project was inspired by public procurement reforms in Georgia ... With the help of commercial platforms, a pilot of the e-procurement system ProZorro was launched in February 2015.
>
> ....
>
> ProZorro, which means 'transparently' in Ukrainian, has ... specific attributes that make it a novelty in the procurement world. Firstly, everything is open. All information related to the tender process, including suppliers' offers, can be accessed and monitored by anyone....
>
> Secondly, ProZorro is a 'hybrid model' e-procurement system, which means the information is stored in one central database, but suppliers and contracting authorities can access the data from a number of different platforms, choosing the one that best serves their needs. Using an API, these interfaces are connected to the central database so that all the information is synchronized across all platforms.

---

[50] World Trade Organization, n. 48.
[51] See Open Contracting Partnership, 'Our Vision', available at https://www.open-contracting.org/about/.
[52] See, Kelman and Yukins, n. 42.

The implementation of ProZorro was extensively influenced by the OCDS. The latter:

> ... enables disclosure of data and documents at all stages of the contracting process by defining a common data model. It was created to support organizations to increase contracting transparency, and allow deeper analysis of contracting data by a wide range of users.[53]
>
> ... the ultimate goal of the OCDS is to help deliver open contracting using standardized open data. The OCDS describes how to publish data and documents for the procurement of goods, works, and services. It makes contracting data available for anyone to use, modify, and share, for any purpose .... The OCDS helps to increase transparency, enables deeper analysis of contracting data, and facilitates the use of data by a wide range of stakeholders.[54]

The ProZorro platform is viewed by Ukraine and its institutional sponsors and partners as a major success. It attracted the participation of almost 1,000 contracting entities within its first three months of operation, saving USD 1.5 million in state budget while increasing competition to an average of three participating bidding companies per tender. With the adoption of the new Public Procurement Law in December 2015, ProZorro became mandatory for the entire public sector procurement in Ukraine and is today used by over 200,000 registered suppliers, including both domestic and international businesses. It has been estimated that, in the first four years of its existence, ProZorro saved Ukrainian taxpayers UAH 100 billion (approximate EUR 3.8 billion)[55] and almost USD 6 billion in public funds since October 2017.[56]

Recognizing this success, an emerging concern is that not all important procurements are necessarily conducted via the ProZorro system.[57] In particular,

---

[53] See Open Contracting Partnership, 'Open Contracting Data Standard', available at https://stand ard.open-contracting.org/latest/en/.

[54] See Open Contracting Partnership, 'What Is the OCDS and Why Use It?', available at https://stand ard.open-contracting.org/latest/en/primer/what/. See also Kelman and Yukins, n. 42.

[55] E. Niewiadomska and C. Nicholas, 'Transformational Change: EBRD-UNCITRAL Public Procurement Initiative Revolutionizes Electronic Public Procurement' (2020) *Law in Transition Journal*, 43–9, available at https://2020.lit-ebrd.com/wp-content/uploads/2020/04/law-in-transition-2020-english-TRANSFORMATIONAL-CHANGE.pdf. See also Open Contracting Partnership, 'Open Contracting: Impact and Evidence', available at https://www.open-contracting.org/impact/evidence/#detail. According to the latter, 'the government's central e-procurement system, ProZorro, helped more than 2000 healthcare organizations that use it save an average of 15% on all their procurements. Where three companies or more bid for contracts, healthcare organizations saved an average of 35%.'

[56] See Kelman and Yukins, n. 42.

[57] See, O. Savran, T. Khavanska, and O. Onysko, 'Corruption, Public Procurement and Competition in Eastern Europe and Central Asia: The Case of the Energy Sector in Ukraine' in Competition Policy in Eastern Europe and Central Asia: Focus on Bid Rigging in Public Procurement (*OECD-GVH Regional Centre for Competition in Budapest*, 2021), available at https://oecdgvh.hu/pfile/file?path=/contents/about/newsletters/focus-on-bid-rigging-in-public-procurement---competition-policy-in-eastern-eur ope-and-central-asia&inline=true. See also Tregle, n. 2, and additional references cited therein.

SPECIFIC MEASURES TAKEN TO COMBAT CORRUPTION   283

military procurements are often excluded from the system, ostensibly on national security grounds. While such exclusions are understandable where legitimate security concerns are at stake (especially in regard, for example, to sophisticated military hardware or software), they need not apply to many of the goods and services that armies routinely require—e.g. food and clothing for soldiers. As we have already seen, the procurement of food supplies by the military in the context of the ongoing war effort is a particular focus of concern in Ukraine, currently.[58]

Ukraine's reliance on ProZorro and its emphasis on pervasive transparency as a central element of its procurement reforms also touch upon questions regarding optimal policy choices for the control and deterrence of corruption and supplier collusion in public procurement. As we have made clear earlier in this book and in previous writings, while transparency is a vital tool in the fight against corruption, there are also potential downsides to 'too much' transparency in public procurement administration and practice. In particular, 'total transparency' with respect to bids received and other parameters of individual procurements can undeniably facilitate supplier collusion.[59]

Nonetheless, our view is that, in the special context in which Ukraine found itself in the aftermath of the 'Revolution of Dignity', it has broadly made the right choices. It made a judgement that, given the pervasiveness of corrupt practices and outright theft of public funds in Ukraine in the post-Soviet period, the only hope of restoring confidence in government and integrity in public procurement lay in implementing a system of sweeping transparency. This is a reasonable and even laudable choice in those circumstances. The approach taken, nonetheless, highlights the need for parallel measures to combat supplier collusion in public procurement in Ukraine.[60]

iii. The engagement of civil society in monitoring outcomes and fighting corruption in public procurement activities in Ukraine

As we have noted separately particularly in Chapter 4, the direct engagement of civil society in framing and monitoring relevant activities can be a powerful tool

---

[58] See also Section C.vi., below.

[59] See this book, Chapter 3; R.D. Anderson, A. Jones, and W.E. Kovacic, 'Preventing Corruption, Supplier Collusion and the Corrosion of Civic Trust: A Procompetitive Program to Improve the Effectiveness and Legitimacy of Public Procurement' (2019) 26(4) *George Mason Law Review* 1233, TLI Think! Paper 5/2019, King's College London Law School Research Paper No. 19–14, available https://ssrn.com/abstract=3289170 or http://dx.doi.org/10.2139/ssrn.3289170; and R.D. Anderson, W.E. Kovacic, and A.C. Müller, 'Ensuring Integrity and Competition in Public Procurement Markets: A Dual Challenge for Good Governance' in S. Arrowsmith and R.D. Anderson (eds), *The WTO Regime on Government Procurement: Challenge and Reform* (Cambridge University Press and the World Trade Organization, 2011), Chapter 22, 681–718.

[60] See Section D, below.

for mitigating corruption in public procurement markets. Indeed, its benefits can be even greater than this: citizen engagement can help directly to steer public procurement to beneficial outcomes. The citizens likely to be impacted by a particular public procurement have the strongest incentive to see it effectively carried out. As such, there is much to be gained from their involvement not only in monitoring but, where possible, in framing and supervising specific public procurement activities.[61]

Consistent with this view, following the 'Revolution of Dignity', Ukraine made a conscious decision to engage the private sector and civil society in the remaking of the country's procurement system. In 2016, DoZorro—a designated watchdog for ProZorro—was launched to create a network of civil society and government buyers to monitor public procurements conducted on the ProZorro platform.[62] Led by Transparency International, the DOZORRO community includes civil society organizations, procuring entities, businesses, and citizens in improving the effectiveness of public procurement, equal access, and fair play among the relevant stakeholders in Ukraine.[63]

DOZORRO aims to realize the possibilities inherent in the ProZorro platform by providing channels for citizens to regularly monitor specific tenders, analyse contracting data, flag high-risk deals and irregularities, and report them to government authorities.[64] Following the response of the affected public agency, results are added to a ranking of procuring entities and watchdog organizations. Typical violations identified include avoidance of competitive bidding, discriminatory requirements for suppliers, unjustified selection of winners, unreasonable disqualification, collusion, and failure to publish complete contract information on ProZorro.[65]

The resulting high level of engagement of civil society in public procurement in Ukraine is commendable and reflects broad interest in eradicating corruption in Ukrainian public procurement markets. This is, very much, consistent with recent literature that emphasizes the importance of public monitoring and engagement, especially in economies seeking to free themselves from legacies of corruption and cronyism.[66] As a result, by equipping the public with both the data and the

---

[61] See A. Mungiu-Pippidi, *The Quest for Good Governance, How Societies Develop Control of Corruption* (Cambridge University Press, 2015), especially at 166–77.

[62] Niewiadomska and Nicholas, n. 55.

[63] Transparency International Ukraine, 'Public Procurement Oversight', available at https://ti-ukra ine.org/en/project/public-procurement-oversight/.

[64] See Kelman and Yukins, n. 42, and Tregle, n. 2.

[65] Transparency International Ukraine, n. 63.

[66] See, for authoritative discussion, Mungiu-Pippidi, n. 61; A. Mungiu-Pippidi, *Europe's Burden: Promoting Good Governance across Borders* (Cambridge University Press, 2019); and A. Mungiu-Pippidi, *Rethinking Corruption* (Edward Elgar Publishing, 2023) and references cited in those publications.

guidance on how to scrutinize it, the government has taken an important step to tackle corruption and waste in public procurement.[67]

iv. The related (and successful) campaign by Ukraine to join the WTO Agreement on Government Procurement

During essentially the same period, Ukraine applied for admission to and was approved as a party to the WTO GPA. As noted in Chapter 4, participation in international accords such as the GPA can serve as an effective complementary tool for promoting integrity in public procurement markets, by: (i) ensuring adherence to heightened standards of transparency and procedural fairness in public procurement markets; and (ii) engaging a wider set of players in monitoring activities in such markets, including foreign companies and governments.[68] GPA participation can also serve the salutary function of helping to 'lock in' related policy reforms, rendering them less susceptible to overturning by subsequent governments.[69]

Ukraine's accession to the GPA provides a paradigm illustration of these possibilities. As stated forthrightly by Ukraine's Deputy Minister of the Economy and Trade at the time of the conclusion of Ukraine's GPA accession negotiation, 'participation in the GPA would help Ukraine strengthen good governance in the area of public procurement, assist in its fight against corruption, and increase the transparency of government procurement practices'.[70] As noted by Anderson and Sporysheva, this is consistent with an emerging pattern of new GPA accession candidates explaining their interest in joining the Agreement by reference not only to 'mercantilist' considerations (i.e. export market opportunities) but to the utility of the GPA as an instrument for motivating, guiding, and 'locking in' policy reforms and initiatives, including anti-corruption campaigns.[71]

---

[67] Open Government Partnership, 'Through the Power of the People: Empowering Citizen Watchdog's' (21 September 2021), available at https://www.ogpstories.org/through-the-power-of-the-people-empowering-citizen-watchdogs/; and Kelman and Yukins, n. 42.

[68] This book, Chapter 4.

[69] B. Hoekman, 'Reducing Home Bias in Public Procurement: Trade Agreements and Good Governance' (2018) 24(2) *Global Governance* 249.

[70] WTO, 'Ukraine and the Republic of Moldova Welcomed to WTO Procurement Pact' (22 June 2016), available at www.wto.org/english/news_e /news16_e/gpro_22jun16_e.htm.

[71] See also R.D. Anderson and N. Sporysheva, 'The Revised WTO Agreement on Government Procurement: Evolving Global Footprint, Economic Impact and Policy Significance' (2019) 28(3) *Public Procurement Law Review* 71. See also R.D. Anderson and N. Sporysheva, 'WTO Accession, Accession to the WTO Agreement on Government Procurement (GPA) and Economic Reform in the Eurasian Region: A Tale of Synergies' (forthcoming 2023).

v. Corruption control in the war context

As already noted, the ongoing war with Russia has placed severe stress on Ukraine's continuing attempts to combat corruption (and supplier collusion) in public procurement.[72] Nevertheless, important efforts have continued. To begin with, ProZorro has continued to serve as an important tool in the fight against corruption, including during wartime procurement.[73] Indeed, in the course of the war, the Government has continued to emphasize the role of ProZorro as a tool to ensure transparency, broaden business participation, and facilitate fair pricing, while reinforcing, overall, confidence in the Ukrainian government.[74] Also enhancing transparency, the Government has committed itself to publish and make 'prompt disclosure of important public control data on goods and prices' in order to 'minimize the risks by installing a safeguard against inflated prices for goods and other manipulations'.[75]

A further development is ProZorro+, a platform that allows the Ukrainian government to address the shortages brought by the war, especially when it comes to essential civilian goods.[76] The system's architecture allows local and state authorities, military and civil administrators, and humanitarian headquarters to leave their needs on the platform and look for suppliers, with the assistance of the ProZorro+ team.[77] The platform also provides an opportunity for businesses to continue selling in the war context, while encouraging the participation of foreign suppliers and donor organizations.[78] ProZorro+ counts with more than 110 categories of goods for humanitarian needs, though it does not search for suppliers of military goods.[79]

Moreover, as observed, the 2021 Anti-Oligarch Law[80] remains in place. The Law avowedly seeks to overcome the conflict of interest caused by the merger of politicians, media, and big business and the undue use of political power to impact national politics and the economy for private benefit.[81] It creates a registry and

---

[72] See also Mungiu-Pippidi, n. 4.

[73] See Kelman and Yukins, n. 42.

[74] See Kelman and Yukins, n. 42.

[75] See Kelman and Yukins, n. 42.

[76] 'Ukraine Launched the ProZorro+ Platform to Find Suppliers for Humanitarian Needs', *UkrRudProm* (31 March 2022) 2022 WLNR 10196303; Press Release, Ministry of Agrarian Policy and Food, 'ProZorro+ Platform Designed to Find Suppliers for the Country's Humanitarian Needs Kicks Off Its Work', *Ukrainian Govt News* (30 March 2022).

[77] 'Ukraine Launched the Prozorro + Platform to Find Suppliers for Humanitarian Needs', n. 76.

[78] Transparency International, 'ProZorro Launches Platform for Procurement during War' (30 March 2022), available at https://ti-ukraine.org/en/news/prozorro-launches-platform-for-procurem ent-during-war/.

[79] Ukrainian Government Portal, Ministry of Agrarian Policy and Food, 'ProZorro+ platform designed to find suppliers for the country's humanitarian needs kicks off its work', available at https:// www.kmu.gov.ua/en/news/minagropolitiki-v-ukrayini-zapustili-platformu-prozorro-z-poshuku-pos tachalnikiv-dlya-gumanitarnih-potreb-krayini.

[80] Ukraine's Anti-Oligarch Law, n. 37.

[81] Ukraine's Anti-Oligarch Law, n. 37.

prohibits 'tycoons' from financing political parties, political campaigns and demonstrations, or taking part in the privatization of state assets. While its long-run impact remains to be seen, the Anti-Oligarch Law provides a potentially important element of Ukraine's legal framework for limiting the role of big business in politics and, thereby for combatting corruption and limiting the corrosive influence of privileged (oligarchic) interests in Ukraine's economy.[82] It, nonetheless, has also been criticized as potentially itself creating scope for corruption by giving a presidential body the authority to determine who is to be considered an oligarch,[83] and curtailing freedom of speech in Ukraine.[84] Without diminishing the apparent need for such measures in Ukraine, these considerations illustrate the complexities entailed in state measures to limit participation by particular persons in the political process.

The Anti-Oligarch Law also has potential implications for the strengthening of competition in Ukraine:[85] though the National Security and Defence Council is the authority in charge of determining who meets the 'oligarch' criteria, the Antimonopoly Committee of Ukraine (AMCU) plays a role as well in submitting potential names for the 'oligarch' registry. Relevant criteria include besides wielding significant economic and political weight in public life and mass media, to be the ultimate beneficial owner of a business entity that is a natural monopoly entity or occupies a dominant position in the market for at least one year. These measures illustrate the clear relevance of competition policy to corruption and related problems in Ukraine. At the same time, the enacted anti-oligarch measures cannot work in a vacuum: to be effective, they must be accompanied by significant judicial reform and strong competition law enforcement.[86]

vi. A mid-war reality check

Despite the above safeguards, as noted at the outset of this chapter, corruption in public procurement continues to threaten both the efficient and effective management of public resources and (at least potentially) the ability of Ukraine to attract

---

[82] President of Ukraine Official Website, 'President Immediately Signed the Anti-Oligarchic Law Passed by the Verkhovna Rada', available at https://www.president.gov.ua/en/news/prezident-nevidkla dno-pidpisav-uhvalenij-verhovnoyu-radoyu-a-71445.

[83] 'Ukrainian Lawmakers Pass Law on Oligarchs after Assassination Attempt', *Reuters* (23 September 2021), available at https://www.reuters.com/world/europe/ukrainian-parliament-passes-law-oligar chs-final-reading-2021-09-23/.

[84] 'Bill on Oligarchs Creates Risks for Freedom of Press in Ukraine – CNN Leading Commentator', *Bykvu* (13 September 2021), available at https://bykvu.com/eng/bukvy/bill-on-oligarchs-creates-risks-for-freedom-of-speech-in-ukraine-cnn-s-host/.

[85] See, generally, Section D, below.

[86] S. Dzamukashvili, 'Why Ukraine's Anti-Oligarch Bill Is so Problematic', *Emerging Europe* (18 November 2021), available at https://emerging-europe.com/news/why-ukraines-anti-oligarch-bill-is-so-problematic/.

288 UKRAINE'S FIGHT AGAINST CORRUPTION AND SUPPLIER COLLUSION

broad-based international support and to effectively transition to a more stable and democratic society. In press coverage of the above-noted crackdown and departure of high-ranking public officials beginning in January 2023, the following details have come to light:

- Deputy Defense Minister Viacheslav Shapovalov has resigned, in the face of allegations concerning a scandal involving the purchase of food for the Ukrainian Armed Forces.[87]
- Valentyn Reznichenko, formerly governor of the Dnipropetrovsk region, has been accused in local media of channelling more than USD 40 million in government contracts to associates, including his girlfriend.[88]
- Ukraine's Deputy Minister for Infrastructure, Vasyl Lozinskiy, has been arrested for allegedly embezzling USD 400,000 in public funds, according to Ukraine's state anti-corruption bureau.[89]
- Vasyl Lozynskyy, Acting Minister for Regional Development, has been accused by the National Anti-Corruption Bureau of Ukraine of receiving USD 400,000 in 'unlawful benefits' for facilitating the allocation of state contracts, including with respect to power generators.[90]
- Separately, President Zelensky accepted the resignation of Kyrylo Tymoshenko, deputy head of the presidential administration, an important member of the President's inner circle.[91]
- Most recently, and as already noted, President Zelensky has replaced Ukraine's Minister of Defence, Oleksii Reznikov, amid continuing concerns regarding alleged 'huge overpayments' relating to food and other military supplies in the course of the ongoing war effort.[92]

Below the level of such 'headline stories', other important enforcement efforts have occurred. As Minakov notes:

… in January 2023, [the National Anti-Corruption Bureau (NABU) and the Special Anticorruption Prosecutor's Office (SAPO)] completed the second part of a sprawling investigation into fifteen persons suspected of operationalizing the so-called 'Rotterdam Plus' formula, a legacy of former president

---

[87] 'Senior Ukrainian Officials Ousted in Corruption Crackdown', *NBC News*, n. 8.
[88] 'Ukraine's Zelensky Removes Top Officials in Bid to Contain Corruption Scandals: Graft Allegations Shake-Up Could Threaten Western Confidence in Kyiv', *Wall Street Journal*, n. 8.
[89] 'Ukraine's Zelensky Removes Top Officials in Bid to Contain Corruption Scandals: Graft Allegations Shake-Up Could Threaten Western Confidence in Kyiv', *Wall Street Journal*, n. 8.
[90] 'Zelensky Shakes Up Ukrainian Government Amid Growing Corruption Scandal', *CNN*, n. 8.
[91] 'Top Ukrainian Officials Quit in Anti-Corruption Drive', *BBC News* (24 January 2023); see also Minakov, n. 8.
[92] See New York Times, n. 10.

QUEST TO STRENGTHEN COMPETITION POLICY IN UKRAINE 289

Petro Poroshenko. Under the terms of the formula, electricity consumers over-paid oligarch-controlled companies more than 400 million USD in 2018–2019. Among those suspected of putting the formula into practice are two former heads and seven members of the National Energy and Utilities Regulatory Commission.[93]

These and related developments illustrate vividly the continuing challenges faced by Ukraine with respect to corruption in public governance, including (very much) in public procurement sector and related activities. Still, the actions taken are also, in many ways, an encouraging sign.[94] President Zelensky appears, thus far, to be unwilling to accept the status quo ante bellum as Ukraine's future. The challenge for Ukraine and the international community is to ensure that his avowed intention is fulfilled.

In sum, despite its history, Ukraine has, in recent years, made major efforts to reduce and prevent corruption in public procurement—and not without important successes. In particular, the ProZorro system and the DOZORRO network both represent important international benchmarks for anti-corruption reform, the former as a tool for achieving greatly enhanced transparency and the latter as an approach for engaging the involvement of interested citizens and relevant civil society groups in monitoring procurement activities. No doubt, the situation will continue to evolve. Still, given Ukraine's history, the recent scandals, and the findings of current surveys[95] and related reporting, it would be naïve to conclude that the country's problems in this area have been resolved.

D. The Internationally Supported Quest to Strengthen Competition Policy in Ukraine

The potential contribution of competition policy to the resolution of Ukraine's economic, political, and governance challenges, including with reference to the specific challenges posed by the public procurement sector, has not been entirely neglected, over the years. Indeed, significant capacity building efforts have been undertaken. This section details relevant developments and experience.

---

[93] Minakov, n. 8.

[94] L. Bershidsky, 'Ukraine's Wave of Graft Scandals Is a Healthy Sign', *Washington Post* (25 January 2023), available at https://www.washingtonpost.com/business/ukraineswave-of-graft-scandals-is-a-healthy-sign/2023/01/25/0dbcecac-9c70-11ed-93e0-38551e88239c_story.html. See also 'Removal of defense Minister shows wartime Ukraine is changing', n. 10.

[95] See, again, Mungiu-Pippidi, n. 4.

i. Competition law and policy in Ukraine: origins, institutional basis, and pre-2014 history

Following the dissolution of the Soviet Union, Ukraine adopted a new competition law system as part of its effort to transition from a centrally planned to a market-based economy. The competition framework has its foundation in the Ukraine's Constitution and is mainly enshrined in Law No. 3659-XII 'On the Antimonopoly Committee of Ukraine' of 26 November 1993 (the competition law). Additionally, other legislations, namely, Law 236/96-VR 'On the Protection from Unfair Competition' of 7 June 1996, and Law No. 2210-III 'On the Protection of Economic Competition' of 11 December 2001 deal tangentially with competition issues.[96]

The AMCU, as the national competition agency, is in charge of implementing the Ukrainian competition law and policy. The tasks of the Antimonopoly Committee include the classic responsibilities of an antitrust enforcement agency, i.e. investigating and resolving complaints in relation to abuse of dominant position, acts of unfair competition, non-competitive actions of public authorities, non-competitive concerted actions of commercial entities, as well as acquisition and merger control.[97] The AMCU is also involved in (i) the drafting of legal texts, within the scope of the law, for later approval and adoption by the Cabinet of Ministers, and (ii) the review of legal acts developed by other branches of the government that could affect competition in the country. The AMCU may independently initiate necessary investigations of anti-competitive practices, without the need of third-party claims or requests.

Despite the difficult political context of the 1990s, including decades-long pervasive state control of the economy and the absence of institutions needed to support a market economy, the beginnings of Ukraine's competition regime and the designated competition authority were encouraging.[98] However, as the AMCU reached its second decade as an active institution, the initial drive slowed down and the national competition law system nearly foundered.[99] Severe political and economic turmoil beset Ukraine in 2013. For an 18-month period, the AMCU was headed with uncertain authority and frail political support. The agency's board functioned with five commissioners, four fewer than the number specified in the competition law and budget cuts of roughly 70 per cent forced experienced managers and professional staff to leave the agency. Furthermore, powerful forces in business and within the government resist the market reforms needed to spur the growth of the economy.[100]

---

[96] See, WTO, 'Trade Policy Review: Ukraine', n. 48.

[97] See, WTO, 'Trade Policy Review: Ukraine', n. 48.

[98] OECD, 'OECD Reviews of Competition Law and Policy: Ukraine' (2016), available at https://www.oecd.org/fr/daf/concurrence/competitionlawandpolicyinukraine2016.htm.

[99] OECD, n. 98, 9.

[100] OECD, n. 98, 9.

Another problem is that, in practice, even when functioning as a viable organization, rather than grappling effectively with the market power of oligarchs and practices that thwart competition, the AMCU historically functioned predominantly as a price-control body. As Aslund observed in 2015:

> In a Ukrainian restaurant, every single page of the menu has the signatures of the restaurant's manager, deputy manager and accountant as well as the restaurant's official stamp. The Antimonopoly Committee has ordered restaurants to do this. It focuses on controlling prices rather than encouraging competition.

Following the 2014 'Revolution of Dignity' and reform efforts supported by the international community, the AMCU is once again effectively in the situation of a start-up institution with a renewed commitment to achieve the aims of the 1990s competition reforms. It has begun the difficult process of restoring lost human capital, rebuilding its substantive programmes, and resuming recommendations set by international organizations and experts,[101] towards the attainment of accepted international standards for competition law implementation.[102] These efforts are vital to establishing a true competitive market economy in Ukraine. Time will tell if they are successful.

ii. Pursuing bid rigging and related conduct in public procurement

As we have emphasized throughout this book, the investigation and prosecution of bid rigging in public procurement is seen by enforcement authorities and scholars around the world as an essential dimension of competition law enforcement, arguably one of the highest-payoff areas for such enforcement in terms of its impact on public welfare. Currently, there are indications that the AMCU has embraced this vision. Overall, in Ukraine, bid rigging is the single most commonly prosecuted horizontal competition offence. Between 2017 and 2019, the AMCU prosecuted and fined almost 600 bid rigging cases, roughly 97 per cent of all horizontal hardcore cartels.[103]

A recent and relevant example includes a 2019 case where suppliers colluded to distort seven tenders for catering across different regions of the country. Based on the analysis and collection of evidence, it was established that the cartel members

---

[101] UNCTAD, 'Voluntary Peer Review of Competition Law and Policy: Ukraine' (2013) UNCTAD/DITC/CLP/2013/3, available at https://unctad.org/system/files/official-document/ditcclp2013d3_overview_en.pdf.

[102] UNCTAD, n. 101.

[103] OECD, 'Fighting Bid-Rigging in the Energy Sector in Ukraine: A Review of Public Procurement at Ukrenergo' (2021), available at http://oe.cd/fbr-nrg-ukr.

participated at two levels, that is, on a general coordination level during the bidding procedure and also within certain regional groups. The AMCU fined the infringers a total of UAH 865 million (almost USD 32 million).[104] The AMCU has also fined foreign firms for rigging a 2015 tender from Ukrainian state enterprise UkrGasVydobuvannya.[105]

Another relevant case highlights how certain measures can be misused to exclude foreign competitors and facilitate bid rigging. In 2015, the state-owned company, NPC Ukrenergo, announced tenders for the purchase of transformers and excluded, unexpectedly, foreign companies under the premise that they were financially risky. A Ukrainian company successfully placed a bid and won at a much higher than average price (it actually exported the same type of transformers to Russia at a price that was almost seven times lower). The possible embezzlement of almost UAH 2 billion created a media scandal and the AMCU annulled the results of the tender.[106] After the tender documentation was revised, qualification requirements were improved so as to stimulate the participation of foreign manufacturers. As a result, the tender value decreased significantly.[107]

The adoption of electronic procurement through the ProZorro platform has contributed importantly to enhancing competition in the public procurement market, by expanding the set of potential suppliers:

> About 90 per cent of registered businesses on ProZorro are small and medium-sized enterprises (SMEs). Monthly, 3.000 to 5.000 new suppliers register in ProZorro. Over 50.000 suppliers registered in the system in 2019. ProZorro is trusted – it is significant that suppliers from more than 40 countries (mainly from the European Union) are registered in ProZorro and participate in Ukrainian public tenders.[108]

Reportedly, the digitalization of public procurement and big data analysis tools have also strengthened the ability of AMCU officials to identify patterns related to supplier collusion, in particular, by identifying relationships between bidders, evaluation of formal signs of corruption, and automatic searches relating to information of prospective suppliers, among others.[109]

---

[104] O. Nechytailo, 'Bid-Rigging in Ukraine: Flavoured Products' in *Competition Policy in Eastern Europe and Central Asia: Focus on Bid Rigging in Public Procurement*, n. 57.

[105] Global Competition Review, 'Ukraine: Antimonopoly Committee of Ukraine', available at https://globalcompetitionreview.com/insight/enforcer-hub/2022/organization-profile/ukraine-antimonopoly-committee-of-ukraine.

[106] See discussion of the role of AMCU as the independent body for review of supplier complaints in public procurement, below.

[107] See, Savran, Khavanska, and Onysko, n. 57.

[108] Niewiadomska and Nicholas, n. 55.

[109] See, Nechytailo, n. 104.

Still, the AMCU needs to further develop and improve key tools considered essential for effective prosecution and deterrence of bid rigging,[110] including the ability to conduct dawn raids in a manner that allows collecting sufficient evidence to build a strong case[111] as well as enhanced powers to seize documents and interview individuals.[112] The AMCU should, additionally, take *full* advantage of the existing e-procurement system as an effective means for detecting and combatting supplier collusion through the monitoring and analysis of public procurement data and the subsequent identification of red flags.[113] Also, close cooperation between the competition authority and other public bodies is necessary to maximize the possibility of detection.[114] Plans are in place to work with the US Department of Justice and other competition agencies to develop appropriate tools.[115]

Another concern is that much of the bid manipulation that has attracted international attention appears to be directed by public officials rather than being organized secretly by the suppliers themselves (which is not to deny that this is also a problem). Several of the corruption allegations that surfaced in January 2023 fall broadly into this category, including bribes to fix contracts related to restoring infrastructure facilities battered by Russian missile strikes and purchases at inflated prices.[116] Also, the mandatory requirement of conducting public purchases through the ProZorro system has, on occasion, been circumvented by the authorities. For example, in the past, the Government of Ukraine has decided, by way of a Decree, to implement a very large infrastructure project outside the ProZorro platform.[117]

A further development that may impact negatively on competition in Ukrainian public procurement markets is the entry into force of the law 'On Amendments to the Law of Ukraine "On Public Procurement" to Create Preconditions for Sustainable Development and Modernization of Domestic Industry'. The law introduces localization requirements for public procurement of certain goods.[118] This new mandate may not only limit competition by narrowing the pool of prospective

---

[110] OECD, n. 98, 7. See, also OECD, 'Fighting Bid Rigging in Public Procurement: Report on Implementing the OECD Recommendation' (2016), available at https://www.oecd.org/daf/competit ion/Fighting-bid-rigging-in-public-procurement-2016-implementation-report.pdf.

[111] OECD, n. 98, 32.

[112] OECD, n. 98, 8.

[113] OECD, n. 110.

[114] Concurrence, 'Bid-Rigging', available at https://www.concurrences.com/en/dictionary/bid-rigging.

[115] Antimonopoly Committee of Ukraine, 'The Role and Tasks of the AMCU in the Process of Rebuilding Ukraine Were Discussed at Meetings with the FTC, the US Department of Justice and the World Bank' (27 June 2022), available at https://amcu.gov.ua/en/news/role-and-tasks-amcu-process-rebuilding-ukraine-were-discussed-meetings-ftc-us-department-justice-and-world-bank.

[116] See, related news and articles, n. 8.

[117] See, Savran, Khavanska, and Onysko, n. 57.

[118] See, Law of Ukraine No. 1977-IX. Also, 'The Law on Production Localization Entered into Force', available at https://www.asterslaw.com/press_center/legal_alerts/the_law_on_production_localiza tion_entered_into_force/.

suppliers but also directly undermine the ability of public authorities to seek out the best available technologies and maximize value for money.

Already in 2008 and 2013 respectively, the OECD[119] and UNCTAD[120], formulated recommendations with respect to the enforcement of competition law and policy in Ukraine's public procurement sector. The OECD advised that the Public Procurement Law should be amended to establish unconditional liability for bid rigging for cartel participants and sanctions in the form of fines and disqualification for violators. Another recommendation referenced the need to enhance transparency in public procurement.[121] Reflecting on these previous recommendations, a 2016 OECD Review reinforced the need to improve the existing legal framework for effective bid rigging detection and prosecution, enabling the AMCU to enforce its decisions directly.[122] Additionally, relevant actions are to be taken in relation to the current limited powers of the AMCU to seize documents and interview individuals, the infeasibility to search private premises, the inadequacy of the existing leniency regime vis-à-vis subsequent applicants, and the lack of individual sanctions for competition law infringements. The Review commended the adoption of ProZorro as a tool to improve transparency in the public procurement system,[123] by allowing the AMCU to visually observe the progress of the procurement procedure and identify signs that may indicate possible bid rigging.[124]

Lastly, following the signing of the EU-Ukraine Association Agreement in 2014, the Ukrainian competition law was amended substantially in the late 2010s to reflect international best practices and further align it with the EU competition standards, including in relation to public procurement.[125] Major reforms were enacted to address, among others, the transparency and publicity of the AMCU's decisions.[126]

In sum, even at present (at least since 2014) the AMCU has, appropriately, made the detection and deterrence of bid rigging an important focus of its activities. However, significant work remains to be done in this area, given the apparent extent of related problems in Ukraine. This observation also highlights the potential contribution of related activities of the AMCU that are detailed below.

---

[119] OECD, 'Competition Law and Policy in Ukraine: An OECD Peer Review' (2008), available at https://www.oecd.org/daf/competition/41165857.pdf.

[120] UNCTAD, n. 101.

[121] OECD, n. 98, 12.

[122] OECD, n. 98, 8.

[123] OECD, n. 98, 58.

[124] See, Nechytailo, n. 104.

[125] Law No. 935-VIII, 'On Amendments to the Law of Ukraine "On Protection of Economic Competition"'.

[126] OECD, n. 98, 18.

iii. The AMCU's role in the debarment of infringing suppliers: a further innovation

Building on the OECD recommendation noted in the preceding section, in 2016 the Public Procurement Law of Ukraine was amended to introduce, among others, a special mandatory ground to exclude a bidder from the tender process if, during the preceding three years, it has been held accountable for supplier collusion.[127] In a related development, the AMCU established a mechanism for the publication of information on undertakings that have engaged in bid rigging. The AMCU web portal contains a Consolidated Table[128] of decisions of the Committee on infringements of the legislation on the protection of economic competition by suppliers.[129] This initiative significantly facilitated the work of procuring entities—now, information related to previous infringements of prospective suppliers is readily available. The summary information also contains the case status, in case of appeals against the decision of the AMCU. Summary information is regularly updated, which allows contracting entities to quickly use such information.

In the fall of 2020, the Consolidated Table was integrated into ProZorro, allowing contracting entities to instantly check previously fined bidders. Thanks to the integration into the system, procuring entities do not need to verify information about bidders with the AMCU; it is enough to open the protocol for consideration of tender proposals, in which the inscription 'The bidder is listed in the Consolidated Information (Table) of the AMCU' appears, in case of a previous infringement. Undertakings on this list are not eligible to participate in public procurement procedures for three years from the date of the AMCU decision on the infringement.

Bid rigging is otherwise subject to the same fines as other concerted practices as set out by the newly implemented AMCU guidelines.[130] Borrowing from EU practices, and in the view of the AMCU, debarment has proven to be more effective than 'blacklisting' cartelized firms as it is often a more effective safeguard against bid rigging than fines.[131]

---

[127] See PPL, n. 31, Article 17, 1(3).

[128] See, the AMCU's Consolidated Table, available at https://amcu.gov.ua/napryami/oskarzhennya-publichnih-zakupivel/zvedeni-vidomosti-shchodo-spotvorennya-rezultativ-torgiv/zvedeni-vidomosti-shchodo-porushnikiv-torgiv-za-2022-rik.

[129] As provided for in paragraph 1 of Article 50, paragraph 4 of part 2 of Article 6 of the Law of Ukraine 'On Protection of Economic Competition'.

[130] OECD, n. 98, 46.

[131] AMCU, 'Bid-Rigging Sanctions and Cooperation with Sector Regulators: AMCU Joined the Meeting of the OECD Competition Committee' (13 December 2022), available at https://amcu.gov.ua/en/news/bid-rigging-sanctions-and-cooperation-sector-regulators-amcu-joined-meeting-oecd-competition-committee.

iv. An additional role: the AMCU as the independent review body for public procurement complaints

The AMCU also plays a significant role in public procurement—it is the designated authority for the review of supplier complaints. The existence of an independent review body is a requirement of the WTO GPA and is an internationally recognized guarantee of fair procedures in the public procurement sector. With the entry into force of the 2014 Public Procurement Law, the functions of the AMCU as appeal body did not become something new as its functions were previously defined in the competition law and the previous Public Procurement Law, however, the terms and the procedure for appeals did change significantly.

Complaints are considered by a Permanent Administrative Board comprised of three state commissioners. From mid-2016, the AMCU fully shifted from the consideration of paper-form complaints to electronic complaints uploaded via ProZorro (the AMCU does not consider complaints filed in paper form). After the complaint and related documents are uploaded to ProZorro (including the payment confirmation, required for consideration), it automatically enters into the register and is also automatically published on the ProZorro online portal. The Permanent Administrative Board may arrive at a decision on the presence or absence of a violation of the procurement procedure by the procuring entity and the actions that it must take to repair the violation.[132] Board decisions enter into force on the date of adoption and may be appealed to a court within one month of notification of the adopted decision.[133] To be clear, the AMCU is not authorized to award contracts, nor to oblige the procuring entity to enter into a contract with certain participants. Rather, it reviews the procurement procedure within the limits of the lodged complaint.[134] This appears to be broadly consistent with good international practices.

Through the use of e-procurement tools, the number of complaints received by the AMCU has grown steadily. For example, in the second half of 2019, participants filed about 1,000 complaints a month while in 2016, the AMCU received fewer than 2,000 complaints in half a year.[135] With respect to the reasons behind the complaints, in the case of open tenders published in English, complaints mainly relate to conditions set forth in the tender documentation. Overall, disputes mostly relate to tenders with high expected value. Following a 2019 amendment of the procurement law, procuring entities are now subject to administrative fines if they

---

[132] O. Fefelov, 'Role of the AMCU as of the Body for Challenging the Public Procurement Procedures', *Chambers and Partners* (23 October 2020), available at https://chambers.com/articles/role-of-the-amcu-as-of-the-body-for-challenging-the-public-procurement-procedures.

[133] See, WTO, 'Trade Policy Review: Ukraine', n. 48.

[134] Fefelov, n. 132.

[135] Transparency International, 'AMCU Granted Almost Half of Complaints by Procurement Participants in 2019', available at https://ti-ukraine.org/en/news/amcu-granted/.

fail to comply with decisions of the AMCU. It is also prohibited to cancel a tender during the period it takes to decide the challenge.[136]

To better ensure transparency in its actions, the AMCU publishes its decisions, provides information about cases considered during the reporting period, provides statistical data on the number of cases reviewed, decisions upheld, and savings made. Additionally, meetings of the Permanent Administrative Board are broadcasted online, providing access to interested stakeholders and civil society, in general.

The role of the AMCU as the designated authority for the review of public procurement supplier complaints is not without precedent: the German Bundeskartellamt (Germany's national competition authority), for example, performs a similar role in that country. This approach, moreover, is logical in that it recognizes and builds directly on the complementarity of competition policy and public procurement policy at a conceptual level.[137]

Nonetheless, our understanding is that, in practice, this role has imposed a significant burden on the AMCU and its top decision-makers, at a time when their attention is needed on multiple other fronts.[138] To ensure the continuing viability of the complaint review mechanism while better enabling the AMCU to tackle the other challenges that it faces, it would be desirable to create, either within or alongside the Commission as it is currently configured, a dedicated and adequately resourced unit to fulfil this function. Both the decision-makers and staff of this unit should have experience/training in public procurement processes in addition to competition enforcement.

v. Competition enforcement in the current war context

At the outset of the current war, in March 2022, the Ukrainian competition authority announced its relocation to Lviv and the suspension of most proceedings. This announcement caused uncertainty for relevant firms and forced their counsels to ask the AMCU for clarifications on Facebook due to the lack of other means to contact the competition authority. Nonetheless, the AMCU has provided guidance on notifications in times of war, especially for merger control. It states that the merger regime in Ukraine does not cease to apply during martial law, and the parties are expected to notify mergers according to the law. It also does not relieve parties from possible fines for violations of the competition law.[139]

---

[136] Transparency International, n. 135.
[137] Recall the discussion in Chapter 3, this book.
[138] Authors' conversations with AMCU leaders.
[139] See, for further details and discussion, D. Lypalo, 'Competition Law in Times of War: Response to the Russian Invasion of Ukraine', Kluwer Law Blog (4 April 2022), available at http://competitionlawblog.kluwercompetitionlaw.com/2022/04/04/competition-law-in-times-of-war-response-to-the-russian-invasion-of-ukraine/.

Reflecting solidarity in the European and international competition law community, the challenges posed by the war have also been the subject of a precedent-setting 'Joint statement by the European Competition Network (ECN) on the application of competition law in the context of the war in Ukraine'. The statement observes, inter alia, that:

> We, the ECN, join the European Council in its statement of 24 February 2022 ... , to condemn in the strongest possible terms Russia's unprecedented military aggression against Ukraine. We stand firmly by Ukraine and its people as they face this war. We are fully aware of the social and economic consequences for Ukraine as well as for the EU/EEA.
>
> ....
>
> The ECN understands that this extraordinary situation may trigger the need for companies to address severe disruptions caused by the impact of the war and/or of sanctions in the Internal Market. This may include for example cooperation in order to (i) ensure the purchase, supply and fair distribution of scarce products and inputs; or (ii) mitigate severe economic consequences including those arising from compliance with sanctions imposed by the EU.
>
> ... it is of utmost importance to ensure that essential products (for example energy, food, raw materials) remain available at competitive prices and that the current crisis is not used to undermine a competitive level playing field between companies. The ECN will therefore not hesitate to take action against companies taking advantage of the current situation by entering into cartels or abusing their dominant position.[140]

The foregoing statement is intriguing and consequential in that it shows both keen awareness on the part of European competition regulators of the broader context in which the AMCU works and their determination to support their sister competition agency in its time of challenge.

vi. International support for strengthening of the competition regime in Ukraine, with a specific focus on public procurement

Competition law and policy have been a focus of capacity building efforts by international organizations, sister competition agencies, and scholars over an extended

---

[140] Press Release of the European Competition Network, 'Antitrust: Joint Statement by the European Competition Network (ECN) on the Application of Competition Law in the Context of the War in Ukraine' (24 February 2022), available at https://competition-policy.ec.europa.eu/system/files/2022-03/202203_joint-statement_ecn_ukraine-war.pdf.

period.[141] These efforts have often, appropriately, had a specific focus on strengthening competition in public procurement markets. For example:

- The OECD has long worked with Ukraine to design public procurement processes that promote competition and to set up methods for detecting collusive agreements. A 2021 review focused on assessing the procurement practices of Ukrenergo, the Ukrainian energy state-owned enterprise (SOE) and national-grid operator, showed that Ukrenergo can still make significant improvements to address both the prevention and detection of bid rigging in its tenders. To this end, the review generated a number of recommendations to benefit not only Ukrenergo's procurement system, but also other SOEs in Ukraine, by benchmarking their own practices and making any necessary adjustments.[142]
- The EBRD also fosters competition and supports anti-corruption efforts in Ukraine. Based on a previous cooperation between the EBRD and the OECD, a project was launched to improve the AMCU's regulatory framework, enforcement procedures, and enhance its capacity to deal with competition cases, in particular bid rigging cases.[143]
- To advance and strengthen the role of the AMCU as the body in charge of reviewing and deciding public procurement complaints, EBRD has also developed a 'Handbook on Key Judicial Skills and Competencies for Members of Procurement Review Tribunals' which has been localized for Ukraine, in cooperation with the AMCU. The Handbook covers such topics as procedural fairness, conflict of interest, evidence and procedure, confidential information, approach to remedies, discretion, and writing decisions.

These initiatives are, very much, in line with the expanded international support for the AMCU's efforts that will certainly be needed in the aftermath of the war.

In sum, efforts to strengthen the role of competition policy in Ukraine have been under way for an extended period, with significant help from the international community. The prevention of bid rigging in public procurement has been an important focus of those efforts. The AMCU has sought to contribute to corruption control and better practices in public procurement in other ways, as well—notably, in its roles in debarring infringing suppliers and acting as a forum for adjudication of supplier complaints. Still, much work remains to be done, including

---

[141] See, for early contributions and overviews of related activity, W.E. Kovacic, 'The Competition Policy Entrepreneur and Law Reform in Formerly Communist and Socialist Countries' (1996) 11(3) *American University International Law Review* 437–74; Y. Stotyka, 'The Role of the Antimonopoly Committee in the Development of Competition in Ukraine' (2004), available at SSRN: https://ssrn.com/abstract=613262 or http://dx.doi.org/10.2139/ssrn.613262; and references cited in those publications.

[142] OECD, n. 103.

[143] See, EBRD's project on 'Digital Transformation of the Competition Law Enforcement Procedures of the Anti-Monopoly Committee of Ukraine', available at https://www.ebrd.com/work-with-us/projects/tcpsd/12860.html.

strengthening of the enforcement tools available to the AMCU with respect to bid rigging in public procurement and competition law enforcement generally. Arguably, Ukraine and the international community have under-invested in competition policy generally, relative to the market power wielded by the country's oligarchs and the high-profile measures that have been taken against corruption.

E. Ukraine's Anticipated Post-War Reconstruction: Major Challenges Ahead

Advance planning regarding the post-war reconstruction of Ukraine is already under way. References are being made to a new 'Marshall Plan for Ukraine'.[144] Concurrently, the EU has granted Ukraine the status of a candidate for accession to the a development which could potentially contribute powerfully to the struggle for better governance.[145] Furthermore, on 14 December 2023, the European Council announced the opening of accession negotiations.[146] These developments signal clearly the high importance that the international community attaches to Ukraine's successful post-war reconstruction. They also create important sources of leverage for the necessary reforms.[147]

Much of the initial discussion has centred on issues concerning macroeconomic stabilization, the removal of war debris, the rebuilding of (often) severely damaged infrastructure and the re-establishment of a viable civilian economy, and/or issues concerning the financial or energy sectors of Ukraine's economy.[148] Increasingly, however, commentators are also stressing the importance of anti-corruption efforts as a centrepiece of the reconstruction efforts.[149] Indeed, from the foregoing sections of this chapter, it is abundantly clear that efforts to eradicate corruption in Ukraine will need to be intensified and carried forward in a systematic way if the country is to survive and establish itself as a sovereign, democratic, and relatively

[144] H.A. Conley, 'A Modern Marshall Plan for Ukraine: Seven Lessons from History to Deliver Hope' (2022), available at https://www.gmfus.org/sites/default/files/2022-10/A%20Modern%20Marsh all%20Plan%20for%20Ukraine.pdf. See also 'Donors Are Already Mulling a Marshall Plan for Ukraine', *The Economist* (8 November 2022), available at https://www.economist.com/international/2022/11/08/donors-are-already-mulling-a-marshall-plan-for-ukraine.

[145] Recall the important role of the EU in establishing necessary institutional foundations for competition, corruption control, and the rule of law in Hungary and Poland (discussed in Chapter 8), notwithstanding the limited access achieved thus far in enforcing relevant standards.

[146] European Council, Ukraine, available at https://www.consilium.europa.eu/en/policies/enlargement/ukraine/#:~:text=Ukraine%20applied%20for%20EU%20membership,EU%20membership%20application.

[147] See 'Briefing Ukraine 2.0: The Battle Within', *The Economist* (24 June 2023) 14–6. See also Tregle, n. 2.

[148] See, e.g., Skidmore, Wessel, and Asdourian, n. 7.

[149] See also T. Becker, J. Lehne, and T. Mylovanov, 'Anti-Corruption Policies in the Reconstruction of Ukraine' in N. Shapoval and G. Spagnolo (eds), *Rebuilding Ukraine: Principles and Policies* (CEPR Press, 2022), available at https://cepr.org/chapters/anti-corruption-policies-reconstruction-ukraine.

non-corrupt polity, potentially more closely aligned with western European countries, in the aftermath of the current war.[150] Moreover, while this need transcends the public procurement sector per se, the prevention of corrupt practices and supplier collusion in public procurement will necessarily be a central part of the effort. Effective measures in this area are also (rightly) critical to the achievement of Ukraine's hope/intention to join the EU. The following outlines specific issues and proposals to be considered in this context.

i. General measures to restore confidence in the Rule of Law and the integrity of related institutions

As we have emphasized in this chapter and throughout this book, the deterrence of corrupt practices and supplier collusion in public procurement cannot be pursued effectively in isolation. Rather, it depends importantly on general respect for the rule of law and on confidence in the independence, impartiality, and integrity of related institutions, including the courts and on national and other prosecution services. Institutional and legal safeguards to limit the ability of ministers and other high-level authorities to 'weigh in' on behalf of cronies are also vital.[151]

In Ukraine, these are particularly compelling needs. As Bohdan Vitvitsky, former Resident Legal Advisor at the US Embassy in Ukraine and Special Advisor to Ukraine's Prosecutor General, has recently observed:

> Ukraine's legal system has been a smouldering crisis situation since independence. When the time comes to begin Ukraine's post-war reconstruction, Ukraine will need to establish a 'legal fire brigade' that will have the authority and the resources to implement the kind of thoroughgoing change and reform of the entire legal system that will be required in order to significantly improve Ukraine's rule of law and facilitate a successful physical reconstruction .... The very real chance of progress toward EU accession provides further additional motivation.[152]

Notwithstanding the direness of the need, in key respects, the reforms needed can build on initiatives already taken. As observed by Rudolph and Eisen in November 2022:

> Ukraine has built the most transparent political-economic system anywhere, featuring the world's first public beneficial ownership registry, most transparent

---

[150] See also 'Creating Ukraine 2.0', *The Economist* (24 June 2023) 8.

[151] See this book, Chapter 4.

[152] B. Vitvitsky, 'Building a Better Ukraine: Rule of Law Is Essential for Post-War Prosperity', *Atlantic Council* (13 July 2022), available at https://www.atlanticcouncil.org/blogs/ukrainealert/building-a-better-ukraine-rule-of-law-is-essential-for-post-war-prosperity/.

public procurement system, most well-enforced and comprehensive asset declarations, first public database of politically exposed persons, and other innovative digital disclosure systems. Cases of grand corruption fall under the jurisdiction of a set of specialized anti-corruption bodies dedicated to investigation, prosecution, high court, and asset recovery. However, three of these new specialized institutions, including the National Anti-Corruption Bureau of Ukraine (NABU), currently lack permanent leadership. Other important areas of the state remain unreformed, such as the ordinary judicial system all the way up to the constitutional court.[153]

With Ukraine's priority currently on winning, or at the very least, coming through the war in reasonably sound condition, the specific reforms to be implemented will undoubtedly require further deliberation. It is important that they be developed with substantial input from Ukrainians themselves, notwithstanding that the international community will and should pay very careful attention, provide all appropriate technical support, and apply pressure, if needed, to ensure the job is done. As a preliminary list, the following points, inter alia, will undoubtedly require attention and appropriate action, most likely to be reinforced by a new Constitution:[154]

- Sweeping political reform to ensure a robust democratic polity, even under times of stress. This will include statutory safeguards for fair and transparent elections, and a peaceful transfer of power. Additional appropriate measures could include: (i) a possible transition to a Parliamentary as opposed to the current presidential system of government; (ii) a move to fully proportional representation; and (iii) increased transparency with respect to the funding of electoral campaigns.[155]
- Fundamental reforms to create a modern, efficient, and transparent state, accountable to Ukraine's citizens. While there will be many dimensions to the necessary reforms, at the top of the list must be new enactments and enforcement mechanisms to ensure the independence, impartiality, and accountability of the national prosecutorial service (a long-running area of concern) and the judiciary, and to eliminate undue discretion.[156] Significant deregulation is also likely to be needed, to limit the state's ability to extract rents and improve the business environment.[157] And, none of this is likely to work unless major attention is devoted to upgrading the quality, professionalism, and (where appropriate) independence of Ukraine's civil service, at all levels.[158]

---

[153] See Rudolph and Eisen, n. 13.
[154] See also Becker, Lehne, and Mylovanov, n. 149.
[155] Aslund, n. 1, Chapter 7.
[156] Aslund, n. 1, Chapter 8. See Rudolph and Eisen, n. 13.
[157] Aslund, n. 1, 150–2.
[158] Aslund, n. 1, 146–50; see also related discussion, below.

ii. Strengthened measures to deter corruption in the public procurement sphere

Turning now to measures specific to the public procurement sphere, these will be vital to the reconstruction effort, not only as a general contribution to a cleaner and healthier economy and society, but also as a specific contribution to reconstruction. In the course of the current war, direct material damage has already reached USD 97 billion.[159] As such, the reconstruction of bombed-out buildings, streets, and general infrastructure will entail very significant public expenditure. Effective corruption control will be vital to obtaining good results for money, and to ensuring the confidence of Ukrainian citizens and the international donor community.

As we have already noted, Ukraine already has significant achievements in this area on which to build. These include: (i) the ProZorro platform, the internationally recognized e-procurement tool developed with international support and based on principles of the OCDS; and (ii) the DoZorro system to enable effective monitoring of procurement activities by civil society organizations. Continuing support for these initiatives is crucial. Still, significantly more can and must be done. Building on the ideas of Mungiu-Pippidi and other authorities, the following ideas merit consideration:

- Extension of citizen involvement to include participation in identifying public procurement needs. As Mungiu-Pippidi aptly observes:

> Public procurement is often corrupted before it has even taken place, by discretionary purchases or distorted terms of reference.... Due consideration needs to be given to avoid the reconstruction turning into either a Samaritan dilemma, where the purchases are driven by the needs of the suppliers rather than the ones of the buyers, or a locally captured process, where higher kickbacks from more concentrated rents get priority over the rest.... This is why the collection of information should rely on civil society (in the broadest sense—including the private sector and communities, not only NGOs), on local government and central government, with findings triangulated in a central mechanism (as an online map with various categories).[160]

> To address this problem, Mungiu-Pippidi advocates a centralized system for the identification of procurement based on an external validation mechanism and a decentralized and pluralistic data collection. This would

---

[159] Open Contracting Partnership, 'Post-War Procurement: How Ukraine Can Ensure the Reconstruction Is Transparent and Effective', available at https://www.open-contracting.org/es/2022/05/26/post-war-procurement-how-ukraine-can-ensure-the-reconstruction-is-transparent-and-effective/.

[160] Mungiu-Pippidi, n. 4.

be complemented by reports on emerging needs to be prepared by international NGOs or other organizations with relevant experience.[161]

- Shifting from the current system of *ex-post* anti-corruption enforcement to preventive anti-corruption measures. Here, Mungiu-Pippidi makes several important points:

> No successful control of corruption has ever worked post-factum except where corruption was already exceptional and isolated and public integrity the norm. Convictions in Courts take years even in countries where they happen, and they can get reversed: recovering assets is highly expensive and takes years. Turning judiciaries which are themselves problems into solutions to corruption is highly unrealistic, although building a non-corrupt and effective judiciary is a worthy goal in itself .... After the war ends, [anti-corruption enforcement in Ukraine] Ukraine should focus on reforms: to eliminate the sources of economic privileges, the monopolies and oligopolies of every sector rather than spend years putting in jail those who profited in earlier times from such political opportunities.[162]
>
> It will be noted that, in addition to corruption control, the foregoing also implicates the role of competition policy and the AMCU (see subsection iii, below). Important additional measures relating to the deterrence and prevention of corruption in public procurement include the following:

- Systematic reform to ensure that all exemptions from normal transparent and competitive tendering procedures in Ukraine are subject to appropriate (and, normally, publicly disclosed) justification. This is a key principle of the EU and US public procurement systems which provide possible models in this respect.[163]
- A strengthening of Ukraine's procurement appeal system. An impartial and independent procurement appeal ('bid protest' or 'domestic review') system is an important tool for the prevention of procurement abuses. Generally, such systems allow challenges arising from any decision or action by the procuring entity allegedly not in compliance with the provisions of relevant national law, by suppliers that believe they have suffered or may suffer loss or injury because of such alleged non-compliance.[164] For example, a key function of such systems can be to prevent/control the unjustified use of non-competitive procedures (also referred to in some systems as 'unlawful direct awards').[165] Support

---

[161] See, for pertinent details, Mungiu-Pippidi, n. 4.
[162] Mungiu-Pippidi, n. 4.
[163] See, for useful discussion of the latter, Tregle, n. 2.
[164] See UNCITRAL, 'Guide to Enactment of the UNCITRAL Model Law on Public Procurement', 378, available at https://uncitral.un.org/en/texts/procurement/modellaw/public_procurement/guide.
[165] See, Article 64 of the 2011 UNCITRAL Model Law on Public Procurement, n. 32.

UKRAINE'S ANTICIPATED POST-WAR RECONSTRUCTION   305

for Ukraine's procurement appeals system should, therefore, be an element of relevant institution-building. At the same time, as noted, the assuming of responsibility for the appeal system by a separate, dedicated and adequately resourced, unit (whether within or alongside the AMCU) is needed to ensure the demands of this function do not impede those of competition policy more generally.

- A strengthening of transparency and related disciplines in the defence sector, subject to reasonable limits based on genuine national security concerns. As we have already noted, military procurements are often excluded from both general transparency measures and the reach of international disciplines on public procurement such as the WTO GPA. Only a portion of such procurements, however, are truly national security sensitive. All others (e.g. food and clothing requirements) should be subject to the relevant disciplines.[166]
- Significant investments in the human resources needed for a clean and effective procurement system. As we have emphasized elsewhere in this book, appropriate investments in human resources are vital to yielding good results from any procurement system. Indeed, much experience suggests that these can partially alleviate the need for costly *ex-post* control systems and deliver better overall value for taxpayers.[167] In Ukraine's case, the need appears to be critical.

iii. Measures to ensure the effective enforcement of competition law, including with respect to public procurement markets

In addition to effective deterrence of bribery and kickbacks, good results in public procurement also require a degree of competition to ensure that best value for money is achieved. Strengthening competition policy in public procurement markets must become part of the support and recovery plan to prevent the monopolization of parts of the economy and ensure that qualified suppliers—either domestic or foreign—are able to participate in tenders not only for works, but also for the provision of essential goods and services. To this end, the following should be prioritized by the AMCU, in cooperation with relevant procuring entities:

- The putting in place of an effective enforcement framework to punish and deter bid rigging with clear rules and effective sanctions.
- A strengthening of tools necessary to address supplier collusion and prosecute cartel members, including the ability to conduct effective dawn raids,

---

[166] See, for useful discussion, Tregle, n. 2.

[167] See this volume, Chapter 4; see also S.L. Schooner and C.R. Yukins, 'Public Procurement: Focus on People, Value for Money and Systemic Integrity, Not Protectionism' in R. Baldwin and S. Evenett (eds), *The Collapse of Global Trade, Murky Protectionism, and the Crisis: Recommendations for the G20* (Centre for Economic Policy Research, 2009) 87, 91.

interview individuals, and further develop the leniency regime for subsequent applicants and whistleblowers.
- The fostering of close cooperation between the AMCU and Ukraine's procuring entities, to maximize the possibility of detection.
- The taking of full advantage of the data made available by the ProZorro platform for detecting and combating supplier collusion through the monitoring and analysis of public procurement data and the subsequent identification of red flags.
- Comprehensive training and professionalization of relevant public officials.
- Outreach to businesses and the wider community to promote the successful creation of a procompetitive procurement system.

iv. The transcendent importance of international support

With all the above, there would seem to be little possibility that Ukraine will succeed in the absence of both unprecedented levels of international support and an appropriate degree of international monitoring and incentivizing of the necessary reforms. As already noted, together with Ukraine's bid to accede to the EU, the anticipated international assistance effort provides not only essential support but crucial leverage to ensure that the necessary sweeping reforms are actually implemented. The donors must use this effectively. As Skidmore, Wessel, and Asdourian observe:

> The overarching goal of reconstruction should be to transform Ukraine's economy and society by modernizing—not only its infrastructure, but also its economic, political, and social institutions, thus providing a decisive break from Ukraine's Soviet past and paving the way for it to join the EU.... Ukrainians should take the lead in setting priorities for reconstruction and implementing it .... *Donor countries and institutions should rigorously and cooperatively oversee their reconstruction assistance to ensure the program's goals are achieved and Ukraine's endemic corruption thwarted.*[168] [Emphasis added.]

F. Concluding Remarks

This chapter has examined and reflected on the ongoing fight against corruption and supplier collusion in public procurement in Ukraine and its relation to the

---

[168] Skidmore, Wessel, and Asdourian, n. 7. See also Blumenthal et al., n. 7, and OECD, 'Public Governance in Ukraine: Implications of Russia's War', *OECD Policy Responses on the Impacts of the War in Ukraine* (2022), available at https://doi.org/10.1787/c8cbf0f4-en.

country's broader existential struggle. It takes the perspective that the fight against corruption in its many forms—including, very much, bribery and supplier collusion in public procurement—is an essential element of the country's efforts to achieve national survival, security, democratic governance, and a decent way of life.

In broader terms, the analysis in this chapter has reinforced and highlighted multiple themes of this book. These include:

- The breadth and tenacity of the problems entailed in cases of 'systemic corruption', and the multifaceted and inter-connected nature of the measures that (potentially) can help;
- The necessity of measures to strengthen competition and competition policy in addition to preventing bribery, kickbacks, and other traditional corrupt practices;
- The centrality of issues concerning the public procurement sector, to efforts to eradicate corruption and foster good governance and effective competition in many countries. In addition to general measures to support and extend the ProZorro and DoZorro systems, a mechanism is needed to ensure that all exemptions from normal transparent and competitive tendering procedures in Ukraine are subject to appropriate (and public) justification;
- The vital importance of those efforts for the viability and credibility of national institutions, sovereignty, and governance;
- The importance of the wider political and institutional context (including the independence, impartiality, and integrity of courts, prosecutors, and other relevant bodies, and politicians' respect for the rule of law) for the success of reform efforts centred on the public procurement sector;
- The extent and difficulty of the institution-building and change management processes that are involved;
- The benefits to be achieved from broader use of digital tools and 'open' contracting systems;
- The overriding importance of engaging civil society in related efforts;
- The interdependence of anti-corruption measures and effective competition policy, particularly in transition economy settings;
- The tendency, at least in some jurisdictions, to under-invest in competition policy as compared to conventional anti-corruption policy and institutions; and
- The importance of international support and multilateral arrangements (including international trade and related agreements) for the struggle against corruption and supplier collusion at the national level.

Beyond this, the experience of Ukraine casts light on a central question considered in this book: whether pervasive transparency as a central element of its procurement reforms is an optimal choice for the control and deterrence of corruption and supplier collusion in public procurement. As we have made clear earlier in this book and in previous writings, while transparency is a vital tool in the fight against corruption, there are also potential downsides to 'too much' transparency in public procurement administration and practice. In particular, 'total transparency' with respect to bids received and other parameters of individual procurements can undeniably facilitate supplier collusion. Still, our view is that, in the special context in which Ukraine found itself in the past decade, it has broadly made the right choices. It made a judgement that, given the pervasiveness of corrupt practices and outright theft of public funds in Ukraine in the post-Soviet period, the only hope of restoring confidence in government and integrity in public procurement, lay in implementing a system of broad transparency. This seems to us to be a reasonable choice in those circumstances, and may well have relevance for other countries in similar situations.

10

Persistent Corruption and Supplier Collusion in Public Procurement in a (Generally) Well-Governed Country: The Case of Canada

A. Introduction	310	
B. Public Procurement in Canada Generally	312	
i. Federal level	313	
ii. Provincial level	313	
iii. The role of Canada's international and internal trade agreements in shaping public procurement policy	315	
C. Early Corruption and Supplier Collusion Scandals in Public Procurement in Canada: A Harbinger of Problems to Come	316	
i. The 'Pacific Scandal'	316	
ii. The 'Hamilton Harbour' dredging scandal	317	
iii. The flour milling bid rigging case of 1990	318	
D. More Recent Examples of Corrupt Practices and/or Supplier Collusion in Public Procurement	319	
i. The 'Sponsorship Scandal'	319	
ii. The 'ETS scandal'	321	
iii. The 'F-35 fighter jet procurement scandal'	321	
iv. Corruption and supplier collusion in the Quebec (Province of Canada) construction sector	322	

v. The 'SNC Lavelin Affair'	324	
vi. The 'WE Charity' scandal	325	
vii. The recent outsourcing debate focusing on contracts issued to McKinsey and Co.	326	
viii. Discerning the common threads: observations relevant to the understanding of corrupt practices and supplier collusion in public procurement globally	327	
E. The Evolution of Canada's Anti-Corruption Framework for Public Procurement	330	
i. Institutional support in fighting corruption	331	
ii. The Canadian 'Integrity Regime' and the role of Public Services and Procurement Canada	332	
iii. Canada and the global fight against corruption	334	
iv. Response to the recent concern over outsourcing and the ballooning contracts issued to McKinsey	335	
F. Evolution of the Canadian Competition Law Framework in Regard to Supplier Collusion and Bid Rigging	336	
G. Concluding Remarks	340	

A. Introduction

Canada has a well-deserved reputation as a moderate, peaceable, and, for the most part, well-governed country. It constitutes an advanced industrial economy and a mature democracy with a well-developed legal system.[1] It is a longstanding member of the G-7 Group of leading industrial economies and the Organisation for Economic Co-operation and Development (OECD).[2] Canada ranks as the 14th least corrupt out of 180 countries surveyed, according to the 2022 Corruption Perceptions Index (CPI) of Transparency International.[3] Famously (at least in Canada), whereas the United States (US) Declaration of Independence enshrines the securing of citizens' rights to 'life, liberty and the pursuit of happiness' as overriding goals of democratic governance, Canada's founding document (the Constitution Act of 1867, formerly the British North America Act) refers instead to the goals of 'peace, order and good government'.[4]

Canada has a relatively sophisticated anti-corruption regime[5] in addition to long experience in competition law enforcement (its competition regime dates back to 1889, a year prior to the passage of the Sherman Antitrust Act in the US).[6] It has been a party to the World Trade Organization (WTO) Agreement on Government Procurement (GPA) since 1995, and previously participated as a member of the Tokyo Round Code on Government Procurement. Canada has also played important roles in relevant work of other international organizations active in the area of public procurement, for example, the OECD's work on Integrity in Government[7] and the development of the UNCITRAL Model Law on Public Procurement.[8]

---

[1] See, for an overview of relevant indicators, Canada's country profile at the World Bank Country Profile gateway, available at https://databank.worldbank.org/views/reports/reportwidget.aspx?Repo rt_Name=CountryProfile&Id=b450fd57&tbar=y&dd=y&inf=n&zm=n&country=CAN and OECD, 'Selected indicators for Canada', available at https://data.oecd.org/canada.htm. This is not to deny that, like most or all countries, Canada faces its own significant challenges and controversies. The point is simply that, in relative terms, Canada on the whole is rightly regarded as a prominent example of a well-governed, prosperous, and advanced industrial economy and polity.

[2] Government of Canada, 'Canada and the G7', available at https://www.international.gc.ca/world-monde/international_relations-relations_internationales/g7/index.aspx?lang=eng.

[3] Transparency International, 'Corruption Perceptions Index' (2022), available at https://www.trans parency.org/en/cpi/2022/index/can. The US, by contrast, ranks 24th out of 180. Canada's score is, however, down by three since 2020.

[4] See Canada, Department of Justice, 'A Consolidation of the Constitution Acts 1867 to 1982', Section 91, available at https://laws-lois.justice.gc.ca/eng/const/const_index.html; and, for thoughtful discussion, P. Hogg and W.K. Wright, 'Peace, Order and Good Government' in P. Hogg and W.K. Wright (eds), *Constitutional Law of Canada* (Carswell, 5th edn, 2021), Chapter 17.

[5] See, for elaboration, Section E, below.

[6] See, for elaboration, Section F, below.

[7] For example, Canada, along with Korea, has served as a co-lead examiner for the OECD Working Group on Bribery. See, OECD, 'Anti-Corruption and Integrity Hub: Canada', available at https://www. oecd.org/corruption-integrity/Explore/Countries/canada.html.

[8] See United Nations Commission on International Trade Law (UNCITRAL), 'UNCITRAL Model Law on Public Procurement' (2011), available at https://uncitral.un.org/en/texts/procurement/model law/public_procurement.

INTRODUCTION 311

Despite these important strengths and efforts, Canada has suffered, from its beginnings, from persistent and well-documented problems with both official corruption and supplier collusion in its public procurement markets.[9] As discussed
in this chapter, in the past two decades extensive corrupt practices and supplier
collusion have been disclosed particularly in the public procurement sector of
the Province of Quebec,[10] but also in other Canadian provinces and (with disturbing regularity) at the central (federal) level of government.[11] In fact, corruption issues in public procurement date back to the early years following Canada's
'Confederation' (i.e. the country's establishment as a (mainly) self-governing polity
in 1867).[12] Related scandals have, on multiple occasions, caused embarrassment
to the country's senior political leadership and impacted the outcome of national
elections.[13] This is despite major efforts being made, over decades, to introduce and
enforce appropriate safeguards to detect, deter, and punish both corrupt practices
and supplier collusion.[14] To some extent, this record, no doubt, reflects structural
and behavioural considerations already flagged in other chapters of this book—e.g.
principal–agent and collective action problems, the temptations posed by the large
sums of money involved, universal human weaknesses, etc. Yet, as will be discussed
below, in other ways, it reflects structural, cultural, and institutional factors that
are unique to Canada.[15] Canada's experience also provides valuable insights into
measures that can be taken to address these issues, over time.

[9] See, for complementary perspectives to those advanced in this chapter, D. Saint-Martin, 'Systemic
Corruption in an Advanced Welfare State: Lessons from the Quebec Charbonneau Inquiry' (2015)
53(1) *Osgoode Hall Law Journal* 66, and S. Chaster, 'Public Procurement and the Charbonneau
Commission: Challenges in Preventing and Controlling Corruption' (2018) 23 *Appeal* 121. A useful
overview of relevant developments in the Canadian Province of Quebec is provided in OECD, 'Integrity
Review of Public Procurement in Quebec, Canada: A Strategic Approach to Corruption Risks', *OECD
Public Governance Reviews* (OECD Publishing, 2020), available at https://doi.org/10.1787/g2g95
000-en.
[10] The official source is Quebec, Commission d'enquête sur l'octroi et la gestion des contrats publics
dans l'industrie de la construction, 'Rapport final de la Commission d'enquête sur l'octroi et la gestion
des contrats publics dans l'industrie de la construction', *CEIC* (2015) (henceforth, 'Charbonneau
Commission Report'). See, for relevant commentary, Saint-Martin, n. 9, Chaster, n. 9, and OECD,
n. 9. A colourful summary of highlights is provided in 'No One Can Deny It Now: Quebec Is Facing a
Corruption Crisis', *Maclean's* (24 November 2015), available at https://www.macleans.ca/news/canada/
quebecs-now-undeniable-corruption-crisis/.
[11] See details of relevant cases set out in Sections C and D, below.
[12] The 'Pacific Scandal' of the 1870s involved allegations of bribes being offered to/accepted by multiple senior members of the Conservative government led by Sir John A. Macdonald (Canada's first
Prime Minister), in an attempt to influence the award of a national railway construction contract. See,
for pertinent details, Canada, Royal Commission Relating to the Canadian Pacific Railway, 'Report
of the Royal Commissioners appointed by commission, addressed to them under the Great Seal of
Canada, bearing date the fourteenth day of August, A.D. 1873', available at https://publications.gc.ca/
site/fra/9.826326/publication.html and, for insightful commentary, 'Pacific Scandal: Canadian History'
Encyclopedia Britannica, available at https://www.britannica.com/event/Pacific-Scandal. See also related discussion, below.
[13] See details of relevant cases set out in Sections C and D, below.
[14] See Sections E and F, below, and references cited therein.
[15] See also Saint-Martin, n. 9.

312 PERSISTENT CORRUPTION AND SUPPLIER COLLUSION

This chapter explores these relationships and phenomena. An effort is made to identify the principal factors underlying the observed patterns of corruption and supplier collusion in public procurement in Canada, notwithstanding the country's generally advanced and well-developed governance systems.[16]

The remainder of the chapter is structured as follows. Section B sets out basic information on the organization and administration of public procurement activities in Canada. Section C discusses some revealing early examples of public procurement scandals in Canada, especially the so-called 'Pacific Scandal', which coincided with the country's founding. Section D examines more recent examples of both bid rigging (supplier collusion) and corrupt practices (e.g. bribery of and kickbacks to government officials in relation to the award of government contracts). Section E reviews the evolution of the statutory and policy frameworks that attempt to deter/control corruption in Canada's public procurement sector. Likewise, Section F examines the evolution of Canada's framework for the investigation and prosecution of bid rigging and related activities, under the federal Competition Act, as amended. Section G concludes by highlighting the principal factors that have incentivized the corrupt and collusive practices, how the anti-corruption and competition law regimes have adapted in response, and what more can be done to preclude such conduct from undermining public procurement processes in the future.

B. Public Procurement in Canada Generally

Public procurement in Canada is generally carried out in a relatively decentralized manner, with substantial portions of procurement being conducted by the governments of Canada's individual provinces, territories, and municipalities, although the federal government remains a key player. As observed by Lalonde:

> Canada's procurement laws ... vary by jurisdiction, and by the entity carrying out the procurement. For example, procurement rules that apply to federal government departments differ significantly from those that apply to provincial government departments, which in turn differ from those that apply to sub-provincial entities such as municipalities. While there are common threads (obligations to compete requirements above certain value thresholds, obligations to publicize opportunities, etc.), the manner in which procurement is carried out, the degree to which procurement activity is regulated, and the extent to which prejudiced suppliers are provided with recourses vary widely across the country.[17]

Pertinent details are discussed below.

---

[16] Again, see, for complementary perspectives, Saint-Martin, n. 9 and Chaster, n. 9.

[17] P. Lalonde, 'The Internationalization of Canada's Procurement' in A.C. Georgopulos, B. Hoekman, and P.C. Mavroidis (eds), *The Internationalization of Government Procurement Regulation* (Oxford University Press, 2017), Chapter 11.

i. Federal level

At the federal level, the authority for disbursement of government funds is derived from the Financial Administration Act (FAA). The majority of government purchasing is conducted through the Department of Public Services and Procurement Canada (PSPC), formerly known as the 'Department of Public Works and Government Services Canada' (PWGSC).[18] The Government Contracts Regulations (GCR), which are promulgated pursuant to the FAA, provide a general obligation to purchase on a competitive basis. They do not, however, provide specific guidelines that must be followed in contracting or in the post-award administration of contracts. The Treasury Board of Canada and the courts exercise important supervisory responsibility for the enforcement of the FAA and the Government Contracts Regulations. PSPC has issued a Supply Manual and Standard Acquisition Clauses and Conditions (SACC) under the auspices of the Department of Public Works and Government Services Act. Together, these provide additional non-statutory guidance on how PSPC officials carry out contracting activities.[19] Important updates to aspects of the guidance provided are currently in progress, in response to, among other developments, concerns expressed regarding an apparent ballooning, in recent years, of government contracts issued to private consulting firms, especially McKinsey and Co., concerning the conduct of government business.[20] In Canada, defence procurement is subject to separate legislation, the Defence Production Act.[21]

ii. Provincial level

Significantly greater diversity of approaches is evident with regard to public purchasing at the provincial level. According to Lalonde:

---

[18] Also known as 'Public Services and Procurement Canada' (PSPC) under the Federal Identity Program.

[19] Lalonde, n. 17; see also B. Swick, 'Public Procurement in Canada: Overview', available at https://content.next.westlaw.com/practical-law/document/I2ef1296f1ed511e38578f7ccc38dcbee/Public-procurement-in-Canada-overview?viewType=FullText&transitionType=Default&contextData=(sc. Default).

[20] Treasury Board of Canada Secretariat and Public Services and Procurement Canada, 'Federal Contracts Awarded to McKinsey & Company (1 January 2011 to 7 February 2023): A Review by the Treasury Board of Canada Secretariat and Public Services and Procurement Canada' (27 June 2023), available at https://www.canada.ca/en/treasury-board-secretariat/corporate/organization/review-fede ral-government-contracts-mckinsey-company/federal-contracts-awarded.html. See also CNW Group, 'The Government of Canada Completes Its Review of Contracts with McKinsey', *Yahoo!Finance* (27 June 2023), and related discussion, below.

[21] Defence Production Act (RSC, 1985, c. D-1), available at https://laws-lois.justice.gc.ca/eng/acts/D-1/. See, for related discussion, A.S. Williams, *Reinventing Canadian Defence Procurement: A View from the Inside* (Breakout Educational Network, 2007), especially Chapter 2, and Section D, below.

Every province is subject to individual provincial legislative frameworks, which have varying degrees of complexity and formality. In Quebec, for example, the province has passed the Act Respecting Contracting by Public Bodies, which details the procurement practices to be used by public bodies in that jurisdiction.

.... Pursuant to the general directives of the Financial Administration Act, the Treasury Board of Ontario (TBO) controls the expenditure of public funds. As part of this mandate, the TBO has issued, among other things, the Supply Chain Guideline (SCG), which provides detailed instructions on how Ontario departments and agencies should carry out procurements. But the SCG is not a statutory instrument and there is no clear sanction or remedy in the event that it is contravened. The SCG also does not apply to the entities that are not departments or agencies of the Government of Ontario but that receive significant public funding, such as school boards, the health care sector, and other government-funded entities (referred to in Ontario as the 'broader public sector').[22]

Perceived abuses and scandals have been significant factors in the evolution of relevant policies and legislation at the federal as well as the provincial level. For example, and as will be elaborated below, at the central government level, the so-called 'Sponsorship Scandal' of the late 1990s/early 2000s drew significant attention to apparent fraudulent practices in the context of procurement conducted at the time of a national election. Subsequently, the far-reaching investigation of corruption and supplier collusion in the Quebec provincial construction sector by the 'Charbonneau Commission' in addition to related activities of the SNC-Lavalin Group (a major Quebec-based international engineering and construction conglomerate that received significant attention in the Charbonneau Inquiry) resulted in a significant tightening of relevant legislation, both in Quebec and at the federal level.[23]

---

[22] Lalonde, n. 17.

[23] See M. Barutciski and M. Kronby, 'Canadian Government Overhauls the Integrity Regime for Suppliers', *Bennett Jones LLP* (6 July 2015), available https://www.bennettjones.com/Publications-Section/Updates/Canadian-Government-Overhauls-the-Integrity-Regime-for-Suppliers; P. Lalonde and S. Stephenson, 'Canada Tightens Fraud and Corruption Controls on Government Procurement', *Mondaq* (23 September 2019), available at https://www.mondaq.com/canada/government-contracts-procurement-ppp/846862/canada-tightens-fraud-and-corruption-controls-on-government-procurement, and, for further discussion of relevant cases, Sections C and D, below. A valuable overview of relevant developments in the Canadian Province of Quebec is provided in OECD, n. 9.

iii. The role of Canada's international and internal trade agreements in shaping public procurement policy

International trade agreements have been another important factor in shaping the Canadian public procurement system, initially at the federal and subsequently at the provincial levels of government. As noted by Lalonde:

> a procurement review process under the terms of the Canadian International Trade Tribunal Act ensures compliance with the GPA and NAFTA (and other agreements). This Act endows the Canadian International Trade Tribunal (CITT) with the power to investigate complaints from suppliers about non-compliance with the trade agreement commitments. The Tribunal's jurisdiction is limited to the procurement process that concern 'designated contracts', which means procurements that are:
> a. by federal departments, agencies, and state enterprises that are specifically listed in prescribed international agreements; and
> b. for purchases above the value thresholds stipulated in the relevant agreements.
>
> Several exemptions further restrict the scope of review where contracts deal with, among other things, national security, shipbuilding, certain transportation equipment, financial services, health services, engineering and architectural services, and certain agricultural arrangements.[24]

It bears noting that, until 2011, Canada, in its coverage commitments under the WTO Agreement on Government Procurement, omitted to cover entities at the sub-central (provincial and municipal) government level. This omission arguably facilitated, in an important way, the corrupt practices and supplier collusion that have been observed in provincial procurement markets, by limiting the number of competitors in relevant markets and shielding related conduct from potential scrutiny. To its credit, Canada undertook to remedy this situation in 2011, pursuant to commitments made initially in Canada-US bilateral negotiations that culminated that year.[25] Lalonde, nonetheless, considers that 'compliance by the provinces [with relevant international agreements and related requirements] is unclear and inconsistent. For example, many provinces have still not adopted formal, effective bid challenge processes'.[26]

---

[24] Lalonde, n. 17.
[25] See D. Collins, 'Canada's Sub-Central Government Entities and the Agreement on Government Procurement: Past and Present' in S. Arrowsmith and R.D. Anderson (eds), *The WTO Regime on Government Procurement: Challenge and Reform* (Cambridge University Press and the World Trade Organization, 2011), Chapter 7.
[26] Lalonde, n. 17.

316 PERSISTENT CORRUPTION AND SUPPLIER COLLUSION

The framework for public procurement in Canada is further underpinned by the country's Agreement on Internal Trade which came into effect in 1995.[27] Chapter 5 of the Agreement incorporates important general commitments pertaining to non-discrimination and transparency in government procurement. Notably, the Agreement also requires defence procurement to be competed unless specific exceptions apply or a 'national security' exemption is invoked.[28]

Most recently, Canada and the European Union (EU) have negotiated a Comprehensive Economic and Trade Agreement (CETA) that includes very significant commitments in the area of government procurement. Pursuant to that agreement, Canada now covers federal, provincial, and local procurement, including goods and services that were previously excluded, such as rolling stock for public transit.[29] Overall, the long-term trend in favour of increased coverage of Canadian public procurements by international trade agreements, buttressed by the Internal Trade Agreement, augurs well for better governance in public procurement markets in Canada.

C. Early Corruption and Supplier Collusion Scandals in Public Procurement in Canada: A Harbinger of Problems to Come

The disclosure of corruption issues in public procurement dates back to the early years following Canada's Confederation, in 1867. These episodes are, by no means, of mere antiquarian interest. Rather, it will be argued, these early examples illuminate tendencies and institutional weaknesses that have persisted (at least) until very recent times. The most pertinent examples are the following.

i. The 'Pacific Scandal'

The 'Pacific Scandal' of the 1870s involved allegations of bribes being offered to/ accepted by senior members of the Conservative government led by Sir John A. Macdonald (Canada's first Prime Minister, and a key architect of Confederation), in an attempt to influence the award of a national railway construction contract.[30] The railway's construction was a central pillar of early economic development and

---

[27] 'Agreement on Internal Trade: Consolidated Version' (2015), available at https://www.cfta-alec.ca/wp-content/uploads/2017/06/Consolidated-with-14th-Protocol-final-draft.pdf. See also Lalonde, n. 17.

[28] See Williams, n. 21, Chapter 2.

[29] Lalonde, n. 17.

[30] Canada, 'Royal Commission Relating to Canadian Pacific Railway', n. 12.

political unification in Canada—i.e. a major exercise in 'nation-building'.[31] The ensuing scandal triggered the defeat of Macdonald's government and delayed the eventual completion of the national railway by more than a decade.[32]

The sequence of events underlying the Pacific Scandal is of interest. According to the Canadian Encyclopedia:

> The Pacific Scandal originated when Prime Minister Sir John A. Macdonald and his Conservative colleagues Sir George-Étienne Cartier and Hector-Louis Langevin went looking for campaign funds for the 1872 general election.... The target of their solicitations was Sir Hugh Allan, a Montreal shipping magnate and railway builder. The Conservatives needed money to compete in the election; particularly in Ontario and Quebec, where it appeared they might lose several seats.
>
> Financed partly by American backers, Allan donated more than [CAD] 350,000 to the Conservative campaign [a huge sum at the time, at least by Canadian standards]. After the election, a railway syndicate organized by Allan was rewarded with the profitable contract to build the Canadian Pacific Railway. Subsequently, [a series of uncovered] letters showed that an agreement existed between Allan and the Conservatives; notably Macdonald, Cartier and minister of public works Hector-Louis Langevin. The deal assured Allan the railway contract in return for campaign funds.[33]

Thus, in its essence, the Pacific Scandal involved the direct award of a huge public infrastructure contract to a designated beneficiary (Sir Hugh Allan) as an explicit quid pro quo for a major contribution of campaign funds. As will be seen below, the exigencies posed by federal election campaigns figure also in more recent government procurement-related scandals in Canada.

ii. The 'Hamilton Harbour' dredging scandal

Hamilton is one of Canada's major industrial cities, in the 'Golden Horseshoe' area of southern Ontario. The 'Hamilton Harbour' dredging scandal[34] was, in many respects, a textbook example of collusive tendering in a market (dredging services)

---

[31] P. Berton, *The National Dream: The Great Railway, 1871–1881* (Anchor Canada, 2001, first published 1970) and P. Berton, *The Last Spike: The Great Railway, 1881–1885* (Anchor Canada, 2001, first published 1971).

[32] Berton, *The National Dream*, n. 31.

[33] See, The Canadian Encyclopedia, 'The Pacific Scandal', available at https://www.thecanadianencyclopedia.ca/en/article/pacific-scandal.

[34] 'Harbourgate Dominated Hamilton Headlines in 1974', *The Hamilton Spectator* (28 August 2021), available at https://www.thespec.com/life/local-history/spec175/2021/08/28/harbourgate-dominated-hamilton-headlines-in-1974.html.

318   PERSISTENT CORRUPTION AND SUPPLIER COLLUSION

known to have figured in procurement scandals in other jurisdictions.[35] Its notoriety grew, importantly, from the overlay of public corruption evidenced by the Harbour Commissioner's acceptance of kickbacks, coupled with the alleged role of a prominent Canadian politician, Health Minister John Munro, in the contracting process (although the extent of Munro's involvement was disputed). Eventually, prominent corporate executives served prison sentences for defrauding the Government of Canada, as did the then Harbour Commissioner, Kenneth Elliot, for accepting bribes/kickbacks.[36] From a legal perspective, it is noteworthy that the significant sanctions that were eventually imposed were derived from relevant provisions of Canada's Criminal Code concerning, for example, fraud on the government as opposed to Canada's then competition law (predecessor of the current legislation), the Combines Investigation Act.[37]

iii. The flour milling bid rigging case of 1990

In 1990, eight Canadian flour milling companies were charged with conspiring to lessen competition and rigging prices over a 12-year period on about CAD 500 million worth of wheat flour sold to the Federal Government for export to developing countries in Africa, Asia, the Caribbean, and Central America, pursuant to a Canadian overseas aid program administered by the Canadian International Development Agency (CIDA).[38] The firms charged represented about half the flour milling companies in Canada. The case vividly illustrates both the harm caused by bid rigging and the usefulness of prevention/deterrence programs focused on raising awareness of suspicious signs. Specifically, the conduct in question undoubtedly resulted in increased misery, and very possibly, deaths in the countries that were the intended beneficiaries of the program, in that the higher (rigged) prices for milled flour directly reduced the quantum of flour that could be purchased and disbursed. Moreover, the conduct was apparently brought to light through concerns voiced by a procurement officer who had

[35] See, e.g., 'Bid Rigging Charged Dredging Projects Focus of State Inquiry', *South Florida Sun-Sentinel* (14 July 1988), available at https://www.sun-sentinel.com/news/fl-xpm-1988-07-14-8802110 143-story.html.

[36] 'Two Prominent Dredging Executives Convicted Two Years Ago in ...', *UPI Archives* (7 April 1981), available at https://www.upi.com/Archives/1981/04/07/Two-prominent-dredging-executi ves-convicted-two-years-ago-in/5955355467600/ and 'Obituary: Elliott Was at Centre of Hamilton's "Harbourgate" Scandal', *The Hamilton Spectator* (2 September 2009), available at https://www.thespec. com/news/2009/09/02/obituary-elliott-was-at-centre-of-hamilton-s-harbourgate-scandal.html..

[37] S.C. 1952 supp. c. 314. See, for related discussion, Section E, below.

[38] See, Director of Investigation and Research, 'Flour Mills Fined $3,225,000 for Bid-Rigging' News Release NR-00090/90-52 (7 December 1990). See also 'Milling Firms May Have Shortchanged Famine Relief', *UPI Archives* (6 March 1990), available at https://www.upi.com/Archives/1990/03/06/Milling-firms-may-have-shortchanged-famine-relief/2408636699600/.

received training from the then Canadian Bureau of Competition Policy (now the Competition Bureau) in the detection of suspicious signs indicative of bid rigging.[39]

To summarize, these early examples pre-figure enduring fault lines and concerns that are also seen in the more recent examples to be discussed below. These include: (i) allegations of outright bribery and other forms of corruption in regard to major public procurement contracts at the central government level; (ii) the comingling of supplier collusion and bribery concerns, at least in the Hamilton Harbour Dredging Scandal; and (iii) at least in the case of the Pacific Scandal, a clear nexus between illicit conduct and the exigencies of a federal election campaign.

D. More Recent Examples of Corrupt Practices and/or Supplier Collusion in Public Procurement

More recently, the incidence of major national scandals involving public procurement in Canada has not diminished. Prominent examples are discussed below. Again, several common features are evident, including a mix of both supplier collusion (i.e. bid rigging) and malfeasance on the part of government officials. Pressures related to federal election or re-election campaigns have continued to play a role. The following examples also showcase the growing importance of the federal Competition Bureau and the essential though not all-powerful roles of Canada's Auditor General and Ethics Commissioner as key institutional safeguards against corruption.

i. The 'Sponsorship Scandal'

The 'Sponsorship Scandal' of 1996–2004 involved misuse and misdirection of public funds intended for procurement of government advertising in Quebec. As explained in an article published in the Canadian Encyclopedia:

> After a razor-thin majority voted in the 1995 Quebec Referendum for Quebec to stay in Canada, the Liberal government of Prime Minister Jean Chrétien responded with various initiatives to promote federalism in the province. A sponsorship program began in 1996. Public money was directed from the Department of Public Works and Government Services to private advertising agencies to

---

[39] Authors' discussions with relevant contacts.

320 PERSISTENT CORRUPTION AND SUPPLIER COLLUSION

promote Canada and the federal government at cultural, community and sports events in Quebec.[40]

On 8 May 2002, then Auditor General Sheila Fraser released a special report on a key set of contracts awarded pursuant to the program. The report found that 'senior public servants responsible for managing the contracts demonstrated an appalling disregard for... policy, and rules designed to ensure prudence and probity in government procurement'. The report provided details of numerous cases in which non-competitive contracts were awarded to firms and individuals in Quebec and payments were made for services that were never delivered.[41] Subsequently, a second report by the Auditor General severely criticized the absence of proper contracting and accountability processes concerning the disbursement of government funds pursuant to the sponsorship program. It showed, as well, that CAD 100 million in public funds had been redirected to the Quebec wing of the federal Liberal Party.[42]

Eventually, key findings of the Auditor General were confirmed in two reports by a Commission of Inquiry led by Quebec Superior Court Justice John Gomery, which also set out recommendations for establishing open and transparent processes for awarding advertising and sponsorship contracts; enhanced funding for parliamentary committees involved in the oversight of government programs; and public service reforms generally.[43] In the meantime, former Prime Minister Jean Chretien, under whose authority the sponsorship program was initiated, had resigned, and his successor, Prime Minister Paul Martin, had been defeated in an election forced by the opposition parties.[44]

The significance of the Sponsorship Scandal has been summarized as follows:

The Sponsorship Scandal helped send the federal Liberals into the political wilderness for a decade. After winning three consecutive majorities in 1993, 1997 and 2000, when they won 172 of 301 seats, they were reduced to a minority of 135 seats in 2004, to 103 seats in 2006, to 77 seats in 2008 and to only 34 seats in 2011.... A series of ineffective leaders struggled to rebrand the party following years of focus on its corruption.... It took a charismatic new leader in Justin Trudeau facing a Conservative government weighed down by

---

[40] See 'Sponsorship Scandal (Adscam)', *The Canadian Encyclopedia*, available at https://www.thecanadianencyclopedia.ca/en/article/sponsorship-scandal-adscam.

[41] See 'Sponsorship Scandal (Adscam)', n. 40.

[42] See 'Sponsorship Scandal (Adscam)', n. 40.

[43] Canada, Commission of Inquiry into the Sponsorship Program and Advertising Activities, 'Who is Responsible? Phase 1 Report' (1 November 2005) and 'Restoring Accountability, Phase 2 Report' (1 February 2006), available at https://publications.gc.ca/site/eng/9.649881/publication.html.

[44] 'Sponsorship Scandal (Adscam)', n. 40.

EXAMPLES OF CORRUPT PRACTICES AND/OR SUPPLIER COLLUSION   321

its own baggage after a decade in power for the Liberals to regain office in 2015.[45]

ii. The 'ETS scandal'

The 'ETS scandal' of the mid-2000s initially involved allegations of wrongdoing by government officials in the award of a CAD 400 million information technology services contract.[46] It subsequently devolved into a major investigation of alleged bid rigging under Canada's Competition Act. Ultimately, however, the nine Ottawa-area defendants were found *not* guilty on sixty charges of bid rigging and conspiracy to rig bids under the Act. The decision was regarded as a major defeat for the federal prosecution service and the Competition Bureau, responsible for related investigations under the Canadian Competition Act.[47]

iii. The 'F-35 fighter jet procurement scandal'

The 'F-35 fighter jet procurement scandal' of the 2010s was initially triggered by an announcement by the then Prime Minister Stephen Harper's government of its intention to sign an untendered, sole-sourced contract with Lockheed Martin to purchase sixty-five F-35 Lightning II aircraft (also known as the 'Joint Strike Fighter' (JSF)). This, together with the government's refusal to provide details of related costing, resulted in a finding of contempt of Parliament and perhaps, to an extent, also contributed to the government's subsequent defeat in a non-confidence vote.[48] Already, at the time, a knowledgeable former official had observed as follows: 'The sole-sourcing of the JSF has highlighted the basic perils connected with sole-sourcing in general. These include ... increased costs, reduced opportunities for Canadian industry, and uncertainty as to whether the best product has been acquired to meet the identified needs.'[49] In April 2012, with the release of a highly

---

[45] 'Sponsorship Scandal (Adscam)', n. 40.

[46] 'Ottawa Tech Company Challenges Awarding of [CAD] 400M Contract', *CBC News* (17 April 2007), available at https://www.cbc.ca/news/canada/ottawa/ottawa-tech-company-challenges-awarding-of-400m-contract-1.673114?ref=rss.

[47] 'Analysis: Bid-Rigging Trial Ends with 60 Not-Guilty Verdicts', *Ottawa Citizen* (27 April 2015), available at https://ottawacitizen.com/news/national/not-guilty-times-60-jury-clears-all-accused-in-federal-bid-rigging-trial and 'Crown Won't Appeal Bid Rigging Trial Verdict', *Ottawa Citizen* (25 May 2015), available at https://ottawacitizen.com/business/local-business/crown-wont-appeal-bid-rigging-trial-verdict.

[48] See A. Coyne, 'Peeling Back the Layers of Misconduct in the F-35 Fiasco', *National Post* (4 April 2012), available at https://archive.ph/20130104003959/http://fullcomment.nationalpost.com/2012/04/04/andrew-coyne-the-f-35-affair-is-a-fiasco-from-top-to-bottom/.

[49] See A. Williams, 'Flying Solo: Canada's Involvement in Developing the Joint Strike Fighter by No Means Compelled Us to Sole-Source It – To Do So Is Unbelievably Bad Business', *Ottawa Citizen* (24 July 2010).

322 PERSISTENT CORRUPTION AND SUPPLIER COLLUSION

critical Auditor General of Canada report on the failures of the government's F-35 program,[50] the procurement was labelled a national 'scandal' and 'fiasco' by the media.[51]

This was, however, far from being the end of the story. Rather, on 19 October 2015, the Liberal Party of Canada, under [its incoming new leader] Justin Trudeau, won a majority in part on a campaign promise to *not* buy the F-35, but instead 'one of the many, lower-priced options that better match Canada's defence needs'.[52] Subsequently, a formal competition was launched to select a new fighter, which included the F-35. On 28 March 2022 (roughly twelve years after the original announcement by the Harper government), the government announced that the competition had selected the F-35A (i.e. a version of the same aircraft that was the subject of the originally foreseen direct award by the Harper government) and that negotiations would begin with Lockheed Martin to purchase eighty-eight aircraft.[53]

The F-35 procurement scandal did not, to public knowledge, involve either outright corruption, such as bribery or kickbacks, or supplier collusion (bid rigging). Rather, the wastage of time and (possibly) of resources observed, seem to be attributable more to mismanagement and political/bureaucratic ineptitude. This is an important distinction. The episode illustrates, nonetheless, the risks associated with any high-value direct contract award (without competition) and the centrality of public procurement decision-making to the political process and to the viability of effective government in a modest-sized country such as Canada.[54]

iv. Corruption and supplier collusion in the Quebec (Province of Canada) construction sector

The definitive example of a public procurement scandal in Canada involving both proven malfeasance on the part of public officials *and* extensive collusion by suppliers in the relevant market(s) consists in the Quebec provincial construction sector

---

[50] M. Fitzpatrick, 'F-35 Program Slammed By Auditor General', *Canadian Broadcasting Corporation* (3 April 2012). The Auditor General's report observed as follows: 'when National Defence decided to recommend the acquisition of the F-35, it was too involved with the aircraft and the JSF Program to run a fair competition. It applied the rules for standard procurement projects but prepared key documents and took key steps out of proper sequence. As a result, the process was inefficient and not managed well. Key decisions were made without required approvals or supporting documentation … National Defence did not exercise the diligence that would be expected in managing a [CAD] 25-billion commitment. It is important that a purchase of this size be managed rigorously and transparently.'

[51] See, e.g., Coyne, n. 48.

[52] Liberal Party of Canada, 'A New Plan For a Strong Middle Class' (5 October 2015).

[53] 'Liberals Launch Negotiations to Buy F-35 Fighter Jets', *CBC News* (28 March 2022), available at https://www.cbc.ca/news/politics/f-35-negotiations-1.6399978.

[54] See, for a compelling overall account, A.S. Williams, 'Canada, Democracy and the F-35' (2012) *Defence Management Studies Program School of Policy Studies, Queen's University*.

EXAMPLES OF CORRUPT PRACTICES AND/OR SUPPLIER COLLUSION 323

corruption/collusion scandal investigated by the 'Charbonneau Commission'.[55] The scandal came to a head in the mid-2010s, though aspects of the conduct involved date back significantly earlier than that (more than a decade), and the repercussions of the scandal are still being felt. The Commission found evidence of extensive corrupt practices and supplier collusion involving Montreal-based engineering and construction firms and public officials. Sewer, water, building, and road projects, and related maintenance work such as snow removal (a major expenditure in Montreal) were directed to firms that would kick back money and gifts to criminal organizations, politicians, and public officials.[56]

In the words of the Commission's chairperson, recorded in a preamble to her 2015 report:

- 'This inquiry confirmed that there is a real problem in Quebec, one that was more extensive and ingrained than we could have thought.'[57]
- '[Testimony] revealed the existence and the workings of types of collusion orchestrated by engineering firms and construction companies in Montreal, in Laval and elsewhere in the province, as well as within [Quebec's] ministry of transport and its municipal affairs ministry.'[58]
- '[The testimony] also showed the huge problem of the accepting of gifts from suppliers to the keepers of the public purse, along with civil servants, their mandarins, and elected officials within the City of Montreal, the ministry of transport and municipal affairs. A culture of impunity developed.'[59]
- '[The witnesses] revealed that the Mafia had infiltrated Quebec's construction industry. Cartels formed so as to prevent other companies from bidding on public contracts. Construction company owners revealed they were victims of threats, intimidation, and assaults. Certain members of organized crime attempted to take control of legitimate companies so as to launder dirty money derived from illegal activities.'[60]
- ' "FTQ-Construction" [the province's largest union federation of construction workers] solicited individuals tied to the Mafia and Hells Angels [a motorcycle gang], who wanted to gain access to the FTQ's finance and investment arm, its real estate arm, and the province's union of electrical workers. These

---

[55] See 'Charbonneau Commission Report', n. 10. See also 'No One Can Deny It Now: Quebec Is Facing a Corruption Crisis', Maclean's, n. 10.

[56] 'No One Can Deny It Now: Quebec Is Facing a Corruption Crisis', Maclean's, n. 10.

[57] Quotation taken from 'No One Can Deny It Now: Quebec Is Facing a Corruption Crisis', Maclean's, n. 10.

[58] Quotation taken from 'No One Can Deny It Now: Quebec Is Facing a Corruption Crisis', Maclean's, n. 10.

[59] Quotation taken from 'No One Can Deny It Now: Quebec Is Facing a Corruption Crisis', Maclean's, n. 10.

[60] Quotation taken from 'No One Can Deny It Now: Quebec Is Facing a Corruption Crisis', Maclean's, n. 10.

324 PERSISTENT CORRUPTION AND SUPPLIER COLLUSION

individuals had close ties with FTQ-Construction's director general, as well as its president.'[61]

The patterns of conduct that were detailed in the Charbonneau Inquiry provide a definitive illustration of the interplay and mutually reinforcing effects of official malfeasance and supplier collusion in public procurement. As observed by Matthew Boswell, then Canada's Senior Deputy Commissioner of Competition, and now the Commissioner of Competition:

> During testimony at the Charbonneau Commission, a retired engineer working for the City of Montreal confessed to accepting over [CAD] 700,000 in payoffs from construction contractors as part of a system of collusion. In his testimony, he said the average cost of the city's sewer, water main, paving and sidewalk contracts jumped by at least 20% as a result of the schemes. In some cases, costs even doubled as a result of the collusion and corruption.... In another case, another engineer working for the City of Montreal testified that he had accepted half a million [CAD] in cash kickbacks and explained that the money he received represented 25% of the total value of false extras added to contracts.[62]

v. The 'SNC Lavelin Affair'

A related scandal, the 'SNC Lavelin Affair', overlaps with but extends beyond the patterns of conduct disclosed in the Charbonneau Inquiry.[63] The SNC-Lavalin Group is a major Quebec-based international engineering and construction conglomerate and a 'national and provincial champion' (a revealing term used in Canada to describe major industrial enterprises that are a focus of government support). It was extensively involved in the conduct examined by the Charbonneau Commission, resulting in a guilty plea for violation of the conspiracy provisions of the Canadian Competition Act and significant related penalties (see details of this and related prosecutions under the Competition Act, in Section F).

An important further dimension of the scandal emerged out of charges that, between 2001 and 2011, SNC-Lavalin/its subsidiaries paid CAD 48 million in bribes to officials of the Libyan government of Muammar Gaddafi and defrauded Libyan

---

[61] Quotation taken from 'No One Can Deny It Now: Quebec Is Facing a Corruption Crisis', Maclean's, n. 10.

[62] M. Boswell, 'Bid-Rigging Detection and Prevention: Ensuring a Competitive and Innovative Procurement Process', Remarks to the Canadian Public Procurement Council Forum 2017: Innovation in Public Procurement (7 November 2017), available at https://www.canada.ca/en/competition-bureau/news/2017/11/bid-rigging_detectionandpreventionensuringacompetitiveandinnovat.html.

[63] See, for background, 'What You Need to Know about the SNC-Lavalin Affair', CBC News (13 February 2019), available at https://www.cbc.ca/news/politics/trudeau-wilson-raybould-attorney-general-snc-lavalin-1.5014271.

EXAMPLES OF CORRUPT PRACTICES AND/OR SUPPLIER COLLUSION   325

organizations of CAD 130 million. Specifically, the firms were charged with one count of fraud under Section 380 of Canada's Criminal Code and one count of corruption under Section 3(1)(b) of the Corruption of Foreign Public Officials Act,[64] relating to attempts to influence the award of major infrastructure procurement contracts.[65]

Subsequently, the Ethics Commissioner of Canada's Parliament, Mario Dion, found that the current Prime Minister, Justin Trudeau, attempted to improperly influence the then Minister of Justice and Attorney General, Jody Wilson-Raybould, to offer the company a deferred prosecution agreement (DPA), as a way of defusing the situation in advance of an anticipated national election. Specifically, the Prime Minister was found to be in violation of Section 9 of the Canadian Conflict of Interest Act.[66] Attorney General Wilson-Raybould resigned in protest—casting the Prime Minister in an unfavourable light and, to many observers, undermining the Liberal Party's performance in a subsequent national election.[67]

vi. The 'WE Charity' scandal

Most recently, in 2020, Canada witnessed the emergence of yet another federal scandal concerning the national administration of the current Prime Minister (Justin Trudeau): the so-called 'WE Charity' scandal. The scandal concerned the direct award of a federal contract to WE Charity to administer the CAD 912 million Canada Student Summer Grant program (CSSG) in 2020. The controversy arose when it was revealed that WE Charity had previously paid close family members of Prime Minister Justin Trudeau to appear at its events, despite making claims to the contrary. Further, not only had the charity employed a daughter of former Minister of Finance, Bill Morneau, but a close relationship existed between the Minister and members of its staff.[68]

In subsequent reports, Prime Minister Trudeau was absolved of personal misconduct in the scandal. In contrast, Minister of Finance, Bill Morneau, was found by the Commissioner of Ethics to have had contravened Sections 6(1), 7, and 21 of

---

[64] See related discussion in Section E, below.

[65] 'What You Need to Know about the SNC-Lavalin Affair', n. 63.

[66] See M. Dion, 'Conflict of Interest and Ethics Commissioner, Trudeau II Report', available at https://ciec-ccie.parl.gc.ca/en/publications/Documents/InvestigationReports/Trudeau%20II%20Report.pdf#search=trudeau%20report%20II and ' "I take responsibility", Trudeau Says in Wake of Damning Report on SNC-Lavalin Ethics Violation', *CBC News* (14 August 2019), available at https://www.cbc.ca/news/politics/trudeau-snc-ethics-commissioner-violated-code-1.5246551.

[67] See 'What You Need to Know about the SNC-Lavalin Affair', n. 63, and '5 Things We Learned from Ethics Commissioner Mario Dion's Report on Justin Trudeau', *CBC News* (14 August 2019), available at https://www.cbc.ca/news/politics/mario-dion-report-justin-trudeau-1.5247209.

[68] See 'Bill Morneau Has Family Ties to WE Charity, Did Not Steer Clear of Cabinet Discussion of Contract', *CBC News* (10 July 2020), available at https://www.cbc.ca/news/politics/we-charity-contract-morneau-1.5644839.

326 PERSISTENT CORRUPTION AND SUPPLIER COLLUSION

the Federal Conflict of Interest Act. In his ruling, Commissioner Dion stated: 'The examination found the relationship between Mr. Morneau and WE included an unusually high degree of involvement between their representatives and afforded WE unfettered access to the Office of the Minister of Finance, which amounted to preferential treatment.' Dion also found that 'this unfettered access to the Office of the Minister of Finance was based on the identity of WE's representative, Mr. Craig Kielburger', who apparently was a close friend and a constituent of Minister Morneau.[69] The scandal was all the more regrettable given the valuable and socially relevant work that WE Charity appeared to be doing.[70]

vii. The recent outsourcing debate focusing on contracts issued to McKinsey and Co.

As noted in the introduction to this chapter, more recently, extensive public concerns have been voiced in Canada over an apparent ballooning of government contracts issued to private consulting firms, especially McKinsey and Co., concerning the conduct of government business.[71] According to one account, the cost of contracts issued to McKinsey increased 30-fold since the time of previous Prime Minister, Stephen Harper.[72] There is, in fact, no doubt that McKinsey has performed very significant work under contract to the Federal Government since Prime Minister Justin Trudeau's Liberal government assumed office in 2015.[73] The subject matter of the contracts has run from the government's response to the COVID-19 pandemic to the provision of extensive advice concerning information technology used by the government and a broad array of other responsibilities relating to the administration of government programs, including immigration

---

[69] See 'Bill Morneau Has Family Ties to WE Charity, Did Not Steer Clear of Cabinet Discussion of Contract', n. 68, and 'Trudeau Cleared of Wrongdoing in WE Charity Scandal by Ethics Watchdog', *Canadian Press* (13 May 2021), available at https://toronto.citynews.ca/2021/05/13/we-charity-ethics-commissioner-trudeau/.

[70] See, for a useful overall account, 'The WE Charity Controversy Explained', *CBC News* (28 July 2020), available at https://www.cbc.ca/news/canada/we-charity-student-grant-justin-trudeau-testimony-1.5666676.

[71] See Treasury Board of Canada Secretariat and Public Services and Procurement Canada, n. 20. See also 'Auditor General to Probe Federal Government Contracts with McKinsey', *CBC News* (24 February 2023), available at https://www.cbc.ca/news/politics/auditor-general-probe-mckinsey-government-contracts-1.6760220.

[72] 'The Value of One Consulting Firm's Federal Contracts Has Skyrocketed under the Trudeau Government', *CBC News* (4 January 2023), available at https://www.cbc.ca/news/politics/mckinsey-immigration-consulting-contracts-trudeau-1.6703626.

[73] 'On February 8, 2023, [Treasury Board Canada] asked departments subject to the Directive on the Management of Procurement to identify and undertake an internal audit of their contracts with McKinsey from January 1, 2011, to February 7, 2023. Ten departments identified that they had either entered into or acted as the contracting authority for 39 contracts with McKinsey. These contracts included 19 that were awarded in the form of call-ups against a non-competitive standing offer established by PSPC with McKinsey for specialized benchmarking services', Executive Summary, Treasury Board of Canada Secretariat and Public Services and Procurement Canada, n. 20.

policy. In addition to the sheer volume of contracts awarded to the company, questions have been raised about apparent undue reliance by the government on an outside source for advice and project implementation/management functions that, in the view of some observers, could or should be carried out by the government itself—even in a time when public service staffing levels have also increased.[74]

To date, no allegations have been substantiated regarding outright corruption (or supplier collusion) in the issuance of the relevant contracts. A major joint report issued by the Treasury Board of Canada Secretariat and Public Services and Procurement Canada concluded that 'departmental audits found no evidence of political interference in the contracts awarded to McKinsey and no evidence that the integrity of the procurement process was not maintained'. Nonetheless, the report also determined that:

> certain administrative requirements and procedures were not consistently followed. For example, some procurement files had insufficient or missing documentation and there were errors in the reporting of contracts according to the requirements for proactive publication.[75]

The above-cited report also confirmed that important updates to aspects of the guidance provided were in progress.[76]

viii. Discerning the common threads: observations relevant to the understanding of corrupt practices and supplier collusion in public procurement globally

The developments referenced above have, to say the least, shown clearly the continuing presence over an extended period of corrupt practices and supplier collusion in public procurement in Canada. The ability of corruption in public procurement to undermine confidence in/potentially bring down national governments has, moreover, been repeatedly demonstrated. At the same time, Canada's experience affirms that corruption and supplier collusion in public procurement markets cannot be understood solely in terms of generic practices that cut across markets without differentiation; on the contrary, in our view the scope and

---

[74] 'John Ivison: Growing Spending on Consultants by Ballooning Public Service Is the Real Scandal', *National Post* (11 January 2023), available at https://nationalpost.com/opinion/liberal-spending-cons ultants-scandal; and 'The Time and Place for Consultants', *Policy Options* (28 February 2023). See also 'Carr: How Contracting Out Hurts the Federal Government—and Canadian Taxpayers', *Ottawa Citizen* (3 February 2023), available at https://ottawacitizen.com/opinion/carr-how-contracting-out-hurts-the-federal-government-and-canadian-taxpayers.

[75] Executive Summary, Treasury Board of Canada Secretariat and Public Services and Procurement Canada, n. 20.

[76] See further discussion below, Section E.iv.

328 PERSISTENT CORRUPTION AND SUPPLIER COLLUSION

incentives for corrupt practices and optimal approaches to their control in all jurisdictions need to be understood, very much, in the context of national political, legal, and business culture.

The report of the Charbonneau Commission and other scandals referenced above have resulted in significant reflection processes, encompassing scholars and officials at the provincial and federal levels of government. Their observations can be sobering. For example, Professor Denis Saint-Martin has observed as follows [citations omitted]:

> My key theoretical point is that the shift of societies from a systemically corrupt social order to a non- or less corrupt one is not irreversible and [is] never achieved definitively as discontinuous models of institutional change lead us to believe. Too often in corruption research, scholars explain change by pointing to exogenous shocks such as wars and revolutions that bring about radical institutional reconfiguration. Enduring historical pathways are thus punctuated by sudden and revolutionary moments of agency and choice. But thinking of change as involving the breakdown of one set of institutions and its replacement with another makes the analysis blind to the [persistent, arguably cyclical] nature of corruption in societies.[77]

In pointing to underlying causes for the observed patterns, Saint-Martin references intrinsic problems associated with the construction industry across jurisdictions:

> Construction is a three trillion dollar industry worldwide, and estimates of financial losses from corruption vary from fifteen to thirty per cent per year. Construction projects are prone to corruption because of their size, uniqueness and complexity, and the fact that projects are structured through various phases and contractual links that disperse accountability among numerous separate agents. Extensive approval processes and multiple layers of contractors afford the greatest opportunities for corruption.[78]

At the same time, in seeking a full explanation, Saint-Martin implicates political, historical, and sociological factors peculiar to the situation of the Province of Quebec. He suggests, in particular, that corruption has been facilitated by: (i) economic nationalism underlying public policies partial towards French-speaking and Quebec-based businesses, notably in the engineering sector; (ii) political 'Jacobinism' descending from historic French models that centralized power at the provincial government level and left Quebec's municipalities underdeveloped in terms of bureaucratic capacity, making them 'easy prey for corrupted interests'; and

---

[77] Saint-Martin, n. 9.
[78] Saint-Martin, n. 9, 72.

EXAMPLES OF CORRUPT PRACTICES AND/OR SUPPLIER COLLUSION   329

(iii) the historical cleavage in Quebec between federalists (sympathetic to a strong central government for the country as whole) and 'Quebec sovereigntists', which, in his view, has enabled party officials to extract rents from businesses in return for ensuring an overall climate of stability.[79]

Without diminishing the intellectual force and relevance of Saint-Martin's insights, additional contributing factors can be noted here. First, the relatively small size of Canada's public procurement markets, especially at the provincial level, has historically been reinforced by significant barriers to both inter-provincial and international trade. This is a well-known problem in Canadian political economy,[80] addressed to an extent by the Agreement on Internal Trade which came into effect belatedly in 1995.[81] Second (and not dissimilar to the situation in many other countries), for decades competition law enforcement in Canada has suffered from inadequate penalties and issues of statutory framing that have only very recently (and arguably) been satisfactorily addressed.[82]

Thirdly, a factor sometimes overlooked is that the exclusion of provincial government procurement activities from the application of the WTO GPA until 2011 undoubtedly facilitated corruption and supplier collusion in those activities. Conversely, the commitment (since 2011) of provincial government procurement activities under the WTO GPA holds significant potential to reinforce competition in markets and to achieve a higher level of transparency/accountability than existed previously, over time. Fourthly, regarding the specific area of defence procurement, Ministerial responsibility is split, with the PSPC responsible for the procurement process and the Minister of National Defence for budgeting and defining relevant technical requirements. This, arguably, has acted as a key impediment to effectiveness and public accountability.[83]

Fifth, and sadly, especially in considering the 'Sponsorship', 'SNC-Lavalin', and 'WE Charity' scandals, it is difficult not to conclude that, notwithstanding its generally good reputation internationally, governance in Canada has suffered from temptations and weaknesses in applicable safeguards at the top level of the central government. Lastly, a sixth and important related observation is that official corruption has often been associated with situations in which high-level decisions

---

[79] Saint-Martin, n. 9.

[80] See, for discussion of the relationship between competition policy and constitutional measures impacting Canada's internal market, R.D. Anderson and S. Dev Khosla, 'Competition Policy, the Canadian Economic Union and Renewal of the Federation' (1991) 12(4) *Canadian Competition Policy Record* 57–77.

[81] See 'Agreement on Internal Trade: Consolidated Version' (2015), available at https://www.cfta-alec.ca/wp-content/uploads/2017/06/Consolidated-with-14th-Protocol-final-draft.pdf and, for related commentary, Lalonde, n. 17.

[82] See T.W. Ross, 'Canada Looks at Revising Its Competition Act', *CPI Columns: US and Canada* (April 2022), and related discussion in Section F, below.

[83] See Williams, n. 21, especially Chapter 5, 'Redressing the accountability muddles: Defence Procurement Canada'.

330 PERSISTENT CORRUPTION AND SUPPLIER COLLUSION

have been made to exclude particular procurement activities from normal competitive award procedures, for example through direct awards.

E. The Evolution of Canada's Anti-Corruption Framework for Public Procurement

In Canada, the legal framework governing bribery and corrupt acts in relation to the award of public contracts is found mainly in the *Criminal Code*[84]—which set out offences related to domestic acts—and the *Corruption of Foreign Public Officials Act*[85] *(CFPOA)*, prohibiting bribes to foreign public officials or to any person for the benefit of a foreign public official. These are supplemented by the Federal *Conflicts of Interest Act* and other instruments and policy statements. As discussed below, this framework has evolved importantly over the past two decades, in response to the scandals and other developments noted above.

To begin with, Canada's Criminal Code establishes a number of domestic bribery and corruption offences that capture mainly the payment of bribes or providing benefits and (undue) advantages to domestic public officials. Under the Criminal Code, potential penalties include fines in an unlimited amount and imprisonment for up to fourteen years. Officials and employees can be convicted personally, and companies can be found liable for offences committed by senior officers. Under certain circumstances, the actions of middle managers may also be sufficient to make a company criminally liable.[86]

The CFPOA, adopted in 1998, implements Canada's international obligations[87] under the OECD's Convention on Combating Bribery of Foreign Public Officials in International Business Transactions (the Anti-Bribery Convention).[88] The Convention criminalizes both the bribery of foreign public officials and the maintaining or destruction of books and records to facilitate or hide the bribing of foreign public officials. Canada also criminalizes a conspiracy or attempt to commit those offences. The implementation of the Act has been criticized for a perceived lack of vigorous enforcement.[89] Further criticism relates, inter alia, to the points that: (i) the offence of bribing a foreign public official in the CFPOA only

---

[84] Criminal Code, RSC 1985, c C-46. Sections 119 through 125.

[85] Corruption of Foreign Public Officials Act, SC 1998, c 34, available at http://laws-lois.justice.gc.ca/eng/acts/C-45.2/index.html.

[86] Chambers and Partners Practice Guide, 'Anti-Corruption: Canada' (2022), available at https://practiceguides.chambers.com/practice-guides/anti-corruption-2022/canada/trends-and-developments.

[87] Government of Canada, 'Canada's Fight against Foreign Bribery', available at https://www.international.gc.ca/trade-agreements-accords-commerciaux/topics-domaines/other-autre/corr-21.aspx?lang=eng.

[88] The OECD Anti-Bribery Convention, available at http://www.oecd.org/daf/anti-bribery/oecdantibriberyconvention.htm. See further information on the Convention, below.

[89] Chambers and Partners Practice Guide, 'Anti-Corruption: Canada', n. 86.

applies to bribes for the purpose of obtaining or retaining an advantage of business carried out in Canada or elsewhere 'for profit'; and (ii) the sanctions applied have been too low to be effective, proportionate, and dissuasive.[90]

At the sub-federal level, in the Province of Quebec, the *Quebec Anti-Corruption Act* deals with corruption, breach of trust, malfeasance, collusion, fraud, and influence peddling in the public sector, as well as misuse of public funds or public property, or gross mismanagement of public contracts. Additionally, individual public officials are also subject to the *Conflict of Interest Act*, which prohibits public office holders, and members of their families, from accepting any gift or other advantage that might influence the individual in the exercise of its duty or function.[91] Related statutes are applicable in other jurisdictions.

i. Institutional support in fighting corruption

A number of federal departments, agencies, and Crown corporations play key roles in Canada's fight against bribery and corruption. They generally work together in close cooperation, focusing on both enforcement and prevention.[92] These agencies include, among others:

- The Royal Canadian Mounted Police (RCMP) Federal Policing Criminal Operations (FPCO) Directorate, which manages the International Anti-Corruption Program. The RCMP International Anti-Corruption Unit, established in January 2008, comprises two anti-corruption teams located in Ottawa and Calgary;[93]
- The Public Prosecution Service of Canada (PPSC), which prosecutes criminal offences under federal statutes, on behalf of the Attorney General of Canada;
- The Financial Transactions and Reports Analysis Centre of Canada (FINTRAC), Canada's Financial Intelligence Unit, which facilitates the detection, prevention, and deterrence of money laundering and the financing of terrorist activities, while ensuring the protection of personal information under its control;
- Public Services and Procurement Canada (PSPC), the central purchasing agency which administers the government-wide Integrity Regime, introduced

---

[90] OECD, 'Phase 3 Report on Implementing the OECD Anti-Bribery Convention in Canada' (2011), available at https://www.oecd.org/daf/anti-bribery/anti-briberyconvention/Canadaphase3reportEN.pdf.

[91] T. Carsten, J. Deering, and A. Sarhan, 'Canada – Global Bribery Offenses Guide', *DLA Piper Publication* (2019), available at https://www.dlapiper.com/en/us/insights/publications/2019/09/bribery-offenses-guide/canada/.

[92] Government of Canada, n. 87.

[93] OECD, n. 90.

in July 2015, to help ensure that Canada conducts business and awards public contracts to ethical suppliers;

- Global Affairs Canada (GAC), which plays a lead role in representing Canada at international anti-corruption fora in outreach efforts with emerging economies regarding corruption, and in coordinating Canada's whole-of-government approach to meeting its international anti-corruption obligations; and
- The Competition Bureau of Canada (see related discussion in Section F, below).

In Quebec, the Unité permanente anticorruption (UPAC) is a Quebec government agency whose aim is to fight corruption, collusion, and other economic crimes involving government procurement.

ii. The Canadian 'Integrity Regime' and the role of Public Services and Procurement Canada

Public Services and Procurement Canada (formerly Public Works and Government Services Canada) is the principal department of the Canadian Federal Government with responsibility for procurement activities. PSPC is responsible for Canada's Integrity Regime,[94] a policy-based instrument broadly analogous to the concept of 'Integrity Pacts' developed by Transparency International.[95] It is enforced through contractual clauses that incorporate by reference the *Ineligibility and Suspension Policy*.[96] The goal of this policy is to protect and safeguard the expenditure of public funds and to maintain the public trust with respect to public procurement, by reducing the instances in which Canada awards contracts to suppliers convicted for unethical behaviour, such as fraud, corruption, bid rigging, and other crimes or relevant regulatory breaches.[97] Since 2012, the Integrity framework has gone through several iterations, reflecting amendments adopted to lessen some of the more severe aspects of the policy, including the length of the ineligibility period and the inclusion of due process enhancements.[98]

Under the Regime, Canada follows a relatively strict approach whereby procurement agencies may suspend a supplier or declare it ineligible to win a contract if it has been convicted of, or charged with, an applicable listed offence (e.g. offences related

---

[94] Government of Canada's Integrity Regime, available at https://www.tpsgc-pwgsc.gc.ca/ci-if/ci-if-eng.html.

[95] See, Transparency International, 'Integrity Pacts', available at https://www.transparency.org/en/tool-integrity-pacts.

[96] See, for further details, PWGSC, 'Guide to the Ineligibility and Suspension Policy', available at https://www.tpsgc-pwgsc.gc.ca/ci-if/guide-eng.html.

[97] Chambers and Partners Practice Guide, n. 86.

[98] J. Tillipman and S. Block, 'Canada's Integrity Regime: The Corporate Grim Reaper' (2022) 53 *The George Washington International Law Review* 475, GWU Legal Studies Research Paper No. 2022-15, GWU Law School Public Law Research Paper No. 2022-15.

to corruption, fraud, or bribery) within the past three years, in Canada or abroad. The names of all ineligible and suspended companies are published on the PSPC website, as well as those who have entered into an administrative agreement with the PSPC.

The Regime has gone through several modifications,[99] including one encompassing an amendment to the federal Criminal Code to include the adoption of deferred prosecution agreements (DPA), also known as 'remediation agreements', an alternative to criminal prosecution and debarment.[100] In particular, the 2015 amendments expanded the application of the Integrity Regime, previously limited to PSPC-managed contracts and real property transactions, to all federal procurement and real property transactions under Schedule I, I.1, and II of the *Financial Administration Act*.[101] In addition, since its introduction, agencies identified in the *Financial Administration Act* have signed Memoranda of Understanding (MOUs) with the procurement central agency to obtain supplier integrity verification services, allowing supplier verification prior to awarding a contract.[102] The PSPC also works closely with the private sector and civil society organizations to promote ethical business culture and integrity in public procurement.

Following a public consultation in 2018, the Government announced that it intended to make several further enhancements to the Integrity Regime, including more flexibility and discretion in debarment decisions and the revision of the Ineligibility and Suspension Policy. To date, the 'revised' Policy has not been released.[103] See Box 10.1.

Box 10.1 The Integrity Regime at a glance

The Integrity Regime applies to:
- goods, services and construction contracts, subcontracts and real property agreements with a transaction value over [CAD] 10,000
- contracts that:
  - o are issued by a federal department or agency listed in Schedule I, I.1 or II of the Federal Administration Act
  - o contain provisions of the Ineligibility and Suspension Policy

---

[99] Tillipman and Block, n. 98.

[100] Budget Implementation Act, 2018, No. 1, S.C. 2018, c 12 (Can.), available at https://laws-lois.just ice.gc.ca/eng/AnnualStatutes/2018_12/page-51.html#h-123 [https://perma.cc/CA4K-VGVQ].

[101] Government of Canada, 'Expanding Canada's Toolkit to Address Corporate Wrongdoing: The Integrity Regime Stream Discussion Guide' (16 December 2020), available at https://www.tpsgc-pwgsc.gc.ca/ci-if/ar-cw/examiner-review-eng.html [https://perma.cc/KYM6-JB2H].

[102] A list of the participating federal agencies is accessible at Government of Canada, 'Departments and Agencies that Follow the Integrity Regime' (16 December 2020), available at https://www.tpsgc-pwgsc.gc.ca/ci-if/pe-mou-eng.html [https://perma.cc/3U73-6K84].

[103] Tillipman and Block, n. 98.

334 PERSISTENT CORRUPTION AND SUPPLIER COLLUSION

Components of the Integrity Regime:

- *Ineligibility and Suspension Policy*, setting out when and how a supplier may be declared ineligible or suspended from doing business with the government.
- *Integrity directives*, providing formal instructions to the federal departments and agencies that follow the policy.
- *Integrity provisions*, clauses that incorporate the policy into solicitations and the resulting contracts and real property agreements.

Ineligibility to conduct business with the Government of Canada

- Supplier or any of its affiliates, convicted of certain offences under the Criminal Code or under the following acts:
  - o Competition Act
  - o Controlled Drugs and Substance Act
  - o Corruption of Foreign Officials Act
  - o Excise Tax Act
  - o Financial Administration Act
  - o Income Tax Act
  - o Lobbying Act
- Supplier entered into a subcontract with an ineligible supplier.
- Supplier provided a false or misleading certification or declaration to Public Services and Procurement Canada.
- Supplier breached any term or condition of an administrative agreement under the policy.

Source: Government of Canada, About the Integrity Regime.[104]

---

iii. Canada and the global fight against corruption

In 1997, Canada signed the above-mentioned *OECD's Convention on Combating Bribery of Foreign Public Officials in International Business Transactions,* an international anti-corruption instrument focused on the 'supply side' of the bribery transaction, i.e. the person or entity offering, promising, or giving a bribe. As a legally binding international agreement, Canada agreed to establish the bribery of foreign public officials as a criminal offence under its laws[105] and to investigate, prosecute, and sanction this offence.[106] The OECD Convention is supplemented

---

[104] Government of Canada, 'About the Integrity Regime', available at https://www.tpsgc-pwgsc.gc.ca/ci-if/apropos-about-eng.html.

[105] The OECD Anti-Bribery Convention is implemented in Canada through the CFPOA.

[106] See, in general, the OECD Anti-Bribery Convention, n. 88.

by a number of companion instruments, namely, the OECD Recommendation for Further Combating Bribery of Foreign Public Officials in International Business Transactions (the 2009 Recommendation) and the OECD Guidelines for Multinational Enterprises (the OECD Guidelines), which contain guidance regarding responsible business conduct aimed at multinational enterprises.

In addition to the OECD Convention, Canada takes part in two other international treaties related to bribery and corruption: the *United Nations Convention against Corruption (UNCAC)* and the *Inter-American Convention against Corruption (IACAC)*. UNCAC reflects the language from the OECD Convention and provides global norms on the criminalization of bribery, complementing enforcement of the CFPOA. After UNCAC came into force, the Parliament passed relevant legislation making Canadian law consistent with the provisions of the Convention.

iv. Response to the recent concern over outsourcing and the ballooning contracts issued to McKinsey

A joint report issued by TBS and PSPC in June 2023 makes clear that further reforms to federal contracting procedures are in progress. Indeed, as of the time of writing, the issuance of new guidance had already commenced:

> TBS and PSPC have taken this opportunity, after considering additional information including the proceedings of the Standing Committee on Government Operations and Estimates (OGGO), to identify broader actions they can take, consistent with their respective mandates, to strengthen procurement policy, guidance and training, as well as implementation practices and contracting approaches across the federal government. Distinct from this review of McKinsey contracts, the federal government also announced in Budget 2023 its commitment to reducing spending on professional services.
>
> TBS and PSPC will continue to work together to ensure that departments and agencies are supported in their ability to procure goods and services, and that appropriate risk-based controls are in place to meet public expectations for procurement across the Government of Canada, which are to achieve best value for Canadians in a fair, open, and transparent manner. Work will also continue to renew the Government of Canada's Integrity Regime.[107]

As a summary observation, notwithstanding and undoubtedly (at least to an extent) in response to the many scandals detailed in Section C and D, Canada has

---

[107] Executive Summary, Treasury Board of Canada Secretariat and Public Services and Procurement Canada, n. 20.

developed a relatively sophisticated legislative and policy framework for the prevention, detection, and deterrence of corruption. This framework has rightly been the focus of (positive) international attention, for example in the context of work at the OECD. It remains to be seen if it will be successful in deterring further procurement scandals which, as we have noted, have tended to occur in situations in which high-level decisions have been made to exclude particular procurement activities from normal competitive award procedures, for example through direct awards.

F. Evolution of the Canadian Competition Law Framework in Regard to Supplier Collusion and Bid Rigging

Canada's Competition Act is an important and longstanding underpinning of the country's commitment to dynamic and competitive markets in the national economy.[108] It originated in predecessor legislation that was first enacted in 1889 and has evolved extensively over the years. Important amendments to the legislation were adopted in 2009, inter alia to strengthen its treatment of horizontal price fixing and related agreements.[109] More recently, the Government of Canada has launched a far-reaching review process on possible revisions to further modernize the legislation to address a broad spectrum of issues, including digitalization, the intersection of privacy, personal information and competition, developments abroad, and the evolving nature of competition itself.[110]

The following analysis focuses on two key elements of the legislation relevant to public procurement and, specifically, supplier collusion, namely the Act's general provisions governing conspiracies between competitors and its specific provision relating to bid rigging. Attention is also given to related advocacy and similar activities.

Canada's treatment of conspiracies, agreements, or arrangements between competitors (i.e. cartel agreements) has a long and interesting history.[111] As outlined recently by Ross:

> One feature [of the competition regime] that was not in alignment with economic principles related to the treatment of cartels. The Canadian law stated that to be illegal an agreement had to 'unduly' limit competition. As is easy to imagine, the

---

[108] R.D. Anderson and S. Dev. Khosla, 'Competition Policy as a Dimension of Economic Policy: A Comparative Perspective', *Industry Canada Occasional Paper No. 7* (1995).

[109] See the following paragraphs, and references cited therein.

[110] See Government of Canada, 'Consultation on the Future of Competition Policy in Canada', available at https://ised-isde.canada.ca/site/strategic-policy-sector/en/marketplace-framework-policy/competition-policy/consultation-future-competition-policy-canada; and Innovation, Science and Economic Development Canada, 'The Future of Competition Policy in Canada' (2022), available at https://ised-isde.canada.ca/site/strategic-policy-sector/sites/default/files/attachments/2022/The-Future-of-Competition-Policy-eng_0.pdf. A list of related submissions received by the government is available at https://ised-isde.canada.ca/site/strategic-policy-sector/en/marketplace-framework-policy/competition-policy/submissions-consultation-future-competition-policy-canada.

[111] Ross, n. 82.

EVOLUTION OF THE CANADIAN COMPETITION LAW FRAMEWORK 337

presence of the qualifier meant that price-fixing, even of the most naked variety, could not be taken as per se illegal. This early failing was at least partly corrected with the 2009 amendments that created two tracks for the review of agreements between competitors supplying products: a per se criminal track for naked collusion [i.e. with no undueness test] and a civil 'rule of reason' track for other horizontal agreements such as joint ventures and strategic alliances.[112]

In sum, following decades of debate, Canadian competition law now contains a clear 'per se' prohibition of cartel activity, subject only to specific defences which are noted in the legislation. This represents a significant strengthening of Canada's competition law as compared to the situation that prevailed over many decades.[113]

In addition to the more general offence of price fixing or conspiracies in restraint of trade, the Competition Act has long incorporated a separate 'per se' offence relating to bid rigging that is directly applicable to collusive practices in public procurement.[114] The prohibition applies only 'where the agreement or arrangement is not made known to the person calling for or requesting the bids or tenders at or before the time when any bid or tender is submitted or withdrawn, as the case may be, by any person who is a party to the agreement or arrangement'. In other words, the prohibition is not applicable in circumstances of 'joint tendering' where the arrangement is disclosed in advance to the appropriate authorities.[115]

Further, following a call by Canada's Prime Minister, Justin Trudeau for a strengthening of the country's competition law,[116] new legislation was adopted by Parliament and came into effect in December 2023.[117] The legislation repeals the efficiencies defence for anti-competitive mergers and business collaborations, and implements other important changes. Further amendments to strengthen the legislation are expected to follow. .[118]

---

[112] Ross, n. 82.

[113] Ross, n. 82.

[114] Competition Act, Section 47(1) and (2). A related provision was incorporated even in the Combines Investigation Act, the predecessor legislation to the 1986 Competition Act.

[115] See M. Katz, 'Bid-Rigging in Canada: Recent Developments', *Kluwer Competition Law Blog* (10 September 2013), available at http://competitionlawblog.kluwercompetitionlaw.com/2013/09/10/bid-rigging-in-canada-recent-developments/.

[116] See Prime Minister of Canada, 'Fighting for the Middle Class' (14 September 2023), available at https://www.pm.gc.ca/en/news/news-releases/2023/09/14/fighting-for-the-middle-class#:~:text=The%20Prime%20Minister%2C%20Justin%20Trudeau,down%20the%20cost%20of%20groceries.#:~:text=The%20Prime%20Minister%2C%20Justin%20Trudeau,down%20the%20cost%20of%20groceries, and for related commentary, A. Banicevic and C. Tingley, 'Canadian Government Announces "First Set" of Competition Act Reforms', *Davies* (19 September 2023), available at https://www.dwpv.com/en/Insights/Publications/2023/Canadian-Government-Announces-Competition-Act-Reforms.

[117] See See, 'An Act to Amend the Excise Tax Act and the Competition Act' Statutes of Canada, Chapter 31 (15 December 2023) (Bill C-56), available at https://www.parl.ca/DocumentViewer/en/44-1/bill/C-56/royal-assent.

[118] See, for insightful commentary and references, J. Bodrug, A. Banicevic, and C. Tingley, 'Canada's Competition Act Reforms Include Expanded Power to Challenge Anticompetitive Agreements', *Davies* (28 September 2023), available at https://www.dwpv.com/en/Insights/Publications/2023/Competition-Act-Reforms-Expanded-Power-Challenge. (Bill C-56) and, for the latest developments, C. Tingley and U. Khandelwal, 'First Set of Major Changes to Canada's Competition Act in Force' Davies (19 December 2023).

338 PERSISTENT CORRUPTION AND SUPPLIER COLLUSION

Recently, there has been extensive enforcement activity implicating the foregoing provisions. Table 10.1 highlights the outcomes of bid rigging schemes targeting public infrastructure contracts in Quebec. Investigations by the Competition Bureau resulted in substantial fines and settlements, reimbursed overpayments, the obligation of maintaining corporate compliance programmes, and guilty pleas by former executives, who received conditional prison sentences totalling five years and eleven months, and court-ordered community service totalling 260 hours.[119]

Table 10.1 Recent bid rigging investigations by the Competition Bureau in relation to bid rigging on municipal infrastructure contracts in Quebec

Investigated firm	Decision	Year
Dessau	Ordered to pay a CAD 1.9 million settlement for its role in the bid rigging scheme. The investigation also resulted in guilty pleas and court-ordered community service.[120]	2019
WSP Canada (formerly Genivar)	Ordered to pay a CAD 4 million settlement for its role in the bid rigging scheme. The investigation resulted in a guilty plea by a former executive, receiving conditional prison sentence and court-ordered community service.[121]	2019
Norda Stelo (formerly Roche)	Ordered to pay a CAD 750,000 settlement for its role in the bid rigging scheme.[122]	2020
SNC-Lavalin	Ordered to pay a CAD 1.9 million settlement for rigging bids on municipal infrastructure contracts in the Province of Quebec as part of a settlement with the Public Prosecution Service of Canada.[123]	2020

[119] See, in general, Competition Bureau Canada, Press Release, 'SNC-Lavalin to Pay $1.9 Million in Fourth Quebec Bid-Rigging Settlement' (19 June 2020), available at https://www.canada.ca/en/comp etition-bureau/news/2020/06/snc-lavalin-to-pay-19-million-in-fourth-quebec-bid-rigging-settlem ent.html; 'Génius Conseil Inc. to Pay $300,000 in Fifth Quebec Bid-Rigging Settlement' (19 June 2020), available at https://www.canada.ca/en/competition-bureau/news/2020/06/genius-conseil-inc-to-pay-300000-in-fifth-quebec-bid-rigging-settlement.html; and Competition Policy International, 'SNC-Lavalin Settles Canadian Bid-Rigging Case' (2020), available at https://www.competitionpolicyintern ational.com/snc-lavalin-settles-canadian-bid-rigging-case/.

[120] Competition Bureau Canada, Press Release, 'Dessau to Pay $1.9 Million in Settlement Over Bid-Rigging on Public Contracts in Quebec' (19 February 2019), available at https://www.canada.ca/en/ competition-bureau/news/2019/02/dessau-to-pay-19-million-in-settlement-over-bid-rigging-on-pub lic-contracts-in-quebec.html.

[121] Competition Bureau Canada, Press Release, 'Engineering Firm to Pay $4 Million in Quebec Bid-Rigging Settlement' (13 March 2019), available at https://www.canada.ca/en/competition-bureau/ news/2019/03/engineering-firm-to-pay-4-million-in-quebec-bid-rigging-settlement.html.

[122] Competition Bureau Canada, Press Release, 'Third Engineering Firm to Pay $750,000 in Settlement for Quebec Bid-Rigging' (5 March 2020), available at https://www.canada.ca/en/competit ion-bureau/news/2020/03/third-engineering-firm-to-pay-750000-in-settlement-for-quebec-bid-rigg ing.html.

[123] 'SNC-Lavalin to Pay $1.9 Million in Fourth Quebec Bid-Rigging Settlement', n. 119.

EVOLUTION OF THE CANADIAN COMPETITION LAW FRAMEWORK   339

Table 10.1   Continued

Investigated firm	Decision	Year
Génius Conseil Inc.	Ordered to pay a CAD 300,000 settlement for bid rigging on municipal infrastructure contracts in Montreal and North Shore municipalities between 2002 and 2012.[124]	2020
Cima+	Ordered to pay CAD 3.2 million over the next four years for bid rigging on municipal infrastructure contracts in the Province of Quebec. The investigation also resulted in a guilty plea by a former executive sentenced to house arrest, and court-ordered community service.[125]	2020

The Competition Bureau has also engaged in significant outreach and advocacy activities relating to the prevention of bid rigging and supplier collusion in public procurement. As an important example, as early as 2013, the Bureau entered into a MOU with the then PWGSC (now PSPC) on the prevention, detection, reporting, and investigation of possible cartel activity. The purpose of the Memorandum is to 'promote cooperation and coordination between the participants in addressing possible cartel activity in procurement processes and real property transaction processes under the responsibility of PWGSC'. Specifically, in addition to other powers and responsibilities, it provides that:

> Where PWGSC [now PSPC] detects possible cartel activity in relation to a pro-
> curement process or a real property transaction process under its responsibility,
> PWGSC will inform the Commissioner about the matter as soon as practicable.[126]

Subsequently, the Bureau entered into multiple other MOUs with other relevant agencies.[127] This represents a highly pertinent example of best practices in anti-collusion enforcement in public procurement markets. The Competition Bureau has also engaged in significant related advocacy activities in relation to detecting and preventing bid rigging.[128] Other pertinent activities include

---

[124] 'Génius Conseil Inc. to Pay $300,000 in Fifth Quebec Bid-Rigging Settlement', n. 119.

[125] Competition Bureau Canada, Press Release, 'CIMA+ to Pay $3.2 Million in Latest Quebec Bid-Rigging Settlement' (8 December 2020), available at https://www.canada.ca/en/competition-bureau/news/2020/12/cima-to-pay-32-million-in-latest-quebec-bid-rigging-settlement.html.

[126] See Government of Canada, 'Memorandum of Understanding between the Competition Bureau and the Department of Public Works and Government Services (PWGSC) Regarding the Prevention, Detection, Reporting and Investigation of Possible Cartel Activity' (30 May 2013), available at https://ised-isde.canada.ca/site/competition-bureau-canada/en/how-we-foster-competition/collaboration-and-partnerships/memorandum-understanding-between-competition-bureau-and-department-public-works-and-government.

[127] See, e.g., Government of Canada, 'Memorandum of Understanding between the Competition Bureau and Defence Construction Canada', available at https://www.competitionbureau.gc.ca/eic/site/cb-bc.nsf/eng/04406.html.

[128] See for instance, the Compliance Bootcamp, available at https://ised-isde.canada.ca/site/competition-bureau-canada/en/how-we-foster-competition/education-and-outreach/compliance-bootc

340 PERSISTENT CORRUPTION AND SUPPLIER COLLUSION

releasing updated guidelines on procurement processes to ensure that these are conducted in a competitive and fair manner,[129] publishing a collusion risk assessment tool for procurement agents, and providing relevant training for procurement professionals.[130]

G. Concluding Remarks

As discussed in this chapter, in the past two decades extensive corrupt practices and supplier collusion have been disclosed particularly in the public procurement sector of the Province of Quebec, but also in other Canadian provinces and (with disturbing regularity) at the federal level of government. In fact, corruption issues in public procurement date back to the early years following Canada's 'Confederation' (i.e. the country's establishment as a (mainly) self-governing polity in 1867). Related scandals have, on multiple occasions, caused embarrassment to the country's senior political leadership and impacted the outcome of national elections. This is despite major efforts being made, over time, to introduce and enforce appropriate safeguards to detect, deter, and punish both supplier collusion and other corrupt practices.

This chapter has explored these relationships and phenomena. An effort has been made to identify the principal factors underlying the observed patterns of corruption and supplier collusion in public procurement in Canada, notwithstanding the country's generally advanced and well-developed governance systems. The following factors are highlighted:

- first, the relatively small size of Canada's public procurement markets, especially at the provincial level, which is a well-known contributing factor to both collusion and corruption problems;
- second, the persistence of significant barriers to both inter-provincial and international trade in public procurement markets over an extended period;
- third, a culture of 'patronage' which developed early in the country's history and has persisted for many decades, at least in certain regions;
- fourth, for many years, inadequate penalties and other problems associated with competition law enforcement; and

---

amp#sec02, and the Competition Bureau's Podcast, 'Bid Rigging Under the Spotlight (COR4-P01)', available at https://www.csps-efpc.gc.ca/podcasts/bid-rigging-spotlight-eng.aspx.

[129] M. Tetrault, 'Competition Bureau Releases Updated Guidelines on Procurement Processes' (10 February 2021), available at https://www.mccarthy.ca/en/insights/articles/competition-bureau-relea ses-updated-guidelines-procurement-processes.

[130] 'Preventing Bid-Rigging: Tips for Tendering Authorities', available at https://ised-isde.canada.ca/ site/competition-bureau-canada/en/bid-rigging-price-fixing-and-other-agreements-between-comp etitors/preventing-bid-rigging-tips-tendering-authorities.

CONCLUDING REMARKS 341

- fifth, evident temptations and weaknesses in applicable safeguards (at times) at the top level of the central government.

Concerning the relevant policy responses, notwithstanding and undoubtedly (at least to some extent) *in response to* the many scandals detailed in Sections C and D of this chapter, Canada has developed a relatively sophisticated legislative and policy framework for the prevention, detection, and deterrence of corrupt practices in public procurement. This framework has rightly been a focus of international attention, for example in the context of work at the OECD. It remains to be seen if it will be successful in deterring further procurement scandals which, as we have noted, have often occurred in situations in which high-level decisions have been made to exclude particular procurement activities from normal competitive award procedures.

With respect to competition law enforcement, Canadian competition law and the Competition Bureau, as the principal enforcement authority, have grappled with the problem of bid rigging and supplier collusion in public procurement in innovative ways. These encompass enforcement, advocacy, and institutional outreach activities. The law of competition in Canada has, itself, been strengthened, over time, in important ways. The MOUs that the Bureau has developed with important federal procuring agencies are models for possible related initiatives in other jurisdictions. Without doubt, Canada is a jurisdiction whose enforcement and related activities in this area merit ongoing study.

At the same time, there appear to be elements of the Canadian public procurement system that cannot be adequately controlled altogether with the standard tools of anti-corruption and competition law enforcement. Corrupt practices in Canada have, all too frequently, occurred with tacit acceptance or even knowing participation of top governmental authorities. This element of the problem can only be controlled—if at all—through stricter auditory and related controls impacting on the top levels of government. For example, given Canada's history, it could be interesting to explore more explicit legislative controls limiting the ability of top government officials to weigh in on major decisions regarding the awarding of important government contracts, and subjecting such decisions to heightened scrutiny. Consideration could also be given to establishing an intergovernmental supervisory mechanism, possibly at the level of the United States-Mexico-Canada Agreement (USMCA), the OECD, or even the WTO, to review related activities and governance structures.[131] As ever, the vigilance and involvement of ordinary citizens, the news media and civil society organizations in the monitoring of public procurement activities remains vital.

---

[131] Recall the discussion on the potential benefits of multi-level governance in Chapter 4, this book. Such a mechanism could, potentially, build upon the comparative analysis and peer review activities that are already undertaken in the OECD. See OECD, 'Public Procurement', available at https://www.oecd.org/governance/ethics/public-procurement.htm#:~:text=OECD's%20work%20on%20Public%20Procurement&text=Undertaking%20hands%2Don%20peer%20reviews,shape%20directions%20for%20future%20reforms.

11
Conclusions

This book examines the topic of corruption and supplier collusion in public procurement and considers their causes and facilitating conditions; their economic and social impact; how they can be prevented and deterred; and the experiences of seven diverse jurisdictions in relation to conduct. It highlights the fundamental importance of efficient and effective public procurement for the prosperity of nations and the well-being of citizens. When public procurement is performed well, it enriches individuals' lives, in particular, by ensuring that they are provided with high-quality public infrastructure, goods and services, and by contributing to economic and human development, and poverty reduction. Good results in public procurement are especially important for society's more vulnerable members. Effective public procurement can also build trust in democratic governance by fostering a belief that the government is committed to such improvements and responsive to the needs of citizens. In contrast, when public procurement processes are undermined by corruption and/or supplier collusion, precious public resources are squandered, and the quantity and quality of public infrastructure, goods and services are reduced to the significant detriment of citizens. This impacts negatively on economic and social development, may cause risk to life, and breeds mistrust in government and its institutions.

The central significance of public procurement, and the need to shield it from corrupt and collusive practices, is generally accepted. Numerous international efforts have led to substantial consensus as to how laws on public procurement, corruption control, and fighting cartels should be constructed. Indeed, all of the jurisdictions focused on in this book have relatively well-composed systems, comprised of robust public procurement, competition and anti-corruption laws which in most cases derive from, or are influenced by, international initiatives such as the UNCITRAL Model Law on Public Procurement, the World Trade Organization's Agreement on Government Procurement (WTO GPA), United Nations and the Organisation for Economic Co-operation and Development (OECD) anti-corruption conventions, and various international initiatives to ensure effective action against cartels.

The book recognizes, nonetheless, the extensive challenges involved in developing, and ensuring the enduring effectiveness of, these systems, and that even comprehensive regimes often fail to realize their goals. Indeed, the discussion reinforces an articulated concern that increased international efforts to combat corruption and collusion since the 1990s have produced limited, or disappointing,

344 CONCLUSIONS

results. Not only does it illustrate that corruption and collusion risks in public procurement remain real in the seven jurisdictions surveyed (and, by logical extension, many other jurisdictions around the world), but that examples of both types of practices continue to be exposed with depressing regularity, even in some of the most advanced industrial economies and even in times of (and taking advantage of) national crises. Further, the analysis suggests that these risks may now actually be increasing in some countries in the light of, for example: the series of recent, global crises which have necessitated, and are continuing to necessitate, rapid procurement responses (and, often, the sidestepping of ordinary procurement procedures); insufficient funding of the public sector and law enforcement agencies; a failure to prioritize investigation of economic crime; a weakening of the rule of law (e.g. where democratic backsliding, or autocratizing, is occurring); or because corruption has become embedded into a system. Although these risks plague all areas of public procurement, they appear to be especially acute in construction, defence, and at the local level. In several chapters of this book, nonetheless, it has also been seen that corruption impacting on public procurement can reach the highest echelons of government and society and be facilitated by leading politicians or businesspeople.

A main aim of the book is, consequently, to seek to understand why (despite international and national efforts) this conduct remains so prevalent, and how public procurement regimes can be bolstered to make them more resilient to them. The discussion indicates that, in addition to well-documented general causes (springing from the volume of money being spent with regularity and the challenge of counteracting the significant incentives and opportunities for corruption and collusion that public procurement creates), a number of common problems arise. In particular, it confirms that risks frequently arise in certain sectors and in emergency purchasing situations when spending increases and ordinary safeguards are reduced, and that in many countries general difficulties may be compounded by the fact that, for example: public procurement rules limit the pool of bidders so facilitating corruption and collusion between a close knit group of players; procurement, or law enforcement agency, workforces lack capacity (or even capability) to meet the significant demands imposed upon them; procurement officials may participate in, or facilitate, misconduct so hampering detection of infringements; it is difficult to control cronyism; in some jurisdictions, it is not easy to preclude political donations that may influence the award of procurement contracts; there is frequently a lack of policy and enforcement coordination between procurement, anti-corruption, and competition agencies or institutions; and anti-corruption or competition regimes often fail to create the deterrent effect they were formed to establish, so contributing to a sense of impunity. Indeed, in many countries law enforcement remains limited and, even where it does occur, it may be resolved through settlements or other plea arrangements that can dilute the full deterrent effect of the law and fail to guard sufficiently against future violations.

CONCLUSIONS   345

Despite these common themes, weaknesses in any individual system inevitably derive from a range of factors which differ from state to state, and which relate to particular national, political, legal, and business environments. In the UK, for example, concerns identified have included the lack of consistent anti-corruption or competition law training for procurers, insufficient monitoring and oversight of procurement processes, rather limited enforcement of cartel and anti-corruption (at the domestic level) laws, relatively weak sanctions with insufficient deterrent effect, and a failure of policy coordination. A particular problem may also be an, arguably misguided, sense that the system is effective and working, as the UK is not generally perceived as a particularly corrupt country.

In both Canada and the US, it is seen that corruption and collusion scandals have repeatedly impacted on public procurement processes for more than a century and have even implicated top-level officials and politicians. This is so in spite of the many cases that have been brought, and numerous (and ongoing) efforts made to improve law and enforcement in the public procurement sphere—rather, tendencies and institutional weaknesses have persisted, and players often seem to have been able to adapt to amended and enhanced regulatory frameworks. In Canada, for example, problems have been associated with the relatively small size of public procurement markets, persistent international and internal trade barriers, a deep culture of patronage at least in certain regions of the country and, as in the UK, weak oversight mechanisms and inadequate deterrents to the prohibited conduct. In the US, difficulties derive from a variety of features of the system, including procurement personnel's lack of capacity, insufficient funding of public agencies, and because US public procurement policy sometimes embraces policies that suppress, rather than stimulate competition, and so facilitate and stabilize corrupt and collusive schemes.

In Brazil, a dominant cause of the extensive problems surveyed has been, in addition to weaknesses in procurement processes, the close links and ties developed between politicians, officials in state-owned enterprises (SOEs) and businesses, the complexities of the political system, and the sense of impunity felt by core players, which combined to create a culture of corruption and kickbacks. Similarly, systemic corruption has been an entrenched problem in Ukraine since its independence; it has taken time for the country to put in place effective public procurement, anti-corruption and competition law systems, and the ongoing war triggered by Russia's invasion has placed substantial additional stress on these systems. Still, significant achievements have been noted (e.g. implementation of the ProZorro platform to strengthen transparency). Further progress will be vital to maintain international support for Ukraine's ongoing war effort and to ensure a secure, prosperous, and democratic future for Ukraine when the war finally concludes.

With respect to Hungary, it is feared that the foundations are being laid for a culture of corruption to emerge as the country autocratizes, checks and balances in the system are reduced, and cronyism, favouritism, and economic nationalism, grow. Backsliding in democracy and the economy have also created challenges in Poland, although it remains to be seen whether, and how quickly, this trend can be reversed by the new government formed at the end of 2023. The two countries' experiences highlight, nonetheless, both the potential contribution and acute relevance of regional organizations or multilateral governance mechanisms (resulting in this case from the overarching role of the European Union institutions) in addressing problems in the public procurement sector, as well as the limits to even quite far-reaching enforcement tools.

The diverse 'roots' of the problems, identified in the jurisdictions examined, confirm that the 'solutions', and mechanisms, for combatting them must be tailored to the particular environment in which they are to be implanted. Specific suggestions have been offered in relation to each of the jurisdictions examined. In addition, a few general themes emerge.

A crucial matter highlighted is the importance, given the costs and difficulties of law enforcement, of preventative means, to avert infringements from arising in the first place. Often, such preventative measures provide more achievable and realistic reform mechanisms, which are likely to attract less opposition from those reluctant to support change than the threat of punitive measures resulting from law enforcement. The book thus recognizes that many (and perhaps all) jurisdictions need to consider bolstering measures to make public procurement a less protected environment for wrongdoing and to reduce opportunities for corruption, cronyism, and collusion during the process, including in emergency purchasing situations. This can be achieved through, for example: reform, where needed, to ensure that all exemptions from normal transparent and competitive tendering procedures are subject to appropriate (and, absent very exceptional circumstances, publicly disclosed) justification, with additional safeguards being built into processes governing emergency purchases; considering how transparency can be increased in relation to defence spending; reducing unnecessary barriers to participation in public procurement processes and markets; enhanced use of e-procurement tools; investing properly in, and training, an independent and meritocratically appointed procurement workforce; strengthening market research and negotiation capabilities in procuring agencies; and ensuring effective internal and external monitoring of processes and adherence to publication rules and codes of conduct.

An important related question touched upon in this book concerns the design of transparency measures for the optimal control of corruption and supplier collusion. Transparency is, to be sure, a vital tool in the fight against corruption, and the adoption of 'open contracting' regimes such as Ukraine's ProZorro system has been a key factor in the progress achieved to date in deterring corrupt practices in relevant jurisdictions. Transparency measures such as the systematic advertising of procurement opportunities and full disclosure of bidding and related procedures can also favour competition in important ways, by drawing additional competitors into the market. Still, economic models and the experience of competition agencies in jurisdictions such as the United States and Canada also show clearly that 'too much transparency' with respect to bids received and other parameters of individual procurements can facilitate supplier collusion. Reflecting on these issues, our view is that the right choices will often depend on the circumstances of particular jurisdictions. In situations where corrupt practices and the misuse of public funds are known to be pervasive, the only hope of establishing integrity in public procurement (and public confidence in government) may lie in implementing a system of relatively complete transparency. In contrast, in jurisdictions in which there is a higher degree of confidence in the integrity of procurement officials and institutions, a less sweeping approach to transparency measures (especially avoiding the disclosure of individual bids) may be appropriate, for the sake of making cartel activity more difficult to organize and enforce. In all circumstances, emphasis should also be placed on measures that can unambiguously help to deter both collusion and corrupt practices—for example, market opening and the elimination of unnecessary barriers to entry, the strengthening of market research capabilities in conjunction with professionalization of the procurement workforce, the successful engagement of civil society in monitoring relevant activities, and the effective enforcement of anti-corruption, competition, and procurement laws.

The integrity of public procurement processes may also be enhanced through the use of integrity pacts and certificates of independent bidding; a carefully constructed debarment or exclusion process for economic operators that create a risk to the process, such as those that have previously engaged in corrupt or collusive practices and which have not gone through a process of self-cleaning; and a rigorously operated and rapid complaints or domestic review procedure that provides the opportunity for effective challenge to procurements wrongfully sidestepping competitive tendering procedures, or otherwise conducted in breach of the rules.

In addition to evaluating public procurement laws and rules, our analysis stresses the need to review the anti-corruption and competition law framework periodically—both the laws themselves and the enforcement structures. One difficulty noted is that many anti-corruption laws do not easily reach cronyism, or favouritism, or the demand side of foreign bribery. Further, few countries have in place laws which acknowledge the interaction between corruption and bid rigging in the public procurement sphere. The introduction of such laws could, however, facilitate investigations and prosecutions of this conduct when they operate together, especially in jurisdictions where complexities arise because different agencies have to challenge what may form part of the same overall illegal scheme, under several distinct offences (this is a problem in the UK, for example).

Problems may also arise if there is inadequate enforcement of anti-corruption and competition laws, and relevant actors feel that they are above the law and that their illegal conduct will go unchallenged. The book consequently emphasizes the importance of enforcement in this area being prioritized and the use of a broad range of detection techniques, including complaints, whistleblowing, direct

348 CONCLUSIONS

referrals, monitoring and screening tools to facilitate ex officio investigations. The potential of digital tools and open contracting systems as mechanisms both, to open up procurement processes to a wider range of bidders, *and* to facilitate scrutiny of procurement is highlighted. Although it is recognized that self-reporting schemes play a valuable role in rooting out hidden conduct which may otherwise be difficult to uncover, their limits are also acknowledged and the risks of over-reliance on these tools emphasized. Moreover, it is noted that in many countries more needs to be done to ensure that a wider range of dissuasive penalties are used to deter infringements, and which extend beyond the use of corporate fines. For example, in some jurisdictions, greater efforts are clearly required to hold responsible individuals to account, to exclude contractors that have participated in offences, and to recover bribes, the proceeds of crime, or damages for harm suffered in consequence of a competition law infringement. Despite the complexities involved in bringing competition law damages actions, these could, in addition to deterring future violations, help to ensure that taxpayer money lost due to inflated contract prices is clawed back.

Another matter stressed is the need in most countries to recognize the interdependence between the three areas of law governing public procurement, corruption control, and competition law, respectively. The book discusses the benefits that can be achieved from the different groups of actors involved cooperating with one another, both positively to achieve their common goals (through training, exchange of information, joint investigations, sharing of relevant information, etc.) and through ensuring that the actions of one set of institutions do not thwart efforts by the others.

Where there is a 'will' for reform at the national level, a number of the changes proposed may be achieved through relatively simply adjustments to training, monitoring, procurement, and enforcement processes, and interagency coordination mechanisms. Although legislative reform is likely to be more difficult, especially if there is pressure on time for legislative processes and reform is not viewed as a high priority by government, it may be required in some cases. In such situations, enhanced advocacy and peer review mechanisms supported by international institutions may help to persuade governments to act to meet objectives or principles they have agreed to in international conventions. Multilateral development banks, the international aid ministries of relevant countries, the UN, the OECD, and the WTO, all of which already recognize public procurement as an important area for their involvement, can help to ensure that issues concerning effective public procurement policy and the prevention of related abuses, whether through corruption or anti-competitive practices, receive the full attention that they deserve, at the international, national, and local levels. As at the domestic level, greater coordination in and mutual support for such activities by the relevant organizations could be helpful.

In countries where corruption arises not from a principal–agent problem but because it is the expected norm and is embedded, or becoming embedded, in the system, the need for a different approach is acknowledged. In such circumstances, direct legal responses (attacking corruption head on) are unlikely to be achievable or sufficient on their own to combat the conduct. They may also provoke claims of bias by those targeted. As indirect responses aimed at changing the moral equilibrium and social contract can be difficult to accomplish in the short run, the book proposes that a number of self-reinforcing steps can be considered to try to break a cycle of corruption. For example, in addition to steps to make public procurement processes more resilient to corruption in the first place and to strengthened, and more coordinated, law enforcement (if necessary, refashioned and reinvigorated to address collective action problems), measures can be adopted to weaken ties between procurers, politicians, and businesses. Trade liberalization, for example via the WTO GPA, may provide a means for diluting cosy relationships between core players that have developed, changing norms and signalling a commitment to a new, more open, and competitive approach.

The wider political and institutional context and the degree to which corruption is entrenched in institutions will, nonetheless, affect the success of any such reform efforts. As is discussed, in particular in Chapters 4, 7, 8, and 9, actions against former government officials may be challenged as politically biased and reform and law enforcement are unlikely to be possible to counter wrongdoing, especially by government insiders, in the absence of separation of powers, independent, and impartial, courts, prosecutors, and other law enforcement agencies, a free media, and respect for the rule of law. Where these, or some of these, features are absent, domestic and international pressure, and support, may be vital to encourage and assist political and institutional reform and capacity building. Engagement of the press and civil society groups may thus be essential not only to monitor for wrongdoing, but to lobby for change and the development of new moral norms and a new social contract. International financial institutions and donors of international aid can also, and do, take steps to ensure that their funds are used for the purposes granted, by working with states to build capacity and to develop anti-corruption initiatives, through overseeing reform efforts and monitoring exercises, through seeking recovery of improperly used money, and by using sanctions systems to protect the funds (for example, through the debarment or exclusion of entities that have engaged in fraud or corrupt practices). Notably, the EU has developed techniques—including the use of financial penalties and the withholding of EU funds—to counter corruption risks arising in EU Member States themselves, and which impact on the EU budget or undermine fundamental EU values, especially the rule of law. These measures have imposed not insignificant pressure on both Poland and Hungary to reverse actions that have been increasing corruption and collusion risks in those countries.

350 CONCLUSIONS

Given the enormous sums of public money that governments spend on public procurement, especially in turbulent political and economic times, it is our view that action on these matters should be a matter of high priority for governments. Additional measures are clearly desirable in all of the jurisdictions examined in this book to ensure that public spending delivers good value for taxpayer money, that citizens receive the highest quality goods, services, and infrastructure that this money can buy, and, crucially, to ensure that public monies are used for the purposes for which they are collected and are not siphoned off by corrupt public officials, politicians and their cronies, or tenderers engaged in corrupt or anti-competitive conduct. Corruption control in public procurement is also essential to foster good governance and effective competition, and to engender trust and belief in government. The measures proposed in this book may, consequently, be essential more broadly to promote confidence in democratic governments and their institutions, and even to ensure their very survival.

Index

For the benefit of digital users, indexed terms that span two pages (e.g., 52–53) may, on occasion, appear on only one of those pages.

accountability
 basic element 5, 21–22, 50
 Brazil 214
 Canada 320, 329
 e-procurement 54–55
 rule of law and 77, 248–49
 individual accountability 43, 50, 79, 88, 89–90, 113
 international development and external policies 135
 transparency and 25, 53
 Ukraine 302
 United Kingdom 168–69
active bribery *see bribery*
anti-corruption laws and conventions
 basic element 67–71, 92–120
 Brazil anti-corruption laws 215
 Canada Criminal Code 330–31
 EU 242–43
 failure to prevent bribery 145
 foreign bribery
  demand side 94–95, 347
  meaning and scope 38–39, 68–71, 94–95, 97–99, 128–29
 Hungary and Poland 244
 need for regular reviews 92, 93–95, 347
 OECD Convention on Combating Bribery of Foreign Public Officials in International Business Transactions 67–68, 70–71, 92–93, 97–98, 145, 242–43, 330–31, 334–35
 Ukraine
  control in the context of war 286–87
  legislative reforms of 2014 280–81
 United Kingdom
  anti-corruption laws 145–46
  cases 152
  foreign bribery cases 153–54
 United Nations Convention against Corruption (UNCAC) vi, 10, 67–69, 92–93, 120–21, 145, 242–43, 335
 United States
  anti-corruption and public integrity laws 205–6

Foreign Corrupt Practices Act 70, 94–95, 191–92, 194, 202, 206
 'War' on corruption 67–69
appeals *see domestic review/appeal procedures*
audits
 basic element 50, 60–61, 92, 128–29
 Brazil 232–33
 Canada 327, 341
 Hungary and Poland 248–49, 255
 United Kingdom 159–60, 168–69, 177–78
 United States 195

barriers to entry
 basic element 25, 50, 51–52, 61, 346–47
 Brazil 230–31
 Canada 340
bid rigging
 Brazil 215
 Canada 316–27, 336–40
 common bid rigging practices 7–9
 harm caused 9, 39–40
 incentives and conditions facilitating collusion in public procurement 23–28
 Hungary and Poland 244
 Operation Car Wash *see Operation Car Wash*
 overlap with corruption 8–9
 Ukraine 291–94
 United Kingdom 143–44, 150–52
 United States 182–98, 199–200, 203–4
bid protest, *see domestic review/appeal procedures*
Brazil
 enduring perception of widespread corruption 227–28
 Operation Car Wash *see also Operation Car Wash*
  large-scale, long-lasting corruption scheme 223
  multi-layered anti-corruption and competition investigation 221–22
  multiple fronts of investigation 215–20
  penalties 222
  political sanctions 221

352   INDEX

Brazil (*cont.*)

powerful lessons for other jurisdictions 238

sense of impunity 224

undermining factors 224–28

widespread involvement of politicians 223

reform proposals

ensuring that players cannot act with impunity 232–37

making public procurement a less protected environment for wrongdoing 230–31

need for, and feasibility of, reform 228–13

need for change of mindset 237–38

weakening links between business, procurement officials, and politicians 229–30

bribery *see also corruption in public procurement and anti-corruption laws and conventions*

active bribery

Brazil 214, 215, 225–26

EU 242–43

facilitation of corruption 21

meaning and scope 5–6

national measures 71, 93–94

United Kingdom 145

United States 94–95

foreign bribery

Canada 330–31

demand side 94–95, 347

Foreign Corrupt Practices Act (US) 202, 206

meaning and scope 38–39, 68–71, 94–95, 97–99, 128–29

OECD Convention on Combating Bribery of Foreign Public Officials in International Business Transactions 67–68, 70–71, 92–93, 97–98, 145, 242–43, 330–31, 334–35

Organisation for Economic Co-operation and Development, *see* **Organisation for Economic Co-operation and Development**

United Kingdom 145, 150, 152, 153–54

United States 70, 94–95, 191–92, 194, 202, 206

passive bribery

Brazil 215

EU 242–43

facilitation of corruption 20–21

meaning and scope 5–6

national measures 71

United Kingdom 145, 164–65

United States 94–95

recovery of bribes 116–18

Canada

anti-corruption framework

Canada's Criminal Code 330–31

global fight against corruption 334–35

institutional support in fighting corruption 331–32

competition laws 336–40

early corruption and supplier collusion scandals

flour milling bid rigging case of 1990 318–19

'Hamilton Harbour' dredging scandal 317–18

'Pacific Scandal' 316–17

'Integrity Regime' 332–34, 333*b*

long standing problems of corruption and collusion 345

more recent examples of alleged corruption, supplier collusion and/or mismanagement

'ETS scandal' 321

'F-35 fighter jet procurement scandal' 321–22

Quebec construction sector 322–24

'SNC Lavelin Affair' 324–25

'Sponsorship Scandal' 319–21

'WE Charity' scandal 325–26

public procurement

Federal level 313

international and internal trade agreements 315–16

Provincial level 313–14

relatively decentralized manner 312

cartels *see bid rigging*

collective action problem 6–7, 15, 22–23, 123–30, 311, 349

competition laws

Brazil 215

Canada 336–40

cartels 71–72

Hungary and Poland 244

national developments 72

need for regular reviews 347

Ukraine

bid rigging and related conduct 291–94

enforcement in current war context 297–98

ensuring enforcement of competition law 305–6

United Kingdom 143–44

United States

antitrust laws 199–200, 203–4

early applications of the Sherman Act 184–85

expansion of criminal antitrust
enforcement 190–91
corporate fines, *see also penalties and*
remedies 78–79, 112–13
corruption in public procurement
Brazil *see Brazil*
Canada *see Canada*
collective action problem 6–7, 15, 22–23,
123–30, 311, 349
different national norms and expectations 5
factors which need to be tackled 41
harm caused
costs of corruption 33–39
corrosion of public trust 10
human well-being 9
impact on democracy 9
Hungary and Poland *see Hungary and Poland*
incentives and conditions facilitating
corruption in public procurement 20–23
importance of combatting corruption 10–11
lack of international success in combatting
problems 11–12
meaning and scope
abuse by public officials 5
particularism 5–6
principal–agent problem 6–7, 14–15, 20–21,
123–25, 138, 311
surveys, risk indicators and examples
agency exposures 30–32
general evidence and risk indicators
suggest 29–30
need to estimate levels of
wrongdoing 28–29
serious allegations across the world 31–32
Ukraine *see Ukraine*
United Kingdom *see United Kingdom*
United States *see United States*
WTO GPA *see WTO GPA*
COVID-19, corruption risks and
mismanagement issues
Canada 326–27
Hungary and Poland 250–51
importance of combatting corruption 10–11
need to improve emergency and crisis
situations 89
unique challenges 2–3
United Kingdom 139, 142–43, 155–56, 158
United Nations 89
United States 194–95, 197

debarment and exclusion
Brazil 215
Canada 333
EU 241–42, 265

definition and importance 58–59, 79–
80, 115–16
penalties 79–80
Ukraine 295
United Kingdom 174–75
United States 204
democracy, impact of corruption on
costs of corruption 35
EU commitment 136
global struggle 1–2
illiberal influence of populist governments
in Hungary and Poland 246–54
rule of law, *see rule of law*
domestic review/appeal procedures
GPA parties 63
EU 241–42, 265, 267
importance and design of 45, 50, 59–60, 347
Ukraine 296–97, 304–5
United Kingdom 142–43, 168–69
United States 205

e-procurement
EU's Tender Electronic Daily 168–69
importance and role in shaping an open,
competitive bidding system 17, 54–55
Korea 106–7
Ukraine 281–83
United Kingdom 159
enforcement, *see also Brazil, Canada, Hungary*
and Poland, Ukraine, United Kingdom
and United States
detection techniques and investigative
tools 74–77
capability, capacity, and prioritization 95–97
detection techniques: overuse of self-reporting
schemes 99–101
detection techniques: red flags, monitoring,
and screening tools 101, 109
effective enforcement
institutions 74
insufficient or under-enforcement of the
laws 95–99
judicial protection of the law 77
optimal deterrence 73–74
importance 347–48
institutions 74, 83–99
judicial protection of the law 77
multi-layered anti-corruption and
competition investigation 221–22
Operation Car Wash *see Operation Car Wash*
optimal deterrence 73–74
European Union (EU)
acting against individual cases of suspected
corruption and bid rigging 257–58

354 INDEX

European Union (EU) (*cont.*)
  bidding by separate companies in the same
    corporate group 91
  compliance with EU law by Hungary
    and Poland
    backsliding and breaches of EU law 255–57
    enforcement, penalties, and financial
      mechanisms 261–64
    greater supervision and oversight of public
      procurement processes 264–65
    procedures against Member States
      for infringement of EU law and
      values 258–61
  enforcement techniques 349
  EU's Tender Electronic Daily 168–69
  trade liberalization 62
  Ukraine 262, 278
    bid to join 306
exclusion *see debarment and exclusion*

foreign bribery *see anticorruption laws and*
    conventions and bribery

golden parachutes 5–6, 20–21
grand corruption 5–6, 114, 249, 252–53,
    301–2

harm from corruption and collusion
  corrosion of public trust 10
  costs of bid rigging
    higher procurement prices 40
    national examples 39–40
    undermining of free market 39
  costs of corruption
    foreign bribery 38–39
    hidden nature 33–34
    impact on democracy 35
    impact on world's gross domestic
      product 37–38
    serious social problem 35
    squandering of resources 35–36
  human well-being 9
  impact on democracy 9
  Operation Car Wash 32–33
Hungary and Poland
  compliance with EU law
    acting against individual cases of suspected
      corruption and bid rigging 257–58
    backsliding and breaches of EU
      law 255–57
    enforcement, penalties, and financial
      mechanisms 261–64
    greater supervision and oversight of public
      procurement processes 264–65

procedures against Member States
  for infringement of EU law and
  values 258–61
illiberal influence of populist governments
  illiberal change in democracy 246–47
  illiberal change in the economy 247–48
  impact on public procurement 248–54
  transformation of post-communist Central
    European countries 245–46
reform proposals
  compliance with EU law 255–65
  initiatives at the national level 254–55

independent bid preparation/determination
  certificates of independent bid preparation/
    determination 60, 114, 200, 230–31, 237
  enhancement of public procurement
    processes 347
  integrity pacts *see integrity pacts and regimes*
  provisions to reinforce the integrity of the
    process 60
integrity pacts and regimes
  Brazil 230–31
  Canada 332–34
  debarment 58–59
  enhancement of public procurement
    processes 60, 347
  EU 240, 265, 267
investigations *see enforcement*

judiciary
  effective enforcement 77
  rule of law, and independence of *see rule of law*
  Ukraine 301–2

money laundering
  Brazil 234
  Canada 331
  importance to fight against
    corruption 130–31

Operation Car Wash
  extent of problems 214–15
  harm caused 32–33
  large-scale, long-lasting corruption
    scheme 223
  lessons for other jurisdictions 238
  main fronts of investigations 215
  most far-reaching corruption and collusion
    scheme 30–31
  multi-layered anti-corruption and
    competition investigation 221–22
  multiple fronts of investigation 215–20
  penalties 224

political sanctions 221
sense of impunity 224
undermining factors
  economic scars 225
  insufficient deterrence 227
  political or improper motivation 224–25
  waning government support 225–26
widespread involvement of politicians 223
Organisation for Economic Co-operation and Development (OECD)
acceptance of an international norm that forbids bribery 202
bid rigging 40
Canada 310, 330–31, 341
Canada's membership 310
encouraging collective action 132–33
enhancement of public procurement processes 343
foreign bribery 94–95
important area for involvement 348
key international cooperation 45–46
OECD Convention on Combating Bribery of Foreign Public Officials in International Business Transactions 67–68, 70–71, 92–93, 97–98, 145, 242–43, 330–31, 334–35
promotion of anti-bribery laws 70–71
Ukraine 278, 299
'War' on corruption 67–68
workforce capacity, capability, and independence 85

passive bribery *see bribery*
penalties and remedies
corporate fines 78–79
debarment/exclusion 79–80, 115–16
individual accountability 79, 113–14
recovery of bribes and damages actions 80, 116–18
personnel *see workforces and personnel*
petty corruption
meaning and scope 5–6
United Kingdom 95–96
Poland *see Hungary and Poland*
principal-agent problem 6–7, 14–15, 20–21, 123–25, 138, 311
prisoner's dilemma 34, 75, 126–27, 129–30
public procurement
bid protest, *see domestic review/appeal procedures*
Brazil, *see Brazil*
Canada, *see Canada*
corruption risk 6–7
  collusion risk 7

debarment and exclusion, *see debarment and exclusion*
detrimental effects of failures 4
domestic review, *see domestic review/appeal procedures*
economic and social importance 1–4
impact on citizens' lives 2–3
maximisation of resources 3–4
Hungary see *Hungary and Poland*
illiberal influence of populist governments in Hungary and Poland 248–54
Poland see *Hungary and Poland*
role of EU in establishing liberal procurement framework for Member States 240–44
Ukraine *see Ukraine*
United Kingdom *see United Kingdom*
United States *see United States*
WTO GPA, *see WTO GPA*

recovery of bribes and damages actions see also *penalties and remedies*
Brazil 215
importance of 80, 116–18
United Kingdom 175–76
United States 116–17
rule of law
effective enforcement 93
independent and effective judicial protection of the law 77
EU commitment to 136, 243–44, 256, 259–60, 261–62
Conditionality Regulation 263–64
Hungary and Poland 245–47, 248–49, 251, 262, 266–67
importance, and the impact of corrupt and collusive practices on 9–10, 11–12, 35, 77, 93, 118, 343–44, 349
separation of powers 118–19
success of any reform mechanisms 18
Trump era scandals and challenges to the rule of law 195–97
Ukraine 271–72, 273–74, 278, 283, 301–2

sanctions *see penalties and remedies*
siloed regimes
policy coordination 119–21
relevant laws 121–22
United Kingdom 164–65
supplier collusion *see bid rigging*
Sustainable Development Goals (SDGs) 10, 34
systemic corruption 21–23combatting endemic, or systemic, corruption 23, 122–30, 137–38
particularism 5–7, 21–22, 81, 84, 122–23, 132
Ukraine 270–71

356 INDEX

trade liberalization
benefits of trade liberalization in the public
procurement sector 65–67
contribution to the fight against corruption 61
role in strengthening the integrity of the public
procurement process 61–62
role of the EU vis-à-vis its Member
States 64–65
WTO GPA *see WTO GPA*
transparency
Brazil 225–26
Canada 320
design of transparency measures 12, 283,
307–8, 346–47
factors rendering public procurement
susceptible to supplier collusion 25
Hungary and Poland 254
Open Contracting Data Standard
(OCDS) 54–55, 281–82
other relevant international
developments 135
shaping an open, competitive bidding
system 54–55
role in addressing systemic corruption 128–
29, *see also systemic corruption*
Ukraine 281–83, 303–5, 307–8
United Kingdom 168–69
Transparency International
Corruption Perceptions Index (CPI) 28–30,
69–70, 140, 155–56, 227–28, 251

Ukraine
causes of problems 270, 345
effect of excessive dependence on Russia 279
legacy of the Soviet Union 275–76
challenges regarding post-war reconstruction
central issues 300–1
ensuring enforcement of competition
law 305–6
restoration of confidence in rule of
law 301–2
strengthening deterrence measures 303–5
continued fight with corruption during
current war 273, 279
corruption and collusion in public procurement
continuing efforts to prevent and deter
corruption 273–74
continuing impact on economic and
national prospects 271–72
essential element of the country's broader
ongoing struggle 270
impact of war with Russia 272–73
systemic and deeply embedded
problem 270–71

DoZorro 278, 284–85
post-2014 reforms 277–78
ProZorro 281–83
role of competition policy and the
Anti-monopoly Committee of
Ukraine (AMCU)
AMCU as independent review body 296–97
AMCU's role in debarment 295
bid rigging and related conduct 291–94
enforcement in current war context 297–98
international support for 298–300
importance 306
pre-2014 history 290–91
strengthening of competition
regime 298–300
specific anti-corruption measures
control in the context of war 286–87
digital transformation with ProZorro
platform 281–83
engagement of civil society 283–85
legislative reforms of 2014 280–81
mid-war reality check 287–89
successful campaign to join WTO GPA 285
UNCITRAL Model Law on Public Procurement
central significance of public
procurement 343
choice of procurement methods 43
description of the subject matter and technical
specifications 55–56
enhancement of public procurement
processes 343
international cooperation 45–46
qualification procedures and conditions for
participation 55
Ukraine 278, 280
United Kingdom
Al Yamamah 92–93, 97–98, 145
competition and anti-corruption law
bid rigging 143–44
corruption 145–46
failure to prevent bribery 145
foreign bribery 145
detection and outcomes 147–49
core cases
bid rigging 150–52
corruption 152–53
foreign bribery 153–54
extent of corruption and collusion
overview 155
perceptions and survey evidence 155–58
siloed regimes 164–65
weaknesses in corruption and competition
laws 160–64
weaknesses in procurement processes 158–60

foreign bribery 145, 153–54
need for improvements 139–40
public procurement law
  competitive tendering procedures 142–43
  post-Brexit overhaul 141
  sophisticated regime 140–41
reform proposals
  fact finding 166–67
  importance 165
  improving anti-corruption and competition laws and enforcement 169–76
  improving public procurement processes 167–69
  increased policy coordination 176–77
  interlinked reforms to raise awareness 177–78
summary of core cartel and corruption offences 149
undetected corruption and bid rigging 177
United Nations
importance of public procurement 348
support for Ukraine 278
Sustainable Development Goals (SDGs) *see* **Sustainable Development Goals (SDGs)**
UNCITRAL Model Law on Public Procurement *see* **UNCITRAL Model Law on Public Procurement**
United Nations Convention against Corruption (UNCAC) vi, 10, 67–69, 92–93, 120–21, 145, 242–43, 335
United States
exceptions to pro-competition procurement policy 208–9
Buy American Act 48–49, 64, 208–9
historical experiences
  Boeing's bribery of Darlene Druyen 193
  COVID-19 194–95
  early applications of the Sherman Act 184–85
  expanded global reach of US foreign policy after the World War II era 189
  expansion of criminal antitrust enforcement in 1970s and 1980s 190–91
  'Fat Leonard' corruption scandal 193–94
  formative developments 182
  marine hose manufacturers 194
  naval build-up at the end of the nineteenth century and in the early twentieth century 183–84
  notable lessons 197–98

Operation Ill Wind 192
'The Gentlemen Conspirators': The Tennessee Valley Authority and the electrical equipment conspiracy cases 189–90
Trump era scandals and challenges to the rule of law 195–97
wartime mobilization: the example of World War II 186–88
Watergate-related scandals and the revelation of foreign bribery schemes 191–92
policy framework and enforcement
  anti-corruption and public integrity enforcement 205–6
  anti-corruption and public integrity laws 201–2
  antitrust enforcement 203–4
  antitrust laws 199–200
  bid protests 205
  Foreign Corrupt Practices Act 202, 206
  interagency collaboration 206–7
  Procurement Collusion Strike Force (PCSF) 206
  public procurement enforcement 204–5
  public procurement law 200–1
  qui tam actions 207–8
  suspension and debarment 215
reform proposals 209–11
support for Ukraine's competition regime 278

workforces and personnel
professionalization and training of the procurement workforce 14, 85–90
well-trained and supported procurement workforce as central component of the procurement system 57–58, 346–47
WTO GPA
choice of procurement methods 43
contribution to public procurement policy internationally 62–63
locking in pro-competitive reforms 130
enhancement of public procurement processes 343
key forum for international cooperation 45–46
qualification procedures and conditions for participation 55
trade liberalization 62, 64
Ukraine's successful campaign to join 285